Innovative Technologies to Benefit Children on the Autism Spectrum

Nava R. Silton
Marymount Manhattan College, USA

A volume in the Advances in Medical
Technologies and Clinical Practice
(AMTCP) Book Series

Managing Director:	Lindsay Johnston
Production Manager:	Jennifer Yoder
Development Editor:	Allyson Gard
Acquisitions Editor:	Kayla Wolfe
Cover Design:	Jason Mull

Published in the United States of America by
Medical Information Science Reference (an imprint of IGI Global)
701 E. Chocolate Avenue
Hershey PA 17033
Tel: 717-533-8845
Fax: 717-533-8661
E-mail: cust@igi-global.com
Web site: http://www.igi-global.com

Library of Congress Cataloging-in-Publication Data

Innovative technologies to benefit children on the autism spectrum / Nava R. Silton, editor.
     pages cm
 Includes bibliographical references and index.
  ISBN 978-1-4666-5792-2 (hardcover) -- ISBN (invalid) 978-1-4666-5793-9 (ebook) -- ISBN 978-1-4666-5795-3 (print & perpetual access) 1. Autistic children--Services for. 2. Assistive computer technology. I. Silton, Nava R., 1981-
  RJ506.A9I56 2014
  618.92'8588200285--dc 3
                    2013050981

This book is published in the IGI Global book series Advances in Medical Technologies and Clinical Practice (AMTCP) (ISSN: 2327-9354; eISSN: 2327-9370)

British Cataloguing in Publication Data
A Cataloguing in Publication record for this book is available from the British Library.

All work contributed to this book is new, previously-unpublished material. The views expressed in this book are those of the authors, but not necessarily of the publisher.

For electronic access to this publication, please contact: eresources@igi-global.com.

Advances in Medical Technologies and Clinical Practice (AMTCP) Book Series

Srikanta Patnaik
SOA University, India
Priti Das
S.C.B. Medical College, India

ISSN: 2327-9354
EISSN: 2327-9370

MISSION

Medical technological innovation continues to provide avenues of research for faster and safer diagnosis and treatments for patients. Practitioners must stay up to date with these latest advancements to provide the best care for nursing and clinical practices.

The **Advances in Medical Technologies and Clinical Practice (AMTCP) Book Series** brings together the most recent research on the latest technology used in areas of nursing informatics, clinical technology, biomedicine, diagnostic technologies, and more. Researchers, students, and practitioners in this field will benefit from this fundamental coverage on the use of technology in clinical practices.

COVERAGE

- Biomedical Applications
- Clinical Data Mining
- Clinical High-Performance Computing
- Clinical Studies

IGI Global is currently accepting manuscripts for publication within this series. To submit a proposal for a volume in this series, please contact our Acquisition Editors at Acquisitions@igi-global.com or visit: http://www.igi-global.com/publish/.

Titles in this Series

For a list of additional titles in this series, please visit: www.igi-global.com

Innovative Technologies to Benefit Children on the Autism Spectrum
Nava R. Silton (Marymount Manhattan College, USA)
Medical Information Science Reference • copyright 2014 • 323pp • H/C (ISBN: 9781466657922) • US $195.00
(our price)

Assistive Technology Research, Practice, and Theory
Boaventura DaCosta (Solers Research Group, USA) and Soonhwa Seok (Korea University, South Korea)
Medical Information Science Reference • copyright 2014 • 342pp • H/C (ISBN: 9781466650152) • US $200.00
(our price)

Assistive Technologies and Computer Access for Motor Disabilities
Georgios Kouroupetroglou (University of Athens, Greece)
Medical Information Science Reference • copyright 2014 • 351pp • H/C (ISBN: 9781466644380) • US $200.00
(our price)

Disability Informatics and Web Accessibility for Motor Limitations
Georgios Kouroupetroglou (University of Athens, Greece)
Medical Information Science Reference • copyright 2014 • 443pp • H/C (ISBN: 9781466644427) • US $200.00
(our price)

Medical Advancements in Aging and Regenerative Technologies Clinical Tools and Applications
Andriani Daskalaki (Max Planck Institute for Molecular Genetics, Germany)
Medical Information Science Reference • copyright 2013 • 333pp • H/C (ISBN: 9781466625068) • US $245.00
(our price)

E-Health, Assistive Technologies and Applications for Assisted Living Challenges and Solutions
Carsten Röcker (RWTH Aachen University, Germany) and Martina Ziefle (RWTH Aachen University, Germany)
Medical Information Science Reference • copyright 2011 • 392pp • H/C (ISBN: 9781609604691) • US $245.00
(our price)

Evidence-Based Practice in Nursing Informatics Concepts and Applications
Andrew Cashin (Southern Cross University, Australia) and Robyn Cook (Sidra Medical & Research Center, Qatar)
Medical Information Science Reference • copyright 2011 • 320pp • H/C (ISBN: 9781609600341) • US $245.00
(our price)

www.igi-global.com

701 E. Chocolate Ave., Hershey, PA 17033
Order online at www.igi-global.com or call 717-533-8845 x100
To place a standing order for titles released in this series, contact: cust@igi-global.com
Mon-Fri 8:00 am - 5:00 pm (est) or fax 24 hours a day 717-533-8661

Editorial Advisory Board

Table of Contents

Section 1
Assistive and Computer Technology for Children with Autism

Chapter 1
Kari Andersen, Fordham University, USA
Lauren Levenson, Fordham University, USA
Fran C. Blumberg, Fordham University, USA

Chapter 2
Brenda Smith Myles, Ohio Center for Autism and Low Incidence, USA
Jan Rogers, Ohio Center for Autism and Low Incidence, USA

Chapter 3
Iva Strnadová, University of New South Wales, Australia
Therese M. Cumming, University of New South Wales, Australia
Cathi Draper Rodríguez, California State University – Monterey Bay, USA

Chapter 4
Frank J. Sansosti, Kent State University, USA
Mary Lynn Mizenko, Kent State University, USA
Allison Krupko, Kent State University, USA

Section 3
Video and Virtual-Based Instruction for Children with Autism

Detailed Table of Contents

Section 1
Assistive and Computer Technology for Children with Autism

The use of assistive technology to enhance skill development among children with autism continues to expand. To date, this technology has been primarily used to remediate deficits in language, social skills, and, to a lesser extent, academic skills. Despite the growing body of literature examining the use of these technologies among children with autism, the success of these interventions has been mixed. The authors review findings concerning available forms of assistive technology and the factors that impact their efficacy among children with autism such as developmental level and severity of impairments.

Access to the common core and the general education environment are attainable goals for learners on the autism spectrum when their autism is clearly understood and meaningful supports and instruction are in place. This chapter focuses on one area that is often not addressed for students with Autism Spectrum Disorders (ASD) yet is critical to academic success: executive function. Specifically, this chapter overviews the executive function challenges related to ASD and technology supports in the executive functions areas of (a) information management, (b) materials management, (c) time management, and (d) self-management.

Chapter 3

Iva Strnadová, University of New South Wales, Australia
Therese M. Cumming, University of New South Wales, Australia
Cathi Draper Rodríguez, California State University – Monterey Bay, USA

This chapter discusses how mobile technology can contribute to the quality of life of children with autism across their school years and through the transition to adulthood. Mobile technology has the potential to support students not just at school, but also across all environments in and throughout their lives. There are a number of educational practices and strategies that have been identified as having a strong evidence base to effectively support students with autism. The theoretical framework underpinning this chapter is the Universal Design for Learning (UDL), which prescribes that these practices be integrated into instruction from the outset to ensure equal access and participation of all students in the classroom. Case studies of students on the autism spectrum with diverse needs and during different stages of their lives (from the school years to the transition to adulthood) are used to demonstrate the benefits of incorporating mobile technology into evidence-based educational practices for people with autism.

Chapter 4

Frank J. Sansosti, Kent State University, USA
Mary Lynn Mizenko, Kent State University, USA
Allison Krupko, Kent State University, USA

In recent years, the number of students with Autism Spectrum Disorder (ASD) in both special and general education classrooms has increased substantially. As such, there may be no greater challenge facing educators than planning for the education of this growing population. One method of instruction that appears to hold great promise for educating these students is the use of computer-based technologies. The purpose of this chapter is to: (a) provide a brief overview of the contemporary research regarding the use of computer-assisted instruction and mobile devices for improving the academic, behavior, and social outcomes of students with ASD within school-based contexts and (b) to provide educators with strategies for collecting data to promote accountability. Taken together, the intent is to call attention to the evidence that supports the use of computer-based technologies for students with ASD in schools, raise awareness of those strategies that appear to be the most effective for such students, and assist service providers in providing defensible education.

Chapter 5

Zandile P. Nkabinde, New Jersey City University, USA

The goal of this chapter is to explore the effective use of information and computer technology to assist individuals with autism. In 1985, the Picture Communication System, also known as PECS, was developed for children who had limited abilities to express themselves verbally. The idea was that by pointing to a picture, the child could communicate what he/she wanted. PECS has been modernized with the development of Apps for the iPad. Now, a child can choose from a wide variety of communication choices simply by touching a screen that will facilitate the process and provide a wide variety of choices never before available. This chapter helps parents and teachers to understand how information and computer technology improves communication for children with autism. In addition, use of the iPad and how it improves communication for children with autism are discussed. The use of iPads by children with autism was chosen because of the interactivity they offer to this population as well as for the range of educational opportunities they provide.

Section 2
Single User Devices for Children with Autism

Chapter 6

Jody M. Pirtle, Northern Arizona University, USA
Elizabeth A. West, University of Washington, USA

Augmentative and Alternative Communication (AAC) is a prominent component in the development of support services for learners with Autism Spectrum Disorders (ASD). In this chapter, the authors provide parents, educators, researchers, academics, and other professionals with the most up to date and innovative information as well as practical resources regarding AAC for learners with ASD. Emphasis will be on school-age children diagnosed with ASD. Features of AAC systems as well as the benefits and challenges are presented to provide the reader with information on the current state of the field. The chapter concludes with directions for future research and provides a comprehensive list of resources and organizations.

Chapter 7

Michael Ben-Avie, SCSU Center of Excellence on Autism Spectrum Disorders, USA
Deborah Newton, Southern Connecticut State University, USA
Brian Reichow, AJ Pappanikou Center for Excellence in Developmental Disabilities
    University of Connecticut Health Center, USA

While the knowledge that has been gained from previous studies has accelerated the understanding of the difficulties facing individuals with Autism Spectrum Disorders (ASDs), there is concern regarding the speed with which and the overall lack of translation of research into interventions that make differences in the everyday lives of individuals with ASDs (Gresham, et al., 2001; Volkmar, et al., 2004; Volkmar, Reichow, & Doehring, 2011). For example, the symptoms of ASDs can greatly impair an individual's ability to navigate independently through everyday events. Translating this knowledge into instructional practice requires, then, the design of methods for easing students' transitions within the school, home, and community. While research has validated the use of low-tech visual supports (e.g., National Autism Center, 2009), little has been done to analyze the utility and appropriateness of high-tech assistive technology, such as those interventions administered through smartphones, tablets, and other handheld devices, which are devices that are being used more frequently in education settings (Gray et al., 2010). This chapter presents the results of federally funded research to determine whether the use of iPrompts— a software application for iOS and Android-based smartphones and tablet computers—assists teachers and other educational professionals as they help students with ASD transition from one activity to the next or from one setting to another.

Chapter 8

Cassidy Lamm, University of Alabama, USA

Lauren Lambert, University of Alabama, USA

Joshua Wolfe, University of Alabama, USA

Jeff Gray, University of Alabama, USA

Angela Barber, University of Alabama, USA

Gary Edwards, United Cerebral Palsy of Greater Birmingham, USA

Smartphone apps are used with increased frequency to teach children a variety of skills and to supplement more traditional forms of instruction. In particular, children diagnosed with Autism Spectrum Disorder (ASD) could benefit from applications suited to help them build social emotional skills that could contribute to more successful social interactions. In the study, the authors first investigated and compiled a list of existing apps to see where gaps exist in topic coverage. From this survey of existing smartphone apps for children with ASD, they developed a new app called LEA (Learning Emotions with Autism) that challenges children to interact in a social setting by responding to emotional cues, and having other children determine the emotion that is expressed. This app provides a new context to help children focus their attention on facial cues in order to recognize and interpret emotions through supported peer interaction. In this chapter, the authors discuss how this app was designed and implemented. They also provide a tutorial on how to develop smartphone apps that can be used for ASD research

Chapter 9

Julie E. N. Irish, University of Minnesota, USA

This chapter considers whether a computer-aided technology, single-user virtual environments, can provide a viable option to teach social skills to children with Autism Spectrum Disorder (ASD). Viability is discussed in terms of key themes found in the literature: evidence-basis, generalizability, cost effectiveness, appropriateness for children with ASD, user experience, teacher's contribution, and usefulness for caregivers. A matrix is developed to provide a viability rating for each theme. The chapter concludes that evidence-basis and generalizability for single-user virtual environments as an intervention to teach social skills to children with autism spectrum disorder is weak but that cost effectiveness, appropriateness to teenage children with ASD, positive experience of the user, and potential usefulness for caregivers is strong, whilst the teacher's contribution is a mixed rating between ease of use for the teacher and the high one-on-one time commitment required.

Chapter 10

Joo Tan, Kutztown University, USA

This chapter introduces the use of software technology that is used to create a Web application system called iPAWS to help individuals with Autism Spectrum Disorder (ASD) accomplish simple tasks. These individuals can repeatedly access tasks for assistance or learning through a mobile tablet. For post-school employment, the use of this software technology can help lessen the burden of supervision needed for individuals with autism. For school age children at different levels, iPAWS can serve as training or as a learning tool. This chapter starts with a review of computer-based interventions that have been used in the past. Next, the overall design of the Web application system is introduced. Sample cases that are suitable for children and post-secondary employment are then discussed. Two case studies that were conducted with individuals on the autism spectrum, follow. Finally, possible future improvements to iPAWS are presented.

Section 3
Video and Virtual-Based Instruction for Children with Autism

Chapter 11

Technology featuring robots is a promising innovative technological intervention for treating and educating children with Autism Spectrum Disorder (ASD). This chapter reviews, critiques, and presents future directions for research on clinical and educational applications of robots for these children. Specifically, this chapter reviews current research on: (1) robots that act as social mediators for children with ASD and (2) robots that assist them in developing social skills such as joint attention and imitation. A critical review of the research suggests that robots may have the capacity to assist some of these children, but additional rigorous studies are necessary to demonstrate their efficacy and effectiveness. Future research must (1) examine whether robots have differential effects for specific subgroups of children with ASD and (2) contribute to a deeper understanding of robots' potential use in educational settings.

Chapter 12

The use of video games as a therapeutic intervention for children with Autism Spectrum Disorders (ASD) has steadily increased over the past years. Children with ASD tend to show a great interest in and affinity for playing video games for leisure. This chapter explores how researchers have sought to determine if this inherent motivation could be utilized to assist children with autism spectrum disorders in increasing beneficial skills needed for daily life. Video games have, therefore, been used to assist these children in improving social competence for communicative purposes, improve executive functioning skills, and increase a variety of personal performance skills. Although the variety of research studies in this subject area is expanding, there continues to be a lack of empirical research in this area, and small sample numbers of participants in the majority of the existing research. A lack of longitudinal studies, moreover, is problematic as the studies cannot demonstrate if a learned and mastered skill on a video game can carryover and transfer from the video gaming setting to everyday activities.

Chapter 13

Individuals with Autism Spectrum Disorders (ASD) will struggle to different degrees with social communication skills. To facilitate the learning of new social skills and to allow for repetition and practice, video modeling is being utilized in the PreK-12 setting. This chapter describes behaviors inherent to individuals with autism spectrum disorders that could benefit from the use of video modeling as an intervention, or part of an intervention, as well as a step-by-step description on how to effectively implement video modeling. Additionally, examples of data collection forms, permission forms, and other helpful resources are provided.

The role of virtual reality technologies to help people with autism has been well documented and is an area of research that continues to develop. While the evidence base is somewhat limited, there are many studies that have started to explore the potential of virtual reality technologies for people with autism. Work conducted by Strickland et al. (1996), Murray (1997), Charitos et al. (2000), Parsons and Mitchell (2002), Parsons et al. (2006, 2007), Cobb (2007), Fabri and Moore (2005), and Fabri et al. (2004) have all added to this positive picture of virtual reality technologies to support people on the autism spectrum, specifically in terms of social interaction and social skills development. This chapter uncovers the evidence base and work of others in relation to virtual reality technologies used by people with autism. This chapter concludes with a view as to what future work might pursue in this field.

This chapter explores Realabilities, a video-based children's television program featuring unique characters, each with a distinct disability. Beyond utilizing video technology to directly teach cognitive and social-emotional skills to children with autism, Realabilities demonstrates how video can be used to foster positive behavioral intentions and cognitive attitudes towards children with autism and other disabilities. Realabilities also reveals how a video medium can promote a stop bullying platform, especially since children with disabilities are at least two to three times more victimized by bullying than their typical peers. One hundred and sixty-six students from schools in Manhattan, NY, and Baltimore, MD, showed more favorable behavioral intentions and cognitive attitudes towards hypothetical peers with disabilities following a three episode viewing of Realabilities. Finally, Realabilities not only showcases the realities of disabilities but shares the potential strengths that children with disabilities possess. This is particularly illuminating, since the Affect/Effort Theory suggests that children are more motivated to interact with others when they possess positive expectancies of their social interaction partners.

Foreword

"Is your son high functioning or low functioning autistic?" I am asked by a well-dressed, well-meaning woman in her 30s, minutes before I am about to offer a keynote about Inclusion. "He's both." I smile and am then whisked on to the podium.

I later explain to the group of 400 that if you put my son in a crowded classroom with 30 students, each clamoring for attention from the teacher, he may run around in circles, hold his hands over his ears, make seemingly bizarre sounds, appear like he is not paying attention, and be deemed "low functioning." However, if you observe him in the Santa Monica Mountains, confidently leading the same 30 teens on a hike, you would think of him as "high functioning." For these main reasons and more, I prefer *not* to use the terms "high functioning" and "low functioning" and instead paraphrase my mentor and dear friend, Dr. Barry Prizant, "Different levels of supports in different environments" (2012).

In a crowded classroom, my son needs considerable support; he wears headphones to block out the excessive noise and unpredictable sounds, and he requires a one-on-one aide to help him stay focused. In nature, as I mentioned, my son needs limited support. He can navigate trails independently and holds a job working in an organic garden. Although he is severely apraxic and cannot verbally express language, he understands everything. Today, thanks to the advent of assistive technology, my son can participate in group discussions by using a voice activated app on his iPad called ProLoquo2Go to express his immediate needs. He can independently order "pasta with butter and cheese, please" at any restaurant by simply locating the food icon on his iPad, and when he shows up to work in the organic garden, dressed in his Shalom Institute Staff T-Shirt, he can proudly choose, "Hi Boss. I'm ready for work." With support from a communication partner, he can type more involved thoughts on his iPad using the app "Speak It."

Since the creation of the iPad and all of the similar tech products now available, individuals like my son, can be seen at an equal intellectual footing with verbal peers. Because of technology, parents are connecting with their children on the spectrum in ways never before possible. Portia Iverson, writes in her book, *Strange Son,* that when she asked her severely challenged nine-year-old son, Dov, what he was doing all of the years before he learned to type, he responded, "Listening" (2006, p. 340).

Technology is truly changing the world for individuals of all ages and all abilities who have autism. The challenge has been that there are so many new and exciting technologies for children with autism across the globe with no "portal" to vet this plethora of information and bring it altogether. Until now.

Enter Dr. Nava Silton, who passionately cares about enhancing the way technology improves communication, socialization, and education for those diagnosed with ASD. Silton has successfully compiled this most needed text to describe many of the innovative technologies that can be employed to improve the lives of individuals with autism while also critically assessing their efficacy. She has highlighted technologies that benefit those with minimal or no language as well as included a discussion of virtual reality, robots, video modeling, video gaming, and various other technologies that appeal to individuals on the autistic spectrum. With the rise of the many usages of technology, Silton's text is extremely important to help benefit the lives of so many.

In The Miracle Project, an inclusive theater arts program, non-verbal children with autism type lyrics to songs that verbal children on the spectrum can sing. When participating in our classes, Ido Kedar (Ido in Autismland), an author, self-advocate, and individual with non-verbal autism, remarks that he hears the songs in his head. Debunking the myth that children with autism prefer to be alone and do not desire friendships, Dashiel Chandler, a minimally fluent fourteen year old, used his iPad to type these lyrics to a song which Katiana Zimmerman, The Miracle Project Music Director, composed. Below are some of the lyrics:

Friends come in all shapes and sizes
Friends are there when you need them
Friends are the most important part of my life
I love my friends so much
I love my friends so much
I love my friends so much
They're the most important part of my life

Technology enhances the lives of verbal kids as well. In my classes, I've witnessed highly verbal teens with Asperger's finding their creative voices leading towards careers using technology. Ezra Fields-Meyer, the subject of his Dad's (Tom Fields-Meyer) book, *Following Ezra,* created the artwork for The Miracle Project t-shirts and show programs. After taking a class in animation, Ezra posted a YouTube animated short about the letters A through Z sharing a home and supporting each other, called "Alphabet House." Children's book writer, Tom Lichtenheld, randomly saw the YouTube clip and contacted Ezra. Together, they then collaborated on the award-winning children's picture book *E-mergeny!*

On April 2, 2013, my son and I were invited to speak at The United Nations in honor of World Autism Awareness Day. After I finished my speech, appealing to the group to focus on the abilities and gifts of autism rather than the deficits, my son was called up to the podium. He calmly opened his iPad, pushed "speak" and played a speech he had typed in school:

I cannot speak. For whatever reason, God has intended for me to be mute. Many people might believe that I cannot think, but despite their thinking, I can. What's more is that I listen. A lot of people may stare at me, and when they do, I listen to their body movements and eye gaze. I listen to their ignorance. I listen because I have no choice but to take in the world in the way I can... I've listened enough. It's time for me to speak, however it may sound. Through an electronic device, my hands, or my mouth. Now it's your turn to listen. Are you ready? (Katz, 2013)

Thank you, Nava Silton for showing the many ways that our kids can "speak." My hope is that this work, *Innovative Technologies to Benefit Children with Autism,* will be read by parents, professionals, educators, and employers to see what is possible. We are ready.

Elaine Hall
Independent Researcher, USA

Elaine Hall *is a motivational speaker, inclusion activist, and founder of the Miracle Project. She was profiled in the HBO film AUTISM: The Musical, is the author of Now I See the Moon (HarperCollins 2010) and co-author of Seven Keys to Unlock Autism: Making Miracles in the Classroom (Wiley 2011).*

REFERENCES

Iverson, P. (2006). *Strange son: Two mothers, two sons, and the quest to unlock the hidden world of autism.* New York: Riverhead Books.

Katz, N. (2013). Inspired by the Shema-To listen. *Jewish Journal for Disability Awareness Month.* Retrieved from http://www.jewishjournal.com/rob_eshman/article/neals_prayer_jewish_disability_awareness_month

Prizant, B. (2012). High and low-functioning autism: A false (harmful) dichotomy. *Autism Spectrum Quarterly,* 31-33.

Preface

As diagnoses of autism continue to rise exponentially, dedicated research, established fundraising arms and fascinating volumes that describe ever more amazing "miracle cures" continue to proliferate; still, autism's mysterious cause and its complex effects on the brain elude our grasp.

Families and school districts are impoverished by their desperate attempts to mitigate the always baffling and often challenging behaviors that the condition wreaks. Even though the parents of these children have exhausted every conceivable therapy modality, often the child remains alone, locked inside his unfathomable world that appears to torment him despite every attempt to break through.

Until the advent of the iPad and related technology. For several years now, children who have no spoken language and whose mental processes are inscrutable have taken note of these colorful mobile devices and have actually taken them in hand. To the amazement of family members and caregivers, they appear to understand, almost intuitively, how to find programs that look or sound pleasing to them. They enjoy manipulating the devices on a cozy corner of a sofa, crouched under a table, or stretched out on the carpet of an unoccupied room. Clearly, these devices are small miracles in instances when nothing else works to calm, interest, or stimulate such a child. According to recent reports in books and online, using an iPad, some fortunate children have actually begun to write out their thoughts and offer us a glimpse into their mysterious world.

Knowing full well that the latest technology has taken our world by storm, informing every nuance of our lives, most of the contributors to this fine collection of research papers have watched with fascination at how these small mobile devices captivate heretofore unreachable children. Some of the devices discussed here are larger than iPads or iPhones but are still eminently mobile, so that they can move easily from classroom to home and back. Why, these researchers have asked, using the latest technology, can we not socialize, educate, and help these children become more comfortable in our world? They have explored this area thoroughly, evaluating the efficacy of assistive technology to enhance academic, behavioral, and social outcomes for children on the Autism Spectrum, exploring augmentative and alternative communication, improving emotion recognition, developing virtual reality technologies, and even providing help to those non-techies who would like to learn to create their own apps. Most of the chapters are directed at enhancing the life experiences of children on the Autistic Spectrum. However, my *Realabilities* program capitalizes on the fine use of various modern technologies to address bullying behavior and to raise typical children's consciousness and acceptance of their peers with special needs.

The collection opens with Andersen, Levenson, and Blumberg's "The Promise and Limitations of Assistive Technology Use among Children with Autism." This piece seeks to enlarge the heretofore limited research on the true efficacy of assistive technology as a remediation tool. Does that efficacy hinge on the nature of the child's presenting symptoms and the severity of his/her impairments? The authors, who have worked with children with autism, write from a deep desire to alleviate some of the significant difficulties they have observed. They strive to gain a deeper understanding of children with autism and of possible intervention techniques.

Myles and Rogers address the possibility of enhancing executive function in the brain through assistive technology. Fully aware that executive function underlies the complexity of everything we do on a daily basis and greatly impacts the quality of our lives, the researchers believe that individuals with autism might have unlimited potential when assistive technology is carefully designed and selected to offer them a unique support system—all the while being supremely cost effective.

"Incorporating Mobile Technology into Evidence-Based Practices for Students with Autism" comprehensively describes multiple uses of mobile technology and their advantages. Authors Strndova, Cumming, and Draper show how students with autism can utilize these devices to learn and practice social skills through video modeling and electronic social stories. Employing case studies, they demonstrate how access to curriculum can be improved through mobile technology applications that provide students with visual schedules, electronic text, academic games, and audio text. The real beauty of these possible solutions lies in their mobility. They can move easily from a school setting to home and community.

In their fine chapter, "The Use of Computer-Based Technologies to Increase the Academic, Behavioral and Social Outcomes of Students with Autism Spectrum Disorders in Schools: Considerations for Best Approaches in Educational Practice," researchers Sansosti, Mizenko, and Krupko present additional key points concerning the advantages of Assistive Technology. They hone in on powerful reasons that students thrive when they are trained with the help of these devices: computer-based technologies emerge as an ideal method of educating students with ASD because they provide a predictable environment, increase student concentration, and render students free from anxiety-provoking demands. These technologies allow support and learning to occur at all times of the day, whether at home or at school; they also permit self-management and self-instruction. A stunningly great feature of these devices is the fact that they are now so commonplace in our society that they can provide a less stigmatizing method for supporting and teaching students with disabilities. The authors list at least two priorities: 1) that computers be infused into a daily curriculum rather than solely for reward or recreation and 2) that current and future educators be carefully trained in the application of computer-based innovations for teaching students with ASD.

Nkabinde ("Information and Computer Technology for Individuals with Autism") has been fascinated with the challenge of autism since growing up in South Africa with a brother who had a severe form of the condition. Her family knew nothing about this condition, and only when she arrived in America could she name the affliction. In this chapter, Nkabinde delves into types of computer technology that are suitable for individuals with autism and some of the limitations that may be encountered. She is especially sensitive to the needs of the parents of these special children and offers them ways to understand the use of computer technology with a special emphasis on the now ubiquitous iPad.

In the chapter titled "Augmentative and Alternative Communication for Learners with Autism Spectrum Disorders," by Pirtle and West, readers will learn the differences between low tech and high tech AAC options and begin to understand the SETT framework and rationale for considering the student, the environment, and the tasks required for active participation. They will deliberate over these options before selecting suitable tools to address specific tasks and encounter systems of support that help meet the challenge of improving the independent life functioning and meaningful relationships for learners with ASD. Pirtle has two nephews with autism, both of whom use AAC options designed for learners with ASD throughout the day.

Before he worked as a psychological researcher at the Yale Child Study Center, Ben-Avie taught students with ASDs and other developmental disorders to work independently at jobs in the community. At the time, research showed which parts of the brain lit up when these students engaged in various tasks. Since that time, Ben-Avie has attempted to translate these research findings into instructional practice. In "Using Handheld Applications to Improve the Transitions of Students with Autism Spectrum Disorders," Ben-Avie, Newton, and Reichow demonstrate how the use of high-tech devices may ease students' transitions from school to home to community. While they are in the community, the use of iPhones is far less stigmatizing than conventional methods of visual supports. The trio acknowledges that, although professionals very much want to utilize this technology, there are barriers such as the lack of teacher follow up, the level of training needed, and assistive technology specialists who are spread too thin.

The impetus for "Improving Socialization and Emotion Recognition for Children with Autism Using a Smartphone App" was the result of a recent collaboration between the United Cerebral Palsy Center for Greater Birmingham and two academic departments at the University of Alabama (Autism Spectrum Disorders Clinic and Department of Computer Science). Here, researchers, students, and clinical professionals united to investigate benefits accruing from smartphone technologies as a context for new educational training ideas. The students' interest in working with young children mixed with their knowledge of app development led to a survey of apps already available for children with ASD. The survey, however, identified a gap in the area of emotion recognition among young children diagnosed with ASD. This observation provided the researchers and students with a target context for deeper investigation and led to the creation of the app described as a case study in this contribution. Here, authors Lamm, Lambert, Wolfe, Gray, Barber, and Edwards offer an overview of Autism Spectrum Disorders (ASD) research and educational opportunities through mobile app technologies and survey-related literature and existing state-of-the-art apps that address various age groups and challenges for those with ASD. Finally, the authors offer a case study that demonstrates how an app can be designed and implemented for either potential clinical usage or as a research instrument. Happily, the authors believe that new software development tools are making it easier for those without a computer science background to develop apps for their own purposes and needs; thus, another objective of the contribution is to encourage those who are not computer scientists to explore app creation for their own clinical or research needs.

As an interior designer whose research interest is how the design of the real world environment could support children with ASD, Irish became intrigued by research into how a virtual world could support children with ASD. With the increasing use of computer-aided design, Irish is sure that more relationships could be explored between the real and the virtual world. In "A Viable Option? Single-User Virtual Environments to Teach Social Skills to Children with ASD," Irish considers recent research about SVEs (Single Virtual Environments); a "viability matrix" provides a visual impression of the viability of SVEs and interesting examples of future research directions.

Tan's chapter, "A Task Assistant for Individuals with Autism," evolved as a result of an opportunity to help a graduate student's sibling work more independently at his place of employment. That experience morphed into an opportunity to assist children with Autism Spectrum Disorder from a young age. This chapter posits that Web application (Webapp) offers a mobile training environment that can enhance learning and provides a consistent setting that produces immediate results. Additionally, the Webapp helps to reduce the amount of supervision necessary for a person with mid-level autism spectrum disorder to complete simple tasks, and it may be used to help children of all ages with learning or training.

Senland ("Robots and Autism Spectrum Disorder: Clinical and Educational Applications") has become interested in conducting research with individuals with ASD as a PhD student in Applied Developmental Psychology at Fordham University. Even though robots were and are an intriguing, exciting, and promising technological approach toward treating, socializing, and educating children with ASD, their efficacy has not yet been sufficiently tested. This chapter is an effort to learn more about integrating robots into educational settings for children with ASD and to examine the efficacy of robots in educating children with ASD. Still, additional larger studies are necessary to evaluate the efficacy of this approach and to determine for whom and under what circumstances these robots are most effective. Senland also introduces NAO, a humanoid robot for children with ASD.

As a speech language pathologist, Mehl noticed that children of various ages with ASD displayed a significant interest in video games for enjoyment and leisure. The notion that children with ASD could be helped in terms of improving social competence skills for effective communication using this modality seemed a good possibility. Mehl and Steinmetz in "Video Games for Children with Autism Spectrum Disorders" include a number of up-to-date research articles (including recent presentations at conferences) to highlight how video games are inherently exciting for most children and might continue to be stimulating when used therapeutically. They discuss whether a skill learned from a video game might generalize or carry over to everyday life.

Children on the Spectrum need realistic models of expected behaviors and social skills. Christine Ogilvie of "Video Modeling for Individuals with Autism Spectrum Disorders" was a middle school teacher of students on the Spectrum. Inspired by Temple Grandin, who said that just telling someone on the Autism Spectrum to "be nice" is not as meaningful as providing concrete examples, she began videoing appropriate, pro-social behaviors to show her students in the classroom and then proceeded to translate this experience into her dissertation research. Here Ogilvie and Whitby explain the origin and research behind video modeling and offer step-by-step directions for creating video models and applications for both the general and special education classroom.

Newbutt proceeds from a deep-seated belief that communication is a fundamental right we all have. In "The Development of Virtual Reality Technologies for People on the Autism Spectrum," the author echoes the findings of other contributors in this collection that the evidence base, while growing, still needs longer and more substantial studies that classroom-based and at-home technology (outside lab-based contexts) needs to be better established to help develop Virtual Reality Technology (VRT) for individuals with autism. Finally, he states that teachers, parents, and caregivers are all vital stakeholders in these developments.

We end this collection of fine chapters with a project that helps children with autism and other special needs from a very different vantage point. After conducting a research study at Sesame Street Workshop and follow-up interviews with parents of children with disabilities, I learned that they were not only interested in a video medium to teach their children cognitive or social-emotional skills (as many of the aforementioned technological tools do) but were yearning for a video medium to teach typical children how to be more sensitive to and socially interested in their special children. Fully aware of the minimal, neutral, or even harmful impact of previous video interventions at enhancing the behaviors and attitudes of typical children towards children with special needs, my research assistants, Senada Arucevic, Rebecca Ruchlin, Vanessa Norkus, and I created *Realabilities,* an animated children's television show and graphic novel series aimed at reversing these negative outcomes. *Realabilities* features five characters with disabilities who harness their special strengths to save their school from bullies. While we allude to each of the character's impairments in our show, our video-based medium focuses on the strengths and unique abilities of these special children. Even though few video mediums have been successful at improving the attitudes and behaviors of typical children towards their peers with disabilities, *Realabilities* has already shown marked success at promoting sensitivity and at changing the perceptions of over 300 typical children, who were tested via pilot studies and in their elementary schools. This chapter reminds us that the potential of technological tools is vast and can be incredibly creative and instrumental in not only directly aiding individuals with disabilities but in changing the perceptions and expectancies of those who populate the special child's environment.

Nava R. Silton
Marymount Manhattan College, USA

Acknowledgment

This book could not have been compiled and edited without the gracious guidance and assistance of various individuals. First and foremost, I want to thank all of the bright and creative authors who contributed their great contemporary work in the area of innovative technologies to benefit individuals with autism. I look forward to working with each of them in the future. Secondly, I'd like to offer my gratitude to the peer reviewers who painstakingly took their time to review the content, syntax and empirical rigor of each chapter.

Next, I am grateful to Kayla Wolfe and Allyson Gard at IGI Global Publishing, who made this editing process a pleasure. I ensured that their inboxes were always jam-packed with my emails! I would also like to thank Marymount Manhattan College for their unflagging support and encouragement. I am especially appreciative of Senada Arucevic, Rebecca Ruchlin, and Vanessa Norkus, my three research assistants at Marymount Manhattan College, who contributed greatly to the early preparations of this text.

I would like to acknowledge my wonderful husband, Dr. Ariel Brandwein, and my two little men, Judah Lior and Jonah Gabriel Brandwein, who afforded me the time and opportunity to complete a project that was so important to me. Ariel's technical expertise, his fathering skills, and most importantly his patience were huge assets in completing this project. I thank my father, Rabbi Paul Silton, and my wonderful siblings, Elana, Michal, Akiva, Tamar, Aviva, and my twin sister Shira, for their constant encouragement and support. Finally, there are no words to describe the level of time, effort, patience, and commitment my mother, Faye Silton, took to help ensure the timely completion of this text. Her creative ideas coupled with her tremendous writing and editing skills were invaluable to me, and the text is all the more dear to me since she was such an integral part of its creation.

I want to offer a final note of thanks to all parents, teachers, special educators, technology specialists, siblings, and family members of children on the autism spectrum. Each of you work tirelessly each day to brighten and expand the world of opportunities for our very special children. My hope is that this text will help you expand their worlds further. My final debt of gratitude goes to children with autism themselves, who have afforded us the challenge and opportunity to broaden our scope of how to further engage their unique and beautiful minds.

Nava R. Silton
Marymount Manhattan College, USA

Section 1
Assistive and Computer Technology for Children with Autism

Chapter 1
The Promise and Limitations of Assistive Technology Use among Children with Autism

Kari Andersen
Fordham University, USA

Lauren Levenson
Fordham University, USA

Fran C. Blumberg
Fordham University, USA

ABSTRACT

The use of assistive technology to enhance skill development among children with autism continues to expand. To date, this technology has been primarily used to remediate deficits in language, social skills, and, to a lesser extent, academic skills. Despite the growing body of literature examining the use of these technologies among children with autism, the success of these interventions has been mixed. The authors review findings concerning available forms of assistive technology and the factors that impact their efficacy among children with autism such as developmental level and severity of impairments.

INTRODUCTION

According to the newly redacted and released Diagnostic Statistical Manual of Mental Disorders-V (American Psychiatric Association, 2013), meeting the criteria for a diagnosis of autism spectrum disorder (ASD) requires that individuals show symptoms early in childhood that collectively limit and hinder everyday functioning.

The scope of symptoms must include deficits in social communication and interaction not caused by general developmental delays. These manifestations of ASD include deficits in social-emotional reciprocity (such as an inability to participate in the give-and-take of a conversation), nonverbal communication, and in creating and maintaining social relationships (including imaginative play and a general interest in others). Individu-

DOI: 10.4018/978-1-4666-5792-2.ch001

als with ASD also show repetitive behaviors as reflected in perseveration or echolalia in speech, highly specific routines and ritualized patterns of behaviors (such as putting items of clothing on in a specific order), and heightened sensitivity/reaction to sensory input (American Psychiatric Association, 2013). Efforts to address these behaviors often require behavioral treatments, most notably applied behavioral analysis [ABA], which uses the techniques and principles of positive reinforcement and structured situations to bring about meaningful and positive change in behavior. Antipsychotic drugs have been used at times to treat related symptoms such as seizures and self-injurious behaviors (CDC, 2013).

One increasingly used form of treatment for mitigating some of the symptoms is that of technology in general and educational or assistive technology in particular (see Goodwin, 2008), these include any form of technology that can be used to enhance the functional independence and quality of life of individuals with disabilities (National Research Council, 2001). These technological interventions have involved, for example, the use of video games designed to improve memory function among children with special needs (See Durkin, 2010; Durkin, Boyle, Hunter, & Conti-Ramsden, 2013). Interest in the promise of technology as a mode of intervention for children with ASD and the limited body of research pertaining to its efficacy have been highlighted in recent reviews of literature by Ploog, Scharf, Nelson, and Brooks (2013) and Ramdoss et.al (2011).

The demands on these technologies are high as they must be adapted for individuals with differing levels of autism severity and of differing development levels. Further, some forms of assistive technology are designed as tools for life-long use, such as augmentative and alternative communication devices (AAC) which are used to facilitate and enhance communication. Others are introduced as a temporary instructional aid to modify or improve behavioral functioning, such as a pictorial schedule of activities to be completed during the day (Goldsmith & LeBlanc, 2004). Although such pictorial schedules commonly make use of notebooks or placards with pictures cueing a sequence of activities, increasingly such interventions are including technological supplements, such as video-enhanced modalities (Kimball, Kinney, Taylor & Stromer, 2004) and computer-based schedules delivered through Microsoft PowerPoint (Rehfeldt, Kinney, Root, Stromer, 2004).

Although the use of technology to ameliorate the symptoms of autism has met with qualified success, it continues to become a more prevalent form of treatment. For example, individuals with autism may now receive computerized instruction concerning how to decode facial expressions of human emotion, practice turn-taking in the context of social interactions, and learn how to establish eye contact. Additionally, technology is used to help improve organizational skills and maintain pace with the classroom curriculum (Charlop-Christy, Le, & Freeman, 2000; Goldsmith & LeBlanc, 2004; Goodwin, 2008; Koch, 2012; Ritterfeld & Weber, 2005). This technology is found in both the school and home environment. To be eligible for use of this technology in the school setting, a child must be given a diagnosis of autism, and the Individualized Education Program (IEP) must stipulate that assistive technology is needed. Briefly, an IEP guides the delivery of special education supports and services for students with disabilities and creates an opportunity for teachers, parents, school administrators, related services personnel, and students (when appropriate) to collaborate to improve children's educational outcomes. According to the National Center for Learning Disabilities (2013), by law, the IEP must include certain information about children such as current performance, annual goals, special education and related services, accommodations, participation in state and district-wide tests, needed transition services, measured progress, and an educational program designed to meet his or her unique needs. The specific types of educational technology devices that children will be able to use in the school or home setting, as stipulated by the IEP, will depend on the severity of their symptoms and the types of special impairments that they present. The severity of these deficits may also affect the types of devices instituted in the home.

Our goal for the chapter is to review education and assistive technology currently available and used most often among children with autism. Special emphasis will placed on those technologies used to address language use, social skills, and academic skills and content.

Educational and Assistive Technology used among Children with Autism

According to the Technology-Related Assistance for Individuals with Disabilities Act of 1988 (Public Law 100-407), assistive technology refers to any item, piece of equipment, or product system (whether acquired commercially, off-the-shelf, modified or customized) that is used to increase, maintain, or improve the functional capabilities of individuals with disabilities. Our review of the literature indicates that assistive technology ostensibly ranges along three levels: low, mid, and high. Low technology refers to visual support strategies, which typically preclude involvement of any type of electronic or battery operated device. Examples may include calendars, checklists, reward cards, dry erase boards, highlight tape, and Velcro. These forms of nuts-and-bolts technologies are often used both in the classroom and at home and are primarily designed to address skills related to organization (e.g. time management), attention (e.g. sustained attention in class), self-help (e.g. independence in personal hygiene and care), following directions (e.g. listening and responding appropriately to multi-step requests given by a teacher or parent), following rules (e.g. staying seated in class), and modifying behavior (Lequia,

Machalicek & Rispoli, 2012). Findings show that low level technology has been effective in promoting the independence and self-management skills of a broad range of individuals with intellectual disabilities (Banda & Grimmett, 2008; Takanori & Hui-Ting, n.d.).

Mid-level technology includes battery-operated devices or electronic devices. Examples of these technologies include simple voice output devices, portable word processors, calculators, tape recorders, and timers. The skills areas addressed by these devices often include receptive language comprehension, expressive communication, social interactions, attention, organization, and classroom performance. Depending on the particular technology and the disability severity level, mid-level technology may be effective in both school and home settings. For example, Voice Output Communication Aids (VOCAs) are a form of mid-level technology used to improve communication skills among children with ASD that have been found to generalize across home and school settings (Schepis, Reid, Behrmann & Sutton, 1998). These communication aids involve activation of a device to provide recorded or synthesized speech that has been found to be readily understood by most individuals (Schepis, Reid, Behrmann & Sutton, 1998). The use of VOCAs has been shown to be effective in facilitating expressive language (Checkley, Reidy, Chantler, Hodge & Holmes, 2012), including making specific requests and initiating communicative interactions (Schepis, Reid, & Behrmann, 1996; Dattilo & Camarata, 1991).

High level technologies refer to more complex technological support strategies, some of which are more costly, thus limiting their use in school and home settings. Examples include video games, virtual reality environments, computer-based learning, robotics, complex voice output devices, and video cameras (Stokes, n.d.). Evidence is abundant that high level technology may be beneficial across a range of diagnoses and ages

(Baxter, Enderby, Evans & Judge, 2012). Specifically, computers, PDAs, and video games have been shown to enhance skills relevant to focused attention and attention span, in-seat behavior, fine motor abilities and generalization of these skills to classroom activities (Jordan, 1995). Similarly, high level technology has also been linked to decreases in agitation, perseverative responses, and self-stimulatory behaviors in both school and home settings. While often more costly than other existing technologies and/or interventions, high level devices are often selected because of the positve outcomes they have been found to yield and the limited training that they require (DiGennaro Reed, Hyman, & Hirst, 2011). As Jacobson and Mulick note (2000), individuals who conduct cost-benefit analyses of interventions for those with ASD need to balance the substantial and sustainable, long-term benefits of technology-based treatments and their fiscal cost.

Overall, the potential for technologies to enhance children's independent functioning skills by reducing the amount of direct support needed from another person is vast, if not relatively unexplored from a research vantage point. We consider below the use of these technologies within the three domains in which they have been primarily used: language, social skills, and academic skills. Unfortunately, enthusiasm for the use of these technologies to facilitate skill development among children with autism may far outstrip the extent and rigor of research conducted to examine the efficacy of these technologies as forms of treatment.

Language Development and Skills

Perhaps the most prevalent and established use of assistive technology in the classroom is that which addresses the language and communication skills of children and adolescents with ASD. Generally referred to as AAC, these emerging technologies are used to promote the generation of communication and stimulate the production of speech (Mil-

lar, Light, & Schlosser, 2006). Technology-based AAC can include visual symbols, two-dimensional communication boards, and speech-generating devices (SGDs).

At the low end of AAC technology are simple visual symbol systems, such as *Boardmaker*, which employs picture communication symbols such as pictures of preferred rewards or desired activities to augment, enhance, support, and develop existing language (Cafiero, 2001). *Boardmaker* is used to create visual or pictorial schedules, that use pictures of activities (i.e. reading, blocks, sensory tables) as cues for upcoming daily activities. These schedules may help children with ASD to better predict their environment, feel some control over what is expected of them, reinforce good behavior, facilitate both the understanding of receptive language (i.e. that which the children understands), and the growth of expressive language (i.e. that which the child can produce). In general, pictorial, written, or object schedules have been shown to be effective for children ages 3-14 and to be associated with favorable outcomes for children with ASD (National Autism Center, 2009).

Parents have also successfully used visual schedules to structure leisure, social interaction, self-care, and housekeeping tasks. For example, in one case study, a student using a photographic activity schedule was successfully taught to point to the appropriate page in the schedule, obtain the materials needed for a given activity, complete the activity, clean up when done, check the schedule again for the next activity, and repeat the sequence (Krantz, MacDuff, & McClannahan, 1993). Further, findings from a meta-analysis showed that, overall, visual schedule technologies enhanced and/or remediated targeted behavioral outcomes in individuals with ASD, including communication skills (e.g., making requests verbally), social interaction skills (e.g., spontaneous social initiations), spelling, and challenging behaviors such as aggression (Ganz et al., 2012).

Other commonly used forms of assistive technology are two-dimensional communication boards. The most popular and established example of this innovation for the classroom is the *Picture Exchange Communication System* (PECS). This system involves an exchange-based approach that uses sentence strips in combinations with pictures ranging in both complexity and potential utility of communication (Bondy & Frost, 1998). When using this system, children are expected to progress through six phases of communication, beginning with learning to select and exchange pictures of desired objects or foods and advancing to a level whereby they can answer and comment in response to questions, and communicate spontaneously without prompting. There is copious evidence indicating that PECS enhances functional communication skills of individuals with disabilities (Bondy & Frost, 1994). For example, Schwartz, Garfinkle, and Bauer (1998) examined the ability of the students with severe communication delays to learn the PECS and actively use the system to communicate. In an initial study, the authors analyzed the PECS acquisition data among 31 preschool children and demonstrated that those with severe communication delays and disorders could quickly and efficiently learn to use the system. In their second study, the authors followed 18 preschool PECS users for a year, evaluating language samples from both structured communication exchanges to determine whether what was learned via PECS would generalize to other settings in which it was not used. Results showed that all participants could use PECS to comment on an event or emotion that they experienced, and that eight students (six with ASD) extended their vocabulary and reciprocal communicative speech as compared to their observed speech before the intervention. In her synthesis of 13 studies, Tien (2008) also verified the effectiveness of PECS for improving the functional communication skills of students with ASD. This verification was made by evaluating the efficacy of PECS among 125 participants with ASD ranging from 1 to 12 years

of age (who, upon baseline assessment, had been identified as having limited or no functional communication skills). Despite variations in training, application, and practice of the system, Tien found strong evidence in favor of the intervention for the ASD population. Specifically, across the studies, participants who received the PECS training experienced positive gains in functional communication skills, including language acquisition, spontaneous use of language, and generalization of vocabulary.

As a mid-level assistive technology, Speech Generating Devices, (SGDs) have also been found to be efficacious in cultivating communication among children with ASD through the use of static-display (e.g., *GoTalk*) and dynamic-display (e.g., *Dynavox V*) devices (Shane et al., 2012). Whereas static-display SGDs use overlays to display text and must be changed manually, dynamic-display SGDs display vocabulary as text and/or graphics on a screen and can be changed to another set of text and/or graphics electronically. SGDs typically are presented on a computer-based processing unit with a visual display that presents pictures of common vocabulary items. The device is programmed to produce a synthetic voice corresponding to each of the vocabulary items (O'Reilly, Lancioni, Lang, & Rispoli, 2011). For example, touching the picture of a cookie could be programmed to produce the noun "cookie." The user would then need to construct the sentence, "I want a cookie." A comprehensive meta-analysis of 35 studies investigating this form of assistive technology among participants ranging in age from 1 to 42 yielded positive outcomes in 86% of the studies (Rispoli, Franco, van der Meer, Lang, & Camargo, 2010).

The development of more sophisticated technologies (such as virtual reality platforms and robotics) and the growing accessibility of mobile devices (such as smartphones and tablets) have increasingly been added to the repertoire of tools such as PECS, *Boardmaker*, and visual schedules, to provide more comprehensive and contextually-appropriate interventions (McMillan, 2008; Horner, Carr, Strain, Todd, & Reed, 2002). Presently, apps such as *Proloquo2go, MyTalk, Steps, First-Then, MyChoiceBoard,* and *PicCalendar* are being used in both home and school settings to address language skill deficits among children with varying severities of ASD (Shane et al., 2012). Research investigating the effectiveness of the app *Proloquo2go*, in particular, has shown positive effects. This application for the iPod or iPad is an AAC tool that provides many natural sounding text-to-speech voices, two complete research-based vocabularies, close to 14,000 up-to-date symbols, powerful automatic conjugations, advanced word prediction, multi-user support, ease of use, and the ability to fully customize vocabularies to meet the needs of individual users from beginning symbolic communication to full literacy. Preliminary research is promising for *Proloquo2Go*. For example, in a study with two adolescents and one adult, who were diagnosed with ASD and had little or no language, use of *Proloquo2Go* facilitated rapid acquisition of communication skills. These skills included participants' ability to request their preferred stimuli from an array of choices (Van der Meer, Sigafoos, O'Reilly, & Lancioni, 2011). For further information about the logistics and aims of the app, we refer readers to Sennott and Bowker (2009) for a review of *Proloquo2Go* in light of the best practices in AAC for individuals with ASD.

To date, research examining the efficacy of new apps such as *Proloquo2Go* remains limited and conducted among small samples of individuals (Van der Meer, Sigafoos, O'Reilly, & Lancioni, 2011) who are characterized as moderate to high functioning. Further, considerable individual variation in outcomes and limited generalization or maintenance of usage is reported in the literature (Baxter, Enderby, Evans, & Judge, 2012; Schlosser & Lee, 2000). Clearly, further research and more rigorous studies are needed to better understand the utility of AAC technology for facilitating language development and skills among children with autism.

Social Skills

Assistive educational technology has also been used extensively to address the social skill deficits that are hallmark characteristics of ASD. Thanks to a considerable and diverse array of tools, there are many technological innovations for the classroom intended to act as buffers and bridges through communication partners (Cafiero, 2008). Because individuals with ASD often experience difficulty integrating complex environmental cues such as receiving verbal and written information at the same time, many facets of communication implicit in social interaction including spoken and body language, facial expressions, and tone of voice, often present as significant obstacles to developing and navigating relationships.

Matson and Wilkins (2007) note that behaviors targeted for treatment in the domain of social skills typically include increasing overall verbal output, smiling at people, increasing eye contact, and using appropriate assertiveness in asking for help. Challenging behaviors have also been subsumed in the genre of social skills, including aggression and stereotypic behaviors (e.g. repetitive rocking back and forth or hand flapping) as many of these behavioral nuances impact both learning and appropriate social interaction (Campbell, 2011). A high level technology form of assistive technology is video modeling, which has often been used to increase the frequency and diversity of social behaviors and is based on Bandura's social learning theory, whereby individuals are presumed to learn through observation (Bandura, 1977). In video modeling, individuals with ASD are shown a videotape of individuals who model different target behaviors. The goal is for the individuals with ASD to use the video modeling videotapes to learn which behaviors to model and which behaviors to refrain from when interacting with others (Walton & Ingersoll, 2012). Accordingly, viewers are then expected to enhance their social skill repertoire and further their ability to negotiate social relationships (Ogilvie, 2011).

Findings using this technique have been promising. For example, Nikopoulos and Keenan (2007) found that video modeling in the form of short video clips successfully helped children with ASD learn social behaviors and initiate social interactions. Notably, they also reported decreases in social isolation and accompanying increases in reciprocal play following this form of intervention. Simpson, Langone, and Ayres (2004) combined video modeling and computer-based instruction to teach social skills to four children with ASD who ranged between 5–6 years of age. All children lacked social skills and had mild to severe speech and language impairments. Their teacher designed a program comprising video clips of typically developing students modeling examples and non-examples of the target behaviors: sharing, following a teacher's directions, and social greetings. Findings showed that all children readily improved in the targeted social skills.

Particularly among high functioning children with autism, video feedback of their stereotypical behavior may be incorporated into social or psycho-educational interventions. Charlop-Christy, Le, and Freeman (2000) compared the effectiveness of video modeling to in vivo modeling for teaching developmental skills to five children with ASD (aged 7 to 11) who were either low or high functioning. The video modeling condition consisted of each child watching a videotape of models performing the target behavior, whereas the in vivo modeling condition consisted of the children observing live models perform the target behavior. The findings indicated that video modeling led to fast acquisition of language use during play, and self-help skills such as independently one's brushing teeth and washing one's face. Video modeling also yielded improvements in conversational speech (such as asking "when," "where," or "who" questions) and independent play (including coloring and card games). In contrast with watching video modeling of the targeted behavior, such generalization of skills was not observed in the in vivo condition. Thus,

positive behavioral changes among all children were found using this form of assistive technology independent of their level of functioning.

Video modeling has also been linked to improvements in spontaneous requesting, such as independently touching a picture for a desired object (Wert & Neisworth, 2003), conversational speech (Sherer et al., 2001), task fluency (Lasater & Brady, 1995), social communication including nonverbal communication such as eye contact (Thiemann & Goldstein, 2001; Bellini & Akullian, 2007), daily living skills (Shipley-Benamou, Lutzker, & Taubman, 2002); and perspective-taking skills (Charlop-Christy & Daneshvar 2003). Across all of these studies, children ranging from no autism to severe autism were included as study participants. Findings showed that although the extent of skill development afforded by video modeling varied based on severity, there were consistent universal improvements in functioning across all participants.

Video modeling has also been adapted for use on iPods and iPads. For example, Cihak, Fahrenkroq, Ayres, and Smith (2009) evaluated the efficacy of video modeling delivered via iPod for transitioning between locations and activities in the school. Through their examination of four elementary students diagnosed with autism, the authors found that all participants began transitioning more independently after the intervention was introduced. Similarly, researchers have shown how videoed stories downloaded to an iPod-touch could facilitate functional social skill development in adolescents (Retherford & Sterling-Orth, 2009). Specifically, this University of Wisconsin-Eau Claire program was found to promote independent transitioning among four students. First, the students were shown videos on an iPod touch of other students transitioning independently. Following the intervention, the students were able to transition independently; their inappropriate behavior decreased, and they maintained their transitioning skills weeks after the intervention.

Computer-based multimedia reflects a high technology form of AAC that has been effectively applied to teach young children with ASD how to think through social situations and conflicts (Bernard-Opitz, Sriram, & Nakhoda-Sapuan, 2001). Smartphones and tablets have also been used to target social skills (Fogg, 2003; Fogg & Eckles, 2007; Tentori & Hayes, 2010). A prominent exemplar of this type of intervention is the *HANDS* project, a web-based flexible toolkit that teachers and parents use to develop support and intervention instructions specific to the needs of a given child (Mintz, 2013). As an intervention tool, the *HANDS* toolkit has proven to be a highly efficient medium of intervention, at least in the short term.

More high-level technology includes the use of virtual reality environments to address social skills deficits among children with ASD. A virtual environment (VE) can be defined as a computer-generated, three-dimensional simulation of a real or imaginary environment (Cobb, Kerr, & Glover, 2001). Two forms of virtual environments can be distinguished: a single-user virtual environment, and a multiuser, collaborative virtual environment (Neale, Cobb, & Wilson, 2002). In both, the user can interact freely with the simulated environment via his or her individual avatar, defined as a representation of the user's identity within the computer environment (Gerhard, 2003; Gerhard, Moore, & Hobbs, 2004). Avatars are key in virtual reality environments because they can be manipulated to facilitate and simplify social interactions and inter-human communication in a virtual world (Moore, Cheng, McGrath, & Powell, 2005).

Virtual reality video modeling techniques have been developed and continue to be honed as a means by which to improve social skills among children with ASD (See Strickland, McAllister, Coles, and Osborne (2007) for a review of the history and use of virtual reality video modeling techniques). Positive gains have been documented for social awareness and social behaviors, especially since children and adolescents report that modern virtual reality settings are authentic enough to allow for realistic simulation of social situations (Mitchell, Parsons & Leonard, 2007; Wallace et al., 2010).

Robotic technology also has been used to promote the social skills of children with ASD. Robotics can allow for the presentation of a simplified social environment and gradual increase in the complexity of social interactions. Robots can be used to teach basic social interaction skills using turn-taking and imitation games. Robots used as facilitators of shared attention can encourage interaction with peers and adults (Goldsmith & LeBlanc, 2004). The *AuRoRA Project* (whereby AuRoRA stands for "Autonomous mobile Robot as a Remedial tool for Autistic children") has utilized robots as constructive tools in facilitating social skills including turn-taking, imitation, recognition of emotional expressions/gestures, appropriate tactile interactions, and general communication and interaction skills that are required in human-human contact (Aurora, 2000). The *AuRoRA Project*, started in 1998, aims to study how robots can become a "toy" that might serve a therapeutic role for children with ASD. One of their first prototypes was a robot that resembled a large toy truck with heat sensors that could detect nearby children and a bumper switch that allowed it to reverse upon impact (Graham-Rowe, 2002). The truck was programmed with several basic commands necessary to play interactive games resembling "tag" and "follow the leader." These games were meant to stimulate imitation and turn-taking behaviors. The truck was later modified to include a central point of focus resembling eyes, so that children would have to face the robot for it to sense their movement and respond accordingly. This behavior was seen as promoting eye contact (Graham-Rowe, 2002).

In follow up studies assessing the efficacy of the robots' facilitation of social interaction, researchers found that the particular kind of social interaction among their 6 child participants in the presence of and during interactions with the robot, reflected their social interactions outside the research setting (Goldsmith &LeBlanc, 2004). For example, there appeared to be an improvement in eye contact and shared attention after interacting with the robot. This finding contributed to the contention that interactions with the robot in the pair-trials were ecologically valid. Findings within the *AuRoRA Project* suggest that robots may become therapeutic playmates designed to teach basic social skills, and to encourage, and facilitate social behavior (Dautenhahn, 2003). However, many of the conclusions concerning the efficacy of this work are largely based on case studies or on very small scale studies (Dautenhahan & Werry, 2004; Diehl, Schmitt, Villano & Crowell, 2011).

Overall, the use of assistive technology as reviewed above presents as effective and applicable to remediating social skills as they are easily adjusted and tailored to the specific needs of the individual. However, the efficacy of these platforms seems to hinge upon the severity and nature of the individual's disability (Mintz, 2013) so that they may be most effective for higher-functioning individuals (Bellini & Peters, 2008). For example, cognitive limitations such as the inability to represent another individual's mental state (or failure to demonstrate a theory of mind) may undermine how efficacious interventions such as the use of robots or virtual reality may be in the development of social skills. Clearly, the need for additional research is warranted to substantiate the virtue of high level technology used to remediate social skills among children with ASD.

Academic Skills

A third domain addressed by assistive educational technology is that of academic skills. Educational technology geared specifically toward enhancing academic skills as opposed to language and social skills among children with ASD appears to be the least developed and most sparsely documented in the literature (Lord et al., 2005; Smith et al., 2007). The reason for this paucity

of research and limited discourse likely reflects a focus on the pervasive and pronounced nature of the hallmark characteristics of autism (including impaired social interaction and verbal and non-verbal communication, and restricted, repetitive or stereotyped behavior) manifest in children and adolescents with ASD rather than on other skill sets (University of Maine Center for Community Inclusion and Disability, 2009). The hallmark characteristics are most likely to be addressed among children with ASD antecedent to skills pertinent to academic performance. Fortunately, with more recent accountability requirements to assess all students in reading, math, and science, research for this population has begun to expand from the functional approach typical of skill acquisition to more in-depth investigations of academic interventions for children with ASD (Browder & Cooper-Duffy, 2003).

When academic skills are addressed in the literature, they are typically addressed in the context of the visual processing strength of children with ASD. Based on this visual strength, individuals with ASD ostensibly respond well to the use of media-based tools and technologies such as low-level technology-based visual schedules, mid-level technology such as Voicepods (digital recording and playback tools that help with sequencing stories, practicing spelling words, math facts, history dates, and key concepts from core subject areas and high level technology computers for online learning or reading games) (Cafiero, 2008; Williams, Wright, Callaghan & Coughlan, 2002). In fact, studies of individuals with ASD using the Wechsler Intelligence Scale for Children (WISC) have revealed an advantage for visual-simultaneous processing (i.e. the Block Design subset) over verbal-sequential processing (i.e. the Comprehension and the Picture Arrangement subsets) irrespective of functional levels or ages (Happe, 1994). Further, research evaluating pictorial versus verbal modalities among children with ASD continue to substantiate a specific cognitive style that benefits from visual presentation

(Kamio & Toichi, 2000). These findings suggest that academic interventions presenting stimuli in visual modalities may be more beneficial for children with ASD than interventions presented in other modalities such as in verbal, auditory, or tactile domains.

With this in mind, academic assistive technology has progressively been developed with the intent of engineering tools specifically geared towards the learning styles of children with ASD. Murray (1997) identified factors characteristic of computer-based systems, which were seen as well-suited to the educational needs of children with autism: (1) setting clear boundaries, (2) controlling and step-by-step presentation of stimuli, (3) facilitating joint attention by selecting a compatible focus of interest; (4) instilling feelings of safety, flexibility, adaptability, and predictability of the learning environment or material; and (5) enhancing development of autonomy, encouraging communication, and boosting self-confidence. Computer-based interventions that have capitalized on these components have facilitated enhanced problem solving (Bernard-Opitz, Sriram, & Nakhoda-Sapuan, 2001), improved vocabulary (Moore & Calvert, 2000), and improved reading and communication skills among children with autism (Heimann, Nelson, Tjus, & Gillberg, 1995).

Perhaps the most formidable evidence supporting computer assisted technology (CAT) for remediation of academic skills among children with ASD is derived from a large-scale project utilizing *TeachTown: Basics*. This program uses comprehensive lessons to address a variety of skills that pertain to daily living, social relationships, and academic performance. The online and offline features of the program also include automatic data collection, tracking, and reporting, a note system for communication with the child's team which aids in supporting IEP goals, and optional home-school connection tools for parents. In a 2006 study conducted by Whalen, Linden, Ingersoll, Dallaire, and Linden, four children with ASD

and four with other developmental disabilities participated with their parents in a two-month treatment program using the *TeachTown: Basics* tool. After using the tool, children showed gains on their post-test scores relative to the pre-test. Further, children with ASD demonstrated a 105% increase in language and social behaviors after using *TeachTown: Basics*. In addition, inappropriate language use and behavior decreased by 61%, and children looked at their parents more and showed more enjoyment (i.e. demonstrated positive affect) while working on the computer, as compared to baseline measures (Whelan, Linden, Ingersoll, Dallaire, & Linden, 2006).

Thus far, the *TeachTown: Basics* program has yielded moderate gains in academic skills across various research studies for children with autism (Whelan & Cernich, 2007; Wyman & Stobbe, 2006). For instance, in an investigation involving 1,100 subscribers, researchers found significant and consistent progress across learning domains in a relatively short time frame (Whelan, Cernich, Lockhart, Liden, & Vaupel, 2009). Similarly, an exploration of an autism program in Los Angeles utilizing *TeachTown: Basics* found significant differences between those students using the software versus those students using other instructional software (Whelan, Moss, Ilan, Vaupel, Fielding, & MacDonald, 2010). Specifically, students in the treatment group using *TeachTown: Basics* evidenced significantly larger improvements than the control group on the Brigance Inventory of Early Development and on the Peabody Picture Vocabulary Test, Third Edition (PPVT-III). The Brigance Inventory of Early Development measures a child's school-readiness skills, such as reading ability, language development, social emotional development, math and science knowledge, and approaches to learning. The PPVT-III primarily measures individuals' receptive (hearing) vocabulary for Standard American English and provides an estimate of individuals' verbal intelligence and scholastic ability (Dunn & Dunn, 1981).

Other forms of academic assistive technology have also boasted positive results for children with ASD similar to those of *TeachTown: Basics*. For example, Bosseler and Massaro (2003) developed and evaluated a computer-animated tutor to improve vocabulary and grammar among children with autism. Specifically, eight children with ASD were given an initial assessment of tests and tutorials, and were then reassessed 30 days following the mastery of vocabulary items. Findings showed that students were able to identify significantly more items during the posttest and recalled 85% of the newly learned items at least 30 days after the completion of training.

Williams, Wright, Callaghan, and Coughlan (2002) showed additional support for increased efficacy of computer-based instruction over more traditional methods. Specifically, they found that after computer assisted learning, five of the eight children with autism that they studied could reliably identify at least three words where other methods had failed to promote similar gains. Further, Fitzgerald, Koury, and Mitchem (2008) reported in their review of the literature on the efficacy of CAT that improvements in academics (i.e., reading, mathematics, writing, social studies, and science) were found following the use of CAT by students with mild or severe disabilities.

Researchers who have examined the academic skills of children with ASD have also examined students' motivation to engage in an academic tasks and their attention to that task (Fogg, 2003). For example, desktop computer games have been effectively used with children with ASD to enhance motivation in educational settings (Davis et al., 2010). Similarly, in the context of the *HANDS* project discussed earlier, Mintz (2013) implemented classroom mobile technology in four schools for children with ASD (ranging in ages from 11–16) located in Denmark, Sweden, Hungary, and the UK. As a result of this work, several factors impacting academic outcomes were identified including motivation level and student awareness of difficulties. For example,

All participants were more motivated to receive the intervention via an app rather than via teacher instruction.

Recently, Vedad and Nirvana (2012) have been developing a learning framework for children with autism (LeFCA) to teach basic skills and concepts. Specifically, their goal is to harness the effectiveness of CAT interventions to increase task motivation. Thus far, they have tested LeFCA in a pilot project with four children with ASD using four games that were developed to promote children's matching, pointing out (based on visual and auditory stimuli), and labeling skills, which are considered requisite skills for learning among this population. This preliminary work has produced positive results for the framework, with all four participants mastering all programs without any further instructional aids. Moreover, the skills developed have shown generalization to other new mediums and environments. Taken together, these studies substantiate the idea that motivation is an important aspect related to academic gains among children with ASD.

Despite the promising results of the handful of studies that have examined the efficacy of CAT for mediating academic skills among children with autism, many have lacked rigorous examination. Pennington (2010) studied the effectiveness of CAT in teaching academic skills to individuals with ASD, and concluded that although it appears that CAT is effective for teaching some academic skills, only a few studies have included a control group necessary for a rigorous assessment of its efficacy. Further, understanding the capacity of these technologies for advancing academic skills is clouded by several issues such as small sample sizes, inconsistencies in how children's behavior is assessed across studies, and heterogeneity in how ASD has been characterized among research participants. Thus, further research and more rigorous studies are needed to better understand the utility of assistive technology for facilitating the development of academic skills among children with autism.

CONCLUSION

Given the complex and heterogeneous constitution of ASD, remedial strategies aimed at alleviating its impairments must often be tailored to address the specific needs of the individual. Among children with autism entering school, targeted skills training and specialized approaches to teaching may be particularly effective in meeting the core challenges—communication, socialization, academic skills— and the corresponding motivation to master these skills. Increasingly, this training and instruction has been offered via educational technologies (Wainer & Ingersoll, 2010). However, as we have repeatedly noted above, the utility of these technologies remains to be rigorously examined. This challenge awaits the research and practice community dedicated to the psychological and academic well-being of children with ASD and with disabilities in general.

REFERENCES

American Psychiatric Association. (2013). *Diagnostic and statistical manual of mental disorders* (5th ed.). Washington, DC: APA.

Aurora. (2000). *The Aurora project*. Retrieved June, 1, 2013 from http://www.aurora-project.com

Banda, D. R., & Grimmett, E. (2008). Enhancing social and transition behaviors of persons with autism through activity schedules: A review. *Education and Training in Developmental Disabilities*, *43*, 324–333.

Bandura, A. (1977). *Social learning theory*. Englewood Cliffs, NJ: Prentice Hall.

Baxter, S., Enderby, P., Evans, P., & Judge, S. (2012). Barriers and facilitators to the use of high-technology augmentative and alternative communication devices: A systematic review and qualitative synthesis. *International Journal of Language & Communication Disorders*, *47*, 115. doi:10.1111/j.1460-6984.2011.00090.x PMID:22369053

Bellini, S., & Akullian, J. (2007). A meta-analysis of video modeling and video self modeling interventions for children and adolescents with autism spectrum disorders. *Exceptional Children*, *73*, 264–287.

Bellini, S., & Peters, J. (2008). Social skills training for youth with autism spectrum disorders. *Child and Adolescent Psychiatric Clinics of North America*, *17*, 857–873. doi:10.1016/j.chc.2008.06.008 PMID:18775374

Bernard-Opitz, V., Sriram, N., & Nakhoda-Sapuan, S. (2001). Enhancing social problem solving in children with autism and normal children through computer-assisted instruction. *Journal of Autism and Developmental Disorders*, *31*, 377–384. doi:10.1023/A:1010660502130 PMID:11569584

Bondy, A. S., & Frost, L. A. (1994). The picture exchange communication system. *Focus on Autistic Behavior*, *9*, 1–19.

Bondy, A. S., & Frost, L. A. (1998). The picture exchange communication system. *Seminars in Speech and Language*, *19*, 373–398. doi:10.1055/s-2008-1064055 PMID:9857393

Bosseler, A., & Massaro, D. W. (2003). Development and evaluation of a computer-animated tutor for vocabulary and language learning in children with autism. *Journal of Autism and Developmental Disorders*, *33*, 653–672. doi:10.1023/B:JADD.0000006002.82367.4f PMID:14714934

Browder, D. M., & Cooper-Duffy, K. (2003). Evidence-based practices for students with severe disabilities and the requirements for accountability in no child left behind. *The Journal of Special Education, 37*, 57–163. doi:10.1177/00224669 030370030501

Cafiero, J. M. (2001). The effect of an augmentative communication intervention on the communication, behavior, and academic program of an adolescent with autism. *Focus on Autism and Other Developmental Disabilities, 16*, 179–189. doi:10.1177/108835760101600306

Cafiero, J. M. (2008). Technology supports for individuals with autism spectrum disorder. *Technology in Action, 3*, 1–12.

Campbell, J. M. (2011). Review supports use of aided augmentative and alternative communication (AAC) systems for improving communication skills for individuals with autism spectrum disorders: The role of moderators is not yet clearly established. *Evidence-Based Communication Assessment and Intervention, 5*, 187–192. doi:10.1 080/17489539.2012.688624

CDC. (2013). *Autism spectrum disorders (ASD)*. Retrieved from http://www.cdc.gov/ncbddd/autism/treatment.html

Charlop-Christy, M. H., & Daneshvar, S. (2003). Using video modeling to teach perspective taking to children with autism. *Journal of Positive Behavior Interventions, 5*, 12–21. doi:10.1177/1 0983007030050010101

Charlop-Christy, M. H., Le, L., & Freeman, K. A. (2000). A comparison of video modeling with in vivo modeling for teaching children with autism. *Journal of Autism and Developmental Disorders, 30*, 537–552. doi:10.1023/A:1005635326276 PMID:11261466

Checkley, R., Reidy, L., Chantler, S., Hodge, N., & Holmes, K. (2012). Black white zebra orange orange: How children with autism make use of computer-based voice output communication aids in their language and communication at school. *Journal of Assistive Technologies, 6*, 245. doi:10.1108/17549451211285744

Cihak, D., Fahrenkroq, C., Ayres, K. M., & Smith, C. (2009). The use of video modeling via a video iPod and a system of least prompts to improve transitional behaviors for students with autism spectrum disorders in the general education classroom. *Journal of Positive Behavior Interventions, 1*, 1–13.

Cobb, S., Kerr, S., & Glover, T. (2001). The AS interactive project: Developing virtual environments for social skills training in users with Asperger syndrome. In K. Dautenhahn (Ed.), *Robotic and virtual interactive systems in autism therapy*. Hatfield, UK: University of Hertfordshire.

Coyle, C., & Cole, P. (2004). A videotaped self-modeling and self-monitoring treatment program to decrease off-task behavior in children with autism. *Journal of Intellectual & Developmental Disability, 29*, 3–15. doi:10.1080/08927020410 001662642

Dattilo, J., & Camarata, S. (1991). Facilitating conversation through self-initiated augmentative communication treatment. *Journal of Applied Behavior Analysis, 24*, 369–378. doi:10.1901/ jaba.1991.24-369 PMID:1890052

Dautenhahan, K., & Werry, I. (2004). Towards interactive robots in autism therapy: Background, motivation and challenges. *Pragmatics & Cognition, 12*, 1–35. doi:10.1075/pc.12.1.03dau

Dautenhahn, K. (2003). Roles and functions of robots in human society: Implications from research in autism therapy. *Robotica, 21*, 443–452. doi:10.1017/S0263574703004922

Davis, M., Dautenhahn, K., Powell, S., & Nehaniv, C. (2010). Guidelines for researchers and facilitators designing software and software trials for children with autism. *Journal of Assistive Technologies*, *4*, 38–48. doi:10.5042/jat.2010.0043

Diehl, J. J., Schmitt, L. M., Villano, M., & Crowell, C. R. (2011). The clinical use of robots for individuals with autism spectrum disorders: A critical review. *Research in Autism Spectrum Disorders*, *6*, 249–262. doi:10.1016/j.rasd.2011.05.006 PMID:22125579

DiGennaro Reed, F. D., Hyman, S. R., & Hirst, J. M. (2011). Applications of technology to teach social skills to children with autism. *Research in Autism Spectrum Disorders*, *5*, 1003–1010. doi:10.1016/j.rasd.2011.01.022

Dunn, L. M., & Dunn, L. M. (1981). *Peabody picture vocabulary test, revised*. American Guidance Service.

Durkin, K. (2010). Videogames and young people with developmental disorders. *Review of General Psychology*, *14*, 122–140. doi:10.1037/a0019438

Durkin, K., Boyle, J., Hunter, S., & Conti-Ramsden, G. (2013). Video games for children and adolescents with special educational needs. *Zeitschrift fur Psychologie mit Zeitschrift fur Angewandte Psychologie*, *221*, 79–89. doi: doi:10.1027/2151-2604/a000138

Fitzgerald, G., Koury, K., & Mitchem, K. (2008). Research on computer-mediated instruction for students with high incidence disabilities. *Journal of Educational Computing Research*, *38*, 201–233. doi:10.2190/EC.38.2.e

Fogg, B. J. (2003). *Persuasive technology: Using computers to change what we think and do*. San Francisco, CA: Morgan Kaufman Publishers. doi:10.1016/B978-155860643-2/50011-1

Fogg, B. J., & Eckles, D. (2007). *Mobile persuasion: 20 perspectives on the future of behavior change*. Stanford, CA: Stanford Captology Media.

Ganz, J. B., Earles-Vollrath, T. L., Heath, A. K., Parker, R. I., Rispoli, M. J., & Duran, J. B. (2012). A meta-analysis of single case research studies on aided augmentative and alternative communication systems with individuals with autism spectrum disorders. *Journal of Autism and Developmental Disorders*, *42*, 60–74. doi:10.1007/s10803-011-1212-2 PMID:21380612

Gerhard, M. (2003). *A hybrid avatar/agent model for educational collaborative virtual environments*. (Unpublished Doctoral Dissertation). Leeds Metropolitan University, Leeds, UK.

Gerhard, M., Moore, D. J., & Hobbs, D. (2004). Embodiment and co-presence in collaborative interfaces. *International Journal of Human-Computer Studies*, *61*(4), 453–480. doi:10.1016/j.ijhcs.2003.12.014

Goldsmith, T. R., & LeBlanc, L. A. (2004). Use of technology in interventions for children with autism. *Journal of Early and Intensive Behavior Intervention*, *1*, 166–178.

Goodwin, M. S. (2008). Enhancing and accelerating the pace of autism research and treatment: The promise of developing innovative technology. *Focus on Autism and Other Developmental Disabilities*, *23*, 125–128. doi:10.1177/1088357608316678

Graham-Rowe, D. (2002). My best friend's a robot. *New Scientist*, *176*, 30–33. PMID:12731520

Happe, F. (1994). Wechsler IQ profile and theory of mind in autism: A research note. *Journal of Child Psychology and Psychiatry, and Allied Disciplines*, *35*, 1461–1471. doi:10.1111/j.1469-7610.1994.tb01287.x PMID:7868640

Heimann, M., Nelson, K. E., Tjus, T., & Gillberg, C. (1995). Increasing reading and communication skills in children with autism through an interactive multimedia computer program. *Journal of Autism and Developmental Disorders*, 25, 459–480. doi:10.1007/BF02178294 PMID:8567593

Higgins, K., & Boone, R. (1996). Creating individualized computer-assisted instruction for students with autism using multimedia. *Focus on Autism and Other Developmental Disabilities*, 11, 69. doi:10.1177/108835769601100202

Horner, R. H., Carr, E. G., Strain, P. S., Todd, A. W., & Reed, H. K. (2002). Problem behavior interventions for young children with autism: A research synthesis. *Journal of Autism and Developmental Disorders*, 32, 423–446. doi:10.1023/A:1020593922901 PMID:12463518

Jacobson, J. W., & Mulick, J. A. (2000). Systems and cost research issues in treatments for people with autistic disorders. *Journal of Autism and Developmental Disorders*, 30, 585–593. doi:10.1023/A:1005691411255 PMID:11261469

Jordan, R. (1995). Computer assisted education for individuals with autism. In *Proceedings from Autisme France 3rd International Conference*. Nice, France: Autisme.

Kamio, Y., & Toichi, M. (2000). Dual access to semantics in autism: Is pictorial access superior to verbal access? *Journal of Child Psychology and Psychiatry, and Allied Disciplines*, 41, 859–867. doi:10.1111/1469-7610.00673 PMID:11079428

Kimball, J. W., Kinney, E. M., Taylor, B. A., & Stromer, R. (2004). Video-enhanced activity schedules for children with autism: A promising package for teaching social skills. *Education & Treatment of Children*, 27, 280–298.

Koch, A. (2012). *Assistive technologies for children with autism spectrum disorders*. Academic Press.

Krantz, P. J., MacDuff, M. T., & McClannahan, L. E. (1993). Programming participation in family activities for children with autism: Parents' use of photographic activity schedules. *Journal of Applied Behavior Analysis*, 26(1), 137–138. doi:10.1901/jaba.1993.26-137 PMID:8473254

Lasater, M. W., & Brady, M. P. (1995). Effects of video self-modeling and feedback on task fluency: A home-based intervention. *Education & Treatment of Children*, 18, 389–408.

Lequia, J., Machalicek, W., & Rispoli, M. J. (2012). Effects of activity schedules on challenging behavior exhibited in children with autism spectrum disorders: A systematic review. *Research in Autism Spectrum Disorders*, 6, 480–492. doi:10.1016/j.rasd.2011.07.008

Lord, C., Wagner, A., Rogers, S., Szatmari, P., Aman, M., & Charman, T. et al. (2005). Challenges in evaluating psychosocial interventions for autistic spectrum disorders. *Journal of Autism and Developmental Disorders*, 35, 695–708. doi:10.1007/s10803-005-0017-6 PMID:16496206

Matson, J., & Wilkins, J. (2007). A critical review of assessment targets and methods for social skills excesses and deficits for children with autism spectrum disorders. *Research in Autism Spectrum Disorders*, 1, 28–37. doi:10.1016/j.rasd.2006.07.003

McMillan, J. M. (2008). Teachers make it happen: From professional development to integration of augmentative and alternative communication technologies in the classroom. *Australasian Journal of Special Education*, 32, 199–211. doi:10.1080/10300110802047467

Millar, D., Light, J., & Schlosser, R. (2006). The impact of augmentative and alternative communication on the speech production of individuals with developmental disabilities: A research review. *Journal of Speech, Language, and Hearing Research: JSLHR, 49*, 248–264. doi:10.1044/1092-4388(2006/021) PMID:16671842

Mintz, J. (2013). Additional key factors mediating the use of a mobile technology tool designed to develop social and life skills in children with autism spectrum disorders: Evaluation of the 2nd HANDS prototype. *Computers & Education, 63*, 17–27. doi:10.1016/j.compedu.2012.11.006

Mitchell, P., Parsons, S., & Leonard, A. (2007). Using virtual environments for teaching social understanding to 6 adolescents with autistic spectrum disorders. *Journal of Autism and Developmental Disorders, 37*, 589–600. doi:10.1007/s10803-006-0189-8 PMID:16900403

Moore, D., Cheng, Y., McGrath, P., & Powell, N. J. (2005). Collaborative virtual environment technology for people with autism. *Focus on Autism and Other Developmental Disabilities, 20*, 231–243. doi:10.1177/10883576050200040501

Moore, M., & Calvert, S. (2000). Brief report: Vocabulary acquisition for children with autism: Teacher or computer instruction. *Journal of Autism and Developmental Disorders, 30*, 359–362. doi:10.1023/A:1005535602064 PMID:11039862

Murray, D. K. C. (1997). Autism and information technology: Therapy with computers. In *Autism and learning: A guide to good practice.* Academic Press.

National Autism Center. (2009). *Evidence-based practice and autism in the schools: A guide to providing appropriate interventions to students with autism spectrum disorders.* Randolph, MA: National Autism Center.

National Autism Center. (2009). *National standards report.* Randolph, MA: National Autism Center.

National Center for Learning Disabilities, Inc. (2013). *Individualized education plan.* National Center for Learning Disabilities. Retrieved July 4, 2013 from http://www.ncld.org/students-disabilities/iep-504-plan/what-is-iep

National Research Council, Committee on Educational Interventions for Children with Autism, Division of Behavioral and Social Sciences and Education. (2001). *Educating children with autism.* Washington, DC: National Academy Press.

Neale, H., Cobb, S., & Wilson, J. (2002). A front-ended approach to the user-centered design of virtual environments. [Los Alamitos, CA: IEEE.]. *Proceedings of IEEE Virtual Reality, 2002*, 191–198.

Nikopoulos, C. K., & Keenan, M. (2007). Using video modeling to teach complex social sequences to children with autism. *Journal of Autism and Developmental Disorders, 37*, 678–693. doi:10.1007/s10803-006-0195-x PMID:16897375

O'Reilly, M. F., Lancioni, G. E., Lang, R., & Rispoli, M. (2011). Teaching functional use of an iPod-based speech-generating device to individuals with developmental disabilities. *Journal of Special Education Technology, 26*(3), 1–10.

Ogilvie, C. R. (2011). Step by step: Social skills instruction for students with autism spectrum disorder using video models and peer mentors. *Teaching Exceptional Children, 43*, 20–26.

Pennington, R. C. (2010). Computer-assisted instruction for teaching academic skills to students with autism spectrum disorders: A review of literature. *Focus on Autism and Other Developmental Disabilities, 25*, 239–248. doi:10.1177/1088357610378291

Ploog, B. O., Scharf, A., Nelson, D., & Brooks, P. J. (2013). Use of computer-assisted technologies (CAT) to enhance social, communicative, and language development in children with autism spectrum disorders. *Journal of Autism and Developmental Disorders*, *43*, 301–322. doi:10.1007/s10803-012-1571-3 PMID:22706582

Ramdoss, S., Lang, R., Mulloy, A., Franco, J., O'Reilly, M., Didden, R., & Lancioni, G. (2011). Use of computer-based interventions to teach communication skills to children with autism spectrum disorders: A systematic review. *Journal of Behavioral Education*, *20*, 55–76. doi:10.1007/s10864-010-9112-7

Rehfeldt, R. A., Kinney, E. M., Root, S., & Stromer, R. (2004). Creating activity schedules using Microsoft PowerPoint. *Journal of Applied Behavior Analysis*, *37*, 115–128. doi:10.1901/jaba.2004.37-115 PMID:15154226

Retherford, K., & Sterling-Orth, A. (2009). Facilitating functional social communication skills in adolescents. *Journal of Autism and Developmental Disorders*, *32*, 535–543.

Rispoli, M., Franco, J. H., van der Meer, L., Lang, R., & Camargo, S. (2010). The use of speech generating devices in communication interventions for individuals with developmental disabilities: A review of the literature. *Developmental Neurorehabilitation*, *13*(4), 276–293. doi:10.3109/17518421003636794 PMID:20629594

Ritterfeld, U., & Weber, R. (2005). Video games for entertainment and education. In P. Vorderer, & J. Bryant (Eds.), *Playing video games - Motives, responses, and consequences* (pp. 399–413). Mahwah, NJ: Lawrence Erlbaum.

Schepis, M. M., Reid, D. H., & Behrmann, M. M. (1996). Acquisition and functional use of voice output communication by persons with profound multiple disabilities. *Behavior Modification*, *20*, 451–468. doi:10.1177/01454455960204005 PMID:8875815

Schepis, M. M., Reid, D. H., Behrmann, M. M., & Sutton, K. A. (1998). Increasing communicative interactions of young children with autism using a voice output communication aid and naturalistic teaching. *Journal of Applied Behavior Analysis*, *31*, 561–578. doi:10.1901/jaba.1998.31-561 PMID:9891394

Schlosser, R., & Lee, D. (2000). Promoting generalization and maintenance in augmentative and alternative communication: A meta-analysis of 20 years of effectiveness research. *Augmentative and Alternative Communication*, *16*, 208–226. doi:10.1080/07434610012331279074

Schwartz, I. S., Garfinkle, A. N., & Bauer, J. (1998). The picture exchange communication system: Communication outcomes for young children with disabilities. *Topics in Early Childhood Special Education*, *18*, 144–159. doi:10.1177/027112149801800305

Sennott, S., & Bowker, A. (2009). Autism, AAC, & Proloquo2Go. *Perspectives on Augmentative and Alternative Communication*, *18*, 137–145. doi:10.1044/aac18.4.137

Shane, H. C., Laubscher, E. H., Schlosser, R. W., Flynn, S., Sorce, J. F., & Abramson, J. (2012). Applying technology to visually support language and communication in individuals with autism spectrum disorders. *Journal of Autism and Developmental Disorders*, *37*, 1228–1235. doi:10.1007/s10803-011-1304-z PMID:21691867

Sherer, M., Pierce, K. L., Paredes, S., Kisacky, K. L., Ingersoll, B., & Schreibman, L. (2001). Enhancing conversation skills in children with autism via video technology: Which is better, "Self" or "Other" as a model? *Behavior Modification*, *25*, 140–148. doi:10.1177/0145445501251008 PMID:11151482

Shipley-Benamou, R., Lutzker, J. R., & Taubman, M. (2002). Teaching daily living skills to children with autism through instructional video modeling. *Journal of Positive Behavior Interventions*, *4*, 165–175. doi:10.1177/10983007020040030501

Simpson, A., Langone, J., & Ayres, K. (2004). Embedded video and computer based instruction to improve social skills for students with autism. *Education and Training in Developmental Disabilities*, *39*, 240–252.

Smith, T., Scahill, L., Dawson, G., Guthrie, D., Lord, C., & Odom, S. et al. (2007). Designing research studies on psychosocial interventions in autism. *Journal of Autism and Developmental Disorders*, *37*, 354–366. doi:10.1007/s10803-006-0173-3 PMID:16897380

Stokes, S. (n.d.). *Assistive technology for children with autism*. Retrieved from http://www.specialed.us/autism/assist/asst10.htm

Strickland, D., McAllister, D., Coles, C. D., & Osborne, S. (2007). An evolution of virtual reality training designs for children with autism and fetal alcohol spectrum disorders. *Topics in Language Development*, *27*, 226–241. doi:10.1097/01.TLD.0000285357.95426.72 PMID:20072702

Takanori, K., & Hui-Ting, W. (n.d.). Review article: Use of activity schedule to promote independent performance of individuals with autism and other intellectual disabilities: A review. *Research in Developmental Disabilities*, *32*, 2235-2242, doi:10.1016/j.ridd.2011.05.03

Tentori, M., & Hayes, G. (2010). Designing for interaction immediacy to enhance social skills of children with autism. In J. Bardram, M. Langhenreich, K. Truong, & P. Nixon (Eds.), *Proceedings of the 12th ACM International Conference on Ubiquitous Computing* (pp. 51–60). New York, NY: The ACM Press. http://dx.doi.org/10.1145/1864349.1864359

Thiemann, K. S., & Goldstein, H. (2001). Social stories, written text cues, and video feedback: Effects on social communication of children with autism. *Journal of Applied Behavior Analysis*, *34*, 425–446. doi:10.1901/jaba.2001.34-425 PMID:11800183

Tien, K. C. (2008). Effectiveness of the picture exchange communication system as a functional communication intervention for individuals with autism-spectrum disorders: A practice-based research synthesis. *Education and Training in Developmental Disabilities*, *43*, 61–76.

University of Maine Center for Community Inclusion and Disability. (2009). *A review of evidence-based practices for students with autism spectrum disorders*. Portland, ME: Kurtz.

Van der Meer, L., Sigafoos, J., O'Reilly, M. F., & Lancioni, G. E. (2011). Assessing preferences for AAC options in communication interventions for individuals with developmental disabilities: A review of the literature. *Research in Developmental Disabilities*, *32*, 1422–1431. doi:10.1016/j.ridd.2011.02.003 PMID:21377833

Vedad, H., & Nirvana, P. (2012). LeFCA: Learning framework for children with autism. *Procedia Computer Science*, *15*, 4–16. doi:10.1016/j.procs.2012.10.052

Wainer, A. L., & Ingersoll, R. (2010). The use of innovative computer technology for teaching social communication to individuals with autism spectrum disorders. *Research in Autism Spectrum Disorders*, 5, 96–107. doi:10.1016/j.rasd.2010.08.002

Wallace, S., Parsons, S., Westbury, A., White, K., White, K., & Bailey, A. (2010). Sense of presence and atypical social judgments in immersive virtual environments. Responses of adolescents with autism spectrum disorders. *Autism*, 14, 199–213. doi:10.1177/1362361310363283 PMID:20484000

Walton, K. M., & Ingersoll, B. R. (2012). Improving social skills in adolescents and adults with autism and severe to profound intellectual disability: A review of the literature. *Journal of Autism and Developmental Disorders*, 43, 594–615. doi:10.1007/s10803-012-1601-1 PMID:22790427

Wert, Y. B., & Neisworth, J. T. (2003). Effects of video self-modeling on spontaneous requesting in children with autism. *Journal of Positive Behavior Interventions*, 5(1), 30–34. doi:10.1177/109830 07030050010501

Whelan, C., & Cernich, S. (2007). *Proceedings from the association for behavior analysis international (ABAI) conference '07: Assessment of motivation during reward games vs. learning trials using TeachTown: Basics*. ABAI.

Whelan, C., Cernich, S., Lockhart, D., Liden, L., & Vaupel, M. (2009). *Proceedings from the international meeting for autism research (IMFAR) '09: Analysis of usage of TeachTown: Basics with 1,100 subscribers*. IMFAR.

Whelan, C., Linden, L., Ingersoll, B., Dallaire, E., & Linden, S. (2006). Positive behavioral changes associated with the use of computer-assisted instruction for young children. *Journal of Speech and Language Pathology and Applied Behavioral Analysis*, 1(1), 11–26.

Whelan, C., Moss, D., Ilan, A. B., Vaupel, M., Fielding, P., & MacDonald, K. (2010). Efficacy of TeachTown: Basics computer-assisted intervention for the intensive comprehensive autism program in Los Angeles Unified School District. *Autism*, 14, 179–197. doi:10.1177/1362361310363282 PMID:20484002

Williams, C., Wright, B., Callaghan, G., & Coughlan, B. (2002). Do children with autism learn to read more readily by computer assisted instruction or traditional book methods? A pilot study. *SAGE Publications and the National Autistic Society*, 6, 71–91. PMID:11918110

Wyman, B., & Stobbe, G. (2006). A case study. Presented at the Association for Behavior Analysis International (ABAI) Conference, Seattle, WA.

Chapter 2

Addressing Executive Function Using Assistive Technology to Increase Access to the 21st Century Skills

Brenda Smith Myles
Ohio Center for Autism and Low Incidence, USA

Jan Rogers
Ohio Center for Autism and Low Incidence, USA

ABSTRACT

Access to the common core and the general education environment are attainable goals for learners on the autism spectrum when their autism is clearly understood and meaningful supports and instruction are in place. This chapter focuses on one area that is often not addressed for students with Autism Spectrum Disorders (ASD) yet is critical to academic success: executive function. Specifically, this chapter overviews the executive function challenges related to ASD and technology supports in the executive functions areas of (a) information management, (b) materials management, (c) time management, and (d) self-management.

INTRODUCTION

The outcomes of adults with autism in terms of independent living, developing and maintaining meaningful relationships, and employment have generally been consistent since the 1960s (Henninger & Taylor, 2012). That is, sadly, the majority do not achieve a high quality of life – a finding that has been validated by self-reports of individuals with high-functioning autism spectrum disorders (HFASD) (Müller, Schuler, & Yates, 2008) as well

as results of the National Longitudinal Transition Study (NLTS2) (Shattuck et al., 2012).

How can this dismal trajectory be changed? Learner outcomes will improve when they are taught meaningful skills. The 21st Century Student Outcomes and Support Systems (Partnership for 21st Century Skills, n.d.) have formally recognized that life success goes beyond academics by incorporating a focus on (a) Life and Career Skills; (b) Learning and Innovation Skills; and (c) Information, Media, and Technology Skills (see

DOI: 10.4018/978-1-4666-5792-2.ch002

Table 1 for a brief description of these areas). In addition, it is important match the skills that need to be taught to evidence-based practices (EBP) – strategies that have been shown to be effective for learners on the spectrum (Centers for Medicare and Medicaid Services [CMS], 2010; National Autism Center [NAC], 2009; National Professional Development Center on ASD [NPDC], 2009) (see overview in Table 2).

While these competencies encompass numerous skills areas, many are related to a core challenge in autism spectrum disorders (ASD): executive function (EF). For the purposes of this chapter, EF skills are defined as those that allow us to (a) manage, organize, and process relevant information while screening out irrelevant stimuli; (b) manage the environment, including materials and space; (c) manage time; and (d) manage self, including regulating our behavior and emotions.

EF skills pose lifelong challenges for individuals with ASD; indeed, rather than decreasing, they increase with age (Rosenthal et al., 2013). That is, it is expected that all individuals, not just those with autism will assume responsibility for organizing themselves, their environment, time, and regulating their own behavior. As a result, when learners on the spectrum do not exhibit these skills, it does not mean that their behavior is willful. Rather, their lack of competence in this area reflects the failure of those who support them to provide appropriate instruction and/or supports in the aforementioned areas. That is, these skills are often assumed to be in place instead of directly taught and supported.

This chapter begins with an overview of AT, and is followed by a discussion of how AT can benefit learners with autism in (a) information management/processing, (b) materials management, (c) time management, and (d) self-management.

Table 1. 21ˢᵗ century student outcomes

Outcomes	Skill Areas
Core Subjects and 21ˢᵗCentury Themes	English, reading or language arts World languages Arts Mathematics Economics Geography History, government, and civics Global awareness Financial, economic, business, and entrepreneurial literacy Civic literacy Health literacy Environmental literacy
Life and Career Skills	Flexibility and adaptability Initiative and self-direction Social and cross-cultural skills Productivity and accountability Leadership and responsibility
Learning and Innovation Skills	Critical thinking Communication Collaboration Creativity
Information, Media and Technology Skills	Information literacy Media literacy Information, communications, and technology

Note. Partnership for 21ˢᵗ Century Skills (n.d.).

Table 2. Evidence-Based Practices (EBP)

Intervention	Centers for Medicare and Medicaid Services (CMS)	National Autism Center (NAC)	National Professional Development Center on ASD (NPDC)
ANTECEDENT INTERVENTIONS **Interventions put in place before the occurrence of a behavior to prevent it from occurring.**			
Antecedent Package	X	X	X
Structured Teaching	X		X
Visual Supports			X
Schedules	X	X	
APPLIED BEHAVIOR ANALYSIS INTERVENTIONS **Interventions based on the science of applied behavior analysis.**			
Comprehensive Behavioral Package	X	X	
Differential Reinforcement			X
Discrete Trial Training			X
Extinction			X
Prompting			X
Time Delay			X
Modeling, Including Video Modeling	X	X	X
Reinforcement			X
Response, Interruption, Redirection			X
Task Analysis			X
Functional Behavior Assessment			X
COGNITIVE INTERVENTIONS **Interventions designed to change negative or unrealistic thought patterns/behaviors to positively influencing emotions/life functioning.**			
Cognitive Behavioral Intervention Package	X		
MULTI-COMPONENT INTERVENTIONS **Interventions involve a combination of multiple treatment procedures that are derived from different fields of interest or different theoretical orientations.**			
Multi-Component Package	X		
NATURALISTIC TEACHING STRATEGIES **Instructional strategies used in the individual's natural environments that focus in play, conversation, providing reinforcement, and direct/natural reinforcement.**			
Naturalistic Teaching Strategies	X	X	X
Pivotal Response Treatment	X	X	X
NONPROVIDER-BASED INTERVENTIONS **Interventions provided by parents and peers.**			
Parent-Implemented Interventions			X
Peer Training Package	X	X	X
SELF-MANAGEMENT **Interventions that teach individuals with ASD to regulate their behavior.**			
Self-Management	X	X	X

continued on following page

Table 2. Continued

Intervention	Centers for Medicare and Medicaid Services (CMS)	National Autism Center (NAC)	National Professional Development Center on ASD (NPDC)
SOCIAL AND COMMUNICATION INTERVENTIONS Psychosocial interventions involve targeting some combination impairments such as pragmatic communication skills and the inability to successfully read social situations.			
Joint Attention	X	X	
Picture Exchange Communication System	X		X
Social Communication Intervention	X		
Social Skills Groups			X
Social Skills Package	X		
Story-Based Intervention Package	X	X	
Social Narratives			X
Speech-Generating Devices			X
TECHNOLOGY-BASED INTERVENTIONS The presentation of instructional materials using the medium of computers or related technologies.			
Technology-Based Treatment	X		
Computer-Aided Instruction			X

Note. NAC = National Autism Center; CMS = Centers for Medicare and Medicaid Services; NPDC = National Professional Development Center.

Overview of AT

Before looking at the various types of technology tools that may support students with difficulties related to EF, it is important to define AT and consider the importance of a comprehensive AT assessment for determining the best AT to meet the student's needs.

The Individuals With Disabilities Education Improvement Act (2004) defines AT as any item, piece of equipment, or product system, commercial, modified, or customized, that is used to increase, maintain, or improve the functional capabilities of a child with a disability. This does not include medical devices that are surgically implanted or the replacement of such devices.

AT is different from educational or instructional technology. Educational or instructional technologies are typically used by all students for the purpose of enhancing general learning. Examples of instructional or educational technologies include interactive white boards, drill and practice educational software, computers, laptops and tablet technologies. AT, however, are those technologies that are specifically needed by a student with a disability to access the curriculum or school activities. As such, it is often a scaffold to help overcome a barrier to participation. Further, since it is required by the student to gain access, it is not an optional support. Therefore, AT is not defined by a specific product or device, but by the way it is used and needed by the student.

Devices, such as a Braille note taker, that are not used by the general population are easy to recognize as AT. However, items such as iPads™ or laptop computers, which are used by the general population, may also be considered AT under certain circumstances: when they allow a learner to access a portion of her life that might not otherwise be available. For example, an iPad that contains customized social narratives may be instrumental in helping a learner with autism develop and maintain relationships or seek help in an appropriate manner.

As for any other aspect of educational programming, assessment must be the starting point when identifying effective technologies to meet the needs of a student. Too often attempts are made to retrofit technology that has already been purchased, is available in the student's environment, or is perceived as the "latest and greatest" new technology. Such attempts, however well-meaning, often lead to a poor match between the true needs of the student and the capacity of the technology to meet those needs.

An AT assessment is best conducted by a team of individuals who know the student well and have the professional expertise to identify his strengths and needs and/or are knowledgeable about AT. The student, family, and other significant others in the student's life should also be included in the assessment process.

To help guide the team's discussion of a student's AT needs, Zabala (2002) has proposed a framework called SETT – an acronym for Student, Environment, Tasks, and Tools. Thus, using the SETT framework, the team discusses the student's strengths and needs, the environments where the student will be engaging in tasks, the tasks the student will engage in, and finally the tools that might meet the needs of the student given the environments and tasks.

While the team does not need to know about all AT tools that are available in the market place, it is essential that team members know about the features offered by AT tools. Thus, it is the matching of these features to student needs, environments, and tasks that ensures that a given AT provides the appropriate type and amount of support for the student and creates the potential for a positive student outcome. Table 3 presents an overview of the SETT framework (Bowser & Reed, 2001; Zabala, 2002). Additional information may be found at http://www.joyzabala.com.

AT Features that are Often Helpful for Students with ASD

The following sections present the features of AT that may be useful for students with ASDs who have difficulties with EF, along with examples of available technologies that contain those features. Technology is rapidly changing, and products come and go; however, many features remain relatively stable over time with additional features being added to products. Therefore, it is important is to gain an understanding of the features and how they match student needs rather than the product examples provided, which are merely a few of the many possibilities. Further, it is likely that a student would need a combination of features to meet her needs, and it is this combination of features that ultimately drives the final product selection. Finally, it is important to conduct product trials before purchase to ensure an effective match.

Information management/processing: Students with autism often have difficulties learning and managing information if the task or information is complex and/or contains multiple components (Sumiyoshi, Kawakubo, Suga, Sumiyoshi, & Kasai, 2011). Though learners with ASD have good rote skills and the ability to interpret discrete or small units of information, difficulties ensue when they are asked to integrate and organize more complex information (Tsatsanis et al., 2010). Further, concomitant deficits often exist in planning, flexibility, and integrating and evaluating multiple variables, particularly when tasks become more difficult (Sachse et al., 2103). Within this context, organization of information and processing thereof is often referred to as the "forgotten executive function" in ASD (Kenworthy et al., 2005). Difficulties in these EF skills have been linked to reading comprehensive deficits (Locascio, Mahone, Eason, & Cutting, 2010), which impact almost all academic areas.

Table 3. SETT framework

Framework	Considerations
Student	What are the learner's functional area(s) of concern? What are the student's current abilities, special needs, and interests? Who is involved in the support of this student? What are staff's talents – individually and collectively? How familiar is the staff with the learner and how comfortable are they with the student? What administrative support is available to the student?
Environments	What is the instructional and physical arrangement of the environment? What supports are available to the learner and the staff? What specific materials and equipment are commonly used by others in the environment(s)? What specific technology, physical, instructional access issues must be addressed? What resources (i.e., time, money, people, furniture, physical resources) should be considered when planning for AT selection and use? What are the attitudes and expectations of the learner, staff, family, and others and how will this impact AT selection and use?
Tasks	What tasks occur in the natural environment(s) that support progress toward mastery of individualized education program (IEP) goals and benchmarks? Which supports and tasks are needed to support active involvement in the areas of communication, instruction, participation, productivity, and environmental control? How will the team implement collaborative and shared planning and delivery of services and training? How, when and where should training occur for staff? How many students are in the environment(s)? How can they be included in AT training and use? Who will be responsible for tool programming, trouble shooting, and maintenance? How will staff learn strategies to integration tools into the learner's program?
Tools	What system of supports, devices and services can be used to facilitate tasks and match student and environmental elements? Which tool(s) within the system are most promising for the natural environment(s)? Does the staff have knowledge of the tool(s)? If not, how will they be trained? What is the role of each staff member and peers regarding the tool(s)? What strategies will be used to ensure that the learner can use the tool(s) independently? What specific changes will the learner exhibit as a result of tool(s) use? What type of data will be collected? Who will collect it and when? When will it be analyzed? How will the analyzed data be used?

Note. Adapted from Bowser & Reed (2001) and Zabala (2002)

Features of technology to support information management include text clarification techniques, visual simplification of content, visual supports such as highlighting, masking, text extraction, and summarizing to emphasize key concepts/content, and provision of information in alternate visual formats such as outlines, graphic organizers, plots and graphs, concept maps, mind maps, webbing, and so on. These types of supports can enhance understanding and consequently storage of information. They fall under the EBP of antecedent, naturalistic, and technology-based interventions (CMS, 2010; NAC, 2009; NPDC, 2009). Below, we will take a closer look at the major categories of information management supports.

Text clarification: Text clarification supports provide additional information to help support the student's understanding of the content through vocabulary supports or restating of the information in alternate ways that are more relevant to the student's understanding. They can be as simple as using low-tech sticky notes to add supporting information for written information or they can be higher tech support such as hyperlinks to supporting information found within in-line dictionaries or embedded digital sticky notes. Such supports typically allow the full content to be viewable by the student, but open a small window with the additional information. Some dictionaries, such as those in Read and Write (Texthelp, 2013), provide picture supports to accompany the text definitions. Most of the higher tech text clarifications supports are found as features in comprehensive reading and writing software programs, such as Kurzweil 3000 Reading Writing Learning Education Software (Kurzweil Educational Systems, 2011) and Read&Write Gold (Texthelp, 2013).

Text clarification supports are likely most useful for students who can manage to process all content presented at one time but need occasional supports for clarification to enhance the understanding of the information provided.

Visual simplification: Text visual simplification supports provide the full text information, but in an on-line environment with reduced visual clutter. These types of supports are useful when students find it difficult to process and manage information presented on a website because of competing pictures and advertisements.

Two examples of visual simplification products include Readability, a Firefox browser extension, and the Reader feature of the Safari browser. When enabled, both transform cluttered web pages into text that contains only pictures that are relevant to the content. The text is also often presented without columns and may be enlarged. Though, these products are limited in that they seem to work best on certain types of web pages that are primarily in a news article format.

Visual supports: When students are unable to manage all the content at once, alternate technologies need to be explored (cf. Schopler & Mesibov, 1995). For example, content can be chunked using a variety of technology supports depending on the student's needs. Such supports include electronic highlighting, masking, text extraction, and text summarization. Most of these supports are found as features in the major reading and writing software noted previously.

Electronic highlighting is used to bring attention to the most relevant information and often offers a selection of colors. Some programs allow for labeling the highlighters (e.g., one highlighter color labels the main idea and another, labels

supporting statements), others allow for text extraction of the highlighted information, placing the information into a separate document in an outline form if desired.

Masking provides the opposite function of highlighting by hiding the non-relevant or allowing the user to view only a limited amount of the text at one time. Electronic masks can generally be custom-set for the amount of information to be made available to the student at one time.

Finally, electronic summarizing extracts the non-relevant text, leaving the most critical text for the student. Older versions of Microsoft Office (MS) contain a summarizing feature that allows a choice of the percentage of information to remain after being summarized, as well as the preferred display of the summarized information (e.g., as a separate document, highlighted within the same document, added as an abstract to the same document). Unfortunately, this feature was recently removed from MS Word. However, the website www.textcompactor.com (Knowledge by Design, 2012) provides some of the same functionality as the MS Word summarization feature. Text can be cut and pasted into the website with the user given a choice of the percentage of information to remain after summarization.

Alternate visual formats: Electronic graphic organizers, such as Inspiration 9 (Inspiration, 2010) and Kidspiration 3 (Inspiration, 2008), allow for information to be displayed in alternate ways rather than using strictly text and can assist in chunking information into more manageable pieces. Most of these types of technologies allow for mind mapping, concepts maps, webbing, and outlines. Information can be associated with images that can be displayed in various hierarchical formats or alternately in outline formats, including pictures and auditory supports.

Visually representing information in various formats allows students to explore and link concepts and understand relationships contained in the information. One of the benefits of electronic graphic organizers is the ease with which the information can be visually altered with minimal effort, often by the click of the mouse or the tap of a touch screen, or by toggling between different visual representations to gain a better understanding of the information and the relationships among the components of the information.

Materials management: Keeping track of the materials needed to participate effectively in the school setting can be challenging. For example, a multitude of items, such as pencils, pens, glue, scissors, papers, textbooks, lunch money, coats, and so on, need to be located quickly during classroom and school activities. The demands of materials management generally become more challenging as the student advances in grades – from a single classroom and individual desks in the elementary years to multiple classrooms at the secondary school level and classrooms in multiple buildings at the college level.

Difficulty in managing materials is related to several areas of EF, including working memory, the ability to actively hold multiple items in mind so that they can be manipulated, as well as distractibility and attention to task (Kenworthy et al., 2005). In addition, many learners with ASD demonstrate a gap between knowledge and the ability to act on that knowledge. That is, while some learners on the spectrum recognize that they need paper and a textbook for a task, they may have difficulty acting on this information. For example, students with ASD may have difficulty formulating a question, managing their anxiety, and/or initiating a motor sequence to obtain needed supplies (Gilotty, Kenworthy, Sirian, Black, & Wagner, 2002).

Problems in organizing materials may also be related to central coherence challenges, which are common among individuals with autism. Central coherence is the innate ability to detect meaningful links across a broad range of stimuli, identify relevant from irrelevant attributes, and make generalizations across contexts (Aljunied & Frederickson, 2013). According to Happé and Frith (2006), weak central coherence leads to

a focus on parts of objects instead of the entire task. It also inhibits the formation of categories. As a result, students with autism may focus on a particular material needed for an assignment but may not have developed an internal category of "supplies needed for science class" or "test-taking materials" (Bock, 1999, 2007).

Technology to enhance materials management skills generally centers around supports to assist students in organizing and locating materials, such as visual cues and containment (i.e., notebooks, pencil boxes); in terms of EBP, they considered antecedent, naturalistic, and technology-based interventions (CMS, 2010; NAC, 2009; NPDC, 2009).

Visual cues include color-coding, numbering, and icon/picture systems. They may be used to label physical containment systems, such as folders, papers, notebooks, and so forth. Other physical containment systems include lockers and backpack organizers and containers and organizers for tools (e.g., pencils, pens, erasers, and scissors).

As computers have become more commonplace in schools, these systems can offer the option of providing digital containment for student materials. That is, they can be used to produce, store, and distribute student work. Thus, it is no longer necessary to keep track of writing utensils, art materials, paper, and so on, as separate items, since they are all contained within the computer system. In turn, this helps reduce the loss of papers and other items that otherwise plague many students, while providing a single location in which to search for missing items. In addition, cloud computing allows storing items in a location that can be easily accessed by multiple pieces of hardware. For example, if a student inadvertently leaves her laptop at school, she can still access her work and information on another computer at home.

Finally, as schools and universities increase their use of learning management systems, it is likely they will discover that these environments provide many benefits for students who struggle with organizational skills. On-line classes provide the ultimate in digital containment by delivering information via a learning management system with little need to work outside of the system. It is possible to house most of all student learning materials and activities within these systems including project assignments, readings, videos and other supporting materials. In addition, students can complete assignments by entering responses into these systems to allow for long-term storage and organization of the student's work and archiving teacher feedback. Students can also participate in discussion boards and interact with a course instructor through text, audio, or video modes that are again managed and organized by the learning management system. Finally, teacher assignments, learning materials or student responses to assignments are easily sorted and retrieved by the student if and when they are needed at a later date.

Time management: Time management includes the ability to (a) set goals and priorities; (b) use mechanics, such as making lists or schedules, to reach these goals; and (c) identify organizational preferences. These skills, in turn, give an individual a sense of control over time which, in turn, leads to less tension, fewer health complaints, a high degree or satisfaction, and high performance levels (cf. Fenner & Renn, 2009; Macan, 1994).

Time management can be difficult for students with autism for a variety of reasons, including difficulty related to (a) understanding traditional clocks and calendars; (b) time perception; (c) working memory, which impacts the ability to monitor elapsed time; (d) planning the steps necessary to complete a project or task to meet timelines; and (e) shifting or maintaining attention from one thing to another to complete tasks to meet time requirements (Kenworthy et al., 2005; Sumiyoshi et al., 2011; Wallace & Happé, 2007).

Features of technology that may assist with time management include (a) various types of timers that visually represent elapsed time; (b) reminders that provide cues over time for events, behaviors, or steps; and (c) schedules or planners with a strong

visual component and built-in reminder features. Capitalizing on the visual learning style of learners with autism (cf. Schopler & Mesibov, 1995), in terms of EBP, these supports are considered antecedent, naturalistic, self-management, and technology interventions (CMS, 2010; NAC, 2009; NPDC, 2009).

Visual timers: Visual timers may assist in understanding elapsed time. Some are designed for a short amount of time, such as the Time Timer (Time Timer, 1991) or the Traffic Light Timer (MaxiAIDS, 1996); others provide information on elapsed time over the course of several days or months, such as the app Big Day (Ahn, 2012), which shows the number of days left until a designated event. Most of these timers are fairly low tech and easy to operate.

The Time Timer (1991) shows a visual representation of elapsed time with the disappearance over time of a colored disk that represents the face and hands of a clock. Versions of the Time Timer include an actual physical timer that is available in three sizes, as well as a personal wristwatch design. Software and app versions can be used on computers or mobile devices. The Traffic Light Timer by MaxiAIDS (1996) shows a changing color alert as time elapses. It changes to green when there is one minute left, yellow with 30 seconds left, and red at 10 seconds remaining.

Reminders: Tools that include reminders provide a timing function, but also allow entering of multiple events over longer periods of time, including hours, days, weeks, months, and even years. An example of a device that provides this type of support is the WatchMinder (WatchMinder, 2013). While looking like a watch, it can be set with a number of different activities with corresponding alerts throughout the day. It provides a discrete vibrating cue, as well as a visual display on the watch face indicating the desired behavior or activity.

The reminder function on smartphones is another example, which may be more readily available and desirable for older students. For example, the reminder app on the iPhone not only provides a reminder for a predetermined time and date, it can also be set to provide a reminder when a person leaves and/or returns to a certain location. The location feature can be particularly useful for reminding a student to pack his homework when leaving home in the morning or to bring home his books when leaving school in the afternoon.

Schedules and planners: Schedules and planners can provide a detailed step-by-step listing of a task done at one sitting, or be broader as for a daily schedule of events or longer term projects such as a calendar of events. As such, these supports show the steps of an activity or event within the overall picture. They can be low tech and include picture supports of the items to be completed or higher tech with digital reminders and cues accompanying the steps or events.

Many types of picture schedules used by individuals with autism are considered low tech. Traditional school planners given to students by their teachers are an example of a low-tech support. These are great for many students who are able to remember to write their assignments in the planners and to look at the planner for cues on upcoming assignments. However, for many students with autism who have difficulty with working memory, low-tech planners are not effective for long-term projects or schedules or even when multi-tasking several steps in a project. For these students, higher tech solutions are often more useful. For example, the Visual Schedule Planner (Good Karma Applications, 2012) app provides a variety of supports, including custom pictures and sounds, timers, checklists, reminders, and notes that are bundled to allow for the creation of custom schedules/calendars. The app iHomework (Element 84, 2009) is specifically designed to help students track their homework assignments. It requires that the student enter the assignment and set up the reminders she needs. It offers iCloud compatibility across multiple devices, so that information entered by the student on one device is available on other iOS devices.

Many commonly available apps can provide schedule and planner support for students. These types of supports work well on mobile devices since they are often needed across various environments, throughout the day and, consequently, need to be with the person at all times. One of the primary advantages of using digital versions of schedules and planners is the independence they offer by eliminating the need for another individual to remind the person to look at the schedule or planner by providing an auditory cue paired with the visual cue.

Self-management: In 2007, the Rehabilitation Services Administration, The Council of State Administrators of Vocational Rehabilitation, and George Washington University issued a report on individuals with autism stating, "Perhaps the greatest challenge to those who interact with those on the autism spectrum is the presence of challenging behavior" (Dew & Allen, 2007, p. 8). Similarly, a recent study (Kanne & Mazurek, 2011) of 1,380 children through age 17 found that 68% exhibited aggression toward families or support personnel and 49% manifested this behavior toward others. Although trends showed a decrease among older adolescents, challenging behaviors were apparent among approximately one quarter of students between the ages of 15 and 17. The presence of challenging behaviors is correlated with a lack of peer relationships, access to the community, employment, and high quality of life (cf. Myles & Southwick, 2005).

While the underpinnings of self-regulation are still poorly characterized (Mazefsky, Pelphrey, & Dahl, 2012), difficulties in managing self are often exhibited as challenging behaviors. Often termed a lack of "self-regulation," the presence of these behaviors results from challenges in emotional adaptation (Attwood 2008; Myles, Grossman, Aspy, Henry, & Coffin, 2007) and reflects a myriad of difficulties, including (a) recognizing emotions in the self; (b) matching emotions to events; and (c) changing the expression and levels of frustration, anxiety, alertness, and related behaviors to match acceptable situational contexts (Myles & Southwick, 2005; Rieffe, Terwogt, Mootz, Van Leeuwen, & Stockmann, 2011; Vermeulen, 2012). Further, self-regulation challenges are often exacerbated by challenges in understanding the thoughts, feelings, perceptions, and emotional states of others as well as interpreting why others act the way they do (cf. Sumiyoshi et al., 2011).

Various interventions and supports, including video modeling, the Mind Reading software University of Cambridge, 2003, the Autism 5-Point Scale app (Autism Help, 2012) and the Hidden Curriculum To Go apps (AAPC Publishing, 2010), and Animal Agentz (Jones, 2008), have been created to address self-regulation. They are considered EBP under the categories of antecedent, applied behavior analysis, naturalistic, self-management and technology interventions (CMS, 2010; NAC, 2009; NPDC, 2009).

Video modeling: Using video modeling, individuals learn to understand themselves and others through videotaping that can be homemade or commercial (i.e., Videojug, Model Me Kids, eHow) (Bellini & Akullian, 2007). A variety of video modeling types exists, including video self-modeling using positive self-review. In this type of video modeling, the learner is taped engaging in a behavior, and the video is used as a reminder

to engage in that behavior. Positive self-review is best employed when the learner has developed a specific skill but is either (a) not using it at the appropriate level because it is newly acquired or (b) not maintaining it in the natural environment (McCoy & Hermansen, 2007). Table 4 overviews the various types of video modeling.

Mind Reading software: Authored by Simon Baron-Cohen and colleagues (University of Cambridge, 2003), the Mind Reading software program teaches human emotions, a challenging area for many individuals with autism. Using this software, learners can see and hear 400 different emotions expressed in diverse people. In addition, the software package contains an emotions library, a learning center with lessons and quizzes, and a game zone that allows practice in a video-game type format.

Self-regulation apps: Based on the work of Buron and Curtis (2012), the Autism 5-Point Scale app was designed to help learners on the spectrum understand themselves and, as a result, better manage or regulate their behavior. The scale is unique in that it has a wide range of applications. For example, it can be used as an obsessional index, a stress scale, and a meltdown monitor. Children and youth with ASD learn to recognize the stages of their specific behavioral

Table 4. Types of video modeling

Type	Description
Adult as Models	Parents, teachers, or adults unknown to the learner model targeted behaviors.
Peers as Models	Typically, peer models are the same age and gender as the student with autism, Similar to "adults as models," peer models can include familiar peers, such as siblings or classmates, unknown individuals.
Self as Model	The observation of oneself engaged in a behavior or series of behaviors. Self-observation generally includes unedited video that depicts both negative and positive aspects of the targeted behavior. Positive self-review occurs when the learner is taped engaging in a behavior, and the video is used as a reminder to engage in that behavior.
Point-of-View Models	This type of model presents the image that would be seen if the learner were engaged in the behavior.
Video Priming	A video preview of a task or experience is provided before the individual engages in that activity.
Video Prompting	Task analyzed steps are recorded separately so that the learner can master one task before moving to the next.
Mixed Models	This combines any of the above video model systems.

challenges and methods to self-calm at each level (Autism Help, 2012).

Two Hidden Curriculum To Go apps are designed to help children, adolescents and adults understand unwritten rules, expectations and assumptions (AAPC Publishing, 2010). Presented as an item per day, these apps can increase understanding of the social world which, in turn, can decrease anxiety and related behavioral challenges (cf. Myles, Endow, & Mayfield; Vermeulen, 2012).

Animal Agentz: This program is designed to help children self-regulate their behaviors. Animal Agentz (Jones, 2008) teaches anxiety reduction, guided imagery, positive affirmations, distraction skills, and breathing through five animals. Skills are task-analyzed and taught sequentially; users earn reinforcers as they progress through this web-based program.

SUMMARY

Researchers and practitioners have recognized that skills beyond academics are required for life success and executive function is central among them for individuals with autism. The EF challenges in autism should not be detractors to life success. The tools are in place to assist learners on the spectrum meet their potential. Assistive technology can provide the supports and skill development that translate directly into the 21st century workplace: (a) information management/processing, (b) materials management, (c) time management, and (d) self-management.

REFERENCES

AAPC Publishing. (2010). *Hidden curriculum to go: Version for kids: Version for adolescents and adults.* Shawnee Mission, KS: Author.

Ahn, C. H. (2012). *Big day.* Cupertino, CA: Author.

Aljunied, M., & Frederickson, N. (2013). Does central coherence relate to the cognitive performance of children with autism in dynamic assessments. *Autism, 17,* 172–183. doi:10.1177/1362361311409960 PMID:21715547

Attwood, T. (2008). *The complete guide to Asperger's syndrome.* London, UK: Jessica Kingsley.

Bellini, S., & Akullian, J. A. (2007). A meta-analysis of video modeling and video self-modeling interventions for children and adolescents with autism spectrum disorders. *Exceptional Children, 73,* 264–287.

Bock, M. A. (1999). Sorting laundry: Categorization application to an authentic learning activity by children with autism. *Focus on Autism and Other Developmental Disabilities, 14,* 220–230. doi:10.1177/108835769901400404

Bock, M. A. (2007). A social-behavioral learning strategy intervention for a child with Asperger syndrome. *Remedial and Special Education, 28,* 258–265. doi:10.1177/07419325070280050101

Bowser, G., & Reed, P. (2001). *Hey can I try that? A student handbook for choosing and using assistive technology.* Retrieved from www.wati.org/products/pdf/heycanitrythat.pdf

Buron, K. D., & Curtis, M. (2012). The incredible 5-point scale: The significantly improved and expanded second ed: Assisting students in understanding social interactions and controlling their emotional responses (2nd ed.). Shawnee Mission, KS: AAPC Publishing.

Centers for Medicare and Medicaid Services. (2010). *Autism spectrum disorders: Final report on environmental scan.* Washington, DC: Author.

Dew, D. W., & Alan, G. M. (Eds.). (2007). *Rehabilitation of individuals with autism spectrum disorders (Institute on Rehabilitation Issues Monograph No. 32)*. Washington, DC: The George Washington University, Center for Rehabilitation Counseling Research and Education.

Element 84. (2009). *iHomework*. Alexandria, VA: Author.

Fenner, G. H., & Renn, R. W. (2009). Technology-assisted supplemental work and work-to-family conflict: The role of instrumental beliefs, organizational expectations, and time management. *Human Relations*, *63*, 63–82. doi:10.1177/0018726709351064

Gilotty, L., Kenworthy, L., Sirian, L., Black, D. O., & Wagner, A. E. (2002). Adaptive skills and executive function in autism spectrum disorders. *Child Neuropsychology*, *8*, 241–248. doi:10.1076/chin.8.4.241.13504 PMID:12759821

Good Karma Applications. (2012). *Visual schedule planner*. San Diego, CA: Author.

Happé, F., & Frith, U. (2006). The weak central coherence account: Detail-focused cognitive style in autism spectrum disorders. *Journal of Autism and Developmental Disorders*, *36*, 5–25. doi:10.1007/s10803-005-0039-0 PMID:16450045

Help, A. (2012). [*-point scale app*. Retrieved from http://www.ausm.org/index.php/autism-apps.html]. *Autism*, *5*

Henninger, N. A., & Taylor, J. L. (2012). Outcomes in adults with autism spectrum disorders: A historical perspective. *Autism*, *17*, 103–116. doi:10.1177/1362361312441266 PMID:22914775

Individuals With Disabilities Education Improvement Act of 2004, Pub. L. No. 108-446.

Inspiration Software Inc. (2008). *Kidspiration 3*. Beaverton, OR: Author.

Inspiration Software, Inc. (2010). *Inspiration 9*. Beaverton, OR: Author.

Jones, M. (2008). *Animal agentz*. Liverpool, UK: Animal Agentz.

Kanne, S. M., & Mazurek, M. O. (2011). Aggression in children and adolescents with ASD: Prevalence and risk factors. *Journal of Autism and Developmental Disorders*, *41*, 926–937. doi:10.1007/s10803-010-1118-4 PMID:20960041

Kenworthy, L. E., Black, D. O., Wallace, G. L., Ahluvalia, T., Wagner, A. E., & Sirian, L. M. (2005). Disorganization: The forgotten executive dysfunction in high-functioning autism (HFA) spectrum disorders. *Developmental Neuropsychology*, *3*, 809–827. doi:10.1207/s15326942dn2803_4 PMID:16266250

Knowledge by Design. (2010). *Text compactor*. Whitefish Bay, WI: Author.

Kurzweil Educational Systems. (2011). *Kurzweil 3000 reading writing learning education software*. Dallas, TX: Cambium Learning.

Locascio, G., Mahone, E. M., Eason, S. H., & Cutting, L. E. (2010). Executive dysfunction among children with reading comprehension deficits. *Journal of Learning Disabilities*, *43*, 441–454. doi:10.1177/0022219409355476 PMID:20375294

Macan, T. H. (1994). Time management: Tests of a process model. *The Journal of Applied Psychology*, *79*, 381–391. doi:10.1037/0021-9010.79.3.381

MaxiAIDS. (1996). *Timer traffic light*. Farmingdale, NY: Author.

Mazefsky, C. A., Pelphrey, K. A., & Dahl, R. E. (2012). The need for a broader approach to emotion regulation research in autism. *Child Development Perspectives*, *6*, 92–97. doi:10.1111/j.1750-8606.2011.00229.x PMID:22639681

McCoy, K., & Hermansen, E. (2007). Video modeling for individuals with autism: A review of model types and effects. *Education & Treatment of Children*, *30*, 183–213. doi:10.1353/etc.2007.0029

Müller, E., Schuler, A., & Yates, G. B. (2008). Social challenges and supports from the perspective of individuals with Asperger syndrome and other autism spectrum disabilities. *Autism*, *12*, 173–190. doi:10.1177/1362361307086664 PMID:18308766

Myles, B. S., Endow, J., & Mayfield, M. (2012). *The hidden curriculum and getting and keeping a job: Navigating the social landscape of employment: A guide for individuals with autism spectrum and other social-cognitive challenges*. Shawnee Mission, KS: AAPC Publishing.

Myles, B. S., Grossman, B. G., Aspy, R., Henry, S. A., & Coffin, A. B. (2007). Planning a comprehensive program for students with autism spectrum disorders using evidence-based practices. *Education and Training in Developmental Disabilities*, *42*, 398–409.

Myles, B. S., & Southwick, J. (2005). *Asperger syndrome and difficult moments: Practical solutions for tantrums, rage, and meltdowns* (2nd ed.). Shawnee Mission, KS: AAPC Publishing.

National Autism Center. (2009). *National standards report: Addressing the need for evidence-based practice guidelines for autism spectrum disorders*. Randolph, MA: Author.

National Professional Development Center on Autism Spectrum Disorders. (n.d.). *Evidence based practice briefs*. Retrieved from http://autismpdc.fpg.unc.edu/content/briefs

Partnership for 21ˢᵗ Century Skills. (n.d.). *Framework for 21ˢᵗ century learning*. Retrieved from http://www.p21.org/overview

Rieffe, C., Terwogt, M. M., Mootz, S., Van Leeuwen, E., & Stockmann, L. (2011). Emotion regulation and internalizing symptoms in children with autism spectrum disorders. *Autism*, *15*, 655–670. doi:10.1177/1362361310366571 PMID:21733959

Rosenthal, M., Wallace, G. L., Lawson, R., Wills, M. C., Dixson, E., Yers, B. E., & Kenworthy, L. (2013). Impairment in real-world executive function increase from children to adolescence in autism spectrum disorders. *Neuropsychology*, *27*, 13–28. doi:10.1037/a0031299 PMID:23356593

Sachse, M., Schlitt, S., Hainz, D., Ciaramidaro, A., Schirman, S., & Walter, H. et al. (2013). Executive and visuo-motor function in adolescents and adults with autism spectrum disorders. *Journal of Autism and Developmental Disorders*, *43*, 1222–1235. doi:10.1007/s10803-012-1668-8 PMID:23011252

Schopler, E., & Mesibov, G. B. (1995). *Learning and cognition in autism*. New York, NY: Plenum Press. doi:10.1007/978-1-4899-1286-2

Shattuck, P. T., Narendorf, S. C., Cooper, B., Sterzing, P. R., Wagner, M., & Taylor, J. L. (2012). Postsecondary education and employment among youth with an autism spectrum disorder. *Pediatrics*, *129*, 1042–1049. doi:10.1542/peds.2011-2864 PMID:22585766

Sumiyoshi, C., Kawakubo, Y., Suga, M., Sumiyoshi, T., & Kasai, K. (2011). Impaired ability to organize information in individuals with autism spectrum disorders and their siblings. *Neuroscience*, *69*, 252–257. PMID:21129422

TextHelp, Inc. (2013). *Read&Write gold*. Antrim, Ireland: Author.

Timer, T. (1991). *Time timer*. Cincinnati, OH: Author.

Tsatsanis, K. D., Noens, I. L. J., Illman, C. L., Paul, D. L., Volkmar, F. R., Schultz, R. T., & Klin, A. (2010). Managing complexity: Impact of organization and processing style on non-verbal memory in autism spectrum disorders. *Journal of Autism and Developmental Disorders*, *41*, 135–147. doi:10.1007/s10803-010-1139-z PMID:21128108

University of Cambridge. (2003). *Mind reading*. Cambridge, UK: Author.

Vermeulen, P. (2012). *Autism as context blindness*. Shawnee Mission, KS: AAPC Publishing.

Wallace, L., & Happé, F. (2008). Time perception in autism spectrum disorders. *Research in Autism Spectrum Disorders*, *2*, 447–455. doi:10.1016/j.rasd.2007.09.005

WatchMinder. (2013). *WatchMinder*. Irvine, CA: Author.

Zabala, J. (2002). *A brief introduction to the SETT framework*. Retrieved from http://www.sbac.edu/~ese?AT/referralprocess/SETTUPDATE.pdf

Zabala, J., & Bowser, G. (2005). SETTing up staff and supporters to promote student achievement. *Closing the Gap: Computer Technology in Special Education and Rehabilitation*, *24*(1), 1–3.

Chapter 3
Incorporating Mobile Technology into Evidence-Based Practices for Students with Autism

Iva Strnadová
University of New South Wales, Australia

Therese M. Cumming
University of New South Wales, Australia

Cathi Draper Rodríguez
California State University – Monterey Bay, USA

ABSTRACT

This chapter discusses how mobile technology can contribute to the quality of life of children with autism across their school years and through the transition to adulthood. Mobile technology has the potential to support students not just at school, but also across all environments in and throughout their lives. There are a number of educational practices and strategies that have been identified as having a strong evidence base to effectively support students with autism. The theoretical framework underpinning this chapter is the Universal Design for Learning (UDL), which prescribes that these practices be integrated into instruction from the outset to ensure equal access and participation of all students in the class-room. Case studies of students on the autism spectrum with diverse needs and during different stages of their lives (from the school years to the transition to adulthood) are used to demonstrate the benefits of incorporating mobile technology into evidence-based educational practices for people with autism.

DOI: 10.4018/978-1-4666-5792-2.ch003

INTRODUCTION

Although mobile technology can be traced back to the early 1990's with the introduction of the personal digital assistant (PDA), it greatly increased in popularity in the early 2000's, through the global widespread adoption of various forms of Smartphones and later, in 2010, with the introduction of the iPad and other digital tablets. Tablets are now the preferred method of accessing the Internet by users globally (White, 2013), and it is predicted that there will be over 1.4 billion smartphones in use worldwide by December 2013 (Leonard, 2013). Interestingly, there has been widespread adoption of mobile devices by parents and teachers as teaching and learning devices, particularly for students with autism (Rothschild, 2011).

Although mobile devices and their applications were not originally created with education and/or students with autism in mind, that sort of repurposing is not new and is theoretically supported by Universal Design for Learning Theory (UDL). Universal Design for Learning is an educational framework based on research in the learning sciences that guides the development of flexible learning environments (CAST, 2011a). The theory of Universal Design for Learning is defined as:

a set of principles for curriculum development that give all individuals equal opportunities to learn. UDL provides a blueprint for creating instructional goals, methods, materials, and assessments that work for everyone--not a single, one-size-fits-all solution but rather flexible approaches that can be customized and adjusted for individual needs.

CAST (2011b) describes the three principals that guide UDL: (a) provide multiple means of representation; (b) provide multiple means of action and expression; and (c) provide multiple means of engagement. These three principles, and the UDL Model are now widely accepted and recommended as part of different teaching models,

especially inclusive practice, as they promote accessibility from the start, rather than as a set of accommodations added later on. Accessibility is preferred over accommodation because accommodation is usually triggered by a request, which can take time. It may also require extra effort in the form of time and resources, or moving to a special location, which is exclusionary (Edyburn, 2010).

MOBILE TECHNOLOGIES

Tablet devices, such as the iPad, and their corresponding applications have the potential to support students with autism by increasing the accessibility of educational materials, enhance the presentation of concepts, improve social skills, as well as giving students a way to communicate in different modalities. The devices are also widely recognized and used by students of all ages, making them more readily adopted by students and adults with autism and their peers. Many schools are already widely employing the devices, making it a matter of just adding the right applications to make classroom instruction more accessible to all students.

There is scant research to support the use of mobile technology as teaching and learning tools for students with autism, but popular literature in magazines, newspapers and online media (blogs, vlogs, etc.) detail the many ways that tablet computers and other mobile devices have had a positive impact on the lives of people with autism. These accounts, as well as the few research studies that exist, focus on incorporating mobile technology into practices that already have a strong evidence base, such as: augmentative and alternative communication (AAC).

Gentry, Wallace, Kvarfordt, and Lynch (2010) examined the efficacy of PDAs as task management tools for 22 high school students with autism. The students were trained by occupational therapists to use the PDAs to manage tasks, and after eight weeks the students demonstrated significant improvement on an occupational performance measure, had learned to use the devices' reminder alarms and could independently program the devices. All of the students reported that the devices had improved their independence in performing functional activities, and had, in fact, improved their satisfaction with everyday life. Gentry, Lau, Molinelli, Fallen, and Kriner (2012) also explored using mobile technology with individuals with autism for organizational purposes. The participants in their study, who were adults with autism, effectively used iPods as PDAs to improve their task completion in the workplace. The results of the study demonstrate the versatility of PDAs to support people with autism spectrum disorder, and these two studies support the supposed efficacy of portable devices as learning and cognitive aids for this population.

Price (2011) explored the efficacy of e-books to improve the reading comprehension of students with autism. This study compared traditional printed books to interactive e-books in 30 students with autism aged 12 to 22. The interactive e-books were presented to students via an iPad, and included audio, text, and color graphics. All but one of the students improved their comprehension scores by up to 50% when using the iPad and interactive e-book, and that one student scored 100 per cent on both comprehension assessments. Teachers reported that in addition to gains in comprehension, students found the iPads to be motivating and that the use of iPads reduced off-task behavior.

The iPod was used as an effective tool to improve the independent transitioning of four elementary school students with autism in inclusive settings (Cihak, et al., 2010). In that study, video modelling delivered via an iPod, combined with a system of least prompts, increased the mean percentage of independent transitions made by students from 7% to 77%. Teachers and students reported satisfaction with the intervention, particularly with the portability of the devices.

Several studies have shown promise in the use of mobile technology in supporting the communication of students with autism. Achmadi (2010) investigated teaching adolescents with autism to use an iPod to facilitate communication. All of the participants in the multiple-baseline across subjects design learned to use a speech-generating application on the iPod to make multi-step requests. Results suggested that the adolescents with autism that participated in the study could successfully use an iPod for expressive communication. Flores, et al. (2012) compared the effects of an iPad with a picture exchange communication system (PECS) on the communication rates of five elementary school students with autism. Their findings provided support for use of the iPad as a communication device. Anecdotal data indicated that the students and the teachers preferred using the iPad to the picture system. The teachers reported that iPads were easy to use, required less preparation time and materials, and increased the speed of the students' communication.

Aided language stimulation was combined with tablet technology to create a communication intervention for students with autism (Logan, 2012). Students who participated in the study made gains in communication as well as social skills. The teachers believed that the technology was engaging and easy for students to use for communication. One benefit was that all of the communication icons could be shown on the same page, allowing for a more natural conversational flow.

The efficacy of using evidence-based practices (EBP) has been demonstrated through research and is a requirement for many schools globally (Hall, 2009). Evidence-based practices are defined as "those where there is a body of research demonstrating effectiveness with students with disabilities as opposed to strategies that have been created on convincing premises but have not been evaluated or assessed" (Yell et al., 2005, p.57). Odom and his colleagues (2010) identified 24 evidence-based practices recommended for students with autism spectrum disorders. The authors will use these practices when suggesting how to align the EBP with recommendations on how to effectively incorporate mobile technology into the learning and teaching of students with autism.

STUDENTS WITH AUTISM: CLASSROOM AND HOME-SCHOOL COLLABORATION

Students with autism spectrum disorder display qualitative impairments in areas of communication, social interaction, and repetitive behaviors (Dodd, 2005). Sensory sensitivities are another important area that needs to be considered when educating students with autism. Many students with autism also experience difficulties during transitions from activity to activity or from one environment to another (Meadan et al., 2011). When educating students with autism, teachers need to be aware of their students' strengths, which should be easily incorporated into the lessons. Many students with autism are visual learners, thus they benefit from visual schedules and timetables (Grandin, 2010). The following text focuses on two of the areas of qualitative impairment in people with autism, communication and social skills. These areas overlap significantly (DSM-IV) and are thus discussed under one subheading. The appropriate apps that can be used when applying evidence-based practices in order to improve communication and social skills are discussed. It is important to remember that the student him/herself needs to be included in the choice of app(s), in order to provide a good fit and an app that s/he will actually use.

Communication and Social Skills

Qualitative impairment in communication manifests itself in diverse ways and across the spectrum, ranging from mild to severe levels of difficulty. Some students with autism remain non-verbal and thus benefit from using AAC (Schlosser, &

Wendt, 2008). Students with high-functioning autism typically do not have issues with verbal communication; however, they tend to discuss only the topics of their interests, and have issues with understanding the nuances of pragmatics, resulting in taking spoken words literally (Loukusa, & Moilanen, 2009). People with autism generally have greater difficulties understanding non-verbal aspects of language (e.g., gestures, facial expressions).

There are a number of evidence-based practices, which support communication in students with ASD. Picture Exchange Communication System (PECS) is helpful for students who are nonverbal or have issues with verbal communication (Lancioni, O'Reilly, Cuvo, Singh, Sigafoos, & Didden, 2007). There are a number of applications (commonly referred to as apps) available through mobile technologies, which can support the use of PECS. *iConverse*™ – *Assisted Communication* is an application that functions similarly to PECS. It contains six communication tiles, which reflect basic human needs (such as health, need to eat and drink, etc.). *iConverse*™ provides both audio and visual representations of the items being presented to the student and the person with whom they are communicating. Social narratives or video modeling can help students with autism to better understand the nuances of pragmatics and non-verbal aspects of social communication (Sansosti, & Powell-Smith, 2008). Students who exhibit challenges with verbal and nonverbal language in regards to social skills and communication can be supported with apps such as: *stories2learn*™, *Social Skills Builder*™, or *iPrompts*™.

The qualitative impairment of social skills in people with autism spectrum disorders varies in severity across the spectrum. Students with autism have difficulties developing and maintaining social relationships; understanding and mimicking appropriate social behaviors; and/or initiating, maintaining and closing conversations (Dodd, 2005). Thus they often tend to be isolated from or are even rejected by their peers (Chamberlain,

Kasari, & Rotheram-Fuller, 2007). Students with high-functioning autism experience difficulties with understanding subtle social cues, and thus might appear in some situations as awkward and self-centered (Carrington, Templeton, & Papinczak, 2003). Their social skills impairments unfortunately contribute to greater vulnerability of students with autism, who often experience bullying (Cappadocia, Weiss, & Pepler, 2012; Humphrey & Symes, 2010).

Evidence-based practices supporting the development of social skills include behavior intervention strategies such as: social narratives, self-management, social skills training groups, or video modeling (Odom et al., 2010). Several apps can be used to practice social narratives: *stories2learn*™, *Social Skills Builder*™ or *QuickCues*™. *Stories2learn*™ allows teachers and parents to create personalized stories about social situations, using photographs, text and audio recordings. The preloaded social narratives cover social skills, such as reciprocal play and turn taking. *Social Skills Builder*™ is a social learning application, which contains real life situations from pre-school to high school settings, as well as to community settings. *QuickCues*™ is a social script application designed for teenagers and young adults with autism. Within five modules, they can learn social skills related to communication, life skills or skills important for gaining and maintaining employment. Students with autism can also successfully use this app for self-management. *Milo: Interactive Storybook*™ can be used with social skills training groups. This interactive storybook application allows students with autism to build storytelling and narrative skills. In addition to the *Social Skills Builder* application, the *iPrompts*™ app can be successfully used for videomodeling. Users can also purchase *VideoPrompts*™ which works in conjunction with the app to demonstrate appropriate behaviors to students with autism. Students with high functioning autism can use the iPad's built in video camera to make their own socially-related stories and video modeling

role plays, or teachers and parents can use the app to video the students' appropriate behavior. *iMovie*™ can be used to edit out any unwanted behavior or footage.

School-Home Collaboration

The collaboration between school personnel and parents of a student with autism has been emphasized as critical for student success (Blair, Lee, Cho, & Dunlap, 2011). Active development of this collaborative relationship allows for sharing information about a student's development, strengths and needs, as well as planning future steps from multiple perspectives. Consistency between school and home, in many ways (e.g., communication, behavior management, self-help skills), is crucial for students with autism for a myriad of reasons, including their preference for sameness and routines.

One of the key features in building an effective school-home collaboration is developing a shared vision, i.e., a vision for the present and future of a student with autism spectrum disorders that is shared by the student, his parents, his teachers and relevant stakeholders. Such a shared vision includes, but is not limited to, academic aspects of a student's life as well as future vocational considerations. Developing a shared vision is an evolving process based on communication and mutual respect. Another important aspect of building an effective school-home collaboration is equal input from all parties. As Salazar (2012) points out, too often parents are only the recipients of information, viewed as parties who agree (or disagree) with suggested plans, instead of being 'decision makers and resources in the elaboration of learning' (p.21). A framework or structure should be created to ensure that all team members have a voice in the planning and implementation process.

There are no simple "one size fits all" rules to establishing and nurturing an effective school-home collaboration. The nature of such collaboration depends on the nature of the parties involved. Individual families differ greatly as they build on diverse resources, come from different backgrounds and/or cultures, have diverse priorities, and cope with challenges in different ways (Salazar, 2012; Strnadová & Evans, 2008). Thus the school team members need to be aware of differences among families and accommodate for these accordingly. Therefore, the team should meet and get to know one another before attempting any planning. This initial team meeting can facilitate this process; the team can get to know each other and then decide together on a style of collaboration that best meets everyone's needs. Once this is established, a system of open communication can be decided upon. This will serve to make individual stakeholders comfortable enough to share their views at any time throughout the planning and implementation process. This is especially important when planning for technology implementation; any technology that is proposed should be acceptable to all parties. It is crucial that everyone involved with the student have the skills to support the student in using the technology.

Successful Implementation of Mobile Technology

The success of both mobile technology implementation and school-home collaboration rests largely on the level of training of the teachers and how well prepared the professionals and parents are for any challenges that may arise during planning and implementation (Merbler, Hadadian, & Ulman, 1999). As with the implementation of any educational strategy, communication is key. This communication begins with, but is not limited to, the student. Although student preference is very important, communication with the entire team will provide a more holistic view. The team should include the student, teacher, parent, and any related service providers such as school psychologists, physical therapists, speech therapists, and occupational therapists.

A needs assessment is the first step in implementation. This can be accomplished by all team members, recording their own data regarding student's needs, then convening a team meeting to share assessment results and plan the best course of action together. A whole team assessment will help to ensure that the student's needs are identified and addressed across all environments that s/he lives, works, and plays in. The student should be included in the assessment and planning meetings so his or her voice can be heard. Student preferences for different applications and types of technology are important. If the student favors a particular app or device, then s/he is more likely to learn to use it and use it consistently (Merbler, et al., 1999).

It is also important to identify any potential barriers in implementation as part of the planning process. Messinger-Willma and Marino (2010) list the following three categories of possible barriers to successful implementation of assistive technology: (a) situational, which includes lack of funding, deficits in teacher knowledge of the technology and how to integrate it into the curricula, available resources, lack of time, lack of collaboration, and a lack of consideration for student or family needs; (b) institutional, including a lack of adequate professional development, lack of technology specialists, unreliable technology, overcomplicated technology features, insufficient funding for the devices and applications; and (c) dispositional, which consists of teacher reluctance, negative attention drawn to the student because of the technology. Low expectations that are sometimes held by teachers or parents of students with autism (Carter, Trainor, Owens, Sweden, & Sun, 2010) can be a particularly damaging dispositional barrier, as these can lead to a failure to teach students with autism the skills needed for living as independent a life as possible. Low expectations can also lead to a limited exploration of available assistive technology, including mobile technology.

Upon identifying any possible obstacles, remedies can be built into the planning process in order to avert any missteps with implementation and integration. Ensuring that teachers and parents have the knowledge they need to effectively implement the technology and support students in its use is a common dilemma. Time, cost, and location of training are common concerns, but site-based training is one solution. Site-based training can be offered to all interested teachers and parents and can be sustained, designed and directed by both. This takes the groups' skills, abilities, and needs into consideration (Messinger-Willma & Marino, 2010). In order to enable teachers and parents to stay abreast of evolving technology in regard to the changing needs of students with autism, ongoing support should be built into training programs from the start. Although this could become expensive, training costs can be eliminated or minimized by drawing on the expertise of teachers and parents who are proficient in the technology. Another option is to build strong relationships with local universities that conduct research in special education and/or technology. These relationships are beneficial to all- teachers, and parents get high quality training and support, while participating in research that benefits not only the university, but also other teachers and parents and the field in general.

Time is a precious commodity for both teachers and parents, and sometimes, when families live far from the school, geography works against collaboration. Online professional development and technology support may be the answer to these potential barriers. Collaborative online tools such as *Skype*™ , *FaceTime*™, *Google+*™, *Google Drive*™, *Youtube*™, *Prezi*™, and *SlideShare*™, as well as blogs, wikis, and vlogs can be used to facilitate these.

Parents of students with autism spectrum disorders are instrumental in the planning process leading to successful implementation of mobile technology. While schools commonly acknowledge this, the need for training and preparation of parents for participation in the planning process, and specifically in designing transition plans (Briel

& Getzel, 2009), is often forgotten. Some parents are well acquainted with mobile technology itself, however they still might not understand the value of this technology for their children, This may be due to lack of knowledge about the myriad of educational and special educational applications available and the lack of exposure to research studies whose results indicated mobile technology's usefulness for increased participation in a classroom as well as at home and in the community. Other parents are not well acquainted with mobile technology. While structured training for parents might not be necessary, teachers should never assume that parents fully understand the role of planning from an educational perspective, and thus should devote a meeting or two to discussing the importance of planning (including the planning of mobile technology adoption and implementation).

It is important to clearly set boundaries between the school and the family, because when boundaries are blurred, there is a great danger that home will be perceived as an extension of school which, in return, can contribute to parents feeling overwhelmed by their child's educational demands and possibly feeling that the school is imposing external control on them (Ludicke, & Kortman, 2012). It is, therefore, of crucial importance to assure parents from the very beginning that the purpose of the collaboration is not to burden parents with even more work, duties and responsibilities, but, on the contrary, to find ways to make their lives easier while improving their child's quality of life. The role of mobile technology in this process is obvious and while it can serve as an effective educational and assistive technology tool for students with autism, it can also make communication between school and parents more effective, decreasing time demands in terms of scheduling face-to-face meetings. There are a number of applications that have been found useful for school-home collaboration, such as the *BuzzMob* ™ app, which allows parents and teachers to connect on a private network and to share tips and photos and discuss new ideas. Parents and teachers can also utilize the variety of *Google Apps*™, such as *Drive*™, to keep in contact and share ideas.

Students with autism spectrum disorders are the ones who matter the most in making decisions on whether and/or how to use mobile technology in order to improve the quality of their lives. Yet it is often these students who are left out of the planning process and who become passive objects rather than active agents. This was an experience of most students participating in a study conducted by Hetherington, Durant-Jones, Johnson, Nolan, Smith, Taylor-Brown, and Tuttle (2010). There might be additional reasons for possible limited engagement of students with autism in the planning process. Given the characteristics of autism spectrum disorders, the team meeting of all involved parties (i.e., teachers, parents, students themselves, and other relevant stakeholders) might be a stressful experience for students with autism. Utilizing mobile technology to express their preferences might be a suitable way to address these issues. As demonstrated in Case Study 3 below, many students with autism prefer to use sms or email to communicate with others (of course not exclusively), and this might be a good option for team planning of mobile technology implementation. For example, having a group chat session via Apple's *iChat*™ for sharing ideas about next steps in supporting a student with autism in the classroom, and preparing him/her for a successful transition to post schooling options can be a suitable option for the team. While the team's meetings would still need to be kept, these could happen less frequently, as part of the planning and communication would happen, using mobile technology. This would greatly benefit some students with autism (particularly those who are nonverbal), their parents (who typically battle with time restrictions due to employment and family duties), as well as teachers (who often have complicated schedules).

MOBILE TECHNOLOGY INTEGRATION IN PRACTICE

The following two case studies demonstrate the extent to which the mobile technology can be effectively used within EBP, and how it can contribute to increased access to curriculum, improved literacy and numeracy, increased self-determination and to a decreased presentation of challenging behaviors. Case Study 1 describes Emily, a student with classic autism, while Case Study 2 presents Zack, a student with high-functioning autism. Both students utilize mobile technology, specifically an iPad, in diverse ways, situations and environments. The role of home-school collaboration when implementing mobile technology for students with autism, is an important part of both case studies, since without this collaboration the mobile technology utilization might not be as effective as it could be.

Case Study 1: Emily

Emily lives with her mother and brother. She likes to spend time outside with the dogs, and on the trampoline. When inside, she plays with toys, reads books, watches DVDs or TV or plays games with family members. Due to her sensory issues, her choice of food is very limited.

Student's Abilities and Challenges in Education

Emily is a 2nd grade student in a self-contained classroom in a public school. She was diagnosed with autism and intellectual disability. Emily can independently complete some classroom tasks, such as taking her bag to the shelf and placing her lunch box and communication books in trays. Emily requires verbal prompts or occasional repeated instructions 80% of the time in order to complete tasks successfully.

Emily practices vocalizing letter sounds, reads simple sentences, matches sight words, matches words to pictures, and independently uses a sketcher to trace letters and words. Emily can also match pictures to their initial letter independently and some pictures to words with minimal verbal prompts. Emily enjoys counting numbers through number songs and has mastered sequencing numbers 1-100 independently. She can also arrange numbers "before" and "after" 1-50 with minimal verbal prompts.

Emily enjoys experimenting with brush strokes and manipulating different colors to create artwork. She displays great interest in music activities and her favorite music activity is playing the drums. Over the last year Emily has made significant improvements in both eye contact and increasing her vocalizations (i.e., responding to greetings by saying 'hello', 'good morning' and 'bye').

Use of Mobile Technology to Improve Student's Access to and Success with the Curriculum

Emily's teacher integrated mobile technology into the class' teaching and learning activities. She created folders for individual students based on their learning goals and included a range of apps to enhance their functional life skills. The iPad is being used to improve Emily's access to and success in the curriculum, particularly in the areas of literacy and numeracy. The most useful literacy apps for Emily are *Starfall Learn to Read*^{TM}, *Elmo Loves ABCs*^{TM}, *First Words*^{TM}, *Dr. Seuss's ABC*^{TM}, and *ABC Christmas Nursery Rhymes Writing*^{TM},. As Emily's mum highlighted in a journal entry to Emily's teacher, *"Her reading has improved as has her speech because of articulation and spelling-type apps."*

Animals Count^{TM}, *Math Train*^{TM}, and *Counting 123-Learn to Count Challenge*^{TM} are the most beneficial apps for Emily's development of skills and knowledge in numeracy. *4 Forms*^{TM} app

increased Emily's ability to identify shapes and size and recognize wider range of colors.

In order to increase her communication skills, Emily uses visual choice boards and the *SPEAKall!*^{TM} application. One of the advantages of this application is that it is fully customizable; thus, her parents in cooperation with her teacher use recorded audio and images suitable for Emily. *Milo: Interactive Storybook*^{TM} is Emily's favorite storybook application. She enjoys that the application includes recorded voiceover, which allows her to 'read' the story on her own. Her dad created her own story in this app. Although her fine motor abilities are weak, since the iPad was introduced in her classroom, she is eager to trace, draw and color using the *Drawing Pad*^{TM} app. This application allows Emily to draw and write words.

Emily's teacher is also very positive about using the iPad in her class, especially for the purpose of assessment,

It was much easier for me to assess student learning on the basis of their learning goals especially in areas like numeracy – addition and subtraction and literacy – vocabulary, writing or tracing. Spelling apps provide a way for teachers to assess student vocabulary when the student is able to independently arrange letters to form words which otherwise is not possible using pen or paper through writing or low tech teaching aids.

School-Home Collaboration

Emily's mother was very excited about Emily's use of the iPad. As she stated: *"My child enjoys using both educational and entertainment apps as well as sensory apps. This keeps her calm and focused and happy"*. Emily's mum especially highlighted the *MeMoves*^{TM} application, which helps Emily with self-regulation by providing calming music and engaging her in guided movements. She also highlighted how using mobile technology contributed to Emily's self-determination:

She will choose which apps she wants to use independently and she works out how to use new apps very quickly.

Both Emily's mum and her teacher meet biweekly not only to discuss Emily's progress in academic and social skills, but also to share tips regarding the use of the iPad and appropriate applications to benefit Emily's development.

Case Study 2: Zack

Zack lives with both biological parents and an older brother. He enjoys playing video games, watching cartoons and reading. While outside, Zack enjoys playing foursquare, water polo and basketball. Zack does not present with any sensory issues, but does exhibit extreme food preferences.

Student's Abilities and Challenges in Education

Zack is a 6th grade student who has been diagnosed with high-functioning autism. As with many students with high-functioning autism, Zack displays average to above-average cognitive and vocabulary skills. This is typically displayed through advanced knowledge of preferred topics (e.g., science, super heroes). Zack demonstrates difficulty with changes to routine, such as assemblies and substitute teachers. At times, his inability to pick up social cues impacts his ability to relate to other students. This may impact his ability to be successful in the future.

Zack struggles with decoding subtle cues and interacting with others. He demonstrates weaknesses in comprehension, abstract thought, organizational skills and inferences. Zack's individualized education plan (IEP) goals focus on social skills, communication, and behavior. Specifically, the goals address working cooperatively with peers in small group settings, identifying breakdowns in communication and making appropriate ad-

justments, identifying various emotional states and asking questions of others regarding topics initiated by self or others to sustain conversation.

Use of Mobile Technology to Improve Student's Access to and Success with the Curriculum

There are several mobile applications, which can support students with high-functioning autism in accessing the curriculum, improving self-regulation, and promoting positive social interactions. Some of the applications are all-in-one apps, providing assistance with all three of the areas listed above, while others have a strong focus in just one or two areas.

In order to reduce the number of Zack's meltdowns, his teachers have implemented the application, *Social Navigator* ™. *Social Navigator* ™ is an application that is designed for students with autism who present with difficulty staying calm, relating to others, solving problems or conflicts, and/or being flexible. *Social Navigator* ™ is designed to be used by both adults and children. The goals of the application are to reduce meltdowns, improve the way adults approach challenging behaviors, teach social skills, improve communication, develop social awareness. The application also documents and collects data. Zack, along with his general education teacher and case manager, uses this application. His teachers use it to teach Zack to engage in appropriate social interactions and to assist them in engaging with Zack if challenging behaviors arise or appear.

Zack's teachers, general education and special education case manager, have used the *Autism Scheduler* ™ application to create custom schedules for Zack. Particular attention is paid to provide Zack time to adjust when there are changes in his typical routine (e.g., assembly schedule, parent/teacher conferences). This application allows the users to create customized schedules for students. There are images pre-loaded in the application and users may also upload their own photos. This application also allows Zack to check off items on his schedule when they are completed. Additionally, alarms can be set up as notifications of upcoming events.

Zack uses the *Micro-Expression Trainer*™ application to better understand facial expressions. As this application has two modes, Time Attack mode and Perfection mode, it appears game-like and is effective as a reinforcer for Zack. The application shows different facial expressions on various types of faces. Zack enjoys playing this game as it is interactive and provides positive reinforcement for correct answers.

In order to provide opportunities for Zack to work on communication and on social and behavioral skills, *AutisMate* ™ is used. This comprehensive application provides opportunities for Zack to work on communication and on social and behavioral skills. This application utilizes many research-based strategies for students with autism. Teachers can set up video modeling, socially-related stories, timers and scheduling. Zack's teachers have used this to supplement other applications.

School-Home Collaboration

One of the most important pieces of Zack's education is communication between Zack's teachers and his parents. Mobile technologies can be useful in this area, as well. *ReQall* ™ .The *reQall* ™ application is designed to helps users remain organized. The program allows users to save thoughts, make to-do lists and make voice, text and email notes. This application is vital for constant communication between Zack's teachers and his parents. The teachers use this device to ensure that Zack's parents are informed about upcoming deadlines, meetings and provide progress reports of his daily behavior plan. Zack's parents use this application to communicate with the teachers about events in the family, and issues that may be pertinent.

ROLE OF MOBILE TECHNOLOGY IN TRANSITIONS TO POST SCHOOLING OPTIONS

Transition from school to post-school life, whether it's further education, employment or independent life, places special demands on students with autism, their families and their teachers. Schools, in close collaboration with families, need to be actively engaged in preparing students for these transitions. As summarized by Hagner, Kurtz, Cloutier, Arakelian, Brucker and May (2012), a number of studies indicate a correlation between family involvement in the transition process and students' positive post school outcomes, thus school-home collaboration is of a crucial importance at this stage of a student's life.

There are several transition programs worldwide, typically focusing on the development of students' functional skills, and preparing them for as independent a life as possible. The following evidence-based behavior intervention strategies support transitions of students with autism: task analysis and chaining, self-management or visual supports (Odom et al., 2010). Mobile technology can play a vital role in these programs in order to enhance access, engagement and social inclusion of students with autism. For instance, the following applications support functional skills: *Able AAC Free* ™, *Activity Timer* ™, *All About Me* ™, *or AutisMate: the iPad App for Autism* ™. The latter allows creation of contextual environments for an individual student.

The following two case studies demonstrate the role of mobile technology as assistive tools in the process of transition from school to post-schooling options. Case Study 3 presents Lisa, a university student with high functioning autism, and Case Study 4 presents Alex, a post-secondary student preparing to transition from high school.

Case Study 3: Lisa

Lisa is a 20-year old university student with high functioning autism. She is a talented musician and artist, with a passion for 20th century music and modern arts. She lives on her own with a companion dog. She has developed several strategies to function in social relationships. Her main area of difficulty is sensory sensitivity, particularly auditory and tactile sensitivities.

The tablet is an important part of Lisa's life, both academically and personally. Academically, Lisa uses her tablet for accessing books, academic journals, blogs and news. She uses her iPad camera to record the images she wishes to capture for her artwork. The *iTalk*™ application is specifically useful for Lisa to record ambient sound in order to create soundscapes for her multisensory artwork. The iPad also helps Lisa to be organized. *Reminders*™, *Evernote*™ and *MyProject*™ applications keep her on track with her tasks and activities. *iCalendar*™ assists with being on time for appointments.

Similar to other people with high functioning autism, Lisa finds personal interaction with other people overwhelming. She prefers emails and text messages as a way to communicate and socially engage with people. She enjoys the fact that she can communicate with her friends from any setting, thus limiting the need to meet friends in noisy crowded places, such as cafeterias, restaurants or clubs. These forms of communication assist her with sensory issues, which allow her to have "social interaction on my own sensory terms." It also provides her with an opportunity to end conversation and pick it up again any time she wishes to do so. Lisa admits that in most situations she would prefer to use emails/sms "to someone sitting across the room than to go over and speak to them in person." This allows her to avoid engaging "in preliminary social niceties or chitchat before and after coming straight to the point of the communication itself."

Lisa sometimes struggles with orientation, and thus needs to use maps when traveling. With the *Maps*™ and *Sygic GPS Navigation: All Regions*™ applications, she can find her way around easily. Besides that, she does not have to approach other people to ask for directions, which is important for her since she dislikes interacting with strangers.

Case Study 4: Alex

Alex was diagnosed with classic autism at the age of 2 ½ years. At that time, he began receiving early intervention services. Alex has had special education services all throughout his schooling. He is just about to turn 22 years of age. His special education team and parents have been preparing for his transition since he was fourteen.

Alex displays delays in his cognitive skills, communication, and social skills. He also exhibits self-stimulatory behaviors that impact his ability to engage in academic tasks. One of Alex's goals for transition is for him to begin residing in a group facility. This goal has been assisted through the use of mobile technologies for communication, health, and data collection.

As part of his transition, Alex's teachers have downloaded his AAC app, *Autism myVoice* ™. Among many other useful functions, this application allows his teachers to upload speech phrases that are specific to events. All his medical information (e.g., medicine allergies, current medications) have been uploaded, so that all entities have the necessary information in a format that can be accessed quickly by people in the group facility that may need to use it.

As communication is difficult for Alex, he uses PECS to communicate. Alex has completed Phases 1 and 2 training in the PECS system. He needs practice in Phase 3. *PECS Phase III*™ is being used to teach Alex more skills and discrimination in his PECS system. The application is used in conjunction with Alex's own PECS device. To facilitate his transition, pictures from his new setting were used during the training.

As with many students, there are many agencies involved in the transition and future planning for Alex. Communication between these entities is vital for a successful outcome. The app *AutismTrack*™, contains a data-tracking tool. This tool allows caregivers to track interventions, behaviors, and symptoms (e.g., eye contact, aggression and echolalia). The app utilizes checkboxes, which are used to record daily therapies, medicine and diet. Also, behaviors and symptoms can be rated in terms of intensity through the use of sliders.

Finally, all members of Alex's team have been given access to Alex's *Google Calendars* ™. All necessary team members can see when Alex has upcoming appointments. They will also be able to use the calendars to invite others to attend the appointments.

CONCLUSION

It is apparent from the literature and the case studies presented here that the educational needs of students with autism are as varied as the spectrum itself. Mobile technology is an advantageous addition to current evidence-based practices, because mobile devices can be individualized for each student through the downloading and use of different applications. These applications can be added or removed as necessary, allowing the devices to adapt to the developing needs of the user as s/he grows and changes.

When implementing mobile technology as an assistive/educational tool for students with autism, various factors need to be considered, such as parents', students', and teachers' exposure to mobile technology and their training needs in this area. Using mobile technology when implementing evidence-based practices in the education of students with autism can be a powerful tool in increasing students' access to the curriculum and the classroom in general. It can further increase their involvement at home and in the community. When deciding about the specific use of mobile

technology and its apps, it is the preferences of the student with autism that need to be considered first and foremost, and s/he needs to be actively involved in making such decisions. Mobile technology can serve as an assistive tool in facilitating a student's involvement in this planning process.

The case studies presented in this chapter demonstrate how mobile technology can be a useful tool for students with autism across the spectrum when accessing the classroom or during the transition process from school to post schooling options. The unique features of mobile technology (mobility, affordability, popularity, ease of use, and ability to customize) give it the potential to become a widely accepted and effective educational and assistive technology for students with autism throughout their lifespans.

ACKNOWLEDGMENT

The authors would like to express their gratitude to the students with autism spectrum disorders and their teachers and parents that they have met and collaborated with on a number of research studies, for it was they who inspired them to write this chapter. They would like to specifically thank Dawn-Joy Leong, a PhD student with Asperger Syndrome at UNSW, College of Fine Arts, who shared with them her experiences with utilizing mobile technology in her everyday life. Though Case Study 3 is partially fictional, it does reflect her experiences with using mobile technology and the cited text is her own.

REFERENCES

Achmadi, D. (2010). *Teaching a multi-step requesting sequence to two adolescents with autism using an iPod-based speech generating device.* (Unpublished master's thesis). Victoria University of Wellington, Wellington, New Zealand.

Blair, K. C., Lee, I., Cho, S., & Dunlap, G. (2011). Positive behaviour support through family-school collaboration for young children with autism. *Topics in Early Childhood Special Education*, *31*(1), 22–36. doi:10.1177/0271121410377510

Briel, L. W., & Getzel, E. E. (2009). Postsecondary options for students with autism. In *Autism and the transition to adulthood: Success beyond the classroom* (pp. 189–207). Baltimore, MD: Paul H. Brookes.

Cappadocia, M. C., Weiss, J. A., & Pepler, D. (2012). Bullying experiences among children and youth with autism spectrum disorders. *Journal of Autism and Developmental Disorders*, *42*(2), 266–277. doi:10.1007/s10803-011-1241-x PMID:21499672

Carrington, S., Templeton, E., & Papinczak, T. (2003). Adolescents with Asperger syndrome and perceptions of friendship. *Focus on Autism and Other Developmental Disabilities*, *18*(4), 211–218. doi:10.1177/10883576030180040201

Carter, E. W., Trainor, A., Owens, L., Sweden, B., & Sun, Y. (2010). Self-determination prospects of youth with high-incidence disabilities. *Journal of Emotional and Behavioral Disorders*, *18*, 67–81. doi:10.1177/1063426609332605

CAST. (2011a). *About UDL*. Retrieved from http://www.cast.org/udl/index.html

CAST. (2011b). *Universal design for learning guidelines – Version 2.0*. Wakefield, MA: Author. Retrieved from http://www.udlcenter.org/aboutudl/udlguidelines/downloads

Chamberlain, B., Kasari, C., & Rotheram-Fuller, E. (2007). Involvement or isolation? The social networks of children with autism in regular classrooms. *Journal of Autism and Developmental Disorders*, *37*(2), 230–242. doi:10.1007/s10803-006-0164-4 PMID:16855874

Cihak, D., Fahrenkrog, C., Ayres, K., & Smith, C. (2010). The use of video modelling via a video iPod and a system of least prompts to improve transitional behaviors for students with autism spectrum disorders in the general education classroom. *Journal of Positive Behavior Interventions*, *12*(2), 103–115. doi:10.1177/1098300709332346

Dodd, S. (2005). *Understanding autism*. Sydney, Australia: Elsevier Australia.

Edyburn, D. L. (2010). Would you recognize universal design for learning if you saw it? Ten propositions for new directions for the second decade of UDL. *Learning Disability Quarterly*, *33*(1), 33–41.

Flores, M., Musgrove, K., Renner, S., Hinton, V., Strozier, S., Franklin, S., & Hil, D. (2012). A comparison of communication using the Apple iPad and a picture-based system. *Augmentative and Alternative Communication*. doi:10.3109/07434618.2011.644579 PMID:22263895

Gentry, T., Lau, S., Molinelli, A., Fallen, A., & Kriner, R. (2012). The Apple iPod touch as a vocational support aid for adults with autism: Three case studies. *Journal of Vocational Rehabilitation*, *37*(2). doi: doi:10.3233/JVR-2012-0601

Gentry, T., Wallace, J., Kvarfordt, C., & Lynch, K. (2010). Personal digital assistants as cognitive aids for high school students with autism: Results of a community-based trial. *Journal of Vocational Rehabilitation*, *32*(2), 101–107.

Grandin, T. (2010). *Thinking in pictures: My life with autism*. New York: Vintage Books.

Hagner, D., Kurtz, A., Cloutier, H., Arakelian, C., Brucker, D. L., & May, J. (2012). Outcomes of a family-centered transition process for students with autism spectrum disorders. *Focus on Autism and Other Developmental Disabilities*, *27*(1), 42–50. doi:10.1177/1088357611430841

Hall, L. J. (2009). Autism spectrum disorders. In *From theory to practice*. London: Jessica Kingsley Publishers.

Hetherington, S. A., Durant-Jones, L., Johnson, K., Nolan, K., Smith, E., Taylor-Brown, S., & Tuttle, J. (2010). The lived experiences of adolescents with disabilities and their parents in transition planning. *Focus on Autism and Other Developmental Disabilities*, *25*(3), 163–172. doi:10.1177/1088357610373760

Humphrey, N., & Symes, W. (2010). Responses to bullying and use of social support among pupils with autism spectrum disorders (ASDs) in mainstream schools: A qualitative study. *Journal of Research in Special Educational Needs*, *10*(2), 82–90. doi:10.1111/j.1471-3802.2010.01146.x

Lancioni, G. E., O'Reilly, M. F., Cuvo, A. J., Singh, N. N., Sigafoos, J., & Didden, R. (2007). PECS and VOCAs to enable students with developmental disabilities to make requests: An overview of the literature. *Research in Developmental Disabilities*, *28*(5), 468–488. doi:10.1016/j.ridd.2006.06.003 PMID:16887326

Leonard, H. (2013). There will soon be one smartphone for every five people in the world. *Business Insider*. Retrieved on June 8, 2013, from: http://www.businessinsider.com/15-billion-smartphones-in-the-world-22013-2?IR=T

Logan, K. (2012, April 4). *Developing communication skills in children with autism spectrum disorder using Proloquo2go on the iPad: An aided language approach*. Paper presented at the ASPECT Research Forum. Sydney, Australia.

Loukusa, S., & Moilanen, I. (2009). Pragmatic inference abilities in individuals with Asperger syndrome or high-functioning autism: A review. *Research in Autism Spectrum Disorders*, *3*(4), 890–904. doi:10.1016/j.rasd.2009.05.002

Ludicke, P., & Kortman, W. (2012). Tensions in home-school partnerships: The different perspectives of teachers and parents of students with learning barriers. *Australasian Journal of Special Education*, *36*(2), 155–171. doi:10.1017/jse.2012.13

Meadan, H., Ostrosky, M. M., Triplett, B., Michna, A., & Fettig, A. (2011). Using visual supports with young children with autism spectrum disorder. *Teaching Exceptional Children*, *43*(6), 28–35.

Merbler, J., Hadadian, A., & Ulman, J. (1999). Using assistive technology in the inclusive classroom. *Preventing School Failure*, *43*(3), 113–118. doi:10.1080/10459889909603311

Messinger-Willma, J., & Marino, M. (2010). Universal design for learning and assistive technology: Leadership considerations for promoting inclusive education in today's secondary schools. *NASSP Bulletin*, *94*(5). doi: doi:10.1177/0192636510371977

Odom, S. L., Collet-Klingenberg, L., Rogers, S. J., & Halton, D. D. (2010). Evidence-based practices in interventions for children and youth with autism spectrum disorders. *Preventing School Failure*, *54*(4), 275–282. doi:10.1080/10459881003785506

Price, A. (2011). Making a difference with smart tablets: Are iPads really beneficial for students with autism? *Teacher Librarian*, *39*(1), 31–34.

Rothschild, B. (2011). *Special tool for special needs*. Retrieved from http://beta.courierpostonline.com

Salazar, M. J. (2012). Home-school collaboration for embedding individualized goals in daily routines. *Young Exceptional Children*, *15*(3), 20–30. doi:10.1177/1096250612446870

Sansosti, F. J., & Powell-Smith, K. A. (2008). Using computer-presented social stories and video models to increase the social communication skills of children with high-functioning autism spectrum disorders. *Journal of Positive Behavior Interventions*, *10*(3), 162–178. doi:10.1177/1098300708316259

Schlosser, R. W., & Wendt, O. (2008). Effects of augmentative and alternative communication intervention on speech production in children with autism: A systematic review. *American Journal of Speech-Language Pathology*, *17*, 212–230. doi:10.1044/1058-0360(2008/021) PMID:18663107

Strnadová, I., & Evans, D. (2007). Coping strategies in mothers of school-aged children with intellectual disabilities. *Australasian Journal of Special Education*, *31*(2), 159–170. doi:10.1080/10300110701716196

White, T. (2013). Tablets trump smartphones in global website traffic. *Adobe Digital Marketing Blog*. Retrieved on June 8, 2013 from: http://blogs.adobe.com/digitalmarketing/digital-index/tablets-trump-smartphones-in-global-website-traffic/

ADDITIONAL READING

Banda, D. R., Matuszny, R. M., & Sultan, T. (2007). Video modeling strategies to enhance appropriate behaviors in children with autism spectrum disorders. *Teaching Exceptional Children*, *39*(6), 47–52.

Blue-Banning, M., Summers, J. A., Frankland, H. C., Nelson, L. L., & Beegle, G. (2004). Dimensions of family and professional partnerships: Constructive guidelines for collaboration. *Council for Exceptional Children*, *70*(2), 167–184.

Brady, L. (2011). *Apps for autism: An essential guide to over 200 effective apps for improving communication, behavior, social skills and more!* Arlington, TX: Future Horizons.

Brooks-Young, S. (2010). *Teaching with the tools kids really use: Learning with web and mobile technologies.* Thousand Oaks, CA: Corwin Press.

Callahan, K., Henson, R. K., & Cowan, A. K. (2008). Social validation of evidence-based practices in autism by parents, teachers, and administrators. *Journal of Autism and Developmental Disorders*, *38*, 678–692. doi:10.1007/s10803-007-0434-9 PMID:17924182

Campigotto, R., McEwen, R., & Epp, C. D. (2013). Especially social: Exploring the use of an iOS application in special needs classrooms. *Computers & Education*, *60*, 74–86. doi:10.1016/j.compedu.2012.08.002

Cihak, D., Fahrenkrog, C., Ayres, K. M., & Smith, C. (2010). The use of video modeling via a video ipod and a system of least prompts to improve transitional behaviors for students with autism spectrum disorders in the general education classroom. *Journal of Positive Behavior Interventions*, *12*(2), 103–115. doi:10.1177/1098300709332346

Cumming, T., & Draper Rodriguez, C. (2013). Integrating the iPad into language arts instruction for students with disabilities: Engagement and perspectives. *Journal of Special Education Technology*, *28*(4).

Cumming, T., Draper Rodriguez, C., & Strnadová, I. (2013). Aligning iPad applications with evidence-based practices in inclusive and special education. In S. Keengwe (Ed.), Pedagogical applications and social effects of mobile technology integration (55-78). Hershey, PA: IGI Global.

Cumming, T., & Strnadová, I. (2012). The iPad as a pedagogical tool in special education: Promises and possibilities. *Special Education Perspectives*, *21*(1), 34–46.

deFur, S. (2012). Parents as collaborators: Building partnerships with school-and community-based providers. *Teaching Exceptional Children, 44*(3), 58–67.

Fernández-López, Á., Rodríguez-Fórtiz, M. J., Rodríguez-Almendros, M. L., & Martínez-Segura, M. J. (2013). Mobile learning technology based on iOS devices to support students with special education needs. *Computers & Education, 61*, 77–90. doi:10.1016/j.compedu.2012.09.014

Grant, K. B., & Ray, J. A. (2012). *Home, school, and community collaboration: Culturally responsive family engagement.* Los Angeles: Sage.

Green, J. (2011). *The ultimate guide to assistive technology in special education: Resources for education, intervention, and rehabilitation.* Waco, TX: Prufrock Press.

Ho, L. H., Hung, C. L., & Chen, H. C. (2013). Using theoretical models to examine the acceptance behavior of mobile phone messaging to enhance parent–teacher interactions. *Computers & Education, 61*, 105–114. doi:10.1016/j.compedu.2012.09.009

Kagohara, D. M., van der Meer, L., Ramdoss, S., O'Reilly, M. F., Lancioni, G. E., & Davis, T. N. et al. (2013). Using iPods and iPads in teaching programs for individuals with developmental disabilities: A systematic review. *Research in Developmental Disabilities, 34*, 147–156. doi:10.1016/j.ridd.2012.07.027 PMID:22940168

Ludicke, P., & Kortman, W. (2012). Tensions in home–school partnerships: The different perspectives of teachers and parents of students with learning barriers. *Australasian Journal of Special Education, 36*(2), 155–171. doi:10.1017/jse.2012.13

Mancil, G. R., Haydon, T., & Whitby, P. (2009). Differentiated effects of paper and computer-assisted social stories tm on inappropriate behavior in children with autism. *Focus on Autism and Other Developmental Disabilities, 24*(4), 205–215. doi:10.1177/1088357609347324

Neitzel, J. (2010). Positive behavior supports for children and youth with autism spectrum disorders. *Preventing School Failure, 54*(4), 247–255. doi:10.1080/10459881003745229

Olender, R. A., Elias, J., & Mastroleo, J. E. (2010). *The school-home connection: Forging positive relationships with parents by rosemary.* Thousand Oaks: Corwin.

Peacock, G. G., & Collett, B. R. (2009). *Collaborative home/school interventions: Evidence-based solutions for emotional, behavioral, and academic problems.* New York: Guilford Press.

Shukla-Mehta, S., Miller, T., & Callahan, K. J. (2010). Evaluating the effectiveness of video instruction on social and communication skills training for children with autism spectrum disorders: A review of the literature. *Focus on Autism and Other Developmental Disabilities, 25*(1), 23–36. doi:10.1177/1088357609352901

Simpson, R. L. (2005). Evidence-based practices and students with autism spectrum disorders. *Focus on Autism and Other Developmental Disabilities, 20*(3), 140–149. doi:10.1177/1088357 6050200030201

van der Meer, L., Kagohara, D., Achmadi, D., Green, V. A., Herrington, C., & Sigafoos, J. et al. (2011). Teaching functional use of an ipod-based speech-generating device to individuals with developmental disabilities. *Journal of Special Education Technology, 26*(3), 1–11.

Williams, P. (2005). Using information and communication technology with special educational needs students: The views of frontline professionals. *Aslib Proceedings, 57*(6), 539–553. doi:10.1108/00012530510634262

KEY TERMS AND DEFINITIONS

Assistive Technology (AT): Includes assistive, adaptive, and rehabilitative devices used by people with disabilities in order to perform tasks that might otherwise be difficult or impossible. AT can include mobility devices such as wheelchairs, architectural innovations such as curb cuts, as well as hardware, software, and peripherals that assist people with disabilities in accessing computers or other information technologies.

Autism Spectrum Disorders (ASD): Neurological spectrum of disorders characterized by qualitative impairment in communication and social interaction, and by stereotyped behaviours. The cause of autism is not known.

Evidence-Based Practices (EBP): Practices that are implemented with students based on consistent benefits presented through sound research studies.

Inclusive Education: Education that is environmentally and instructionally designed to support the needs of all students.

Mobile Application (App): Software applications designed to run on smart phones or tablets.

Mobile Technology: Various types of portable technology, including mobile smart phones, personal digital assistants (PDAs), and tablet devices such as the iPad.

School-Home Collaboration: The communication and cooperation between the educators and the family of the student, which fosters consistency between the two environments.

Schooling Transitions: Points within a student's school career during which the team serving the student will collaborate to ensure successful change.

Tablet: A mobile computer that the user operates by touching the screen.

Chapter 4

The Use of Computer–Based Technologies to Increase the Academic, Behavioral, and Social Outcomes of Students with Autism Spectrum Disorders in Schools:
Considerations for Best Approaches in Educational Practice

Frank J. Sansosti
Kent State University, USA

Mary Lynn Mizenko
Kent State University, USA

Allison Krupko
Kent State University, USA

ABSTRACT

In recent years, the number of students with Autism Spectrum Disorder (ASD) in both special and general education classrooms has increased substantially. As such, there may be no greater challenge facing educators than planning for the education of this growing population. One method of instruction that appears to hold great promise for educating these students is the use of computer-based technologies. The purpose of this chapter is to: (a) provide a brief overview of the contemporary research regarding the use of computer-assisted instruction and mobile devices for improving the academic, behavior, and social outcomes of students with ASD within school-based contexts and (b) to provide educators with strategies for collecting data to promote accountability. Taken together, the intent is to call attention to the evidence that supports the use of computer-based technologies for students with ASD in schools, raise awareness of those strategies that appear to be the most effective for such students, and assist service providers in providing defensible education.

DOI: 10.4018/978-1-4666-5792-2.ch004

BACKGROUND AND SIGNIFICANCE

Within the past two decades, the number of individuals identified as having an autism spectrum disorder (ASD) has increased substantially. Traditionally, ASD was considered a low-incidence disability, occurring in approximately 1 in 1,600 live births (Lotter, 1967). However, the most recent estimates indicate that ASD may occur in as many as 1 in every 50 births (Centers for Disease Control and Prevention; CDC, 2013). Given these increases, it follows logically that state departments of education also have reported significant increases in the number of students with ASD receiving special education and/or related services. The Individuals with Disabilities Education Improvement Act (IDEIA, 2004) requires each state's Department of Education (DOE) and the U.S. Department of Education to record specific childhood disabilities, including ASD, for each school year. From 1992 (the first year autism statistics were reported) to 2011 (the most recent data available), the total number of students provided with special education under the autism category of IDEA grew from 15,580 to 458,209, a cumulative increase of 2,953% (Data Accountability Center; DAC, 2013). From the available information, it is likely that all educational agencies have observed significant impacts in the number of students with ASD.

While there has been an increase in the number of students receiving special education services under the IDEA category of autism, it is possible that the increase is an underestimate of the actual frequency of services necessary to support the education of students with ASD. This is due to the fact that some children with classic autism and most children with more higher-functioning ASD are not included in IDEIA counts because they attend private schools, are home schooled, or do not meet a state's eligibility criteria for the autism disability category. For example, Bertrand et al. (2001) found that 66% of students with classic autism and only 50% of students with higher functioning ASD had autism listed as their special education designation. In a similar study, Yeargin-Allsopp et al. (2003) discovered that only 41% of children with ASD were receiving special education services under the autism category of IDEIA. This underreporting may be due to the fact that states have different eligibility criteria for the autism disability category and that children with higher functioning ASD may not qualify for any services. Because of their elevated cognitive and language abilities children with higher functioning ASD may receive services under a different IDEA category such as other health impaired, specific learning disability, or emotional disturbance, if they qualify for any services at all. Regardless of which special education category is chosen, the potential exists that children with ASD represent a large underserved student population (Safran, 2008).

Aside from the issue of the exact number of students served, placement in general education settings continues to be a predominant service delivery issue for students with ASD. Data from the Office of Special Education Programs (OSEP; 2011) suggests that children with ASD are served increasingly in inclusive classroom settings. Specifically, participation of students with ASD in the general education curriculum (defined as more than 80% of the day) increased at a faster pace than that of all disability categories combined. Whereas only 4.8% of students with ASD were included in 1991-1992, nearly 34% were in general education for 80% or more of their day in 2006-2007, representing a growth rate of 580%. Aside from the reported statistics, educators frequently comment on the increasing numbers of students with ASD characteristics within general education classrooms (Myles, 2005). With this in mind, developing and implementing effective programming for students with ASD becomes a challenge for educators.

USING COMPUTERS TO FACILITATE KNOWLEDGE FOR STUDENTS WITH ASD

As a group, individuals with ASD demonstrate strong skills in responding to visual media (Wetherby & Prizant, 2000). This affinity to visual materials underscores the success of interventions that use picture-based cues to help students with ASD organize daily events and activities, communicate more effectively, imitate appropriate behaviors, and/or acquire both academic and functional skills. In fact, strategies that incorporate visual presentation and that allow for repeated imitation of skills and/or behaviors are considered to be one of the most effective methods for educating individuals with ASD (NRC, 2001; Nikopoulos & Nikopoulou-Smyrni, 2008). Moreover, it is important that instruction for students with ASD steadily expose them to cues, prompts, and interesting and motivating stimuli, as well as employ consistent feedback and repeated exposure to stimuli (Iovannoe, Dunlap, Huber, & Kincaid, 2003; Travers et al., 2011). One such method that builds upon the visual learning strengths of students with ASD, incorporates methods of best practices for teaching, and can be adapted to fit within a variety of educational contexts is the use of computers, including mobile technologies.

Benefits of Using Computers in School-Based Settings

The success of using computer-based technologies to facilitate learning for students with ASD rests upon the understanding that such individuals have a strong affinity for responding to visual media. In fact, researchers have identified that individuals with ASD not only demonstrate significant skill acquisition when taught via computers, but also have a preference for instruction delivered through such devices (e.g., Bernard-Opitz, Sriram, & Nakhoda-Sapuan, 2001; Moore, McGrath, & Thorpe, 2000; Shane & Albert, 2008). Students

with ASD may prefer the learning environment that is created when utilizing computer-based technologies for several main reasons. First, students with ASD often find the world confusing and unpredictable, and have difficulty dealing with changes. As such, instructional efforts for students with ASD need to provide routines, describe expectations, and present immediate and consistent responding. Computer-based technologies not only provide a predictable learning environment for students with ASD, but also produce consistent responses in a manner that likely will maintain interest and, possibly, increase motivation. Second, viewing of instruction through electronic media allows individuals with ASD to focus their attention on relevant stimuli (Charlop-Christy & Daneshvar, 2003; Shipley-Benamou, Lutzker, & Taubman, 2002), which, in turn, prevents high levels of inattention due to distractions in the environment, such as noises (e.g., the ticking of a clock), objects (e.g., bulletin boards, instructional manipulatives), and overstimulation of the senses (e.g., the flickering of fluorescent lights). Since students with ASD have difficulty screening out unnecessary sensory information (Gomot & Wicker, 2012; Ornitz, 1989), focusing on a computer, where only necessary information is presented, likely maximizes their attention to the instructional task(s); thereby, increasing their time spent engaged academically. Third, the use of computer-based devices likely creates an environment for learning that appears to be less threatening, to individuals with ASD because it removes the complexity of social demands/contexts placed on the student (Sansosti, Powell-Smith, & Cowan, 2010). Taken together, the environment that is created through the use of computer technologies appears to be more effective for instructing students with ASD, since it capitalizes on their strengths and obviates the possibility for inattention, distraction, and anxiety from interrupting learning.

Aside from the underlying mechanisms by which computers assist the facilitation of learning for students with ASD, there are more obvious systemic variables that promote their use within school-based contexts. Most educational programs for students with ASD design instruction to promote independence and self-efficacy within naturalistic environments (i.e., community-based instruction). For example, an educational program may take students with ASD to a store in the local community, have students purchase an item and pay for it on their own. While such a lesson is admirable, it would need to be repeated countless times throughout the year in order for students to learn appropriately, making it both cost and time inefficient. Moreover, to facilitate both maintenance and generalization of the skill across settings, educators would need to repeat this instruction within a variety of natural environments, such as a classroom, the home, and/or a play setting (Snell & Brown, 2011). In an era of reduced budgets for education, community-based instruction at best is limited, if not eliminated altogether (Dymond, 2012; Steere & DiPipi-Hoy, 2012). Limited occasions for such instruction will not permit a sufficient number of opportunities for practice required for students with ASD to learn. However, computer-based technologies can provide near-natural stimuli and increased opportunities to respond and can be both cost and time efficient. Moreover, by using a computer-based approach, educators are better able to design instruction that incorporates strategies to facilitate generalization. That is, educators can augment their teaching by incorporating computer-based lessons, activities, and/or models of appropriate behavior that are simulated to occur within a variety of settings (e.g., classrooms, home environment, community) and that can be implemented by various people (e.g., parent, paraprofessional, lunchroom monitor).

Challenges of Using Computers within School-Based Settings

Despite the many perceived benefits of using computers within schools, there exist significant challenges. The most apparent of these challenges appears to be the unpreparedness of educators to implement computer-based strategies within the classroom (Lee & Templeton, 2008; Schrum & Glassett, 2006). Although the most recent generations of teachers have had more exposure to technology and may be more confident and comfortable working with it, mere exposure has not translated into higher levels of usage in the classroom (Russell, Bebell, O'Dwyer, & O'Conner, 2008). Such limited competence likely is the result of pre-service training that focuses on how to use technology rather than how to teach with technology (Rosenfield, 2008). That is, pre-service trainers may not provide adequate instruction that prepares students with an understanding of both the broad aspects of technological applications and, as it relates to this chapter, the more narrow application of educational support for students with ASD. In addition to the limitations of current pre-service training, there remains a tremendous need for current practitioners to receive similar ongoing professional development focused on the use of computer-based support strategies for students with ASD.

Aside from the aforementioned training issues, there remain logistical issues in an era of budgetary constraints within education. First, the limited amount budget available to schools and school districts could translate into inadequate support for purchasing new equipment, software, and/or other devices. As such, educators may be challenged with integrating new educational strategies/programs with equipment that is insufficient (or incompatible) in capacity. Second, with tight budgets for ongoing professional development, educational staff may be left to teach themselves through trial and error because they receive limited continuing support/technical assistance. Such limited organizational commitment could result in educators "giving up" on using technological supports within the classroom. While such obstacles can be overcome, it requires the dedication and commitment of the educational program to allocate appropriate time and resources to ensure that technology usage is successful and benefits students.

DEFINITIONS AND ROLES FOR COMPUTER-BASED TECHNOLOGIES IN SCHOOL-BASED DELIVERY

The understanding and use of computer-based technologies within the realm of education is not new. In fact, the broad term *Assistive Technology Device* was first codified under the Technology-Related Assistance for Individuals with Disabilities Act, of 1988, and was defined as "any item, piece of equipment, or product system, whether acquired commercially off the shelf, modified, or customized, that is used to increase, maintain, or improve the functional capabilities of individuals with disabilities." This definition was modified further by the IDEA of 2004 to exclude any surgically implanted medical devices. This definition captures just about any technological device. However, with the widespread and continually emerging use of technology-based instruction and intervention for supporting students with ASD, we will provide more precision of the definition. Traditionally, the term "computer" has been used to refer to personal desktop and laptop devices that most people use. While the personal computer is still the most popular type of device, advancing technology has broadened our view of what a computer looks like. Today, computers represent any electronic device that accepts, processes, stores, and/or outputs data at high speeds. As such, computers have come to represent an array of gadgets beyond desktop and laptop computers and now include mobile devices like smartphones (e.g., Android; iPhone) and tablets (e.g., iPad, Kindle Fire). Beyond the way computers may be defined, they have become a ubiquitous part of the global world, and their use will continue to grow in the future. For purposes of this chapter, we offer the following definitions:

- **Computer-Assisted Instruction (CAI):** Refers to the use of desktop or laptop computers and/or computer software programs that can be implemented within classroom settings to supplement or replace the instruction of obvious academic, behavioral, and/or social skills.

- **Mobile Devices (MD):** Refer to a variety of technological instruments such as iPads, iPhones, iPods, or Android tablets and phones that can be used in a variety of locations to permit access to specific programs and/or apps designed to encourage the use of academic, behavioral, and/or social skills taught via CAI. The defining characteristic of a MD is that it is portable and can blend into the environment.

Granted, there is considerable overlap in the definitions provided. However, what differs is the role and application of each of these technologies in practice. CAI most often is used to teach explicit skills or provide a supplement for teaching skills that a student does not possess. For example, a software program (either purchased or designed) intended to teach a student with ASD how to join in a conversation on the playground would be an example of a CAI, as it intends to teach a specific skill. A MD, on the other hand, most often plays a role in providing ongoing, long-term support for the student. For example, after successful teaching using CAI of how to join in a conversation, a student would have a MD that provides triggers (i.e., a vibrating alarm) and prompts (i.e., list of steps for joining in) during opportunities for practice in both educational and/or community-based settings. Combining and interweaving these two ideas into how computer-based technologies can be applied to students with ASD can assist in conceptualizing how best to build an instructional program (Ayres, Mechling, & Sansosti, 2013).

CONTEMPORARY RESEARCH UTILIZING COMPUTER-BASED TECHNOLOGIES IN SCHOOLS

In recent years, there has been a proliferation of studies investigating the use of computer-based instruction and interventions (Goldsmith & LeBlanc, 2004), including MD (Mechling, 2011). Due to the recent proliferation of research investigating both CAI and MD with students with ASD, it is imperative to be well-informed about the significant gains these students may exhibit in the classroom. While it is not the intent of this chapter to synthesize all of the extant literature within this area, we provide an overview of more relevant applied research that can be used to support the development of similar programs by educators in a variety of educational contexts. Specifically, we provide a glimpse into some of the contemporary findings regarding the use of CAI and MD for promoting the development of academic, behavioral, and/or social skills among students with ASD.

Computer-Based Instruction for Improving Academic Skills

In the realm of academic skill instruction, research investigating the use of CAI and MD is limited. However, there appear to be significant gains that can be made by students with ASD when taught via computers. Research has demonstrated that both CAI and MD can be used to teach basic academic skills across a variety of subjects. For example, Schlosser and Blischak (2004) demonstrated that computers could be used to improve the percentage of correct spelling words. Specifically, they used the LightWRITER-SL35™ (a MD that features talk to text speech) and DECtalk™ (a computer-based device/software that allows the student to communicate with a partner on dual computer screens) to administer a group of target spelling words to a sample of four elementary-aged students with ASD (ages 8 to 12) who had little or no func-

tional speech. Results indicated that all students increased their correct spelling sequences/words from zero levels during baseline conditions to 75% and 100% during the intervention. Similarly, Pennington, Stenhoff, Gibson, and Ballou (2012) demonstrated that CAI paired with prompting was effective for teaching a 7-year-old with autism to write sentences and improve story writing. That is, the student was able to acquire story construction skills following the implementation of the CAI. More recently, Smith, Spooner, and Wood (2013) investigated the effectiveness of using an iPad to teach essential scientific terms to students with ASD. Specifically, instructional information was delivered to the student in a model-test explicit instruction format using a slideshow presented via the iPad. Results of this study demonstrated that following the introduction of the iPad, the number of correctly identified science terms increased significantly for each participant.

In addition to teaching basic academic skills, the use of computer-based technologies appears to be useful for teaching more complex academic skills that require integration and/or synthesis of multiple pieces of information or following multi-step tasks. For example, Coleman-Martin, Heller, Cihak, and Irvine (2005) demonstrated that using PowerPoint to introduce and teach decoding skills without teacher instruction improved the ability of three students with ASD (ages 11 to 16) to identify and read words correctly. Results of their study also indicated that the use of the computer produced less variability in student performance and a slightly higher percentage of correctly identified words than teacher instruction alone. Williams, Wright, Callaghan, and Coughlan (2002) also used a computer to present digital versions of instructional material to teach reading skills. Specifically, eight students with ASD (ages 3 to 5) were assigned randomly to one of two groups (traditional book method versus CAI), where they participated in 10 weeks of reading skill instruction. Results indicated that children in the CAI group were able to recall two times as many words compared to the traditional group, and, anecdotally, were reported to be more engaged during instruction. Similarly, Travers et al. (2011), compared the effectiveness of traditional, teacher-led instruction and CAI for teaching early literacy skills to 17 preschool-age students with ASD. Results of their study indicated that significant gains were made for students in each condition. However, no significant difference between the gains exhibited in each group was indicated when comparing performance within the two conditions.

Taken together, results of studies examining the impact of CAI and MD for improving academic outcomes for students with ASD are limited but promising. In the published research to date, all studies have demonstrated improved academic skills, abilities, and outcomes. Moreover, the majority of the studies evidence increased academic engagement when using CAI and MD as opposed to traditional, teacher-led instructional practices. Despite some findings that suggest there is limited or no significant comparative differences between teacher-led and CAI (e.g., Travers et al., 2011), there is reason to believe that such findings are the result of other moderating variables. That is, CAI and MD (or technology, more broadly) are no different from any other tool. The power of their effectiveness comes not from what these tools are, but rather how they are used. It is quite possible that limited differences found in some prior literature are more indicative of skilled application of teaching and/or adaptation of technology to support learning, as well as implementation by teachers and educational staff.

Computer-Based Instruction for Improving Behavior

Generally speaking, effective strategies for improving the behavior of students with ASD build on or shape behavior. The rationale for such a focus is that positive, educational instruction/interventions build skills in students with ASD, who likely have restricted behavioral repertoires. As such,

simply applying behavior reduction strategies (e.g., time-out) is less desirable because it likely does not result in lifelong behavior changes that improve the student's quality of life. Even when the purpose of a behavioral intervention is to reduce inappropriate behavior(s), efforts should be made to teach rather than to punish. As such, the use of CAI and/or MD emerges as an appropriate means for improving behavioral skills in students with ASD for two primary reasons. First, it provides an educational approach, since a computer or other device is used predominantly to teach specific skills or sets of skills (e.g., strategies for regulating and/or controlling behavior teaching effective replacement behaviors that make engaging in inappropriate behaviors ineffective). Second, students with ASD likely view computer-based devices as less aversive, which may lead to the devices increased likelihood of long-term success.

With regard to reducing inappropriate behavior in students with ASD, several computer-based applications have been utilized. For instance, Soares, Vannest, and Harrison (2009) used a computer to reduce the self-injurious and tantrum behaviors of a 13 year-old student with ASD. Specifically, the student used a computer to self-monitor academic task completion by using a digital sticker chart (copying and pasting an image of Mickey Mouse's face to represent tasks completed). The results of this study demonstrated a large degree of change between baseline and intervention phases, as well as a strong relationship between the increase in task completion and a decrease in rates of inappropriate behaviors (self-injury and tantrums). The authors hypothesized that the structure of the program (computer-based) was an effective feature that engaged and attracted the learner. Similarly, Mancil, Haydon, and Whitby (2009) used computer-based Social Stories™ to decrease pushing behaviors (i.e., grabbing, touching, and shoving other children) in three elementary-aged students with ASD (ages 6 to 9). The computer-based format consisted of a slideshow presentation with interactive text.

There have been a greater variety of approaches for using CAI and MD to teach or improve appropriate behavioral responses in students with ASD. For example, Cihak, Fihrenkrog, Ayres, and Smith (2010) used iPods to improve transitioning behaviors among four elementary-aged students with autism. Specifically, educators developed videos depicting a role model displaying positive behavior during transition periods within the classroom or when they switched rooms/activities (e.g., going to the playground, classroom to bus). Each student was instructed on how to turn on the iPod and how to play the video prior to each transition. Results indicated that the mean number of independent transitions increased from 7% to 77% following the introduction of the handheld device. Not only is such a change dramatic, it also required less teacher assistance when transitioning students between activities and classrooms. Berenzak, Ayres, Mechling, and Alexander (2012) also used iPhones to present skill-based videos and self-prompts to three students with ASD (ages 15 to 18) and demonstrated their effectiveness for increasing the acquisition and independence of functional living skills (e.g., using the washing machine). More recently, Carlile, Reeve, Reeve, and DeBar (2013) used an iPod to teach four elementary-aged students with ASD (ages 8 to 12) to follow independent leisure time activity schedules in a classroom. Prior to using the iPod, none of the participants engaged in appropriate, on-task leisure activities. After training, all of the students were able to use the iPod to follow their activity schedules independently and to increase their on-task behavior.

Results of studies investigating the use of CAI and MD for improving behavioral functioning of students with ASD appear to be very promising. Not only does the extant literature indicate that computer-based technologies are useful for teaching functional skills, but that they are also beneficial for teaching the vocational skills necessary for individuals with ASD to become more independent. This leads to the conclusion that this type of intervention can be effective within the classroom as well as within community and home-based environments.

Computer-Based Instruction for Promoting and Enhancing Social Skills

With regard to teaching social skills, an assortment of CAI and MD approaches have been employed. First, CAI can be used to teach basic discrimination tasks to children. For example, computers have been used to teach students with ASD how to recognize basic emotions and/or facial cues (e.g., Faja, Aylward, Bernier, & Dawson, 2008; Hopkins et al., 2011; Weinger & Depue, 2011). Within this format, a student may be presented with a collection of photographs, videos, avatars, and/or other digital images depicting facial expressions or emotions and prompted to select those that correspond to appropriate feeling words. Faja and colleagues (2008) found that it took eight hours of computerized training to improve the holistic processing of information necessary for basic social recognition skills. Moreover, Lacava, Golan, Baron-Cohen, and Myles (2007) found that the use of the Mind Reading program (a multimedia software program designed to teach emotional recognition) improved the understanding of both basic and complex emotions in faces and voices. Second, computer-based approaches can be used to create multimedia interventions that provide students with an opportunity to read about and observe social interaction events. For example, Sansosti and Powell-Smith (2008) demonstrated positive outcomes of a multimedia intervention for three students with higher functioning ASD (ages 6 to 10) that used PowerPoint to display video-modeled Social Stories™. Using this packaged intervention, participants followed along with the story as it was read to them by the computer and watched a video clip demonstrating the appropriate social interaction behavior. Third, computer-based technologies offer a unique opportunity to teach social problem solving through the use of interactive videos and/or educational games. For example, Hopkins et al. (2011) used FaceSay, a computer-based social skills program that uses interactive, realistic avatar assistants in life-like scenarios for teaching social skills to children with ASD. Within their study, Hopkins et al. demonstrated that FaceSay was effective for improving emotion recognition, social interactions, facial recognition, emotion recognition, and social interactions in children with low-functioning and higher-functioning ASD, respectively. Of particular importance were the significant findings in improved social interactions skills of both groups within naturally occurring environments following training.

The use of computer-mediated approaches also appears to be effective for teaching more abstract social skills to students with ASD. For example, Glenwright and Agbayewa (2011) used CAI with 14 children with ASD (ages 9 to 16) to improve their understanding of verbal irony. Specifically, students were shown differing social scenarios—three that ended with a speaker implying ironic criticism in response to another person's failure at performing a task and three that ended with a literal compliment for task completion and a job well done. Overall, results of their investigation indicated that although students with ASD had difficulty tracking and recalling the information that occurred during social exchanges depicted in the scenarios, they were able to navigate and decode situations in which verbal irony was used. More recently, Bauminger-Zviely et al. (2013) used a combined approach of CAI and cognitive-behavioral therapy with 22 students with ASD to increase social understanding and social engagement with peers in a school-based setting. Specifically, the intervention consisted of twelve 45-minute social skills lessons (six lessons on social task collaboration and six lessons on social conversation) focused on the explanation of social constructs and cognitive reconstruction (e.g., cor-

recting distorted perceptions of the social world). With each lesson, students were not only taught social cognitive skills via the designed software but also practiced each skill with a peer using behavioral learning principles of role-playing and feedback and reinforcement (i.e., behaviors were positively reinforced and feedback on skill execution was provided). As a result, students with ASD were able to increase their understanding of the social world and interact more meaningfully post intervention.

Summary of Research Using Computer-Based Instructional Strategies

From the preceding discussion, it is apparent that computer-based technologies have positive claims that suggest they are a promising strategy for supporting skill acquisition of students with ASD in school-based contexts. The growing body of literature has begun to provide data suggesting that CAI and MD have noteworthy potential for improving the academic, behavioral, and social outcomes of students with ASD within school-based contexts. Such findings are arguably due to the fact that computer-assisted technologies capitalize on the visual learning strengths of students with ASD and offer a distraction free environment in which the child did not need to participate in obsessions or self-stimulatory behaviors as a method of reducing anxiety. As such, many students with ASD will find CAI and MD approaches to be both engaging and rewarding. Moreover, the use of CAI and MD appears to be accepted increasingly by educators as an acceptable approach for teaching. In fact, Flores et al. (2012) found that educators preferred to use CAI or MD to implement interventions due to: (a) their ease of use in the classroom setting, (b) less preparation time required to provide lessons, (c) fewer materials needed to implement interventions, and (d) students' increased preference and noticeably rapid improved performance when using such devices. Still, although they are promising, the results of the various studies cannot be generalized across the entire ASD population without more research.

IMPLICATIONS FOR EDUCATIONAL PRACTICE

The Importance of Collecting Data on Student Outcomes

Of the steps involved in the assessment of and intervention for academic, behavioral, and social difficulties in students with ASD, data collection is the one step that is most often ignored or performed irregularly (Sansosti, Powell-Smith, & Cowan, 2010). However, there are several undeniable reasons for frequently collecting data as a critical part of demonstrating student improvement when using computer-based technologies. First, through data collection, it is possible to determine if the effects of particular computer-based approaches/strategies are favorable. Without data, educators may not be able to notice a student's improvements from his or her initial performance to his/her current behavior. This is likely the result of a student's making progress but still performing outside the range of what is expected. Data gathered regularly not only serve to illustrate a student's, sometimes minor, improvement but also encourages educators to continue their efforts (Crone & Horner, 2003).

Second, systematic data collection allows for formative evaluation. That is, data collected while a strategy or an intervention is being implemented, allows educators to identify problems early on in the process and make changes during the course of the intervention rather than waiting to see if it was successful after several weeks or months (Alberto & Troutman, 2008). For example, Michael's team wanted to increase his ability to join in activities appropriately. To accomplish this task, the team created a computer-based social skills intervention. Data collection demonstrated initial success

for the first several days of the intervention, followed immediately by a regression in skills and, in some instances, aggression towards his peers (see Sansosti & Powell-Smith, 2008 for a full review of this example). As might be expected, Michael's teachers were ready to eliminate this strategy, since they assumed it was a failure. However, Michael's team reviewed the data, made hypotheses as to why he was not using the skills appropriately, and conducted several qualitative observations on the playground. His teachers' further examination revealed that Michael, in fact, was using his skills appropriately. It was his peers who were not providing Michael with opportunities to practice his skills. Based on this knowledge, Michael's team made a few adjustments to the intervention to include prompts and child confederates. These minor modifications resulted in an abrupt improvement in Michael's behavior that was modestly maintained modestly after the intervention was terminated. From this example, it is clear that had it not been for careful analysis of the data collected, Michael's team would have completely abandoned the intervention, thinking that their efforts did not make a difference.

Third, collecting data is the ultimate tool for accountability! As a result of educational reform efforts, beginning with the No Child Left Behind Act (NCLB; 2001) and extended by the IDEA (2004), educators are required to select appropriate instruction strategies that are evidence-based. As such, it is essential that data be gathered for *all* aspects of instruction. In this era of evidence-based accountability, educators are responsible for results and educational planning. This is particularly true when implementing computer-based technologies for students with ASD, which, relatively speaking is still 'new' and constantly emerging. Therefore, it is vital to have reliable and valid data demonstrating that the use of a software program, computer, or some other mobile device is effective at creating change in student academic, behavioral, and/or social performance. Quality data not only permit educators and educational teams to make appropriate programming decisions for students with ASD, but also deliver legally defensible practices.

Steps in the Data Collection Process

As has been indicated, accurate and functional data collection is key in demonstrating student performance, improving accountability, and creating an effective working relationship among staff, parents, and students. Thus, it is critical to identify high quality data collection by detailing the process for collecting meaningful data.

Step 1: *Define the Target Behavior.* Defining the target behavior is a crucial feature of effective data collection. Without an accurate definition of a target behavior(s), data collection will likely be irrelevant. The key principle is to identify a behavior that is observable, measurable and relevant. A well-written target behavior definition includes an element that can be recognized easily by all educational staff. For example, "Daniel thinks about football constantly" is not an observable definition. While the student may appear to be thinking, one cannot be sure that he is actually engaging in that activity or in the specific material. "Daniel spends significant instructional time staring off into space," is a more observable target. A target behavior should be one that is easily measurable. Targets definitions such as "James always speaks out of turn," are ineffective, as they do not define any specific form of behavior. For instance, "James talks out of turn without raising his hand in 80% of classroom discussions," is a more accurate definition as it provides the setting and frequency of the behavior. A target behavior should also be relevant, often referred to as the "so what" factor. Behaviors that are the source of intervention should be educationally or socially relevant to the student. For example,

"Parker colors outside of the lines on 9 out of 10 coloring sheets each week," is not an appropriate target behavior. It is not highly relevant to the child's life and furthermore, it may be common for students his age. Behaviors such as, "Parker knows 1 of 8 basic colors on 4 out of 5 trials," is a more educationally and socially relevant goal.

Step 2: *Determine What Data Collection Procedure to Use.* In determining which data collection system to employ, the first step is to determine whether the instance of occurrence or time engagement is the outcome to measure. The type of behavior defined as the target behavior also is a factor to consider in choosing which data collection system to utilize. Discrete behaviors are those that have a clear beginning and a clear conclusion. Continuous behaviors are those that are constant. An example of a continuous behavior could be a student who is out of his/her seat and rarely sits down. Once these factors have been established, a system can be chosen based on the specifics of the target behavior. Figure 1 provides a decision tree for determining what data collection method to use (interested readers should see Sansosti, Powell-Smith, & Cowan, 2010 for a more thorough description of data collection procedures, as well as data collection reproducibles that can be used within the classroom).

When interested in evaluating the number of times a student with an ASD engages in a target behavior, either a simple frequency count or an interval recording method can be used. *Frequency Recording,* in its simplest form, is marking each instance in which the behavior occurs. Frequency recording is best for discrete behaviors (which have a clear beginning and end) that occur on a more limited basis. *Interval Recording* is noting each instance a behavior occurs during a particular interval of time. Within the category

Figure 1. Decision tree for determining what data collection method to use

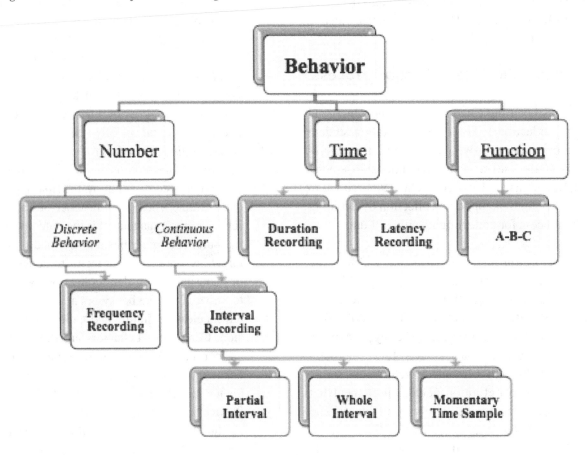

of interval recording, there is whole interval recording (noting a behavioral occurrence only when it is present for the entire time interval) and partial interval recording (documenting an instance of the target behavior when it is present for a portion of a specified time interval).

If an educational team is interested in recording time, then either duration recording or latency recording should be used. *Duration recording* is a data collection system that simply records the length of a target behavior. For example, if a child regularly has prolonged tantrums, duration recording can be used to track the length of each tantrum and provide a basis from which to reduce the extent of outbursts. On the other hand, *latency recording* monitors the time between a directive or a specific trigger and the onset of the target behavior. For example, Mrs. Simpson is concerned with the amount of time it takes Carter to begin in-class assignments. When recording elements of time, instructors should take care to identify how time will be consistently monitored (e.g., timer, clock, wristwatch).

Step 3: *Develop an Action Plan*. After establishing an appropriate data collection system, it is important to develop a plan for collecting data consistently and frequently (this will ensure accountability). Specifically, the action plan should address who will collect data, when (or how often) data will be collected, and where data will be collected (e.g., school, home, community). All such information should be highlighted within an action plan document with the entire educational team responsible for providing services to a student with ASD. The action plan also should include scheduled meetings whereby the educational team can meet to review the student's data and determine whether instruction/intervention is effective or needs to be altered. In preparation for such meetings, progress reports should be created. Progress reports are most effective when graphs of the data are included, as the simplest graphs often speak the loudest to student performance. Graphs convey the data and data trends in a concise manner that leads to a clear understanding. Creating graphs can seem like a daunting task; they are, however, relatively easy to construct (see Sansosti, Powell-Smith, & Cowan, 2010 for detailed information)

Methods for Evaluating Data

Collection of data for the mere sake of collecting data is a fruitless activity unless the data are evaluated. For the most part, visual inspection of a graph will indicate whether or not the desired treatment effects were obtained. As part of a visual inspection of graphs, educators will want to provide information regarding changes in the mean data that occur from baseline to intervention. More recently, Parker and Hagan-Burke (2007) and Parker, Vannest, and Brown (2009) suggested using the improvement rate difference (IRD) to supplement visual inspection of graphs and for calculating effect size. IRD has been used for decades in the medical field (referred to "risk reduction" or "risk difference") to describe the absolute change in risk that is attributable to an experimental intervention. This metric is valued within the medical community due to its ease of interpretation, as well as the fact that it does not require specific data assumptions for confidence intervals to be calculated (Altman, 1999). IRD represents the difference between two proportions (baseline and intervention). More specifically, it is the difference in improvement rates between

baseline and intervention phases (Higgins & Green, 2009; Parker, Vannest, & Brown, 2009). By knowing the absolute difference in improvement, practitioners can determine the effect of an intervention and if the change in behavior is worth repeating. To calculate IRD, a minimum number of data points are removed from either baseline or intervention phases to eliminate all overlap. Data points removed from the baseline phase are considered "improved," meaning they overlap with the intervention. Data points removed from the intervention phase are considered "not improved," meaning they overlap with the baseline. The proportion of data points "improved" in baseline is then subtracted from the proportion of data points "improved" in the intervention phase ($IR_I - IR_B = IRD$). The maximum IRD score is 1.00 or 100% (all intervention data exceed baseline). An IRD of .70 to 1.0 indicates a large effect size, .50 to .70 a moderate effect size, and less than .50 a small or questionable effect size (Parker et al., 2009). An IRD of .50 indicates that half of the scores between the baseline and treatment phases were overlapping so there is only chance-level improvement. One distinct advantage of IRD is that it affords the ability to calculate confidence intervals. Practitioners can interpret the width of a confidence interval as the precision of the approach (large intervals indicate that the IRD is not trustworthy, whereas narrow intervals indicate more precision).

IMPLICATIONS FOR EDUCATIONAL PRACTICE

Pre-Service Training Considerations

University trainers should provide more training and direct instruction to develop teacher competence in classroom technology use, in general, as well as the more specific application for students with ASD as it relates to this chapter. However, such training should be embedded among coursework pertaining to curriculum, instruction, and intervention rather than within technology specific courses. Technology specific courses may be insufficient to train future practitioners how best to use technology to support learning because, in these courses, technology may become an abstraction without specific regard to the practices or context of instructing students with ASD. Instead, trainers should model and explain a traditional instructional approach and/or intervention and then demonstrate and/or incorporate technology-based examples of that same instruction/intervention. In so doing, trainees stand a better chance of understanding the relationship and value of the technological application and, in turn, are better equipped to justify the inclusion of technology.

In addition to instruction, trainers should require specialized, "hands-on" projects during student teaching, practicum, and/or internships that require students to utilize various technologies with students in the classroom. Such projects should focus on the development, implementation, data collection, and evaluation of the use of computer-based technologies. This application not only has the benefit of teaching students the logistics of intervention development and implementation, but also has the added benefit of demonstrating to those in the field how the research conducted at the university level can be applied effectively within a classroom context.

Ongoing Professional Development Needs

Given the increased use of technology in classrooms, combined with requests by parents and advocates for educators to use a variety of technological supports for students with ASD within the school context, current practitioners need to engage in a host of ongoing professional development activities. As such, educational staff must continually seek to strengthen and broaden their skill-set to remain relevant and effective. Perhaps the quickest way to gain immediate information

about emerging technologies is through attendance at professional conferences. Although conference sessions typically excel at providing attendees breadth, they often fall short in delivering in-depth information and practice with technological tools. Given this limitation, technology-specific conferences likely will offer workshops and trainings allowing attendees an opportunity to explore the available technologies and observe applications of such within a variety of contexts. However, there is a danger in the technology becoming an abstraction, where the focus is more on the technology than on how it relates to practice.

Another, less structured, strategy is to allot time over the year to explore software demonstrations that are often available free of charge online or in device-specific "app stores." This clearly places the onus on the educator to seek out different mobile technology applications (not to mention that the practitioner needs to have the basic skills to load the software, etc.).

Finding potential interventions is not likely the greatest challenge. Instead, the challenge rests in separating those that are likely to work from those that are unlikely to benefit a student.

Finally, efforts should be made to create collaborative projects that benefit both researchers and educators. That is, researchers/consultants who have familiarity with computer-based technologies may work with educators/schools to develop a supportive infrastructure. Both the school psychologist and researcher/consultant can work together to identify the needs of buildings (or the larger district) and align those technologies that best meet the needs of students. Once the needs are identified, the researcher/consultant can provide ongoing training/coaching with educational staff and other student support services personnel. Once this small team of individuals has the foundation, they can provide a trainer-of-trainers approach to others within their building(s). While the building (district) teams are implementing computer-based technologies with students, the researcher/consultant can provide ongoing, supportive technical assistance (e.g., troubleshooting difficulties, modeling application of strategies, observing the schools progression). In so doing, it is likely that schools can increase their capacity to use computer-based technologies such as CAI and MD to support the education of students with ASD, as well as provide the much-needed applied research.

CONCLUSION

Computers have become a ubiquitous part of our culture, and it is likely that there are endless opportunities for the application of computer-based innovations for teaching students with ASD. To date, computer-based technologies have been used to increase the academic, behavioral, and social functioning of students with ASD within a variety of school-based contexts. Moreover, students with ASD appear to be more attentive and motivated when using a computer than when interacting with a human instructor. As such, an effort to increase the use of a variety of computer-based applications for students with ASD across a variety of educational contexts is warranted. In so doing, educators may be able to provide higher quality instruction that has a greater likelihood of long-term success.

REFERENCES

Ayres, K. M., Mechling, L., & Sansosti, F. J. (2013). The use of mobile technologies to assist with life skills/independence of students with moderate/severe intellectual disability and/or autism spectrum disorders: Considerations for the future of school psychology. *Psychology in the Schools*, *50*, 259–271. doi:10.1002/pits.21673

Bauminger-Zviely, N., Eden, S., Zancanaro, M., Weiss, P., & Gal, E. (2013). Increasing social engagement in children with high-functioning autism spectrum disorder using collaborative technologies in the school environment. *Autism*, *17*, 317–339. doi:10.1177/1362361312472989 PMID:23614935

Bereznak, S., Ayres, K., Mechling, L., & Alexander, J. (2012). Video self-prompting and mobile technology to increase daily living and vocational independence for students with autism spectrum disorders. *Journal of Developmental and Physical Disabilities*, *24*, 269–285. doi:10.1007/s10882-012-9270-8

Bernard-Opitz, V., Sriram, N., & Nakhoda-Sapuan, S. (2001). Enhancing social problem solving in children with autism and normal children through computer-assisted instruction. *Journal of Autism and Developmental Disorders*, *31*, 377–398. doi:10.1023/A:1010660502130 PMID:11569584

Bertrand, J., Mars, A., Boyle, C., Bove, F., Yeargin-Allsopp, M., & Decoufle, P. (2001). Prevalence of autism in a United States population: The Brick Township, New Jersey investigation. *Pediatrics*, *108*, 1155–1161. doi:10.1542/peds.108.5.1155 PMID:11694696

Carlile, K. A., Reeve, S. A., Reeve, K. F., & DeBar, R. M. (2013). Using activity schedules on the iPod touch to teach leisure skills to children with autism. *Education & Treatment of Children*, *36*, 33–57. doi:10.1353/etc.2013.0015

Centers for Disease Control and Prevention. (2013). Changes in prevalence of parent-reported autism spectrum disorder in school-aged U.S. children: 2007 to 2011-2012. *National Health Statistics Reports, 5*.

Charlop-Christy, M. J., & Daneshvar, S. (2003). Using video modeling to teach perspective taking to children with autism. *Journal of Positive Behavior Interventions, 5*, 12–21. doi:10.1177/10983007030050010101

Cihak, D., Fahrenkrog, C., Ayers, K. M., & Smith, C. (2010). The use of video modeling via a video iPod and a system of least prompts to improve transitional behaviors for students with autism spectrum disorders in the general education classroom. *Journal of Positive Behavior Interventions, 12*, 103–115. doi:10.1177/1098300709332346

Coleman-Martin, M. B., Heller, K. W., Cihak, D. F., & Irvine, K. L. (2005). Using computer-assisted instruction and the nonverbal reading approach to teach word identification. *Focus on Autism and Other Developmental Disabilities, 20*, 80–90. doi:10.1177/10883576050200020401

Data Accountability Center. (2013). *Individuals with disabilities education act (IDEA) data.* Retrieved from www.ideadata.org

Dymond, S. (2012). Community participation. In P. Wehman, & J. Kregel (Eds.), *Functional curriculum for elementary and secondary students with special needs* (3rd ed., pp. 351–387). Austin, TX: Pro-Ed.

Faja, S., Aylward, E., Bernier, R., & Dawson, G. (2008). Becoming a face expert: A computerize face-training program for high functioning individuals with autism spectrum disorders. *Developmental Neuropsychology, 33*, 1–24. doi:10.1080/87565640701729573 PMID:18443967

Flores, M., Musgrove, K., Renner, S., Hinton, V., Strozier, S., Franklin, S., & Hil, D. (2012). A comparison of communication using the Apple iPad and a picture-based system. *Augmentative and Alternative Communication, 28*, 74–84. doi:10.3109/07434618.2011.644579 PMID:22263895

Glenwright, M., & Agbayewa, A. S. (2012). Older children and adolescents with high-functioning autism spectrum disorders can comprehend verbal irony in computer-mediated communication. *Research in Autism Spectrum Disorders, 6*, 628–638. doi:10.1016/j.rasd.2011.09.013

Goldsmith, T. R., & LeBlanc, L. A. (2004). Use of technology in interventions for children with autism. *Journal of Early and Intensive Behavior Intervention, 1*, 166–178.

Gomot, M., & Wicker, B. (2012). A challenging, unpredictable world for people with autism spectrum disorder. *International Journal of Psychophysiology, 83*, 240–247. doi:10.1016/j.ijpsycho.2011.09.017 PMID:21968196

Hopkins, I. M., Gower, M. W., Perez, T. A., Smith, D. S., Amthor, F. R., Wimsatt, F. C., & Biasini, F. J. (2011). Avatar assistant: Improving social skills in students with an ASD through computer-based intervention. *Journal of Autism and Developmental Disorders, 41*, 1543–1555. doi:10.1007/s10803-011-1179-z PMID:21287255

Individuals with Disabilities Education Improvement Act of 2004, 20 U.S.C.§ 614 *et seq.*

Iovannone, R., Dunlap, G., Huber, H., & Kincaid, D. (2003). Effective educational practices for students with autism spectrum disorders. *Focus on Autism and Other Developmental Disabilities, 18*, 150–165. doi:10.1177/10883576030180030301

Lacava, P. G., Golan, O., Baron-Cohen, S., & Myles, B. (2007). Using assistive technology to teach emotion recognition to students with Asperger syndrome: A pilot study. *Remedial and Special Education, 28*, 174–181. doi:10.1177/07419325070280030601

Lee, H., & Templeton, R. (2008). Ensuring equal access to technology: Providing assistive technology for students with disabilities. *Theory into Practice, 47*, 212–219. doi:10.1080/00405840802153874

Mancil, R. G., Haydon, T., & Whitby, P. (2009). Differentiated effects of paper and computer-assisted Social Stories™ on inappropriate behavior in children with autism. *Focus on Autism and Other Developmental Disabilities*, *24*, 205–215. doi:10.1177/1088357609347324

Mechling, L. C. (2011). Review of twenty-first century portable electronic devices for persons with moderate intellectual disabilities and autism spectrum disorders. *Education and Training in Autism and Developmental Disabilities*, *46*, 479–498.

Moore, D., McGrath, P., & Thorpe, J. (2000). Computer-aided learning for people with autism: A framework for research and development. *Innovations in Education and Training International*, *37*, 218–228. doi:10.1080/13558000050138452

Myles, B. S. (2005). *Children and youth with Asperger syndrome: Strategies for success in inclusive settings*. Thousand Oaks, CA: Corwin Press.

National Research Council. (2001). *Educating children with autism*. Washington, DC: National Academy Press.

Nikopoulos, C. K., & Nikopoulou-Smyrni, P. (2008). Teaching complex social skills to children with autism: Advances in video modeling. *Journal of Early and Intensive Behavior Intervention*, *5*, 30–43.

Office of Special Education Programs. (2011). *30th annual report to congress on the implementation of the individuals with disabilities education act, 2008*. Washington, DC: U.S. Department of Education.

Ornitz, E. M. (1989). Autism at the interface between sensory and information processing. In G. Dawson (Ed.), *Autism: Nature, diagnosis, and treatment* (pp. 174–207). New York: Guilford Press.

Rosenfield, B. (2008). The challenges of teaching with technology: From computer idiocy to computer competence. *International Journal of Instructional Media*, *35*, 157–166.

Safran, S. P. (2008). Why youngsters with autistic spectrum disorders remain underrepresented in special education. *Remedial and Special Education*, *29*, 90–95. doi:10.1177/0741932507311637

Sansosti, F. J., Powell-Smith, K. A., & Cowan, R. J. (2010). *High functioning autism/Asperger syndrome in schools: Assessment and intervention*. New York: Guilford.

Schlosser, R. W., & Blischak, D. M. (2004). Effects of speech and print feedback on spelling in children with autism. *Journal of Speech, Language, and Hearing Research: JSLHR*, *47*, 848–862. doi:10.1044/1092-4388(2004/063) PMID:15324290

Schrum, L., & Glassett, K. F. (2006). Technology integration in P-12 schools: Challenges to implementation and impact of scientifically-based research. *Journal of Thought*, *41*, 41–58.

Shane, H. C., & Albert, P. D. (2008). Electronic screen media for persons with autism spectrum disorders: Results of a survey. *Journal of Autism and Developmental Disorders*, *38*, 1499–1508. doi:10.1007/s10803-007-0527-5 PMID:18293074

Shipley-Benamou, R., Lutzker, J. R., & Taubman, M. (2002). Teaching daily living skills to children with autism through instructional video modeling. *Journal of Positive Behavior Interventions*, *4*, 165–175. doi:10.1177/10983007020040030501

Smith, B. R., Spooner, F., & Wood, C. L. (2013). Using embedded computer-assisted explicit instruction to teach science to student with autism spectrum disorder. *Research in Autism Spectrum Disorders*, *7*, 433–443. doi:10.1016/j.rasd.2012.10.010

Snell, M., & Brown, F. (2011). *Instruction for students with severe disabilities* (7th ed.). Boston, MA: Pearson.

Soares, D. A., Vannest, K. J., & Harrison, J. (2009). Computer aided self-monitoring to increase academic production and reduce self-injurious behavior in a child with autism. *Behavioral Interventions*, *24*, 171–183. doi:10.1002/bin.283

Steere, D. E., & DiPipi-Hoy, C. (2012). When you can't get out: Strategies for supporting community-based instruction. *Teaching Exceptional Children*, *45*, 60–67.

Travers, J. C., Higgins, K., Pierce, T., Boone, R., Miller, S., & Tandy, R. (2011). Emergent literacy skills of preschool students with autism: A comparison of teacher-led and computer-assisted instruction. *Education & Training in Autism & Developmental Disabilities*, *46*, 326–338.

Weinger, P. M., & Depue, R. A. (2011). Remediation of deficits in recognition of facial emotions in children with autism spectrum disorders. *Child & Family Behavior Therapy*, *33*, 20–31. doi:10.1080/07317107.2011.545008

Wetherby, A. M., & Prizant, B. M. (2000). *Autism spectrum disorders: A transactional developmental perspective*. Baltimore, MD: Brookes.

Williams, C., Wright, B., Callaghan, G., & Coughlan, B. (2002). Do children with autism learn to read more readily by computer assisted instruction or traditional book methods? *Autism*, *6*, 71–91. doi:10.1177/1362361302006001006 PMID:11918110

Yeargin-Allsopp, M., Rice, C., Karapurkan, T., Doernberg, N., Boyle, C., & Murphy, C. (2003). Prevalence of autism in a US metropolitan area. *Journal of the American Medical Association*, *289*, 49–55. doi:10.1001/jama.289.1.49 PMID:12503976

Chapter 5

Information and Computer Technology for Individuals with Autism

Zandile P. Nkabinde
New Jersey City University, USA

ABSTRACT

The goal of this chapter is to explore the effective use of information and computer technology to assist individuals with autism. In 1985, the Picture Communication System, also known as PECS, was developed for children who had limited abilities to express themselves verbally. The idea was that by pointing to a picture, the child could communicate what he/she wanted. PECS has been modernized with the development of Apps for the iPad. Now, a child can choose from a wide variety of communication choices simply by touching a screen that will facilitate the process and provide a wide variety of choices never before available. This chapter helps parents and teachers to understand how information and computer technology improves communication for children with autism. In addition, the use of iPad and how it improves communication for children with autism are discussed. The use of iPads by children with autism was chosen because of the interactivity they offer to this population as well as for the range of educational opportunities they provide.

INTRODUCTION

This chapter focuses on how people with autism benefit from information and computer technology. While autism is said to confine people afflicted by it to problems in social interaction, communication, and cognitive and motor difficulties, modern computer technology has become a valued asset that can assist them to live productive lives. Simpson (2005) reported that fifty percent of children with autism will not develop functional speech, instead they may either have no speech or they may use echolalia, often in what appears to be nonsensical forms.

Porter and Cafiero (2009) stated that individuals with autism spectrum disorders (ASD) are severely challenged by their difficulties with language and communication. According to these authors language and communication are the core challenges faced by individuals with autism spectrum disorder (ASD).

DOI: 10.4018/978-1-4666-5792-2.ch005

Thus, information and computer technology becomes necessary for this population. Ganz, Hong, and Goodwyn (2013), reported that currently, handheld devices, including tablet computers, smart phones, and personal digital assistants, are gaining popularity in U.S. society, and researchers are beginning to investigate their effects as AAC systems for individuals with ASD on improving their academic, social, behavior, and communication skills.

AUTISM SPECTRUM DISORDERS DEFINED

Autism is defined by Putman and Chong (2008) as a pervasive developmental disorder diagnosed by the age of three. According to the Diagnostic and Statistical Manual of Mental Disorders (DSM-IV-TR), the disorder is characterized by qualitative impairment in social interaction, qualitative impairment in communication and restricted, repetitive and stereotypic patterns of behavior, interest and activities. Ennis-Cole and Smith (2011) stated that within the Autism Spectrum, several classifications of disorders exist: Rett's Disorder, Asperger's Disorder, Pervasive Developmental Delay Not Otherwise Specified (PDD-NOS), Autistic Disorder, and Disintegrative Disorder. According to these authors each of these has its own particular attributes, though there are common denominators such as deficits in communications skills, deficits in social skills, and restrictive and/or repetitive behaviors.

Prevalence

The National Institute of Mental Health (2010) reported that 3.4 of every 1, 000 children 3-10 years old had autism. The effects of autism vary from child to child. Autism Spectrum Disorders affect 1 in 88 children, with a higher prevalence in boys (1 in 54), than girls (1 in 252) (The Center for Disease Control and Prevention as cited in

Rigo (2013). According to Holstein (2013) even more alarming is the rate at which the disease is becoming more prevalent. It is reported that there are more than 1.5 million Americans presently diagnosed with autism (Holstein, 2013).

The degrees of severity vary from person to person. Bryant and Kratz (2012) stated that 70% of individuals with autism have impaired intellectual abilities while the other 30% fall within the normal range of intellectual ability.

Characteristics of ASD

It is well documented that the population of individuals with ASD is heterogeneous (Ennis-Cole, Smith 2011). According to these authors, individuals in the spectrum vary in their intellect, functional ability, preferences, language ability, motor skills, and cognitive ability. The degree of severity also varies from person to person. Some individuals are nonverbal with severe cognitive deficits while others have normal or average intelligence. Ennis-Cole and Smith (2011) described some individuals in the spectrum as possessing skills that make them a genius in a narrowly defined area, which relies on memorization, pattern recognition, computation, musical, or artistic talent.

Autism is characterized by impaired language function, idiosyncratic speech, and an inability to maintain conversations coupled with cognitive and motor difficulties (Holstein, 2013). The following possible indicators of ASD were cited on the report by the National Institute of Mental Health:

- Does not bubble, point, or make meaningful gestures by 1 year of age
- Does not speak one word by 16 months
- Does not combine two words by 2 years
- Does not respond to name
- Loses language or social skills
- Poor eye contact
- Does not seem to know how to play with toys
- Excessively lines up toys or other objects

- Is attached to one particular toy or object
- Does not smile
- At times seems to be hearing impaired (p.1).

THE iPAD DEFINED

According to Fan (2012) the iPad was introduced to consumers in January 2010. It is a touch screen device for consuming media in all its forms: video, music, the Web, electronic books and magazines, and video games (Fan, 2012). Thus, information and computer technology when used with children with autism do support their strongest processing modality, which can include visual cues and visual schedules (Fan, 2012).

iPad users find its flexibility and portability more advantageous over laptops or PCs. The touch screen and layout make the iPad more accessible for children with coordination or learning disabilities; these children may find sliding and tapping easier than either typing or writing (The ipad: A Useful Tool for Autism, 2013). The iPad is also capable of being physically used in multiple environments due to its portability.

Bryant and Kraft (2012) reported that some augmentative communication devices can be quite cumbersome and may be difficult to use in some environments such as in restaurants, grocery stores, and or on the bus. Unlike other assistive devices that are bulky and hard to transport, the iPad is more popular with everyone and thus do not stigmatize its users by making them stand out in public. Grandin (2012) suggested that to be effective, the tablet's use must be facilitated by a teacher or parent in order to keep the child engaged and on tasks as well as to prevent the child from stimming by moving the icons. Grandin (2012) warns that the iPad must not turn into another opportunity for stims. Other concerns about the iPad are that it may inhibit children's interactions with others.

WHY USE INFORMATION AND COMPUTER TECHNOLOGY FOR INDIVIDUALS WITH AUTISM?

Research studies support the notion that individuals with ASD process visual information more effectively than auditory information (Cafiero, 2008; Fan, 2012; Grandin and Scariano, 2005; Putman and Chong, 2008 ;). Some of the difficulties that are faced by individuals who have autism can be minimized through the use of computer technology. These difficulties as cited by Cafiero (2008) include but are not limited to:

- **Difficulty with communication:** Communication as defined by Smith and Tyler (2010) is the process of exchanging knowledge, ideas, opinions, and feelings through the use of verbal or nonverbal language. Communication is also the core deficits in ASD. Bryant and Kraft (2012) reported that approximately 50% of children with autism never learn to speak. Therefore, early interventions to increase appropriate communication are necessary for children with autism. Thus, Computer technology becomes a very viable strategy and a useful tool in the areas of reading, writing, speaking, and using augmented speech supports. Most children with autism have complex communication deficits and are generally unable to communicate spontaneously at a level near that of their typically developing peers using speech (Ganz, Hong and Goodwyn, 2013).
- **Difficulty with complex cues:** Individuals with ASD have global sensory processing difficulties, translating into localized and fragmented processing of the stimuli around them. These processing difficulties often are related to challenges in understanding multiple or complex cues. Computer technology offers the capability for creating a range of symbols to multiple and more complex symbols (Cafiero, 2008).

- **Difficulty with affective and social learning:** Affective and social learning are developed in relationships with others. Computer technology can act as a buffer and a bridge between communication partners (Cafiero, 2008, p. 2).

The main goal in using information and computer technology for children with autism is to provide a means for them to spontaneously and effectively communicate in generalized situations (Webber and Scheuermann, 2008).

THE ROLE OF INFORMATION AND COMPUTER TECHNOLOGY FOR CHILDREN WITH AUTISM

Computers can be effective tools for children with autism in facilitating communication and in aiding their learning. People diagnosed with autism have varied strengths and weaknesses in both their social and academic skills. Some are verbal and others are nonverbal. Many individuals with autism are visual thinkers and have strong technological and/or artistic skills (The iPad: a Useful Tool for Autism, 2013).

Information and computer technology are considered to be effective tools for children with autism. Putman and Chong (2008) cited the following reasons for the easy acceptance and effectiveness given by researchers investigating technology solutions designed for people with ASD:

- Software programs accommodate the ASD need for sameness by being predictable and familiar.
- Tasks can easily be repeated with very little change from one exercise to the next. In other words, software does not get impatient with repetition and can be implemented to provide prompts and reinforcement consistently.

- Most software and technologies are delivered through a visual medium, for example desktop computers and iPads, which capitalizes on what many consider a strength of the audience.
- Much of software delivered in computer-based training eliminates the social complexities of interactions with others and allows users to work at their own pace.
- Educational software for the personal computer platform can deliver a one-on-one structured learning environment which is often required for children with ASD to effectively learn a topic.
- Software delivered on technology devices may provide readily available and affordable teaching tools which augment off-line learning that children and adults can access at home or school, thereby addressing the shortage of instructors needed for intensive one-on-one teaching (p.2).

It must be pointed out that computer technology is more expensive than nonelectronic devices such as traditional PECS, nonelectronic communication boards, eye gaze displays and communication books. However, computers are still viewed as motivating to children with autism due to their predictability and consistency, compared to the unpredictable nature of human responses (Habash, 2005). Research on the use of computers with students with autism as cited by Habash (2005) proved to be effective for the following reasons:

- Increase in focused attention
- Increase in overall attention span
- Increase in in-seat behavior
- Increase in fine motor skills
- Increase in generalization skills (from computer to related non-computer activities)
- Decrease agitation
- Decrease in self-stimulatory behaviors
- Decrease in perseverative responses (p.4).

Plowman and Stephen (in press) as cited by Bouck, Okolo, and Courtad (2008) stated that children's interaction with computers can offer three advantages: (a) development of students' dispositions to learn, (b) increases in students' motivation and engagement, and (c) knowledge of the world, including the academic content that students are expected to master in school (p. 48).

TYPES OF COMPUTER TECHNOLOGY THAT IS SUITABLE FOR INDIVIDUALS WITH AUTISM

According to the Wisconsin Assistive Technology Initiative (2009), computer technology involves the use of complex, typically high-cost equipment as well as some training for effective use (e.g., video cameras, computer software, adaptive computer hardware, complex voice output devices, etc. (p.2).

- **Computer games and software programs:** It is reported that some individuals with ASD find sensory regulation in various computer software and programs. A report by the Wisconsin Assistive Technology Initiative (2009) contended that programs or games that are highly visually stimulating and have a relatively fast pace are often popular for some individuals with ASD. According to this report, for others, programs that are accompanied by music or other auditory stimuli are preferred. This report also indicated that although not always appropriate in all environments, video game systems are often a popular recreation choice for individuals with ASD because of their rapid pace and high stimulation levels (Wisconsin Assistive Technology Initiative, 2009).
- **Touch screens:** Many students who are unable to use a traditional keyboard to access information from the computer can make

use of the touch screen. This is described as a device that is placed on the computer monitor and permits direct selection by merely touching the screen (Bryant and Bryant, 2012). The touch screen allows students to take notes or complete written assignments without the added stress of typing.

- **Videotaping:** The Wisconsin Assistive Technology Initiative (2009) reported that many individuals with ASD seem to enjoy repetitive viewing of videos due to the "predictability" of the information given, that is: knowing what's coming up next. Furthermore, this medium can serve as an excellent tool to teach a variety of skills to students with ASD who show a particular interest in this piece of technology. Social skills can be taught via videotaping so are vocabulary skills and other life skills.
- **E-books:** Electronic books are digitally recorded books designed for individuals with print disabilities, including those with learning disabilities, visual impairments, cognitive disabilities, and physical disabilities (Bryant and Bryant, 2012). While these books were designed for individuals with different types of disabilities, they are quite popular among nondisabled consumers.
- **Interface devices:** These devices according to Bryant and Bryant (2012) provide the use of switches, alternate keyboards, and other input devices such as joysticks and speech synthesizers, to access the keyboard and keyboard functions. According to these authors interface devices can make communication boards accessible by a switch or alternate keyboard, connect a switch to a computer with scanning options, and permit multiple input devices to be connected, such as several switches that can activate keyboard functions.

- **Switches:** Switches can be used to offer students with autism access to information and computer programs. Johnson, Beard and Carpenter (2007) described switches as input and output devices that facilitate interactions with their environments. Bryant and Bryant (2012) reported that switches are often found in early childhood programs to help students with physical and cognitive difficulties to engage in play activities in early childhood programs, at home, and in day care settings. These authors further stated that because the use of switches can promote developmental learning such as cause and effect, social activities such as play, and communication, it is critical that younger children have multiple opportunities to use switches as needed in their learning, social, and home environments.

- **Joysticks:** Some students with ASD, who have significant physical and/or fine motor skill deficits, can use the joysticks as an alternative keyboard input device. Bryant and Bryant (2012) described joysticks as a popular input device for game machines such as Nintendo, and are found on wheelchairs to promote mobility; thus, they are readily available. According to Bryant and Bryant (2012), some joysticks can be plugged into the mouse port, while others require special software for the computer to accept them.

- **Trackballs:** These are mouse alternatives. Dell, Newton, and Petroff (2008) described a trackball as a mouse lying on its back. According to these authors the base of the trackball remains in one place; to move the mouse pointer, the ball is rotated with a thumb, fingers, and the palm of the hand, a foot, or other body part.

- **Pointing devices:** Pointing devices are generally used by individuals with physical disabilities and those who may have limited use of their hands or fingers. These devices may be controlled by hand movement or movement of the head (Dell, Newton and Petroff, 2008). Some pointing devices are mouth sticks, headsticks, and chinsticks that are controlled with head movement. According to Dell et al. (2008), both headsticks and chinsticks require a headpiece to hold the selecting/pointing device in position.

- **Alternate keyboards:** There are a wide variety of alternative keyboards that make the computer accessible to almost every student (Dell et al., 2008). There are enlarged or oversized keyboards which are ideal for students with poor fine motor control, who need a large target area to accurately make key strokes whether they are using their hand, foot, or typing aid (Dell et al. 2008).

- **Voice recognition:** This technology permits a user to speak into a microphone to operate the computer or to create text (Dell et al., 2008). These authors suggested that this medium be used to provide access to the computer and computer applications for people with disabilities.

- **Speech synthesis/screen reading:** Screen-reading software programs, according to Dell et al., (2008) provide auditory output for some or all of the elements that are visible on a computer monitor. According to these authors full- featured screen readers speak the contents of dialog boxes and menus, identify toolbar buttons and the presence of graphic images, alert users to new windows, and speak the text found in word processing documents and other applications.

iPAD AS A TOOL FOR LEARNING FOR CHILDREN WITH AUTISM

Stokes (2013) identified the following areas in which assistive technology including an iPad can be used for children with autism to increase or improve their:

- Overall understanding of their environment;
- Expressive communication skills;
- Social interaction skills
- Attention and motivation skills;
- Organization skills
- Academic skills;
- Fine motor skills;
- Self help skills;
- Overall independent daily functioning skills (p.1).

Overall Understanding of their Environment

Hammond and Whatley (2010) described how video technology such as video modeling and prompting have been successfully used to teach a variety of functional skills to children with moderate intellectual disabilities including those with autism. These skills include the following, withdrawing money from an ATM, purchasing items in a store, daily life skills such as brushing teeth, setting the table, cooking and vocational skills

These authors described video modeling as the presentation of the entire target behavior, whereas video prompting refers to playing a video clip of each step in the target behavior being completed in isolation.

AutisMate is one of the apps which allow parents or caretakers to take and upload photos of the child's surrounding environment. The child can then use those images to express his/her needs (Innovative Ways the Autism Community Uses iPads). AutisMate according to Horowitz (2013) allows children with autism to use the iPad's GPS features to learn about scenes based on their current location, such as the kitchen or bedroom in their home, or scenes around a school.

Expressive Communication Skills

Porter and Cafiero (2009) reported that between 30 and 50% of individuals in the autism spectrum will never have spoken language that is adequate to meet their most simple daily needs. While advances in the use of assistive technology to overcome language and communication deficits for individuals with ASD have been made, according to Porter and Cafiero (2009), there is little research available to guide practitioners to match assistive technology or strategies with individual needs.

Temple Grandin (1996) asserted that children with autism think in pictures rather than words. What Temple Grandin meant is that most people with autism have relative strengths in visual thinking. For example, a child with autism can create a sentence or even a story using a series of images. This in turn will result in a child being able to communicate with peers, parents, teachers and his/her caretakers without any challenges.

The use of visual graphic symbols aimed at supporting learning and communication for persons on the autism spectrum has shown tremendous growth over the past decade. However, despite this growth, according to Shane, O'Brien and Sorce (2009), current visual supports do not yet comprise a cohesive, rule-bound visual language system: rather, they usually are presented as independent visual cues. The authors cited Shane and Weiss-Kapp (2008) who proposed a comprehensive framework that includes three modes of visual supports:

- **The Visual Expressive Mode (VEM):** Visual cues used for the purpose of expressive communication;

- **The Visual Instructional Mode (VIM):** Visual cues used for the purpose of comprehension, which are imposed as an alternative to, or in conjunction with, speech;
- **The Visual Organizational Mode (VOM):** Visual cues used to represent the organization of an activity, routine, script, or schedule (p.130).

Shane et al. (2009) suggested that this logical framework accounts for the multiplicity of ways that visual supports can be used to strengthen communication and learning for children with autism.

Uxbridge Public Schools (2013) reported that there are many apps that allow for text to speech, graphic organizers, and story builders.

Social Interactive Skills

There are many good programs available for the iPad aimed at encouraging positive social interactions. Shamah (2013) describes tasks such as solving puzzles, which require a team as being good for children with autism. According to this author the same cooperation/interaction principle can work with games, virtual storytelling, or even schoolwork.

Mason and Stroud (2012) cited the following social skills apps:

- **Face-cards C:** This app is a resource for exploring feelings and the faces that go with them. Face –cards portray the ten most common emotion expressions. People on the autism spectrum use face-cards to identify and explain feelings.
- **iCreate Social Skill Stories:** The app is designed to make unlimited personalized social skill story books by importing personal photos, adding titles, text and audio to unlimited pages in the story.
- **iGet My Classmates Photo Album:** This app gives picture, text and audio support to individuals learning about classmates. Add

photo album with up to thirty icons that can be personalized by the user. Text statements and audio recording can be added to each photo.

- **Model Me Going Places 2:** This app provides social stories for students who may have difficulty navigating going places in the community. Stories include going to the mall, play ground, doctor, hairdresser, restaurant, and grocery store.
- **Quick Cues:** This app helps teens and young adults on the autism spectrum to handle new situations and learn new skills. The five modules include: communication, life skills, socialization, coping, and on the job.
- **Social Skill Builder:** This app is a series of interactive videos that teach social thinking, language and behavior that are critical to everyday living. Focus is on: friendship/ life skills, critical thinking, emotions, and consequences.
- **Social Skills Sampler HD:** This app is a complement to the Functional Skills System software. Each app contains digital videos that focus on functional life, literacy, math, social, health, transportation and work skills.
- **Super Duper "What are They Thinking?"** Use the app to improve your students' inferencing, reasoning, and conversational skills. The student then gives a verbal response. You score their response as correct or not.
- **Touch and Learn – Emotions:** This app focuses on helping kids read body language and understand emotions by looking at gorgeous pictures and figuring out which person is expressing a given emotion.
- **The Social Express:** This app is designed to teach users how to think about and manage social situations, helping them to develop meaningful social relationships

and succeed in life. Based on the work of Michelle Garcia Winner.

- **What Would You Do at School if Fun Deck:** Select the cards you want students to see, and have them work on solving problems and practicing good social skills as they discuss situations in and around school. The prompts include questions like, "What would you do if.."

- **What Would You Do at Home if Fun Deck:** Select the cards you want students to see, and have them work on solving problems and practicing good social skills as they discuss situations in and around home. The prompts include questions like, "What would you do if (p.26).

Attention and Motivation Skills

Due to its predictability an iPad seems to be a good learning tool for children with autism. Project Autism (2013) contended that children with autism seem to naturally gravitate to technology and computers thus, it seems logically to give them opportunities to learn using technology. An iPad encourages students to focus and to become independent learners. Rigo (2013) in his study of using an apple ipad for self-monitoring of students with autism found that the use of iPad reduced the off task behavior such as: calling out, looking around, playing with objects, and drifting off and increased the on task behavior.

It has been documented that because of the customization options and because the iPad is a "cool tech device" that does immediately mark a child as different, many see it as a more attractive option than the more traditional devices (The iPad: a Useful Tool for Autism, 2013).

Organization Skills

iPads are making a difference for children with autism can access apps aimed at teaching them organization skills. The use of video modeling

provides individuals with autism step by step instructions on how to perform daily tasks. There are apps that with financial management tools that can help an individual by teaching them how to manage their finances. The following apps listed by Mason and Stroud can be useful in teaching organization skills:

- **Corkulous Pro:** Collect, organize and share your ideas on this virtual corkboard. Includes notes, labels, photos, contacts, tasks, index cards and arrow flags. Save your board as a photo and email it to a friend.

- **Evernote:** This app helps keep organized across devices. Create and edit text notes. Record voice notes. Organize notes by notebook tags. Sync your notes with your computer.

- **Educreations Interactive Whiteboard:** Turn your iPad into a recordable whiteboard. Create video tutorials for students. Walk students through math problems or essay writing (p.29).

Academic Skills

Other uses for iPads include but are not limited to Math and English games; making music and or listening to music; making videos and or watching videos; using customized pictures; writing stories and or listening to stories; and in creating or exploring art.

Mason and Stroud listed the following language and math apps:

- **A Novel Idea:** This app helps with story writing elements: characters, setting, and plot. Create scenes and characters in no time.

- **Ace Learn 2 Bee:** Sight Words: This app provides a fun environment for children to learn essential English words. Sight words can be grouped into pre-primer up to third grade.

- **I Like Books:** Enjoy 37 I Like Children's picture books. Children learn about the world around them while learning how to read.
- **Math Kid:** Build foundation skills in Math through visual supports. Add, subtract, multiply, divide, and figure out fractions and percents. Rewards are built in.
- **Math Terms:** This app contains 1000 visual definitions of math terms for middle school students.
- **Quick Graph:** Quick Graph makes graphing equations easy in 2D and 3D. Up to 6 equations can be visualized at the same time
- **Edit Text Notes:** Record voice notes (p. 24-25).

Fine Motor Skills

The iPad is said to be effective for children with autism especially those with fine motor deficits since it utilizes a touch and swipe procedure. According to Rigo (2013), The iPad is popular because of its portability and a touch screen capability which allows its users to manipulate and respond to visual and audio content without a mouse or stylus required.

The iPad can be tailored to the child's specific needs thus making it more effective. Children with autism prefer sameness thus apps can be organized to provide predictability and easy accessibility. The iPad is said to provide multi-modal delivery methods for those students who have difficulty reading or those who have difficulty following the spoken word

Horowitz (2013) reported that SpecialNeedsWare has recently developed an app for the iPad that incorporates images and video to acclimate kids with autism to daily tasks. This company provides a customized library of images, sounds, signs and symbols to ease behavioral processing

for children with autism. According to Horowitz (2013) video modeling aids children in developing social, communication, functional and behavioral skills.

Since many individuals with autism are visual learners the iPad makes visual images more accessible. Another positive aspect of an iPad is that it involves less writing and more touching which may aid learning for an individual with poor fine motor skills. Regardless of the computer technology being used for this population, it is essential to determine the child's level of interest as well as his/her level of comprehension. According to Wisconsin Assistive Technology Initiative (2009), visual representation systems may include a variety of visual supports, such as objects, photographs, realistic drawings, line drawings, and written words.

Mason and Stroud (2012) listed the following apps that are suitable fine motor:

- **ABC Cursive Writing:** This is a fun way for kids learning the basics of cursive writing. Trace big letters with guiding strokes.
- **ABC Easy Writer-Printing:** This app provides upper and lower cases tracing. Audio is included so students learn the letter names.
- **ABC Letter Tracing:** Students learn to trace letters and are guided. Feedback is provided for proper letter stroke.
- **Absolute Board:** This app allows students to sketch and take notes with their finger. They can share and save their ideas then email their work.
- **All-in-One Big Trace Combo:** Students can trace oversized letters and numbers. Both print and cursive are offered.
- **Big Number Trace HD:** Students learn the proper strokes with large numbers and as well are provided with audio of each number name.
- **Build It Up:** This app develops visual-perceptual skills as well as fine motor skills.

Students will also learn math concepts such as size, top, bottom and before and after.

- **Colors Dots:** This visual tracking game will build student's visual tracking and fine motor skills. Very fun to play (p.28).

Overall Independent Daily Functioning Skills

iPads also promote independent learning for high functioning students with autism. Immediate feedback can also make iPads more appealing to individuals with autism. Picture prompts can help individuals with autism in completing daily tasks while iPad apps such as cooking tutorials can allow an individual with autism not to be dependent on others for their immediate needs. There are also apps such as visual timers which may help individuals with autism learn time management. Others like visual schedule planner provide visual schedule with an ability to view daily, weekly and monthly events (Chase, 2012).

Holstein (2013) listed the following examples of autism applications: TapToTalk™, JabTalk™, iAugComm™, Quick Talk AAC™, AAC Speech-Buddy™, Voice4U™, My Talk™, Proloquo2Go™, EZ Speech™, More apps are said to be found at the iAutism and Apps for AAC web sites.

ADVANTAGES OF INFORMATION AND COMPUTER TECHNOLOGY FOR INDIVIDUALS WITH AUTISM

Bryant and Kraft (2012) identified the advantages of information and computer technology as tools that increased independence and options of speech output. According to these authors, while children may not be able to operate an electronic device without assistance, adults are usually capable of independent use. The iPad, like other computer technology can be used for varied purposes by children with autism. It can be used as a communication device as well as a tool to manage behavior through the use of video modeling and video prompting.

When choosing AAC system, Webber and Scheuermann (2008) cited the following questions to be asked by parents and professionals who work with individuals with autism:

- Is the system portable? Is it easy for the student to access the system at all times?
- Does the system accommodate a wide variety of vocabulary and language functions?
- Can others easily understand the system?
- Is it easy to prompt responses with the system?
- Is the student motivated to use the system? (p.190).

Some of the advantages of computer technology as cited by the Wisconsin Assistive Technology Initiative (2009) are to:

- Increase the student's overall understanding of his or her environment
- Increase attention and motivation
- Improve organizational skills, social skills, and self help skills
- Allow the student to focus on the content of academic materials and tasks; and most importantly
- Increase independent functioning in all aspects of the student's life, which typically results in an overall decrease in the occurrence of challenging behaviors (p.2).

LIMITATIONS ASSOCIATED WITH THE USE OF COMPUTER TECHNOLOGY FOR CHILDREN WITH AUTISM

The computer technology may not be accessible to all children who need it. Cost can be one reason while compatibility could be another reason. Not every individual with autism will respond positively towards assistive technology. Another negative aspect associated with assistive technology is the fact that some fear that working on computers will further isolate children with autism who are already suffering from social deficits or the computer might further increase their obsessive compulsive behaviors (Putman and Chong, 2008). Bouck et al. (2008) contended that extensive computer use can lead to physical problems and injuries such as eyestrain; wrist, neck, and back pains; poor posture; and repetitive injury. The authors also stated that the visual stimulations provided by computers and iPads may be more salient than the images children create for themselves through creative play and art.

Bryant and Kraft (2012) stated that the added weight and size of electronic communication systems can add difficulty to making the equipment readily accessible to the user. Portability is also mentioned by Bryant and Kraft (2012) as being a negative factor. If the person has to use the device in multiple settings it may pose a problem.

WHAT PARENTS MUST KNOW ABOUT INFORMATION AND COMPUTER TECHNOLOGY FOR INDIVIDUALS WITH AUTISM

Parents must know that information and computer technology are not a cure-all tool. However if these tools are used effectively they can facilitate learning and provide independence to children with autism. The following strategies for use of AAC devices were identified by Johnston, Beard and Carpenter (2007):

- **Provide a supportive environment:** Teachers, parents, and service providers should all work together to evaluate the student's needs on a regular basis. This will facilitate the student's communication.
- **Challenge the student:** Adults who work with the student should challenge the indi-

vidual to use the device. A system of gentle reinforcement should also be used when the student succeeds.
- **Keep communication open among team members:** Common goals and consistent strategies should be developed by members to implement the AAC device.
- **Take an active role:** All team members must be knowledgeable of the system the student is using to make sure the student is successful.
- **Check the IEP/IFSP and the transition plan language:** Make sure the IEP/IFSP and the transition goals are followed. The IEP/IFSP and the transition plan guide the process that allows for various strategies and devices as the students develop communication skills.
- **Try simple strategies first:** Try more light-tech devices and get into the more sophisticated devices later (p. 109-110).

Bryant and Bryant (2012) stated that a team of professionals including the family and person with autism should be involved in selecting the AAC strategy and communication goals. In addition, the authors suggested that professionals must follow up with the family and person with autism on an ongoing basis to ensure that the technology is being adequately used and to determine whether retraining or alternative goals or strategies are necessary. The cost of information and computer technology including iPads may be beyond financial reach for some families, thus, it is important to ensure that families have adequate resources to purchase and maintain such technology (Bryant and Bryant, 2012).

CONCLUSION

Computers and iPads have afforded students with autism new ways of learning and communicating in both school and home environments. However, it must be noted that while information and computer technology have opened new doors for children with disabilities including those with ASD, one must not forget the fact that these technologies require training for both the users as well as the professionals implementing them. Speech pathologists, special education teachers and parents of children with autism must be proficient in the use of the iPad before they even consider it as a viable option for this population. An iPad may work for one child and not for all children with autism. The successful use of information and computer technology for children with cognitive deficits may not yield positive results as quickly as anticipated. It must be noted that AAC devices may require longer trials and errors before positive results are achieved.

Teachers, family members, support personnel, and peers should encourage student independence through the use of information and computer technology. The use of information and computer technology including the use of iPad must facilitate communication and independence across settings. Seven Tips for using iPads with Kids with Autism (2013) suggested the following tips for implementation:

- **Set learning goals for your child:** This will help parents to align the goals with the child's needs.
- **Read app reviews with your specific goals in mind:** This will eliminate information overload and will allow parents and or teachers to choose what will be helpful to a child.
- **Adjust the iPad setting based on your child's needs:** The more confusing the iPad settings are the less likely the child will use the tool to his/her advantage.
- **Rotate the apps on your iPad:** Allowing the child to use one application over and over might encourage obsessive behavior. Thus once the skill is mastered it is important to work on a different goal.

- **Monitor how long your child uses the iPad:** The child must be exposed to other learning tools to diversify his/her learning experiences.
- **Customize the settings and preferences for your child:** This allows the child to be engaged and to be kept interested and motivated.
- **Select the apps that you can use along with your child:** A good learning program is designed to allow interactive opportunities between the learner and the teacher (p.2).

Computer technology as well as iPad use holds great potential for children with autism and their families. According to Bouck et al. (2008) it is not difficult to envision ways in which information and computer technology can reinforce and enhance learning, communication, social opportunities, and leisure activities for children and youth with autism. Research on this topic is still lacking but technology and its use is growing. Teachers and parents must embrace the new possibilities that technology provide for children with disabilities including those with autism.

REFERENCES

American Psychiatric Association. (2000). *Diagnostic and statistical manual of mental disorders* (4th ed.). Washington, DC: APA.

Bouck, E. C., Okolo, C. M., & Courtad, C. A. (2008). Technology at home: Implications for children with disabilities. *Journal of Special Education Technology*, 22(3), 43–56.

Bryant, B. R., & Kraft, G. (2012). Assistive technology devices to enhance speech communication. In D. P. Bryant, & B. R. Bryant (Eds.), *Assistive technology for people with disabilities* (pp. 104–125). Boston: Pearson Publishers.

Cafiero, J. M. (2008). Technology supports for individuals with autism spectrum disorders. *Technology in Action*, 3(3), 1–12.

Chase, J. (2012). *A list of apps for social skills and autism spectrum disorders*. Academic Press.

Dell, A. G., Newton, D. A., & Petroff, J. G. (2008). *Assistive technology in the classroom: Enhancing the school experiences of students with disabilities*. Upper Saddle River, NJ: Pearson/Merrill Prentice Hall.

Ennis-Cole, D., & Smith, D. (2011). Assistive technology and autism: Expanding the technology leadership role of the school librarian. *School Libraries Worldwide*, 17(2), 86–98.

Fan, T. (2012). *Enhancing learning with the use of assistive technology for children on the autism spectrum*. (Unpublished thesis for Master of Science in Education). Dominican University of California, San Rafael, CA.

Ganz, J. B., Hong, E. R., & Goodwyn, F. D. (2013). Effectiveness of the PECS phase 111 app and choice between the app and traditional PECS among preschoolers with ASD. *Research in Autism Spectrum Disorders*, (7): 973–983. doi:10.1016/j.rasd.2013.04.003

Grandin, T. (2006). *Thinking in pictures: My Life with autism*. New York: Vintage Books.

Grandin, T. (2012). *Tablet computers: What they're good for, what they're not*. Autism Asperger's Digest.

Grandin, T., & Scariano, M. M. (2005). *Emergence labeled autistic*. New York: Warner Books.

Habash, M. A. (2005). Assistive technology utilization for autism an outline of technology awareness in special needs therapy. In *Proceedings of the Second International Conference on Innovations in Information Technology*. Retrieved from http://www.autismarabia.com

Hammond, D. L., & Whatley, A. D. (2010). Effectiveness of video modeling to teach iPod use to students with moderate intellectual disabilities. *Education and Training in Autism and Developmental Disabilities*, 45(4), 525–538.

Holstein, J. (2013). *Tablets for autism: Tablet computers provide a voice for the autistic*. ViewSonic Corporation. Retrieved from www.viewsonic.com

Horowitz, B. (2013). *iPad app helps children with autism learn life skills*. Posted on the internet 2013-05-14.

Innovative Ways the Autism Community Uses iPads. (2013). Retrieved online 9/5/13.

Johnston, L., Beard, L. A., & Carpenter, L. B. (2007). *Assistive technology access for all students*. Upper Saddle River, NJ: Pearson/Merrill Prentice Hall.

Male, M. (2003). *Technology for inclusion: Meeting the special needs of all students*. Boston: Allyn and Bacon.

Mason, T., & Stroud, D. (2012). iPads to support students with autism spectrum disorders: One districts' implementation. Academic Press.

National Institute of Mental Health. (2010). *What is autism spectrum disorders?* Retrieved from http://www.nimh.nih.gov/health/publications/autism/what-are-theautism...

Porter, G., & Cafiero, J. M. (2009). Pragmatic organization dynamic display (PODD) communication books: A promising practice for individuals with autism spectrum disorders. *Perspectives on Augmentative and Alternative Communication*, 18(4), 121–129. doi:10.1044/aac18.4.121

Putman, C., & Chong, L. (2008, October). Software and technologies designed for people with autism: What do users want?. *Assets*.

Rigo, E. E. (2013). *Using an Apple iPad for self-monitoring of students with autism.* (Unpublished Masters of Arts Thesis). Department of Language, Literacy & Special Education at Rowan University, Rowan, NJ.

Seven Tips for Using iPads with Kids with Autism. (2013). Retrieved online 6/17/13.

Shamah, D. (2012, August 16). iPads and tablets could help autistic kids learn social skills. *Times of Israel.*

Shane, H. C., O'Brien, M., & Sorce, J. (2009). Use of visual graphic language system to support communication for persons on the autism spectrum. *Perspectives on Augmentative and Alternative Communication,* 130-136.

Simpson, R. L. (2005). *Autism spectrum disorders: Interventions and treatments for children and youth.* Thousand Oaks, CA: Corwin Press. doi:10.1177/10883576050200030201

Smith, D. D., & Tyler, N. C. (2010). *Introduction to special education: Making a difference.* Upper Saddle River, NJ: Merrill.

Stokes, S. (n.d.). *Assistive technology for children with autism.* Retrieved from http://www.specialed.us/autism/assst/asst10.htm

The iPad: A Useful Tool for Autism. (n.d.). Retrieved online 6/17/13.

Uxbridge Public Schools. (2013). *iPad initiative.* Retrieved Online 9/15/13.

Webber, J., & Scheuermann, B. (2008). *Educating students with autism: A quick start manual.* Austin, TX: Pro-Ed.

Wisconsin Assistive Technology Initiative. (2009). *Assistive technology supports for individuals with autism spectrum disorder.* Author.

Section 2
Single User Devices for Children with Autism

Chapter 6
Augmentative and Alternative Communication for Learners with Autism Spectrum Disorders

Jody M. Pirtle
Northern Arizona University, USA

Elizabeth A. West
University of Washington, USA

ABSTRACT

Augmentative and Alternative Communication (AAC) is a prominent component in the development of support services for learners with Autism Spectrum Disorders (ASD). In this chapter, the authors provide parents, educators, researchers, academics, and other professionals with the most up to date and innovative information as well as practical resources regarding AAC for learners with ASD. Emphasis will be on school-age children diagnosed with ASD. Features of AAC systems as well as the benefits and challenges are presented to provide the reader with information on the current state of the field. The chapter concludes with directions for future research and provides a comprehensive list of resources and organizations.

INTRODUCTION

Most recently, *disability* is being conceptualized through a social-ecological lens, with the emphasis on the interaction between personal characteristics and environmental demands (Fisher & Shogren, 2012). Conceptualizing disability in this manner shifts the focus of supports and services from remediating deficits within the person to addressing the match (or mismatch) between environmental demands and personal competencies. When there

is a mismatch between personal competencies and the demands of the environments in which individuals live, work, learn, and play, a need for support is created. Luckasson and Schalock (2012) defined supports as, "resources and strategies, that aim to promote the development, education, interests and personal well-being of a person and that enhance individual functioning" (p. 660). Creating systems of supports for people with disabilities helps improve their independent life functioning and promotes valued outcomes, including meaningful relationships. AAC is a

DOI: 10.4018/978-1-4666-5792-2 .ch006

form of support that can positively influence the lives of learners with ASD.

Learning Objectives

After completing this chapter, the reader should be able to:

1. Define and describe AAC options for learners with ASD
2. Describe the history of and legislation to support AAC
3. Explain the differences between 'low-tech' and 'high-tech' AAC options
4. Understand the features of unaided and aided AAC systems
5. Discuss the SETT framework and rationale for considering the student, the environment and the tasks required for active participation before selecting the tools needed to address the tasks
6. Describe the benefits and challenges of AAC systems

BACKGROUND

There is much heterogeneity in the speech, language, and communication characteristics of learners diagnosed with ASD (NRC, 2001). A main characteristic of learners with ASD is a delay in receptive and expressive communication, and approximately half of these individuals do not develop speech to the degree required to meet their basic needs (Alpert & Rogers-Warren, 1985; American Psychiatric Association [APA], 2000; Cafiero, 2001; Ganz et al., 2011). These deficits, combined with increasing numbers of individuals diagnosed with ASD, have led to a need for identification of evidence-based practices. AAC systems have been implemented to compensate for deficits in functional communication and language skills in individuals with communication needs (Ganz, Davis, Lund, Goodwyn, & Simpson, 2012).

AAC systems, which are frequently implemented with individuals with ASD to enhance current communication skills or provide a primary means of communication, are empirically supported interventions; however the literature lacks clarity regarding participant specificity related to what works and for whom (Cafiero, 2001).

Children with autism have been found to have strong visual processing skills, making them good candidates for an AAC approach. One of the general trends identified in children with autism is that they are visual learners and thinkers (Dettmer, Simpson, Myles, & Ganz, 2000; Edelson, 1998; Grandin, 1995a; Mesibov, 1998; Prizant & Rubin, 1999; Quill, 1997; Wheeler & Carter, 1998). It is now widely accepted that the use of visual supports and strategies are of benefit to many individuals with autism. Qualities of visual systems for communication appear to match the cognitive strengths of students with autism (Quill, 1995). Use of AT, specifically AAC, is of great benefit to learners with ASD given their visual strengths and the communication difficulties they may experience. The use of visual supports and symbols as receptive and expressive components of an AAC system has been established as an evidence-based practice for individuals with ASD (Mirenda & Iacono, 2009).

Visual systems have been used in a variety of ways to assist children with autism- specifically aiding communication, language comprehension, self-management, and skill acquisition. Visual stimuli can be presented in a variety of forms, such as photographs, symbols, and drawings. Visuo-spatial symbols have been successfully used with children who have limited speech or who are nonverbal. Use of a graphic system may provide the child with concrete choices without a reliance on linguistic recall. Use of technology, specifically technology that relies heavily on visual input, may be of particular benefit for learners with ASD.

Defining AAC: What is AAC?

AT (assistive technology) is a set of tools, including AAC, which can be used to help students with disabilities access curriculum and other activities. AT devices are defined as "any item, piece of equipment, or produce system, whether acquired commercially off the shelf, modified or customized, that are used to increase, maintain, or improve functional capabilities of a child with a disability" (34 C.F.R. 300.5). AT services are defined as "any service that directly assists a child with a disability in the selection, acquisition, or use of an AT device" (34 C.F.R. 300.6). AAC devices are a subcategory of the broad range of AT devices and services. An AAC system is defined as an "integrated group of components, including the symbols, aids, strategies, and techniques used by individuals to enhance communication" (American Speech-Language-Hearing Association, 1991, p. 10). AAC is a form of AT that supplements speech for individuals who have little to no verbal communication (Reichle, Beukelman & Light, 2002). Supplements that are primarily used include gestures and graphics. Gestures can be sign language, natural gestures or sign systems. Graphics include line drawings, orthography and photographs (Reichle et al., 2002). A variety of symbol types are available for inclusion in AAC systems. These include graphic, auditory, gestural and textured or tactile symbols, which can be unaided or aided." (Beukelman & Mirenda, 2005, p. 4). In a review, Wendt (2009) found that the use of graphic symbols for requesting has the most extensive evidence base for people with ASD.

AAC systems can range from relatively low-tech systems (i.e., simple adaptations with no batteries or electronics, such as communication boards, conversation books, and visual schedules) to high-tech devices (i.e., complex electronic or computer-driven technologies).

AAC systems can be classified into one of two categories: unaided communication systems and aided communication systems (Beukelman & Mirenda, 1998; Romski & Sevcik, 1988). Unaided AAC systems may include sign language, facial expressions, gestures, and non-symbolic vocalizations and do not require any type of external communication device for production of expressive communication. Aided systems require an external device for expressive communication production and include the use of picture communication boards and systems and voice output devices (Beukelman & Mirenda, 1998; Miller & Allaire, 1987). For example, if a student uses a speech-generating device (SGD) that speaks a message when she pushes a button, her language is considered aided (Heflin & Alaimo, 2007).

The ultimate goal of an AAC system is functional and effective communication for the learner with ASD (Heflin & Alaimo, 2007). Given the communicative needs of students with ASD, practitioners have relied upon AAC to assist students to become functional communicators both in the present and with a vision toward the future (Beukelman & Mirenda, 1998). A wide variety of AAC systems exist (i.e., Picture Exchange Communication System) and have been demonstrated to be an evidence-based practice for learners with ASD. For the purpose of this chapter, the authors will primarily focus on high-tech, innovative AAC technologies for learners with ASD.

Overview of Law and Policy Related to AAC

AAC emerged in the 1950s and 1960s as an avenue for communication for those individuals (largely people with significant disabilities) who had not developed the more traditional communication skill of speech. During its brief history, AAC has undergone remarkable changes. For example, the fundamental nature of assessment in AAC has evolved from a candidacy model, in which persons were to demonstrate eligibility for an AAC system by attaining certain prerequisite skills, to the contemporary universal model based on the premise that anyone can communicate and benefit from

AAC services. Similarly, the essential philosophy of AAC service provision has evolved from a focus on isolated skills taught during pullout therapy to an inclusive model, one in which functional communication skills are taught within natural environments. Perhaps the most dramatic change in AAC technologies has been the explosion in the availability and capabilities of technology. These advances have led to communication options and possibilities for learners with ASD unavailable even a decade ago (Hourcade, Everhart, West & Parette, 2004).

The Assistive Technology Act was first passed by Congress and signed by the President as the Technology-Related Assistance Act of 1988. It is often called the Tech Act for short and it was reauthorized in 1994, 1998, and 2004. The most current version of the Act was authorized through 2010 (NICHCY, 2013). The following is a brief summary of laws/legislation to support AT and ultimately, AAC:

- **P.L. 94-142 (1975):** Did not include assistive technology devices and services.
- **1990 Individuals with Disabilities Education Act (IDEA) Amendments:** Added the terms "assistive technology devices" and "assistive technology services."
- **1992:** Allowed AT devices and services to be considered special education, related services, and supplementary aids and services.
- **1997 IDEA Amendments:** Required that AT devices and services be considered for each student when developing his/her Individualized Education Plan (IEP).
- **2004:** IDEA reauthorization upheld AT requirements.

Features of AAC Systems

Whether one considers new, innovative, high-tech equipment or low-tech systems, you have to understand the features of these tools to best serve potential AAC users. Two of the most important advances in AAC technology over the past decade have been the development of high-quality synthesized voice output and dynamic displays that automatically change the visible options in response to user input. This section highlights the following features related to AAC for learners with ASD: output features, access methods, selection set features, message composition features, and physical features (Dowden, n.d.).

Output features include the types of speech, visual, and/or electronic methods by which a message is communicated to a partner and includes devices that produce auditory output as well as devices and techniques that use visual output for the partner.

Access methods refer to the way in which the AAC user makes selections for communication, e.g. pointing, single-switch scanning, etc. The methods used can be direct or indirect. This is sometimes called the "Selection Method."

The "Selection Set" refers to the types of vocabulary, messages and/or symbols that are available to AAC users for communication. This includes the features that characterize different selection sets, including types of symbols, vocabulary capacity and the message retrieval method. Vocabulary selection strategies may highlight the visual strengths of learners with ASD and include:

- **Vocabulary for Emerging Communication:** How to choose powerful vocabulary as you search for that first, reliable means of symbolic communication.
- **Vocabulary for Context-Dependent Communication:** Whether the individual communicates with only a few people in a few contexts or with many people in many contexts, vocabulary selection remains a major task.
- **Vocabulary for Independent**

Communication: Vocabulary has an entirely different purpose for the Independent Communicator who can spell anything. Words and phrases are selected primarily to enhance rate and reduce fatigue.

Message composition is related to encoding, dynamic display, and rate enhancement features that permit the AAC user to compose the message he wants to communicate in the most efficient manner.

Physical features of AAC must be considered, factors such as size, portability, and durability.

Innovative AAC Technologies

Edyburn (2013) discusses issues and trends in innovation and suggests that research follows innovation. The field has been innovative – creating advances at an incredible rate. Many of these innovative technologies exist and do not have the research to back their effectiveness. The field is at the stage where innovation is occurring at a rapid pace and now research must follow to establish a technology as an evidence-based practice. In addition, what is innovative one day may not be in a few weeks or months as the field shifts at a rapid pace (Edyburn, 2013). We highlight a few of the innovations below.

A recent increase in accessible handheld media devices with applications have promoted opportunities for access to visual content and appropriate instructional materials (Shane et al., 2012). The AAC field has witnessed the explosion of mobile technologies (e.g., touch screen phones and tablets such as the iPad™) with a plethora of "apps" (i.e., software applications), including those intended to support communication (RERC on Communication Enhancement, 2011). The arrival of mobile technologies has resulted in enhanced potential to meet the increased scope of communication needs for learners with ASD who require AAC (RERC, 2011).These types of technology (e.g., Apple iPad and Proloquo2go) can enhance language and communication in learners with ASD. At times, a technology can serve both as an instructional technology and as an AT and both types can serve as supports for learners with ASD within the educational context. Everyday technologies (smart phones, iPod touches, tablets) may be more cost effective for learners with ASD and may be more motivating than traditional AT devices.

A wide range of tools, devices, and technologies exist that can be used to help increase, supplement, or "augment" a person's ability to communicate. Numerous AAC devices exist, focusing on output and input methods. Voice output communication aids (VOCAs), also referred to as speech-generating devices (SGDs) are portable AAC devices that produce synthesized or digitized speech. Van Der Meer and Rispoli (2010) performed a review of communication interventions involving SGDs for children with autism, and identified that they are a viable communication option for children with autism; especially given their visual modality. Recently, meta-analyses have aggregated results of numerous single-case studies, indicating that SGDs have moderate to large effects on communication skills in young children with ASD (e.g., Ganz, Davis et al., 2012; Ganz, Earles-Vollrath et al., 2012; Ganz et al.,2011). Single-case researchers have investigated the efficacy of use of SGDs for improving language and communication skills of children with ASD, finding increased functional communication as a result (Olive et al., 2007, 2008; Schepis, Reid, Behrmann, & Sutton, 1998; Schlosser et al., 2007).

A few frequently used AAC systems are highlighted below:

- **Simple voice output devices:**
    - **BIGmack:** The BIGmack Communicator's large activation surface helps simplify the selection process. It is designed for those with motor, visual or cognitive impairments and comes in four different colors: red, yellow, green and blue.

- ○ **Cheap Talk:** Excellent for early speech development and remedial work with older individuals. The Cheap Talk 8 allows the user to record and re-record eight different messages with up to 37.5 seconds per message.
- **Voice output devices with levels**:
  - ○ **Tech Speak:** User-friendly Tech/Speak 32 provides up to 12 levels of communication with 32 messages per level. "Time-Lock" technology controls recording to enhance the operating experience. "Real-Voice" technology provides speech playback at high audio quality. The water resistant membrane operates with a light touch.
  - ○ **MACAW:** Pictures or words are used to make an overlay (or a display) which represents the messages stored in each key. A person with speech records the desired messages onto the MACAW. The person using the MACAW selects the message by pressing a button and the MACAW speaks it. The many keyboard set-ups of the MACAW can accommodate physical challenges that may affect access and the potential need for different displays over time. As the user's needs change and abilities grow, the MACAW 5 can grow with him/her, up to 32 keys on 32 levels on the MACAW 5 and 128 keys on 63 levels on the MACAW 5 Green or DACtyl model.
- **Voice output device with icon sequencing**:
  - ○ **AlphaTalker II:** A simple, lightweight communication device that is anything but basic. Its sleek, durable case houses more capabilities than any other device in its class. It comes

with enough digitized speech to record hundreds of words and can be set up with 4, 8, or 32 locations.

- ○ **Chatbox:** A beginning-level device that introduces a non-speaking person to electronic voice aids. ChatBox can be programmed for the appropriate vocabulary, voice and native tongue of the user.
- **Voice output devices with dynamic displays**:
  - ○ **Speaking Dynamically with laptop computer:** Builds on the foundation of Boardmaker.
- **Device with speech synthesis for typing**:
  - ○ Cannon Communicator, Link, Write Out Loud with laptop computer.
  - ○ **iPad/iPhone/iPod Touch:** There has been a lot of buzz about the iPad's potential as an AAC device. For many users with speech disabilities, the iPad's portability, varied functionality, large touch screen and relatively cheap price — not to mention the "cool" factor — make it an attractive alternative to more traditional communication devices.
- **Mobile apps**:
  - ○ **Proloquo2Go™:** Proloquo2Go® is an award-winning Augmentative and Alternative Communication (AAC) solution for iPad, iPhone and iPod touch for people who have difficulty speaking or cannot speak at all. Providing a "voice" to over 50,000 individuals around the world, Proloquo2Go enables people to talk using symbols or typed text in a natural-sounding voice that suits their age and character. Proloquo2Go can be adapted to suit the needs of a wide range of users with varying literacy levels. Featuring natural-sounding voices, speech can

be generated by tapping buttons with symbols, selecting buttons using an adaptive switch or typing using the on-screen keyboard with word prediction.

Benefits of AAC

Numerous benefits of AAC exist. Giving individuals diagnosed with ASD access to communication can help enrich their lives and encourage and support engagement with families, friends and the community. AAC has been demonstrated to have positive effects in a variety of areas including behavior, literacy, quality of life, and inclusion and access.

Behavioral Support: Walker and Snell (2013) conducted a meta-analysis of 54 studies on the effects of AAC on challenging behavior and found AAC interventions had positive effects in decreasing challenging behaviors for individuals with varying disabilities. Thirty-nine of the studies had participants who were diagnosed with ASD. Given the behavior challenges learners with ASD present with, these results are encouraging. Additionally, Walker and Snell suggested AAC intervention may be more beneficial when applied to younger persons with disabilities.

Literacy skills: Literacy skills provide vocabulary access via AAC systems such as alphabet boards and computer-based speech-generating devices. Literacy skills also facilitate access to mainstream technologies such as the Internet that may be used to bypass communication limitations in face-to-face conversations, enhance education, and expand employment opportunities. With appropriate instruction, individuals who require AAC can achieve improved literacy skills and will be able to maximize their educational and vocational outcomes (Light & McNaughton, 2012).The development of literacy skills in individuals who use AAC requires the collective efforts of collaborative literacy teams who have expertise in language, literacy, and AAC (Fallon & Katz, 2008).

Quality of life (QOL): Hapeman, Krzynefski, Randazzo, Youells, Reed, and Anson (2004) found that individuals with communication disorders (e.g. individuals with autism), upon receiving and integrating AAC into their lives, perceive an improved quality of life (QOL) as a result of an increased ability to participate in functional life activities.

Inclusion and access: There have been huge advances in AT over the years. These advances have helped students access the curriculum and more fully participate in general education classes (Reed & Lahm, 2005). Three main benefits of inclusion in general education for children who require AAC, have been identified including: (a) the satisfaction and enjoyment that the child who requires AAC and his/her parents feel as a result of participating academically with typically developing peers; (b) the academic achievements and skill that are acquired by the child who requires AAC in the inclusive education classroom; and (c) the child who requires AAC benefits from inclusion in general education classrooms because of his/her increased interaction with typically developing peers during classroom activities (Kent-Walsh & Light, 2003).

Challenges Related to AAC

Several challenges related to AAC do exist and a few important ones are highlighted below.

Literacy challenges: Literacy teams who are responsible for teaching reading and writing skills to students with ASD who have complex communication needs, face many challenges including students who often cannot participate in conventional literacy activities (e.g., reading aloud), a lack of materials and resources, and poor professional preparation in the area of AAC and literacy. In the ongoing effort to improve the quality and effectiveness of literacy services provided to students who use AAC, it is important to evaluate the professional expertise of personnel involved in literacy assessment and intervention (Fallon & Katz, 2008).

Lack of expertise: In their credentialing program, teachers are not being properly trained about the different types of AT tools available and how to use them in the classroom with students (Bausch & Hasselbring, 2004; Chimiliar & Cheung, 2007). In fact, teachers report that they feel inadequately prepared to use AT with their students (Chimiliar & Cheung, 2007). This lack of training has been exacerbated by several additional barriers to effective AT integration in the classroom found at the district and teacher level. At the district level, the extensive quantity and diversity of AT devices available for use, makes it difficult for the consumer to be knowledgeable. Second, teachers are often not trained in the available AT services that can be found within their school and district. Third, there is a shortage of trained school district personnel that can recommend, obtain, and/or train teachers to provide students with appropriate technology supports and services (Bausch & Hasselbring, 2004; Copley & Ziviani, 2004).

High rate of abandonment: Nearly one third of the AT devices that are purchased nationwide are abandoned during the first year after they were recommended and implemented. Philips and Zhao (1993) found four factors significantly related to abandonment—lack of consideration of user opinion in selection, easy device procurement, poor device performance, and change in user needs or priorities. Their findings suggest that technology-related policies and services need to emphasize consumer involvement and the long-term needs of consumers to reduce device abandonment and enhance consumer satisfaction.

Lack of funding: Local school districts are mandated by state and federal law (the Individuals with Disabilities Education Act - IDEA) to provide AT to all students with disabilities if it is required for them to receive a free appropriate public education (FAPE). Each Individualized Educational Program (IEP) team must consider and determine if AT is needed for that student. If AT is deemed necessary, it will be written into the student's IEP. In an effort to make AT more available to individuals with disabilities, the federal government has created several specific entitlements. These entitlements, or funding streams, include the public schools under IDEA and Vocational Rehabilitation under the Rehabilitation Act of 1993. IDEA requires AT to be provided as part of early intervention services, and as part of the special education, related services, or supplementary aid or service by local school districts. This is easier said than done as many parents find it difficult to obtain the necessary devices and services to support their child with ASD.

Changing technology: Rapidly changing technology presents a myriad of challenges to AAC users—in fact, one can describe the pace at which technology changes as exponential. Careful consideration must be given to the AAC tools or devices selected for learners with ASD—long-term support is critical to the success of the AAC system.

A Practical Framework for Decision-Making in AT

A typical AT delivery system consists of: assessment, acquisition, application and an evaluation. Service delivery should include a detailed, systematic process for examining a student's abilities and difficulties and the demands of the environments and tasks. When considering AT, the environment and the tasks must be considered before tools are selected. To support this belief, the SETT Framework has been developed to aid in gathering and organizing data which can be used to make appropriate decisions. The SETT Framework developed by Dr. Joy Zabala (more information at: http://www.joyzabala.com/) considers, first, the student, the environment(s) and the tasks required for active participation in the activities of the environment, and, finally, the tools needed for the student to address the tasks. Information about the student, the environments, and the tasks, must be gathered and thoughtfully considered before an appropriate system of tools can be proposed and acted upon.

The outline of questions to consider in each area of the SETT Framework was developed as a guideline and a place to start. Teams gathering and acting upon this data may wish to seek answers to numerous additional questions. In virtually every situation, however, any questions which arise will relate to one of the areas of the SETT Framework. Refer to Table 1 for specific questions related to the framework.

Cultural, Familial, and Linguistic Considerations

Since the early 1990s, familial, cultural, and linguistic issues have had greater prominence in the AAC process than ever before. Language interventionists understand more completely that providing an augmentative communication system impacts not only the child, but the entire family (Parette, Brotherson, & Huer, 2000; VanBiervliet & Parette, 1999). More specifically, while professionals understandably tend to focus on positive outcomes, there is increasing professional recognition that the introduction of AAC systems can have a negative impact on the family as well (Hourcade, Parette, & Huer, 1997).

Familial considerations: In the excitement over the possibilities represented by an augmentative communication system, both parents and professionals can fail to recognize the potential stress this system may introduce into the home (Parette & Angelo, 1996). Use of an AAC device or system may result in disruptions or limitations on familiar family routines or environments (Parette, Brotherson, Hourcade, & Bradley, 1996). Training often places additional stress upon the family. Transportation to and from therapy and training sessions can further compound this problem (Hourcade, Parette, & Huer 1997; Parette et al.). Additionally, the stress of introducing a particular AAC device into the family can result in technol-

ogy abandonment or rejection of the device and/or system (Hourcade et al.).

Cultural and linguistic sensitivity: Similarly, a variety of cultural issues can significantly impact the AAC system selection process. The explicit and implicit rules of language and communication are strongly rooted in cultural norms (Hetzroni & Harris, 1996). Culture may affect a family's acceptance or rejection of certain communication devices and systems, or their willingness to use AAC systems in public settings (Hourcade et al., 1997). Ongoing refinements in AAC technology have led to devices capable of being programmed in multiple languages, thus making AAC available to persons from a wide variety of cultures (Zangari et al., 1994). As a result of growing awareness of culture and family issues and greater availability of technology, contemporary assessment and intervention practices have become more culturally sensitive and family oriented. Selection of an AAC system without substantial incorporation of cultural, familial, and linguistic considerations may result in less than optimal outcomes (Hetzroni & Harris, 1996).

Sociocultural factors are important in learning, and teaching methods must be used that meet the needs of culturally and linguistically diverse (CLD) students with autism. Researchers have suggested that an ecological assessment of communication needs in the natural environment is important for students with limited communication (Westling & Fox, 1995). Further, such an assessment will assist in making decisions regarding language interventions, such as what vocabulary the family believes is important for their child to learn in their native tongue. In 1989, the American-Speech-Language-Hearing Association (ASHA) released a statement advocating for SLPs (speech language pathologists) involved in AAC delivery to include family involvement in interventions. Andrews and Andrews (1990) argue that in order for an intervention to be successful, it needs to be congruent with family dynamics. Researchers and practitioners must learn about the cultural groups with whom they desire to work. It is important to question whether the dynamics of a program are a good fit for participants of various culturally and linguistically diverse backgrounds and how that fit might influence the effectiveness of the program with those participants. Familiarity with participants can allow for adaptations of interventions in ways that are most appropriate and relevant to those particular populations.

Future Research Directions

Lorah, Tincani, Dodge, Gilroy, Hickey and Hantula (2013) suggest that additional research investigating the iPad as a speech-generating device (SGD) is warranted. Importantly, future research should address discrimination of the acquired mand (request) repertoires with multiple pictures and extended SGD vocabularies, and generalization of mand responses across trainers and environments. Finally, future research should investigate the collateral effects of the acquisition of a mand repertoire using the iPad as a SGD such as the effects of the acquired repertoire on vocalizations and/or disruptive behaviors, relations with peers and on teacher/instructional aide behavior toward the child.

Although there is evidence that aided AAC is effective for individuals with ASD, there are questions remaining regarding the relative effectiveness of different AAC systems and the relationship of participant preference to effectiveness. A small number of studies have compared acquisition of different AAC systems (Adkins & Axelrod, 2001; Gregory, DeLeon, & Richman, 2009; Tincani, 2004) and preferences of individuals with ASD for different AAC systems (Cannella-Malone, DeBar, & Sigafoos, 2009; Son, Sigafoos, O'Reilly, & Lancioni, 2006; van der Meer et al., 2012; van der Meer, Sigafoos, O'Reilly, & Lancioni, 2011). Preference regarding AAC system appears to vary by individual (van der Meer et al., 2011, 2012).

Currently, handheld devices, including tablet computers, smart phones, and personal digital assistants, are becoming more ubiquitous in U.S. society, and researchers are beginning to investigate their effects as AAC systems for individuals with ASD on improving their academic, social, and communication skills (e.g., Gal et al., 2009; Madsen, Kaliouby, Goodwin, & Picard, 2008; Tentori & Hayes, 2010). Although studies involving the use of handheld devices have demonstrated improvements in targeted outcomes of individuals with ASD (Kagohara et al., 2012, 2013), the role of the participants' preference for AAC systems, particularly including handheld devices, has only begun to be investigated. Additional research to determine these effects is a priority.

CONCLUSION

The goals of communication interventions for learners with ASD are to support and promote the attainment of critical developmental skills such as reciprocal social interaction skills, joint attention skills, and imitation and play skills, as well as the development of specific communication and social skills required to have successful conversations with others. The acquisition of effective communication and social skills often has a positive impact on interfering behaviors—behaviors that get in the way of the child's ability to access curriculum and/or participate in the classroom—since individuals learn more effective ways of expressing wants and needs (Carr, Levin, McConnachie, Carlson, Kemp, & Smith, 1994). Likewise, many of the strategies and techniques described in this chapter promote development in multiple skill areas and domains, making them efficient as well as effective. To implement specific communication intervention practices, careful attention should be paid to guiding principles for instruction, foundational instructional strategies and optimal learning environments, assessment of individual skills and needs, Individual Family Service Plan (IFSP) or Individual Education Plan (IEP) goals and objectives, as well as other considerations such as state and local standards and requirements. With a solid foundation, the specific practices highlighted in this chapter may be implemented with great confidence in their intended outcomes.

Resources and AAC Apps

- **Apps for Children with Special Needs:** www.a4cwsn.com
- **Babies with iPads:** http://babieswithipads. blogspot.com/
- **Hottest Apps Used by Apple Distinguished Educators:** http://www. adesontheweb.com/ADEs_on_the_Web/ ADE_Hottest_Apps_Blog/ADE_Hottest_ Apps_Blog.html
- **iPod and iPad Resources LiveBinders:** http://livebinders.com/play/ play_or_edit/36989
- **Junior's Voice:** http://juniorsvoice. blogspot.com/
- **Leo's iPad:** http://www.squidalicious. com/2010/11/leos-ipad-apps-for-kids- with-autism.html
- **Lillie's Pad:** http://www.lilliespad.com/
- **There's a Special App for That:** http:// www.inov8-ed.com/2010/10/theres-a- special-app-for-that-part-1-5-apps-to-im- prove-organizational-skills-for-students- with-learning-disabilities/
- **Speech-Language Pathology Sharing:** http://slpsharing.com/app-resources/

Organizations

- **American Speech, Hearing & Language Association:** www.asha.org
- **American Speech, Hearing & Language Association: Introduction to AAC Association of Tech Act Projects:** ATAP Homepage

- **Augmentative & Alternative Communication Connecting Young Kids:** YAACK Homepage
- **Augmentative Communication, Inc.:** Augmentative Communication News
- **Augmentative Communication On-Line Users Group:** ACOLUG Homepage
- **Barkley Augmentative & Alternative Communication Center (University of Nebraska, Lincoln):** Barkley Homepage with Barkley AAC Presentations (available for viewing on the web)
- **International Society of Augmentative & Alternative Communication:** ISAAC Homepage
- **National Center for Disability Services:** NCDS Homepage
- **Nathaniel H. Kornreich Technology Center:** http://www.viscardicenter.org/ services/nathaniel-h-kornreich.html
- **Rehabilitation Engineering Research Center on Communication Enhancement:** AAC-RERC Homepage
- **Special Education Technology Center (WA State):** SETC Homepage
- **UW Augcomm Website:** UW Augcomm Homepage
- **Dynavox:** For over 25 years, Dynavox has developed technology through clinical research and customer feedback and has helped thousands of individuals who have limited or no speech due to a variety of causes including stroke, autism, CP, ALS or traumatic injury.
- **Mayer-Johnson:** DynaVox Mayer-Johnson is the leading provider of speech generating devices and symbol-adapted special education software used to assist individuals in overcoming their speech, language and learning challenges. Their line of speech generating devices (SGDs) gives a voice to people who are unable to speak as a result of severe cognitive and physi-

cal limitations due to amyotrophic lateral sclerosis (ALS or Lou Gehrig's Disease), stroke, traumatic brain injury, cerebral palsy, autism, intellectual disabilities, and other conditions. Their *Boardmaker* line of special education software is used as a publishing and editing tool to create interactive, symbol-based educational activities and materials for special education students.

- **PRC:** Prentke Romich Company (PRC) is a member of a consortium of companies that are pioneers in the field of assistive technology and augmentative communication. The group includes Prentke Romich Company (USA), Saltillo Corporation (USA), Liberator Ltd. (UK), Prentke Romich Deutchland (Germany) and Liberator Pty Ltd. (Australia). These companies bring a broad range of products and services to provide the most comprehensive line of AAC devices in the industry.

- **For an additional list of equipment vendors, please visit:** http://depts.washington.edu/augcomm/00_general/resources.htm

REFERENCES

Adkins, T., & Axelrod, S. (2001). Topography-versus selection-based responding: Comparison of mand acquisition in each modality. *Behavior Analyst Today, 2*, 259–266.

Alpert, C. L., & Rogers-Warren, A. K. (1985). Communication in autistic person: Characteristics and intervention. In S. Warren & A. K. Rogers-Warren (Eds.), Teaching functional language: Generalization and maintenance of language skills (pp. 123–155). Academic Press.

American Psychiatric Association. (2000). *Diagnostic and statistical manual of mental disorders* (4th ed.). Washington, DC: American Psychiatric Association.

American Speech-Language-Hearing Association. (1991). Report: Augmentative and alternative communication. *ASHA, 33*(Suppl. 5), 9–12. PMID:1660275

Andrews, J., & Andrews, M. (1990). *Family based treatment in communicative disorders*. Sandwich, IL: Janelle.

Bausch, M. E., & Hasselbring, T. S. (2004). Assistive technology: Are the necessary skills and knowledge being developed at the preservice and inservice levels? *Teacher Education and Special Education, 27*, 97–104. doi:10.1177/088840640402700202

Beukelman & Mirenda. (2005). *Augmentative and alternative communication: Supporting children and adults with complex communication needs* (3rd ed.). Baltimore, MD: Brookes Publishing Co.

Cafiero, J. M. (2001). The effect of an augmentative communication intervention on the communication, behavior, and academic program of an adolescent with autism. *Focus on Autism and Other Developmental Disabilities, 16*(3), 179–189. doi:10.1177/108835760101600306

Cannella-Malone, H. I., DeBar, R. M., & Sigafoos, J. (2009). An examination of preference for augmentative and alternative communication devices with two boys with significant intellectual disabilities. *Augmentative and Alternative Communication, 25*, 262–273. doi:10.3109/07434610903384511 PMID:19883289

Carr, E. G., Levin, L., McConnachie, G., Carlson, J. I., Kemp, D. C., & Smith, C. E. (1994). *Communication-based interventions for problem behavior: A user's guide for producing behavior change*. Baltimore, MD: Paul H. Brookes.

Chimiliar, L., & Cheung, B. (2007). Assistive technology training for teachers – Innovation and accessibility online. *Developmental Disabilities Bulletin, 35*(1-2), 18–28.

Copley, J., & Ziviani, J. (2004). Barriers to the use of assistive technology for children with multiple disabilities. *Occupational Therapy International, 11*(4), 229–243. doi:10.1002/oti.213 PMID:15771212

Dettmer, S., Simpson, R. L., Myles, B. S., & Ganz, J. B. (2000). The use of visual supports to facilitate transitions of students with autism. *Focus on Autism and Other Developmental Disabilities, 15*, 163–169. doi:10.1177/108835760001500307

Dowden, P., & Cook, A. (2002). Choosing effective selection techniques for beginning communicators. In *Implementing an augmentative communication system: Exemplary strategies for beginning communicators*. Baltimore, MD: Paul H. Brookes Publishing Co.

Dowden. (n.d.). *UW augcomm*. Retrieved from http://depts.washington.edu/augcomm/02_features/00_features_intro.htm

Edelson, S. M. (1998). *Learning styles and autism*. Retrieved January 16, 1998, from www.autism.org

Edyburn, D. L. (2013). Critical issues in advancing the special education technology evidence-base. *Exceptional Children, 80*(1), 7–24.

Fallon, K. A., & Katz, L. A. (2008). Augmentative and alternative communication and literacy teams: Facing the challenges, forging ahead. *Seminars in Speech and Language, 29*(2), 112–119. doi:10.1055/s-2008-1079125 PMID:18645913

Fisher, K. W., & Shogren, K. A. (2012). Integrating augmentative and alternative communication and peer support for students with disabilities: A social-ecological perspective. *Journal of Special Education Technology, 27*(2), 23–62.

Gal, E., Bauminger, N., Goren-Bar, D., Pianesi, F., Stock, O., & Zancanaro, M. et al. (2009). Enhancing social communication of children with high-functioning autism through a co-located interface. *AI & Society, 24*, 75–84. doi:10.1007/s00146-009-0199-0

Ganz, J. B., Davis, J. L., Lund, E. M., Goodwyn, F. D., & Simpson, R. L. (2012). Meta-analysis of PECS with individuals with ASD: Investigation of targeted versus nontargeted outcomes, participant characteristics, and implementation phase. *Research in Developmental Disabilities, 33*, 406–418. doi:10.1016/j.ridd.2011.09.023 PMID:22119688

Ganz, J. B., Earles-Vollrath, T. I., Mason, R. A., Rispoli, M. J., Heath, A. K., & Parker, R. I. (2011). An aggregate study of single-case research involving aided AAC: Participant characteristics of individuals with autism spectrum disorders. *Research in Autism Spectrum Disorders, 5*, 1500–1509. doi:10.1016/j.rasd.2011.02.011

Ganz, J. B., Earles-Vollrath, T. L., Heath, A. K., Parker, R., Rispoli, M. J., & Duran, J. (2012). A meta-analysis of single case research studies on aided augmentative and alternative communication systems with individuals with autism spectrum disorders. *Journal of Autism and Developmental Disorders, 42*, 60–74. doi:10.1007/s10803-011-1212-2 PMID:21380612

Grandin, T. (1995a). How people with autism think. In E. Schopler, & G. Mesibov (Eds.), *Learning and cognition in autism: Current issues in autism* (pp. 137–156). New York: Plenum Press. doi:10.1007/978-1-4899-1286-2_8

Gregory, M. K., DeLeon, I. G., & Richman, D. M. (2009). The influence of matching and motor-imitation abilities on rapid acquisition of manual signs and exchange based communicative responses. *Journal of Applied Behavior Analysis, 42*, 399. doi:10.1901/jaba.2009.42-399 PMID:19949531

Heflin, L. J., & Alaimo, D. F. (2007). *Students with autism spectrum disorders: Effective instructional practices*. Upper Saddle River, NJ: Pearson Education, Inc.

Hetzroni, O. E., & Harris, O. L. (1996). Cultural aspects in the development of AAC users. *Augmentative and Alternative Communication, 12*, 52–58. doi:10.1080/07434619612331277488

Hourcade, J., Everhart, T., West, E., & Parette, P. (2004). A history of augmentative and alternative communication (AAC) for individuals with severe and profound disabilities. *Focus on Autism and Other Developmental Disabilities, 19*(4), 235–244. doi:10.1177/10883576040190040501

Hourcade, J. J., Parette, H. P., & Huer, M. B. (1997). Family and cultural alert! Considerations in assistive technology assessment. *Teaching Exceptional Children, 30*(1), 40–44.

Kagohara, D. M., van der Meer, L., Achmadi, D., Green, V. A., O'Reilly, M. F., & Lancioni, G. E. et al. (2012). Teaching picture naming to two adolescents with autism spectrum disorders using systematic instruction and speech-generating devices. *Research in Autism Spectrum Disorders, 6*, 1224–1233. doi:10.1016/j.rasd.2012.04.001

Kagohara, D. M., van der Meer, L., Ramdoss, S., O'Reilly, M. F., Lancioni, G. E., & Davis, T. N. et al. (2013). Using iPods and iPads in teaching programs for individuals with developmental disabilities: A systematic review. *Research in Developmental Disabilities, 34*, 147–156. doi:10.1016/j.ridd.2012.07.027 PMID:22940168

Kent-Walsh, J. E., & Light, J. C. (2003). General education teachers' experiences with inclusion of students who use augmentative and alternative communication. *Augmentative and Alternative Communication, 19*, 104–124. doi:10.1080/0743461031000112043

Light, J., & McNaughton, D. (2012). The changing face of augmentative and alternative communication: Past, present, and future challenges. *Augmentative and Alternative Communication, 28*, 197–204. doi:10.3109/07434618.2012.7370 24 PMID:23256853

Lorah, Tincani, Dodge, Gilroy, Hickey, & Hantula. (2013, February). Evaluating picture exchange and the iPad™ as a speech generating device to teach communication to young children with autism. *Journal of Physical and Developmental Disabilities.*

Luckasson, R., & Schalock, R. L. (2012). Human functioning, supports, assistive technology, and evidence-based practices in the field of intellectual disability. *Journal of Special Education Technology, 27*(2), 3–10.

Madsen, M. E., Kaliouby, R., Goodwin, M., & Picard, R. (2008). Technology for just-in-time in-situ learning of facial affect for persons diagnosed with an autism spectrum disorder. In *Proceedings of the 10th International ACM SIGACCESS Conference on Computers and Accessibility* (pp. 19–26). ACM.

Mesibov, G. B. (1998). *Learning styles of students with autism.* Retrieved January 16, 1998, from http://www.autism-soceity.org/packages/edkids_learning-styles.html

Miller, J. F., & Allaire, J. (1987). Augmentative communication. In M. A. Snell (Ed.), *Systematic instruction of persons with severe handicaps* (3rd ed., pp. 273–296). Upper Saddle River, NJ: Merrill.

Mirenda, P., & Iacono, T. (2009). *Autism spectrum disorders and AAC.* Baltimore, MD: Paul H. Brookes.

National Research Council. (2001). *Educating children with autism.* Washington, DC: National Academies Press.

Olive, M. L., de la Cruz, B., Davis, T. N., Chan, J. M., Lang, R. B., & O'Reilly, M. F. et al. (2007). The effects of enhanced milieu teaching and a voice output communication aid on the requesting of three children with autism. *Journal of Autism and Developmental Disorders, 37*, 1505–1513. doi:10.1007/s10803-006-0243-6 PMID:17066309

Olive, M. L., Lang, R. B., & Davis, T. N. (2008). An analysis of the effects of functional communication and a voice output communication aid for a child with autism spectrum disorder. *Research in Autism Spectrum Disorders, 2*, 223–236. doi:10.1016/j.rasd.2007.06.002

Parette, H. P., & Angelo, D. H. (1996). Augmentative and alternative communication impact on families: Trends and future directions. *The Journal of Special Education, 30*, 77–98. doi:10.1177/002246699603000105

Parette, H. P., Brotherson, M. J., Hourcade, J. J., & Bradley, R. H. (1996). Family centered assistive technology assessment. *Intervention in School and Clinic, 32*, 104–112. doi:10.1177/105345129603200206

Parette, H. P., Brotherson, M. J., & Huer, M. B. (2000). Giving families a voice in augmentative and alternative communication decision-making. *Education and Training in Mental Retardation and Developmental Disabilities, 35*, 177–190.

Phillips, B., & Zhao, H. (1993). Predictors of assistive technology abandonment. *Assistive Technology, 5*(1), 36–45. doi:10.1080/10400435.1993.10132205 PMID:10171664

Prizant, B. M., & Rubin, E. (1999). Contemporary issues in interventions for autism spectrum disorders: A commentary. *The Journal of the Association for Persons with Severe Handicaps, 24*, 199–208. doi:10.2511/rpsd.24.3.199

Quill, K. A. (1995). Visually cued instruction for children with autism and pervasive developmental disorders. *Focus on Autistic Behavior, 10*, 10–20.

Quill, K. A. (1997). Instructional considerations for young children with autism: The rationale for visually cued instruction. *Journal of Autism and Developmental Disorders, 27*, 697–714. doi:10.1023/A:1025806900162 PMID:9455729

Reed, P., & Lahm, E. A. (2005). *A resource guide for teachers and administrators about assistive technology.* Oshkosh, WI: Wisconsin Assistive Technology Initiative. Retrieved February 3, 2006 from http://www.wati.org

Reichle, J., Beukelman, D., & Light, J. (2002). *Exemplary practices for beginning communicators: Implications for AAC.* Baltimore, MD: Brookes Publishing Company.

RERC on Communication Enhancement. (2011, March 14). *Mobile devices and communication apps: An AAC-RERC white paper.* Retrieved from http://aac-rerc.psu.edu/index.php/pages/show/id/46

Romski, M. A., & Sevcik, R. A. (1988). Augmentative and alternative communication systems: Considerations for individuals with severe intellectual disabilities. *Augmentative and Alternative Communication, 2*, 83–93. doi:10.1080/07434618812331274667

Schepis, M. M., Reid, D. H., Behrmann, M. M., & Sutton, K. A. (1998). Increasing communicative interactions of young children with autism using a voice output communication aid and naturalistic teaching. *Journal of Applied Behavior Analysis, 31*(4), 561–578. doi:10.1901/jaba.1998.31-561 PMID:9891394

Schlosser, R. W., Sigafoos, J., Luiselli, J. K., Angermeier, K., Harasymowyz, U., & Schooley, K. et al. (2007). Effects of synthetic speech output on requesting and natural speech production in children with autism: A preliminary study. *Research in Autism Spectrum Disorders, 1*, 139–163. doi:10.1016/j.rasd.2006.10.001

Shane, H. C., Laubscher, E. H., Schlosser, R. W., Flynn, S., Sorce, J. F., & Abramson, J. (2012). Applying technology to visually support language and communication in individuals with autism spectrum disorders. *Journal of Autism and Developmental Disorders, 42*, 1228–1235. doi:10.1007/s10803-011-1304-z PMID:21691867

Son, S. H., Sigafoos, J., O'Reilly, M., & Lancioni, G. E. (2006). Comparing two types of augmentative and alternative communication systems for children with autism. *Developmental Neurorehabilitation*, 9, 389–395. doi:10.1080/13638490500519984 PMID:17111565

Tentori, M., & Hayes, G. R. (2010). Designing for interaction immediacy to enhance social skills of children with autism. In *Proceedings of the 12th ACM International Conference on Ubiquitous Computing* (pp. 51–60). ACM.

Tincani, M. (2004). Comparing the picture exchange communication system and sign language training for children with autism. *Focus on Autism and Other Developmental Disabilities*, 19, 152–163. doi:10.1177/10883576040190030301

van der Meer, L., Kagohara, D., Achmadi, D., O'Reilly, M. F., Lancioni, G. E., & Sutherland, D. et al. (2012). Speech-generating devices versus manual signing for children with developmental disabilities. *Research in Developmental Disabilities*, 33, 1658–1669. doi:10.1016/j.ridd.2012.04.004 PMID:22554812

van der Meer, L., Sigafoos, J., O'Reilly, M. F., & Lancioni, G. E. (2011). Assessing preferences for AAC options in communication interventions for individuals with developmental disabilities: A review of the literature. *Research in Developmental Disabilities*, 32, 1422–1431. doi:10.1016/j.ridd.2011.02.003 PMID:21377833

van der Meer, L. A. J., & Rispoli, M. (2010). Communication interventions involving speech-generating devices for children with autism: A review of the literature. *Developmental Neurorehabilitation*, 13, 294–306. doi:10.3109/17518421003671494 PMID:20629595

VanBiervliet, A., & Parette, H. P. (1999). *Families, cultures, and AAC*. [CD-ROM]. Little Rock, AR: Southeast Missouri State University and University of Arkansas for Medical Sciences.

Walker, V., & Snell, M. (2013). Effects of augmentative and alternative communication on challenging behavior: A meta-analysis. *Augmentative and Alternative Communication*, 29, 117–131. doi:10.3109/07434618.2013.785020 PMID:23705814

Wendt, O. (2009). Research on the use of manual signs and graphic symbols in autism spectrum disorders: A systematic review. In P. Mirenda, & T. Iacono (Eds.), *Autism spectrum disorders and AAC* (pp. 83–140). Baltimore, MD: Paul H. Brookes.

Westling, D. L., & Fox, L. (1995). *Teaching students with severe disabilities*. Englewood Cliffs, NJ: Prentice-Hall, Inc.

Wheeler, J. J., & Carter, S. L. (1998). Using visual cues in the classroom for learners with autism as a method for promoting positive behavior. *B.C. The Journal of Special Education*, 21, 64–73.

Zangari, C., Lloyd, L. L., & Vicker, B. (1994). Augmentative and alternative communication: An historic perspective. *Augmentative and Alternative Communication*, 10, 27–59. doi:10.1080/07434619412331276740

ADDITIONAL READING

Autism Internet Modules. http://www.autisminternetmodules.org/

National Professional Development Center on ASD. http://autismpdc.fpg.unc.edu/content/briefs

Principles for Speech-Language Pathologists in Diagnosis, Assessment, and Treatment of Autism Spectrum Disorders Across the Life Span [Technical Report]. Available from www.asha.org/policy. doi: 10.1044/policy. TR2006-00143, pp. 7 -12.

The National Dissemination Center for Children with Disabilities. www.nichy.org

KEY TERMS AND DEFINITIONS

Assistive Technology (AT): An umbrella term that includes assistive, adaptive, and rehabilitative devices for people with disabilities and also includes the process used in selecting, locating, and using them.

American Sign Language (ASL): A sign language for the deaf in which meaning is conveyed by a system of articulated hand gestures and their placement relative to the upper body.

Augmentative and Alternative Communication (AAC): Includes all forms of communication (other than oral speech) that are used to express thoughts, needs, wants, and ideas. We all use AAC when we make facial expressions or gestures, use symbols or pictures, or write.

Communication: The act or process of using words, sounds, signs, or behaviors to express or exchange information or to express your ideas, thoughts, feelings, etc., to someone else.

Echolalia: The often pathological repetition of what is said by other people as if echoing them.

Gestures: A movement of your body (especially of your hands and arms) that shows or emphasizes an idea or a feeling.

Language: The system of words or signs that people use to express thoughts and feelings to each other.

Mand: A request.

Speech: A spoken expression of ideas, concerns, opinions, etc.

Verbal: Relating to or consisting of words; spoken rather than written.

APPENDIX

Table 1. SETT Questions

1. The Student
• What does the student need to do?
• What are the student's special needs and current abilities?
2. The Environments
• What are the instructional and physical arrangements? Are there special concerns?
• What materials and equipment are currently available in the environments?
• What supports are available to the student and the people working with the student on a daily basis?
• How are the attitudes and expectations of the people in the environment likely to affect the student's performance?
3. The Tasks (Be as specific as possible)
• What activities occur in the student's natural environments which enable progress toward mastery of identified goals?
• What is everyone else doing?
• What are the critical elements of the activities?
• How might the activities be modified to accommodate the student's special needs?
4. The Tools
• What no tech, low tech, and high tech options should be considered for inclusion in an assistive technology system for a student with these needs and abilities doing these tasks in these environments?
• What strategies might be used to invite increased student performance?
5. How might the student try out the proposed system of tools in the customary environments in which they will be used?

Chapter 7
Using Handheld Applications to Improve the Transitions of Students with Autism Spectrum Disorders

Michael Ben-Avie
SCSU Center of Excellence on Autism Spectrum Disorders, USA

Deborah Newton
Southern Connecticut State University, USA

Brian Reichow
AJ Pappanikou Center for Excellence in Developmental Disabilities University of Connecticut Health Center, USA

ABSTRACT

While the knowledge that has been gained from previous studies has accelerated the understanding of the difficulties facing individuals with Autism Spectrum Disorders (ASDs), there is concern regarding the speed with which and the overall lack of translation of research into interventions that make differences in the everyday lives of individuals with ASDs (Gresham, et al., 2001; Volkmar, et al., 2004; Volkmar, Reichow, & Doehring, 2011). For example, the symptoms of ASDs can greatly impair an individual's ability to navigate independently through everyday events. Translating this knowledge into instructional practice requires, then, the design of methods for easing students' transitions within the school, home, and community. While research has validated the use of low-tech visual supports (e.g., National Autism Center, 2009), little has been done to analyze the utility and appropriateness of high-tech assistive technology, such as those interventions administered through smartphones, tablets, and other handheld devices, which are devices that are being used more frequently in education settings (Gray et al., 2010). This chapter presents the results of federally funded research to determine whether the use of iPrompts—a software application for iOS and Android-based smartphones and tablet computers—assists teachers and other educational professionals as they help students with ASD transition from one activity to the next or from one setting to another.

DOI: 10.4018/978-1-4666-5792-2.ch007

CHARACTERISTICS OF AUTISM SPECTRUM DISORDERS

Children with autism spectrum disorders (ASD) have difficulties with social interactions and social communication, and have restricted, repetitive, or stereotyped behaviors (American Psychiatric Association, 2013). Once thought to be a rare condition, the most recent prevalence estimates for autism spectrum disorders from the Centers for Disease Control and Prevention (CDC, 2012) estimate that 1 in 88 children in the United States has an autism spectrum disorder. Although it is common and recommended practice for students with ASDs to be educated in general education settings with their like-aged peers, modifications and adaptations are needed to optimize learning opportunities in general education settings for these students. Major difficulties in social interactions are consistently identified as a central feature of ASD (Carter et al., 2005) and can be a powerful predictor of educational outcomes (Malecki & Elliot, 2002; Myles et al., 2005; Welsh et al., 2001). Thus, the underlying social deficits in ASD likely hinder the developmental, cognitive, communicative, academic, social, behavioral, and functional outcomes of students with ASDs (Loveland & Tunali-Kotoski, 2005).

When entering new or unfamiliar social and physical environments, individuals with autism spectrum disorder (ASD) often experience a high level of anxiety that may result in inappropriate behavioral manifestations (e.g., tantrums, crying) and/or social withdrawal. The high level of anxiety and resulting inappropriate behaviors make it difficult for these students to transition to a new environment or setting and to immediately engage in educational and social tasks. Moreover, students with ASD may feel lost or anxious, if daily activities are not clearly indicated, or if the sequence of events is not understood. Students may become prompt-dependent if adults are constantly required to move them from activity to activity, and students may want to shut down (Hume, 2009).

Students with ASDs struggle with the rapid comprehension required for spoken communication. The fleeting nature of verbal language (i.e., once spoken, the words disappear) is especially problematic, when the information is complex and/or lengthy (Hume, 2009). On the other side of the equation, research has consistently shown that individuals with ASD have superior visuo-spatial skills, and learn easier and faster with visual presentation of materials (Garreston, Fein, & Waterhouse, 1990). Therefore, in order to accommodate students with ASD in classroom settings, visual supports will be necessary.

Therefore, developing methods to assist students with ASD transition has been a major focus of educational interventions for individuals across the autism spectrum. There is not one specific intervention that will be effective at reducing problem behavior and social withdrawal during transitions for all students with ASD, and there has not been a great deal of research focusing specifically on transitions. However, our clinical experience and knowledge of how individuals with ASD best learn leads us to believe that visual supports, including visual schedules, "first/then" displays, social narratives, and countdown timers can be used effectively for this purpose. All of these supports can be delivered using both low- and high-tech mediums, the latter of which will be the focus of this chapter.

ASSISTIVE TECHNOLOGY

Visual supports can be considered assistive technology using the definition of assistive technology (AT) provided in the Individuals with Disabilities Education Act (IDEA) of 2004, 20 U.S.C. § 1401:

1. Assistive Technology Device
   a. In general – the term 'assistive technology device' means any item, piece of equipment, or product system, whether acquired commercially off the shelf,

modified, or customized, that is used to increase, maintain, or improve the functional capabilities of a child with a disability

b. Exception – the term does not include a medical device that is surgically implanted, or the replacement of such a device (Public law 105-394 [29 USC 2201]).

Assistive technology encompasses a wide array of devices and conceptualizing such devices in terms of a spectrum ranging from low-tech to high-tech devices may be helpful. Low-tech devices do not use electronic components, whereas high-tech devices are often based on computer technology. High-tech devices are typically more complicated to operate than low-tech devices, and often require more training, and expenses, as well. However, relative to low-tech devices, high-tech devices may offer unique benefits that make their monetary and training demands worthwhile (Dell, Newton & Petroff, 2008).

The value of assistive technology in the education of students with disabilities is recognized by federal legislators. When IDEA was reauthorized in 1997 it mandated that the assistive technology needs of every student receiving special education services be considered during the process of developing their Individualized Educational Plan. This requirement was maintained in the 2004 reauthorization.

Belief in the benefits of AT is echoed by the results of a 2010 survey that we conducted of assistive technology specialists, speech language pathologists, special education teachers, occupational therapists, and school guidance counselors (Ben-Avie et al., 2010). Two salient themes emerged in the data analysis. The first was that assistive technology increases students' level of success and independence in the classroom and community. Representative statements included,

"Assistive technology expands students' ability to communicate with as well as understand the world around them and the choices they have," "Assistive technology helps students become more independent and to participate more fully in daily routines and classroom activities," and "Assistive technology opens the door to life experiences. It gives them an opportunity to be active participants in their learning." The second theme was that assistive technology provides students with disabilities with access to the curriculum and educational opportunities that are more on par with their typical peers. This theme was derived from comments such as, "Assistive technology provides equal access to the curriculum and life," "Assistive technology provides educational and communicative opportunities that greatly enhance that child's world, and would not exist otherwise," and "Assistive technology gives students access to the general education curriculum and participate in ways that may be different but equally effective in learning amongst peers." The teachers and related service providers in the study also identified such advantages of assistive technology for students with ASDs as providing access to the curriculum, communication, myriad life experiences both in school and out of school.

This chapter will focus on how visual supports delivered using assistive technology (AT), especially high-tech AT, can facilitate transitions for students with ASDs. First several evidence-based practices that can be employed using assistive technology will be presented. This will be followed by additional evidence-based practices that are dependent upon mid- or high- assistive technology, where mid-assistive technology refers to devices that use batteries to power voice, text, or light output (Desch & Gaebler-Spira, 2008) and high-assistive technology consists of more complex devices. Finally, considerations for the successful implementation of assistive technology based on our research will be presented.

VISUAL SUPPORTS

As mentioned earlier, students with ASD typically learn better with the use of visual supports (Hayes, Hirano, Marcu, Monibi, Nguyen, & Yeganyan, 2010). Current research has found the use of visual supports to be an evidence-based practice to support individuals with ASD across many behaviors and activities. The National Research Council (2001) defines visual supports as

... any tool presented visually that supports an individual as he or she moves through the day. Visual supports might include, but are not limited to pictures, written words, objects within the environment, the arrangement of the environment or visual boundaries, schedules, maps, labels, organization systems, timelines, and scripts. They are used across settings to support individuals with ASD (p. 1).

Visual supports can be created in a variety of formats and for a variety of different purposes. They may provide an analysis of a complex task, a label showing where to find or place materials required to complete a task, they may serve as a static reminder of the expectations of a situation (e.g., sit during circle time, raise your hand to ask the teacher a question), or offer a schedule to help a student understand where to go or what to do next, among other things. Visual supports can help to build independence, because in the presence of visual supports the student needs fewer prompts from adults.

Visual supports facilitate students' comprehension of the environment and transitions. Studies pertaining to support strategies for school-aged students with ASD provide evidence that priming to reduce disruptive-transition behavior and social narratives to support transitions are effective strategies (Briody & McGarry, 2005; Cihak, 2011; Dettmer, Simpson, Myles, & Ganz, 2000;

Massey & Wheeler, 2000; Schreibman, Whalen, & Stahmer 2000).

Visual supports are encountered frequently in everyday life by all of us; they help individuals with and without disabilities to navigate and comprehend the world around them. Examples of visual supports encountered in everyday life include visual schedules such as train schedules and calendars or day planners. Specifically designed visual supports can help individuals with ASD anticipate daily events and better understand the often complex social milieu surrounding them, thus reducing anxiety and facilitating transitions from one task to the next or from one environment to another.

Visual supports can compensate, in part, for the problems students with ASDs encounter due to the preponderance of information that is conveyed by speech within school settings. Visual schedules provide access to information by focusing on students' strengths in processing visual information, and provide a static reminder of expectations (whereas verbal instructions are often fleeting and only provided once). When students with ASD fail to comprehend orally-presented messages or forget the information, the student can refer to the visual schedule to be reminded of the next step in a task sequence, the next task to be completed, or the next environment to which they need to move. This can be a tremendous help in reducing the anxiety, stress level, and inappropriate behaviors that can result when students with ASDs do not understand the expectations of the environment (Illinois Autism Training & Technical Assistance Project, undated).

Mesibov, Schopler, and Hearsey (1994) indicate that visual supports, are beneficial because they help to compensate for problems students with ASDs have with sequential memory, organization of time, and attentional issues, as well as receptive language deficits that make comprehending oral directions difficult. Visual picture schedules provide predictability; students know what events, activities, environments, etc. to expect and in what order they will be encountered. These schedules can be especially beneficial to ease transitions from preferred to non-preferred activities (Downing & Peckham-Hardin, 2001).

VISUAL SCHEDULES

Current research validates the use of low-tech visual supports, such as visual picture schedules drawn or printed on paper, to facilitate students' comprehension of the sequence in which events will occur or the order in which the steps of a specific task need to be completed. Visual picture schedules support successful transitions from task-to-task or from environment-to-environment (Banda & Grimmett, 2008). Many teachers currently create visual supports, including visual schedules using printed media, often with the assistance of special software, computers and printers (e.g., symbols are selected from a picture library, printed on to paper, cut out with scissors, and then laminated to increase durability). This process can be time-consuming and requires that the visual supports be constructed in advance. This can result in large, physical products (e.g., notebooks containing printed symbols) that may be cumbersome to carry and stigmatizing to use. Typically, these visual picture schedules use graphics that are generic, rather than representative of the actual social or physical environment in which the child is expected to function (e.g., a generic image of a dentist, rather than the actual dentist the child will be visiting; or a generic line illustration of a gymnasium, rather than the actual gymnasium to which the child is expected to transition). The use of generic graphics can be especially problematic for students with ASDs who benefit from the concrete presentation of information, and requires teaching the child the meaning of

each abstract symbol – another time-consuming process. While low-tech visual picture schedules that incorporate actual photographic images are more readily comprehensible, constructing them requires even more pre-planning, can be more time consuming, and offers even less flexibility when plans change or unexpected situations are encountered.

Given the proven benefit of visual schedules (National Autism Center, 2009) it is not surprising that those supporting individuals with ASD would seek to capitalize on the portability and multi-functionality of smartphones and other handheld technology to construct high-tech visual picture schedules. The significant data storage capacity of handheld technology permits an almost limitless number of images to be stored – without adding bulk or weight. Photographic images are easily captured in advance or on an "as needed" basis using the built-in cameras. Connectivity to the Internet via Wi-Fi or cell capability provides access to a virtually unlimited supply of visual images that can be downloaded. The visual supports can then be presented to the student with ASD on a device that has a "cool factor" and is used by typical peers instead of using low-tech laminated cut-outs which are secured with Velcro to a cardboard square and often look out of place and atypical.

One method that can be used to incorporate these visual images in a visual schedule is the use of an "app," a software program/application designed for handheld devices. The number of apps that can be used to create a visual picture schedule has increased along with the increased use of smartphones and other handheld technology; a recent App Store search for "visual schedule" resulted in a display of 39 apps. The features available within each app vary as does the complexity of creating schedules, accessing them when needed, and using them with students. To maximize the benefits derived from high-tech visual schedules within a school setting, they must work reliably, consistently, and be easy to use. Regardless of the specific app, the use of high-tech visual schedules that are reliable and easy to use is a promising practice. Within the school setting, these visual supports can be used in a variety of ways to promote student success. Visual schedules that use pictures, optionally accompanied by supportive text, indicating a sequence of events can support transitioning from one class to another or from one activity to another as well as for completing a specific task. For example, a visual picture schedule to support transition might show the following:

- A picture of a math textbook, notebook, and pencil (with or without text such as "Get your textbook, notebook and pencil for math class"),
- A picture of students standing in line (with or without text such as "Line up for math class"),
- A picture of students walking in line in a school hallway (with or without text such as "Walk quietly, in line down the hallway to Mrs. Green's room"), and
- A picture of a teacher standing in her classroom doorway (with or without text such as "Math lesson").

A visual picture schedule to support completion of a specific task might show the individual steps of the task. For example a visual picture schedule to support washing one's hands might include all the discrete steps in the process. Depending upon the app, users may be able to customize the visual supports by selecting (a) illustrations and/or digital pictures included in a digital library within the app, (b) digital pictures taken with the handheld device's camera, and/or (c) images downloaded from the Internet. It is important to have a range of image options available to meet the needs of individual students.

CASE STUDY 1: FEASIBILITY OF USING HIGH-TECH VISUAL SCHEDULES IN SCHOOL SETTINGS

A study undertaken by researchers from our Center of Excellence on Autism Spectrum Disorders at Southern Connecticut State University sought to determine the feasibility of using high-tech visual schedules created with the iPrompts® app effectively in actual classroom settings. iPrompts® developed by HandHold Adaptive LLC, includes three main features, each corresponding to a different type of visual support commonly used to meet the needs of individuals with ASDs: Schedules, Choices, and Countdown:

- **Schedules**: Educators create sequences of pictures, guiding those they care for through activities of any sort. Captions can be edited for each image, allowing users to create social narratives. Caregivers can also create simple "First this, then that" picture prompts using only two images.
- **Choices:** Educators present choices between images for those who cannot vocalize their preferences.
- **Countdown:** Educators show students a graphical countdown timer (set to any duration).

iPrompts was originally conceived as an app to use in didactic interactions (e.g., caregiver and child) to make it easier for users to create visual supports in advance or "on-the-go" in response to unexpected situations and schedule changes or to take advantage of the "teachable moment." Each of the visual supports available within iPrompts can help individuals with ASDs transition from one activity to the next, understand upcoming events, and/or to focus on the task at hand. This study sought to examine the use of iPrompts in classroom settings.

To launch the study, 25 teachers were trained to use iPrompts and the iPhone and/or iPodTouch. Participants were asked to incorporate iPrompts during their work with students; no directives were given regarding specific visual supports to use or how frequently to use them. Participants were simply asked to use iPrompts how and when they deemed appropriate. Data collection was accomplished through direct observation, video recordings, surveys, and through a focus group.

A scoring rubric for analyzing the 33 videotaped observations was developed by the interdisciplinary research team at the Center for Excellence on Autism Spectrum Disorders ("Autism Center"). The scoring rubric is comprised of three sections: (1) the reliability and ease of use of iPrompts; (2) the teachers' use of iPrompts with the students, including specific features; and (3) the students' responses to iPrompts. Prior to the use of the scoring rubric for analyzing the videos, inter-rater reliability was calculated and disagreements were resolved through mediation. The process of establishing inter-rater reliability was as follows: (1) four raters observed all of the videos independently; and (2) the raters discussed amongst themselves the reasoning behind the scores that they assigned to each variable. An inter-rater reliability analysis using the Kappa statistic was performed to determine consistency among the raters. For example, the inter-rater reliability for the Chair of the Department of Special Education and Reading and the Senior Research Analyst from the Office of Assessment and Planning was found to be Kappa = .865 with ($p = .001$). Inter-reliability training continued among the raters until all had achieved at least a Kappa of .85 with one another. For example, the Director of the Autism Center and the Chair of the Department of Special Education and Reading started with Kappa = .842 with ($p = 001$) and this increased to almost identical scores after that. All data collected in this feasibility research suggested iPrompts could be used successfully to ease students' transitions within the school set-

ting (Newton, Eren, Ben-Avie, & Reichow, 2013; Zamfir, Tedesco, & Reichow, 2012).

The videos were scored by multiple faculty of the Autism Center for a total of 61 scored rubrics that captured the work of all the teachers using visual schedules to help their students with transitions. The videos showed that the teachers were able to use graphics from the picture library within the app, and some used pictures taken with the iPhone to further individualize the visual schedules. In almost a third of the videotapes (31%), an exemplary score was given to the teachers' use of the assistive technology to ensure students' "smooth transitions to the next activity."

We administered our *Self-Reflection on Teaching Index* to the teachers. The index is a 30-item scale that measures the teachers' reflections on the use of iPrompts in their teaching. The teachers responded on a 5-point scale ranging from "strongly disagree" to "strongly agree." The internal consistency reliability was found to be .825. The teachers were asked to reflect on their teaching using iPrompts. The section opened with this statement: "No matter how unprepared my student may be to attend to iPrompts, I can always find a way..." Eighty-three percent strongly agreed or agreed that they could always find a way to engage their students' attention. Ninety-five percent strongly agreed or agreed that they could always find a way to review part of the schedule with the students.

The focus group discussion that occurred after the study confirmed the feasibility of using iPrompts within a school setting. It also provided evidence that visual schedules created in the iPrompts app contributed to smooth transitions. Teachers indicated they preferred using the iPrompts scheduler to help prepare students for transitions versus using a computer program to create hard copy (low-tech AT) visual schedules. The ease of use of the scheduler application, the amount of time and effort that was saved using the scheduler, and the ability to create schedules "on the fly" as needs arose made it more convenient for the teachers to create and then use the schedules to support students' transitions. Overwhelmingly, the teachers agreed that they would use iPrompts in their classrooms.

TIMERS AND COUNTDOWN SYSTEMS

Many students with ASD have time perception impairments making it difficult for them to assess how much time has passed (Martin, Poirier, & Bowler, 2010). This impairment may make it difficult for students with ASD to distinguish between the passage of minutes, hours, days, and even whole seasons. This impairment in time perception may explain why verbal cues such as, "In five minutes it will be time to go to lunch" or "You have to stop playing with the blocks in five minutes," may not be effective in helping students with ASD transition from one activity to another. Hume (2008) states that "Presenting information related to time visually can assist in making the concepts more meaningful" (para. 8). Timers and countdown systems can be useful visual support strategies; they provide salient cues that can help students with ASDs comprehend the amount of time remaining until the one task ends or a new task begins. Timers and countdown systems can provide this support regardless of students' ability to tell time in the conventional sense.

The portability of handheld devices makes it possible to use timers and countdown systems "on the go" and across multiple environments. Time and countdown apps use a graphic to depict the passage of time; the graphic helps to make this concept more concrete and understandable. Depending upon the app, graphic representations or actual photographs of the specific activities in which students are to engage or the activities to which they are to transition can be included along with the timer or countdown image. These activity images provide a reference to which students can refer to help them remain on task or anticipate the next event.

CASE STUDY 1, CONTINUED: THE VISUAL TIMER

The focus group elicited details regarding how, specifically, the use of iPrompts contributed to smooth transitions. Many declared that the visual support they used most often was the visual timer. The visual timer (the "Countdown" feature) provides a colored square that loses color in sync with the displayed numerical countdown. When time is up, the numerical countdown displays 00:00, a tone sounds, and the square has no color left. The user can include a graphic image to support students' understanding. To help transition from one activity to another, for example, a picture of art supplies could be used to indicate that when the timer sounds, it will be time for art. To help maintain focus on a task, a picture of a math worksheet could be displayed to let students know they must continue working until the allotted time is up, for example.

The visual timer was utilized to support whole group transitions, and several teachers commented on its effectiveness. The teachers mainly used the timer tool to indicate when whole group activities would be ending. The timer tool helped students to keep working until time was up and to stop working at the appropriate time. One teacher commented that the students in her group responded to the visual in the iPrompts timer tool more than to the teacher's verbal prompts.

Similar to its use with whole groups, the Countdown was used to help individual students transition from one activity to another. Also, this feature helped students to keep engaged in tasks. Several teachers commented on the effectiveness of the iPrompts Countdown tool for both of these purposes. One pair of teachers illustrated the effectiveness of the visual timer by explaining that they had a student who would not sit at the table and work on individual or groups tasks; rather, he would wander around the classroom or try to leave the room. When the iPrompts timer tool was set and the iPodTouch or iPhone was positioned next to him so he could view the timer, he would calmly sit at the table and engage in an individual fine motor task for the requisite amount of time assigned by the teacher.

Visual timer apps on handheld devices can support transitions as well as students' time-on-task as illustrated in the case study. Analog, digital clocks and countdown timers present the passage of time in ways that require students to have a good understanding of certain mathematical concepts. Timers that employ a visual image (e.g., the colorized and animated iPrompts Countdown timer) show the passage of time in an easily understood and concrete manner.

In a third of the videos, teachers received "exemplary" scores in the use of the visual timer to frame an activity and/or indicate the end of an activity and thereby facilitate the students' attention to the activity. In 66% of the videos, iPrompts had an exemplary score with respect to positive impact on students' time-on-task behavior.

On the *Self-Reflection on Teaching Index* that the teachers completed, they were asked to describe how their students responded to the use of iPrompts to help with transitions. The following are selected comments:

- The Countdown specifically helped our kids to prepare for what could be difficult transitions; the timer helped ease their anxieties.
- The Countdown helped students transition. When presented with the timer, and it went off, two children would verbalize "all done" and transition to the next activity. I watched them be more compliant rather than melting down.
- The visual timer was very successful for my students; they understood that they had to stop working when the timer read zero and the green bar was all done. They would periodically check to see how much time was left.

- The student I am working with using iPrompts, likes to watch the timer "tick" down and this seems to help him provide a clearer understanding of when an activity will be done and when we will be moving to the next one.
- They become excited when they see the green "disappear" on the timer.
- While working with high functioning 8/9 years old boys, I have found that the timer is very beneficial to keep them on task and helps them better understand the beginning and end to activities.

CASE STUDY 2: USING DIFFERENT VISUAL SUPPORTS TO AID STUDENTS AS THEY TRANSITION

A teacher wrote on her *Self-Reflection on Teaching Index* that "The students have responded well to the timer, schedule, and choice maker. When a child is having a difficult time transitioning, it has been nice to set the timer. When the timer is done, I had the students make a choice of what they would like to do next. I then added the choice into the schedule so they would see when the choice activity will happen." Another teacher wrote, "The timer and choice maker help students to clearly visual the time left in an activity or choice available." One teacher wrote, "The timer and scheduler were both used to help the students and they reacted positively be transitioning to activities smoothly."

To determine the extent to which the different features of an app for a smartphone could effectively aid teachers and other educational professionals as they help their students with transitions, a field study was conducted in mid-2012. The sample consisted of 31 teachers of students with ASD from three school districts in Connecticut.

For this study, we preloaded iPrompts onto Samsung Galaxy Tab 7 Plus devices running Android version 3.2 (i.e., Android-compatible tablets with a 7 inch display screen). The teachers were given a Samsung tablet and a printed user guide containing information on how to use the device, how to implement visual supports, and how to use the iPrompts application. We then instructed the teachers to use visual supports with their students during their normal educational routines. We conducted one 30-minute live observation of each teacher between three to eight weeks after receiving the device. After eight weeks, we convened focus groups and collected the devices.

Flurry Analytics is a built in statistical analysis tool that provides information on user interactions with the application. The tool automatically maintains a log of data, updating each time users select certain screens, features, and images. Data were made available to the research team through a password-protected Web portal in which user information was coded. This analytic tool allowed us to ascertain which features were most popular, the frequency of use, the duration of use, and which specific user commands resulted in software crashes, among other things.

The Flurry Analytic data revealed that teachers used iPrompts for a median of 3.8 uses per day (range 1-20+) during which the median length of each session was 1.7 min (31% of sessions were > 3 min). The breakdown of usage by feature was as follows: 14% of usage was devoted to Choices, 66% of usage was devoted to Schedules, and 10% of usage was devoted to the Timer (the remaining 10% was devoted to set-up). Errors were only encountered in 7 of 238 sessions 2.9%), indicating that the app had strong reliability of use.

Observations were conducted in the classrooms as teachers used iPrompts with their students. Observers were trained by faculty from our Center of Excellence on Autism Spectrum Disorders who had demonstrated excellent reliability in previous studies. The observers noted when the teachers used iPrompts to help with students' transitions. The following are representative notes:

- Students could move through activity schedule independently. They were excited to see the times and change in schedule.
- Student turned on device to check schedule sporadically. Student was able to complete classwork and move with class to new academic activities. Student independently transitions to different activities.
- Student looks at the app and responds when asked, "What will happen next?"
- Several students used the app at snack to monitor time left until snack was over.
- Student was uninterested in the app when using it in class. When in the bathroom, however, student requested the app to be used as a timer.
- Student was able to follow multi-step directions.

Analysis of the observational data provided further confirmation that teachers were able to use iPrompts to assist their students with ASD prepare for transitions. In 71% of the observations, the teachers' use of the iPrompts scheduler for transitions received an exemplary score.

The most salient themes from the focus groups study were the high levels of student interest and engagement with the application, which teachers felt led to increased student independence. Teachers reported that, "Students paid attention to the student who was handling the device," and that their students "responded with curiosity and excitement" when the application was being used. Other teachers commented on improvements in student behavior such as increases in on-task behavior ("When my student used the scheduler, she was 'right on the ball'), reduced anxiety, ("Timer reduced anxiety"), and better transition behavior, ("My student recognized that the sound meant that the activity was done [and time to transition]"). Representative comments for increasing student independence included: "My student was able to complete his task independently with iPrompts," "He was so much more independent," "He was focused and motivated," and "He could do it independently, but it kept him more focused, less prompting was needed."

VIDEO MODELING

Research shows video modeling to be an evidence-based practice (Franzone & Collet-Klingenberg, 2008; Reichow & Volkmar, 2010) for individuals with ASD. Video modeling is an instructional strategy, in which students view videos that depict the targeted behavioral skill. Depending upon the objective of the video and the functional level of the individual, the model in the video might be the student himself or herself (known as video self-monitoring), a typical peer, or an adult.

Video modeling can be used effectively to address behaviors of students with ASDs across all domains. Communication, participating appropriately within the school setting, completing self-care activities, and engaging in leisure and recreation activities are among the functions that video model may target. Research has shown that video modeling can support students' smooth transition between locations and activities within a given school as well as to major transitions such as moving from one school to another (Cihak, Fahrenkrog, Ayres, & Smith, 2010; Ganz, Earles-Vollrath, & Cook, 2011).

Video modeling provides visually supported instruction within a limited area that can increase attention and focus and in a way that requires little social interaction. This capitalizes on the strength of students with ASDs as visual learners, while minimizing learning challenges such as inattention and the demand for social engagement. Being able to view the recorded video numerous times and in a context that students typically associate with recreation may also contribute to the effectiveness of video modeling (Corbett & Abdullah, 2005).

Unlike many visual support strategies that can be implemented using low-tech through high-tech assistive technology this is not the case for video modeling. Sophisticated equipment is required for recording video clips that can be played back at a later time, either edited or unedited. In the past, this could require several pieces, one for recording the video and another for viewing it. Often this would restrict the environment in which the video could be watched. Today, handheld assistive technology provides a compact, all-in-one solution that both captures videos and plays them back. The videos can be played and viewed as often as required and in any environment. Handheld assistive technology makes it possible for students to view videos in multiple environments, including the actual environment in which they will need to practice or imitate the modeled skill.

Commercial video modeling apps are available for purchase and for use on handheld devices. Some of these apps include premade videos, which can be a convenience and timesaver. However, most handheld devices today have a built in camera to record videos that can then be viewed directly on the device, so a dedicated app is not an absolute necessity.

While video modeling was not directly studied in the research described below, the ability to show videos on an iPhone or equivalent when students with ASD are in the community or "on the fly" is a considerable advantage over previous methods in which a video could be shown only on a desktop computer.

SOCIAL NARRATIVES

Once they arrive at school, students have to cope with transitions between tasks, at various locations within the classroom, and at multiple locations within the school. Students with ASDs also need to cope with transitioning from working with one teacher to another teacher, paraprofessionals, and special service providers. There are also unexpected and/or less frequent transitions and events for which social narratives can prepare students such as leaving the classroom quickly when the fire alarm sounds. Social narratives can also help student with ASDs to transition at the end of the school day to home. For example, social narratives might help them to independently pack up to go home and transition without disruptive behavior to an awaiting bus or car.

Social narratives are evidence-based treatments that provide a narrative description of what occurs during a social situation; what participants of the situation might be thinking or feeling, and the appropriate behavior for participating in the social interactions. The National Professional Development Center (NPDC) on ASD has indicated that social narratives "are aimed at helping learners adjust to changes in routine and adapt their behaviors based on the social and physical cues of a situation, or to teach specific social behaviors or skills." Social narratives were pioneered for students with ASD by Carol Gray (i.e., Social Stories; Gray, 2010) and have been shown to be beneficial for improving social and behavioral outcomes for individuals with ASDs (Reynhout & Carter, 2006; Sansosti et al., 2004), and have been identified by multiple sources as an evidence-based practice (NPDC and NAC):

Social narratives are interventions that describe social situations in some detail by highlighting relevant cues and offering examples of appropriate responding. They are aimed at helping learners adjust to changes in routine and adapt their behaviors based on the social and physical cues of a situation, or to teach specific social skills or behaviors (http://autismpdc.fpg.unc.edu/content/social-narratives 6/25/13).

Social narratives presented in a printed format require the student to be able to read the text of the story independently or that an adult be available to read the text to the student. For the social narratives to be effective, students also must be able to attend to them. Photographs or other illustrations are often used to increase salience and attention when presenting social narratives to students with ASD. When social narratives are presented with the use of higher-tech assistive technology such as handheld technology, they become accessible to students regardless of users' reading ability. Depending on the particular app for handheld devices, it is possible to have the text read aloud using a computer generated voice or a digital recording of a human voice. Depending upon the options available within a specific app the text may be read aloud automatically upon accessing the social narrative, or students can initiate reading by executing a command (e.g. clicking on or touching the text; clicking or touching an onscreen READ button). High-tech assistive technology makes it easy to create an accessible, individualized social narrative that incorporates images in the format to which students best respond (e.g. generic pictures, photographs). Handheld AT can contribute to the efficient and effective creation and implementation of social narratives because they are easily portable and can be conveniently used with or by students with ASDs in a broad array of settings. As a high tech assistive technology solution, social narratives on a handheld device make it possible to support student success in a wide variety of situations and environments. A virtually limitless number of social narratives can be stored on the easily transported devices and are available "on demand" whenever and wherever they are needed. Stored social narratives can be quickly and easily modified, if necessary, to adjust to unexpected changes or to new situations. For instance, a social narrative created to facilitate a smooth transition from a student's classroom to the art room is easily altered when an unanticipated schedule changes occurs and the student will be going to the library instead of the art room.

CASE STUDY 3: EVALUATING THE USE OF SOCIAL NARRATIVES TO GUIDE TRANSITIONS

Our research compared the creation and delivery of social narratives using the StoryMaker app, by Handhold Adaptive, LLC to standard practice (e.g., low-tech, paper-based materials, desktop computers, etc.). The participants were 31 teachers of students with ASD from three school districts in Connecticut. StoryMaker allows users to create and present social narratives, including Social Stories™, using pictures, text, and audio. StoryMaker was installed on ten iPhones and 11 iPad2s. Five teachers were given iPhones, six teachers received an iPad, five teachers received both an iPhone and an iPad, and the 15 teachers using standard practice (control group) received no technology. The teachers using high-tech AT were provided with a printed user guide containing information on how to use an iPhone and/or iPad, how to create and use social narratives, and how to use the StoryMaker application. The control group received a printed guide that contained information only related to how to create and use social narratives. All teachers were instructed to create at least one social narrative to use with at least one of their students during their normal educational routines. Data collection was accomplished via direct observation and focus groups.

Observational data focused on the reliability of the StoryMaker app, the teachers' ability to effectively use a handheld device to present social narratives to students with ASDs, and the students' level of attention to the social narratives. Overall, StoryMaker was used successfully on all of the devices and functioned reliably in almost 100% of the examined cases. All teachers were able to use the assistive technology competently for presenting social narrative – accessing the app, then holding or placing the device to allow the student(s) to see or read the social narrative. We also observed and rated students' engagement with social narratives created and presented with StoryMaker. The vast majority (91.7%) of the students were rated as exhibiting acceptable levels of engagement. Annotations written by the observers indicated that engagement was frequently indicated by moving closer to the device (e.g., leaning in) as well as following along and focusing on the presented social narratives: "The student held the device closely and maintained concentration." The observational data provides evidence of the feasibility of using StoryMaker efficiently and effectively on handheld devices in school settings.

Regardless of the app that teachers elect to use or the handheld device on which the app is running, high-tech social narratives can be implemented to achieve the same goals as low-tech social narratives. They can help students with ASDs adjust to changes in routine, adapt their behaviors based on the social and physical cues of a situation, and teach specific social skills or behaviors. They are well suited to helping students respond appropriately to transitions. For example, teachers might create social narratives addressing the transitions students must go through to just get to school - leaving parents and ride the bus to school and leaving the school bus to enter the school and/or classroom.

An example of one such social narrative would be the following, which occurred in one of the classrooms under observation. A teacher used StoryMaker to help a student learn to put on a helmet before riding his bike so that he could engage with his peers during recess. The teacher reflected on a student with severe sensory needs who enjoyed riding his bike but refused to wear a helmet. Without the helmet, the student was unable to participate in the activity at school, resulting in missed opportunities to interact with his peers. Using StoryMaker, the teacher created a four page story that included pictures of the student, his helmet, and his bike (this is the story that is shown in the figure below with a slight modification to remove the student's name and image). After creating the story, the teacher showed and read the story to the student. He was "beaming from ear to ear" when he saw himself on the screen. After hearing the story, the student commented that, "I must put on my helmet to ride my bike," walked over and grabbed his helmet from the shelf, put it on his head, hopped on his bike, and began riding his bike with his peers. The teacher reported both she and her student were very excited and that he continued to enjoy listening to the story while looking at the pictures. He continued to use his helmet, which allowed him to regularly interact with his peers at school (see Figure 1).

BARRIERS TO ASSISTIVE TECHNOLOGY

The professionals with whom we consulted with our survey on assistive technology wrote about conditions that facilitate and impede the use of assistive technology in schools. The professionals indicated that assistive technology tends to be the responsibility of one professional, and not the responsibility of all those who work with the students. Consider the following representative comment: "Assistive technology is something that needs to be embraced by all educators, not just one staff member such as the Assistive Technology provider. The entire team that works with a child should be looking at the needs of the child and understanding the impact that the AT equipment could have on the child. This will help the entire team to use the equipment and have a great impact on the child's life and learning."

Why does this tend to occur? Time is clearly the most pressing limitation, as assistive technology devices tend to require training; Moreover, they tend to require time to set up the devices and/or software, as many are not intuitive or user-friendly. Another impediment is teachers' follow-up. As one professional explained, "Teachers and speech language pathologists do not always see the need to implement the technology. They were part of the team to assess and agree with the technology.

They received training but still do not utilize the devices or systems." This, too, appears to be due to the level of training needed—and availability of an assistive technology specialist. As one professional stated, "My district has a great Assistive Technology (AT) Team, but they are often stretched thin. Initiation of AT across the district is highly varied and often depends on a given IEP team's knowledge, experience, and comfort with AT." When an AT specialist or team functions well, teachers are supported in learning how to use the assistive technology and they receive follow-up training—time permitting. As one professional mentioned, "Time is the challenge. I am now working on e-mailing teachers and therapists and trying to follow up on the student. This is not easy but it is a start." Another stated, "I go to 10 schools with a caseload of 45—all students who use alternative and augmentative communication devices."

EFFECTIVE IMPLEMENTATION OF ASSISTIVE TECHNOLOGY

According to ABI Research (2013), smartphone usage will total 1.4 billion by the end of 2013 and 268 million tablets will be in active use. As these handheld devices have become ubiquitous in public usage, increasing attention has been focused on the potential these devices, with appropriate apps, to be used for supporting individuals with disabilities. While the body of research related to the use of handheld assistive technology is increasing, as late as 2010 Gray and colleagues indicated that little had been done to analyze the utility and appropriateness of high-tech, handheld assistive technologies in education settings. Despite the lack of research, school districts have purchased iPads, sometimes hundreds of them, due to their beliefs in the potential these devices offer, and without any idea what they will actually do with them (Bowser, 2011; Zabala, 2011).

Figure 1. Screenshots from social narrative created using StoryMaker

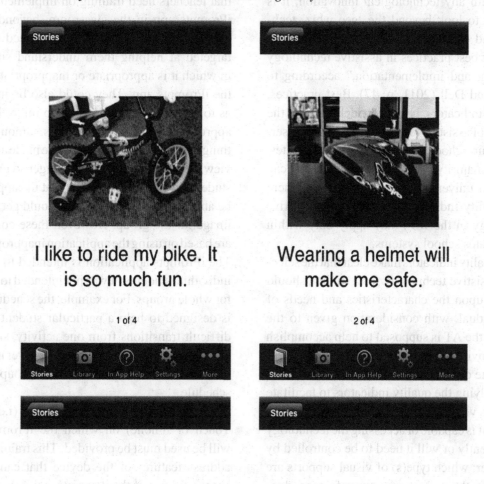

"As with any technological innovation, it is important to look beyond the 'gee whiz' technology and examine mobile devices within the context of best practices in assistive technology assessment and implementation," according to Newton and Dell (2011, p. 47). Best practices, or quality indicators, have been identified for the provision of assistive technology devices and services within school settings in the United States. The vast majority of the quality indicators can be applied universally, although some of them (e.g., Quality Indicators for Including Assistive Technology in the IEP) may apply only within United States school systems.

The quality indicators make clear that the selection of assistive technology for a student should be based upon the characteristics and needs of the individual, with consideration given to the tasks that the AT is supposed to help accomplish and the environments in which the AT is used. Among the questions that need to be considered when applying the quality indicators to facilitate transitions with assistive technology are whether the student is capable of accessing the technology independently or will it need to be controlled by a caregiver; which type(s) of visual supports are effective for the student; what type of images does the student respond to; what size visual display is required; and in which environments will transitions occur. The answers to these questions will help to determine whether a handheld device is a feasible solution; what size device (e.g., iPad, a smaller tablet, or a smartphone) is required or preferable; and which visual support apps should be installed and available to the student.

Just as with any other assistive technology, in order for the potential benefits of handheld devices to be realized, an implementation plan needs to be developed. It is necessary to clearly identify any individuals who will need training, the type of training each one needs, and who will provide the training.

The teachers in our studies felt that they needed additional training in three areas. First, it was clear that teachers need training on implementing the iPrompts app in the classroom, beyond knowing how the app works. Teachers need training targeted at helping them understand situations in which it is appropriate or inappropriate to use the iPrompts app. They could also be informed as to which tools within the app might be most appropriate in given situations, among other things. Numerous comments were made about the viewing screen needing to be bigger so groups of students could see it better or that the app should be able to be projected so they could get a larger image for the group. However, these comments are based on using the application inappropriately. The iPrompts application is intended to support individual students; it was not intended to be used for whole groups. For example, the scheduler tool is designed to help a particular student though difficult transitions from one activity, situation, environment, etc. to another. It was never intended to be used for or replace a whole group picture schedule.

Secondly, training on the device (i.e., iPod-Touch or iPhone) on which the iPrompts app will be used must be provided. This training must address features of the device that can impact successful use of the iPrompts app. Specifically, several teachers mentioned that the image on the screen would disappear and the screen would be black. One student commented that she did not even realize this happened until she watched a video of herself using the app with her students. She was talking to the students about what they were seeing, and when she saw the video she realized they weren't seeing anything but a black screen.

The third area in which training needs to be provided relates to clearly differentiating between the device (i.e., iPodTouch or iPhone) on which the app runs and the iPrompts app itself. This became obvious as many of the SCSU teachers would say things such as, "I always had the iPrompts with me," or "I would leave the iPrompts on the desk." Another teacher discussed using iPrompts to take pictures of the students' expressions and show them to the students right away. With probing, it was determined that she took the pictures with the iPhone and then showed them the pictures. The iPrompts app wasn't used at all in this process.

Being able to take photos and incorporate them into the iPrompts app was identified by teachers as an important feature of the app. For this reason they preferred using the iPhone, which has a built in camera, rather than the iPod Touch, which does not have a camera. Many teachers commented on the value of being able to take photographs. One teacher commented that being able to take pictures on the spot could help avoid meltdowns. The teachers believed that students responded to the photographs more than the visual images in the iPrompts library.

It is worthwhile to also note that the effective implementation of handheld devices depends upon planning. For example, the handheld device will need to be charged and ready at the start of each day; depending upon the device and the amount of usage, recharging during the day may be necessary. Customized visual supports take time to create – photos must be taken, images located, the text of social narratives developed, etc. The individuals responsible for creating the visual supports must be specifically identified. Explicit identification of roles and responsibilities is especially important when a student will be using assistive technology in a variety of environments and with a variety of educational personnel; assuming that someone else is attending to the details can result in underutilization or non-utilization of the AT. This, in turn, can result in the potential benefits of the assistive technology never being realized.

An additional, vital component of any implementation plan is data collection and analysis. The data will provide insights into the effectiveness of the assistive technology in meeting the needs of students. The data can help to pinpoint what is working, what is not working, and what modifications or updates are needed related to the technology, strategies for technology use, and the implementation plan itself.

The importance of an implementation plan cannot be overstated. This planning is vital for the successful use of visual supports on handheld devices to support the transitions of students with ASDs. It is just as Winston Churchill admonished, "He who fails to plan is planning to fail."

CONCLUSION

As smartphones and other handheld devices have become more ubiquitous in usage, there has been increasing attention on the potential of translating research findings about how this technology benefits students with ASD into instructional practice through the use of high-tech devices. However, little has been done to analyze the utility and appropriateness of these high-tech, handheld assistive technologies in education settings (Gray et al., 2010). The research described in this chapter lends support that the use of high-tech devices may ease students' transitions within the school, home, and in the community.

REFERENCES

ABIresearch. (2013, January 31). *45 million Windows phone and 20 million BlackBerry 10 smartphones in active use at year-end, enough to keep developers interested*. Retrieved from http://www.abiresearch.com/press/45-million-windows-phone-and-20-million-blackberry

American Psychiatric Association. (2013). Autism spectrum disorder. *DSM-5 Autism Spectrum Disorder Fact Sheet*. Retrieved from http://www.dsm5.org/Documents/Autism%20Spectrum%20Disorder%20Fact%2Sheet.pdf

Banda, D. R., & Grimmett, E. (2008). Enhancing social and transition behaviors of persons with autism through activity schedules: A review. *Education and Training in Developmental Disabilities, 43*, 324–333.

Ben-Avie, M., & Reichow, B. (2010). *Assistive technology national survey.* New Haven, CT: Center of Excellence on Autism Spectrum Disorders.

Bowser, G. (2011, May 5). *Posting to QIAT listserv.* Retrieved from http://natri.uky.edu/assoc_projects/qiat/listserv.html

Briody, J., & McGarry, K. (2005). *Beyond the journal: Young children on the web.* Retrieved from http://www.naeyc.org/files/tyc/file/TYC_V4N1_Briody McGarry.pdf

Carter, A. S. et al. (2005). Social development in autism. In F. R. Volkmar, R. Paul, A. Klin, & D. Cohen (Eds.), *Handbook of autism and pervasive developmental disorders* (3rd ed., pp. 312–334). Hoboken, NJ: Wiley.

Centers for Disease Control and Prevention. (2007). Prevalence of autism spectrum disorders—Autism and developmental disabilities monitoring network, six sites, United States, 2000. *Surveillance Summaries, 56*(SS-1), 1–11.

Centers for Disease Control and Prevention. (2009). Prevalence of autism spectrum disorders–Autism and developmental disabilities monitoring network, United States, 2006. *Surveillance Summaries, 58*(SS10), 1–20.

Centers for Disease Control and Prevention. (2012). Prevalence of autism spectrum disorders – Autism and developmental disabilities monitoring network, 14 sites, United States, 2008. *Surveillance Summaries, 61*(SS03), 1–19. PMID:22456193

Cihak, D., Fahrenkrog, C., Ayres, K., & Smith, C. (2010). The use of video modeling via a video iPod and a system of least prompts to improve transitional behaviors for students with autism spectrum disorders in the general education classroom. *Journal of Positive Behavior Interventions, 12,* 103–115. doi:10.1177/1098300709332346

Cihak, D. F. (2011). Comparing pictorial and video modeling activity schedules during transitions for students with autism spectrum disorder. *Research in Autism Spectrum Disorders, 5,* 433–441. doi:10.1016/j.rasd.2010.06.006

Corbett, B. A., & Abdullah, M. (2005). Video modeling: Why does it work for children with autism. *Journal of Early and Intensive Behavior Intervention, 2*(1), 2–8.

Dell, A. G., Newton, D. A., & Petroff, J. G. (2008). *Assistive technology in the classroom: Enhancing the school experiences of students with disabilities.* Upper Saddle River, NJ: Pearson Merrill Prentice Hall.

Desch, L. W., & Gaebler-Spira, D. (2008). Prescribing assistive-technology systems: Focus on children with impaired communication. *Pediatrics, 121*(6), 1271–1280. doi:10.1542/peds.2008-0695 PMID:18519500

Dettmer, S., Simpson, R., Myles, B., & Ganz, J. (2000). The use of visual supports to facilitate transitions of students with autism. *Focus on Autism and Other Developmental Disabilities, 15,* 163–170. doi:10.1177/108835760001500307

Downing, J. E., & Peckham-Hardin, K. D. (2000). Daily schedules: A helpful learning tool. *Teaching Exceptional Children, 33,* 62–68.

Franzone, E., & Collet-Klingenberg, L. (2008). *Overview of video modeling.* Madison, WI: The National Professional Development Center on Autism Spectrum Disorders, Waisman Center, University of Wisconsin.

Ganz, J. B., Earles-Vollrath, T. L., & Cook, K. E. (2011). Video modeling: A visually based intervention for children with autism spectrum disorder. *Teaching Exceptional Children, 43*(6), 8–19.

Garreston, H. B., Fein, D., & Waterhouse, L. (1990). Sustained attention in children with autism. *Journal of Autism and Developmental Disorders*, *20*(1), 101–114. doi:10.1007/BF02206860 PMID:2324050

Gray, C. (2010). *The new social story book*. Arlington, TX: Future Horizons.

Gray, L., Thomas, N., & Lewis, L. (2010). *Teachers' use of educational technology in U.S. public schools: 2009 (NCES 2010-040)*. Washington, DC: National Center for Education Statistics.

Gresham, F. M., Sugai, G., & Horner, R. H. (2001). Interpreting outcomes of social skill training for students with high-incidence disabilities. *Teaching Exceptional Children*, *67*, 331–344.

Hayes, G. R., Hirano, S., Marcu, G., Monibi, M., Nguyen, D. H., & Yeganyan, M. (2010). Interactive visual supports for children with autism. *Personal and Ubiquitous Computing*, *14*(7), 663–680. doi:10.1007/s00779-010-0294-8

Hume, K. (2008). *Transition time: Helping individuals on the autism spectrum move successfully from one activity to another*. Retrieved from http://www.iidc.indiana.edu/?pageId=399

Hume, K. (2009). *Visual schedules: How and why to use them in the classroom*. Retrieved from http://www.education.com/reference/article/visual-schedule-classroom autismASD/

Illinois Autism/PDD Training and Technical Assistance Project. (n.d.). *Visual supports fact sheet*. Retrieved from http://autism.pbisillinois.org/iattap_Visual_Supports_Fact_Sheet_1_.pdf

Loveland, K. A., & Tunali-Kotoski, B. (2005). The school-aged child with autistic spectrum disorder. In F. R. Volkmar, R. Paul, A. Klin, & D. Cohen (Eds.), *Handbook of autism and pervasive developmental disorders* (3rd ed., pp. 247–287). Hoboken, NJ: Wiley. doi:10.1002/9780470939345.ch9

Malecki, C. K., & Elliot, S. N. (2002). Children's social behaviors as predictors of academic achievement: A longitudinal analysis. *School Psychology Quarterly*, *17*, 1–23. doi:10.1521/scpq.17.1.1.19902

Martin, J. S., Poirier, M., & Dowler, D. M. (2010). Brief report: Impaired temporal reproduction performance in adults with autism spectrum disorder. *Journal of Autism and Developmental Disorders*, *40*(5), 640–646. doi:10.1007/s10803-009-0904-3 PMID:19924521

Massey, G., & Wheeler, J. (2000). Acquisition and generalization of activity schedules and their effects on task engagement in a young child with autism in an inclusive preschool classroom. *Education and Training in Mental Retardation and Developmental Disabilities*, *35*, 326–335.

Mesibov, E., Schopler, G. B., & Hearsey, K. A. (1994). Structured teaching. In E. Schopler, & G. B. Mesibov (Eds.), *Behaviorial issues in autism* (pp. 195–207). New York: Plenum Press. doi:10.1007/978-1-4757-9400-7_10

Myles, B. S. et al. (2005). *Life journey through autism: An educator's guide to Asperger syndrome*. Arlington, VA: Organization for Autism Research.

National Autism Center. (2009). *National standards report*. Randolph, MA: Author.

National Research Council. (2001). *Educating children with autism*. Washington, DC: National Academy Press.

Newton, D., & Dell, A. G. (2011). Mobile devices and students with disabilities: What do best practices tell us? *Journal of Special Education Technology*, *26*(3), 47–49.

Newton, D., Eren, R., Ben-Avie, M., & Reichow, B. (2013). Handheld technology for visual supports. *Journal of Special Education Technology*, *27*(4), 53–56.

Reichow B., Volkmar F.R. (2010). Social skills Interventions for individuals with autism: Evaluation for evidence-based practices within a best evidence synthesis framework. *Journal of Autism and Developmental Disorders*. *40*(2), pp. 149-166. doi: 10.1007/s10803-009-0842-0

Reynhout, G., & Carter, M. (2006). Social stories for children with disabilities. *Journal of Autism and Developmental Disorders*, *36*, 445–469. doi:10.1007/s10803-006-0086-1 PMID:16755384

Sansosti, F. J. et al. (2004). A research synthesis of social story interventions for children with autism spectrum disorders. *Focus on Autism and Other Developmental Disabilities*, *19*, 194–204. doi:10.1177/10883576040190040101

Schreibman, L., Whalen, C., & Stahmer, A. C. (2000). The use of video priming to reduce disruptive behavior in children with autism. *Journal of Positive Behavior Interventions*, *2*, 3–11. doi:10.1177/109830070000200102

Volkmar, F. R., Lord, C., Bailey, A., Schultz, R. T., & Klin, A. (2004). Autism and pervasive developmental disorders. *Journal of Child Psychology and Psychiatry, and Allied Disciplines*, *45*, 135–170. doi:10.1046/j.0021-9630.2003.00317.x PMID:14959806

Volkmar, F. R., Reichow, B., & Doehring, P. (2011). Evidence-based practices in autism: Where we are now and where we need to go. In *Evidence-based practices and treatments for children with autism* (pp. 365–391). New York: Springer. doi:10.1007/978-1-4419-6975-0_14

Welsh, M. et al. (2001). Linkages between children's social and academic competence: A longitudinal analysis. *Journal of School Psychology*, *39*, 463–482. doi:10.1016/S0022-4405(01)00084-X

Zabala, J. (2011, March 11). *Posting to QIAT listserv*. Retrieved from briohttp://natri.uky.edu/assoc_projects/qiat/listserv.html

Zamfir, B., Tedesco, R., & Reichow, B. (2012). Handheld app offering visual support to students with autism spectrum disorders (ASDs). In *Computers helping people with special needs* (pp. 105–112). Berlin: Springer. doi:10.1007/978-3-642-31534-3_16

Chapter 8
Improving Socialization and Emotion Recognition for Children with Autism Using a Smartphone App

Cassidy Lamm
University of Alabama, USA

Jeff Gray
University of Alabama, USA

Lauren Lambert
University of Alabama, USA

Angela Barber
University of Alabama, USA

Joshua Wolfe
University of Alabama, USA

Gary Edwards
United Cerebral Palsy of Greater Birmingham, USA

ABSTRACT

Smartphone apps are used with increased frequency to teach children a variety of skills and to supplement more traditional forms of instruction. In particular, children diagnosed with Autism Spectrum Disorder (ASD) could benefit from applications suited to help them build social emotional skills that could contribute to more successful social interactions. In the study, the authors first investigated and compiled a list of existing apps to see where gaps exist in topic coverage. From this survey of existing smartphone apps for children with ASD, they developed a new app called LEA (Learning Emotions with Autism) that challenges children to interact in a social setting by responding to emotional cues, and having other children determine the emotion that is expressed. This app provides a new context to help children focus their attention on facial cues in order to recognize and interpret emotions through supported peer interaction. In this chapter, the authors discuss how this app was designed and implemented. They also provide a tutorial on how to develop smartphone apps that can be used for ASD research.

DOI: 10.4018/978-1-4666-5792-2.ch008

INTRODUCTION AND MOTIVATION

One in 88 children in the United States has an Autism Spectrum Disorder (Centers for Disease Control, 2012), which is characterized by deficits in social communication and social interaction, and by the presence of repetitive and ritualistic behaviors that are present in early childhood and impair everyday functioning. Specifically related to social deficits, an individual with ASD may demonstrate impairments in social-emotional reciprocity, using and interpreting nonverbal communicative behaviors, and developing and maintaining relationships. These impairments may range in presentation and severity. Social functioning is a highly prioritized goal for individuals with ASD (Rogers & Dawson, 2010). Recently, clinicians, parents, and teachers have begun incorporating technology into intervention and educational plans to enhance social communication. In fact, Autism Speaks[1], a leading national resource for information on ASD, lists over 200 mobile apps that may be appropriate for individuals with ASD, though very few studies have examined the efficacy of technological applications used to enhance social interactions (DiGennaro Reed, Hyman, & Hirst, 2011).

The adoption rate of mobile computing, in the form of smartphones popularized by Android and iPhone platforms, continues to increase and has recently passed the number of desktop computer sales (Gartner, 2013). Despite the growth and interest in mobile computing devices, few apps have been developed to directly improve social-emotional recognition and response within natural contexts including school, home, and social environments. Though the utility of these types of programs has not been established, apps offer promise to enhance social communication within social situations for which smart phones are already commonplace. Smartphone apps are used with increased frequency to teach children with ASD a variety of skills. In our research, we first investigated and compiled a list of existing apps to see where gaps exist in topic coverage. From this survey of existing smartphone apps geared towards children with ASD, we developed a new app that encourages children to interact in a social setting by responding to emotional cues, and having other children determine the emotion expressed by their peers. Our app, called LEA (Learning Emotions with Autism) provides a new context to help children learn about their emotions through peer interaction. This chapter summarizes the findings from our literature and tool survey, identifies a missing gap in current app offerings, and provides an introduction as to how others can create their own mobile app to initiate additional research within the field.

STATE OF THE ART IN MOBILE APPS FOR CHILDREN WITH ASD

Children with ASD demonstrate poorer social attention when compared to typically developing children (Dawson et al., 2004). Further, previous research has indicated that children with ASD have difficulty recognizing emotions (Golan, Ashwin, Granader, McClintock, Day, Leggett, & Baron-Cohen, 2010; Kuusikko et al., 2009) that may be related to more severe social impairments (Borston et al., 2007, Downs & Smith, 2004). Studies suggest that individuals with ASD are less proficient and slower at matching emotional expressions (Bormann-Kischkel, Vilsmeier, & Baude, 1995; Celani et al., 1999; Hobson et al., 1988; Sawyer et al., 2012) and some individuals make abnormal social judgments based on facial processing (Adolphs, Sears, & Piven, 2001). Some children with ASD have been found to prefer visually examining geometric figures compared to social images (Pierce, Conant, Hazin, Stoner, Desmond, 2011). Further, individuals with ASD use different strategies and focus on different cues to recognize emotion than typically developing individuals (Downs & Smith, 2004; Hobson, Ouston, & Lee, 1988). For example, Klin et al. (2002), used eye tracking technology in social scenes to determine that individuals with ASD focus more on the mouth region of a face and less time on the eye region than age, gender, and cognitively matched peers, indicating an abnormal visual fixation pattern. A lack of social motivation may reduce attention to faces early in development of individuals with ASD (Dawson et al., 2002; Klin et al., 1999), which may deprive the child from having important early social learning experiences resulting in an imbalance in attending to social vs. non-social stimuli (Chevallier et al., 2012). In individuals with ASD, this lack of social motivation leads to a decreased attention to faces that may result in a failure to develop perceptual interpretation of faces. Although most individuals are able to process complex nonverbal emotions, this can be quite challenging for many who have been diagnosed with an ASD (Tracy, Robins, Schriber, & Solomon, 2011). Most individuals employ gaze perception and facial cues to understand emotions, both simple and complex (Ashwin, Ricciardelli, & Baron-Cohen, 2009). However, individuals with ASD may have trouble using gaze socially to decode the emotions of others (Ashwin et al., 2009), in part due to poor social motivation. While there is some debate about why this happens for individuals with ASD, the fact remains that emotion recognition is a challenge for many children. The app discussed in this chapter may contribute to improved emotional recognition by assisting individuals with ASD to attend to salient facial expressions that signal particular emotions.

BENEFITS OF TECHNOLOGY AS A TEACHING TOOL

"Technology's goal," says Bölte, Golan, Goodwin, & Zwaigenbaum, (2010), "is to provide an avenue through which people can be better equipped for their environment." Technology is being used more frequently as a teaching tool (Ploog, Scharf, Nelson, & Brooks, 2013). Many researchers also

believe new technology has great potential to be an effective approach to learning (Bölte et al., 2010). In addition to helping individuals learn new skills and concepts, a variety of forms of technology are becoming more commonly integrated into clinical and educational interventions for individuals with an ASD. While some treatments require expensive machinery, others have been developed for computers and even for smartphone applications. With technology improvements also comes the promise of efficient, accessible, and effective technology-based interventions for individuals with ASD. Current devices are portable, cost effective, easily accessible, and socially acceptable and, therefore, can be used to support and enhance social communication for individuals with ASD (Shane et al., 2012).

The recent integration of technology into intervention and educational plans for children with ASD has spurred more studies that incorporate various permutations of technology in treatments such as robotics, virtual reality; many implement computer training (Bölte et al., 2010). This offers a new, potentially successful support for those who have a diagnosis of ASD and their families. Computers may be able to assist individuals with ASD in ways that were not possible before, or were only possible with expensive, sometimes cumbersome computerized devices. Some research has even suggested that individuals with ASD are innately good at working with computers and see them as an effective opportunity for learning (Ploog et al., 2013). Ploog (2013) chronicled many studies involving computer assisted training and suggests that their success is as good or is even better than non-technical learning approaches. Not only do computer-based treatments promote learning, but many studies have found a lasting impact of computer-based approaches with some skills generalizing to real life situations (Ploog et al., 2013).

Research on ASD and technology has been conducted across a wide age group. Kuusikko, Haapsamo, Jansson-Verkasalo, Hurtig, Mattila,

Ebeling, and Moilanen, (2009) studied children and adolescents with ASD compared with typical children and adolescents. Bölte et al. (2010) cited several studies that surveyed children between four to eight years of age, eight to eleven years of age and in one case children as young as three years of age. Golan and Baron-Cohen (2006) hypothesized about adults from 21 to 43 and how this age group can best learn. Ploog et al. (2013) studied computer technology usage in children with a mean age of eight, but a mean mental age of three. While there is much to be researched concerning older adults with ASD, early intervention research has proven to be very successful in many cases (Dawson, Jones, Merkle, Venema, Lowy, Faja, & Webb, 2012).

GROWING UTILIZATION OF SMARTPHONE TECHNOLOGY

Closely related to the aforementioned computer studies are new ways of using smartphone technology to help children with ASD. With recent advances in technology, smartphone apps have been utilized in many innovative ways. As this field of smartphone technology grows, the potential for their impact on children with ASD increases. Smartphone applications are being developed with the aim of helping individuals with ASD communicate more effectively, gain knowledge and skills, and participate in functional and meaningful settings such as school and with peers. Small in size and relatively common for families in the United States, smartphones are a viable option as a learning support platform for children with ASD. School-aged children can hold a smartphone or tablet in their own hands. Many applications that teach a wide variety of skills can be downloaded from an online app store. This type of smartphone aided support can be accessed anywhere by individuals with a range of skills and symptom severity. While the impact of smartphone apps as a support for children with

ASD is encouraging, very little research exists to support the efficacy of specific apps or categories of apps designed to address a particular skill-set (DiGennaro Reed, Hyman, & Hirst, 2011).

The future of learning through smartphone technology is already being studied as an aid for teaching assistants to help students with ASD (Tunney & Ryan, 2012). Some apps help by incorporating video-modeling to display actions common in daily life (Bereznak, Ayres, Mechling, & Alexander,, 2012). Other apps are interactive and involve individuals in their own learning. Just as there is a variety of ways to use smartphone apps to teach children with ASD, there are also a plethora of different areas that are being taught through applications. One important area for children with ASD represents an opportunity to improve the social attention skills related to facial cues that may to ultimately improve emotion recognition. The question has been posed as to whether or not smartphone technology can help close the gap in emotion recognition for this specific population. Many of the challenges that individuals with ASD encounter fall under the broad categorization of social skills (Ryan & Charragáin, 2010).

There are many apps on the market that are designed for children with ASD. However, through our research of existing apps and a compilation of those that specifically addressed social issues, we found a lack of applications that dealt with social attention and emotion. Many of these applications are marketed specifically for children with ASD and serve only as a calendar reminder of activities of the day. Other apps offer tools such as a mood meter. Some of the apps for small children with ASD were concerned with teaching basic pre-academic skills (e.g., spelling, number recognition). Most commonly, apps are used to augment communication skills. Overall, the topic of emotion recognition was not addressed. Although there are a few social apps, many of these are "social stories" and are not interactive (Murdock, Ganz, & Crittendon, 2013). While being labeled as social learning tools, these kinds of apps simply mimic the situation of a child with ASD at a social event. These stories very rarely ask the child to be involved in the social choices offered by the app.

Before setting out to create our own app, we first searched those that are already on the market to help children with ASD. We sought to understand what has already been created so that we could identify a gap in research coverage using smartphone apps for children with ASD. Some apps, such as Number Sequence[2], focus on teaching a child to recognize numbers. Although Number Sequence has been shown to offer benefits, we decided that we wanted to focus on helping children in an area that is more specifically related to ASD. Thus, our project definition evolved into an app that assists children with ASD in recognizing and responding to social cues. One related app is called iConverse[3], which allows a child to communicate with his or her peers through pictures and text. It encourages the child to express common ideas such as "I want to eat," through a phone if the child is unable to express the words verbally. Although this app encourages social interaction, we believe that it would be useful to focus on the most crucial and foundational aspects of social interaction with more basic ideas such as emotions. Another app on the Android market called Emotions and Feelings[4] is geared towards helping children express emotions through social stories. Social stories are a common type of application for children with ASD. These apps show the child in a social situation with events unfolding in storybook fashion. Sometimes the child might be asked for input; however, it may be just a simple animation for the child to watch. This category of app often provides a contextual situation and asks the child how he or she most likely feels in that situation. Though this can be helpful, we wanted to make LEA more interactive. Although Emotions and Feelings allows the child to read about how they would feel in different situations, we wanted LEA to allow the child to recognize certain emotions and assist them in acting out

the emotions in real-life social settings, perhaps even with peers. Through further research on apps created specifically to help children with emotion recognition, we soon recognized an area that was lacking. From realizing the foundational focus of our new app, we began the planning process to design and implement the app.

Our research has focused on an interactive way for children with ASD to recognize emotions by attending to important social cues. Although there is a lack of applications that help children learn about social interactions in a fun and challenging way, we sought to combine what was good about the other apps while improving upon it for our own app. Reviewing related apps, we found that it was beneficial to show children with ASD what a typical social or emotional experience would look like. We also believe that it is important for the children to be assessed on what they learned, which allows us to measure the efficacy of the app over time. Not only should the children be watching, they should be actively involved in choosing the actions that seem appropriate or fitting for an emotion or social interaction. Although it was beneficial for other apps to show emotional responses, we believe it is helpful to start at the beginning and assist children with ASD in identifying the basic six emotions (e.g., happy, sad, angry, scared, surprised, and disgusted) with words that describe emotions and facial expressions. These six emotions are the universally recognized basic emotions (Ekman, 1957). Each of these six has a distinct facial expression pattern that is consistent across the population. These are the first emotions to come online in childhood, and will remain throughout an individual's life span.

Although other previous apps, as well as our own, use smartphones as a support for teaching a child with ASD about social and emotional functioning, it should never stop with just technology. A child who is working hard to be an active participant in social situations in his or her everyday life also needs to act out and experience those feelings and situations first-hand. To address this most important, real-world gap between existing apps and reality, we also considered the potential for a charades feature within LEA. Such a feature can assist children with ASD to interact with other children while being facilitated by a teacher or adult, thereby further increasing opportunities for children to practice attending to important social cues. This phase encourages children to explore an emotion deeper than just the word that represents it and the basic facial appearance.

CASE STUDY: AN APP FOR SOCIALIZATION AND EMOTION RECOGNITION

We developed a smartphone app called LEA (Learning Emotions with Autism) to investigate the difficulties in understanding facial cues and

gaze for children with ASD. Our goal is to help children with ASD to become more proficient in recognizing emotions. Specifically, LEA focuses on the six basic emotions mentioned in the last section. To accomplish this, the app uses pictures of faces expressing basic emotion faces and asks children to identify the emotion with the word associated with it. This section will summarize the app and provide a lead-in for the next section that will demonstrate how researchers who are not computer scientists can develop similar apps for their own investigations.

LEA is used in three phases: the recognition phase (Figure 1), the quiz phase, and the charades phase. The recognition phase of the app provides a child with an introduction to each of the six emotions. In the current version of the app, we use pictures of the same cartoon to express the different emotions in each picture. This allows

Figure 1. The recognition phase

the child to see different emotions expressed by the same character on the screen. After the child clicks the link for the recognition phase, a single image appears on the screen expressing one of the six emotions. A label displaying the text: "This emotion is:" is shown beneath the picture along with the name of the emotion such as "Sad" or "Angry." After the child has viewed that image, he or she can click on the "previous" or the "next" button to progress through all six emotions. There is no score kept because the child is simply learning to match an emotion word with the facial expressions of that emotion in this phase. He or she may iterate through the emotions as many times as needed. Each emotion is displayed randomly for each execution of the app to remove the tendency to memorize the order in which an emotion is presented in the app.

The quiz phase (Figure 2) of the app allows a child to test his or her emotion recognition skills. In this phase, for consistency, we use the same pictures as those from the recognition phase for consistency. When the child enters into the quiz phase, the screen displays one of the emotion images. Beneath the image, there are six buttons, each displaying one of the emotion words. In the quiz phase the child is prompted to press the button containing the name that corresponds with the image. The app keeps track of how many emotion words to faces the child matched correctly and how many he or she matched incorrectly. The score is later displayed in a label below the buttons at the end of the quiz phase. After the child has pressed the button he or she believes is associated with the image, the app then displays whether or not the answer was correct. The child then presses the next button to continue to the next image. Each picture is displayed at random and is displayed only once per session. After all six images have been displayed and guessed, the quiz phase ends and the score is displayed. This phase offers the child a fun way to practice recognizing the various basic emotions.

One way to extend the two phases is to add a third one that would allow children to apply what they have learned into practice in real life situations. This third phase, called the charade phase, could be played in a group setting with other children. Led by an adult supervisor, this phase allows the children to recognize the same six emotions as expressed by other children, as well as act out the emotions themselves. This can

Figure 2. The quiz phase

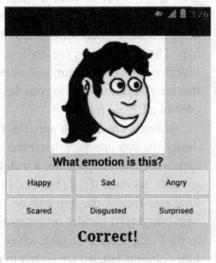

encourage social interaction among other children using what the child learned previously through individual interaction with the app. This phase requires each participant to have a phone. There are two parts to this phase: one person would be prompted with an emotion to act out, and the other players would be prompted to guess which emotion was being acted out. After the participants individually selected the emotion word that they think is being suggested, the information would be stored in a database or sent to the phone of the supervisor to review how each child performed. It would also be helpful if, after each child pressed the button to choose which emotion he or she thought was being acted out, the app would display if he or she was correct or incorrect. This phase would allow the supervisor to track the progress of their students as they are also informed about which emotion the children guessed. The score can also be recorded for each child based on how many emotions he or she matched correctly.

Future work will include experimenting with different ways to display the emotions. Instead of the images being cartoons, it may be more useful to use images of real people displaying the emotion. Perhaps a series of photographs of someone familiar to the child acting out the six different emotions would allow the child to recognize the emotions in real-life more easily. The app could also be extended by adding more features for better accessibility. For example, if the child was unable to press the buttons, the app could be extended to use voice recognition to quiz the child instead. This would allow the child to speak the emotion word that goes with the image in the quiz phase and may work better for some children.

CREATING APPS FOR ASD SPECTRUM DISORDER RESEARCH

The app described in the previous section was created using App Inventor, which is a visual, drag-and-drop tool for building mobile apps on the Android platform. The creation of an app can be thought of as a progression through three development steps. First, the user interface that defines the visual appearance of an app is designed using a web-based graphical user interface (GUI) builder. The second step is to specify the app's behavior and functionality by piecing together "blocks" of code, similar to placing puzzle pieces or Lego blocks together. The last step in building an app is to test it on an Android device or on App Inventor's emulator. The emulator is a tool in App Inventor that emulates the functionality of an Android phone and can be used to demonstrate how an app works without having to load the app onto a real phone. If during the testing process there emerges a need to change anything that was created, it is possible to go back and edit any of the two previous steps and see the changes take immediate effect on the device or emulator. App Inventor was initiated at Google and is now maintained by the MIT Center for Mobile Learning. It is freely available at http://appinventor.mit.edu.

App Inventor is unique because it doesn't require a deep extensive knowledge about computer programming, a computer scientist or a software engineer. With easy to configure pre-programmed blocks, all the app creator has to do is drag-and-drop blocks into the correct places. Thus, App Inventor does not require extensive computing knowledge. In fact, with a little initiative and imagination, those from other research areas can bring a fun and interesting idea to life through an app. The possibilities are endless because App Inventor can create a range of apps from games that are simple and fun, to complex apps that can control a LEGO robot.

To begin creating an app, the first step is to design the user interface that represents the visual appearance of an app using a web-based graphical user interface (GUI) builder. In this step, the look and feel of the app can be specified. The web-based GUI builder is commonly referred to as the Component Designer, which is made up of four columns labeled (from left to right) palette, viewer, components, and properties (please see Figure 3). The Palette column contains all of the available components that may be used in an application, ranging from labels, buttons, and pictures, to speech recognizer, barcode scanners, and much more. The viewer column provides a rough, unformatted view of what the app looks like as it is being designed. The components column shows the hierarchy of components that are being used in the app. Lastly, the properties column gives the ability to alter and customize any component to the desired look.

To operate the Component Designer, a component (e.g., Button, Label, TextBox, etc.) is selected from the Palette and dragged onto the screen preview located in the Viewer column. After the component is dropped on the screen preview, it should appear in the Components column. If it is not already automatically selected, clicking on the component in the Components

column will allow the component to be customized in the Properties column. In the Properties column, the properties of the component (e.g., font size, width, and height) can be changed and adjusted as desired.

After the design of an app is created in the Component Designer, it is time to move to the next step, which is building the functionality of the app. At any point in time, the design can be altered in any way by returning to the Component Designer. The functionality and behavior of the app is created in the Blocks Editor, where the actual "programming" of the app is done. The Blocks Editor (Figure 4) is available by simply clicking on the "Open the Blocks Editor" at the top-right of the Component Designer.

The left column of the Blocks Editor has three tabs categorizing the different types of blocks. The "Built-In" tab contains basic blocks to logically control the functionality of an app. Using

Figure 3. An empty Component Designer

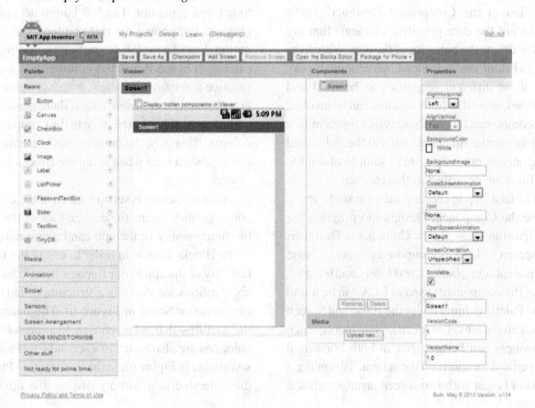

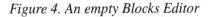

Figure 4. An empty Blocks Editor

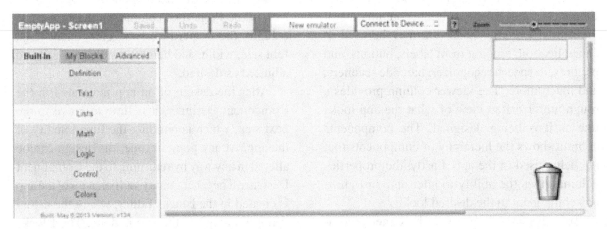

these blocks it is possible to define variables and procedures, create functionality for lists, and logically control the app's behavior with control statements. The "My Blocks" tab contains the functions associated with components that were specified in the Component Designer. With these blocks, the unique functionality can be programmed visually for each component that was specified in the Component Designer. These blocks are the core primitive elements that are used to define the behavior of the app. Within the Blocks Editor, the "Advanced" tab contains blocks that allow different properties to be used and modified, as well as functions that can be invoked on a component block. There is rich functionality available in the Advanced tab and the individual components, but only a small sample of the capabilities are described in this chapter.

The first step in creating the case study app is to use the Component Designer to program the Recognition Phase. In the Component Designer, the screen of LEA is composed of several basic components (e.g., buttons, text labels, and images). All of the components used in LEA can be found in the Palette column under the Basic and Screen Arrangement tabs. The specific placement of each component can be arranged in both horizontal and vertical locations on the screen. This phase's creation began with two screen arrangements, a

vertical arrangement above a horizontal arrangement. An image component is added inside the vertical arrangement (top arrangement) along with two labels below the image. The top label is set to "This emotion is" and the bottom label to the emotion name. These properties can be set in the Properties column. Next, two buttons were added, and an empty label between them to act as a separator. The left button acts as the previous button and the right button as the next button. Just like the labels, the buttons' properties can be set in the Properties column. It is a good practice to rename the labels, buttons, and screen arrangements used, especially if there are similar components. This can be done in the Components column. This way, the components can easily be distinguished later when using the Blocks Editor (Figure 5).

After the screen is set up with all of the correct components to create the desired look of the app, the functionality of the app can be programmed in the Blocks Editor. In order to create the functionality of the app in our Recognition Phase, the six emotions are stored in a structure called a list (see EmotionName in Figure 6). The names of the pictures that were chosen to represent the emotions are also added to a second list (PicturesAvailable in Figure 6). In the Recognition Phase, the objective is to simply display the emotion

Figure 5. Case study's recognition phase Component Designer

name with its corresponding picture. Creating these two lists will allow the app to recognize which picture corresponds to a specific emotion.

Though the items in the created lists are in a fixed order, the app can display them in a random order by creating a variable that allows the app to keep track of a specific value (CurrentPicture in Figure 6). In this case, the app needs to keep track of how many pictures have not yet been displayed. The app then picks a random picture to display each time so that the child does not memorize any particular order. The app also creates a variable to save the previous picture shown (Previous in Figure 6), in case the child wants to go back and view that picture again.

Although the app has lists to display the pictures and emotions, and a way to ensure that they appear in a random order, there are still several actions of the app that need to be programmed. For example, the actions that are to be taken when each button is pushed must be programmed. When the child presses the Next button, the app needs a new picture to pop up with the corresponding emotion displayed beneath it. In order to accomplish this, a new procedure can be defined that provides app-specific functionality. When creating an app in App Inventor, the programmer can create a customized procedure to accomplish certain tasks. When the Next button is pressed, the app needs to display a random picture from the list of

Figure 6. Case study's recognition phase Blocks Editor

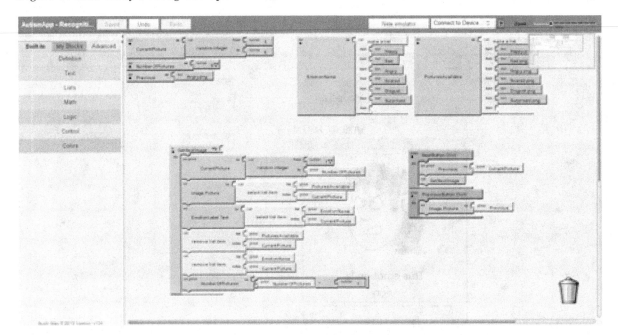

pictures (see NextButton.Click in Figure 6). This is accomplished by setting a variable that stores the placement of the current picture to a random number in between one and the number of pictures that have not been shown. If the app instead choses a random number between one and the total number of pictures, there is a high probability that a picture will appear twice. The random number generated by our variable represents where the picture is located in the list. Because the order of the picture list and the emotion list is exactly the same, this number also represents the placement of the emotion word in the second list. The app can look at that location in both lists to display the picture and emotion word on the screen.

After each picture and emotion word are displayed, they should not be displayed again. To ensure that this happens, the app must remove both items from their respective lists. This also decreases the number of pictures that have not been displayed (i.e., the number of items left in the list) by one (GetNextImage in Figure 6). Also, when the next button is clicked, the variable storing the previous picture needs to be assigned as

the current picture. This ensures that when the "Previous" button is clicked (Previous.Click), the previous picture is displayed. This completes the functionality for the Recognition Phase. With this functionality, the child will be able to click through the emotions with the touch of a button.

In the Quiz Phase, the first step is to use the Component Designer to create the appearance. A new screen (using the "Add Screen" button in the Component Designer) provides an empty space on which components can be placed. Next, the screen is comprised of three arrangements (please see Figure 7). A vertical arrangement is specified that has two horizontal arrangements inside of it. An image and label component are added inside the vertical arrangement and placed above the two horizontal ones. Three buttons are added to each horizontal arrangement; totally, six in all. These buttons will act as the answer choices for the child. After all of the components have been added, the properties of each component are configured to the desired appearance. This includes setting the label to "What emotion is this?" and setting each button's label to an appropriate answer option.

Figure 7. Case study's quiz phase Component Designer

The blocks editor for the Quiz Phase functions much the same way as the Recognition Phase, with a few extra steps. However, unlike the first phase, the app only needs a list to store the pictures for this phase. Because the six buttons displaying the emotions remain constant, the app only needs to keep track of the pictures that are displayed. After creating the list storing all six pictures, the app also creates the variable to store the placement of the current picture. Just like as before, the app sets the variable to a random number between one and the number of pictures left in the list. Similarly, the app also defines a procedure to retrieve the next picture. This procedure is identical to the one in the previous blocks editor, except that the app only needs to look up and remove items in one list instead of two.

In the Quiz Phase, the app must deal with six buttons instead of two. With the ability to change pictures, the app must make sure that the child can press a button to guess the emotion associated with each picture. When the button is pressed, the app needs to compare the button pressed to the picture displayed on the screen in order to check if the answer provided by the child is correct. The app also needs to keep track of how many questions the child has missed (NumberMissed in Figure 8), as well as display whether the answer is correct or incorrect. To do this, a procedure is created to process the button click (ProcessButtonClick in

Figure 8. Case study's quiz phase Blocks Editor

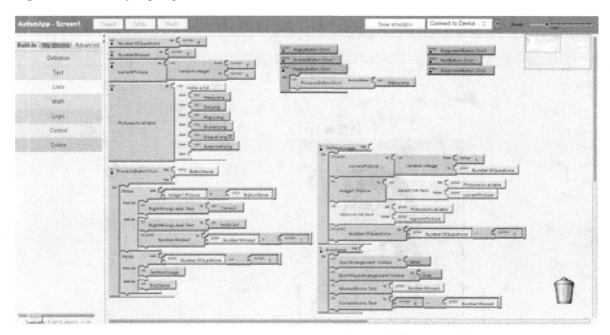

Figure 8). This method looks at the button name and compares it to the name of the picture being displayed. If they match, the app sets the text to display "Correct!" Otherwise, the text is displayed as "Incorrect" and NumberMissed is increased by one. Because this is a quiz that keeps score, the app eventually needs to be able to determine when the game is over (i.e., when all six pictures have been shown). After the app compares the pictures with the button, it needs to check whether or not there are more pictures to be displayed. If the number of questions left is greater than or equal to one, GetNextImage is invoked to get the next picture. However, if there are no more pictures to be displayed, the EndGame procedure is executed.

Creating the process to end the game is simple. The app simply makes the screen and buttons invisible and displays the number of questions that the child answered correctly or incorrectly. This completes the Block Editor programming for the Quiz Phase. When making a quiz-like app for children with ASD, App Inventor makes it easy.

As stated in the previous section, this app can also be expanded in a wide variety of ways. App Inventor has several other capabilities, such as sending text messages, making quizzes, turning text into speech, and much more. Using App Inventor, the possibilities for app development in the area of support for children with ASD are endless.

CONCLUSION

In conclusion, we have shown how the adoption of smart phones over the past decade has been used in both educational and clinical contexts for children of all ages. In particular, we have described our use of mobile applications to assist children with ASD. Although there are many mobile applications developed in the general area of ASD, our research has discovered that mobile applications are lacking in the area of social-emotional development for young children with ASD. In our research, we developed our set of requirements and features for the apps that were designed to help with emotion recognition and social skills in young children with ASD. Using these requirements, we were able to filter through the apps already on the market and find a gap where further development was required.

We then introduced an app that we created to fill the gap in current apps designed to improve aspects of social communication in individuals with ASD. Specifically, this app will assist individuals in focusing their attention on facial cues in order to accurately recognize emotions within peer interactions. This app provides a way for children with ASD to be introduced to emotions as they relate to facial expressions. We chose the six main emotions for the child to identify because these are emotions that will be important throughout their life. In the first phase of the app, a child is facilitated in learning the different emotions and recognizing the facial cues that correspond to each emotion. Through the second phase of this app, children can also practice viewing a facial expression and pairing it with its correct emotion name in a quiz-like setting. Children will get feedback from the app and learn as they progress in using the app. The app can also be adapted to a context of usage by a group of children and an adult facilitator who would play a game of charades together, acting out the emotions. This will help children to not only to recognize an emotion and pair it with a word, but also to be able to relate to their peers and practice making the facial expressions that are tied to the six basic emotions. There are also various ways to extend and change the app as we have described in previous sections.

In addition, we also explain the process for developing such apps. We introduced MIT's App Inventor to show how others working in any area, who are not computer scientists, can develop prototypes related to their own research interests. After an overview of the Components Designer and Blocks Editor, we demonstrated how App Inventor can be applied to extend our own app, as well as for development for other research contexts. We encourage others to create an app for children with ASD using this platform and to develop some new capabilities within the ASD research community.

As future work, we plan to empirically investigate the different configurations in which LEA can be used to determine the level of benefit offered to children with ASD. An experimental or application group will play our application game, and a control group will not. The study will analyze the benefits of a longer intervention of eight weeks over the benefits after just four weeks. If our emotion recognition app is successful in teaching children with ASD to recognize and match emotion words and facial expressions, better scores should be observed on an Emotions Recognition test after playing than before. We will evaluate these assumptions through our collaborations with local organizations that assist children with ASD.

REFERENCES

Adolphs, R., Sears, L., & Piven, J. (2001). Abnormal processing of social information from faces in autism. *Journal of Cognitive Neuroscience*, *13*(2), 232–240. doi:10.1162/089892901564289 PMID:11244548

Ashwin, C., Ricciardelli, P., & Baron-Cohen, S. (2009). Positive and negative gaze perception in ASD spectrum conditions. *Social Neuroscience*, *4*(2), 153–164. doi:10.1080/17470910802337902 PMID:18726820

Bereznak, S., Ayres, K. M., Mechling, L. C., & Alexander, J. L. (2012). Video self-prompting and mobile technology to increase daily living and vocational independence for students with ASD spectrum disorders. *Journal of Developmental and Physical Disabilities*, *24*(3), 269–285. doi:10.1007/s10882-012-9270-8

Bölte, S., Golan, O., Goodwin, M. S., & Zwaigenbaum, L. (2010). What can innovative technologies do for autism spectrum disorders? *Autism, 14*(3), 155–159. doi:10.1177/1362361310365028 PMID:20603897

Boraston, Z., Blakemore, S. J., Chilvers, R., & Skuse, D. (2007). Impaired sadness recognition is linked to social interaction deficit in ASD. *Neuropsychologia, 45*(7), 1501–1510. doi:10.1016/j.neuropsychologia.2006.11.010 PMID:17196998

Cardon, T. A. (2012). Teaching caregivers to implement video modeling imitation training via iPad for their children with ASD. *Research in ASD Spectrum Disorders, 6*(4), 1389–1400. doi:10.1016/j.rasd.2012.06.002

Centers for Disease Control and Prevention. (2012). *Prevalence of ASD spectrum disorders — ASD and developmental disabilities monitoring network, 14 sites, United States, 2008.* Washington, DC: Author.

Chevallier, C., Kohls, G., Troiani, V., Brodkin, E. S., & Schultz, R. T. (2012). The social motivation theory of autism. *Trends in Cognitive Sciences, 16*(4), 231–239. doi:10.1016/j.tics.2012.02.007 PMID:22425667

Dawson, G., Carver, L., Meltzoff, A. N., Panagiotides, H., McPartland, J., & Webb, S. J. (2002). Neural correlates of face and object recognition in young children with autism spectrum disorder, developmental delay, and typical development. *Child Development, 73*(3), 700–717. doi:10.1111/1467-8624.00433 PMID:12038546

Dawson, G., Jones, E. H., Merkle, K., Venema, K., Lowy, R., Faja, S., & Webb, S. J. (2012). Early behavioral intervention is associated with normalized brain activity in young children with ASD. *Journal of the American Academy of Child and Adolescent Psychiatry, 51*(11), 1150–1159. doi:10.1016/j.jaac.2012.08.018 PMID:23101741

Dawson, G., Toth, K., Abbott, R., Osterling, J., Munson, J., Estes, A., & Liaw, J. (2004). Early social attention impairments in Autism: Social orienting, joint attention, and attention to distress. *Developmental Psychology, 40*(2), 271–283. doi:10.1037/0012-1649.40.2.271 PMID:14979766

DiGennaro Reed, F. D., Hyman, S. R., & Hirst, J. M. (2011). Applications of technology to teach social skills to children with ASD. *Research in ASD Spectrum Disorders, 5*(3), 1003–1010. doi:10.1016/j.rasd.2011.01.022

Downs, A., & Smith, T. (2004). Emotional understanding, cooperation, and social behavior in high-functioning children with ASD. *Journal of ASD and Developmental Disorders, 34*(6), 625–635. doi:10.1007/s10803-004-5284-0

Ekman, P. (1957). A methodological discussion of nonverbal behavior. *The Journal of Psychology, 43*, 141–149. doi:10.1080/00223980.1957.9713059

Ekman, P., & Friesen, W. V. (1976). *Pictures of facial affect.* Palo Alto, CA: Consulting Psychologist Press.

Gartner. (2013). *Gartner says worldwide PC, tablet and mobile phone combined shipments to reach 2.4 billion units in 2013.* Retrieved from http://www.gartner.com/newsroom/id/2408515

Gastgeb, H. Z., Rump, K. M., Best, C. A., Minshew, N. J., & Strauss, M. S. (2009). Prototype formation in autism: Can individuals with autism abstract facial prototypes? *Autism Research, 2*(5), 279–284. doi:10.1002/aur.93 PMID:19877157

Golan, O., Ashwin, E., Granader, Y., McClintock, S., Day, K., Leggett, V., & Baron-Cohen, S. (2010). Enhancing emotion recognition in children with ASD spectrum conditions: An intervention using animated vehicles with real emotional faces. *Journal of ASD and Developmental Disorders, 40*(3), 269–279. doi:10.1007/s10803-009-0862-9

Golan, O., & Baron-Cohen, S. (2006). System-izing empathy: Teaching adults with Asperger syndrome or high-functioning ASD to recognise complex emotions using interactive multi- me-dia. *Development and Psychopathology, 18,* 591–617. doi:10.1017/S0954579406060305 PMID:16600069

Harms, M. B., Martin, A., & Wallace, G. L. (2010). Facial emotion recognition in ASD spectrum disorders: A review of behavioral and neuroimaging studies. *Neuropsychology Review, 20*(3), 290–322. doi:10.1007/s11065-010-9138-6 PMID:20809200

Hobson, R. P., Ouston, J. J., & Lee, A. A. (1988). What's in a face? The case of ASD. *The British Journal of Psychology, 79*(4), 441. doi:10.1111/j.2044-8295.1988.tb02745.x

Klin, A., Jones, W., Schultz, R., Volkmar, F., & Cohen, D. (2002). Visual fixation patterns during viewing of naturalistic social situations as predic-tors of social competence in individuals with ASD. *Archives of General Psychiatry, 59*(9), 809–816. doi:10.1001/archpsyc.59.9.809 PMID:12215080

Klin, A., Sparrow, S. S., de Bildt, A., Cicchetti, D. V., Cohen, D. J., & Volkmar, F. R. (1999). A normed study of face recognition in autism and related disorders. *Journal of Autism and Developmental Disorders, 29*(6), 499–508. doi:10.1023/A:1022299920240 PMID:10638462

Kuusikko, S., Haapsamo, H., Jansson-Verkasalo, E., Hurtig, T., Mattila, M., Ebeling, H., & Moil-anen, I. (2009). Emotion recognition in children and adolescents with ASD spectrum disorders. *Journal of ASD and Developmental Disorders, 39*(6), 938–945. doi:10.1007/s10803-009-0700-0

Murdock, L. C., Ganz, J., & Crittendon, J. (2013). Use of an iPad play story to increase play dialogue of preschoolers with ASD spectrum disorders. *Journal of ASD and Developmental Disorders, 43*(9), 2174–2189. doi:10.1007/s10803-013-1770-6

Pierce, K., Conant, D., Hazin, R., Stoner, R., & Desmond, J. (2011). Preference for geometric patterns early in life as a risk factor for autism. *Archives of General Psychiatry, 68*(1), 101–109. doi:10.1001/archgenpsychiatry.2010.113 PMID:20819977

Ploog, B. O., Scharf, A., Nelson, D., & Brooks, P. J. (2013). Use of computer-assisted technolo-gies (CAT) to enhance social, communicative, and language development in children with ASD spectrum disorders. *Journal of ASD and Develop-mental Disorders, 43*(2), 301–322. doi:10.1007/s10803-012-1571-3

Rogers, S. J., & Dawson, G. (2010). *Early start denver model for young children with autism: Promoting language, learning, and engagement.* New York: Guilford.

Ryan, C., & Charragáin, C. (2010). Teaching emotion recognition skills to children with ASD. *Journal of ASD snd Developmental Disorders, 40*(12), 1505-1511.

Shane, H. C., Laubscher, E. H., Schlosser, R. W., Flynn, S., Sorce, J. F., & Abramson, J. (2012). Applying technology to visually support lan-guage and communication in individuals with ASD spectrum disorders. *Journal of ASD and Developmental Disorders, 42*(6), 1228–1235. doi:10.1007/s10803-011-1304-z

Tracy, J. L., Robins, R. W., Schriber, R. A., & Solo-mon, M. (2011). Is emotion recognition impaired in individuals with ASD spectrum disorders? *Journal of ASD and Developmental Disorders, 41*(1), 102–109. doi:10.1007/s10803-010-1030-y

Tunney, R., & Ryan, M. (2012). Can iDevices help teaching assistants support pupils with ASD? *Journal of Assistive Technologies, 6*(3), 182–191. doi:10.1108/17549451211261308

KEY TERMS AND DEFINITIONS

App Inventor: A visual programming environment from the MIT Center for Mobile Learning; assists in the construction of Android smartphone apps for those who may not be trained formally as Computer Scientists.

Autism Spectrum Disorder: According to the Diagnostic and Statistical Manual of Mental Disorders, ASDs are a group of pervasive developmental disorders typically characterized by difficulties in social interactions and communications.

Emotion Recognition: The ability to understand social and physical cues of emotional states in others.

Graphical User Interface (GUI): An interface allowing an individual to respond to a prompted question or dialogue through use of icons or buttons.

Smartphone App: An application that can be run on a smartphone and may be found and downloaded through an online application store.

User Interface: The place where a human can interact with technology.

ENDNOTES

1 http://www.autismspeaks.org/
2 https://play.google.com/store/apps/details?id=air.Numbersequence
3 https://itunes.apple.com/us/app/id304852637?mt=8
4 https://play.google.com/store/apps/details?id=com.TouchAutism.Emotions-Feelings

Chapter 9
A Viable Option?
Single-User Virtual Environments to Teach Social Skills to Children with ASD

Julie E. N. Irish
University of Minnesota, USA

ABSTRACT

This chapter considers whether a computer-aided technology, single-user virtual environments, can provide a viable option to teach social skills to children with Autism Spectrum Disorder (ASD). Viability is discussed in terms of key themes found in the literature: evidence-basis, generalizability, cost effectiveness, appropriateness for children with ASD, user experience, teacher's contribution, and usefulness for caregivers. A matrix is developed to provide a viability rating for each theme. The chapter concludes that evidence-basis and generalizability for single-user virtual environments as an intervention to teach social skills to children with autism spectrum disorder is weak but that cost effectiveness, appropriateness to teenage children with ASD, positive experience of the user, and potential usefulness for caregivers is strong, whilst the teacher's contribution is a mixed rating between ease of use for the teacher and the high one-on-one time commitment required.

INTRODUCTION

Statistics indicate that the numbers of children diagnosed with autism spectrum disorder (ASD) are increasing. Current estimates from the Centers for Disease Control and Prevention suggest that as many as one child in eighty-eight has ASD (Baio, 2012). This is an increase from figures released a few years earlier by the same authority which estimated that around one child in one-hundred-

and-ten had an ASD (Rice, 2006). There are flaws in these estimates as increases could represent increased awareness and diagnosis of the condition as well as, by its own admission, anomalies in the reporting of data used in these estimates (Rice, 2006). Overall, however, it is difficult to refute that there is an upward trend in the numbers of children diagnosed with the condition. Indeed, the Centers for Disease Control and Prevention is concerned enough to term ASD "an urgent public health concern" (Rice, 2006, p.1).

DOI: 10.4018/978-1-4666-5792-2.ch009

As the number of children diagnosed with ASD is growing, the actual diagnosis is also changing. ASD, and Asperger's Syndrome, a less serious disorder, were previously classified by the American Psychiatric Association as one of a number of childhood developmental disorders under the umbrella of "Pervasive Developmental Disorders" (APA, 2000). However, as of May 2013, the association dispensed with these separate diagnoses and classified the range of developmental disorders previously known collectively as Pervasive Developmental Disorders under the term "Autism Spectrum Disorder" (APA, 2013). The term "spectrum" is used to indicate the wide spectrum of difficulties which individuals can have, from high functioning people diagnosed with the disorder who are able to operate at levels at the top of the spectrum, to lower functioning individuals, many with additional learning disabilities and a lack of speech, who operate at much lower levels at the opposite end of the spectrum (Simpson, Myles, & LaCava, 2008).

ASD is defined by the American Psychiatric Association in terms of two major difficulties in functionality which those with the condition exhibit, namely difficulties in socializing, and a tendency to perform restrictive, repetitive behaviors (APA, 2013). Difficulties in socializing are defined as "persistent communication and social interaction deficits in multiple situations" (APA, 2013, p. 31). The World Health Organization, which might be considered as having a global view of ASD, describes the trait as "a lack of modulation of behaviour according to social context, or a weak integration of social, emotional and communicative behaviours" (World Health Organization, 1993, p. 180). These definitions indicate that the inability to communicate and socialize in a typical, acceptable manner with other people is a serious defect that warrants diagnosis and is also something that many of those diagnosed with ASD are acutely aware of. Authors with ASD describe the effect it can have on their lives. Temple Grandin, a renowned scholar and writer with high functioning ASD writes movingly, "I had to think about every social interaction . . . I wanted to participate, but I did not know how," (Grandin, 1996, p. 153). Sinclair (1992), another writer with ASD, explains "social interactions involve things that most people know without having to learn them" (p. 299).

It appears, then, that the number of children diagnosed with ASD is rising and that there are advances in defining and recognizing the symptoms of ASD as more becomes known about the condition. With this evolving background it is not surprising that treatments for children with ASD are also evolving: both medical treatments to treat the physical and mental symptoms associated with ASD, and educational interventions to support the learning and behavioral issues associated with the condition. Adams' 2013 publication lists numerous potential dietary, nutritional, and medical treatments which may alleviate symptoms for some children with ASD. They include administering a supplement of melatonin which my help children with ASD with sleep problems, to hyperbaric oxygen therapy, where oxygen levels are increased in the patient's body via an oxygen chamber to assist some with ASD who have decreased blood flow in the brain. In addition to biomedical treatments, there is a plethora of educational interventions designed to support children with ASD. Well-established treatments include applied behavior analysis, an intervention that investigates the cause and effect of problem behaviors, and TEACCH (Treatment and Education of Autistic and other Communication handicapped CHildren), a structured teaching method that advocates changing the environment to suit the individual with ASD (Simpson, Myles, & Ganz, 2008). One of the aims of these and other interventions is to increase the skill level of children in a particular area to address their challenges in social communication, interaction and functionality. Indeed, Reichow and Volkmar (2010) found sixty-six published studies on social skills interventions which they agreed met evidence-basis criteria for potential intervention. As might be expected, many treatments designed to support children with ASD with their difficulties in communication utilize assistive technology. Recent developments include applications (apps) for mobile technology, (iPad, iPhone, iTouch), such as the "Autism Emotion" app which uses music and photographs to help children learn a number of emotions (http://www. autismspeaks.org/autism-apps/autism-emotion), and "The Urinal Game" an app to test "public men's room etiquette" (http://www.autismspeaks. org/autism-apps/urinal-game). The SenseCam, a wearable video recording device developed by Microsoft, has been used by therapists to study how non-verbal children with ASD could use the technology to communicate with their carers (Marcu & Hayes, 2010). In the classroom, interactive smart board technology has been successfully used to stimulate the learning of children with ASD (Ellwood, 2009).

Another recent area of research to help children with ASD learn social skills is the use of virtual computer environments. Cobb (2007) describes a virtual environment as a 3D computer space which can be set up with graphic objects to look like a real life scene. Real life operations can be performed on objects in the scene and a three dimensional character, known as an avatar, can be navigated through the virtual scene controlled by either a mouse or a joystick (Cobb, 2007). Scenes can be varied allowing children to learn and practice acceptable social skills in a variety of settings. Virtual environments can be either fully immersive virtual environments, where the users wear headsets to help them feel part of the environment (Strickland, 1996); or single-user virtual environments, where the users work independently on their own, with support from a teacher to manipulate their character in the virtual computer space (Cobb, 2007). There are also collaborative virtual environments, where a number of users can interact together via their avatar in shared virtual space to practice social skills (Cobb, 2007).

The purpose of this chapter will be to review the current research into the use of single-user virtual environments (SVEs) to teach social skills to children with ASD and consider whether it offers a viable treatment option. A definition of viability will be offered and a viability matrix produced to adjudge the key themes found in the research in terms of whether each is viable. The overall viability of the SVE as an intervention will be discussed, and, finally, directions for future research will be suggested.

BACKGROUND

Research into the general field of virtual environments to support children with ASD is still developing. Most researchers credit Strickland as the early pioneer of virtual environment techniques (Neale, Cobb, & Wilson, 2002; Parsons et al., 2000; Parsons, Mitchell, & Leonard, 2004). Strickland, however, conducted research involving fully immersive virtual environments (IVEs). In her experiments, children with ASD wore a headset with viewing capability to watch a simulated street scene. The object of the research was to identify a car and ultimately learn to safely cross the road (Strickland, 1996). Strickland's participants were on the low end of the autism spectrum with little speech but, despite this, she reported that both children in her research accepted the headsets and made progress in learning during the forty learning opportunities given to them, and she felt that the potential for virtual environments was promising (Strickland, 1996). Some researchers have criticised Strickland's approach because video evidence indicates that one of the children was uncomfortable wearing the headgear and tried to remove it (Parsons et al., 2000; Parsons, 2005). Obtaining institutional review board approval for similar experiments could, therefore, be an issue. With that background in mind, most research has not centered on immersing the user in the virtual three dimensional scene as if it were real life, but rather on the user viewing the virtual three dimensional scene and having an awareness that they are viewing it and not part of it, either as a single-user or as one of multiple users in a collaborative environment, described earlier.

In reviewing the research into the use of SVEs to teach social skills to children with ASD to date, the bulk of research has been conducted by a team terming themselves the AS Interactive Project Team, (AS being the abbreviation for Asperger's Syndrome, a high-functioning form of ASD). This project was set up in the United Kingdom by the University of Nottingham, supported by the National Autistic Society, the foremost organization promoting ASD awareness in the United Kingdom, and funded by the Shirley Foundation, a charitable foundation (Cobb et al., 2002). The team conducted a number of experiments between 2000 and 2003 and have published many papers describing their research. Much of the research focused on teaching children with ASD how to behave in a socially acceptable manner in a virtual café environment. Thus users would be taught the social conventions of sitting at an empty table rather than at a stranger's table and, as the degrees of difficulty in the scenario progressed, how to ask a stranger whether they could sit at their table if there were no free tables available (Cobb et al., 2002). The other common social scenario used by the same researchers is that of boarding a bus and finding a seat on a bus. Again, researchers built varying degrees of difficulty into the program, from teaching the social niceties of sitting in an empty seat when available, to asking someone if they could sit next to them if there were no empty seats available (Leonard, Mitchell, & Parsons, 2002).

Other researchers have been slow to follow but there is an emerging body of research. A recently published pilot study describes investigations using SVEs to teach a range of social skills to adolescents with ASD, including conversational skills (Kandalaft, Didehbani, Krawczyk, Allen, & Chapman, 2013). The researchers, using older teenagers and adolescents as participants, set up several scenarios including a café as well as additional scenarios more suited to an older age group, such as an office scene to practice job interview skills and shopping in a number of different stores (Kandalaft et al., 2013). In addition to the participant having an avatar to negotiate the social scenarios, each participant was coached by a clinician with their own avatar supported by another clinician, described as a "confederate," whose role was to change avatar characters in the virtual world to suit the learning objectives (Kandalaft et al., 2013). Lányi and colleagues at the University of Pannonia in Hungary have conducted much research into virtual environments for people with a disability, some using children with ASD as participants. One paper describes the use of a virtual environment to teach shopping skills to children with ASD, which includes an element of social skills training (Lányi, Geiszt, Károlyi, Tilinger, & Magyara, 2006).

Researchers have trialled SVEs to teach skills in other areas, such as Strickland and colleagues' work on life safety training for children, including those with ASD (Strickland, McAllister, Coles, & Osborne, 2007), Self and colleagues used a SVE to teach fire safety and tornado safety training to a group of children with ASD (Self, Scudder, Weheba, & Crumrine, 2007). The focus of this chapter, however, will be on the research concerned with teaching social skills to children with ASD. The question asked in the opening pages was whether SVEs can provide a "viable option" as an intervention to teach social skills to children with ASD. The dictionary definition of viable is "feasible; practicable especially from an economic standpoint" (Allen, 1990). To provide some way to define whether SVEs provide a feasible, practicable option, key themes are explored based on findings in the literature as follows:

1. Does the SVE provide an evidence-based intervention?
2. Are the skills taught using the SVE generalizable, either to teach social skills from one virtual scenario to another or from one virtual scenario to a real life scenario?
3. Is the SVE a cost effective intervention?
4. Is the SVE an appropriate intervention to teach social skills to children diagnosed with ASD?
5. What is the user's experience of using the SVEs?
6. What contribution is required from the teacher to administer the SVE intervention?
7. Is the SVE as an intervention to teach social skills useful to caregivers of children with ASD?

The positive and negative aspects of each of these key themes will be explored. A matrix is proposed to rate the viability of each key theme on a scale of 1-5, with 1 being a low rating scale and 5 being a high rating scale. Lastly, the implications of the viability of these key themes will be discussed.

Role of Author

In common with many writers, I have my own potential for bias. Who cannot write about a potential intervention for children with ASD without a hope and a wish for its success? To balance this, I have not personally carried out research into the domain of SVEs as an intervention so am without self-interest. In summary, I am aware of my potential for bias and have immersed myself in the literature and carried out frequent bias checks whilst writing to ensure I provide an impartial view.

SVEs TO TEACH SOCIAL SKILLS TO CHILDREN WITH ASD

Overview

There are sound reasons why there is a growing amount of research into the use of virtual environments to teach social skills to children with ASD. Cobb et al. (2002) explain that children can learn by their mistakes in the virtual world without fear of failure. Mitchell, Parsons, and Leonard (2007) advocate that it can "allow an authentic simulation of situations, potentially helping participants to perceive the relevance to the real world, which maximizes the likelihood of generalized learning" (p. 589). Kandalaft et al. (2013) also report that the ability to continually practice a particular scenario is an important part of treatment in general for people with ASD who may have to practice the skills they are taught many times over before they can remember and repeat them. With this background, the following key themes found in the literature are considered in relation to the potential of SVEs, namely evidence-base, generalizability, cost effectiveness, appropriateness to users with ASD, user experience, teacher's contribution, and usefulness to caregivers.

Evidence-Basis

Perhaps the highest accolade of whether a treatment is viable for children with ASD is whether it can provide a practicable and suitable treatment in the long term, whether it can be considered as an evidence-based intervention. What is considered evidence is open to discussion. The What Works Clearinghouse™ (WWC), set up by the U.S. Department of Education to provide educators in all fields with "a central and trusted source of scientific evidence for what works in education," includes a section on strategies for children with a disability (What Works Clearinghouse™, 2013, p. 1). It has a rigorous protocol for analysing research papers to decide whether a paper meets its evidence-based standard, and also provides a list of rejected papers that do not meet its evidence-based standard, including the reasons why. A search of the WWC website in June, 2013, did not find any research into virtual learning environments to teach social skills to the age group five to eighteen. In early childhood, defined by WWC as children in the age group three to five who do not attend school but may be in a preschool program, forty-six studies were listed as providing social skills training. Only three of these studies met WWC's evidence-based standards, none of them using the virtual environment as a training intervention (WWC, 2013), and no research involving SVEs was reported as rejected. So, although the SVE as an intervention is not considered an evidence-based strategy by the WWC, it should be noted that there are many interventions for children with ASD in use by practitioners and educators which are not included for a variety of reasons.

Another reputable organization, an initiative of several universities, is the National Professional Development Center on ASD. They, too, have their own tightly controlled criteria for establishing whether there is an evidence-base for an intervention strategy, requiring a high quality designed study, free of confounding variables, that has been published in a peer-reviewed science journal (National Professional Development Center on ASD, 2013). The National Professional Development Center on ASD does not include any interventions using computer-aided instruction with a SVE to teach social skills among the six evidence-based strategies which they cite, but this may be because they have not yet evaluated any research on this topic. They do list a computer-aided program to teach adolescents with ASD to recognize and understand emotions in other people as an evidence-based intervention (National Professional Development Center on ASD, 2010).

None of the researchers investigating SVEs to teach social skills to children with ASD claim that their research provides an evidence-based intervention. Parsons et al. (2000) refer to "a paucity of direct evidence to support the idea" (p. 165). Parsons and Cobb (2011) consider virtual environments in general as "significantly underexplored in research terms" and acknowledge that children with ASD will be best served by a strong evidence-based intervention. Authors generally conclude that much more research needs to be carried out before any such claim can be made. Kandalaft et al. (2013) bemoan the lack of evidence-based interventions for adolescents but are prepared to assert that their study provides "preliminary evidence" of the success of improving social skills in young adults (p. 41). In a survey of literature reviewing social skills training technologies in general for children with ASD, Reed, Hyman, and Hirst (2011) found that there was good reliability of dependent variables in the studies reviewed but poor reliability of independent variables. There is also a balance to be found as criteria for establishing an evidence-basis could deter researchers from experimenting in a new field (Simpson et al., 2008). As the authors remind us, "At one time even behavioral methodologies, which are widely accepted now, were considered cutting edge and without a research base behind them" (Simpson et al., 2008, pp. 39-40.

In summary, the above indicates that it is not yet possible to establish the viability of the SVE as an evidence-based intervention, perhaps unsurprising, given that the field is new and research to date has been limited.

Generalizability

Another key aspect which interventionists seek in a treatment for children with ASD is whether it can be generalized from one situation to another. That is, whether the child can take what he or she learns in one situation and transfer those skills to another situation (Simpson, Myles, & LaCava, 2008). Generalizability is important because it can speed up the learning process without the child having to be taught each situation separately. Several authors considered generalizability as part of their study. Leonard et al. (2002) reported a lack of generalizability when they trained children in the social skills involved in using a café environment with a SVE and then tried to generalize that experience to that of boarding and finding a seat on a bus. Mitchell et al. (2007) investigated whether children could transfer the social skills taught in the SVE sessions to find a seat in a café and a bus to a video clip of a café and a bus. They found some generalization in participants discussing a video of the scenario immediately following training in the SVE environment but a lack of generalizability if the video session did not follow the SVE session (Leonard et al., 2002). Kandalaft et al. (2013) noted that, although their results were promising, they were not generalizable due to the small sample size used in their study (eight participants) and the fact that they did not use a control group in their experiment. Howlin (1998) goes as far as saying that social skills training should be carried out in real life situations because the generalization ability of those with ASD is so poor. This is contradictory to other researchers who remind us that there are valid reasons for carrying out training in a virtual environment, including the ability to learn by mistakes and to practice repeatedly, discussed earlier (Cobb et al., 2002; Mitchell et al., 2007).

Interestingly, one of the few indicators that SVE training may be generalizable comes from a participant in one of the research studies. Parsons, Leonard, and Mitchell (2006) carried out a follow-up interview with two individuals three months after they had taken part in a research study using the SVEs in a café scenario and a bus boarding scenario to establish whether they had remembered and used the skills they had been taught. One participant reported that he had used his newly acquired knowledge both on an overland

train journey and on an underground train trip. However, researchers expressed concern that in both instances he had asked the respective passenger if he could sit in the free seat next to them (Parsons et al., 2006). Whilst this might have been appropriate on an overland train journey, it would not be normal practice on an underground train where travellers rarely speak to strangers; if a seat is not taken the traveller would assume it was free and just sit down. This could be a peculiarity of the British underground system, nevertheless, it is an important convention to learn if the traveller is to fit in with social convention, indicating that the particular convention of underground travel may need to be taught in a specific scenario.

It should be noted that generalizability is difficult for people with ASD (Simpson et al., 2008). Grandin (2011) writes that she had to learn "by rote – how to act in different situations" (p. 158). The need to repeatedly practice new skills until they are learned is supported by the SVE as an intervention, but it also has a potential drawback. Neale et al. (2002) reported that children using the virtual café scenario had "visually memorised the environment" from one session to the next without fully understanding or realizing the social implications (p. 261).

To summarize, the current research indicates that the potential of SVEs to provide a generalizable intervention for children with ASD is poor and specific social scenarios may need to be set up in the SVE.

Cost Effectiveness

Cost effectiveness is an important consideration in assessing whether the SVE is viable, not only in terms of the cost of the "treatment" (the hardware and software) but also the cost of administering the treatment. Goodwin (2008, p. 2) states that virtual environments "may provide a relatively low cost way for individuals with autism to practice rule learning and repetition of tasks across contexts." The hardware used in the SVE intervention consists of a standard personal computer. Most teachers have ready access to a computer either in their classroom or in a dedicated computer suite. The software used by researchers working on the AS Interactive Project, Superscape, is currently available for download from the project website free of charge (VIRART, 2013). Kandalaft et al. (2013) used Second Life™ software which is also freely available for download. Lányi and Tilinger (2004) developed virtual environments using DirectX API software, but no costs are provided for this. Peripheral equipment includes a joystick and a mouse, both relatively inexpensive.

The cost of the teacher's time is another factor to consider. The software is touted as relatively easy to use and some researchers recount training teachers and pupils in a relatively short time (Parsons, Mitchell, & Leonard, 2004). If the program is easy to use, the teacher can concentrate on teaching the social skills so their time input will be more cost effective. A downside to the SVE program is that it requires a one-on-one pupil teacher ratio to be most effective, discussed further under 'Teacher's Contribution,' However, most classes with children with ASD have additional para educational staff available that could support the class teacher in the SVE initiative. Also, one of the most highly rated interventions from an evidence-basis, applied behavior analysis, uses an intense, one-on-one therapy so the SVE mirrors this individual teaching approach.

Against the costs of the SVE as an intervention are the costs of supporting a person with ASD during their lifetime. Estimates are just that, but Goodwin (2008) cites a figure of $3.2m per person per annum to treat and care for someone with ASD. There is also data to suggest that these costs could be reduced by two thirds with intervention (Autism Society, 2011). It is not only the financial costs but the human costs of ASD that need to be considered. A person with better developed social skills will be more confident, and could become more independent requiring less support (Andersson, Josefsson, & Pareto, 2006). Depression is a serious side effect of ASD (Parsons et al., 2000; Parsons & Mitchell, 2002), and, worse, there is also a high suicide rate in people with ASD (Parsons et al., 2000). Parsons et al. (2000) explain that many people at the higher end of the autism spectrum do not have sufficient skills to know how they should behave socially but they have enough skills to know that they do not behave in a socially acceptable manner. An intervention that could help provide these social skills and mitigate the hidden human costs of ASD could be truly cost effective.

One cost that we cannot estimate from the research is how long the treatment, the SVE program, has to be administered for it to be successful. Also, we do not know how often the intervention needs to be re-applied or the learning "topped up," if at all. Even if further research indicates that prolonged treatment is required, overall the SVE seems to offer a viable option in terms of cost-effectiveness.

Appropriateness to Users with ASD

Another issue to consider regarding viability is how appropriate SVEs are to teach social skills to children with a profile of ASD, particularly with regard to their age, sex, and diagnosis. If we consider the profile of users who have participated in the research so far, a review of literature into SVE's found that studies included teenage children aged 13-19 (Irish, 2013). Researchers do not generally state why teenage participants were suited to the SVE training but it could be assumed that this age group is more aware of the skills involved in socializing than younger children. Parsons and Mitchell (2002) advocate using older children as participants because they may have missed the opportunity to take part in interventions at a younger age. Kandalaft et al. (2013) focused their research on older teenagers and young adults aged 18-26. Their study was carried out using eight participants aged 18-26, three of whom were teenagers. Their research has been included here as a crossover in the literature to fit the question of whether children with ASD can be taught social skills using SVEs. Kandalaft et al. (2013) selected this age group for research since they are the group setting out into society, the community and the workforce, so social skills are fundamentally important.

Although research has been focused on teenagers, SVEs may be an appropriate intervention for younger children, particularly as the social skills taught could be modified to suit a younger age group. In a summary of its findings for computer-aided interventions, the National Professional Development Center on ASD reported that various strategies have been successful with various age groups. Its findings concluded that, "In short, depending on the targeted skill and the needs/preferences of the learner, CAI [computer-aided instruction] may be used with nearly any age" (National Professional Development Center on ASD, 2013, p.1). Although the National Professional Development Center on ASD did not report specifically on interventions using a SVE to teach social skills, it did report on a number of computer interventions including an intervention to recognize emotions, so their reasoning could be applicable to SVEs.

Participants in the research include males and females (Irish, 2013), and research has not yet been conducted to ascertain whether there is a gender preference and male or female students prefer the SVE method. At present it could be concluded that SVE as an intervention is equally appropriate for males and females. The current virtual scenarios, such as the café and bus, are not gender biased and gender bias is something to be aware of when setting up future scenarios.

Another important consideration is the level of understanding that a pupil with ASD needs to have in order to understand the social skills that the SVE program is aiming to teach. Research to date has been carried out using participants high on the autism spectrum. Some researchers describe participants as having Asperger's

Syndrome (Mitchell et al., 2007; Neale et al., 2002), and some as participants presenting with high-functioning autism (Kandalaft et al., 2011; Neale et al., 2002). Neale et al. (2002) specifically state that their participants had no other learning disabilities. Parsons et al. (2004) refer to their participants as being "non retarded" according to the classification given by the American Psychiatric Association (APA, 2000). They further reported that children with both a low verbal IQ and weak thinking skills experienced more difficulties when practicing with the SVE. Clearly, a child's level of ASD needs to be such that they have a concept of socialization and the verbal ability to communicate with others to benefit from what the SVE can teach. Parsons et al. (2004) acknowledged that SVEs may not suit all children with ASD, because they have so many varied characteristics. This could be said for most interventions. One child may respond better to a particular intervention than another and even the interventionist may not be able to say why. Neale et al. (2002) stressed that the SVE is an unsuitable training program for students with a learning disability. The Centers for Disease Control and Prevention (2010) reported that between 30% and 51% of children with ASD have intellectual disabilities with a low IQ. Conversely, this indicates that some 50% of children with ASD do not have an intellectual disability so are more likely to appreciate and learn from the SVE as an intervention. The SVE could, therefore, be suitable for half the teenage population diagnosed with ASD.

To complete the consideration of whether the SVE is an appropriate intervention for children with ASD, we can also compare it against the weaknesses, and strengths, that children characteristically have. The weakness in communication skills which can cause anxiety in the real world, discussed earlier, can be alleviated by first practicing and learning social skills in the virtual world. Parsons et al. (2002) state that a virtual environment "offers a stable and predictable environment in which interaction can take place without the anxiety-inducing plethora of non-verbal and verbal information that characterises social interactions" (p. 169). Rutten et al. (2003) suggest that the "consistency and predictability of computers and the low level of social contact required for interaction" makes them a suitable intervention. A final aspect of SVEs and their appropriateness to learners with ASD is that they support visual thinking (Lányi & Tilinger, 2004; Rutten et al., 2003). Visual thinking is a trait of many people with ASD, as well documented by Grandin, who states, "I think in pictures" (Grandin, 2006, p.3). There are detractors of the SVE as an intervention who believe it is inappropriate to teach social skills to children with ASD. Howlin (1998) expresses concern that a virtual environment only encourages isolation and a lack of real social contact, which is another trait of some of those with ASD.

Overall, from the research to date, we can conclude that the SVE intervention could be a viable option for teenage children of both sexes who are at the higher end of the autism spectrum. It is not possible to be more specific in a particular diagnosis of ASD that the SVE could treat as, generally, researchers did not have access to the medical records of participants and so are unable to report more fully on the particular diagnoses of ASD that the SVE may be applicable to. Indeed, Parsons et al. (2004) specifically disclaim promoting the SVE for a specific diagnosis.

User Experience

Another criterion to use in considering whether an intervention is viable is what the user feels about the experience. If the user has a good experience and enjoys using the software, then they will be more motivated to learn from it. Several researchers note how people with ASD enjoy using computers in general (Goodwin, 2008; Mitchell, Parsons, & Leonard, 2007; Parsons & Cobb, 2011). Indeed Grandin (2013) wryly suggests that Silicon Valley is full of computer geniuses with undiagnosed Asperger's Syndrome. Many researchers who

investigated the SVE as an intervention report that students with ASD seemed to enjoy using it (Cobb et al., 2002; Neale et al., 2002; Kandalaft et al., 2013). Parsons et al. (2006) describe how participants laughed and joked with the trainer during the SVE sessions. Enjoyment is strongly linked to motivation in the virtual environment as Lányi et al. (2006) write "it can be a source of joy and motivation for success" (p. 65).

Perhaps the strongest advocates for the possibilities of SVEs are the participants themselves. Parsons et al. (2006) carried out a qualitative case study with two participants who had previously taken part in their research to ascertain what they felt about the SVE sessions and whether they had used the social skills taught. One participant reported feeling pride when he was able to ask a fellow passenger if he could sit next to him on a train and felt that the SVE helped him learn "what polite and sensible things to do in public places" (Parsons et al., 2006, p. 195). Interestingly, in their study with older teenagers and young adults, Kandalaft et al. (2013) found that the technical data did not substantiate that participants had improved in their social skills but users themselves felt that they had improved. This again points to enjoyment and a positive user experience. If more evidence of enjoyment is needed readers are encouraged to view Strickland et als. 2007 study, one photograph of the happy, smiling face of a young boy with ASD enjoying fire safety training in a virtual environment endorses this positive experience.

Of course, despite the positive attitude participants report, we cannot just assume that children with ASD easily learn the social skills concepts they are being taught using the software. As one participant phrases it, "I'm still very timid when I'm coming to ask people 'can I sit there please?' It's something that's difficult for me" (Parsons et al., 2006, p. 198).

As a viable option, the SVE demonstrates an ability to provide a motivating and enjoyable experience for users. This feature is important because children with ASD have a tendency to exhibit challenging behaviors if they do not want to participate in a learning activity; so one that is motivating and enjoyable can benefit the child, the teacher, and the whole class.

Teacher's Contribution

The ideal intervention might be considered one in which the child can work by him or herself to learn new skills with minimal input from the teacher, allowing the teacher to carry out other work. To explore this aspect we could consider that an intervention requiring the least contribution in time and effort from the teacher was a more successful intervention than an intervention requiring a high contribution in time and effort. However, a virtual environment intervention with little or no input from a facilitator meets criticisms in other areas. For example, some researchers argue that putting a child who is reluctant to socialize with others in front of a computer where they are encouraged to socialize with screen characters and not with real people is exacerbating their problems (Howlin, 1998). The alternative view is that creating a social skills virtual program that children can use by themselves is positive as it can give them more "self-esteem and independence" (Andersson et al., 2006, p. 41). Most researchers consider that the role of the teacher is an essential contribution to the success of the SVE intervention. Rutten et al. (2003) feel that the SVE will probably always need input from a teacher to make sure that "reflection on learning takes place" (p. 239). In a similar finding, Cobb (2007) states that "teaching expertise is required to ensure appropriate use for individual learners" (p. 221). Mitchell et al. (2007) believe that the SVE should "create a forum for the teacher to communicate in an optimal and contingent manner" (p. 598), stressing the importance of the interaction between the teacher and the pupil. Indeed, one researcher goes as far as suggesting that it could be the teacher providing the learning in tandem with the SVE which is successful rather than the

SVE of itself (Parsons, 2005). Researchers also refer to the importance of scaffolding: that the teacher can build on what the student has learned, explaining why, for example, some actions or words are suitable or inappropriate in a social situation (Kerr, 2002). Learners also need to learn by their mistakes in the virtual environment and the teacher can explain why a certain action or statement is not socially acceptable (Kerr, 2002). Researchers also stress that the SVE is not to be used alone as an intervention but in conjunction with other established interventions (Neale et al., 2002). Kerr (2002) explains that the SVE intervention should be integrated into the overall learning goals in the classroom otherwise it could become "just another gimmick that passes without delivering a positive impact" (p. 89).

This report considered earlier whether users, the children, enjoyed learning in the SVE and should also consider what teacher's felt about the experience, whether they felt it was beneficial to students and how easy they found it to administer. This is important because teachers of children with ASD have to meet many competing demands. The SVE does not require complicated setting up. Lányi and Tilinger (2004) reported that teachers found the software program useful. Neale et al. (2002) trained teachers in the SVE software and observed them using it in practice. They reported how teachers grew in confidence using the software and were able to innovate ways to incorporate social skills technology into the lessons. In terms of effort, Cobb (2007) exhorts that, for the SVE to be a successful intervention, teachers must "take ownership" of it (p. 222). To achieve this, many researchers advocate involving teachers in the development of the virtual environment software so that it functions in a meaningful way to achieve the learning goals teachers view as important for their pupils (Cobb et al., 2002; Rutten et al., 2003). Parsons and Cobb (2011) also note that training needs to be consistent for teachers so that they can use the program effectively and tailor it to the needs of the individual child.

To review, SVEs can be a viable option in terms of the teacher's contribution because it is easy to use and administer, but it does demand the teacher's time one-to-one, discussed earlier under 'cost effectiveness. This is crucial to support the students and scaffold their learning and could be considered as time well spent.

Usefulness for Caregivers

One final criterion considered is whether the SVE constitutes a viable option to teach social skills to children with ASD from the perspective of their caregivers. The stress on parents with a child with ASD has been documented, even when the child functions at the higher end of the autism spectrum (Rao & Beidel, 2009). Taking a child with ASD out in public can be stressful for both parties, and it may reduce the parents' inclination to socialize (Rao & Beidel, 2009). An intervention that can help alleviate anxiety for parent and child in this situation is beneficial. . That the SVE can be used at home by caregivers is an additional benefit. Parsons et al. (2002) believe that caregivers and parents could participate in the SVE intervention in lieu of school teachers. The software used in the AS Interactive Project is downloadable, free of charge, by parents who thus have the ability to practice exercises in social skills with their child at home. It might be assumed that computer access is readily available at home as it is in school but Putnam and Chong (2008) found differently. In an on-line survey which they conducted they reported that only 7% of 114 responders, 79% of whom were parents, had used technological interventions with their child with ASD. They do not expand on whether the parents had access to a computer but had not used it for interventions or whether they did not have ready access to a computer. Putnam and Chong (2008) did report that teaching social skills was viewed as of paramount importance by 21% of respondents, quoting one respondent who requested a software technology to teach "something that engages him to communicate more, teach him on social skills" (p. 6). Putnam and Chong (2008) also reported "a strong desire to be social" (p. 9) as the collective views of 14% of respondents writing about a child with ASD. These comments enforce the view that technological interventions such as SVEs to teach social skills could be both beneficial and desirable for parents.

The ability to use an educational tool such as the SVE at home to teach social skills could also help improve generalizability, discussed earlier, as well as help save on money which caregivers may otherwise have spent on professional therapists (Goodwin, 2008). Established interventions such as TEACCH, and SCERTS (Social Communication, Emotional Regulation, & Transactional Support) call for an integrated approach between home and school because it reinforces learning and repetition (Mesibov, Shea, & Schopler, 2004; Ogletree, 2008). SVEs could be an important aid to reinforce appropriate social skills between home and school, something that Lányi et al. (2006) describe as "distributed learning" (p. 64). Kandalaft et al. (2013) also note that SVEs have the potential to "increase accessibility of interventions" (p. 41). Parents and caregivers are also better placed to practice real-life social skills outside the home which is logistically more difficult for teachers to carry out.

Overall, SVEs to teach social skills could provide a good bridge for reinforcing learning between home and school as well as providing a significant benefit to parents and caregivers trying to maintain a "normal" family life.

Summary

This chapter considered whether SVEs provide a viable option to teach social skills to children with ASD. Viability was considered in terms of key features found in the literature namely, whether SVEs provide an evidenced-based intervention; whether the social skills taught were generalizable; whether SVEs are cost effective; how appropriate

SVEs are to teach social skills to children diagnosed with ASD; how users with ASD found the SVE experience; what contribution is required of the teacher to teach social skills using the SVE; and, lastly, how useful SVEs are as an intervention to caregivers to help teach social skills to their children. To assess the viability of each of the key features discussed a simple matrix has been devised (Figure 1.) rating each on a scale of 1-5, 1 being least viable, and 5 being most viable.

From the matrix it can be seen that SVEs to teach social skills are judged as a weak option as an evidence-based intervention so it is rated 1. Insufficient research has been carried out to confirm whether SVEs could be a viable option, but researchers feel that it is promising. Leonard et al. (2002) report "a sense of optimism" (p. 256), Mitchell et al. (2006) believe in its "great promise" (p. 598), and Parsons et al. state that it "could be extremely powerful" (2000, p. 169). Despite this promise, as recent as 2011 Parsons and Cobb bemoan that SVEs as a plausible intervention to teach social skills to children with ASD are still spoken of in terms of their "potential" (p. 356). Irish's literature review of 2013 confirms this hope that researchers feel and yet there is not enough research to confirm its efficacy. It remains "applicable technology with unique potential" (Parsons & Cobb, p. 8).

Generalizability for any intervention designed for children with ASD is important to aim for but difficult to achieve. It has been rated as 2 in the matrix, recognizing that, whilst there was insufficient research to confirm generalizability, and some studies report not finding any generalizability, researchers found some generalization from the software to video scenario, and participants report a modicum of success using their skills in real life situations. As a viable option to teach social skills to children with ASD, the SVE shows limited ability to support generalization in a population that is notoriously difficult to teach by generalization. It may be that children need to be taught individual scenarios. What this lack of generalizability means in practice is that training will be more time consuming for the teacher.

Figure 1. Viability matrix

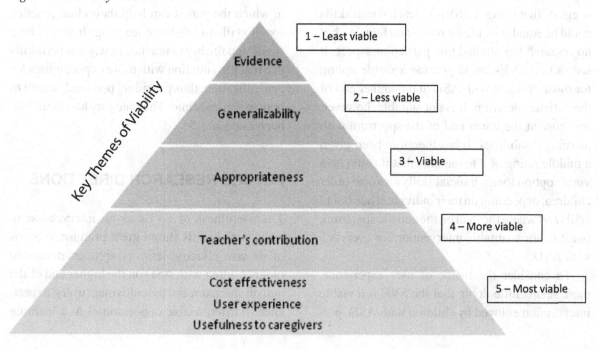

155

In terms of cost effectiveness, the viability of SVEs to teach social skills to children with ASD has been rated highly with a 5. Computer hardware is generally readily available in schools, and at least one of the software programs used by researchers is available free of charge with supportive training materials. On the one hand, SVE is negative in terms of dedicated time which the teacher has to provide on a one-to-one basis to support the learner in the social skills training, but on the positive side, the teacher is scaffolding and building on the knowledge to suit the learner's pace. Also, although the general term "teacher" has been used, a sufficiently trained para-professional substituting for the class teacher, who knows the child well, can help scaffold his learning and enable him to maximize the opportunities to learn social skills.

Another consideration is how viable and appropriate the SVE is to teach social skills to those with the condition of ASD. To date research has been carried out with teenage participants (and older adolescents). This seems the right age group to target because these young people have more awareness of their place in society and need more sophisticated social skills. Currently, research suggests that using the SVE to teach social skills could be equally viable for males and females, but no research has studied this particular aspect. It seems that SVEs could provide a viable option for those children with ASD at the higher end of the autistic spectrum. It is not suitable, however, for those at the lower end of the spectrum with learning disabilities. It has therefore been given a middle rating of 3 to indicate that it could be a viable option to teach social skills for some older children, depending on their individual needs and skills and where they fall on the autistic spectrum, but it is not a suitable intervention for everyone with ASD.

To consider the theme of user experience, there seems little doubt that the SVE is a viable intervention enjoyed by children with ASD, per-haps because they can practice their social skills in safety, perhaps because they have a tendency to enjoy computers and thus a motivation to learn, using a computer. User experience has received a high viability rating of 5.

The teacher's contribution is clearly essential. This criteria has been given a 4 rating to reflect that set up and training time for teachers and children is minimal but it does require great one-on-one support from the teacher. This could be viewed as negative or positive, negative if you, like many other researchers, consider the children should work on their own initiative to become more independent, but positive if you consider that individual attention is important in scaffolding the learning as part of the intervention. This fits with the applied behavior analysis approach which is regarded as an evidence-based intervention, and uses intensive one-on-one training to teach various skills.

The needs of the caregiver of a child with ASD are often overlooked, and this is the final theme that was considered: whether the SVE could provide a viable option to teach social skills. The literature affirms that SVEs could provide a solid bridge between school and home in which the parent can help their child practice social skills to reinforce learning. It would be a small step further to practice newly learned skills in a real life situation with more opportunities for generalization, thus providing potential benefit to both parent and child. This category has, therefore, been rated as a 5.

FUTURE RESEARCH DIRECTIONS

The usefulness of SVEs as an intervention to teach social skills shows great promise in terms of its cost effectiveness, its appropriateness to older children with ASD on the higher end of the autism spectrum and the enjoyment users' experience. It offers viable opportunities as a learning tool for teachers and could offer tangible benefits to caregivers. What has not been established is the evidence-basis for SVEs as an intervention to teach social skills. More research is required to establish whether participants can learn social skills using the SVE, and whether they can retain the knowledge gained over a period of time. More research also needs to be carried out to establish whether the social skills learned in one specific scenario can be generalized to a different social scenario or to real life. The research impetus must continue if SVEs to teach social skills are to become viable in all aspects.

Another future area of research discussed in the literature is the need for a suitable assessment tool to gauge how much children have learned during the SVE sessions (Reed, Hyman, & Hirst, 2011; Kandalaft et al., 2013). Kandalaft et al. (2013) discuss this difficulty due to the lack of published standards generally for measurement of social skills performance. In a pilot study, Kandalaft et al. (2013) conducted a number of tests to ascertain how much participants had learned from the SVE sessions, including a test of social perception skills and a test of conversational skills. They reported promising results for the viability of SVEs as an intervention for older teenagers and adolescents with ASD. Hopefully, their work in this area will continue.

Another new area of research is the use of a "Blue Room" virtual environment (Parsons & Cobb, 2011). Blue Room technology has the benefits of an IVE but without the need for the user to wear a headset as images and scenes are projected directly onto the walls and ceilings, offering the user the perception of being in a real scene (Parsons & Cobb, 2011). This could provide a more realistic and therefore potentially more generalizable intervention with future research (Parsons & Cobb, 2011).

CONCLUSION

This chapter began by asking whether SVEs were a viable option to teach social skills to children with ASD. A simple matrix was created measuring issues of viability found in the literature, the evidence-basis, generalizability, cost effectiveness, appropriateness for users with ASD, user experience, teacher's contribution, and usefulness to caregivers. In conclusion, SVEs are viable as an option in many key aspects but current research indicates a weakness in evidence-basis and generalizability. This is a common theme with possible interventions for children with ASD. Goodwin (2008) complains that many research experiments are abandoned each year because researchers cannot find participants. Funding for research will always be an issue, since there are so many competing demands. The figures show that the number of children with ASD is rising. Now more than ever it is imperative to drive forward research into interventions which could benefit these children. There will probably be no one "magic intervention" to suit every child with ASD, but SVEs could offer a viable option to teach social skills to some children with ASD, and that is why it is important for the research to continue. Hopefully this chapter, this book, will raise some awareness and the impetus to do so. The SVE to teach social skills still "offers the potential" (Strickland, 1997, p. 85), and, until more research is carried out, it will remain only a potential.

REFERENCES

Adams, J. B. (2013). *Summary of dietary, nutritional, and medical treatments for autism-based on over 150 published research studies*. Arizona State University, Autism Research Institute.

Allen, R. E. (Ed.). (1990). *The concise Oxford dictionary of current English* (8th ed.). Oxford, UK: Clarendon Press.

American Psychiatric Association. (2000). Disorders usually first diagnosed in infancy, childhood, or adolescence. In *Diagnostic and statistical manual of mental disorders* (4th ed.). Washington, DC: American Psychiatric Association.

American Psychiatric Association. (2013). *Diagnostic and statistical manual of mental disorders* (5th ed.). Arlington, VA: American Psychiatric Publishing.

Andersson, U. Josefsson, & Pareto, L. (2006). Challenges in designing virtual environments training social skills for children with autism. In *Proceedings of the 6ᵗʰ International Conference on Disability, Virtual Reality, & Associated Technologies,* (pp. 35-43). Academic Press.

Autism Emotion. (n.d.). Retrieved from http://www.autismspeaks.org/autism-apps/autism-emotion

Autism Society. (2011). *Facts and statistics.* Retrieved 6/25/2013 from http://www.autism-society.org/about-autism/facts-and-statistics.html

Baio, J. (2012). *Prevalence of autism spectrum disorders – Autism and developmental disabilities monitoring network, 14 sites, United States, 2008.* Atlanta, GA: Centers for Disease Control and Prevention.

Centers for Disease Control and Prevention. (2010). *Autism spectrum disorders (ASDs) data & statistics.* Retrieved 02/12/2011 from http://www.cdc.gov/ncbddd/autism/data.html

Centers for Disease Control and Prevention. (2012). *Autism spectrum disorders (ASDs) data & statistics.* Retrieved 10/28/2012 from http://www.cdc.gov/ncbddd/autism/data.html

Cheng, Y., Moore, D., & McGrath, P. (2002). Virtual learning environments for children with autism. In *Proceedings of the 6ᵗʰ Human Centred Technology Postgraduate Workshop,* (pp. 32-35). Academic Press.

Cobb, S. (2007). Virtual environments supporting learning and communication in special needs education. *Topics in Language Disorders, 27*(3), 211–225. doi:10.1097/01.TLD.0000285356.95426.3b

Cobb, S., Beardon, L., Eastgate, R., Glover, T., Kerr, S., & Neale, H. et al. (2002). Applied virtual environments to support learning of social interaction skills in users with Asperger's syndrome. *Digital Creativity, 13*(1), 11–22. doi:10.1076/digc.13.1.11.3208

Ellwood, H. (2009). *Oh-my-goodness-moments.* Calgary, Canada: SMART Technologies ULC.

Fornasari, L., Chittaro, L., Ieronutti, L., Cottini, L., & Dassi, S., Cremaschi, Brambilla, P. (2013). Navigation and exploration of an urban virtual environment by children with autism spectrum disorder to children with typical development. *Research in Autism Spectrum Disorders, 7*(8), 956–965. doi:10.1016/j.rasd.2013.04.007

Goodwin, M. (2008). Enhancing and accelerating the pace of autism research and treatment. *Focus on Autism and Other Developmental Disabilities,* 1–4.

Grandin, T. (1996). *Thinking in pictures.* New York, NY: Vintage Books.

Grandin, T. (2013). *The autistic brain: Thinking across the spectrum.* New York, NY: Houghton Mifflin Harcourt.

Howlin, P. (1998). Practitioner review: Psychological and educational treatments for autism. *Journal of Child Psychology and Psychiatry, and Allied Disciplines, 39*(1), 307–322. doi:10.1017/S0021963097002138 PMID:9670087

IES. (n.d.). Retrieved from http://ies.ed.gov/ncee/wwc/default.aspx

Irish, J. E. N. (2013). Can I sit here? A review of the literature supporting the use of single-user virtual environments to help autistic adolescents learn appropriate social communication skills. *Computers in Human Behavior*, (29): A17–A24. doi:10.1016/j.chb.2012.12.031

Kandalaft, M. R., Didehbani, N., Krawczyk, D. C., Allen, T. T., & Chapman, S. B. (2013). Virtual reality social cognition training for young adults with high-functioning autism. *Journal of Autism and Developmental Disorders*, *43*(1), 34–44. doi:10.1007/s10803-012-1544-6 PMID:22570145

Kerr, S. J. (2002). Scaffolding – Design issues in single and collaborative virtual environments for social skills training. In *Eighth eurographics workshop on virtual environments*. Academic Press.

Lányi, C. S., & Geiszt, Z., Károlyi,Tilinger, A., & Magyar, V. (2006). Virtual reality in special needs early education. *The International Journal of Virtual Reality*, *5*(4), 55–68.

Lányi, C. S., & Tilinger, A. (2004). Multimedia and virtual reality in the rehabilitation of autistic children. *Lecture Notes in Computer Science*, *3118*, 22–28. doi:10.1007/978-3-540-27817-7_4

Leonard, A., Mitchell, P., & Parsons, S. (2002). Finding a place to sit: A preliminary investigation into the effectiveness of virtual environments for social skills training for people with autistic spectrum disorders. In *Proceedings of the 4th International Conference on Disability,* (pp. 249-257). Academic Press.

Marcu, G., & Hayes, G. R. (2010). Use of a wearable recording device in therapeutic interventions for children with autism. In *Proceedings of the First International Workshop on Interactive Systems in Healthcare,* (pp. 113-116). Academic Press.

Mesibov, G. B., Shea, V., & Schopler, E. (2004). The TEACCH approach to autism spectrum disorders. New York, NY: Springer Science+Business Media, Inc.

Mitchell, P., Parsons, S., & Leonard, A. (2007). Using virtual environments for teaching social understanding to 6 adolescents with autistic spectrum disorders. *Journal of Autism and Developmental Disorders*, *37*, 589–600. doi:10.1007/s10803-006-0189-8 PMID:16900403

National Professional Development Center on Autism Spectrum Disorders. (2010). *Evidence-base for computer-aided instruction*. National Professional Development Center on ASD, University of North Carolina, University of California, and the University of Wisconsin.

Neale, H., Cobb, S., & Wilson, J. (2002). A front ended approach to the user-centred design of VEs. In *Proceedings of the IEEE Virtual Reality,* (pp. 191-198). IEEE.

Neale, H. R., Kerr, S. J., Cobb, S. V. G., & Leonard, A. (2002). Exploring the role of virtual environments in the special needs classroom. In *Proceedings of the 4th International Conference Disability, Virtual Reality & Associated Technology,* (pp. 259-266). Academic Press.

Ogletree, B. T. (2008). The communicative context of autism. In R. Simpson, & B. Myles (Eds.), *Educating children and youth with autism* (pp. 223–265). Austin, TX: PRO-ED, Inc.

Parsons, S. (2005). Use, understanding and learning in virtual environments by adolescents with autistic spectrum disorders. In B. K. Wiederhold, G. Riva, & A. H. Bullinger (Eds.), *Annual review of cybertherapy and telemedicine* (pp. 207–215). Academic Press. doi:10.1037/e705572011-075

Parsons, S., Beardon, L., Neale, H. R., Reynard, G., Eastgate, R., Wilson, J. R., & Hopkins, E. (2000). Development of social skills amongst adults with Asperger's syndrome using virtual environments: the 'AS interactive' project. In *Proceedings of the 3rd International Conference on Disability, Virtual Reality and Associated Technology* (pp. 163-170). Academic Press.

Parsons, S., & Cobb, S. (2011). State-of-the-art of virtual reality technologies for children on the autism spectrum. *European Journal of Special Needs Education*, *26*(3), 355–366. doi:10.1080/08856257.2011.593831

Parsons, S., Leonard, A., & Mitchell, P. (2006). Virtual environments for social skills training: Comments from two adolescents with autistic spectrum disorder. *Computers & Education*, *47*, 186–206. doi:10.1016/j.compedu.2004.10.003

Parsons, S., & Mitchell, P. (2002). The potential of virtual reality in social skills training for people with autistic spectrum disorders. *Journal of Intellectual Disability Research*, *46*(5), 430–443. doi:10.1046/j.1365-2788.2002.00425.x PMID:12031025

Parsons, S., Mitchell, P., & Leonard, A. (2004). The use and understanding of virtual environments by adolescents with autistic spectrum disorders. *Journal of Autism and Developmental Disorders*, *34*(4), 449–466. doi:10.1023/B:JADD.0000037421.98517.8d PMID:15449520

Parsons, S., Mitchell, P., & Leonard, A. (2005). Do adolescents with autistic spectrum disorders adhere to social conventions in virtual environments? *Autism*, *9*, 95–117. doi:10.1177/1362361305049032 PMID:15618265

Putnam, C., & Chong, L. (2008). Software and technologies designed for people with autism: What do users want? In *Proceedings of the 10th International ACM SIFACCESS Conference on Computers and Accessibility*. ACM.

Rao, P. A., & Beidel, D. C. (2009). The impact of children with high-functioning sutism on parental stress, sibling adjustment, and family functioning. *Behavior Modification*, *33*(4), 437–451. doi:10.1177/0145445509336427 PMID:19436073

Reed, F. D. D., Hyman, S. R., & Hirst, J. M. (2011). Applications of technology to teach social skills to children with autism. *Research in Autism Spectrum Disorders*, *5*(3), 1003–1010. doi:10.1016/j.rasd.2011.01.022

Reichow, B., & Volkmar, F. R. (2010). Social skills interventions for individuals with autism: Evaluation for evidence-based practices within a best evidence synthesis framework. *Journal of Autism and Developmental Disorders*, *40*, 149–166. doi:10.1007/s10803-009-0842-0 PMID:19655240

Rice, C. (2006). Prevalence of autism spectrum disorders – Autism and developmental disabilities monitoring network, United States, 2006. *MMWR. Surveillance Summaries*, *58*(10), 1–20.

Rutten, A., Cobb, S., Neale, H., Kerr, S., Leonard, A., Parsons, S., & Mitchell, P. (2003). The AS interactive project: single-user and collaborative virtual environments for people with high-functioning autistic spectrum disorders. *The Journal of Visualization and Computer Animation*, *14*, 233–241. doi:10.1002/vis.320

Self, T., Scudder, R. R., Weheba, G., & Crumrine, D. (2007). A virtual approach to teaching safety skills to children with autism spectrum disorder. *Topics in Language Disorders*, *273*(3), 242–253. doi:10.1097/01.TLD.0000285358.33545.79

Simpson, R. L., Myles, B. S., & Ganz, J. B. (2008). Efficacious interventions and treatments for learners with autism spectrum disorders. In R. Simpson, & B. Myles (Eds.), *Educating children and youth with autism* (pp. 477–512). Austin, TX: PRO-ED, Inc.

Simpson, R. L., Myles, B. S., & LaCava, P. G. (2008). Understanding and responding to the needs of children and youth with autism spectrum disorders. In R. Simpson, & B. Myles (Eds.), *Educating children and youth with autism* (pp. 1–59). Austin, TX: PRO-ED, Inc.

Sinclair, J. (1992). Bridging the gaps: an inside-out view of autism. In E. Schopler, & G. B. Mesibov (Eds.), *High-functioning individuals with autism* (pp. 1–59). New York, NY: Plenum Press.

Strickland, D. (1996). A virtual reality application with autistic children. *Presence (Cambridge, Mass.)*, *5*(3), 319–329.

Strickland, D., McAllister, D., Coles, C. D., & Osborne, S. (2007). An evolution of virtual reality training designs for children with autism and fetal alcohol spectrum disorders. *Topics in Language Disorders*, *27*(3), 226–241. doi:10.1097/01. TLD.0000285357.95426.72 PMID:20072702

United States Department of Education. (2012). *What works clearinghouse play-based interventions*. Washington, DC: Author.

Urinal Game. (n.d.). Retrieved from http://www. autismspeaks.org/autism-apps/urinal-game

VIRART. (n.d.). Retrieved from https://www. virart.nott.ac.uk/asi/b_design.htm

Wing, L., & Gould, J. (1979). Severe impairments of social interation and associated abnormalities in children: epidemiology and classification. *Journal of Autism and Developmental Disorders*, *9*(1), 11–29. doi:10.1007/BF01531288 PMID:155684

Works Clearinghouse, W. (2013a). *Early childhood education interventions for children with disabilities – Social skills training*. Washington, DC: Institute of Education Sciences.

Works Clearinghouse, W. (2013b). *Procedures and standards handbook, version 3.0*. Washington, DC: Institute of Education Sciences.

Works Clearinghouse, W. (2013c). *WWC evidence review protocol for early childhood education interventions for children with disabilities, version 2.0*. Washington, DC: Institute of Education Sciences.

Works Clearinghouse, W. (2013d). *WWC evidence review protocol for K-12 students with learning disabilities, version 2.0*. Washington, DC: Institute of Education Sciences.

World Health Organization. (1993). *The ICD-10 classification of mental and behavioural disorders diagnostic criteria for research*. Geneva, Switzerland: World Health Organization.

ADDITIONAL READING

Brown, D., Neale, H., Cobb, S., & Reynolds, H. (1998). Development and evaluation of the virtual city. *The International Journal of Virtual Reality*, *3*(4), 27–38.

Cheng, Y., & Ye, J. (2010). Exploring the social competence of students with autism spectrum conditions in a collaborative virtual learning environment – the pilot study. *Computers & Education*, (54): 1068–1077. doi:10.1016/j. compedu.2009.10.011

Earles-Volrath, T. L., Cook, K. T., Robbins, L., & Ben-Arich, J. (2008). Instructional strategies to facilitate successful learning outcomes for students with autism spectrum disorders. In R. Simpson, & B. Myles (Eds.), Educating children and youth with autism (pp. 93-178).

Hayes, G. R., Hirano, S., Marcu, G., Monibi, M., Nguyen, D. H., & Yeganyan, M. (2020). Interactive visual supports for children with autism. *Pers Ubiquit Comput, 14,* 663-680.

iSET: Interactive social-emotional toolkit for ASD. Retrieved 10/29/2012 from http://iset.media.mit.edu/#goals

iSocial 3D Virtual Learning: helping youth with Autism Spectrum Disorders develop social competence. Retrieved 9/24/2012 from http://isocial.missouri.edu/iSocial??q=projectsummary

KEY TERMS AND DEFINITIONS

Collaborative Virtual Environment (CVE): A virtual computer scene for used by multiple users.

Immersive Virtual Environment (IVE): A computer scene in which real life is simulated by the user wearing headgear.

Intervention: A treatment or tool to improve skills.

Single-User Virtual Environment (SVE): A virtual computer scene for use by a single user.

Chapter 10
A Task Assistant for Individuals with Autism Spectrum Disorder

Joo Tan
Kutztown University, USA

ABSTRACT

This chapter introduces the use of software technology that is used to create a Web application system called iPAWS to help individuals with Autism Spectrum Disorder (ASD) accomplish simple tasks. These individuals can repeatedly access tasks for assistance or learning through a mobile tablet. For post-school employment, the use of this software technology can help lessen the burden of supervision needed for individuals with autism. For school age children at different levels, iPAWS can serve as training or as a learning tool. This chapter starts with a review of computer-based interventions that have been used in the past. Next, the overall design of the Web application system is introduced. Sample cases that are suitable for children and post-secondary employment are then discussed. Two case studies that were conducted with individuals on the autism spectrum, follow. Finally, possible future improvements to iPAWS are presented.

INTRODUCTION

Individuals with autism often require structure and systematic procedures in order to learn. These comprise the basis for discrete trial training (Smith, 2001), which is both difficult and tedious for a human teacher to replicate. In general, software technology fits well with this learning method to simplify instruction for children on the autism spectrum. By transferring academic teaching to a computer instructor, individuals with ASD can receive the structure and repetition they need to learn. Customized mobile technology (Hourcade, 2012) can be created to meet the needs of individuals with autism of all ages. Researchers (Shane, 2008) found that "individuals on the autism

DOI: 10.4018/978-1-4666-5792-2.ch010

spectrum have a preference for instruction to be delivered by computers."

BACKGROUND

Today, 1 in every 88 children (DSM IV, 2013) is diagnosed with some form of autism. Computer-supported activities have been used for many years to enhance the abilities of children with ASD. More specifically, software applications (apps) have been developed for mobile devices such as smart phones and tablets. While the behaviorist approach (Bailey, 2002; Elkeseth, 2009) to intervention for children with ASD has gained increasing positive results over the years, other studies (Bill et al, 2005; Eaves & Ho, 2008; Howlin, 2004) have shown that the number of adults with ASD who are able to live independently is still relatively low. Furthermore, many of these individuals have not been able to achieve a high quality of life (Müller, Schuler, & Yates, 2008; Shattuck et al., 2012). The integration of mobile computing into the daily lives of individuals with autism may be able to help them live a fuller life (Wehman, 2012). Software apps utilize visual and intuitive interfaces which may be matched well to an individual with autism's visual learning style. Furthermore, mobile technology cuts down on the costs of bulky devices that often lack portability. Not only has mobile technology increased the portability of the tools, but also has the effectiveness of techniques for learning. Research (Dettmer, 2000; Hayes, et al., 2010) suggests that learning strategies which include visual presentation can greatly enhance the lives of people with ASD. Grace Picture Exchange and Picture Exchange Communication System (Charlop-Christy, 2002) are examples of two popular apps which utilize this technique for instruction.

For years, different methods for teaching children with ASD have been adapted to computer software format (Cafiero, 2008; Hess 2008; Koch,

2012). There is, however, a noticeable shortage of software intended for post-school life usage. There is a definite lack of software for adults who might be capable of being employed. This is important because the transition from academia to post-school life, such as employment, can be stressful, both economically and socially. To this end, a web application system (Duncan, 2012) that is targeted towards individuals with mid-level autism spectrum disorders (MLASD) was designed and a prototype system developed. The system aims to help lessen the amount of supervision necessary for a person with MLASD to perform tasks. This was accomplished by creating a web application (webapp) that can, in many ways, act as the coach or supervisor. Although this system was originally targeted towards adults with MLASD for post-school employment, it can easily be adapted for use by children with ASD. Therefore, it has the potential to become a helpful tool for parents as well as educators.

MOBILE WEB TECHNOLOGY

Mobile technology in the form of smartphones and tablets uses various modes of interaction that can greatly enrich the lives of people with autism, including children in school as well as post-school life such as higher education or employment. In an article published at SheKnows.com (Beaudry, 2013), Webber states that "the iPad has become a great tool when working with students on the autism spectrum, because it gives them the ability to control a piece of their environment and an opportunity to communicate (Page 1)." Mobile learning through the creation of a web application system that meets the goals of offering visual and auditory modalities of learning makes it ideal for usage by learners on the autism spectrum. Keefe (1991) describes how learning styles differ among different people and how each individual has a distinct and consistent preferred way of learning.

Some people are better visual learners; others are better as auditory learners; yet some learn best using a mixed style. Since mobile devices already cater to a large portion of the population of people with autism, the web application system leverages mobile devices in support of individuals on the spectrum.

Consider the example of an individual with MLASD who works in a library. This person often needs the help of a supervisor who provides assistance in the form of coaching for specific tasks such as how to shelve books onto stacks or how to record new books that have arrived at the library. The need for a supervisor to be physically present can be a burden on valuable resources that are needed in the library. The web application system will aid individuals with MLASD so that they may successfully complete their work with minimal direct supervision. By allowing a supervisor the ability to easily enter tasks and instructions (steps) into the system, they can later be assigned to individuals with MLASD who would view them on mobile devices such as an Apple iPad tablet. This system would therefore free the supervisor to work on other assignments.

Mobile tablets are now designed to be very intuitive to use, so much so that children as young as two years old have been observed using them for educational purposes. In an article published in PARENTS, Bende (2011) reported that "fully half of all kids under 8 had access to mobile device like smart phone, a video iPod, or an iPad or other tablet (Page 1)." As such, it is easy to adapt mobile technology towards the learning needs of toddlers and young children. If we are able to use software technology such as iPAWS to assist individuals with ASD from a young age, perhaps the outcomes of adults with autism in terms of independent living or employment for adults with

MLASD can be improved. To understand how the web application system may be able to help individuals with autism, we need first to know how it works. This is explained in the next section.

Personal Assistant Web Application System

The web application system that has been developed to assist individuals with autism is named iPAWS which stands for interactive Personal Assistant Web Application System. The goal of this system is to introduce software technology for mobile tablets that includes various choices of learning modalities while at the same time allowing a consistent and repeatable environment for learning or training (Tan & Conway, 2012). The system includes a frontend component (named Task Manager) that allows tasks to be viewed from mobile tablets and a backend component (named Task Developer) which manages the tasks that are constructed for individuals with MLASD. Figure 1 shows the design of iPAWS. Since the system must be made accessible to individuals with autism, their families, and potentially even employers and supervisors, it is crucial to have a simple and intuitive application so that all users feel comfortable while accessing the application through mobile tablets. Furthermore, the interfaces need to be easy to use and navigate so as to reduce the learning time necessary to use the application effectively. Dawe (2009) mentioned that meeting these goals will create an easily adoptable assistive application. The Task Manager provides a mobile training environment that enhances learning, and offers a consistent setting that produces immediate responses. This allows the individual with autism to focus his/her attention on relevant material as

Figure 1. System design of iPAWS

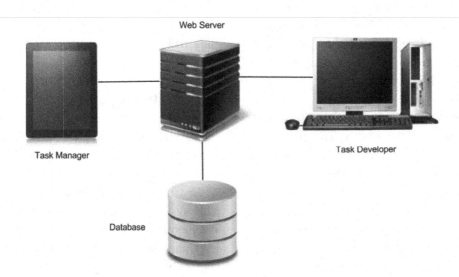

well as maintain his/her interest while working on a task.

Three types of users may access the system: managers, supervisors, and users (these are the individuals with autism). Users view task instructions in the web application through the Task Manager. They will utilize tablets to access the tasks that they need to successfully complete their assigned work. Tasks are entered into the system by coaches or supervisors via the Task Developer. Note that they may use web browsers for this purpose. Both the Task Manager and Task Developer interact through a Web Server. The Web Server saves all tasks into a database that can be retrieved later for updates or modifications. Using a database makes it easier for the supervisor since s/he can simply enter instructions into the task and update them later, if necessary.

After understanding how the system functions, it is helpful to look at sample use cases that are appropriate for individuals with autism of different ages. In the next few sections, use cases are presented for children on the autism spectrum in two different age groups as well as adults with MLASD in post-school employment.

Use Case for Employment

Individuals with MLASD who have completed school and are ready for post-school employment often need help with their given tasks at work. Consequently, a supervisor or coach is frequently assigned to the person. This is where the system would come in handy. The web application provides these individuals with assistance in the form of instructions that are accessible from mobile tablets. This helps them acquire functional skills while at work which can often lead to increased self-confidence. In this example use case, the individual with MLASD is assigned a job of replacing books back onto shelves in a library. This particular task will be named "Shelving Books." The task has five main steps with an appropriate number of detail steps within each of the main steps, as can be seen in Table 1. For example, main step 1 has one detail step; main step 2 has two detail steps; however, main step 5 may not have any. It is up to the supervisor to determine the level of granularity (the number of detail steps) that is necessary for the individual with ASD to complete his/her work successfully.

Table 1. Shelving books in a library

Main Step	Detail Step
1. Check the spine label on the book	Library systems with catalog staff will attach a spine label to each book with the catalog number first.
2. Read the labels on the book shelf ends.	a. The number ranges tell you the classification of books in that row. In a library b. The shelves are placed parallel to each other to make browsing and shelving materials in the collection easier.
3. Locate the correct section by comparing the numbers by the hundreds column.	a. When you find a match b. Go down that row and look for a match of the number in the tens columns and then the ones column.
4. Match all three letters of the author's last name within the numerical section.	This is the correct place to shelve the book. Accurate shelving is an essential part of any library.
5. Shelve journals or newspapers by arranging in order by date, with the most recent edition on the top, and the older issues below.	None

The supervisor or coach will use the Task Developer to enter the instruction steps in Table 1 into iPAWS. From the Task Manager, the individual with MLASD will be able to access the Shelving Books task from a mobile tablet. S/he can simply follow instructions on the screen to help him/her complete the work. After selecting the Shelving Books task from a task listing, the instruction for main step 1 will be presented. Figure 2 shows main step 1 of this task as seen by the user. Note that both video and audio (shown as images) can be included with the main step

instruction by the supervisor. These serve as visual and auditory aids for the individual who is working on the task. If the user needs help, s/he can look at the detail steps. By opening the detail step (tapping on the line that says "Tap here for step by step instructions"), more explanation will made available to assist him/her in completing the current step.

When the user is done with the current main step, s/he simply has to touch the checkbox located at the right side of the instruction on the tablet. Once the checkbox is selected, a prompt

Figure 2. Main step in shelving books task

will appear and the user can then proceed to the next main step. The prompt serves as an encouragement (reinforcement) mechanism for the individual with autism. In the bottom half of the page, all main steps for the current task are listed. This serves a visual clue to the user of how many steps are expected for this task. When the user is at main step 2, a green checkmark will appear next to Step 1 in the completed steps listing. This provides a means of confirmation that previous step (main step 1) has been completed. Note that instructions are self-contained within each step and they can be as clear and simple as necessary for the individual with autism to understand.

By accessing this web application system through tablets, the person with MLASD just has to read the instructions on each step and follow them to complete his/her assigned task. This provides focus for his/her job and the individual is therefore given more freedom to work on his/her own.

Use Case for Elementary School Children

Next, we shall consider how iPAWS might be used to help children on the spectrum in learning. Due to its consistency and user friendly interface, the web application is particularly suited for training purposes since it can be accessed repeatedly. Today, the younger generation is very comfortable with using mobile devices such as computer tablets and smart phones. Therefore, the convenience and availability of tasks designed for use on tablets makes this system very appropriate for children from a young age. Imagine a child with autism who needs to do or learn something on a regular and repetitive basis. The system can act as a 'tutor' that provides training while at the same time presents different modes of assistance, including text as a written aid, images as visual aid, and sound as auditory aid. In addition to these modes of learning, a video presentation can also be added for better understanding.

Although the previous use case was directed towards a person with MLASD who is ready for employment, the web application can easily be adapted for learning by children with autism. The next example task illustrates how to teach a child who is in early elementary school to recognize and name shapes. Since each individual learns best using a particular of mode of operation, it is important to provide different modes of learning. One child may learn best using a visual mode of instruction while another child might do better with verbal mode of instruction.

In main step 1 of this use case (see Figure 3), instructions are provided to teach the child with ASD five different shapes; circle, triangle, square, star, and rectangle. The shapes are introduced using both text and pictures. A verbal (audio) description to explain the shapes can easily be included if desired. Each shape is elaborated further in separate detail steps. In each accompanying detail step, an image (acting as visual stimulant) is used for visual presentation. Video can also be included to further reinforce the shape. In subsequent main steps (2 through 6), the child will be asked a question about the shapes that were introduced in the 1st main step. Included on each of these main steps will be several different shapes for selection. The child will need to choose from one of the shapes provided as the answer to the particular question. If the correct answer is selected, an auditory confirmation will be given. Otherwise, a negative audio response is given. Table 2 shows all the steps for this use case. In main steps 2 through 6, an accompanying detail step will deliver the correct answer to the respective question. This will serve as reinforcement for the child who is learning. As an example, the detail step of main step 2 will show the image of a square along with an auditory answer.

The different modes of learning available on the web application help the child with ASD maintain interest in the subject matter. They also help to focus their attention on the relevant stimuli.

Figure 3. Learning shapes use case

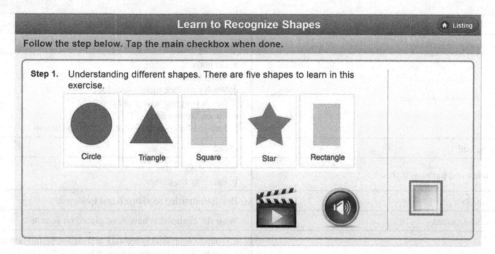

Use Case for Middle School Children

The previous use case provides an example of using iPAWS for learning by children on the spectrum at an early school age. This section will demonstrate another use case, "Getting Ready for School," to assist with instructing children with autism at the middle school age level. Note that the granularity of steps for each task should be considered to cater to the needs of each individual.

Mornings can be stressful for parents with school age kids. This is even more so with a child with ASD in the family. Because children with autism need structure to help with their daily rou- tine, this use case provides order for the morning routine of getting a child ready for school. Photo and audio prompts are used to help kids with life skills. Step instructions along with their respective detail steps are shown in Table 3.

This use case illustrates one particular order- ing of steps for the specified task. Since the needs of each child with autism may differ, instructions for main steps and detail steps can be altered by his/her coach (in this case, likely his/her mother) to suit that particular individual's need. If the child with autism needs help in understanding the in- struction in a main step, s/he can touch (tap) the "Show detail steps" line to see more instructions

Table 2. Learn to recognize shapes

Main Step	Detail Step
1. Understanding different shapes. There are five shapes to learn in this exercise.	a. This is an example of a Circle. b. This is an example of a Triangle. c. This is an example of a Square. d. This is an example of a Star. e. This is an example of a Rectangle
2. Which is a square?	This is a Square.
3. Which is a circle?	This is a Circle.
4. Which is a star?	This is a Star.
5. Which is a triangle?	This is a Triangle.
6. Which is a rectangle?	This is a Rectangle.

Table 3. Getting ready for school

Main Step	Detail Step(s)
1. Good morning and wake up	Say good morning
2. Go to the bathroom and wash up	a. Go potty b. Wash hands c. Wash your face using washcloth d. Brush your hair using hair comb e. Put on Deodorant f. Turn the lights off before leaving the bathroom
3. Make your bed	None
4. Eat breakfast and put away dishes	a. Eat breakfast that is on the table b. Put away the dishes
5. Go to bathroom	Brush teeth using toothbrush and toothpaste
6. Put on school clothes	Wear the clothes that have been placed on your bed
7. Prepare backpack for school	a. Collect completed homework and signed permission slips b. Get books and notebooks according to school schedule c. Check your school stationery d. Collect lunch or lunch money e. Place your backpack by the door that you will exit through
8. Put on socks, shoes and jacket	a. Wear your jacket b. Put on shoes c. Put on gloves if hands are cold
9. Say "Have a good day," and head for the door	None

under the detail steps section. A screenshot of sample detail steps for main step 2 is shown in Figure 4. After finishing each detail step, s/he only has to tap each row to signify its completion. A checkmark will appear in the box on the right to indicate that action for each completed detail step. Notice that an image may be added as a visual clue for greater effect.

This use case further demonstrates the effectiveness of using software technology to provide structure to morning routines. The upshot of having a child with autism use a mobile tablet to check on the things that s/he must do after waking up in the morning helps build character and could potentially motivate independence for the individual.

CASE STUDIES

To understand the usability of the web application and benefits of using mobile technology, case studies were conducted and feedback was collected to help improve the Task Manager component of iPAWS. As a result, the user interface of the Task manager can better cater to the needs of individuals with ASD. For the purpose of these experiments, individuals on the autism spectrum were classified into three general categories of severe (classic) autism, mid-level functional autism, and Asperger. These case studies were carried out during the design of iPAWS, and they are explained next.

Case Study One

The first case study was conducted on an initial prototype of the Task Manager to verify its usability and practicality. Testing was carried out on an Apple iPad tablet by a twenty-two year old

Figure 4. Detail steps in use case

male individual (referred to as test subject X) who is considered to have mid-level functional autism. Normally, he would not be able to complete tasks without the help of a coach which in his case was his mother. Subject X was not sure what to do when initially presented with the web application on an iPad. Not given any initial instructions, subject X seems lost as to how to proceed with the task. He stared at the screen for almost 5 minutes before touching the task listing at the bottom of the screen. This was incorrect, of course, as nothing would happen with that action. The "Steps completed" section simply shows a listing of steps that has been completed which are indicated by a checkmark next to each step. His mother prompted him to focus on the main step instruction at the top instead. After some initial prompting, subject X was able to proceed further, including opening up the detail steps section for more instructions.

Based on subject X's testing, several modifications were made to improve the Task Manager's user interface. Changes to the user interface include enlarging the checkbox next to the main step, placing a green outline box around the main step for emphasis on the step instruction, changing the completed steps section at the bottom from black to gray (for less emphasis), and making both the audio and visual aids more prominent (using bigger images for easier selection). After these changes were made, subject X was again presented with the improved web application for a second round of testing. After several rounds of testing with different tasks, he became more comfortable with how the web application worked. Eventually, he was able to use the Task Manager, even without any prompting from his mother. This shows the potential of using the Task Manager Web application for training.

It should be noted that the learning curve for using this web application was relatively short. Also, subject X was observed to enjoy using the web application even after employing it many times. His mother also reported that subject X got a huge sense of satisfaction from being able to complete tasks successfully while using the web application. He was even able to prepare dinner for the family (for the first time) simply by following instructions which were entered by his mother.

Table 4 Results of Asperger testing

Test Subject	# Tasks Completed	Audio Help	Video Help	Detail Steps Opened	# Prompts
A	5	0	0	3	2
B	5	0	0	2	3
C	5	0	0	0	2
D	5	0	1	5	8
Average score	5	0	0.25	2.5	3.75

Case Study Two

The second case study involves testing with four individuals (college students) who were considered to be in the Asperger category. A total of five tasks were designed for this experiment using the improved model. The task listing was separated into three categories: easy, intermediate, and challenging. Each test subject was asked to complete as many tasks as possible in a period of 30 minutes. The tests were conducted by two observers who took notes on several points of interest. First, did the test subject make use of either the audio or video options for assistance? Second, did the test subject tap on the detail steps for more help while using the app? If so, how often was this done? Third, did the test subject require prompts or help from an observer? Table 4 shows the outcome of these observations. Results from testing indicate that the average number of detail steps opened (2.5) and average number of prompts required (3.75) was relatively low. Once again, the Task Manager webapp showed promise. After using the Task Manager, the test subjects were asked to rate the webapp on three categories: ease of use, practicality, and potential for client training. Results of this survey are shown in Table 5. All test subjects were able to complete all five tasks within the allotted time frame. The average time to complete the five tasks was 16 minutes. Results suggest that the webapp is deemed very usable, with an average score of 9 out of 10. It was considered practical (8.25/10) and has tremendous potential for client training (8.75/10).

FUTURE RESEARCH DIRECTIONS

The iPAWS web application system that is presented in this chapter is flexible enough to accommodate tasks for individuals of all ages on the autism spectrum. Minor modifications to the user interface of Task Manager can be made to cater to the needs of specific groups such as children, youths, or adults. Although the current system targets the community of individuals with autism, this web application can be adapted for use by other demographic groups as well. One particular community that the author has in mind is senior citizens who may be able to use it as a checklist for daily activities. With this in mind, a large sample of test subjects in each group will be needed for continuous improvement to the web application.

Due to ever changing computer technology, the system must be able to adapt to new changes for mobile tablets. Because of the Task Manager's present layout design, the best type of mobile device to use this web application is tablet computers.

Table 5 Evaluation of web application

Test Subject	Ease of Use	Practicality	Client Training
A	10	9	9
B	10	10	10
C	8	7	8
D	8	7	8
Average score	9	8.25	8.75

Future changes to the layout would involve adapting this system to fit on smaller mobile devices like mini-tablets or smart phones.

Improvements to the Task Developer component can be made on the existing features to dynamically allow options for specifying various types of choices (lists, checkboxes, radio buttons, etc.) within a step. For example, the web application might allow the individual's coach the ability to stipulate a specific number of choices when entering steps for a task.

The ability to automatically track usage of tasks would be useful. Ideally, the web application system should be able to record different measures such as how many times details steps are opened for each main step, the number of times audio or video aids are accessed, the number of steps that were completed for each task, and the amount of time needed to complete a specific task. This serves as a type of report that can later be used for analysis.

Currently, the web application system is hosted on a local web server. Service may be interrupted in the event of a server failure which would result in the individuals not being able to access the tasks that they need. A possible improvement from the current model would be to port the system to the cloud, thereby decreasing the possibility of not being able to access the system when needed.

CONCLUSION

This chapter introduced software technology that creates a simple and intuitive web application system to train individuals on the autism spectrum or help them learn. The web application system provides the ability for a coach or supervisor to enter instructions through the easy-to-use Task Developer. Individuals with ASD can access these tasks through an intuitive Task Manager by using mobile tablets. The structured and consistent nature of the web application with its clear step by step instructions is suitable for use by individuals

of all ages on the spectrum. Different modes of instructions (textual, audio, visual) can be made available in the tasks to better assist users understand task steps. Through the use of tablets, autistic individuals become more engaged and focused on their tasks. As seen by the example use cases, this web application provides a mobile learning environment that can be employed for assisting users with autism including children.

To determine the system's usability and practicality, two case studies were conducted with individuals on the autism spectrum. The case studies were explained and results obtained were then presented. Feedback from these studies shows that there is good potential for training and learning.

REFERENCES

American Psychiatric Association. (2013). *Diagnostic and statistical manual of mental disorders* (5th ed.). Washington, DC: Author.

Bailey, J. S., & Burch, M. R. (2002). *Research methods in applied behavior analysis*. Thousand Oaks, CA: SAGE Publications.

Beaudry, N. (2013). Best iPad apps for children with autism. *SheKnows Parenting*. Retrieved from http://www.sheknows.com/parenting/articles/953661/best-ipad-apps-for-children-with-autism

Bende, R. (2011). Kids and mobile devices: Half of kids under 8 use them. *PARENTS*. Retrieved from http://www.parents.com/blogs/red-hot-parenting/2011/10/25/health/kids-and-mobile-devices-half-of-kids-under-8-use-them/

Billstedt, E., Gillberg, I. C., & Gilbert, C. (2005). Autism after adolescence: population-based 13-22-year follow-up study of 120 individuals with autism diagnosed in childhood. *Journal of Autism and Developmental Disorders*, *35*(3), 351–360. doi:10.1007/s10803-005-3302-5 PMID:16119476

Cafiero, J. M. (2008). Technology supports for individuals with autism spectrum disorders. *Technology in Action, 3*(3), 1–12.

Charlop-Christy, M. H., Carpenter, M., Le, L., LeBlanc, L., & Kellet, K. (2002). Using the picture exchange communication system (PECS) with children with autism: Assessment of PECS acquisition, speech, social-communication behavior, and problem behavior. *Journal of Applied Behavior Analysis, 35*(3), 213–231. doi:10.1901/jaba.2002.35-213 PMID:12365736

Dawe, M. (2006). Desperately seeking simplicity: how young adults with cognitive disabilities and their families adopt assistive technologies. In *Proceedings of the SIGCHI Conference on Human Factors in Computing Systems,* (pp. 1143-1152). ACM.

Dettmer, S., Simpson, R., Myles, B. S., & Ganz, J. B. (2000). The use of visual supports to facilitate transitions of children with autism. *Focus on Autism and Other Developmental Disabilities, 15*(3), 163–169. doi:10.1177/108835760001500307

Duncan, H., & Tan, J. (2012). A visual task manager application for individuals with autism. *Journal of Computing Sciences in Colleges, 27*(6), 49–57.

Eaves, L. C., & Ho, H. H. (2008). Young adult outcome of autism spectrum disorders. *Journal of Autism and Developmental Disorders, 38*(4), 739–747. doi:10.1007/s10803-007-0441-x PMID:17764027

Elkeseth, S. (2009). Outcome of comprehensive psycho-educational interventions for young children with autism. *Research in Developmental Disabilities, 30*(1), 158–178. doi:10.1016/j.ridd.2008.02.003 PMID:18385012

Hayes, G. R., Hirano, S., Marcu, G., Monibi, M., Nguyen, D. H., & Yeganyan, M. (2010). Interactive visual supports for children with autism. *Personal and Ubiquitous Computing, 14*(7), 663–680. doi:10.1007/s00779-010-0294-8

Hess, K. L., Morrier, M. J., Heflin, L. J., & Ivey, M. L. (2008). Autism treatment survey: Services received by children with autism spectrum disorders in public school classrooms. *Journal of Autism and Developmental Disorders, 38*(5), 961–971. doi:10.1007/s10803-007-0470-5 PMID:17929155

Hourcade, J. P., Bullock-Rest, N. E., & Hansen, T. E. (2012). Multitouch table applications and activities to enhance the social skills of children with autism spectrum disorders. *Personal and Ubiquitous Computing, 16*(2), 157–168. doi:10.1007/s00779-011-0383-3

Howlin, P., Goode, S., Hutton, J., & Rutter, M. (2004). Adult outcome for children with autism. *Journal of Child Psychology and Psychiatry, and Allied Disciplines, 45*(2), 212–229. doi:10.1111/j.1469-7610.2004.00215.x PMID:14982237

Koch, A. (2012). *Assistive technologies for children with autism spectrum disorders*. Minneapolis, MN: Division of Science and Mathematics, University of Minnesota.

Müller, E., Schuler, A., & Yates, G. B. (2008). Social challenges and supports from the perspective of individuals with Asperger syndrome and other autism spectrum disabilities. *Autism, 12*(2), 173–190. doi:10.1177/1362361307086664 PMID:18308766

Shane, H. C., & Albert, P. D. (2008). Electronic screen media for persons with autism spectrum disorders: Results of a survey. *Journal of Autism and Developmental Disorders, 38*(8), 499–508. doi:10.1007/s10803-007-0527-5 PMID:18293074

Shattuck, P. T., Narendorf, S. C., Cooper, B., Sterzing, P. R., Wagner, M., & Taylor, J. L. (2012). Postsecondary education and employment among youth with an autism spectrum disorder. *Pediatrics, 129*(6), 1042–1049. doi:10.1542/peds.2011-2864 PMID:22585766

Smith, T. (2001). Discrete trial training in the treatment of autism. *Focus on Autism and Other Developmental Disabilities, 16*(2), 86–92. doi:10.1177/1088357601016000204

Tan, J., & Conway, T. (2012). iPAWS – Personal assistant web application system for autistic adults. Pennsylvania Computer and Information Science Educators, E. Stroudsburg.

Wehman, P. B. (2012). *Life beyond the classroom: Transition strategies for young people with disabilities*. Brookes Publishing Company.

ADDITIONAL READING

Cohen, M. J., & Sloan, D. L. (2007). *Visual supports for people with autism: a guide for parents and professionals*. USA: Woodbine House.

Cramer, M., Hirano, S. H., Tentori, M., Yeganyan, M. T., & Hayes, G. R. (2011). Classroom-based Assistive Technology: collective use of interactive Visual Schedules by Students with Autism, *Proceedings of the SIGCHI Conference on Human Factors in Computing Systems*, 1-10

Escobedo, L., Nguyen, D. H., Boyd, L., et al. MOSOMO: (2012) A Mobile Assistive Tool to Support Children with Autism Practicing Social Skills in Real-Life Situation. *Proceedings of the SIGCHI Conference on Human Factors in Computing Systems,* 2589-2598

Grynszpan, O., Martin, J., & Nadel, J. (2007). What influences human computer interaction in Autism? *Proceedings of the SIGCHI Conference on Human Factors in Computing Systems*, 1-10.

Hayes, G. R., & Abowd, G. D. (2006). Tensions in designing capture technologies for an evidence-based care community. *Proceedings of the CHI 2006*, 937-946

Hourcade, J. P. (2008). Interaction design and children. *Foundations and Trends Human-Computer Interaction, 1*(4), 277–392. doi:10.1561/1100000006

Hurst, A., & Tobias, J. (2011). Empowering individuals with do-it-yourself assistive technology, *Proceedings of the 13th international ACM SIGACCESS conference on Computers and Accessibility*, 11-18.

Kientz, J. A., Hayes, G. R., Westeyn, T. L., Starner, T., & Abowd, G. D. (2007). Pervasive Computing and Autism: assisting caregivers of children with special needs. *IEEE Pervasive Computing / IEEE Computer Society [and] IEEE Communications Society, 6*(1), 28–35. doi:10.1109/MPRV.2007.18

Leo, G. D., & Leroy, G. (2008). Smartphones to facilitate communication and improve social skills of children with severe autism spectrum disorder: Special Education Teachers as proxies. *Proceedings of the Interaction Design and Children*, 45-48.

Massaro, D. W., Bosseler, A., & Light, J. (2003). Development and evaluation of a computer-animated tutor for language and vocabulary learning, *15th International Congress of Phonetic Sciences*, Barcelona, Spain, 3-9.

Milne, M., Powers, D., & Leibbrandt, R. (2009). Development of a software-based social tutor for children with autism spectrum disorders, *Proceedings of the 21st Annual Conference of the Australian Computer-Human Interaction Special Interest Group: Design*, 265-268.

Rajendran, G., & Mitchell, P. (2008). Computer mediated interaction in Asperger's syndrome: the Bubble Dialogue program. *Computers & Education, 35*(3), 187–207.

Riemer-Reiss, M., & Wacker, R. (2000). Factors associated with assistive technology discontinuance among individuals with disabilities. *Journal of Rehabilitation, 66*(3).

Tartaro, A. (2005). Storytelling with a virtual peer as an intervention for children with autism. *Proceedings of the ASSETS 2005*, ACM Press, 42-44.

KEY TERMS AND DEFINITIONS

Cloud: A variety of different types of computing concepts that involve a large number of computers connected through a real-time communication network such as the Internet.

Mobile Technology: Refers to the use of mobile devices, such as smart phones and tablet computers, for purpose of communication.

Software Technology: A collection of software programs and related data that provides the instructions to perform specific operations.

Task: A job that is assigned to an individual Use Case: A sequence of actions/events that results in the completion of a task Visual Aid: A visual aid may include images or video.

Web Application: A computer program that is accessible over the Internet that allows the user to access data using a web browser.

Section 3
Video and Virtual–Based Instruction for Children with Autism

Chapter 11
Robots and Autism Spectrum Disorder:
Clinical and Educational Applications

Amie Senland
Fordham University, USA

ABSTRACT

Technology featuring robots is a promising innovative technological intervention for treating and educating children with Autism Spectrum Disorder (ASD). This chapter reviews, critiques, and presents future directions for research on clinical and educational applications of robots for these children. Specifically, this chapter reviews current research on: (1) robots that act as social mediators for children with ASD and (2) robots that assist them in developing social skills such as joint attention and imitation. A critical review of the research suggests that robots may have the capacity to assist some of these children, but additional rigorous studies are necessary to demonstrate their efficacy and effectiveness. Future research must (1) examine whether robots have differential effects for specific subgroups of children with ASD and (2) contribute to a deeper understanding of robots' potential use in educational settings.

INTRODUCTION

During recent decades, the prevalence of autism spectrum disorder (ASD) has increased dramatically (Centers for Disease Control and Prevention, 2012) and technology has become progressively influential and widespread in society. Once considered an uncommon disorder consistently characterized by intellectual disability, poor social skills, and an inability to speak (Lord & Bishop, 2010), the heterogeneity of ASD is now recognized; some individuals remain non-verbal and dependent on supports throughout life, and others continue to struggle with social communication skills despite adequate language and intelligence (U.S. Department of Health and Human Services, 2011). Regardless of varied symptoms and outcomes, all children with ASD have impaired social communication and restricted, repetitive behavior, interests, or activities (American Psychological

DOI: 10.4018/978-1-4666-5792-2.ch011

Association, 2013). The current prevalence rate for ASD is 1 in 88 children (Centers for Disease Control and Prevention, 2012), ten times that of the 1990s (U.S. Department of Health and Human Services, 2011). As prevalence rises, the societal and familial cost of ASD also increases. The annual cost to society for ASD is approximately $90 billion, and in addition to the typical costs of raising a child, a family of a child with ASD pays an extra $3 to $5 million across the child's lifespan (Lord & Bishop, 2010).

Given the considerable rising impact of ASD on children, families, and society, the U.S. Department of Health and Human Services (2011) has continued to emphasize the need for evidence-based interventions for children with ASD. Alongside its broader societal advances, technology has become increasingly important in treating and educating children with ASD (Bölte, Golan, Goodwin, & Zwaigenbaum, 2010; Ploog, Scharf, Nelson, & Brooks, 2013), with robots proposed as one of many innovative technological interventions for such children. Robots might be a valuable intervention because many of these children are interested in computers (Ploog et al., 2013), and the simplicity and predictability of robots might be particularly effective in engaging such children (Bölte et al., 2010; Scassellati, Admoni, & Matarić, 2012; Thill, Pop, Belpaeme, Ziemke, & Vanderborght, 2012). Excitement about the potential use of robots for children with ASD is reflected in the media (Diehl et al., 2012). Since 2012, news clips about robots for these children have been featured on the *NBC Today Show*, *PBS News Hour*, *The Stan Simpson Show*, and *ABC News*, and numerous news articles have been written about the topic. Furthermore, in April 2013, a French robotics company, Aldebaran Robotics, announced their ASK (Autism Solution for Kids) NAO initiative (Aldebaran Robotics, 2013). This initiative allows schools and special education teachers to acquire NAO, a commercial robot, for use with students with ASD. NAO comes equipped with games designed to enhance social

and communication skills in children with ASD (Aldebaran Robotics, 2013).

While the potential for using robots in treating and educating children with ASD is exciting, larger more rigorous studies are necessary to evaluate the efficacy and effectiveness of this approach and to determine whether robots have differential effects for specific subgroups of these children (Diehl et al., 2012). Most current research on robots and children with ASD originates from the field of socially assistive robotics (Diehl et al., 2012). Socially assistive robotics is a relatively new interdisciplinary field that uses robots to help people through social interaction (Feil-Seifer & Matarić, 2009; Scassellati et al., 2012; Tapus, Matarić, & Scassellati, 2007). For example, in socially assistive robotics, robots are used to facilitate social interaction and/or emotional expression, teach social skills, and/or provide companionship (Feil-Seifer & Matarić, 2009; Scassellati et al., 2012; Tapus et al., 2007). This field has several application areas, such as using robots as companions for the elderly or assistants in post-stroke recovery, but one of its largest potential application areas is ASD (Tapus et al., 2007). For children with ASD, social robots, or robots that use verbal and/or body language to socially interact with people, could potentially facilitate social interaction or foster social skills such as joint attention and/or imitation (Dautenhahn, 2003; Scassellati et al., 2012).

Accordingly, various types of social robots have been used in research with children with ASD, including mobile robots, creature-like robots, dinosaur robots, and humanoid robots (robots built to resemble humans) such as NAO. Some research teams develop and design their own robots (e.g., Duquette, Michaud, & Mercier, 2008; Vanderborght et al., 2012), while others program and adapt commercially available robots (e.g., François, Powell, & Dautenhahn, 2009; Kim, Berkovits, Bernier, Leyzberg, Shic, Paul, & Scassellati, 2013). Examples of robots used in ASD research are shown in Figures 1 and 2, including a creature-like robot, Keepon (Figure 1), and a humanoid robot, NAO (Figure 2).

Figure 1. Keepon, a creature-like robot used in ASD research (© 2007, Elsevier. Used with permission)

Figure 2. NAO, a humanoid robot used in ASD research, developed by Aldebaran Robotics (© 2012, Elsevier. Used with permission)

Most social robots used in ASD research are controlled through a Wizard of Oz (WOZ) technique, where the experimenter controls the robot without the participant's knowledge, providing the impression that the robot is acting autonomously (Kim et al., 2013; Vanderborght et al., 2012). This control allows the experimenter to direct the robot's responses so that it reacts correctly, flexibly, and contingently to each participant (Kim et al., 2013). Bekele, Lahiri, Swanson, Crittendon, Warren, and Sarkar's (2013) work is an

exception. Instead of using the WOZ technique, Bekele et al. developed an Adaptive Robot-Mediated Intervention Architecture (ARIA) that enabled the robot in their study to autonomously respond accurately and contingently to participants.

In general, when social robots are used in clinical and educational settings for children with ASD, "the hope [is] that a robot might be used as a 'social crutch' which engages children, teaches them social skills incrementally, and assists in the transfer of this knowledge to interaction with humans" (Tapus et al., 2007, p. 2). Scholars have also explored robots' capacity to assist in the diagnosis of ASD (Diehl, Schmitt, Villano, & Crowell, 2012 and Scassellati et al., 2012 provide excellent overviews of the topic), but space limitations prevent a significant discussion of this application. This chapter focuses on social robots' potential use in clinical and educational interventions for children with ASD. If robots can encourage such children to socially interact and/or to develop social skills, they could be integrated into existing therapies or educational practices to provide individualized support to children with ASD (Bekele et al., 2013). Specifically, this chapter concentrates on 1) studies investigating the use of robots as social mediators or facilitators of social interaction between or among people (Dautenhahn, 2003) and 2) studies examining the use of robots to help children with ASD develop social skills such as joint attention and/or imitation (Diehl et al., 2012). These small, predominately exploratory studies indicate that robots encourage social interaction (e.g., François et al., 2009; Kozima, Nakagawa, & Yasuda, 2007) and facilitate social skills for some of these children (e.g., Bekele et al., 2013; Vanderborght et al., 2012).

While using robots to intervene with children with ASD is a promising new technique, evaluating this innovative technology is crucial to ensure its benefit to such children. The majority of research on robots and children with ASD has emerged from the robotics field (e.g., computer science and engineering) as researchers build robots for use in educating and treating these children (Diehl et al., 2012). Most of these studies are feasibility studies conducted to develop robots and determine whether they function as planned with a limited number of children. These studies have been crucial in demonstrating that robots can be created with the potential to aid children with ASD, but further evidence is needed to demonstrate their efficacy and effectiveness in intervening with such children. Efficacious interventions are those that work under ideal experimental settings; effective interventions are those that work in everyday settings such as treatment centers or schools (Rossi, Freeman, & Lipsey, 2004). Specifically, assessing the efficacy of robots for children with ASD and determining for whom they work would require studies with adequate control and larger samples with sufficiently described participants (Diehl et al., 2012). This chapter will review current research on robots and children with ASD with the following objectives:

1. To review current research investigating a) robots as social mediators for children with ASD (Dautenhahn, 2003) and b) robots that attempt to help these children develop social skills such as joint attention or imitation (Scassellati et al., 2012).
2. To critique current research and propose that additional studies are necessary to a) evalu-

ate robots' efficacy in treating and educating children with ASD, and b) examine whether robots have differential effects for specific subgroups of these children (Diehl et al., 2012).
3. To discuss future and emerging trends in using robots for intervening with children with ASD, such as a) developing increasingly autonomous robots, and (Scassellati et al., 2012) b) conducting further studies about robots' educational implications for these children.

BACKGROUND

Researchers are excited about the possibility of using robots for children with ASD partly because such children have generally shown a preference for robots. Studies have demonstrated that these children are more successful at imitating a robotic than human hand (Pierno, Mari, Lusher, & Castiello, 2008), direct more attention and eye gaze to a mobile robot than a toy truck (Dautenhahn & Werry, 2004), and show a preference for looking at a robot compared to a therapist (Bekele et al., 2013). While these children may be enthusiastic about robots (at least initially), it is challenging to design clinical and educational interventions capitalizing on this engagement to facilitate their socio-emotional growth.

This section focuses on two broad clinical and educational applications for using robots with children with ASD: 1) as social mediators (Dautenhahn, 2003) and 2) as facilitators and/or teachers of social skills such as joint attention and imitation (Scassellati et al., 2012). Studies are predominately exploratory and do not yet have the sample size or control necessary to demonstrate the efficacy of this technique for these children (Diehl et al., 2012). After current research is presented, it will be critiqued, allowing for the discovery of solutions and recommendations, as well as future research directions.

Robots as Social Mediators for Children with ASD

A number of initial feasibility and exploratory studies show the potential for robots as social mediators for at least some children with ASD (e.g., François et al., 2009; Kozima et al., 2007). When a robot acts as a social mediator for a child with ASD, it facilitates interactions that are dyadic (between the child and another person) or triadic (among the child and two other people). Some researchers also consider a child's interaction with the robot to be a dyadic interaction and a child's interaction with the robot and another person (e.g., therapist or parent) to be a triadic interaction (e.g., François et al., 2009; Kozima et al., 2007).

Kozima et al. (2007) conducted an observational pilot study of a robot as a social mediator for children with ASD. Keepon, a simple creature-like robot capable of demonstrating attention and emotion (shown in Figure 1) facilitated dyadic and triadic interactions for young children with ASD. As another toy for children to play with, Keepon was placed in the playroom of a day-care center for children with ASD (aged 2 to 4-years-old) with intellectual disabilities. Parents and therapists were also present to interact with the children. Kozima et al. observed children's interactions with Keepon and described three prototypical case studies (two girls and one boy) of these exchanges. Keepon facilitated triadic interactions for two children, fostering shared topics of conversation between the children and their therapist and/or parent. The other child engaged in spontaneous dyadic interactions with Keepon (Kozima et al., 2007). These results suggest that Keepon acted as a social mediator for the three children with ASD presented in the case studies. However, Kozima et al. explained that over three years, they observed 30 children with ASD or other developmental disabilities interacting with Keepon. It is not clear whether the 27 other children, who were also observed interacting with Keepon, lost interest in the robot over time or failed to engage in dyadic or triadic interactions despite the robot's presence.

Similar to Kozima et al. (2007), François et al.'s (2009) exploratory study examined whether playing with a robotic mobile dog, Sony Aibo ERS-7, fostered social interaction for children with ASD. François et al. conducted case studies of six children with ASD selected by their teacher to participate (five boys and one girl, aged 7 to 10-years-old). Information about intellectual ability was not provided. Children played with the robotic dog for a maximum of ten sessions; children directed the play and could choose whether to draw the experimenter into the play. François et al. found that children responded individually to the robot, highlighting the importance of determining whether robots are most effective for specific subgroups of these children. Of the six children, two engaged in solitary play without the robot, one engaged in dyadic play with the robot, and three engaged in triadic play with the robot and experimenter (François et al., 2009).

Kozima et al. (2007) and François et al. (2009) focused on whether a robot could assist in facilitating social play for a child with ASD. In contrast, Wainer, Ferrari, Dautenhahn, and Robins's (2010) exploratory study examined whether programming robots in an after-school program could foster collaboration in a group of children and adolescents with ASD. Participants included seven boys with ASD without intellectual disabilities (aged 8 to 14-years-old), who chose to attend a robotics class and already knew each other from the after-school program. Only participants completing 60% of the robotics classes were included. During each robotics class, children received a lesson about programming a robot and then programmed the robot (LEGO-NXT-G) in groups organized by those responsible for the after-school program. To assess whether collaboration skills transferred to a non-structured environment, children also completed three drawing activities where they worked with the same group of students to draw robot images. Wainer et al. argued that children enjoyed the robotics class, showed greater collaboration with peers while programming robots, and demonstrated some increased collaboration from the first to last drawing sessions. About 60% of parents indicated that the robotics class assisted their child during social situations beyond the robotics class or had the capacity to do so in the future (Wainer et al., 2010).

Wainer et al.'s (2010) study demonstrates the potential for a robotics class to foster collaboration among children with ASD but also has significant limitations. First, children who signed-up for and persisted through a robotics class were presumably more fascinated by robots than those who chose not to attend or continue the class. Results might not generalize to children less enthusiastic about robots. Second, Wainer et al. investigated the generalization of collaboration skills to a non-structured environment with the same groups of students who programmed the robots together. Collaboration skills might not generalize to a non-structured environment with unknown children. Third, there was no control group; thus, one does not know whether the robotics class facilitated collaboration or spending increased time together did so.

Finally, Kim et al. (2013) conducted the largest study to date examining the use of robots as social mediators for children with ASD. Participants included 24 children (21 boys and 4 girls, aged 4 to 12-years-old) with ASD without intellectual disabilities. Kim et al. compared the number of utterances children made and to whom they spoke when relating to three interaction partners in random order: a) Pleo, a commercially available robotic dinosaur, b) a human, and c) a nonsocial touch-screen computer game. During each experimental condition, the child could also speak with a researcher in the room (a confederate). When children interacted with the robot, they made significantly more utterances in general and also spoke significantly more to the confederate. Children made comparable utterances to the robot and human but significantly more to the robot

than the computer. Results indicate that the robot facilitated more utterances than another human or computer, with such increased speech used to initiate social interaction with the confederate (Kim et al., 2013). However, questions remain about whether this effect would generalize outside of the laboratory, how children with ASD and intellectual disabilities would respond to the robot, and whether this effect would remain for the long-term (Kim et al., 2013).

In general, these studies suggest robots' potential to serve as social mediators for some but perhaps not all children with ASD. Crucial next steps include designing larger more adequately controlled studies to further evaluate the efficacy of this approach and determine whether it is most effective for specific subgroups of these children.

Robots that Assist Children with ASD with Social Skills

In addition to examining robots' capacity to act as social mediators, several researchers have investigated robots' ability to assist children with ASD in developing social skills such as joint attention and imitation (e.g., Diehl et al., 2013; Tapus et al., 2013). The overarching goal of these studies is to investigate whether robots can assist in addressing core social communication deficits in ASD such as joint attention (i.e., when two people focus on the same object or event) and imitation (i.e., when one person observes and then copies another person's actions, words, or behaviors) (Scassellati et al., 2012).

Accordingly, Duquette et al. (2008) conducted four exploratory single-subject studies investigating whether children's social engagement with the mobile robot, Tito, could facilitate social learning, including imitation. Participants included four children with ASD and intellectual disabilities (three boys and one girl, aged 4 to 5-years-old). Half the children engaged in imitation play scenarios with the robot Tito, and half did so with another person (the experimenter). Results indicated that interaction with Tito facilitated more shared attention and interest than engagement with another person. However, compared to children interacting with another person, those interacting with the robot were significantly more likely to engage in ASD rituals and to leave the communication area, as well as significantly less likely to imitate words (Duquette et al., 2008). Despite robots' capacity to socially engage children with ASD, researchers continue to grapple with how best to capitalize on this sense of engagement to teach social skills, such as imitation.

Tapus et al.'s (2012) research on robots and children with ASD further highlights the complexities of utilizing robots to facilitate social skills in these children. Tapus et al. conducted four exploratory single-subject studies to examine whether NAO (shown in Figure 2) could facilitate more motor imitation and social engagement than a human. Participants included four boys with ASD and intellectual disabilities, aged 2 to 6-years-old. A baseline was established (A), children interacted with NAO (B), a second baseline was established (A), and finally children interacted with a human (C) (ABAC single-subject design). The number of imitations (without prompts) and duration of eye gaze, smiles, and laughter were recorded (Tapus et al., 2012).

Children's responses to NAO varied widely (Tapus et al., 2012). NAO had the most success with one child, who demonstrated significantly more eye gaze, smiles/laughter, and shared eye gaze when interacting with NAO than with another human or during baseline. This child also experienced significantly more motor imitation in the NAO and human conditions than baseline but the amount of imitation in the NAO and human conditions were comparable. Another child showed significantly increased eye gaze and smiles/laughter in response to NAO but no change in motor imitation. NAO had no impact on motor imitation or social engagement for the other two children (Tapus et al., 212). Children's individual responses to NAO further highlight the value of

investigating robots' effectiveness for specific subgroups of children with ASD.

Vanderborght et al. (2012) had more consistent results than Tapus et al. (2012) when conducting four exploratory single-subject studies to examine whether using a robot to tell a social story could enhance the social success of children with ASD. Participants included four children with ASD and intellectual disabilities aged 4 to 9-years-old (two boys and a set of twin girls). Individualized social stories were created for the children based on their therapeutic needs (e.g., learning to say thank you). A therapist and Probo (a soft creature-like robot) read children the social stories in a counterbalanced single-subject design. A counterbalanced design controlled for order of treatment: half the children received the therapist intervention prior to the robot intervention and half received the robot intervention before the therapist intervention. The number of promptings necessary to elicit the social behavior in the story from the children was counted. Children needed fewer prompts when Probo told the social story than when the therapist did, but this was only significant for one participant (Vanderborght et al., 2012). Vanderborght et al. explained that results would have been significant for two of the four children if statistical tests had not been conducted with a conservative Bonferroni correction. These results further demonstrate the individual and varied responses of children with ASD to robots.

While Duquette el al. (2008), Tapus et al. (2012), and Vanderborght et al. (2012) designed single-subject studies investigating robots' capacity to assist children with ASD in developing social skills, Bekele et al. (2013) conducted a larger well-controlled feasibility experiment utilizing a robot to aid such children in practicing joint attention. The researchers programmed NAO with capabilities for joint attention cues such as pointing, gazing, talking, and head movements, as well as the ability to react contingently to children's responses of joint attention. Participants included six children with ASD aged 2 to

5-years-old with a range of cognitive abilities and six same-aged typically developing children. Both groups, matched on sex (five boys and one girl per group) and age, engaged in counterbalanced joint attention tasks with NAO and a human therapist (Bekele et al., 2013).

Both groups preferred looking at the robot over looking at the therapist, suggesting a preference for the robot (Bekele et al., 2013). The therapist and robot were about as effective at eliciting joint attention for both groups (the therapist was always successful for both groups; the robot succeeded 95.83% of the time for the ASD group and 97.92% of the time for the typically developing group). However, both groups took significantly longer to engage in joint attention with the robot than the human and required significantly more prompts to do so (14.58% more for the ASD group and 9.37% more for the typically developing group). Bekele et al. (2013) explained that this could have been because of children's excitement about the robot; however, this enthusiasm could decline over time, reducing the additional time needed for joint attention. Although this study is well controlled, one still does not know whether joint attention skills would generalize outside of the laboratory and whether preference for the robot would remain over time (Bekele et al., 2013).

Diehl et al. (2013) also conducted a larger well-controlled study. Diehl et al. examined whether using NAO as a co-therapist during applied behavior analysis therapy could help children with ASD develop social behaviors such as asking appropriate questions. Participants included 19 children with ASD (aged 6 to 13-years-old with varying cognitive and language abilities) who received 12 sessions of applied behavior analysis (six sessions with NAO and six with a trained therapist). Participants were pair-wise matched; whether one initially received the robot or therapist session was counterbalanced across pairs. Children's social behaviors progressed significantly during sessions with NAO but did not improve significantly during sessions without NAO. Children generalized

such skills to their natural environment. Diehl et al. noted that children's responses to the robot varied both behaviorally and eletrophysiologically, further highlighting the crucial need to determine for whom robots are most successful.

Collectively, these studies suggest that robots can potentially facilitate social skills for some but perhaps not all children with ASD. Additional larger controlled studies are necessary to determine the complexities of this approach, including for whom it works, the specific components of interventions with robots, and whether results generalize to the real-world.

EVALUATING CURRENT RESEARCH ON ROBOTS AND ASD

Limitations, Problems, and Issues of Current Research on Robots and ASD

Technological advances have made interventions with robots possible for children with ASD, and the field of socially assistive robotics has demonstrated its capacity to create and design robots for this purpose. However, technological capacities have preceded understanding of the efficacy and effectiveness of robots in the treatment and education of children with ASD. Larger more rigorous studies are necessary to evaluate the efficacy and effectiveness of robots in intervening with these children (Diehl et al., 2012; Ploog et al., 2013). Technology, including robots, will become increasingly accessible to clinicians and educators, as demonstrated by the recent availability of NAO in schools. Clinicians and educators' ethical responsibility to provide children with effective interventions highlights the need to critically evaluate all innovative technologies, including robots (Ploog et al., 2013).

While using robots for children with ASD is a promising innovative technique, at least three major problems and issues are evident in current research about this approach. These include: 1) methodological limitations of current research restrict knowledge about the efficacy and effectiveness of this approach for children with ASD (Diehl et al., 2012), 2) clinicians and researchers are beginning to understand how robots can be incorporated into therapy for children with ASD (see Diehl, 2012), but less is known about integrating robots into educational settings for such children, and 3) robots need to become affordable and technologically feasible for therapists and educators to operate (Scassellati et al., 2012).

Current studies share significant methodological limitations (Diehl, 2012) when one's goal is to evaluate the usefulness of robots in intervening with children with ASD. Studies share these limitations because most studies come from the robotics rather than clinical literature (Diehl, 2012), and robotic and clinical researchers differ in their research approaches and study designs (Kim, Paul, Shic, & Scassellati, 2012). Robotic researchers focus on technological innovation and a robot's feasibility; clinical researchers concentrate on obtaining evidence demonstrating a robot's effectiveness for children with ASD (Kim et al., 2012). A small sample is sufficient to verify feasibility of robot systems for robotic researchers; in contrast, clinical researchers need large well-characterized samples and control groups to examine robots' efficacy and to determine for whom this approach is most effective (Kim et al., 2012). Since most studies originate from the robotics field, they primarily focus on developing robots for children with ASD rather than on examining the clinical and educational utility of this approach (Diehl et al., 2012). When one tries to examine the literature to determine clinical utility of this approach, a number of methodological limitations emerge, highlighting the need for: 1) more rigorously controlled studies, 2) larger samples, 3) more longitudinal studies, and 4) further examination of whether effects generalize to real-world clinical and educational settings (Diehl et al., 2012).

Feasibility of robot systems can be tested with uncontrolled studies, but rigorous control is necessary to determine robots' effectiveness in intervening with children with ASD. As Reichow, Volkmar, and Cicchetti (2008) indicated, both group and single-subject studies should be rigorously controlled. In addition to evaluating efficacy and effectiveness, controlled studies are necessary to compare this innovative approach with current therapeutic and educational methods.

Studies investigating the use of robots as social mediators (e.g., François et al., 2009; Kozima et al., 2007) have predominately been uncontrolled, resulting in several limitations. For one, robots appear to facilitate dyadic and/or triadic interaction for some children with ASD (e.g., François et al., 2009; Kozima et al., 2007) but little is known about whether another toy or activity could also encourage such interaction. The few studies that do compare children's reactions to a robot versus another toy have weaknesses. For example, Kim et al. (2013) found that Pleo, the robotic dinosaur, more effectively facilitated speech for children with ASD than a nonsocial computer game, but did not compare children's responses to Pleo versus a socially engaging game. Considering the cost and complexities of robot interventions, it is crucial to further compare the capacity of robots versus traditional toys and activities to serve as social mediators for these children. Controlled studies are also necessary to rigorously evaluate interventions using robots for children with ASD. To illustrate, Wainer et al. (2010) concluded that a robotics class facilitated group collaboration, but a control group would have been necessary to confirm that the class, rather than spending increasing time together, promoted collaboration.

In contrast to initial exploratory studies examining the use of robots to teach social skills to children with ASD, recent studies with this aim (e.g., Bekele et al., 2013; Diehl et al., 2013; Duquette et al., 2008) have been better controlled and suggest important ways that robots can be integrated into therapy with these children. Comparing robots to more traditional therapy tentatively suggests that incorporating robots into existing therapies as co-therapists (as in Diehl et al.'s 2013 study) might benefit children with ASD, but robots might be less effective than therapists at facilitating social skills (e.g., joint attention, imitation) when used in isolation (as in Bekele et al.'s 2013 and Duquette et al.'s 2008 studies). Robots might elicit shared attention and interest in children with ASD, but human therapists might assist in maintaining this enthusiasm over time so that the robot can be useful in facilitating social skills. Future well-controlled studies comparing robots to human therapists are necessary to examine this possibility.

While small samples may be sufficient to develop robots, larger more well-characterized samples are necessary to examine the efficacy and effectiveness of robots for children with ASD (Diehl et al., 2012). Studies must have enough power to determine whether robots are positively impacting these children. Larger samples are also critical because preliminary evidence suggests that children show individual differences in their responses to robots (e.g., François et al., 2009; Tapus et al., 2012; Vanderborght et al., 2012), but this evidence does not yet indicate for whom robots are most effective (Diehl et al., 2012). To illustrate, as described previously, Tapus et al. found that NAO had a positive impact on one child, no impact on two others, and a mixed impact on a fourth child. With larger more adequately characterized samples, researchers could examine robots' differential effects to establish the specific subgroups of children with ASD for whom they worked best. Children for whom robots were not likely to be effective could receive another intervention.

Furthermore, feasibility studies indicate that robots can be developed that interest children with ASD (e.g., Bekele et al., 2013; Duquette et al., 2008), but one does not yet know whether their engagement with a robot can be sustained for the long-term or if it is a short-term preference due to the robot's novelty (Bekele et al., 2013). Kanda,

Hirano, Eaton, and Ishiguro's (2004) school-based research with a robot and typically developing children suggests that children's interest in the robot may be temporary. Kanda et al. conducted a two week field trial with a social robot and children in the first and sixth grade. A few children continued to engage with the robot but most became less excited about the robot over time. Most current studies are short-term (e.g., Bekele et al., 2013; Duquette et al., 2008; Vanderborght et al., 2012), and one does not know whether children's enthusiasm about the robot occurred because of its novelty or a more meaningful fascination with the robot that could be maintained.

Several studies (e.g., Diehl et al., 2013; Kozima et al., 2007; Wainer et al., 2010) do examine children's long-term responses to a social robot, but these studies have significant limitations. As described previously, Wainer et al. (2010) only included children who attended 60% of the robotics classes; this means that children who stopped attending classes (possibly because they lost interest in the robot over time) were not included in their study. Similarly, Kozima et al. (2007) reported case studies on three children at a daycare; these children might have been the only ones who ultimately remained interested in the robot. Finally, Diehl et al.'s (2013) research suggests that children's interest in a robot can be maintained over time (i.e., over six sessions of applied behavior analysis therapy); however, a human co-therapist, as in Diehl et al.'s research, might be necessary to maintain such interest. Since most therapeutic and educational interventions are long-term, additional research is needed on the contexts that facilitate sustaining children's interest in a robot over time.

Finally, little is known about how skills learned through engagement with a robot generalize to the real-world (Diehl et al., 2012). For example, Bekele et al.'s (2013) research suggests that a robot can teach children joint attention skills, but one does not know whether children are able to utilize these skills outside of a laboratory setting is not yet clear. Kozima et al.'s (2007) research indicates that a robot can encourage dyadic and triadic interactions for some children with ASD, but one does not know whether these children are able to engage in such interactions in different contexts, without the robot. Diehl et al. (2013) examined whether children with ASD could generalize social skills learned in applied behavior analysis therapy with and without a robot as a co-therapist. These children were significantly more likely to engage in the targeted social behaviors in a real-life environment from pre-test to post-test (Diehl et al., 2013). Although this shows that children generalized skills, it does not specifically show that they generalized skills learned from a robot since both the human and robot interventions occurred between pre-test and post-test. Future research is needed to establish that children with ASD can generalize skills learned through their interactions with a robot.

A second major weakness of current research on robots and children with ASD is that while researchers are starting to understand how robots can be integrated into clinical interventions for children with ASD (see Diehl et al., 2012 for a review), less is known about robots' potential use in educating these children. Since NAO is available to educators and additional robots will likely become accessible soon, it is crucial to develop a deeper understanding of robotic use in educational settings for children with ASD. While NAO has been released to educators, there is no published research (to my knowledge) on the use of NAO in educational settings for these children. Conceivably, educational robots for children with ASD could have similar purposes as therapeutic robots, such as acting as social mediators and teaching social skills, but preliminary results from clinical studies might not generalize to educational settings. Wainer et al. (2010) and Kozima et al. (2007) conducted their research in school settings, but these were exploratory feasibility; studies and additional rigorously controlled studies with larger

samples are necessary to show the efficacy of robots in educational settings for children with ASD.

Lastly, a final concern with current research is that robots used in treating and educating children with ASD need to be affordable and simple to operate (Scassellati et al., 2012; Tapus et al., 2007). Foster, Dodge, and Jones (2003) emphasize the importance of approximating the implicit and explicit costs of interventions. A single NAO robot costs approximately $16,000 without accessories (e.g., battery, battery charger, case) (Robotshop Distribution, 2013). Robots' cost underscores the importance of objectively evaluating the efficacy and effectiveness of robots for children with ASD and determining whether there is a subgroup of children with ASD for whom this approach is most useful. If robots benefit some children with ASD more than others, interventions with robots could be targeted toward such children, containing costs by limiting the number of robots each treatment or educational center needs, and ensuring that other children have access to interventions and techniques most effective for them. Further, many robots are operated by WOZ technology. Since educators and therapists need to focus on their clients and students, more automated, simple to use robotic systems would assist therapists and educators in integrating robots into interventions (Scassellati et al., 2012).

Solutions and Recommendations to Strengthen Research on Robots and Children with ASD

As discussed previously, research on robots for children with ASD needs to progress from exploratory and feasibility studies focused on developing robots for children with ASD to larger well-controlled studies evaluating the efficacy of robots in treating and educating these children (Diehl et al., 2013; Ploog et al., 2013). Kim et al. (2012) explained that addressing the methodological limitations of prior research requires collaboration between roboticists and clinicians who have different research approaches, study designs, and standards for publication and dissemination. By extension, it also requires cooperation between roboticists and educators, who would also differ in their research goals and standards. Kim et al. proposed that collaborators design studies that address questions of mutual interest, meet clinical standards for large controlled studies, and engage in open discussion about publication prior to collaboration. Kim et al.'s approach is one tactic that could address some of the methodological limitations of current research, leading to the larger well-controlled studies necessary for evaluating the efficacy of robots for children with ASD.

As another approach, clinicians and educators could design larger well-controlled studies with commercially available robots. Clinicians or educators could lead research teams, that include roboticists familiar with the robot. Diehl et al. (2013) achieved a larger sample ($N = 19$ children with ASD) with NAO, a commercial robot available to researchers and educators. Kim et al. (2013) also obtained a larger sample ($N = 24$ children with ASD) with Pleo, a commercially produced robot. Since NAO is now available to educators, it could be used to develop a research-based understanding of the efficacy of robots in educational settings for children with ASD.

Given evidence that children with ASD respond individually to robots (e.g., Diehl et al., 2013; Tapus et al., 2012), participants in larger well-controlled studies must be described in detail (Diehl et al., 2012) and include groups of children with ASD differing by sex, cognitive ability, age, and social ability. Developing a deeper understanding of which children with ASD are most likely to benefit from therapeutic or educational robots will allow clinicians and educators to cost-effectively target this innovative approach. Due to the cost and complexities of this approach, roboticists will also want to continue conducting feasibility studies that assist in making robots more affordable and simple for clinicians and educators to operate.

FUTURE RESEARCH DIRECTIONS

Robots are one of many innovative technologies with the potential to benefit children with ASD. As explained throughout this chapter, future research needs to address the efficacy and effectiveness of robots for intervening with these children. Guerra, Boxer, and Cook's (2006) statement, "Rather than asking, 'What works . . . ?' we suggest that it is most important to ask: (a) what works and does not work, (b) for whom, and (c) under what circumstances" (p. 60), is relevant to current research about robots and children with ASD.

Larger well-controlled studies are necessary to evaluate the clinical and educational utility of robots for children with ASD and to determine for whom and under what circumstances this approach is most effective. Preliminary evidence that robots may work for some but not all children with ASD (e.g. François et al., 2009; Tapus et al., 2012) highlights the importance of determining for whom robots are most effective. Well-characterized samples are necessary to examine whether children's responses to the robot vary by age, social capacities, cognitive and/or language abilities, or sex (Diehl et al., 2012). Robots may also work for some children but only under certain circumstances. To illustrate, robots may be effective in clinical but not educational settings, children may maintain interest in the robot over time with the assistance of a human co-therapist (as in Diehl et al.'s 2013 study) but not independently, or children may be able to generalize skills learned from some robot interventions but not others.

A second major future direction in research with robots with children with ASD will involve developing a deeper understanding of robots' possible roles in educating children with ASD. Diehl et al.'s (2012) review of robots' clinical applications for children with ASD highlights current knowledge about robots' potential roles in therapeutic interventions with children with ASD and how to integrate robots into such interventions. Less is known about robots' prospective roles in educating these children and/or how to incorporate them into educational interventions. Some therapeutic and educational interventions with robots might be similar but not all results would generalize to educational settings. Current research also predominately focuses on robots' capacity to facilitate social interaction or social skills for children with ASD rather than robots' ability to enhance their cognitive growth (Scassellati et al., 2012). NAO is available to and adopted by educators working with children with ASD but further research is needed to examine its efficacy in educating such children.

Third, most modern robots are designed to be operated by WOZ techniques. This technique requires a human controller. Scassellati et al. (2012) explained that the current trend is to develop robots controlled with architecture capable of sensing and responding to the behaviors and actions of a child with ASD, allowing such robots to contingently react to a child without human control. For example, in Bekele et al.'s (2013) study, NAO was controlled by an Adaptive Robot-Mediated Intervention Architecture, which enabled it to respond contingently to children's responses without human intervention. Although roboticists are currently progressing toward designing robots that respond autonomously and contingently to children, long-term goals also include creating robots capable of identifying and reacting to children's moods and preferences (Scassellati et al., 2012) and adapting to the needs of children with ASD as they change and grow (Thill et al., 2012). This may be crucial for intervening with children with ASD, who often have diverse needs and sensitivities to incorporate into therapeutic and educational interventions (Scassellati et al., 2012).

Finally, as Scassellati et al. (2012) suggested, it is important to investigate why robots captivate the interest of children with ASD. Scholars have hypothesized that robots' simplicity and predictability engage these children but do not yet know what causes them to attend to robots. Insights about the cause of this fascination with robots will assist roboticists in designing robots for this population, as well as aid clinicians and educators in sustaining these children's interest in robots over the long-term.

CONCLUSION

Robots are one of several emerging innovative technologies for children with ASD. Enthusiasm about the potential use of robots in treating and educating these children is evident in media attention to these robot interventions (Diehl et al., 2012), as well as the launching of the ASK NAO program in educational settings. Despite the potential for robots to benefit such children, the field needs to take an objective view toward evaluating their efficacy and effectiveness for children with ASD (J. J. Diehl, personal communication, August 7, 2013).

Feasibility studies dominate most current research on robots and children with ASD. These studies have been important for demonstrating that robots can be developed for use with these children. However, additional larger well-controlled studies are necessary to evaluate robots' efficacy and effectiveness in educating and treating children with ASD (Diehl et al., 2012). Furthermore, initial research suggesting that robots may work for some children with ASD but not others (e.g., Tapus et al., 2012) highlights the importance of examining factors moderating children's responses to robots (e.g., age, severity of ASD, cognitive ability). Although researchers and clinicians are beginning to understand how robots can be used in treating children with ASD, little is known about robots' potential role in educating these children or whether results from clinical studies generalize to an educational setting. Further research on robots in educational settings is necessary.

Robots have the potential for exciting clinical and educational applications, but caution is necessary until the efficacy and effectiveness of this approach is evaluated objectively. Collaborations between roboticists and clinicians, as well as the increased availability of commercial robots, should facilitate the larger well-controlled studies essential to investigating the efficacy and effectiveness of this approach. Continuing technological advances will also assist roboticists in designing increasingly autonomous robots capable of responding contingently to users, which will be easier to integrate into educational and therapeutic settings.

REFERENCES

Aldebaran Robotics. (2013). *Aldebaran robotics' NAO robot goes to school to help children with autism: ASK NAO initiative to revolutionalize special education for children with autism.* Retrieved from http://asknao.aldebaranrobotics.com/media/article/download/Press%20release%20ASK%20NAO_RFB.pdf

American Psychiatric Association. (2013). *Diagnostic and statistical manual of mental disorders: DSM-5* (5th ed.). Washington, DC: Author.

Bekele, E. T., Lahiri, U., Swanson, A. R., & Crittendon, J., A., Warren, Z. E., & Sarkar, N. (2013). A step towards developing adaptive robot-mediated intervention architecture (ARIA) for children with autism. *IEEE Transactions on Neural Systems and Rehabilitation Engineering, 21*(2), 289–299. doi: doi:10.1109/TNSRE.2012.2230188 PMID:23221831

Bölte, S., Golan, O., Goodwin, M. S., & Zwaigenbaum, L. (2010). What can innovative technologies do for autism spectrum disorders? *Autism, 14*, 155–159. doi: doi:10.1177/1362361310365028 PMID:20603897

Centers for Disease Control and Prevention. (2012). Prevalence of autism spectrum disorders—Autism and developmental disabilities monitoring network, 14 sites, 2008, United States. *Morbidity and Mortality Weekly Monitoring Report, 61*(SS-3), 1–19.

Dautenhahn, K. (2003). Roles and functions of robots in human society: Implications from research in autism therapy. *Robotica, 21*, 443–452. doi: doi:10.1017/S0263574703004922

Dautenhahn, K., & Werry, I. (2004). Towards interactive robots in autism therapy: Background, motivation and challenges. *Pragmatics & Cognition, 12*, 1–35.

Diehl, J. J., Cromwell, C. R., Villano, M., Wier, K., Tang, K., & Flores, J. … Van Ness, M. (2013). *Humanoid robots as co-therapists in ABA therapy for children with autism spectrum disorder.* Paper presented at the International Society for Autism Research. San Sebastián, Spain.

Diehl, J. J., Schmitt, L. M., Villano, M., & Crowell, C. R. (2012). The clinical use of robots for individuals with autism spectrum disorders: A critical review. *Research in Autism Spectrum Disorders, 6*, 249–262. doi: doi:10.1016/j.rasd.2011.05.006 PMID:22125579

Duquette, A., Michaud, F., & Mercier, H. (2008). Exploring the use of a mobile robot as an imitation agent with children with low-functioning autism. *Autonomous Robots, 24*, 147–157.

Feil-Seifer, D., & Matarić, M. J. (2009). Toward socially assistive robotics for augmenting interventions for children with autism spectrum disorders. *Experimental Robotics, 54*, 201–210.

Foster, E. M., Dodge, K. A., & Jones, D. (2003). Issues in the economic evaluation of prevention programs. *Applied Developmental Science, 7*(2), 76–86. PMID:20228955

François, D., Powell, S., & Dautenhahn, K. (2009). A long-term study of children with autism playing with a robotic pet: Taking inspirations from non-directive play therapy to encourage children's proactivity and initiative-taking. *Interaction Studies: Social Behaviour and Communication in Biological and Artificial Systems, 10*, 324–373. doi: doi:10.1075/is.10.3.04fra

Guerra, N. G., Boxer, P., & Cook, C. B. (2006). What works (and what does not) in youth violence prevention: Rethinking the questions and finding new answers. *New Directions for Evaluation, 110*, 59–71. doi: doi:10.1002/ev.187

Kanda, T., Hirano, T., Eaton, D., & Ishiguro, H. (2004). Interactive robots as social partners and peer tutors for children: A field trial. *Human-Computer Interaction, 19*, 61–84.

Kim, E. S., Berkovits, L. D., Bernier, E. P., Leyzberg, D., Shic, F., Paul, R., & Scassellati, B. (2013). Social robots as embedded reinforcers of social behavior in children with autism. *Journal of Autism and Developmental Disorders, 43*, 1038–1049. doi: doi:10.1007/s10803-012-1645-2 PMID:23111617

Kim, E. S., Paul, R., Shic, F., & Scassellati, B. (2012). Bridging the research gap: Making HRI useful to individuals with autism. *Journal of Human-Robot Interaction, 1*(1), 26–54. doi: doi:10.5898/JHR1.1.1.Kim

Kozima, H., Nakagawa, C., & Yasuda, Y. (2007). Children–robot interaction: A pilot study in autism therapy. *Progress in Brain Research, 164*, 385–400. doi: doi:10.1016/S0079-6123(07)64021-7 PMID:17920443

Lord, C., & Bishop, S. L. (2010). Autism spectrum disorders: Diagnosis, prevalence, and services for children and families. *Social Policy Report, 24*(2), 1–26.

Pierno, A. C., Mari, M., Lusher, D., & Castiello, U. (2008). Robotic movement elicits visuomotor priming in children with autism. *Neuropsychologia, 46*, 448–454. doi: doi:10.1016/j.neuropsychologia.2007.08.020 PMID:17920641

Ploog, B. O., Scharf, A., Nelson, D., & Brooks, P. J. (2013). Use of computer-assisted technologies (CAT) to enhance social, communicative, and language development in children with autism spectrum disorders. *Journal of Autism and Developmental Disorders, 43*, 301–322. doi: doi:10.1007/s10803—12-1571-3 PMID:22706582

Reichow, B., Volkmar, F., & Cicchetti, D. V. (2008). Development of the evaluative method for evaluating and determining evidence-based practices in autism. *Journal of Autism and Developmental Disorders, 38*, 1311–1319. doi: doi:10.1007/s10803-007-0517-7 PMID:18095149

Robotshop Distribution. (2013). *Aldebaran robotics*. Retrieved from http://www.robotshop.com/aldebaran-robotics-en.html

Rossi, P., Freeman, H., & Lipsey, M. (2004). *Evaluation: A systematic approach* (7th ed.). Thousand Oaks, CA: Sage.

Scassellati, B., Admoni, H., & Matarić, M. (2012). Robots for use in autism research. *Annual Review of Biomedical Engineering, 14*, 275–294. doi: doi:10.1146/annurev-bioeng-071811-150036 PMID:22577778

Tapus, A., Matarić, M., & Scassellati, B. (2007). The grand challenges in socially assistive robotics. *IEEE Robotics & Automation Magazine, 4*, 35–42.

Tapus, A., Peca, A., Aly, A., Pop, C., Jisa, L., & Pintea, S. et al. (2012). Children with autism social engagement in interaction with nao, an imitative robot: A series of single case experiments. *Interaction Studies: Social Behaviour and Communication in Biological and Artificial Systems*, *13*(3), 315–347. doi: doi:10.1075/is.13.3.01tap

Thill, S., Pop, C., Belpaeme, T., Ziemke, T., & Vanderborght, B. (2012). Robot-assisted therapy for autism spectrum disorders with (partially) autonomous control: Challenges and outlook. *Palaydn: Journal of Behavioral Robotics*, *3*(4), 209–217.

U.S. Department of Health and Human Services, Interagency Autism Coordinating Committee. (2011). *2011 strategic plan for autism spectrum disorder research* (NIH Publication No. 10-7573). Retrieved from http://iacc.hhs.gov/strategic-plan/2011/index.shtml

Vanderborght, B., Simut, R., Saldien, J., Pop, C., Rusu, A. S., & Pintea, S. et al. (2012). Using the social robot Probo as a social story telling agent for children with ASD. *Interaction Studies: Social Behaviour and Communication in Biological and Artificial Systems*, *13*(3), 348–372. doi: doi:10.1075/is.13/3/02van

Wainer, J., Ferrari, E., Dautenhahn, K., & Robins, B. (2010). The effectiveness of using a robotics class to foster collaboration among groups of children with autism in an exploratory study. *Personal and Ubiquitous Computing*, *14*, 445–455. doi: doi:10.1007/s007/s00779-009-02660z

ADDITIONAL READING

Benitti, F. B. V. (2012). Exploring the educational potential of robotics in schools: A systematic review. *Computers & Education*, *58*, 978–988. doi: doi:10.1016/j.compedu.2011.10.006

Billard, A. (2003). Roberta: Clever toy and educational tool. *Robotics and Autonomous Systems*, *42*(3-4), 259–269.

Bird, G., Leighton, J., Press, C., & Heyes, C. (2007). Intact automatic imitation of human and robot actions in autism spectrum disorders. *Proceedings. Biological Sciences*, *274*, 3027–3031. PMID:17911053

Boccanfuso, L., & O'Kane, J. M. (2011). CHARLIE: An adaptive robot design with hand and face tracking for use in autism therapy. *International Journal of Social Robotics*, *3*(4), 337–347. doi: doi:10.1007/s12369-011-0110-2

Dautenhahn, K., Nehaniv, C. L., Walters, M. L., Robins, B., Kose-Bagci, H., Mirza, N. A., & Blow, M. (2009). KASPAR: A minimally expressive humanoid robot for human-robot interaction research. *Applied Bionics & Biomechanics*, *6*(3/4), 369–397. doi: doi:10.1080/11762320903123567

Dautenhahn, K., Werry, L., Rae, J., Dickerson, P., Stribling, P., & Ogden, B. (2002). Robotic playmates: Analyzing interactive competencies of children with autism playing with a mobile robot. In K. Dautenhahn, A. Bond, L. Canamero, & B. Edmonds (Eds.), *Socially intelligent agents: Creating relationships with computers and robots* (pp. 117–124). Dordrecht, Netherlands: Kluwer Academic.

Druin, A., & Hendler, J. (2000). *Robots for kids: Exploring new technologies for learning*. San Francisco, CA: Morgan Kaufmann.

Feil-Seifer, D., Skinner, K. M., & Matarić, M. J. (2007). Benchmarks for evaluating socially assistive robotics. *Interaction Studies: Psychological Benchmarks of Human-Robot Interaction*, *8*(3), 423–439.

Fong, T., Nourbakhsh, I., & Dautenhahn, K. (2003). A survey of socially interactive robots. *Robotics and Autonomous Systems*, *42*, 143–166. doi: doi:10.1016/S0921-8890(02)00372-X

Fujimoto, I., Matsumoto, T., Kobayashi, M., Higashi, M., & de Silva, P. R. S. (2011). Mimicking and evaluating human motion to improve the imitation skill of children with autism through a robot. *International Journal of Social Robotics*, *3*(4), 349–357. doi: doi:10.1007/s12369-011-0116-9

Giannopulu, I., & Pradel, G. (2010). Multimodal interactions in free game play of children with autism and a mobile toy robot. *NeuroRehabilitation*, *27*, 305–311. doi: doi:10.3233/NRE-2010-0613 PMID:21160119

Giannopulu, I., & Pradel, G. (2012). From child-robot interaction to child-robot-therapist interaction: A case study in autism. *Applied Bionics and Biomechanics*, *9*(2), 173–179.

Goodrich, M. A., Colton, M., Brinton, B., Fukiki, M., Atherton, J. A., & Robinson, L. et al. (2012). Incorporating a robot into an autism therapy team. *IEEE Intelligent Systems*, *27*(2), 52–59. doi: doi:10.1109/MIS.2012.40

Jordan, K., King, M., Hellersteth, S., Wiren, A., & Mulligan, H. (2013). Feasibility of using a humanoid robot for enhancing attention and social skills in adolescents with autism spectrum disorder. *International Journal of Rehabilitation Research. Internationale Zeitschrift fur Rehabilitationsforschung. Revue Internationale de Recherches de Readaptation*, *36*(3), 221–227. doi: doi:10.1097/MRR.0b013e32835d0b43 PMID:23328816

Kahn, P. H., Gary, H. E., & Shen, S. (2013). Children's social relationships with current and near-future robots. *Child Development Perspectives*, *7*, 32–37. doi: doi:10.1111/cdep.12011

Kahn, P. H., Kanda, T., Ishiguro, H., Freier, N. G., Severson, R. L., & Gill, B. T. et al. (2012). Robovie, you'll have to go into the closet now: Children's social and moral relationships with a humanoid robot. *Developmental Psychology*, *48*(2), 303–314. doi: doi:10.1037/a0027033 PMID:22369338

Kozima, H., Michalowski, M. P., & Nakagawa, C. (2007). Keepon: A playful robot for research, therapy, and entertainment. *International Journal of Social Robotics*, *1*(1), 3–18. doi: doi:10.1007/s12369-008-0009-8

Lee, J., Nagai, C., Takehashi, H., Obinata, G., & Stefanov, D. (2012). Which robot features can stimulate better responses from children with autism in robot-assisted therapy? *International Journal of Advanced Robotic Systems*, *9*, 72–77. doi: doi:10.5772/51128

Leite, I., Martinho, C., & Paiva, A. (2013). Social robots for long-term interaction: A survey. *International Journal of Social Robotics*, *5*(2), 291–308.

Lui, C., Conn, K., Sarkar, N., & Stone, W. (2008). Online affect detection and robot behavior adaptation for intervention of children with autism. *IEEE Transactions on Robotics*, *24*(4), 883–896. doi: doi:10.1109/TRO.2008.2001362

Michaud, F., & Caron, S. (2002). Roball, the rolling robot. *Autonomous Robots*, *12*(2), 211–222.

Michaud, F., Salter, T., Duquette, A., & Laplante, J. F. (2007). Perspectives on mobile robots used as tools for pediatric rehabilitation. *Assistive Technology*, *19*, 14–29. PMID:17461288

Michaud, F., & Théberge-Turmel, C. (2002). Mobile robotic toys and autism. In K. Dautenhahn, A. Bond, L. Cañamero, & B. Edmonds (Eds.), *Socially Intelligent Agents* (pp. 125–132). Dordrecht, Netherlands: Kluwer Academic Publishers.

Miyamoto, E., Lee, M., & Okada, M. (2007). Robots as social agents: Developing relationships between autistic children and robots. *Japanese Journal of Developmental Psychology*, *18*(1), 78–87.

Palsbo, S., & Hood-Szivek, P. (2012). Effect of robotic-assisted three-dimensional repetitive motion to improve hand motor function and control in children with handwriting deficits: A nonrandomized phase 2 devise trial. *The American Journal of Occupational Therapy.*, *66*(6), 682–690. PMID:23106988

Pioggia, G., Igliozzi, R., Sica, M. L., Ferro, M., Muratori, F., & Ahluwalia, A. et al. (2008). Exploring emotional and imitational android-based interactions in autistic spectrum disorders. *Journal of CyberTherapy and Rehabilitation, 1,* 49–62.

Pop, C. A., Petrule, A. C., Pintea, S., Peca, A., Simut, R., Vanderborght, B., & David, D. O. (2013). Imitation and social behaviors of children with ASD in interaction with Robonova: A series of single case experiments. *Transylvanian Journal of Psychology, 14*(1), 71–91.

Reed, F. D. D., Hyman, S. H., & Hirst, J. M. (2011). Applications of technology to teach social skills to children with autism. *Research in Autism Spectrum Disorders, 5,* 1003–1010. doi:doi:10.1016/j.rasd.2011.01.022

Rick, L. D. (2012). Wizard of oz studies in HRI: A systematic review and new reporting guidelines. *Journal of Human-Robot Interaction, 1*(1), 119–136.

Ricks, D. J., & Colton, M. B. (2010). Trends and considerations in robot-assisted autism therapy. *2010 IEEE international conference on robotics and automation (IRCA),* 4354-4359. doi:10.1109/ROBOT.2010.5509327

Robins, B., Dautenhahn, K., & Dubowski, J. (2006). Does appearance matter in the interaction of children with autism with a humanoid robot? *Interaction Studies: Social Behaviour and Communication in Biological and Artificial Systems, 7,* 509–512.

Robins, B., Dautenhahn, K., Ferrari, E., Kronreif, G., Prazak-Aram, B., & Marti, P. et al. (2012). Scenarios of robot-assisted play for children with cognitive and physical disabilities. *Interaction Studies: Social Behaviour and Communication in Biological and Artificial Systems, 13*(2), 189–234. doi:doi:10.1075/is.13.2.03rob

Robins, B., Dautenhahn, K., te Boekhorst, R., & Billard, A. (2004). Effects of repeated exposure to a humanoid robot on children with autism. In S. Keates, J. Clarkson, P. Langdon, & P. Robinson (Eds.), *Designing a more inclusive world* (pp. 225–236). London: Springer Verlag.

Robins, B., Dautenhahn, K., te Boekhorst, R., & Billard, A. (2005). Robotic assistants in therapy and education of children with autism: Can a small humanoid robot encourage social interaction skills? *Universal Access in the Information Society, 4,* 115–120.

Robins, B., Dickerson, P., Stribling, P., & Dautenhahn, K. (2004). Robot-mediated joint attention in children with autism: A case study in robot–human interaction. *Interaction Studies: Social Behaviour and Communication in Biological and Artificial Systems, 5,* 161–198.

Salter, T., Michaud, F., & Larouche, H. (2010). How wild is wild? A taxonomy to categorize the wildness of child-robot interaction. *International Journal of Social Robotics, 2*(4), 405–415. doi:doi:10.1007/s12369-010-0069-4

Scassellati, B. (2007). How social robots will help us diagnose, treat, and understand autism. *Robotics Research, 28,* 552–563.

Welch, K., Lahiri, U., Warren, Z., & Sarkar, N. (2010). An approach to the design of socially acceptable robots for children with autism spectrum disorders. *International Journal of Social Robotics, 2*(4), 391–403.

Werry, I., Dautenhahn, K., Ogden, B., & Harwin, W. (2001). Can social interaction skills be taught by a social agent? The role of a robotic mediator in autism therapy. *Cognitive Technology: Instruments of the Mind, 2117*, 57–74.

KEY TERMS AND DEFINITIONS

Dyadic Interaction: Interaction between two people; or between a child and a robot.

Effectiveness: How well an intervention works in everyday settings such as schools or treatment centers.

Efficacy: How well an intervention works under ideal conditions such as controlled experimental settings.

Feasibility Study: A study conducted to determine whether an innovative idea works as planned.

Humanoid Robot: A robot physically built to look like a human.

Socially Assistive Robotics: Using robots to help people through social interaction by, for example, facilitating social interaction or fostering social skills such as joint attention and imitation.

Social Mediator: An object, such as a robot, that facilitates social interaction between or among people.

Social Robots: Robots that use verbal and/or body language to socially interact with people.

Triadic Interaction: Interaction among three people; or among a child, therapist/educator, and robot.

Wizard of Oz Technique: When this technique is used, an experimenter controls a robot's actions and responses so that the participant perceives the robot's responses as autonomous.

Chapter 12
Video Games as a Form of Therapeutic Intervention for Children with Autism Spectrum Disorders

Toby Mehl-Schneider
City University of New York, USA

Shimon Steinmetz
Brooklyn College, City University of New York, USA

ABSTRACT

The use of video games as a therapeutic intervention for children with Autism Spectrum Disorders (ASD) has steadily increased over the past years. Children with ASD tend to show a great interest in and affinity for playing video games for leisure. This chapter explores how researchers have sought to determine if this inherent motivation could be utilized to assist children with autism spectrum disorders in increasing beneficial skills needed for daily life. Video games have, therefore, been used to assist these children in improving social competence for communicative purposes, improve executive functioning skills, and increase a variety of personal performance skills. Although the variety of research studies in this subject area is expanding, there continues to be a lack of empirical research in this area, and small sample numbers of participants in the majority of the existing research. A lack of longitudinal studies, moreover, is problematic as the studies cannot demonstrate if a learned and mastered skill on a video game can carryover and transfer from the video gaming setting to everyday activities.

INTRODUCTION

Video game playing has been noted as both a beneficial and problematic form of leisure for children (Gentile, Choo, Liau, Sim, Li, Fung & Khoo, 2011; Gentile, 2009; Smyth, J.M., 2007;

Nally, Houlton & Ralph, 2000). Playing video games has also been associated with increased sensitivity to visual stimuli (Appelbaum, Cain, Darling & Mitroff, 2013). It has been determined that the playing of video games actually assisted individuals with various medical diagnoses, in-

DOI: 10.4018/978-1-4666-5792-2.ch012

creasing the mood and psychological fitness of these individuals as well as decreasing the level of their physical stress. Video gaming technology has, furthermore, been utilized to address improving physical fitness (Lotan, Yalon-Chamovitz & Weiss, 2009; Quinn, 2013). In their study on casual video games and its effect on heart rate variability (HRV) and Electrocephalography (EEG), Russoniello, O'Brien & Parks (2009) determined that video games had positive and beneficial effects on individuals with medical disorders ranging from cardiovascular disease to diabetes and depression. Furthermore, the authors recommended examining the potential benefits of video games for individuals with autism spectrum disorders (Russoniello, O'Brien & Parks, 2009).

Video games are used by a variety of disciplines in therapeutic situations. Speaking about the utilization of video games in therapy, Dr. Ceranoglu (Ceranoglu, 2010, p. 233), a psychiatrist at the Massachusetts General Hospital, stated that, "In psychiatric practice, video games aid in social skills training of children with developmental delays and in cognitive behavioral therapy (CBT)". Since video games are a motivating tool for many children, the idea of using video games to enable children to learn new skills or to increase positive behaviors is of interest to many parents, teachers and therapists alike. Utilizing video game technology for therapeutic purposes is, therefore, a beneficial tool for professionals assisting children with a variety of different deficits and challenges.

AUTISM SPECTRUM DISORDER (ASD)

The use of video game technology to assist children with ASD is considered to be a beneficial tool for a therapist to use in the therapeutic intervention setting. Autism Spectrum Disorder (ASD) is a disorder classified in the Diagnostic and Statistical Manual of Mental Disorders, Fifth Edition (DSM-V). The diagnostic criteria for this disor-

der include these five characteristics (Note: See the Diagnostic and Statistical Manual of Mental Disorders, Fifth Edition, 2013 for the complete diagnostic criteria):

Persistent deficits in social communication and social interaction across multiple contexts, as manifested by the following: Deficits in social-emotional reciprocity; Deficits in nonverbal communicative behaviors used for social interaction; Deficits in developing, maintaining, and understanding relationships.

Restricted, repetitive patterns of behavior, interests, or activities, as manifested by at least two of the following, currently or by history (examples are illustrative, not exhaustive; see text): Stereotyped or repetitive motor movements, use of objects, or speech; Insistence on sameness, inflexible adherence to routines, or ritualized patterns of verbal or nonverbal behavior; Highly restricted, fixated interests that are abnormal in intensity or focus; Hyper- or hyporeactivity to sensory input or unusual interest in sensory aspects of the environment.

Symptoms must be present in the early developmental period (but may not become fully manifest until social demands exceed limited capacities, or may be masked by learned strategies in later life).

Symptoms cause clinically significant impairment in social, occupational, or other important areas of current functioning.

These disturbances are not better explained by intellectual disability (intellectual developmental disorder) or global developmental delay. (DSM-V, 2013, 50-51)

The DSM-V diagnosis of 'autism spectrum disorder' updated and modified the previous diagnoses for individuals with these characteristics, designating that all "individuals with a well-established DSM-IV diagnosis of autistic disorder, Asperger's disorder, or pervasive developmental disorder not otherwise specified should be given the diagnosis of autism spectrum disorder," (Diagnostic and Statistical Manual, Fifth Edition, 2013). The majority of the research studies included within this chapter were conducted with children with ASD who had received a diagnosis under the DSM-IV; all of the study participants with ASD, however, are now included under the DSM-V new diagnosis of 'autism spectrum disorder'.

VIDEO GAMES: A FORM OF LEISURE FOR CHILDREN WITH ASD

The varied patterns of activity of children with ASD have been a subject of study for many researchers (Reynolds, Bendixen, Lawrence & Lane, 2011; Pan & Frey, 2006). One such activity that has been studied in the literature regarding children with ASD is the playing of video games. Various studies have assessed the amount of time that children with ASD play video games as opposed to their typically developing peers (Mazurek & Engelhardt, 2013; Mazurek & Wenstrup, 2013). In a research study conducted by Mazurek & Wenstrup (2013), the researchers determined that children with ASD spent a greater amount of time per day playing video games when compared to their typically developing peers. In assessing 202 children with ASD and 179 typically developing children, all between the ages of eight to eighteen, Mazurek & Wenstrup (2013) noted that male children with ASD spent an average of 2.4 hours per day playing video games as opposed to typically developing children, who spent 1.6 hours per day playing video games. Furthermore, female children with ASD were found to play video games 1.8 hours per day, as opposed to typically developing female children who played video games for 0.8 hours per day.

The playing of video games for leisure purposes has also been established as a negative and problematic behavior for children with ASD. In a recent sample of 169 males, aged eight to eighteen, Mazurek & Engelhardt (2013) determined that there was a high correlation between oppositional behavior and difficulty attending with video game use. There was a great variety in video game genre utilized by Mazurek & Engelhardt's study, and it was determined that "the most reliable predictors of problem behaviors were shown to be video game genre and problematic, or addictive, qualities of play," (Mazurek et al., 2013, p. 321) resulting in significantly greater inattention and oppositional behaviors on the part of the children with ASD.

Whereas social media technology was not as attractive for children with ASD, non-social media-based technology, like television and video games, were very much a part of life for a child with ASD (Mazurek, Shattuk, Wagner & Cooper, 2012). Based on their research into the use of video games, television and social media by typically developing children and children with ASD, Mazurek & Wenstrup (2013) determined that the "strong evidence for preference" for video games may be used as an "effective reinforcer that can be built into intervention programs to increase positive behaviors" (Mazurek & Wenstrup, 2013, p. 1267). For children with ASD, "a digital environment provides stimuli that are more focused, predictable, and replicable than conventional tools (Bartoli, Corradi, Garzotto & Valoriani, 2013, p.2)." The utilization of video games by this population "also reduces the confusing, multi-sensory distractions of the real world that may induce anxiety and create barriers to social communication (Bartoli et al., 2013, p. 2)."

Anderson-Hanley, Tureck and Schneiderman (2011, p. 130) stated that the, "Growing research literature demonstrates the benefits of virtual reality computer programs for improving social skills in ASD". Ploog, Scharf, Nelson & Brooks (2013) include an excellent, comprehensive chart of numerous computer-assisted technologies (CAT) that have been utilized within the research studies to aid children with autism spectrum disorders in developing a variety of different skills. On the list, video games are included as one form of computer assisted technology.

Overall, numerous research studies have determined that video games can and should be created and modified to reflect areas in which a child with ASD requires intervention, as this mode of therapy is interesting and exciting for the child with ASD. Since the reality is that "videogames and virtual reality exergames (eg, Wii) are widely utilized by youth today and specifically, are often attractive to children with pervasive developmental disorders such as ASD" (Anderson-Hanley, Tureck & Schneiderman, 2011, p. 130), these are motivating tools that can be utilized for intervention purposes to accomplish a variety of therapeutic goals.

The following sections will review current research demonstrating how video games have been utilized to assist the child with ASD increase social competence, improve facial recognition skills, increase executive function abilities, decrease repetitive behaviors, improve attention and increase responses to multiple cues in an environment. These skill sets, though varied in nature, all aim to provide an opportunity for the child with ASD to increase his or her personal performance skills via use of an engaging and motivating medium—the video game.

Social Competence Skills

As characterized by the Diagnostic and Statistical Manual of Mental Disorders, Fifth Edition (DSM-V, 2013), children with ASD demonstrate deficits in their social competence skills. Social interactions are very challenging for children with ASD and often they require assistance to improve their social communication and social play with family and peers (Baker, 2000).

Individuals with ASD often experience difficulty attending to the faces of their communication partners and maintaining appropriate eye contact during conversational exchanges (Senju & Johnson, 2009). Therapy for individuals with ASD

includes assisting each individual with this difficulty to demonstrate appropriate eye gaze during an interaction, suggesting his or her involvement and interest in the communication partner and in the conversation at hand. Eyes convey considerable meaning in communicative interactions, as "cues to the person's mental states" (Baron-Cohen, Wheelwright & Jolliffe, 1997, p. 315). Eye contact, or eye gaze, does not need to remain consistent throughout the communication exchange but does have to be intermittently reestablished.

The Autism Research Group at The Catholic University of America recognized the importance of utilizing technological advances with individuals with ASD. The group has conducted various projects using virtual reality and computer technology to increase and expand the social skill competence and proficiency of these individuals (Trepagnier, Sebrechts, Finkelmeyer, Coleman, Stewart & Werner-Adler, 2005).

Trepagnier et al. (2005) utilized a virtual environment to assess the face gaze of the individual with ASD, determining if the individual established appropriate eye gaze via a virtual reality (VR) headset with an eye tracking device. Their assessment determined that individuals with ASD tended to look at the periphery of a person's face rather than at the eyes; this resulted in the loss of information from the eye area. Based on this evaluative study, the Autism Research Group presented a therapeutic intervention to assist individuals with ASD in improving their eye gaze by creating an early intervention tool for this purpose. An eye tracker will evaluate if children aged 24 to 54 months can attend to the eye area of a face, gaining appropriate and meaningful cues from the gaze and will provides awards for each child based on his or her performance.

Virtual reality has evolved over the years as a tool for assisting children with ASD (Strickland, McAllister, Coles & Osborne, 2007). The Autism Research Group additionally developed a virtual reality game for the purpose of assisting individuals with ASD in approaching, navigating and dealing with social challenges within a busy environment. Trepagnier et al. (2005) developed a virtual mall, in which the individual with ASD controllled and manipulated an avatar to navigate a dynamic and hectic mall setting. Using a joystick, the individual controlled his or her avatar throughout the virtual reality mall setting, avoiding obstacles along the way, to arrive at a predetermined destination. The players were, moreover, prompted to describe the actions of their avatar aloud.

This virtual reality experience was tested by The Autism Research Group on eight adult participants, four females and four females, one of whom had an ASD diagnosis (mean age: 20.9). First-person exclamations expressed to describe the movements of the avatar as well as a subsequent review of the avatar's path through the mall demonstrated the players' cognizance and recognition of the social challenges of the virtual reality setting.

An interesting result of this assessment centered around the differences between the participants who played Version I of the Virtual Mall, which was a virtual reality setting presented without speech, and Version II, which was the identical setting with augmented speech. In navigating the mall in Version I, each of the four players walked his or her avatar between two virtual people in the mall, who were facing one another, presumably engaged in a communicative interaction as easily as walking between two inanimate objects on the screen.

In Version II, however, the addition of speech between the two virtual reality characters on the screen prompted the individual player to move his or her avatar around the two characters facing each other, rather than between them. On the other hand, each player using Version II did allow his or her avatar to walk between inanimate objects, demonstrating that the addition of speech to the virtual reality setting increased the socially appropriate nuances of the game.

The Autism Research Group is also undertaking a conversational interaction simulation project to assist individuals with ASD in increasing their pragmatic language and social communication skills. In collaboration with SIMmersion LLC™,, The Autism Research Group provides a scenario for an individual with ASD to communicate with a simulated character on a computer screen, enabling the individual to initiate and maintain an appropriate conversational exchange. SIMmersion LLC™, technology is an interactive simulation in which the individual user with ASD can interact with an individual on the screen, a preprogrammed video response performed by a professional actor. As the individual player speaks to the onscreen persona, the technology implements a tremendous variety of potential responses from the actor, enabling a new conversational exchange with each juncture. This practical conversational experience will assist an individual adult with ASD in pragmatic conversational language skills, including initiating and maintaining a conversational topic, turn-taking between communication partners and identifying and interpreting verbal communicative cues within the communicative interaction (Trepagnier et al., 2005).

Weiss, Gal, Eden, Zancanaro & Telch (2011) utilized multi-touch tabletop surface games to conduct a field study with children with autism spectrum disorders to augment the children's social competence skills. These video games, titled the Join-In Suite includes a cohort of games that are played and manipulated by two or three users simultaneously, necessitating social cooperation and interaction between players. This tool provided an opportunity for a child with ASD to partake in a leisurely activity with a peer, in which the peer's interaction is crucial for the program to work.

The Join-In Suite, an application to assist in learning the concept of social competence based on Cognitive-Behavior Therapy (CBT), requires active participation by users, necessitating that users interact with one-another to play the game (Guisti, Zancanaro, Gal & Weiss, 2011). The application was designed to support the work of multi-disciplinary therapists and teachers in assisting children with ASD in learning crucial social skills. In the field study by Weiss et al., (2011), three varied games were chosen to address the collaborative skills of joint performance (in the game, 'Apple Orchard'), mutual planning (in the game, 'Save the Alien') and sharing (in the game, 'Bridge'). These three goals were addressed within the application, addressing, "Joint Performance where collaboration is the performance of joint actions, Sharing where collaboration is the sharing of personal resources to achieve a common objective and Mutual Planning where collaboration requires formulation and performance of a joint plan" (Weiss et al., 2011, 73). Each of the objectives of the game was implemented to assist individuals with ASD in acquiring these skills via the game requirements. These skills are achieved via "constraints on objects" within the game to provide a situation to accomplish joint performance goals, "constraints on ownership" to accomplish sharing goals and "constraints on roles" within the game to accomplish mutual planning goals (Weiss et al., 2011, 73).

The study assessed eight boys aged nine to thirteen years old who were diagnosed with high functioning ASD. The subjects were divided into pairs, to play these social competence games with the assistance of two occupational therapists. This was a field study, providing the therapists with three questionnaires to evaluate each child's enjoyment of the games, the child's learning experience as well as each child's individual motivation. The occupational therapists, furthermore, provided feedback regarding the usability of the application.

The results of this field study determined that children enjoyed the gaming experience, rating the 'Bridge' game, which focused on increasing the children's sharing skills, as the best of the three game options; it was also determined to be the game that was easiest to use.

Based on the questionnaires which delineated the participants' overall enjoyment of the gaming experience, children preferred the 'Bridge' and 'Save the Alien' games to the Apple Orchard game. Additionally, in the two preferred games, the children exhibited greater control and success with their partners than during the 'Apple Orchard' game. Moreover, the children exhibited high cooperation for both the 'Bridge' and 'Save the Alien' game, in contrast to the 'Apple Orchard' game. In displaying their learning skills, the children determined that the three games appeared similar in their instructional functionality (Weiss et al, 2011). The therapists appreciated the inherent functionality of the Join-in Suite game system, lauding the games' ease of use and expressing interest in utilizing the tool in further therapeutic intervention sessions.

Join-In Suite and TalkAbout, two technologies using collaborative designs to increase social competence abilities were presented at the 2011 International Conference on Virtual Rehabilitation in Zurich, Switzerland (Weiss, Gal, Cobb, Millen, Hawkins, Glover, Sanassy, Zancanaro, Giusti & Eden, 2011). TalkAbout is a collaborative virtual environment (CVE) program which aims to assist users in practicing and improving their social communication abilities. Using a virtual environment, two users can interact in a social conversation with the aid of a communication facilitator, often a therapist or teacher. TalkAbout utilizes a virtual reality setting via a laptop through which the users can communicate with one another via his or her avatar within the game. The users work on increasing their individual skills in all aspects of a social communication interaction, such as Greet, Initiate, Maintain, Switch and Exit (Weiss et al., 2011).

Gotsis, Piggot, Hughes & Stone (2010) described another intervention for children with ASD: a video game for training social skills. The Social Motivation Adaptive Reality Treatment Games (SMART-Games) suite, developed through technology at the University of Southern California, aims to identify social skill difficulties of a specific child with ASD and assist him or her in increasing social competence for this area of difficulty. A notable aspect of this specific video technology is that it is designed to assist children with ASD at various levels of cognitive and language development, rather than solely addressing the high functioning children with ASD.

The SMART-Games suite includes a stuffed toy which connects technologically to an identically presented character on the computer screen. Using a Flash™ game on a portable computer and controlled by a Plush Interface Device (PID), namely a plush stuffed toy with connecting sensors, the child can play and manipulate the toy to change the onscreen version's reactions. The onscreen character's mood will visually change as the video game user interacts with the PID, displaying a happy, sad, irritable etc. mood, due to the child's manipulation of the stuffed PID. While the character displays emotion, he does not speak. The video game enables the player to both play with and train the character onscreen by simply manipulating the PID (Gotsis et al., 2010).

A pilot study of three children with ASD, two males aged eight and one female aged ten, determined that the video game was both user-friendly and accessible by all of the children. All three children demonstrated positivity and enjoyment with the tactile PID controller; utilizing it in the correct manner to effectively keep the onscreen PID character's mood positive. Following these preliminary results, Gotsis et al. (2010) proposed further development of this technology, aiming to develop the SMART-Games suite to assist children with ASD in improving a variety of social deficits.

While the majority of the video games in use today for children with ASD address increasing the social competence skills of these children, there are a variety of other video games that aim to improve other performance skills, which will be discussed in the following sections.

Facial Recognition and Facial Expression

Children with ASD have been known to display difficulties in face discrimination; even distin-

guishing familiar faces is a challenging task for some individuals with ASD. A study was conducted utilizing the facial recognition program suite Let's Face It! ™ to determine if children with ASD can enhance their face recognition skills (Tanaka, Wolf, Klaiman, Koenig, Cockburn, Herlihy, Brown, Stahl, Kaiser, Schultz, 2010). Using a treatment group (N = 42) and a control group (N = 37), they demonstrated that the twenty hour use of the facial recognition program suite Let's Face It! ™ over a period of two to four months enhanced the facial recognition skills of children with ASD. Additionally, a study by Grynszpan, Martin, & Nadel (2008, 632) used computer software to train individuals with ASD how to recognize understated and elusive pragmatic features in communication interactions "to examine the impact of emotional facial expressions on dialogue disambiguation".

Improving Attention

An example of a study which assessed the usage of previously existing and popular video games is that of Bartoli, Corradi, Garzotto & Valoriani (2013) who presented their findings at the Interaction Design and Children 2013 convention. In their study, researchers used the Xbox 360 Kinect to evaluate the attentional skills of five children with ASD. The Kinect video games included an array of virtual environments, such as Bump Bash ™ and Body Ball, ™ both virtual beach volleyball games requiring the user to coordinate his or her movements with the video game avatar playing the game on the visual screen. Other games within this study included 'Pin Rush'™, a virtual reality bowling environment and Target Kick, ™ a virtual reality soccer setting. The fifth game included in the research study is the game titled, 'It's not what you think! Honest'™, a virtual environment in which the child has to both identify and create specific appropriate body postures, via use of his or her avatar in virtual reality.

Bartoli et al. (2013) concluded that the use of the Xbox 360 Kinect video games in this research study presented evidence to support the belief that motion-based video games can advance the attention skills for children with autism. However, the authors recognize the limitations of their study, acknowledging numerous flaws in their study, among them the difficulty in measuring the causality of the noted improvements (Bartoli et al., 2013).

Multiple Cue Responding

Video games have also been created to assist and train children with ASD to responding to multiple cues in the environment simultaneously. Hiniker, Wong Daniels & Williamson (2013) created video games to assist children with multiple cue responding, based on the Pivotal Response Treatment (PVT) technique. The Pivotal Response Treatment technique has been discussed in many research papers on autism spectrum disorders (Koegel, R. L., Fredeen, Kim, Danial, Rubinstein, & Koegel, L., 2012; Bellini & Peters, 2008; Koegel, R. L., Koegel, L. K. & McNerney, E., 2001; Koegel, L. K., Koegel, R. L., Harrower, & Carter, 1999; Koegel, L., Koegel, R. L., Shoshan, & McNerney, 1999). One of PVT's targeted areas of intervention is the ability of the individual to respond to multiple cues; the 'Go Go Games' therapeutic suite of games is based on this targeted area (Hiniker, Wong Daniels & Williamson, 2013, 463).

'Multiple cue responding' refers to identifying different pieces of information and maintaining the features concurrently in order to make a specific decision. Hiniker et al. (2103, 463) provides the example of viewing a green, left turn arrow as a signal to turn when driving as multiple cue responding, since the driver needs to both notice the color and the shape of the arrow to respond correctly; had either of the two cues been different, the driver's decision would have been altered. It is a crucial skill for children with ASD to learn to notice multiple cues simultaneously and not to focus and attend to solely one cue at a time.

The author's goal in creating a game for children with ASD was to use evidence-based practice therapies in game creation (Hiniker et al., 2013); hence, their use of 'multiple cue responding' as a target feature of the PVT behavioral intervention. The suite of games which they developed, including Build - a –Train ™, Wheels and Roads ™ and Out of this World ™, all require the user to designate a particular choice from a number of presented options. In Build - a –Train ™, the user must construct a train on the screen, choosing the train cars from presented choices; in 'Wheels and Roads', the user must drive a vehicle down a particular road marked by various signs; in Out of this World ™, the user constructs a robot, utilizing body pieces presented on an assembly line. In each game, users can choose the correct item by using multiple cues simultaneously presented to identify the targeted item.

Although 'Go Go Games' have been created with the feedback of thirty children with ASD, the authors of the paper state their intent of using the suite of games for an efficacy study. Hiniker et al. (2013) aim to evaluate the level of involvement of children with ASD in playing the video games and assessing their skills in responding to multiple cues.

Carlile, Reeve, Reeve and DeBar (2013) taught four eight to ten-year-old children with ASD how to use an activity schedule on an iPod touch without prompts. Typically, a written schedule is cumbersome and may even be a socially stigmatizing format for a child with ASD in a school setting. Utilizing participants who had some prior experience using an iPod touch, but had been unable to follow a written schedule or exhibit on-task behavior, these children learned to follow their schedule and increased on-task behavior. The students were able to generalize this skill even without the experimenter present.

Prosody and Content

In a research study by Ploog, Banerjee & Brooks (2009), a video game was used to observe the attention of children with ASD towards prosody and content and to determine if there were any differences between how typically developing children and children with ASD perceived intonation and content in presented sentences.

In this study, the results indicated that children with autism spectrum disorders displayed no demonstrated preference for the presented content in the sentences over the presented intonation of the sentences, while typically developing children displayed a preference for the content of the sentences over the intonation of the sentences. Children with autism spectrum disorders are noted to demonstrate interesting attending behavior patterns, and the research data supported the notion that children with ASD have weak central coherence, in which they process peripheral sensory details as opposed to the general informational framework presented (Ploog et al., 2009).

Although this study did not utilize the video game for the expressed purpose of teaching a particular skill to children with ASD, but rather as an assessment tool, the authors of this research study suggest that the game could be used for therapeutic intervention purposes. Ploog et al. (2009, p. 754) recommend that the game could be utilized to improve the child with ASD's attending behaviors, "by scheduling specific contingencies that provide extra reinforcers for attention to a given neglected stimulus dimension".

Increasing Executive Function and Decreasing Repetitive Behaviors

Varied studies have demonstrated the relationship between executive function and individuals with ASD. Lopez, Lincoln, Ozonoff & Lai (2005) determined that varied executive function processes were highly correlated with restricted and repetitive symptoms of ASD. The terminology, "executive function" refers to numerous brain functions, such as "working memory, planning, impulse control, inhibition, and the shifting and control of attention (Johnson, 2012, p. 454)." It can also include cognitive flexibility, creativity and initiating action (Sachse, Schlitt, Hainz, Ciaramidaro, Schirman, Walter, Poustka, Bolte, & Freitag, 2013; Hill, 2004). Although "executive dysfunction in children with ASDs is not universal," (Rosenthal, Wallace, Lawson, Wills, Dixon, Yerys, & Kenworthy, 2013, p. 14) it does affect many children on the spectrum.

Anderson-Hanley, Tureck & Schneiderman (2011) conducted a study to utilize exergaming activities to both attempt to increase executive function abilities in individuals with ASD as well as, simultaneously, attempting to decrease their repetitive behaviors. Exergaming is terminology for video and virtual reality games in which the individual player can exercise in a variety of different ways. Examples of exergaming activities include tennis, bowling and other activities on the Wii console (Anderson-Hanley et al., 2011) as well as the PCGamerBike™, a bike connected to the computer screen, in which the individual user's pedal motion on the bike controls the character's motion of the vehicle on the computer screen (See www.pcgamerbike.com, for more information). Exergaming is considered a fun and exciting mode of exercise, as the exergame user is focused on accomplishing a goal on the screen and must exercise accordingly in order to attain and achieve the objective of the onscreen game.

Dance Dance Revolution™ (DDR) is a popular exergame developed by Konami in 1998, last updated in 2013. This exergame requires the user to stand on a dance platform which features colored arrows on the stage. The objective of the game is for the user to imitate the dance moves on the screen, dancing on the appropriate arrows of the dance platform. DDR™ has been utilized in varied school research studies, which have promoted and advocated increased physical activity among the students. For instance, Dance Dance Revolution™ technology has been utilized as a means of intervention to counter childhood obesity in the school setting (Quinn, 2013). Anderson-Hanley et al. (2011, p. 131) states that, "Since compliance with exercise can be challenging at any age, but especially among clinical populations with ASD, exergaming holds particular promise as an exercise intervention given the research previously noted on increased motivation, enjoyment, and energy expenditure."

In Anderson-Hanley's (2011) pilot study, twelve subjects (mean age: 14.8) participated in the Dance Dance Revolution™ exergame. The repetitive behaviors as well as the executive function skills were assessed prior to the twenty minute exergaming session and again following the exergaming experience.

To evaluate the repetitive behaviors of the individual participant, a videotape was made for the five minutes prior to and following the control and exergaming activities. To assess executive function, three tasks were administered: Digit Span Forward and Backward, Color Trails Test and Stroop task; each of these tasks were administered using the standardized approach, in order to determine the executive function abilities or difficulties of the individual study participant. Furthermore, the Gilliam Autism Results Scale, 2nd edition (GARS-2) was administered by each participant's parent or guardian, in order to assess the individual participant's severity of ASD.

Results of this pilot study indicated that there was a significant decrease in repetitive behaviors following the exergaming session, compared with the control group. Furthermore, following the exergaming session, the subjects' performance on the Digits Backwards task improved. However, in assessing the Stroop task, the subjects' performance decreased in the time taken to complete the task, both for the control and for the exercise conditions, indicating a weaker performance following the exergaming session.

Anderson-Hanley et al. (2011) conducted a second pilot study, assessing twenty-two participants (mean age: 13.2) in performing a cybercycling exergame, in which a stationary bike is connected to a video game on a computer screen. The objective of the exergame is to enable the user to pedal and steer the bike according to the simultaneous onscreen virtual reality site. This cybercycling game was connected to Dragon Chase™ in which the player endeavors to earn game points while accomplishing different onscreen chases and missions (Anderson-Hanley, 2011). Similar to the first pilot study, assessing the effect of the DDR™ exergame on executive function skills, the results of the cybercyling study indicated that there was a significant decrease in repetitive behaviors following the cybercycling and improvement was noted in the Digits Backwards task as well (Anderson-Hanley, 2011).

Video Games for Leisure: Improving Engagement

Leisure activities are an important part of socialization, and increasing and expanding one's leisure skill abilities enables the individual to connect with another individual over a relaxing or enjoyable activity. Numerous studies have investigated the potential benefits of leisure activities for children with autism, as some of these children tend to demonstrate deficits in this area (Matson, Hattier & Belva, 2012). Oppenheim-Leaf, Leaf & Call (2012) instructed two children with ASD in learning how to play a variety of age appropriate card games and board games, while Charlop-Christy & Freeman (2000) taught a child with ASD how to play card games using video modeling and in-vivo (live) modeling.

Blum-Dimaya, Reeve, Reeve & Hoch (2010) instructed four children with ASD on how to play Guitar Hero II™, a guitar simulation video game. The objective of their study was to teach children with ASD how to participate appropriately in an age-appropriate leisure skill, following use of an activity schedule, for the purpose of increasing quality of life.

In Guitar Hero II™, the player is provided with a guitar-shaped controller to utilize with the video game simulation. Each time a specific music note is auditorily and visually presented on the television screen, the player is required to press the corresponding, matching button on the guitar controller. The aim of the video game is to allow the player to be the guitarist of the virtual band in the video game; the player can do this by carefully following the notes on-screen and pressing and strumming on the controller accordingly.

In the study by Blum-Dimaya et al. (2010), the video game mode was set to "practice", providing each child with the simplest and slowest setting, to increase the ease of the activity. The accuracy of the children was not assessed; rather, each child was assessed based on his or her ability to utilize a photographic activity schedule which evaluated the child's ability to set up the video game and controller, select a setting for the game, play the song and complete the game.

The results of this study indicated that all of the children participating in the study were able to successfully demonstrate efficiency in playing the Guitar Hero II™ game. An unforeseen result of the study occurred as well, as the children demonstrated abilities in carrying over and generalizing this game playing skill to their home setting. Moreover, the children demonstrated significant accuracy and appropriate playing of another song as well, suggesting that the skill generalized to another similar task. Blum-Dimaya et al. (2010, p. 367) explains that the "generalization of game playing to the home setting in the current study increases the functionality of this leisure skill."

LIMITATIONS OF INTERVENTION

A plausible limitation of utilizing video games for children with ASD as an intervention or therapeutic tool to teach a specific concept or concepts is that the individual manipulating the game is confined to the various solutions that the game presents. An important part of increasing the competence skills of a child with ASD is providing the child with opportunities to learn how to interact appropriately in a variety of settings; many of these situations are significantly challenging for the individual with ASD due to extensive social nuances that are present in our everyday socialization. While some video experiences aim to "encourage children to create and insert their own alternative solutions, and not rely solely on those presented by the software," (Weiss et al., 2011, p. 74), the very nature of video gaming technology binds the user to the choices therein, decreasing their ability to attempt numerous solutions to social problems, and ultimately learning how to truly increase their social competence skills.

The use of video games by children with ASD to acquire a variety of social skills can be developed as one part of a therapeutic strategy. Mazurek & Wenstrup (2013, p. 1267) state that, "Care must also be taken to develop strategies for building generalization from solitary screen-media formats to real-world social situations, particularly given the current evidence that children with ASD do not appear to commonly initiate socially interactive screen-based media use". Although children with ASD show great interest in video gaming technology, the same children demonstrate markedly less interest in social media, such as email and communication over various social media forms. Therefore, it is crucial that any research including video games must endeavor to carry over the skill to the interactive technological arena, assisting children with ASD in using their technological skills to communicate socially through a technological medium.

FUTURE RESEARCH

There is a significant need for future studies in the area of video games as an intervention tool for children with autism spectrum disorders. Future research is needed on the carryover and generalization of any social skills to the real-world situations which the video games target. Although children may demonstrate improvements in social skills using video game technology, the real test of a child's skill enhancement is if he or she can generalize the learned skill into reality settings.

Moreover, it is important to determine if video games are providing an efficacious and beneficial form of treatment, as compared to measurable gains made in conventional therapeutic intervention. Ploog et al. (2013), in their comprehensive overview of the research conducted on computer-assisted technology (CAT) utilized by children with autism spectrum disorders, concluded that "although many studies illustrate the tremendous promise of CAT to enhance skills of individuals with ASD, most lack rigorous, scientific assessment of efficacy relative to non-CAT approaches" (Ploog et al., 2013, p. 301). This determination extends to video games, a novel technology utilized recently as a tool for therapeutic intervention purposes.

This is due to the fact that the majority of the research in this area uses a significantly small number of participants to test the variety of video games and their effects—or lack thereof—on the target population of children with ASD. Utilizing only a small sample of children with ASD to assess any particular video game does not fully demonstrate the possible effectiveness or benefits of a specific form of technology. Longitudinal studies, moreover, as well as studies with numerous subjects are needed to replicate many of the previous studies conducted on the beneficial nature of video games for therapeutic intervention for children with ASD.

Many studies in this subject area, furthermore, included background data about the child with ASD solely from parental reports about the child's social and behavioral history. In future studies, it would be beneficial for the researchers to directly assess the child with ASD themselves and to evaluate the varied exhibited behaviors on a case-by-case basis, prior to conducting the research.

Moreover, therapists should be involved in the design process for the various video games utilized for intervention, with the purpose of improving the games to better suit the needs of the user and the assisting therapist (Annema, Verstraete, Abeele, Desmet & Geerts, 2010). The collaborative process between therapists and game designers is crucial in creating appropriate therapeutic video games for children (Ceranoglu, 2010) to better assist the children in making valuable therapeutic gains.

Overall, a 2010 editorial in *Autism* stated that, "Technological advances can potentially lead to novel and more effective treatment strategies and enhance the quality of life for people with ASD and their families" (Bolte, Golan, Goodwin & Zwaigenbaum, 2010, p. 155). Although this is the overriding, present understanding, there is still much work to be done before this dream can become a reality.

REFERENCES

American Psychiatric Association. (2013). *Diagnostic and statistical manual of mental disorders* (5th ed.). Arlington, VA: American Psychiatric Publishing.

Anderson-Hanley, C., Tureck, K., & Schneiderman, R. L. (2011). Autism and exergaming: Effects on repetitive behaviors and cognition. *Psychology Research and Behavior Management, 4*, 129–137. PMID:22114543

Annema, J. H., Verstraete, M., Abeele, V. V., Desmet, S., & Geerts, D. (2010). *Videogames in therapy: A therapist's perspective.* Paper presented at Fun and Games 2010. Leuven, Belgium.

Appelbaum, L. G., Cain, M. S., Darling, E. F., & Mitroff, S. R. (2013). Action video game playing is associated with improved visual sensitivity, but not alterations in visual sensory memory. *Attention, Perception & Psychophysics, 75*, 1161–1167. PMID:23709062

Baker, M. J. (2000). Incorporating the thematic ritualistic behaviors of children with autism into games: Increasing social play interactions with siblings. *Journal of Positive Behavior Interventions, 2*(2), 66–84.

Baron-Cohen, S., Wheelwright, S., & Jolliffe, T. (1997). Is there a language of the eyes? Evidence from normal adults, and adults with autism or asperger syndrome. *Visual Cognition, 4*(3), 311–331.

Bartoli, L., Corradi, C., Garzotto, F., & Valoriani, M. (2013). *Exploring motion-based touchless games for autistic children's learning.* Paper presented at the Interaction Design and Children '13. New York, NY.

Bellini, S., & Peters, J. K. (2008). Social skills training for youth with autism spectrum disorders. *Child and Adolescent Psychiatric Clinics of North America, 17*(4), 857–873. PMID:18775374

Blum-Dimaya, A., Reeve, S. A., Reeve, K. F., & Hoch, H. (2010). Teaching children with autism to play a video game using activity schedules and game-embedded simultaneous video modeling. *Education & Treatment of Children, 33*(3), 351–370.

Bolte, S., Golan, O., Goodwin, M. S., & Zwaigenbaum, L. (2010). Editorial: What can innovative technologies do for autism spectrum disorders? *Autism, 14*(3), 155–159. PMID:20603897

Carlile, K. A., Reeve, S. A., Reeve, K. F., & DeBar, R. M. (2013). Using activity schedules on the iPod touch to teach leisure skills to children with autism. *Education & Treatment of Children, 36*(2), 33–57.

Ceranoglu, T. A. (2010). Star Wars in psychotherapy: Video games in the office. *Academic Psychiatry, 34*, 233–236. PMID:20431107

Ceranoglu, T. A. (2010). Video games in psychotherapy. *Review of General Psychology, 14*(2), 141–146.

Charlop-Christy, M. H., Le, L., & Freeman, K. A. (2000). A comparison of video modeling with in vivo modeling for teaching children with autism. *Journal of Autism and Developmental Disorders, 30*(6), 537–552. PMID:11261466

Gentile, D. (2009). Pathological video-game use among youth ages 8 to 18: A national study. *Psychological Science, 20*(5), 594–602. PMID:19476590

Gentile, D. A., Choo, H., Liau, A., Sim, T., Li, D., Fung, D., & Khoo, A. (2011). Pathological video game use among youths: A two-year longitudinal study. *Pediatrics, 127*, e319–e329. PMID:21242221

Giusti, L., & Zancanaro, M. Gal, E., & Weiss, P. L. T. (2011). Dimensions of collaboration on a tabletop interface for children with autism spectrum disorder. In *Proceedings of Conference on Human Factors in Computing Systems* (CHI 2011). Vancouver, Canada: ACM.

Gotsis, M., Piggot, J., Hughes, D., & Stone, W. (2010). SMART-games: A video game intervention for children with autism spectrum disorders. In *Proceedings of the 9th International Conference on Interaction Design and Children.* ACM.

Grynszpan, O., Martin, J., & Nadel, J. (2008). Multimedia interfaces for users with high functioning autism: An empirical investigation. *International Journal of Human-Computer Studies, 66*, 628–639.

Hill, E. L. (2004). Evaluating the theory of executive dysfunction in autism. *Developmental Review, 24*, 189–233.

Hiniker, A., Wong Daniels, J., & Williamson, H. (2013). *Go go games: Therapeutic video games for children with autism spectrum disorders.* New York, NY: IDC.

Johnson, M. H. (2012). Executive function and developmental disorders: The flip side of the coin. *Trends in Cognitive Sciences, 16*(9), 454–457. PMID:22835639

Koegel, L. K., Koegel, R. L., Harrower, J. K., & Carter, C. M. (1999). Pivotal response intervention I: Overview of approach. *Research and Practice for Persons with Severe Disabilities, 24*(3), 174–185.

Koegel, L. K., Koegel, R. L., Shoshan, Y., & McNerney, E. (1999). Pivotal response intervention II: Preliminary long-term outcome data. *Research and Practice for Persons with Severe Disabilities, 24*(3), 186–198.

Koegel, R. L., Fredeen, R., Kim, S., Danial, J., Rubinstein, D., & Koegel, L. (2012). Using perseverative interests to improve interactions between adolescents with autism and their typical peers in school settings. *Journal of Positive Behavior Interventions, 14*(3), 133–141. PMID:24163577

Koegel, R. L., Koegel, L. K., & McNerney, E. (2001). Pivotal areas in intervention for autism. *Journal of Clinical Child Psychology, 30*(1), 19–32. PMID:11294074

Lopez, B. R., Lincoln, A. J., Ozonoff, S., & Lai, Z. (2005). Examining the relationship between executive functions and restricted, repetitive symptoms of autistic disorder. *Journal of Autism and Developmental Disorders, 35*(4), 445–460. PMID:16134030

Lotan, M., Yalon – Chamovitz, S., & Weiss, P. L. (2009). Improving physical fitness of individuals with intellectual and developmental disability through a virtual reality intervention program. *Research in Developmental Disabilities, 30,* 229–239. PMID:18479889

Matson, J. L., Hattier, M. A., & Belva, B. (2012). Treating adaptive living skills of persons with autism using applied behavior analysis: A review. *Research in Autism Spectrum Disorders, 6,* 271–276.

Mazurek, M. O., & Engelhardt, C. R. (2013). Video game use and problem behaviors in boys with autism spectrum disorders. *Research in Autism Spectrum Disorders, 7,* 316–324.

Mazurek, M. O., & Engelhardt, C. R. (2013). Video game use in boys with autism spectrum disorder, ADHD, or typical development. *Pediatrics, 132*(2), 260–266. PMID:23897915

Mazurek, M. O., Shattuck, P. T., Wagner, M., & Cooper, B. P. (2012). Prevalence and correlates of screen-based media use among youths with autism spectrum disorders. *Journal of Autism and Developmental Disorders, 42,* 1757–1767. PMID:22160370

Mazurek, M. O., & Wenstrup, C. (2013). Television, video game and social media use among children with ASD and typically developing siblings. *Journal of Autism and Developmental Disorders, 43,* 1258–1271. PMID:23001767

Nally, B., Houlton, B., & Ralph, S. (2000). Researches in brief: The management of television and video by parents of children with autism. *Autism, 4*(3), 331–337.

Oppenheim-Leaf, M. L., Leaf, J. B., & Call, N. A. (2012). Teaching board games to two children with an autism spectrum disorder. *Journal of Developmental and Physical Disabilities, 24,* 347–358.

Pan, C. Y., & Frey, G. C. (2006). Physical activity patterns in youth with autism spectrum disorders. *Journal of Autism and Developmental Disorders, 36,* 597–606. PMID:16652237

Ploog, B. O., Banerjee, S., & Brooks, P. J. (2009). Attention to prosody (intonation) and content in children with autism and in typical children using spoken sentences in a computer game. *Research in Autism Spectrum Disorders, 3*(3), 743–758.

Ploog, B. O., Scharf, A., Nelson, D., & Brooks, P. J. (2013). Use of computer-assisted technologies (CAT) to enhance social, communicative, and language development in children with autism spectrum disorders. *Journal of Autism and Developmental Disorders, 43*, 301–322. PMID:22706582

Quinn, M. (2013). Introduction of active video gaming into the middle school curriculum as a school-based childhood obesity intervention. *Journal of Pediatric Health Care, 27*(1), 3–12. PMID:23237611

Reynolds, S., Bendixen, R. M., Lawrence, T., & Lane, S. J. (2011). A pilot study examining activity participation, sensory responsiveness, and competence in children with high functioning autism spectrum disorder. *Journal of Autism and Developmental Disorders, 41*, 1496–1506. PMID:21221753

Rosenthal, M., Wallace, G. L., Lawson, R., Wills, M. C., Dixon, E., Yerys, B. E., & Kenworthy, L. (2013). Impairments in real-world executive function increase from childhood to adolescence in autism spectrum disorders. *Neuropsychology, 27*(1), 13–18. PMID:23356593

Russoniello, C. V., O'Brien, K., & Parks, J. M. (2009). The effectiveness of casual video games in improving mood and decreasing stress. *Journal of CyberTherapy & Rehabilitation, 2*(1), 53–66.

Senju, A., & Johnson, M. H. (2009). Atypical eye contact in autism: Models, mechanisms and development. *Neuroscience and Biobehavioral Reviews, 33*, 1204–1214. PMID:19538990

Smyth, J. M. (2007). Beyond self-selection in video game play: An experimental examination of the consequences of massively multiplayer online role-playing game play. *Cyberpsychology & Behavior, 10*(5), 717–721. PMID:17927543

Strickland, D. C., McAllister, D., Coles, C. D., & Osbourne, S. (2007). An evolution of virtual reality training designs for children with autism and fetal alcohol spectrum disorders. *Topics in Language Disorders, 27*(3), 226–241. PMID:20072702

Tanaka, J. W., Wolf, J. M., Klaiman, C., Koenig, K., Cockburn, J., & Herlihy, L. et al. (2010). Using computerized games to teach face recognition skills to children with autism spectrum disorder: The let's face it! program. *Journal of Child Psychology and Psychiatry, and Allied Disciplines, 51*(8), 944–952. PMID:20646129

Trepagnier, C. Y., Sebrechts, M. M., Finkelmeyer, A., Coleman, M., Stewart, W. Jr, & Werner-Adler, M. (2005). Virtual environments to address autistic social deficits. *Annual Review of Cybertherapy and Telemedicine, 3*, 101–107.

Weiss, P. L. T., Gal, E., Cobb, S., Millen, L., Hawkins, T., & Glover, T. … Eden, S. (2011). Usability of technology supported social competence training for children on the autism spectrum. In *Proceedings of International Conference on Virtual Rehabilitation 2011.* Zurich, Switzerland: Academic Press.

Weiss, P. L. T., Gal, E., Eden, S., Zancanaro, M., & Telch, F. (2011). Usability of a multi-touch tabletop surface to enhance social competence training for children with autism spectrum disorder. In *Proceedings of the Chais Conference on Instructional Technologies Research 2011: Learning in the Technological Era.* Raanana, Israel: The Open University in Israel.

Chapter 13
Video Modeling for Individuals with Autism Spectrum Disorders

Christine R. Ogilvie
University of West Florida, USA

Peggy Whitby
University of Arkansas, USA

ABSTRACT

Individuals with Autism Spectrum Disorders (ASD) will struggle to different degrees with social communication skills. To facilitate the learning of new social skills and to allow for repetition and practice, video modeling is being utilized in the PreK-12 setting. This chapter describes behaviors inherent to individuals with autism spectrum disorders that could benefit from the use of video modeling as an intervention, or part of an intervention, as well as a step-by-step description on how to effectively implement video modeling. Additionally, examples of data collection forms, permission forms, and other helpful resources are provided.

INTRODUCTION

According to the National Autism Center (NAC) (2009), video modeling is a research-based intervention that can be used to enhance communication, cognitive functions, personal responsibility and play/social skills, it can also decrease problem behaviors and sensory/emotional difficulties. There are several types of video modeling techniques, often times video modeling is combined with other types of strategies such as prompting and reinforcement. In order for video modeling to serve as an effective intervention, teachers, parents, and Individualized Education Program (IEP) teams must first understand the research behind the effectiveness, the types and components of video modeling, and how to create and then implement the intervention with fidelity. The purpose of this chapter is to describe the behaviors inherent in individuals with autism spectrum disorders that could benefit from the use of video modeling as an intervention or part

DOI: 10.4018/978-1-4666-5792-2.ch013

of an intervention as well as a step by step description on how to effectively implement video modeling interventions. Additionally, examples of data collection forms, permission forms, and other helpful resources will be provided. Finally, a comprehensive list of further reading and web resources highlighting the research-base behind video modeling is included.

Why use Video Modeling?

Video modeling capitalizes on the strengths and preferred interests of individuals with ASD while addressing the skill deficit area. Many individuals with ASD have strengths in visual processing and a preference for visual media along with deficits in social communication/interaction.

Strengths of individuals with ASD include "visual discrimination skills, and visual spatial processing, and the capacity to focus or sustain attention for static visual information" (Tsatsanis, 2004, p. 62). Numerous studies also document relative strengths in visual processing (Fullerton, 1996; Huang & Wheeler, 2006; Quill, 2000; Rubin & Lenin, 2004). The National Autism Center (NAC) (2009) lists visual strategies as an established intervention. Learning social skills through watching videos with clearly defined action steps capitalizes on visual strengths of individuals with ASD. Visual media, such as video models, is a type of visual strategy. A well-constructed video model intervention captures and maintains the attention of individuals with ASD, allowing for more in-depth learning of new skills because of the absence of unnecessary distractions (Bellini & Akullian, 2007; Wilson, 2013).

Technology is highly reinforcing and preferred activity for many individuals with ASD (Bellini & Akullian, 2007; Sherer et al., 2001). Stumey (2003) reported that "video technology has proven useful as a tool for modeling appropriate behavior, providing feedback, and creating discriminating opportunities for the child's own behavior and as a medium for presenting basic instruction that many children find engaging (p. 168; in Goldsmith & LeBlanc, 2004). Moore, Cheng, McGrath, and Powell (2005) reported that people with ASD often have a natural affinity for technology, often thrive in the controlled environment offered by the computer, and often value the repetitive nature of some computer tasks. Moreover, Moore, McGrath, and Thorpe (2000) as cited in el Kaliouby, Picard, and Baron-Cohen (2006), reported that "many persons with ASD prefer to communicate with and through computers because they are predictable and place some control on the otherwise chaotic social world" (p. 237).

Shane et al. (2011) describe the role of technology in society as "burgeoning" while more and more professionals working with individuals with ASD and their families adopt new technologies to facilitate not only every day communication but also social and functional skills. Video technology is among the most cost-effective, readily available technology is for individuals working or living with someone with ASD (Goldsmith & LeBlanc, 2004; Huang & Wheeler, 2006; Nikopoulos, Canavan, & Nikopoulou-Smymi, 2009). Access to simple

Box 1. Case study part 1: Introducing Noah

Noah is a twelve year old boy with a diagnosis of Asperger's syndrome. He is currently starting sixth grade and is in mostly general education classes with the exception of a study/social skills class in the resource room setting and a gifted math class. Since transitioning from elementary to middle school, Noah has experienced a lot of changes in his daily schedule, some of which resulted in a full meltdown at school due to his difficulty in handling unexpected changes. Last week in the cafeteria, Noah's lunch period was interrupted by a fire drill. Noah refused to leave the cafeteria with his classmates and began to pace up and down near the lunch table. When approached by a peer who asked Noah to walk outside with him, Noah became upset and yelled to "Leave me alone and let me eat my lunch!" Noah put his hands over his ears and hummed. He was approached by his math teacher who spoke softly to Noah and was able to lead him out of the cafeteria with the rest of his class. Outside, Noah continued to block his ears and hum and refused to stand with his class.

recording devices has become more widespread. Most hand-held media devices include a video function and the prices of digital cameras have become more reasonable as new technologies emerge (Shane et al., 2011).

Video modeling incorporates the modeling strategies first introduced in the 1970s by Bandura (Bandura, 1977). Bandura demonstrated that modeling has a profound impact on the development of children and that children acquire skills through observing other people performing the skills (Bandura, 1977). However, even Bandura agreed that if a person can't direct and maintain attention to the relevant features of a model, learning may not occur. Video modeling for students with ASD addresses the issue of directing and maintaining attention by using a highly preferred mode of instruction and through carefully designing the model to include only relevant stimuli by removing the distractions in the environment. Video modeling simplifies the modeling process in terms of ease of repetition (i.e., pressing "play" for video is much faster than getting the same group together to replay the desired behavior). The ease of repetition allows intervention teams to use the video model as a prime. Priming consists of previewing the behavior in less demanding settings before the behavior should occur. Video modeling involves a child watching a video of specific behaviors and then imitating the behavior(s) in the

video (Bellini & Akullian, 2007). Video modeling can be utilized across many settings and for individuals of varying abilities.

The research on video modeling for students with ASD has increased in recent years. The National Autism Center (NAC) (2009) published a report in recent years that included video modeling as an established practice for communication, higher level cognitive functions, interpersonal skills, personal responsibility skills, and play skills for children aged 3-18. The 50 studies upon which this report was based were held to high standards of rigor in their research design, implementation, data collection, and results. Additionally, video modeling meets the Council for Exceptional Children's criteria for evidence-based practices (Bellini & Akullian, 2007). To become an evidence-based practice, a program/intervention must have data to support its use as beneficial to individuals with exceptional needs. It is important to note, also, that the data must have been derived / collected from rigorously designed research projects.

For individuals with ASD, difficulties in social interactions may include impairment of nonverbal behaviors such as facial expression, eye gaze, and posture (American Psychiatric Association, 2004). Additionally, deficits in social functioning associated with an ASD include a failure to create and maintain developmentally appropriate relationships with peers (Volkmar & Tidmarsh,

Box 2. Case study part 2: Determining the need and intervention

Noah's recent incident at lunch has prompted his Individualized Education Program (IEP) team to get together and plan an intervention to help Noah better handle unexpected schedule changes. Since his behavior was also a safety risk (i.e., if it hadn't been a drill), the team discussed the necessity of providing Noah with adaptive instructions on safe and acceptable behaviors during fire drills. The first goal of the team, which included Noah, was to create a video model of a coping strategy that Noah could use when there was an unexpected change in his schedule. The team started by determining the steps of the coping strategy. They decided on the following steps for Noah to take to cope with unexpected schedule changes:

1. When an unexpected schedule change occurs, I can stop, take a deep breath, and count to ten before I react.
2. Think to myself, "What are my choices right now?"
3. In my head, list the choices.
4. Squeeze my stress ball when I think about my choices.
5. Act on the best choice for that situation.

The team decided to create a video model of Noah acting out the steps of the skill that he could watch on his iPod at the beginning of each day to practice this coping strategy.

2003). Any skill that can be divided into distinct steps for a task analysis can be developed into a video model. However, the type of video model chosen should be based upon the skill need and level of the student.

HOW TO CHOOSE WHICH TYPE OF VIDEO MODEL IS APPROPRIATE

There are three main types of video modeling: video prompting, video modeling, and video self-modeling. According to Wilson (2013), while considerations for age, gender, race/ethnicity, and preferences should be taken:

Research has not documented any difference between the effectiveness of video modeling when conducted with self or other as the model (Bellini & Akullian, 2007; Sherer et al., 2001), and the intervention has been proven effective using all types of models, including peers, adults, and self (McCoy & Hermansen, 2007). Consideration of an individual student's traits (e.g., age, gender) and preferences, as well as the nature of the target skill, will dictate the character (p. 108).

Video prompting involves showing a video clip of one step of a task then allowing the students to complete the step before the next step is shown (Bereznek, Ayres, Mechling, & Alexander, 2012; Cihak, Alberto, Taber-Doughty, & Gama, 2006). This technique is frequently used to model job and daily living skills. In a study by Bereznek, Ayres, Mechling, and Alexander (2012), three high school-age male students with diagnoses of an ASD were taught using video self-prompting via an iPhone. Two of the three students learned how to self-prompt with the iPhone and went on to teach themselves the targeted skills.

Video modeling involves creating of a video of someone performing a target behavior, then showing the video to a student and prompting him/her to engage in the behavior. In 2000, Charlop-Christy,

Le, and Freeman compared video modeling with in vivo modeling and reported that video modeling can be more effective in promoting generalization of skills because it increases the amount of time the child maintains focus, utilizes a "user-friendly" format to present skills in systematic steps, and is a less emotional way for individuals with ASD to learn. Video modeling can be used for any skill. It is best to use a model of the same age and gender. Many times friends or siblings will agree to be the video model. Video models must be used when the student cannot perform the skill with prompts or the prompting is so complex, they cannot be edited out of the video.

Similar to video modeling, video self-modeling involves the creation of a video of someone performing a target behavior, except in this case, the individual imitates the target behavior by observing him/herself engaged in the target behavior. In a 2010 study by Bellini and McConnell, a case for video self-modeling was made. Video self-modeling, as stated in Bellini and McConnell (2010), "deluges the child with visual representations of personal success" (p. 221). Dowrick (1999) reported that video self-modeling interventions produced significant intervention effects on participants and these effects were transferred across settings. Video modeling can be used when a child is able to perform the task with prompts and the prompts can be easily edited out of the final product.

Identifying Target Behaviors

One benefit of video modeling is that it can be used to impact a multitude of behaviors (Table 1). Any behavior that can be broken down into individual steps can be easily adapted to video modeling. However, many social skills curricula have already provided task analysis of specific behaviors.

One resource available to teach social skills is the *Skillstreaming* series by Goldstein and McGinnis (1997). While not specifically designed for

Table 1. Skills and sample behaviors impacted by video modeling

Skill Type	Sample Behaviors
Social Interaction Skills	Introducing oneself (Kagohara et al., 2013) Initiating conversation (Shukla-Mehta, Miller, & Callahan, 2010) Interpreting nonverbal cues (Bellini & Akullian, 2007)
Academic Skills	Solving word problems (Burton, Anderson, Prater, & Dyches, 2013) Completing work (Prater, Carter, Hitchcock, & Dowrick, 2012) Spelling (Kinney, Vedora, & Stromer, 2003)
Functional Skills	Attending / focusing (Plavnick, 2012) Completing tasks in the workplace (Mechling & Ayres, 2012) Hand washing (Rosenberg, Schwartz, & Davis, 2010)
Communication Skills	Asking for help (Wert & Neisworth, 2003) Peer directed social language (Maione & Mirenda, 2006) Offering to help (Sansosti & Powell-Smith, 2008)
Daily Living Skills	Brushing teeth (Bereznek, Ayres, Mechling, & Alexander, 2012) Shaving (Banda, Matuszny, & Turkan, 2011) Making a meal (Shipley-Benamou, Lutzker, & Taubman, 2002)
Play Skills	Taking turns (macdonald, Clark, Garrigan, & Vangala, 2005) Sharing toys (Apple, Billingsley, & Schwartz, 2005) Pretend play (macdonald, Clark, Garrigan, & Vangala, 2005)
Perspective Taking Skills	Recognizing the feelings of others (leblanc et al., 2003) Accepting differing opinions (Charlop-Christy & Daneshvar, 2003) Navigating the hidden curriculum (Smith Myles, Trautman, & Schelvan, 2004)

people with ASD, the curriculum is used by many schools and is therefore readily available. The curriculum provides task analysis of 40 skills, many of which the student with ASD will need to learn to develop appropriate social relationships. Three research studies have tested the utility of *Skillstreaming* on the social skill development of individuals with ASD and report positive results (Lopata, Thormeer, Volker, Nida, & Lee, 2007; Ogilvie & Dieker, 2010; Tse, Tagalakis, Meng, & Fombonne, 2007).

There are three levels in the Skillstreaming collection including Skillstreaming in Early Childhood (McGinnis, 2011a), *Skillstreaming the Elementary School Child* (McGinnis, 2011b), and *Skillstreaming the Adolescent* (Goldstein & Mc-Ginnis, 1997). The early childhood book contains forty skills broken down into concrete, measurable steps. Both the elementary and adolescent books contain sixty skills each, also broken down into concrete, measurable steps. Individuals working with students on the autism spectrum can utilize

the steps to create video models that may be viewed repeatedly for learning and practice. The *Skillstreaming* series includes an observation checklist to gather information about the sixty social skills detailed in each book (forty skills in the early childhood version).

It is important for those working with individuals with ASD to realize that it's not necessary to use only one specific curriculum, such as *Skillstreaming*. Resources about different social skills and activities can be gleaned from a myriad of resources currently available. Table 2 provides a few examples of commercially published social skill curricula.

CREATING THE INTERVENTION

So, you're ready to do some video modeling? Ogilvie (2012) provides ten easy steps to create video models using peers. The ten steps outlined will walk you through the process from beginning

Table 2. Commercial social skills curricula

Designing Comprehensive Interventions for High-Functioning Individuals with ASD: The Ziggurat Model (Aspy & Grossman, 2011)	Includes information on modeling, video supports, and also includes an underlying characteristics of ASD checklist that would be good to use for assessing social functioning
Social Skills Training (Baker, 2003)	Breaks down social skills into distinct steps; provides information on role playing and modeling
Building Social Relationships (Bellini, 2008)	User-friendly handbook on creating video models and providing social skills instruction including a social skills assessment
The Five Umbrellas (Ortiz, 2011)	Provides information on targeting skills for intervention
The Hidden Curriculum: Practical Solutions for Understanding Rules in Social Situations (Smith Myles, Trautman, & Shelvan, 2004)	Focuses on Hidden Curriculum skills (unwritten social rules) and how to break the skills down to create video models

to end. Table 3 provides a summary of Ogilvie's (2012) steps to creating video models. Keep in mind that Table 3 delineates the steps when using peers for video modeling and adaptations will need to be made for video prompting and video self-modeling due to the absence of the peer mentor.

APPS FOR VIDEO MODELING

With Smartphones, iPods, iPads, Tablets, and other handheld technology becoming readily available, innovative professionals, parents, and educators have created a multitude of applications, or "apps" to facilitate video modeling. Given the number of apps available and the evolving nature of technology, it is important that consumers of new and exciting app technology know how to effectively evaluate apps before investing time (or money) in one specific application.

Vincent (2012) created a rubric for use in evaluating apps on a one-to-four rating scale. The categories included in the rubric are curriculum connection, authenticity, feedback, differentiation, user friendliness, and student motivation. Curriculum connection focuses on the connection between the function of the app and the targeted skills, concepts, or standards. Authenticity refers to how the skills are practiced; whether in a contrived, rote way or in a problem-based learning environment. The third category, feedback, is meant to evaluate the type of feedback / data the app provides and to what level (i.e., table, graph, email, etc.) that data can be available to the user. The flexibility of the settings of the apps is measured in the differentiation category of the rubric. The last two categories, user-friendliness and student motivation focus on the student. User-friendliness refers to how independent the user can be to launch and operate the app, while student motivation evaluates how excited/motivated the student is to use the app. Although all of these categories may be important in evaluating some apps, it is important to note that not all apps will be able to be evaluated

Box 3. Case study part 3: Creating the video model

Noah asked a friend of his in math class to help him make the video. They decided to film the video in a few different places and to meet the next day after school to discuss the video. Mr. Lucian, Noah's special education teacher, sent a note home with Charlie, Noah's peer mentor and friend, to ask his parents' permission to participate in the video.

The next day, Noah and Charlie met after school in the resource room to create the video. Noah, always the joker, had created big "thinking bubbles" to hold up when he was "thinking about his options." Noah taught Charlie the steps of the coping strategy and they brainstormed ideas for the video. They decided to film in their math classroom and in the cafeteria.

Table 3. Ten steps for video modeling (Ogilvie, 2011)

Step	Description	Resources
Identify the Target Behavior	Get input from all stakeholders: parents, teachers, the child (depending on the age), paraprofessionals, extra service providers, etc.	Bellini, S. (2008). Building social relationships: A systematic approach to teaching social interaction skills to children and adolescents with autism spectrum disorders and other social difficulties. Shawnee Mission, KS: Autism Asperger Publishing. Constantino, J. N., & Gruber, C. P. (2005). Social responsiveness scale. Los Angeles: Western Psychological Services. Goldstein, A. P. & McGinnis, E. (1997). Skillstreaming the adolescent: New strategies and perspectives for teaching prosocial skills. Champaign, IL: Research Press.
	Focus on skills that can be used at home, in school, and in the community	Bellini, S. & Akullian, J. (2007). A meta-analysis of video modeling and video self-monitoring interventions for children and adolescents with autism spectrum disorders. *Exceptional Children, 73*, 264-287
	Complete a task analysis on the skill to break it into distinct steps	Functional Skills Assessment Checklist - http://media.mindinstitute.org/education/ADEPT/Notes/SelfHelpChecklist.pdf
Collect Baseline Data	Collect data at consistent times in consistent settings to ensure validity in frequency data	Data Collection Folder See Appendix 1 and 2, Tables 6 and 7, "How to Create a Data Collection Folder"
	Prepare data forms in advance	Bellini, S., Peters, J. K., Benner, L., & Hopf, A. (2007). A meta-analysis of school-based social skills interventions for children with autism spectrum disorders. *Remedial and Special Education, 28*, 153-162
	Collect data in several different settings	Data Collection Resources https://sites.google.com/a/ghaea.org/challenging-behavior-team/data-collection-resources-1 http://www.escambia.k12.fl.us/pbis/data/Data%20Collection%20Guide_10-11-10.pdf
Choose Appropriate Peer Mentors to Help Create the Videos	Use similar age peers to increase the chances that the student with ASD will relate / identify with the video model	Provide peers with information / simulations on ASD
	Seek out peers through service-oriented school clubs or peer mentoring programs	Dunn, M. (2006). *S.O.S. Social skills in our schools.* Shawnee Mission: Asperger Publishing Company
	Choose socially appropriate peers	Peer Mentoring Resource Booklet http://www.csun.edu/eop/htdocs/peermentoring.pdf
Secure Parent/ Guardian Permission as well as Student Assent	Permission for the student with ASD may be obtained earlier at an IEP meeting	See Appendix 3, Table 8, for an example permission letter
	Be sure to notify your administrators that you will be filming students	Smith Myles, B. & Simpson, R. L. (2001). Understanding the hidden curriculum: An essential social skill for children and youth with Asperger's syndrome. *Intervention in School and Clinic, 6*, 279-286
	Consider filming before or after school hours to minimize chances of accidental filming	Be sure to explain the activity to the peer models and the student with ASD
Prepare the Peer Mentors	Discuss the importance of peer mentors and what their role is	Brainstorm ideas with peer mentors so they're prepared to help the student with ASD think of ideas
	Review the steps of the skills with the peers	Ganz, J. B., Cook, K. E., Earles-Vollrath, T. L. (2006). *How to write and implement social scripts.* Austin, TX: PRO-ED
	Practice role playing different scenarios	Consider making two videos: one self model and one peer model

continued on following page

Table 3. Continued

Step	Description	Resources
Prepare the Environment	Select the setting where the skill is most needed / most likely to be utilized	Film in the location where you most want to see the skill to start; then film in other settings to promote generalization
	Write the steps of the skill on a small whiteboard or pieces of paper to show at the beginning of the video	Wilson, K. P. (2013). Incorporating video modeling into a school-based intervention for students with autism spectrum disorders. *Language, Speech, and Hearing Services in Schools, 44, 105*-117
	Consider using props or other visuals	Be sure to gather enough power cords Charge batteries Check memory
Create the Video	Short, simple steps work best	Consider creating a video library of "how to" videos for common social skills
	Videos should be 3-5 minutes in lengths	Buggey, T. (2005). Video self-modeling applications with students with autism spectrum disorder in a small private school setting. *Focus on Autism and Other Developmental Disabilities, 20, 52-63.*
	Be sure to introduce the skill and note the steps	Try out video editing programs like iMovie or Windows Movie Maker and apps for video modeling
Implement the Intervention	First, explain the social skill to the student. Be sure to review where and when they might need to use the skill. Show the student the video model. After the student has watched the video, it's time for him/her to practice the skill. Showing the video repeatedly is recommended	Some options for reviewing the skill include writing the steps on a piece of paper or white board or creating a poster. The written procedures allow the student to hear and see the words of the each step in the skill. The student should review the video before going into the social setting in which they need to use the skill. This could be done every morning before school, immediately before recess or lunch, or several times throughout the day. Contrive situations in which the student needs to use the new skill to promote practice of the skill
Gather Data	Collect data across multiple settings to check for generalization of the skills	Remember to collect data one month, three months, etc, after the intervention to check for maintenance of the skills
	Data should be collected at least three times per week and assessed weekly	Gresham, F. M. (2002). Best practices in social skills training. In A. Thomas. & J. Grimes (Eds.), *Best practices in school psychology* (4th ed.). Bethesda, MD: NASP.
	If a student is not making progress, the intervention can then be adapted	Make sure your target behaviors are well defined and that you are collecting data during the same times as baseline. This allows you to compare your effectiveness between baseline and intervention.
Assess the Intervention and Reflect	If progress, celebrate. If not, meet with your intervention team to thoroughly assess the data and implementation. It is okay to modify your intervention.	Consider new apps or software for future video modeling projects
	Questions to think about: What worked well? What would I do differently next time?	Gresham, F. M., Sugai, G., & Horner, R. H. (2001). Interpreting Outcomes of Social Skills Training for Students with High-Incidence Disabilities. *Teaching Exceptional Children, 67, 331-344.*
	Did the intervention match the behavior? Would you use this intervention again?	Create a training for other people working with / living with individuals with ASD in your area

in all categories. The person evaluating the app would choose which categories fit the app s/he is using. See Table 4 for the app evaluation rubric.

There is currently an abundance of apps to facilitate video modeling using hand-held technology. Table 5 includes information on selected apps. The applications available range from visual schedulers to talking pictures and also to video clips and tools to create your own video models.

FUTURE RESEARCH DIRECTIONS

Current research on video modeling has been extensive and the intervention has been well established. However, more research is needed on selecting the type of video model based upon student needs and characteristics. A few studies have assessed the differences between video modeling and video self-modeling with mixed results. However, more research is needed in this area to examine factors that lead to the best outcomes

for children with ASD based upon their particular needs (Bellini & Akullian, 2007). Given the evolving nature of video based technology, there will be a continued need for researchers to test the efficacy of new technology.

CONCLUSION

Video modeling is an established intervention for teaching people with ASD skills across social and academic functioning. However, just as with all interventions, great care must be taken in the assessment of the target behavior, careful consideration when choosing an intervention that can be implemented with fidelity, appropriate development of the intervention and fidelity of implementation of the intervention, to increase the likelihood of video modeling success.

There are three types of video modeling: video prompts, video peer modeling and video self-modeling. Each type of video model is based upon the same theory. While research has not

Table 4. App evaluation rubric (Vincent, 2012; www.learninginhand.com)

Domain	1	2	3	4
Curriculum Connection	Skill(s) reinforced in the app are not clearly connected to the targeted skill or concept	Skill(s) reinforced are prerequisite or foundation skills for the targeted skill or concept	Skill(s) reinforced are related to the targeted skill or concept	Skill(s) reinforced are strongly connected to the targeted skill or concept
Authenticity	Skills are practiced in a rote or isolated fashion (e.g., flashcards)	Skills are practiced in a contrived game/simulation format	Some aspects of the app are presented an authentic learning environment	Targeted skills are practiced in an authentic format/problem-based learning environment
Feedback	Feedback is limited to correctness of student responses	Feedback is limited to correctness of student responses and may allow for student to try again	Feedback is specific and results in improved student performance (may include tutorial aids)	Feedback is specific and results in improved student performance; Data is available electronically to student and teacher
Differentiation	App offers no flexibility (settings cannot be altered)	App offers limited flexibility (e.g., few levels such as easy, medium, hard)	App offers more than one degree of flexibility to adjust settings to meet student needs	App offers complete flexibility to alter settings to meet student needs
User Friendliness	Students need constant teacher supervision in order to use the app	Students need to have the teacher review how to the use the app on more than one occasion	Students need to have the teacher review how to the use the app	Students can launch and navigate within the app independently
Student Motivation	Students avoid the use of the app or complain when the app is assigned by the teacher	Students view the app as "more schoolwork" and may be off-task when directed by the teacher to use the app	Students will use the app as directed by the teacher	Students are highly motivated to use the app and select it as their first choice from a selection of related choices of apps

Table 5. Sample apps for video modeling

	iModeling	• Create a title, record footage, add images • Cost: $14 • Website: https://itunes.apple.com/us/app/imodeling/id457539171?mt=8
	My Pictures Talk – Video Modeling Tool	• Catalog, share, and teach social skills by adding text and audio to photographs • Cost: $5 • Website: https://itunes.apple.com/us/app/my-pictures-talk-video-modeling/id368388315?mt=8
	Social Skill Builder Lite	• Interactive video focused on five areas: friendship/life skills, understanding emotions, problem solving, critical thinking, and perspective taking • Cost: $3 (lite version); $15 (full version) • Website https://itunes.apple.com/us/app/social-skill-builder-lite/id486116417?mt=8
	InPromptU	• Watch video clips of people doing common tasks • Clips are broken into short distinct steps to aid in skill mastery • Cost: Free • Website: https://itunes.apple.com/us/app/inpromptu/id473450377?mt=8

established whether one type is better than the other, there are factors that should be taken into consideration when choosing the type of video model. Video self-modeling may be used for those who can perform the steps of the skill with prompts, video peer modeling and video prompts should be used with those who can't perform the steps even with prompts or the prompts cannot be edited out.

Social validity of the target behaviors should always be assessed before beginning an intervention. If the child with ASD, the parents, the teacher, and peers believe the skill is relevant and necessary, the likelihood of the behavior receiving natural reinforcement across settings increases. The goal for children with ASD is to be able to perform the skills they need when they need them, have the skill be effective and efficient, as well as

Box 4. Case study part 4: Implementing the intervention and student outcome

Noah and Charlie had a good time creating the video model. After they showed it to the teacher, they practiced the coping strategy and role-played a variety of different situations where Noah might need the skills.

Noah and his teacher had decided that Noah should watch the video on the way to school or immediately when he arrived at school. Later in the week, Noah arrived at school as usual and was surprised to see a big sign featuring a "special activity period schedule." Noah groaned and started to storm towards the front office to see what the sign was all about. As he reached for the door to the office, he remembered the video he had watched on the bus ride to school. He stopped and took a deep breath, counted to ten, and started to list his choices in his head.

Grabbing his stress ball out of his backpack, Noah considered storming into the office and demanding to know what the activity schedule was all about. Next, he thought about turning around and seeing if he could get back on the bus and go home. "The day would be ruined anyway," he thought, "because the schedule would be mixed up." Finally, he added the option of going to his homeroom early and asking his teacher about it.

Noah reached once again for the doorknob and turned it. He walked directly up to the desk and said in a strong, clear voice, "May I please have a pass to go to my homeroom early?" For Noah, the coping strategy combined with the reinforcement of the video model was beneficial and resulted in being in control of his emotions when faced with an unexpected schedule change. There were other times during the school year when Noah chose to utilize the coping strategy in stressful situations. The number of complete meltdowns decreased and Noah's peers began to invite him to join them at lunch more often because he wasn't behaving so unpredictably. On those days when even the coping strategy wasn't helping, Charlie would give Noah a pep talk to remind him about the steps of the coping strategy.

reinforced by their peers so the behavior continues in a natural setting. Video Modeling can be a fun, effective intervention to teach children with ASD.

REFERENCES

American Psychiatric Association. (2004). *Diagnostic and statistical manual of mental disorders* (4th ed.). Washington, DC: Author.

Apple, A. L., Billingsley, F., & Schwartz, I. S. (2005). Effects of video modeling alone and with self-management on compliment giving behaviors of children with high functioning ASD. *Journal of Positive Behavior Interventions*, 7, 33–46. doi:10.1177/10983007050070010401

Banda, D. R., Matuszny, R. M., & Turkan, S. (2011). Video modeling strategies to enhance appropriate behaviors in children with autism spectrum disorders. *Teaching Exceptional Children*, 39, 47–52.

Bellini, S. (2008). *Building social relationships: A systematic approach to teaching social interaction skills to children and adolescents with autism spectrum disorders and other social difficulties*. Shawnee Mission, KS: Autism Asperger Publishing.

Bellini, S., & Akullian, J. (2007). A meta-analysis of video modeling and video self-monitoring interventions for children and adolescents with autism spectrum disorders. *Exceptional Children*, 73, 264–287.

Bellini, S., Peters, J. K., Benner, L., & Hopf, A. (2007). A meta-analysis of school-based social skills interventions for children with autism spectrum disorders. *Remedial and Special Education*, 28, 153–162. doi:10.1177/07419325070280030401

Bereznek, S., Ayres, K. M., Mechling, L. C., & Alexander, J. L. (2012). Video self-prompting and mobile technology to increase daily living and vocational independence for students with autism spectrum disorders. *Journal of Developmental and Physical Disabilities*, 24, 269–285. doi:10.1007/s10882-012-9270-8

Buggey, T. (2005). Video self-modeling applications with students with autism spectrum disorder in a small private school setting. *Focus on Autism and Other Developmental Disabilities*, 20, 52–63. doi:10.1177/10883576050200010501

Burton, C. E., Anderson, D. H., Prater, M. A., & Dyches, T. T. (2013). Video self-modeling on an iPad to teach functional math problems to adolescents and intellectual disability. *Focus on Autism and Other Developmental Disabilities*, 28, 67–77. doi:10.1177/1088357613478829

Charlop-Christy, M. H., & Daneshvar, S. (2003). Using video modeling to teach perspective taking to children with autism. *Journal of Positive Behavior Interventions*, 5, 12–21. doi:10.1177/10983007030050010101

Charlop-Christy, M. H., Le, L., & Freeman, K. A. (2000). A comparison of video modeling with in vivo modeling for teaching children with autism. *Journal of Autism and Developmental Disorders*, 30, 537–552. doi:10.1023/A:1005635326276 PMID:11261466

Clark, E., Kehle, T. J., Jenson, W. R., & Beck, D. E. (1992). Evaluation of parameters of self-modeling interventions. *School Psychology Review*, 21, 246–254.

Constantino, J. N., & Gruber, C. P. (2005). *Social responsiveness scale*. Los Angeles, CA: Western Psychological Services.

Dowrick, P. W. (1999). A review of self modeling and related interventions. *Applied & Preventive Psychology*, 8, 23–39. doi:10.1016/S0962-1849(99)80009-2

Dunn, M. (2006). *S.O.S. social skills in our schools*. Shawnee Mission, KS: Asperger Publishing Company.

el Kaliouby, R., Picard, R., & Baron-Cohen, S. (2006). Affective computing and autism. *Annals of the New York Academy of Sciences, 1093*, 228–248. doi:10.1196/annals.1382.016 PMID:17312261

Escambia County Public Schools. (2013, July 7). Retrieved from www.escambia.k12.fl.us/pbis/data/Data%20Collection%20Guide_10-11-10.pdf

Fullerton, A. (1996). Who are higher functioning young adults with autism? In A. Fullerton (Ed.), *Higher functioning adolescents and young adults with autism* (pp. 1–20). Austin, TX: PRO-ED, Inc.

Ganz, J. B., Cook, K. E., & Earles-Vollrath, T. L. (2006). *How to write and implement social scripts*. Austin, TX: PRO-ED.

Goldstein, A. P., & McGinnis, E. (1997). *Skillstreaming the adolescent: New strategies and perspectives for teaching prosocial skills*. Champaign, IL: Research Press.

Greenhills, A. E. A. (2013, July 7). *Data collection resources*. Retrieved from https://sites.google.com/a/ghaea.org/challenging-behavior-team/data-collection-resources-1

Grembe, Inc. (2013, February 28). *My pictures talk modeling application information*. Retrieved from https://itunes.apple.com/us/app/my-pictures-talk-video-modeling/id368388315?mt=8

Gresham, F. M. (2002). Best practices in social skills training. In A. Thomas, & J. Grimes (Eds.), *Best practices in school psychology* (4th ed.). Bethesda, MD: NASP.

Gresham, F. M., Sugai, G., & Horner, R. H. (2001). Interpreting outcomes of social skills training for students with high-incidence disabilities. *Teaching Exceptional Children, 67*, 331–344.

Huang, A. X., & Wheeler, J. J. (2006). High-functional autism: An overview of characteristics and related issues. *Journal of International Special Education, 21*, 109–123.

Kagohara, D. M., Achmedi, D., Meer, L., Lancioni, G. E., O'Reilly, M., & Lang, R. et al. (2013). Teaching two students with Asperger syndrome to greet adults using Social Stories™ and video modeling. *Journal of Developmental and Physical Disabilities, 25*, 241–251. doi:10.1007/s10882-012-9300-6

Kinney, E. M., Vedora, J., & Stromer, R. (2003). Computer-presented video models to teach generative spelling to a child with an autism spectrum disorder. *Journal of Positive Behavior Interventions, 5*, 22–29. doi:10.1177/10983007030050010301

LeBlanc, L. A., Coates, A. M., Daneshvar, S., Charlop-Christy, M. H., Morris, C., & Lancaster, B. M. (2003). Using video modeling and reinforcement to teach perspective-taking skills to children with autism. *Journal of Applied Behavior Analysis, 36*, 253–257. doi:10.1901/jaba.2003.36-253 PMID:12858990

MacDonald, R., Clark, M., Garrigan, E., & Vangala, M. (2005). Using video modeling to teach pretend play to children with autism. *Behavioral Interventions, 20*, 225–238. doi:10.1002/bin.197

Maione, L., & Mirenda, P. (2006). Effects of video modeling and video feedback on peer directed social language skills of a child with autism. *Journal of Positive Behavior Interventions, 8*, 106–118. doi:10.1177/10983007060080020201

McGinnis, E. (2011a). *Skillstreaming the elementary school child: A guide for teaching prosocial skills* (3rd ed.). Champaign, IL: Research Press.

McGinnis, E. (2011b). *Skillstreaming in early childhood: A guide for teaching prosocial skills*. Champaign, IL: Research Press.

Mechling, L. C., & Ayres, K. M. (2012). A comparative study: Completion of fine motor office related tasks by high school students with autism using video models on large and small screen size. *Journal of Autism and Developmental Disorders, 42,* 2364–2375. doi:10.1007/s10803-012-1484-1 PMID:22354709

Mighty Kingdom. (2012, December 4). *iModeling application information.* Retrieved from https://itunes.apple.com/us/app/imodeling/id457539171?mt=8

Mind Institute. (2013, July 7). *Self help and functional skills checklist.* Retrieved from http://media.mindinstitute.org/education/ADEPT/Notes/SelfHelpChecklist.pdf

Moore, D., Cheng, Y., McGrath, P., & Powell, N. J. (2005). Collaborative virtual environment technology for people with autism. *Focus on Autism and Other Developmental Disabilities, 20,* 231–243. doi:10.1177/10883576050200040501

Moore, D., McGrath, P., & Thorpe, J. (2000). Computer-aided learning for people with autism- a framework for research and development. *Innovations in Education and Training International, 37,* 218–228. doi:10.1080/13558000050138452

National Autism Center. (2009). *National standards project: Addressing the need for evidence-based practice guidelines for autism spectrum disorders.* Randolph, MA: National Autism Center.

Nikopoulos, C. K., Canavan, C., & Nikopoulou-Smyrni, P. (2009). Generalized effects of video modeling on establishing instructional stimulus control in children with autism: Results of a preliminary study. *Journal of Positive Behavior Interventions, 11,* 198–207. doi:10.1177/1098300708325263

Nikopoulos, C. K., & Keenan, M. (2004). Effects of video modeling on social initiations by children with autism. *Journal of Applied Behavior Analysis, 37,* 93. doi:10.1901/jaba.2004.37-93 PMID:15154221

Ogilvie, C. R. (2011). Ten steps to creating video models for students with autism spectrum disorders. *Teaching Exceptional Children, 43,* 8–19.

Ogilvie, C. R., & Dieker, L. A. (2010). Video modeling and peer-mediated instruction of social skills for students with autism spectrum disorders. *Journal on Developmental Disabilities, 16,* 48–59.

Ohio State University. (2011, November 15). *InPromptu application information.* Retrieved from https://itunes.apple.com/us/app/inpromptu/id473450377?mt=8

Omatsu, G. (2013, July 8). *Peer mentoring resource booklet.* Retrieved from http://www.csun.edu/eop/htdocs/peermentoring.pdf

Ortiz, J. M. (2011). *The five umbrellas: A strength-based framework for Asperger's, high functioning autism, and non-verbal learning disorder.* Dillsburg, PA: The Asperger's Syndrome Institute.

Plavnick, J. B. (2012). A practical strategy for teaching a child with autism to attend to and imitate a portable video model. *Research and Practice for Persons with Severe Disabilities, 37,* 263–270. doi:10.2511/027494813805327250

Prater, M. A., Carter, N., Hitchcock, C., & Dowrick, P. (2012). Video self-modeling to improve academic performance: A literature review. *Psychology in the Schools, 49,* 71–81. doi:10.1002/pits.20617

Quill, K. (2000). *Do-watch-listen-say: Social and communication intervention for children with autism.* Baltimore, MD: Brookes Publishing.

Rosenberg, N. E., Schwartz, I. S., & Davis, C. A. (2010). Evaluating the utility of commercial videotapes for teaching hand washing to children with autism. *Education & Treatment of Children, 33,* 443–455. doi:10.1353/etc.0.0098

Rubin, E., & Lennon, L. (2004). Challenges in social communication in Asperger syndrome and high-functioning autism. *Topics in Language Disorders, 24,* 271–285. doi:10.1097/00011363-200410000-00005

Sansosti, F. J., & Powell-Smith, K. A. (2008). Using computer-presented social stories and video models to increase the social communication skills of children with high-functioning autism spectrum disorders. *Journal of Positive Behavior Interventions, 10,* 162–178. doi:10.1177/1098300708316259

Shane, H. C., Laubscher, E. H., Schlosser, R. W., Flynn, S., Sorce, J. F., & Abramson, J. (2011). Applying technology to visually support language and communication in individuals with autism spectrum disorders. *Journal of Autism and Developmental Disorders, 42,* 1228–1235. doi:10.1007/s10803-011-1304-z PMID:21691867

Sherer, M., Pierce, K. L., Paredes, S., Kisacky, K. L., Ingersoll, B., & Schreibman, L. (2001). Enhancing conversation skills in children with autism via video technology: Which is better, self or other as a model? *Behavior Modification, 25,* 140–158. doi:10.1177/0145445501251008 PMID:11151482

Shipley-Benamou, R., Lutzker, J. R., & Taubman, M. (2002). Teaching daily living skills to children with autism through instructional video modeling. *Journal of Positive Behavior Interventions, 4,* 165–175. doi:10.1177/10983007020040030501

Shukla-Mehta, S., Miller, T., & Callahan, K. J. (2010). Evaluating the effectiveness of video instruction on social and communication skills for children with autism spectrum disorders: A review of the literature. *Focus on Autism and Other Developmental Disabilities, 25,* 23–26. doi:10.1177/1088357609352901

Smith Myles, B., & Simpson, R. L. (2001). Understanding the hidden curriculum: An essential social skill for children and youth with Asperger's syndrome. *Intervention in School and Clinic, 6,* 279–286. doi:10.1177/105345120103600504

Smith Myles, B., Trautman, M. L., & Schelvan, R. L. (2004). *The hidden curriculum: Practical solutions for understanding unstated rules in social situations.* Shawnee Mission, KS: Autism Asperger Publishing.

Social Skill Builder, Inc. (2011, October 24). *Social skill builder lite information.* Retrieved from https://itunes.apple.com/us/app/social-skill-builder-lite/id486116417?mt=8

Tasse, M. J., Aman, M. G., Hammer, D., & Rojahn, J. (1996). *The Nisonger child behavior rating form.* Columbus, OH: The Nisonger Center for Mental Retardation and Developmental Disabilities.

Tsatsanis, K. D. (2004). Heterogeneity in learning style in Asperger syndrome and high functioning autism. *Topics in Language Disorders, 24,* 260–270. doi:10.1097/00011363-200410000-00004

Tse, J., Strulovitch, J., Tagalakis, V., Meng, L., & Fombonne, E. (2007). Social skills training for adolescents with Asperger syndrome and high functioning autism. *Journal of Autism and Developmental Disorders, 37,* 1960–1968. doi:10.1007/s10803-006-0343-3 PMID:17216559

Vincent, T. (2012). *Evaluation rubric for iPod apps.* Retrieved from http://learninginhand.com/static/50eca855e4b0939ae8bb12d9/50ecb58ee4b0b16f176a9e7d/50ecb595e4b0b16f176aaab8/1288148200553/AppRubric.pdf on 07-08-2013

Wert, B. Y., & Neisworth, J. T. (2003). Effects of video self-modeling on spontaneous requesting in children with autism. *Journal of Positive Behavior Interventions, 5,* 30–34. doi:10.1177/1098300703005001050 1

Wilson, K. P. (2013). Incorporating video modeling into a school-based intervention for students with autism spectrum disorders. *Language, Speech, and Hearing Services in Schools, 44,* 105–117. doi:10.1044/0161-1461(2012/11-0098) PMID:23087158

ADDITIONAL READING

Acar, C., & Diken, I. H. (2012). Reviewing instructional studies conducted using video modeling to children with autism. *Educational Sciences: Theory and Practice, 124*(4), 2731–2735.

Aman, M. G., Singh, N. N., Stewart, A. W., & Field, C. J. (1989). The aberrant behavior checklist: A behavior rating scale for the assessment of treatment effects. *The American Journal of Mental Deficiencies, 89*(5), 485–491. PMID:3993694

Banda, D. R., Copple, K. S., Rajinder, K. K., Sancibrian, S. L., & Bogschutz, R. A. (2010). Video modeling interventions to teach spontaneous requesting using AAC devices to individuals with autism: A preliminary investigation. *Disability and Rehabilitation, 32*(6), 1364–1372. doi:10.3109/09638280903551525 PMID:20465397

Bellini, S. (2006). The development of social anxiety in high functioning adolescents with autism spectrum disorders. *Focus on Autism and Other Developmental Disabilities, 2,* 138–145. doi:10.1177/10883576060210030201

Boudreau, E., & D'Etremont, B. (2010). Improving the pretend play skills of preschoolers with autism spectrum disorders: The effects of video modeling. *Journal of Physical and Developmental Disabilities, 22,* 415-431.

Boudreau, J., & Harvey, M. T. (2013). Increasing recreational initiations for children who have ASD using video self-modeling. *Education & Treatment of Children, 36,* 49–60. doi:10.1353/etc.2013.0006

Brinkley, J., Nations, L., Abramson, R. K., Hall, A., Wright, H. H., Gabriels, R., & Cuccaro, M. L. (2007). Factor analysis of the aberrant behavior checklist in individuals with autism spectrum disorders. *Journal of Autism and Developmental Disorders, 37,* 1949–1959. doi:10.1007/s10803-006-0327-3 PMID:17186368

Cihak, D., Alberto, P. A., Taber-Doughty, T., & Gama, R. I. (2006). A comparison of static picture prompting and video prompting simulation strategies using group instructional procedures. *Focus on Autism and Other Developmental Disabilities, 21,* 89–99. doi:10.1177/10883576060210020601

Cihak, D., Fahrenkrog, C., Ayres, K. M., & Smith, C. (2010). The use of video modeling via a video iPod and a system of least prompts to improve transitional behaviors for students with autism spectrum disorders in the general education classroom. *Journal of Positive Behavior Interventions, 12,* 103–115. doi:10.1177/1098300709332346

Cihak, D. F., Smith, C. C., Cornett, A., & Coleman, M. B. (2012). The use of video modeling with the picture exchange communication system to increase independent communicative initiations in preschoolers with autism and Developmental Delays. *Focus on Autism and Other Developmental Disabilities, 27,* 3–11. doi:10.1177/1088357611428426

Dauphin, M., Kinney, E. M., & Stromer, R. (2004). Using video-enhanced activity schedules and matrix training to teach socio-dramatic play to a child with autism. *Journal of Positive Behavior Interventions, 6,* 238–250. doi:10.1177/10983007040060040501

Ganz, J. B., Earles-Vollrath, T. L., & Cook, K. E. (2011). Video modeling: Visually based intervention for children with autism spectrum disorder. *Teaching Exceptional Children*, *43*, 8–19.

Gelbar, N. W., Anderson, C., McCarthy, S., & Buggey, T. (2012). Video self-modeling as an intervention strategy for individuals with autism spectrum disorders. *Psychology in the Schools*, *49*(1), 15–22. doi:10.1002/pits.20628

Gray, C. (2000). *The New Social Story Book: Illustrated Ed*. Arlington, TX. *Future*.

Kagohara, D. M. (2010). Is video-based instruction effective in the rehabilitation of children with autism spectrum disorders? *Developmental Neurorehabilitation*, *13*(2), 129–140. doi:10.3109/17518420903329281 PMID:20222774

Marcus, A., & Wilder, D. A. (2009). A comparison of peer video modeling and self video modeling to teach textual responses to children with autism. *Journal of Applied Behavior Analysis*, *42*, 335–341. doi:10.1901/jaba.2009.42-335 PMID:19949521

Mazurek, M. O., & Wenstrup, C. (2012). Television, video game and social media use among children with ASD and typically developing siblings. *Journal of Autism and Developmental Disorders*, *43*, 1258–1271. doi:10.1007/s10803-012-1659-9 PMID:23001767

Rumsey, J. M. (1992). Neuropsychological studies of high-level autism. In E. Schopler & G. B. Mesibov (Eds.), High-functioning individuals with autism (pp. 41-64). New York: the Plenum Press.

Shrestha, A., Anderson, A., & Moore, D. W. (2013). Using point-of-view video modeling and forward chaining to teach a functional self-help skill to a child with autism. *Journal of Behavioral Education*, *22*, 157–167. doi:10.1007/s10864-012-9165-x

KEY TERMS AND DEFINITIONS

Application: Also known as an "app"; a specialized program that can be downloaded onto a computer or handheld device.

Peer Mentor: An individual in the same grade or around the same age of the individual with a disability who assists in learning new skills or practicing learned skills.

Research-Based Intervention: An intervention that has strong empirical base as to its effectiveness.

Task Analysis: Breaking a skill down into a series of distinct steps.

Video Modeling: An established intervention that can be used to increase communication, cognitive functions, personal responsibility and play/social skills and decrease problem behaviors and sensory/emotional difficulties.

Video Self-Modeling: Creating a video, using the student in need of the skill, of a desired skill and using it as all or part of an intervention.

Video Prompting: Creating video displaying specific steps of a task to be completed by an individual.

APPENDIX 1

Table 6. Creating a data collection folder

1. Open the manila folder and position it lengthwise in front of you. 2. Using your ruler, divide the folder into six columns; one column for each day of the week plus one more column for other notes. 3. Divide each column into six rows. The end result will be a blank six by six table. - Note: It's a good idea to laminate the folder after you have the grid drawn on it to preserve the folder and also so you can use dry erase markers to write the dates of the month in each square. 4. Once the folder is prepped, you can fill in the dates according to when you are starting data collection to when you will finish collecting data. 5. To collect data using the folder data collection tool, the teacher carries around a pack of small post-it notes during the day. 6. Each time you observe the target behavior, write it on a post-it note with the student's initials and place it in the correct space on the folder. At the end of the day or week, you will have a collection of data about your students' behaviors. See Table 7 for a picture of the Data Collection Folder

APPENDIX 2

Table 7. Example data collection folder

MONDAY	TUESDAY	WEDNESDAY	THURSDAY	FRIDAY	NOTES / TO DO
10-03-10 J.R. – answered 4 questions in science class					1. Call R.F.'s Mom 2. Send out IEP notices 3. Check-in with OT & PT
	10-11-10 S.M. – late to class; fidgety in seat; did not participate				*To Do List Write in pencil, use post-its, or laminate folder.*
			10-21-10 H.O. - CALL-OUTS IN MATH CLASS: /////////// (11)	10-22-10 H.O. – CALL-OUTS IN MATH CLASS: //////// (7)	
Quick Data! Write down anything that you might need to recall later – Positive Behaviors, Negative Behaviors, Concerns, Successes, etc.	10-27-10 A.S. – REMEMBERED ENGLISH HOMEWORK				
	11-04-10 L.Y. – INCIDENT IN HALLWAY (SEE REPORT)				

APPENDIX 3

Table 8. Example letter of consent

Dear Mr. and Mrs. Murray,

In the next few weeks, we are going to be creating some video models of social skills in our class. Your son, Larry, has been chosen to be a peer mentor in the videos. He will role play social skills with a student who has autism.

All videos will remain in the school in a secure location and will only be used for our classroom. Please sign the form below and have Larry return it to me by October 28, 2013. You can keep the top half for your own records.

Please feel free to call or email me with any questions. You can reach me via e-mail at TeacherName@emailprovider or 123-456-7890.

All my best,

Ms. Flibberty Widget

_____ Yes! I give my permission to video my child for the purpose of social skills training. I understand that the videos will be kept in the school.

_____ No. I do not give permission to video my child.

_____ Child Name

_____ Parent/Guardian Name

(Please Print)

_____

Parent / Guardian Signature

_____

Date

Chapter 14
The Development of Virtual Reality Technologies for People on the Autism Spectrum

Nigel Newbutt
Bath Spa University, UK

ABSTRACT

The role of virtual reality technologies to help people with autism has been well documented and is an area of research that continues to develop. While the evidence base is somewhat limited, there are many studies that have started to explore the potential of virtual reality technologies for people with autism. Work conducted by Strickland et al. (1996), Murray (1997), Charitos et al. (2000), Parsons and Mitchell (2002), Parsons et al. (2006, 2007), Cobb (2007), Fabri and Moore (2005), and Fabri et al. (2004) have all added to this positive picture of virtual reality technologies to support people on the autism spectrum, specifically in terms of social interaction and social skills development. This chapter uncovers the evidence base and work of others in relation to virtual reality technologies used by people with autism. This chapter concludes with a view as to what future work might pursue in this field.

INTRODUCTION

This chapter seeks to explore and present the use and role of virtual reality technologies (VRTs) for people on the autism spectrum. Although still at a very early stage of providing an evidence-base, VRTs have been used as a way to help enable people with autism to communicate, express emotion, develop social skills and test various social situations. The evidence-base for the role of VRTs has, to date, mainly been conducted in un-naturalistic environments (i.e. research labs, technology centres,) and with small groups of participants. However, and this chapter will reveal, the evidence-base has provided a multi-faceted picture of the benefits VRTs can bring to autism user groups, and some successful outcomes have been reported. This chapter therefore seeks to

DOI: 10.4018/978-1-4666-5792-2.ch014

outline some of the key work in the area of VRTs (including; virtual worlds, virtual environments, collaborative virtual environments and virtual reality), and will provide some analysis of studies carried out to date. Finally, the chapter will consider possible future areas of research and development within the context of VRTs and how the evidence-base could be reinforced; addressing some of the gaps in knowledge and work still to be done in this field.

OVERVIEW

Investigation into supporting children with autism using a variety of computer platforms and technology is growing as the evidence-base increases within research domains. While research has focused on providing evidence for the role technology can play in the lives of people with autism (i.e. social skills training, emotional recognition, developing language skills), there has been less focus or research conducted in off-the-shelf computer technology. Moreover research into the area of technology and autism tends to be measured in terms of positivist paradigms. Several studies have considered a greater level of interpretivist analysis but the views and opinions of the users of technology (in this case users with autism), is an area requiring a greater emphasis and further research. It is argued that by understanding these views and by gathering evidence through, perhaps case studies will enable designers, technologists and researchers to better develop material that is beneficial and appropriate to this specific user group.

This chapter provides an examination of the benefits and limitations of virtual environments (and more broadly computer technology) developed for and used with people with autism and ASCs. Through this review several key gaps in knowledge are identified and future directions outlined.

WHAT IS AUTISM: A BRIEF OVERVIEW

Autism is described as a "spectrum" disorder, ranging from "classic" autism, involving severe learning difficulties, to high-functioning autism and Asperger's syndrome, where typical levels of cognitive ability can be expected (Scott, 2002). However, all children and adults with an ASC experience difficulties with social understanding and communication skills. Baron-Cohen and Bolton (1993) state that autism is a condition that can affect children from birth or early childhood, and is a condition that leaves them unable to form typical social relationships or typical communication (Scott et al., 2002; Bolton et al., 1994). As a result of this, the child may become isolated from human contact and absorb the world in a repetitive, obsessive manner (Baron-Cohen and Bolton, 1993). Baird et al. (2003) describe autism as a "behaviorally defined disorder, characterised by qualitative impairments in social communication, social interaction and social imagination" (p1). Haswell et al. (2009, p.970) define children with autism as having "defects in motor control, imitation and social function". Autism has a range in terms of diagnosis, and can be classified as high- or low-functioning; it can be located within the broader field of spectrum disorders (Bolton et al., 1994).

VIRTUAL REALITY TECHNOLOGY USED BY PEOPLE WITH AUTISM

In reinforcing the need to develop technological tools for people with autism, the international journal of research and practice *Autism* published a special edition in May 2010 – *Autism and Technology*, edited by Bolte et al. In this edition, the editors argue that "technological advances can potentially lead to novel and more effective treatment strategies and enhancing quality of life for people with ASD and their families" (Bolte et al., 2010, p.155). They go on to state how the lives of many have already begun to change as a result of successful computer technology initiatives. It is based on this type of statement that this work aims to provide a starting point for developing a virtual world for children on the autism spectrum.

This section aims to discuss virtual technologies (VTs) as a possible way to augment communication for people with autism, and as an aid in learning how to interact and develop social skills.

Strickland et al. (1996) presented an early study that assessed the effectiveness of Virtual Reality (VR) as a learning tool to engage children with autism; their study was primarily designed to determine if children with autism would tolerate VR equipment and respond to a computer-generated world. They considered the differences between VR and computer programs; the level of interaction with computer-generated images; and independence in determining motion and objects in a VR world as a way to present real-life experiences. The use of VR for children with autism was considered, based on: sensory problems, lack of generalisation, visual thought patterns, individualised treatment and responsiveness to computer technology. The aim of the study was to help children with autism learn how to cross a road safely. They used VR helmets to immerse the users in a 3D environment, so that users could identify cars, the colours of objects and how they were moving. The children were presented with various scenarios to determine generalisation, and were asked to "walk" into the scene and interact with signs. Conclusions gained from the study suggested that the two participants (with ASC) were able to interact with the environments successfully (accepting the virtual helmet, tracking in-world objects; moved their bodies and heads, located in-world objects and moved towards them). In addition the study suggested that the participants appeared to become immersed (labelling in-world objects and moving their bodies interactively). These aspects tended to suggest that

VR afforded far-reaching advantages to children with autism, including encouraging interaction, exploring and learning. A limitation of the study was the small number of participants included; while two children accepted the use of VR devices (helmet, joystick, gloves, etc.), it does not follow that others would.

Building on the work of Strickland et al. (1996), Charitos et al. (2000) designed a virtual environment that was controlled by virtual-reality input devices, to aid the organisational skills of people with autism. The study aimed to teach social skills through providing a virtual interface for people with autism to navigate through. Charitos et al. provided a series of reasons why computer-based systems are well suited for people with autism, based on the work of Murray (1997). Examples cited by Murray included being able to set clear boundaries and controlling the stimuli (through a step by step process). These both allowed for greater control and focus of material in the presentation and learning. Another advantaged cited by Murray links to joint attention and restrictive context. These both, in some ways, play to the strengths of people on the autism spectrum in that focus of interest can be taken into account in addition to restricting other sources of information. Overarching these aspects, Murray suggests that safety, flexibility and adaptability can all be instilled along with a sense of prediction. Again these aspects play to the strengths of people on the autism spectrum. Developing these theories a stage further there is potential to enhance the development of autonomy encouraging communication; through which self-confidence can be heightened.

On this basis, Charitos et al. (2000) proposed designing a virtual environment to aid children with autism in undertaking everyday tasks. This, more specifically, pertained to "returning home" and builds on a traditional teaching practice used within the school. It was an aim of the project reported in this paper to "improve the potential for effective teaching" (Charitos et al., 2000, p.150).

Interestingly, although not surprisingly, Charitos et al. arrived at similar conclusions to those of Strickland et al., including the notion that structured environments go some way to help users feel confident, and that a range of input devices could be used. The work presented by Charitos et al., while including more participants than that of Strickland et al., still has limited participant detail which would help provide useful contextual data, helping us to better understand the study in the exploratory manner it is intended.

Further studies exploring the use of VEs have shown improved communication for users (children) with autism. In particular, Fabri and Moore (2005) discussed the use of collaborative virtual environments (CVEs) to enhance and improve communication and emotional recognition in people with autism. They put forward a case for introducing emotional expressiveness in CVEs, as a way to aid interpersonal communication, generally, and specifically for children with autism. Part of their project involved creating an interface that included a 3D avatar, which could express emotion to help communicate through a text-based two-way tool. They implemented the theories of Ekman and Friesen (1978), using the six "universal" facial expressions of emotion – happiness, surprise, anger, fear, sadness and disgust – and a neutral expression. In using an avatar, Fabri and Moore also proposed reasons for involving a virtual head in their work. A previous study (Fabri et al., 2004) highlighted three points that relate to virtual faces and emotions (in the context of Ekman and Friesen, 1978) six universal facial expressions): (1) emotions can be represented with limited facial features; (2) recognition rates (of virtual faces) are comparable to real-life images; and (3) some expressions are easily recognisable and potentially build a basis for emotionally expressive avatars in CVEs. However, Fabri et al. also concluded that this is not the case for all emotions. For example, disgust was not well understood by participants in their study, largely because expression of this emotion requires wrinkling of the nose – and thus

more detailed avatar models. These conclusions are presented through an experiment involving a pre-test questionnaire, a recognition exercise and a post-test questionnaire. During the recognition task, each participant was shown 28 photographs and 28 corresponding virtual head images and was asked to select an emotion category they felt the virtual head displayed. The study included 29 participants who have not used animation programmes before or who had any experience of classifying facial expressions. We presume the participants were typically developing and the article describes the age range from 22 to 51 and with a male to female split of 12:17.

Fabri and Moore (2005) argued that interaction through CVEs can benefit children with autism, and presented three areas where this could be of particular use: as an assistive technology; as an educational technology; and as a means of helping to address theory of mind (ToM) impairment. The authors reached these conclusions by developing a multimedia program whereby users could interact with emotionally expressive avatars with the potential to engender empathy, therefore being of value for people with autism. In testing this, the authors sent CD-ROMs to one hundred potential participants, in the United Kingdom, diagnosed with autism. The mean age of the 34 who replied was reported as 9.96. While the level and confirmation of diagnosis of autism is less clear, the characteristics of the participants are described as "18 participants were reported as children with Asperger Syndrome, 16 as children with severe autism" (p.5). The CD-ROM (materials including questionnaires and instructions) were sent to the participants who then proceeded to navigate through the three stages of the CD; the first was avatar representations (facial emotions in isolation), the second attempted to elicit possible emotions in context (social scenario). Finally, stage three, presented the user with an avatar representation of one emotion and asked them to select a number of given events that may have caused this emotion. The data sources were the completed questionnaires and data collected in log files from the computer. In analysing these, the authors suggest that emotions were well recognised and applied in context. They note that four participants did not perform well in the tasks, but also suggest that it could have been their diagnosis (reported as "severe autism") that caused this concern; although this does not account for the other 12 participants reported as having "severe autism". Finally, Fabri and Moore concluded that such virtual tools are understood emotionally, and used appropriately, by some individuals with autism.

Elsewhere, Moore et al. (2005) argued the case for using CVEs to help people with autism understand emotion, building on the work presented in Fabri and Moore (2004). They developed a simple platform that integrates the use of images (avatar representations) and animated facial-expression sequences, to help in the understanding of facial emotion and communication for users with autism. Moore et al. present three stages to their product: (1) avatar representations in isolation, to help initial emotional understanding; (2) prediction of emotions in contextual situations – own feelings and feelings of others; and (3) avatar emotional representation, paired with a selection of events. The tasks involved recognition of an emotion from a facial expression, selection of an expression to represent an emotion and prediction of an expression. The user at stage three is required to select an event that may have caused an emotional response, and is asked to infer their own emotion to that of another (cause and effect). In order to identify whether participants were successful in selecting appropriate emotional avatars for each section of their programme, Moore et al. compared the observed responses of the participants to the questions against chance responding. The results showed that over 88% of participants performed above the level of chance. Moore et al. conclude that the study offers evidence that the majority of participants involved were able to interpret and understand the emotions of the avatars appropriately. This study demonstrates that people with autism

have both the ability and predisposition to use CVEs, and that they can, via this medium, identify emotion, apply emotion and predict emotion from facial expressions (Moore et al., 2005). Some areas that are a little unclear are the demographic of the participants, the settings in which the study was carried out, and whether the skills gained could be generalised. These limitations were in part due to the fact CDs (with the application) were posted to participants and returned, meaning that the participants were not directly observed. This means that high variability would have been likely in the implementation and application of the CD to participants. The authors, while providing materials to help 'control' the variability, might have overcome this limitation by inviting participants to their research base. This study does, however, offer clear evidence that using virtual animated facial expression can help users with autism to understand and recognise emotion. The study recognises that a small minority of participants found it difficult to understand the emotions represented by the avatars, and for this reason, more details on the individual participants would have been useful, allowing greater insight into who CVEs could be most beneficial for.

Cheng and Fan (2008) also used a CVE to experiment with the representation of emotions for children with autism. This study included 2D image representations of 3D avatars, rather than 3D avatars as used in Parsons et al (2005). In Cheng and Fan's study ten participants ranging from 5 to 17 years old were selected; they all had a local (school) diagnosis of autism. The study was focused on considering the role of expressive avatars used in conjunction with text chat communication or computer-medicated communication (CMC). To investigate this aspect of CMC, the authors conduced an interview with the ten participants via the CMC programme created for the purpose of the study. One of the primary aims was to judge how the participants with autism responded with text *and* expressive avatars throughout the communication process. In other words they provided an interface that allowed users to talk one-to-one, through the medium of text and visual representations of faces. Each of these faces displayed a different emotion. They were modeled in 3D, then rendered and exported as 2D images. Cheng and Fan conclude that eight of the ten of participants were able to successfully use the system to identify emotion as represented by a graphic. Moreover, the participants were able to interpret the emotions of others through the system. This study considered, and builds upon, the work of Moore et al. (2005) and Fabri et al. (2004), and helps to reinforce the idea that avatar representation, used as part of the communication processes, can prove useful for users with autism. However, the work of Cheng and Fan (2008), Moore et al. (2005) and Fabri et al. (2004) are limited in that none of them draw directly on users' views or experiences of the environments provided. Moreover, there is little information presented regarding the broader application of the findings in other contexts (although schools and education were mentioned) where situating the CVEs within a school, for example, could provide a benefit to or application in an applied context. This could then involve teachers and participants further in the design and development of the process (Kerr, 2005).

Cromby et al. (1996) posit the use of VEs to aid people with learning difficulties (which would include people with autism). They consider the use of a pre-programmed VE to help people with severe disabilities in learning how to shop independently. A control group of participants was tasked with shopping for four items, putting them in a trolley and taking this to the checkout. Another group of participants would do the same, but firstly simulate the task using a VE. The mean age was 15 years old, with 5 male and 6 female participants. The experimental group performed better than the control group when shopping for real after the VE intervention. Moreover, the experimental group correctly identified more items on the shopping list, when repeating the task a second time. What this study fails to make clear are the participants' issues with performing the task in the "real" world, other than having "mental retardation" (p.104). The study examines a population of participants who all met set criteria – they had good motor skills and sufficient visual ability to use an input device (joystick); they could carry out a real shopping trip with little supervision; they had used a VE before; and finally, they had given consent to take part in the research. This study is important for its contribution to VEs and how these have been set up for, and used by, people with intellectual and developmental disabilities. Furthermore, this study makes a clear case for the successful generalisation of learning gained in a VE into a real-world scenario.

Through the studies already reviewed the role VEs can play to support people with autism lie mainly in the issues related to their condition. For example, people with autism could present with repetitive and obsessive behaviours in addition to issues with imagination and changes to their environments. It has been shown, through the review so far, that computers can offer a sense of predictability and structure that people with autism may be drawn to. Several studies have addressed this with positive results; the impact computers can have could prove a fruitful opportunity for researchers working with people who have an ASC.

The following sections address more specific studies in the area of VEs for users with autism, specifically picking up on social skills and communication. However very few of these early studies (from Strickland et al., 1996 to Moore et al., 2005) engage with participants as either co-designers or evaluators of the technology used in the studies. This means limited information regarding preferences or an understanding of users needs are considered. Aspects such as these may have provided further insights to the use of technology it was implemented.

Another study that builds on the work carried out by Strickland et al. (1996) and Cromby et al. (1996), and adds to limited knowledge in the field, is that of Parsons et al. (2006); where newer and different technology is applied. The study of Parsons et al. (2006) involved the creation of a virtual environment (VE) for the purpose of improving social skills in two children with autism. This study included two children within the high-functioning range, as Fabri and Moore (2005) and Fabri et al. (2004) do. However, Parsons et al. introduce a VE that involves navigating through simple scenes (a café and a bus stop), rather than presenting a one-to-one communication tool (building on the findings of Cobb et al., 2002). In other words, the users were able to navigate through an environment or space as part of the simulation. The scene includes other characters, who are passive, but are pre-programmed to respond to user input. In their analysis, Parsons et al. consider five areas for review and discussion: (1) repetition of response; (2) physical and literal interpretations; (3) treating the VE like a game; (4) putting learning into practice; and (5) recognising changes and usefulness. Repetition of response was an area of the research that provided mixed results. Both users would navigate through the café scene in exactly the same way, individually, each time they approached the tasks, although one of the participants would maintain their route through the scene despite encounters with chairs, tables and other objects. Parsons et al. also report some repetitive statements/verbal responses, although the participants did change some responses in the VE, in particular choices of food ordered and when asking if they could sit down to eat their food. Furthermore, the participants sat in different places each time they used the environment, suggesting that they were "responding differently to the changing demands of the VE" (Parsons et al., 2006, p.13). Literal interpretations were an issue for the participants: one of them could not understand why, for example, they could not sit in an empty chair when the person sitting at the table said, "Excuse me, that seat is taken." The participant thus highlighted a problem with accepting that a seat can belong to a person socially.

However, after repeating this several times, and with some help from the facilitators, the participant was able to understand the need to ask if a seat is taken, out of courtesy.

One of the main difficulties in using VEs, and in particular for users with ASCs, is in creating the perception of reality, so that the user can identify and provide natural responses. It was noted by Parsons et al. (2005) that the participants viewed the VE as a game, and would not therefore interact as they might in real-life. However, it was observed that there were occasions when the participants would apply real-world and appropriate actions to the VE. A specific example relates to the choice of seats on a bus – the participant chose a seat that had enough leg-room, and one that was facing in the preferred direction. This perhaps shows how immersed the participant had become, and that they did view the VE as a "real world". A similar finding, but with more participants, was reported in an earlier study by Parsons et al. (2005).

The efficacy of a VE in helping to teach social skills is also evident to some degree. Parsons et al. (2005) concede that VEs take some time to get used to, and allow for errors to be made, but they also observed that such mistakes (taking a seat without asking if it was being used, for example) were absent from later sessions. From this they conclude that more scaffolding could be used, depending on the IQ profiles of users, to help direct people in such social situations, meaning that a range of learners could benefit from VEs. Further reinforcing the value of VEs, Parsons et al. observe that the participants recognised changes in the levels of difficulty that could be set in the VE. Participants were aware of the level changes, identifying that it was busier (with more people), for example. Users also demonstrated an awareness of the implications of the changes on subsequent social decisions in the VEs (Parsons et al., 2006; Parsons et al., 2005). This study also observed that the participants would sometimes test the boundaries/responses of the VE, rather than necessarily behaving as they would in real-life.

Parsons et al. identify this as an important aspect of VEs "because 'testing out' the possibilities affords crucial learning opportunities that may be missed if the participant learns only to click all the correct buttons [clicking buttons in the correct order, for example]" (Parsons et al., 2006, p.201). This contributes to an enjoyment of the tasks, and also, as Parsons et al. suggest, reduces the anxiety or social worry experienced in real-life. In addition, the participants wanted to continue with the tasks, and continued to use the VE long after the study had concluded.

One area of interest that arises in the work of Parsons et al. (2005) and Parsons et al. (2006) is that of avatar and environment design. The work of Parsons et al. (2005; 2006) hypothesised that simplified graphics meant that the complexities of facial detail, for example, were lessened and that the users were thus more able to deal with and process information presented. The research of Fabri and Moore (2005) and Fabri (2006) concurs with this – that less expressive faces are not only preferred, but are equivalent in terms of being able to extract information for users with autism. However, not many, if any, have examined the use of more complex graphics (avatars and scenery), or assessed users' needs other than in the particular tasks within these studies. Therefore it could be argued that the use of more complex and attractive imagery might help to facilitate immersive experiences, while still providing a safe, manageable, predictable and understandable environment. This sentiment is echoed by Parsons et al. (2006), who found that participants in their study suggested the virtual figures (avatars) in the scene could have been more detailed and 'human'.

In summary, Parsons et al. suggest future collaborative virtual environments "could potentially allow grater behavioural realism through incorporation of 'embodied avatars' ... and improved features such as gaze direction and facial expressions...". Although Parsons et al. made this claim in 2006, very limited work since has explored embodied avatars, facial expression or gaze direction; no work has considered artificial intelligent agents in virtual environments either.

It is becoming clear that there is a greater definition in the avatars, a more organic feel to the environment and a greater level of detail overall in Second Life. Moreover, aspects such as lip-synced avatars (when used with a microphone to input speech) and facial expression highlight the potential virtual worlds have, especially in relation to the recommendations of Parsons et al. (2006). This may facilitate a greater level of immersion and remains a gap in current knowledge. Moreover, the more realistic surrounding environments may enable a greater level of recognition (especially with commonly recognised shops, eateries, buildings, etc.).

Cheng and Ye (2010) consider the use of collaborative virtual environments in a broader context, that of learning. Cheng and Ye explore and examine the use of a collaborative virtual learning environment (CVLE) to help improve social competence, and to increase abilities in social interaction in people with autism. To this end, the authors developed a tool that integrates both expressive avatars and animated social situations (i.e. understanding of perception and expressive feelings; recognition of non-verbal behaviours such as facial expressions of the avatar appropriately). As an intervention, this study considers increased positive social competence (social interaction and behavioural performance) as a measure; at baseline, intervention and maintenance stages. The results of the work are presented mainly as quantitative data, though there are also some qualitative data captured from teachers and parents. Three main findings are presented: firstly, that a visual assistant (in the form of a virtual character) may help people with autism to learn; secondly, that visually mediated teaching and written text cues decrease inappropriate social behaviours; and finally, that 3D expressive avatars and sound effects can be highly motivating for users with autism. This work highlights some potentially vital factors in the way a virtual world should be designed: firstly, that careful consideration needs to be given to visual cues; secondly, that the inclusion of text can be useful (to decrease real-world "inappropriate social behaviours" p.1075); and finally, how important audio (sound effects and voice) can potentially be, although all of this will be dependent on particular groups of children and their specific needs.

Leading on from this study, Cheng et al. (2010) developed a tool to test some of the points raised in their earlier 2010 article (Cheng and Ye, 2010). Here a CVLE is designed specifically for the purpose of enhancing empathy instruction. Through an experimental methodology, the authors consider a CVLE to promote the understanding of empathy in users on the autism spectrum. It would have been overly ambitious to consider all empathic traits, so the authors consider expressive empathy – kindness, tolerance and respect – rather than all eight components of empathy discussed by Williams (1996). To test empathic responses from participants, Cheng et al. designed a 3D virtual interface that displayed a restaurant where four social scenes were presented. Each of these scenes (someone cuts into the restaurant queue; a drink is spilled on the floor; a passerby slips and falls; someone comes and sits next to the participant's avatar) could elicit empathic responses from typical users. Through a baseline, intervention and maintain experiment, the authors were able to show an increased ability to recognise empathy in users and others. The study was conducted within a school setting, and participants were all assessed to have good verbal IQ, performance IQ and full-scale IQ (scoring greater than 70 on the Wechsler Abbreviated Intelligence Scale III). Though there were only three participants involved in this study, some key points emerge: that 3D (visualised) applications can help in the learning process; that visual assistance may help users on the autism spectrum; that VE interfaces can help users on the spectrum in performing appropriate behaviours when interacting with others; that creating appropriate scenes can help to generalise

learning; and that computerised systems are appealing to users with autism.

Further reinforcing the use of virtual environments to help teach people with autism, Rutten et al. (2003) explore the use of single-user virtual environments (SVEs). In this study they consider the use of SVEs to help teach, to support learning, and to enhance social skills in people on the autism spectrum. This study uses the same infrastructure and software as Parsons et al. (2005), and considers some of the same issues. Rutten et al. conclude that SVEs can be used successfully to help teach transferable skills, but that this requires support from facilitators/teachers to enable constant reflection and learning. Moreover, say Rutten et al., the safety that SVEs and CVEs provide, and the opportunity they give to practise skills away from real-life contexts, means that they are valuable tools for users with ASCs. Rutten et al. also compare the use of CVEs and SVEs, concluding that CVEs provide less structure, and so become more challenging to use, but conversely that they offer increased flexibility for social-skills training that does not rely on fixed protocol, and that they are more adaptable across cultures. Rutten et al. suggest that SVEs would be best employed as a progressive training package, whereby users learn particular skills, followed by CVE use, where learned skills can be practiced collaboratively.

In addition to using collaborative virtual environments to help people with autism, Schmidt and Schmidt (2008) highlight why and how virtual environments can be successful for people with autism. They examine the use of computers for individuals with ASCs, stating that they are an ideal platform to help people with ASC improve their difficulties, social skills. Computers are predicable, routine and free from social demands; they provide immediate feedback and clear expectations (Schmidt and Schmidt, 2008). This is similar to the points raised by Murray (1997) reinforcing the theoretical potential for virtual environments for this user group. All of this argue Schmidt and Schmidt, provides means to help children to learn and develop social and emotional skills. Within their review, Schmidt and Schmidt note that VEs can help because they allow users to make mistakes, and, in the case of children with autism, to make mistakes without suffering real consequences (Schmidt and Schmidt, 2008). In addition to this, VEs can be modified, customised and simplified to suit individual needs (Schmidt and Schmidt, 2008).

More recently, Millen et al. (2010) and Cobb et al. (2010) have investigated design issues in VEs, specifically for people with autism. Millen et al (2010) consider the current situation as regards methodologies and human–computer interaction (HCI) guidelines for the development of technology for children with autism. They point to research carried out by Grandin (2002) and Van Rijn and Stappers (2008), who provide some guidelines for the use of ICT tools in teaching students with autism. These include: avoiding sudden loud sounds, limiting the use of line drawings, placing the keyboard close to the screen, providing structure, letting users feel in control and utilising users' eye for detail. However, these principles are a little 'scattered' in terms of context, that is, age and abilities are not specified; and so it is difficult to know for whom these recommendations are being made. Concluding, Millen et al. suggest that the following issues need further clarification and discussion in regard to design of VEs for ASC users: how to engage users with ASCs with the design process; what age and ability level users need to be in order to participate; at what stage of the process should users be consulted; what barriers exist to involvement; and how evaluation of prototypes can occur.

Also considering the design of virtual environments, Wallace et al. (2010) consider the role of immersive virtual environments (IVEs) for children with ASCs. The authors argue that immersive virtual environments – essentially the same as virtual reality environments, but without the headsets and input devices – can offer a greater level of 'immersion' for the end user, compared to desktop VEs, by surrounding them (from the side, front, bottom and top) with life-sized, realistic representations. This creates a "naturalistic and direct experience" (Wallace et al., 2010, p.202). The focus of this study is to examine: (1) whether children with ASCs experience IVEs in different ways to their typically developing peers; and (2) whether children with ASCs show atypical social judgments in IVEs, compared to typically developing children. The authors assess the first point by using the *ITC Sense of Presence Inventory* (ITC-SoPI) questionnaire, followed by the *Social Attractiveness* Questionnaire. Data are presented that illustrate how a typically developing group and an ASC group were comparable in terms of the ITC-SoPI. The ITC-SoPI is broken into four-subsections, and the authors report on each of these in turn. They identify that there were "similar levels" of spatial presence and engagement between the two groups, and "no group differences" on the ecological validity or negative effects. On the whole, the typically developing (TD) and ASC groups both performed at similar levels. This supports the notion that children with ASCs are able to make links between images, and to become immersed within a virtual reality set-up (Strickland et al., 1996), in addition to achieving this on par with their TD peers. Moreover, Wallace et al. (2010, p.212) state that "… IVEs can be realistic enough to simulate and assess social situations" for users with ASCs. In verifying the second part of the study, the authors introduce an animated character into the IVE, to test whether children with ASCs make atypical social judgments. Upon testing this (measuring socially desirable and undesirable interactions), the authors conclude that, just as in the real world, children with ASCs are significantly more likely to misjudge a socially unacceptable situation than their typically developing peers.

The work of Wallace et al. (2010) provides further evidence that VEs are meaningful and non aversive for young people with autism spectrum conditions. Key points to be taken from this study include: the successful use of high-quality imagery accepted by participants; verification of data through the qualitative means of questionnaires; and evidence that children with autism can feel the same level of presence as their typically developing peers. Through the work of Wallace et al. it can be seen that the use of high-quality images in a virtual environment could help to provide a positive feeling of presence for users with ASCs. However, the context in which this technology was used might have provided opportunity to work with key stakeholders; one being teachers and schools. In other words the role that this technology can play in educational contexts could have been explored to help provide greater links between technology and educational provision. In addition, there are potentially limited benefits to this type of research in that working in labs (as with the work of Strickland et al., 1996) can only produce results applied in that context. Further work is needed that sees context and generalisation in applied settings.

So far and in sum, the studies reviewed to this point have involved virtual environments of sorts specifically to enable users with autism to either gain emotional recognition skills or rehearse social skills. In addition more complex interfaces are being developed as time progresses (from Strickland et al. in 1996 through to Wallace et al in 2010), and the quality of graphics are be made to resemble 'real-life'. It can therefore be concluded that VEs and VR technologies provide a means to interact without real-world consequences, but more than this, slow communication to a pace users with autism seem to prefer. In addition some encouraging results seem to suggest that undertaking activities in VEs can be generalised to real world contexts; further reinforcing the benefit for users who have an ASC. However, gaps in knowledge still pertain to the preferred types of communication in VEs and in-world appearance through an avatar. In addition, as this is still an emerging field of research, research has remained focused on small samples and limited contextual information meaning that

'tried and tested' technologies are not yet fully explored or realised for this, or many other user groups. Specifically, there is limited understanding of these technologies for users with autism, in the classroom, although Cobb (2007), Cobb et al. (2010) and Parsons and Cobb (2011) have raised this issue.

Cobb et al. (2010) describe a European project, implementing shared active surfaces and collaborative virtual environments for children with autism. Focusing on CVEs the authors argue that there are many reasons for choosing these techniques including: customisability, controllability, predictability, structure, engagement, variability and evaluation. Research design challenges relate to: embodiment, viewpoint control, representation of actions, interface, complexity of graphics, structure, real world location and content. Beyond identifying these justifications and issues, the authors make clear the importance of including stakeholders in the design of interfaces for children with different needs (especially ASC users). They state that: "schools and teachers [as well as] pupils [will be] important design partners on the project" (Cobb et al., 2010, p380). The work of Cobb et al. and Millen et al. may well pave the way in future directions of VE design and evaluation, including careful consideration of what users might require (or even like). While this present study will not focus on the evaluation of the design per se, there will be design considerations that include input from users. These include teachers, pupils (direct users) and parents.

In a related article, Parsons and Cobb (2011) review the literature on the application of VR for autism (encompassing VEs). They highlight the potential for virtual reality interventions for children on the autism spectrum, stating that benefits include: "... simulations of authentic real-world situations in a carefully controlled and safe environment" (Parsons and Cobb, 2011: 355). Parsons and Cobb add that other benefits can include social and life skills training. All of these benefits to users with autism reinforce the case for the use of virtual tools – that they may help children to develop and test skills that otherwise might seem daunting, triggering anxious and inappropriate responses to communication within social situations. However, Parsons and Cobb suggest that there still exists a challenge in developing robust and usable technologies that can make a difference in a real-world classroom. This conclusion is reached through a literature review that extracts successful implementation of virtual reality and virtual environments, whilst also considering some of the areas that have not been covered yet. Parsons and Cobb suggest that there is (1) limited application of VR for educational purposes; (2) a lack of applications for everyday classrooms; and (3) a lack of effective design (specifically user-centred design). Further, it is suggested that integrating the points raised above, would help to establish effective ways of integrating VR into an applicable context. For example, Parsons and Cobb explore the notion that facilitators (or teachers) can be 'designed in' to the VR use in order to help scaffold and support learning more effectively. In providing future directions, Parsons and Cobb's article suggests further research in the areas of representations of self; how the realism of VR contexts helps in the transfer of generalised learning; and collaboration opportunities in-world, to help generate independence within a learning group. This leads us to believe that more evidence and research, of a diverse nature, is really needed to help argue a case for

THE USE AND ROLE OF VIRTUAL WORLDS FOR PEOPLE WITH AUTISM

By examining studies and practice in virtual worlds, this section intends to firstly present some studies that have used virtual worlds with the purpose of developing skills (e.g. group work, reflection) within medical and health domains. From these, this chapter will discuss work in the

domains of virtual worlds used specifically with and by users with ASCs.

Boulos et al. (2007) considered the use of Second Life in medical and health education. This article helps to provide a clear indication of the potential of VWs in health-related conditions – in an educational context. The authors discuss and present two case studies of recent and successful VW endeavours, in Second Life (Healthinfo Island and VNEC – Virtual Neurological Educational Centre), and are able to present a detailed insight into the advantages afforded by the platform. These include the use across a distance-learning education model and for older people and people with physical disabilities; real-time social networking and state-of-the-art graphical representations are also highlighted. Boulos et al., in addition, identify several challenges pertaining to the use of VWs. These include Internet addiction, gambling, violence, trust, identity, copyright and vandalism. These all relate to ethical concerns, and are something all VW studies need to address and consider for their user groups, more broadly.

Virtual worlds (VWs) also offer potential for users with ASCs, and in fact one of the largest, Second Life, has many registered users who have such conditions (Salman, 2006). However, to date few, if any, formal studies have been carried out to assess the impact such environments are having on users with autism, even though virtual worlds have contributed to this field of study and could provide a form of assistive technology.

In a brief correspondence, Fusar-Poli et al. (2008, p.980) hypothesise that Second Life could be used to "develop social and communicative skills of autistic people". They go on to outline the same affordances as Cobb, Parsons, Moore and Fabri, stating that "… it allows anonymous social interactions, and provides high levels of social interactivity but without complex linguistic and social-behavioural processing necessary for face-to-face conversations" (Fusar-Poli et al., 2008, p.980). Further, Fusar-Poli et al. suggest that it "levels the playing field for autistic people", in that it offers a new space to rehearse social skills. This last statement, although a value statement, does suggest that people with autism and related conditions can enter VWs without any preconceptions or assumptions placed upon them. Fusar-Poli et al. also say that a secure and safe space is needed in which social mistakes can be made so that a sense of collaboration and community can be established. The authors propose Second Life as an ideal tool for allowing participants with autism to benefit from the affordances mentioned. Notwithstanding these advantages, the authors may be assuming that structured and autonomous learning is something valued by and relevant for all people on the autism spectrum. Further, they do not identify age ranges or clusters that might be most suitable for using VWs. Nevertheless, this is one of few papers that argue for such an application, for people on the autism spectrum.

As previously mentioned, many users with autism and/or Asperger's are forming groups within Second Life in which they can liaise and communicate. Identities are kept secret – users can be whoever they want to be. One article that examines this is Salman (2006), which highlights how one particular user (who has Asperger's and uses a wheelchair) finds it helpful to enter Second Life as an avatar and become immersed. It is "… easier engaging in conversation … I can participate in activities that I'd otherwise mourn" (Salman, 2006, p.1). The virtual space that this article considers is called Brigadoon, a "self-help group for those affected by Asperger's syndrome or other forms of autism". There are several spaces and groups in Second Life created to support users with ASCs, all of which provide a good illustration of people developing technology and resources for their own purpose. Moreover, the work of Salmon highlights how it is important to listen to what users have to say about their experiences, especially when working with, and designing, technology.

More recently, DeAngelis (2009) discusses the therapeutic potential of virtual worlds, and reports on ways in which researchers are using

Second Life with users who have ASCs. For this case study, the researchers have developed a 'private' island where users can interact with one another, with therapist intervention if and when needed, to help guide and encourage the users. However, the article describes the intervention in little detail, and results from the work have not been published, so again this work lacks any empirical data. Nevertheless one of the researchers points out: "It's only by real-life experiences, by training the brain in social situations, that people can develop some competence in these areas" (DeAngelis, 2009, p.1). Bignell (2008) also points to further opportunities afforded in Second Life for users with autism. Bignell discusses and has highlighted several aspects of virtual worlds that align to many of the findings of Parsons et al., (2006) and Strickland et al., (1996). These include factors related to collaboration, social skills rehearsal and safety in making mistakes. Going further Bignell suggests that virtual worlds could "be a place to share information and simulate social interactions" (slide 28). Here he is eluding to the fact VWs in fact offer a more dynamic and flexible space for their users, and as a result, VWs may well be able to support the strengths of this population. The current study seeks to examine this in further detail though visual representation and communication.

Many of the above affordances of VWs are also reflected in VEs and CVEs (see: Parsons et al. (2006), Cobb et al. (2002), Strickland et al. (1996)). However, it could be argued that some of the main advantages and opportunities offered by VWs over VEs include avatar customisation, multiple users and a more expansive real-time communication process. In addition VWs tend to be more 'off-the-shelf' and readily available to use in less research-focused contexts (out of research labs and in natural settings; bedroom, home, classroom).

Leading on from this, Craig (2011) reports on how children with ASCs are using Second Life to enable a sense of "control". Craig's article explores a project that encourages children with autism and Asperger's to play online games. Part of this initiative involved creating a drop-in centre where Second Life was installed and ready for children with ASCs to use. A case study within the report explores how a young child (aged 12) with high-functioning autism uses the virtual world. It is reported that this individual at one time struggled to make friends and to communicate with his peers, and was "severely anxious". However, through the intervention of a virtual world and online games, the child seems to have overcome some of these issues, is better able to communicate and is "happier in himself". These are the words of the child's parent, who attributes the use of computers and Second Life to this change in her child. Project organisers report that: "in Second Life these [ASC] users understand their environment … you know what the rules are, you can make things, all without having to refer to other people" (Paragraph 10). Interestingly, and perhaps most importantly, the project organisers notice that by sharing passions in-world, users were able to share passions in the real world. Common interests would allow for this generalisation to happen. Another participant noted that using a virtual world had helped him to "make friends with like-minded children" (Paragraph 17). Craig goes on to suggest that the use of computers in this way allows a connection with people who are "non-judgemental", who can be interacted with via the Internet. The report attributes some core components as affordances of virtual worlds for users with autism that are relevant for the current study including having control over the environment, so much so that the participants with autism seems more interested in the environment than communicating with one another. However, the role of an avatar was reported as providing a sense of safety and security; leading us to think that an avatar (within a virtual world) could prove to be a link between CMC and expressiveness (linking the work of Benford, 2008 and Fabri et al. 2004 together). Finally Craig, reports that common

interests can be embedded and generalised out from the virtual world; suggesting that perhaps some form of user-centred approach is appropriate for users with autism, when considering a virtual world.

The article provides a useful insight into how users with ASCs (and their parents) perceive the use of virtual worlds, through which several implications arise: avatar customisation and the role of an avatar in the communication process, in addition to understanding the behaviours of users with autism in virtual worlds. In addition the initiative reported could have been developed in partnership with stakeholders – school and teachers – to a greater degree. This might have provided a means for the project to become more embedded into a structured and secure environment. Notwithstanding this, this project clearly highlights the benefits VWs can offer the ASC community and presents some data in the form of parent and project organisers to support its findings.

In developing social skills in virtual worlds for people with autism, partners in a European Funded Project (ECHOES; Guldberg et al., 2010) have published results of their project on the use of technology-enhanced learning environments for children with autism. Alcorn et al. (2011) report that users with ASC were able to follow a virtual character's gaze and gesture cues. Alcorn et al. frame their study through joint attention, and whether children with autism are able to follow joint attention cues in a virtual environment. The authors were concerned with the accuracy and reaction time of the participants in following a virtual characters gaze and/or pointing. Participants in their study included thirty-two 5 to 14 year olds all diagnosed with an ASC. Participants undertook a simple selection task each involving three flowers (two distractions and a target) to which the virtual character, displayed on-screen, tried to direct the child's attention. For this study participants would touch the screen; a screen that was the size of a television (28-32 inches across) and were presented with a virtual environment on the screen. Measurements were classified as accurate (first touch after the character's indication was to the target flower) or an error (a touch to any non-target area). Through analysis of quantitative data relating to the joint attention task, Alcorn et al. conclude that young people with an ASC could learn how to follow a virtual character's gaze and gesture cues, in addition to responding through a touch screen interface.

These findings are positive in relation to the current study as Alcorn et al. provide information related to communication with a virtual character in a virtual environment. Although this is not achieved through an avatar (the person themselves interacted via a touch screen interface), it provides data that is encouraging about the willingness and ability to interface with virtual characters in a positive manner; which is best evidenced through the qualitative data collected and evaluated by the authors. In collecting video (recording the experiments) several instances of enthusiastic and successful engagements with the virtual character were witnessed leading the authors to conclude that there were examples of social sharing (i.e. spontaneous gaze to adults directly after a child had made a flower choice). This study identifies several advantages of using virtual environments for children with autism that are relevant for this current study. Firstly, the finding that young people with autism are able, and willing, to interact with virtual characters on a screen (with the possible addition of the benefit of joint attention), and secondly that conclusions related to positive social behaviours are reached in part with help from qualitative data (observations). This proves a rich and thick description getting close to reality, as does Thomas (2011), while reporting the views and reactions of participants themselves, in a similar manner to that of Parsons et al (2006). It could also be suggested that this approach and data type (qualitative view of participants with autism) are underrepresented in the study of virtual environments utilised for users with autism. Understanding the views and

opinions of these users within virtual environments (and very specifically collaborative virtual environments) can add to literature and research of computer-mediated communication of ASC users, especially in terms of avatar representation and online (in-world) communication.

In a more recent article, Second Life was utilised to enable social cognition training for young adults with HFA (Kandalaft et al., 2012). The authors of this study considered the perspectives of 8 young adults with HFA over the course of 5 weeks, in a total of 10 sessions. The focus of the study was to examine the viability of VR intervention for social-cognition training. Social performance and skill measures were used to judge social change in the participants. Tasks carried out in-world included social introductions and interactions with friends; meeting strangers and friends; negotiating with a salesman; a job interview; and working with co-workers. Through these activities the following measures were taken and considered in a pre- and post-testing intervention experiment: (1) verbal and non-verbal emotion recognition; (2) social perception subtest; (3) theory of mind; (4) conversational skills; and (5) functional measure (follow-up survey). Scores for many of the measures increased after the intervention, with some displaying a significant increase. Verbal and non-verbal recognition measures showed significant improvement at post-testing, and the ToM and conversational skills measures increased, although not significantly. A broader set of data elicited from questionnaires with participants identified the VR platform as providing a basis on which they could develop skills in maintaining a conversation, establishing a relationship and understanding others' points of view.

Participants, however, were less positive or enthusiastic about the following aspects: expressing emotion, introducing themselves, academic functioning, and negotiation skills. The study addressed and examined some important aspects of virtual worlds as used by people with HFA, providing data that will encourage the use of virtual worlds as a form of therapy or intervention to aid social skills development in users with ASCs. However this study does not address avatar customisation, user-centred design or communication via text-input, aspects that that continue to be missing from the literature. Kandalaft et al. also do not identify what the most appropriate forms of communication for this group are. Finally, it is difficult to judge the severity of autism characteristics, where further diagnosis data could have usefully been presented. The avatars were pre-designed by researchers and presented to the users, where providing some information on how to customise an avatar within the virtual world might have proven of benefit to the participants.

Discussion of various studies, above, suggests that while there are several hypotheses being examined and informal studies being undertaken in virtual worlds, there are limited data to support the benefits of communication methods or avatar representation in virtual worlds for users with autism. There is also limited research that considers how best to deploy or develop technology with users, for users. It follows that there is limited uptake of said technology in schools, the home or any other settings where this technology is potentially best placed for people with disabilities to access, support and become comfortable with technology to support their daily needs. It is also the case that much of the research to date has left limited legacies; certainly in terms of technology infrastructure. This aspect of the research is severely lacking, where limited focus is placed on the technology, per se, but rather the outcomes. While focusing on outcomes is vitally important, especially in this emerging field of research, greater emphasis could and should be placed on the lasting impact of the technology after research is completed. Moreover, few studies provide a rich description of classroom integration of a virtual world, or in-depth users' perspectives. Thus, whilst there is clear evidence, for the application of VRTs for people on the spectrum (Kandalaft et

al., 2012; Parsons et al., 2007; Fabri and Moore, 2006; Parsons and Cobb, 2011; Wallace et al., 2010), the use of virtual worlds warrants further investigation in several areas. These include communication patterns in-world, avatar design and customisation (representation of self), peer-to-peer activity and relationships between multiple users. Finally, 3D representational fidelity, as Parsons and Cobb (2011) discuss, could be investigated, to discover if and how fidelity is important to ASC user groups.

FUTURE RESEARCH DIRECTIONS

The evidence-base for VRTs used for and by people with autism is a growing one and an area of research that continues to grow. While much of the earlier work (i.e. Strickland et al. 1996) consisted of small samples and some basic graphics, they were vitally important in helping to establish an acceptance for VRT technology and allow insights to how people with autism dealt with various input and visualization devices. While the research to-date has added to, and helped to develop an evidence-base, more research could be completed to help move the state-of-the-art to the next level. For example using VRTs in applied settings and apply evaluation methodologies to include greater emphasis on qualitative approached would enrich and widen the work carried out to-date.

Another strand that future research might consider relates to the design and pedagogical aspects of virtual reality technology, and specifically virtual world technology used with, and by, people with autism. This strand should focus on considering representation of self, self-awareness, communication and the role of communication tools available in VRT interfaces (Newbutt, 2013). For example, the importance of the role of avatar customisation in embodiment, communication and interactions experienced and generated in VRTs (specifically VWs and CVEs) is clear: it is important for users of virtual worlds to invest time in designing their avatars in order to facilitate the full potential of CMC in these environments (Newbutt, 2013). The work of Newbutt (2013) highlighted that avatar customisation by users with autism appears to be limited (when compared to a typically developing group, and users in other studies in the area of avatar design). Future work, therefore, might explore this further; investigating in greater detail the reasons for this and its impact on virtual world communication. It may also be of interest for future scholars to investigate avatars used by people with autism over a longer period of time, and perhaps in more natural settings (at home, for example). Moreover, future studies could reflect on the role of avatar design in more depth, perhaps enriching *their* accounts and conclusions reached in relation to in-world interactions (Schmidt et al., 2012; Kandalaft et al., 2012).

Future work in this area could also consider the deployment and set up of VRTs; helping to make the set-up and use as easy as possible for various stakeholders. Stakeholders within this context might include; parents, teachers, carers or support workers (to name a few). While technology has and will continue to help support a variety of people, it could be argued that unless users and key stakeholders are able to understand the technology in question and how to best use, develop or apply the technology, barriers may continue to exist. The term 'continue' is used here, as there are currently very few applications within the use of VRTs that have continued to exist in the place they were first tested or researched. Therefore, a need to provide ownership to end-users and key stakeholders remains a research priority, if the full potential of VRTs is to be realised. In doing so, a greater level of customisation/bespoke applications and VRT scenarios can be developed; perhaps providing one way to help make VRTs more meaningful and useful; aimed at specific outcomes (Kandalaft et al., 2012).

Future work might also consider more closely the needs for bespoke solutions to aid the day-to-day lives of people with autism. As Parsons et al. (2006) highlight: "... comments from Mike suggested he had some ideas about what VEs he would like to see developed in the future: *I know what would be useful for me.* 'Cause I'm wanting to learn how to walk safe from ... my house to my Grandma's house ... It's something that's a starter really. [emphasis added]" (Parsons et al., 2006, p.200).

This quote clearly identifies a need for research to focus on specific outcomes and the needs of individuals. It would therefore be useful within this research domain to consider a set of generic encounters and situations that users could rehearse in virtual-world environments. Such environments could include artificially intelligent agents (known as "chat-bots"), to help enable social encounters and situations to occur without other "players" being present. Customisable social situations could be set by teachers or carers who understand what might be useful for specific users.

Finally, longer and more sustained research could be introduced to enable greater comprehension of how VRTs can impact and enable people with autism. Longitudinal studies considering mixed-methods would be a welcomed addition to the field, as would consideration of off-the-shelf technologies. Although VRTs are able to offer clear affordances for people with autism, -- and there is much to be excited about -- more research and greater application (within context) is required to provide more definitive and substantial conclusions in this area.

CONCLUSION

The increase of multimedia computing within the area of educational support for children with autism has been the focus of much research; from the early work of Colby (1973) and Heimman et al. (1995) to the work of Silver and Oakes (2001).

These published works examined specific skills that multimedia could address in the educational development of children with autism. Through such studies, an argument has been constructed, for the use of virtual environments in providing a unique affordance for users with ASCs. Scholars such as Strickland et al. (1996), Rutten et al. (2003), Parsons et al. (2005; 2006), Wallace et al. (2010) and Cheng et al. (2010) have each explored the role of immersion, realism, engagement and learning within virtual environments. Building on this, Kandalaft et al. (2012), have provided a specific example of the role virtual worlds can play in social-cognition training. Yet, there remains a limited understanding in the literature of users' perspectives; the role virtual worlds can play in social skills training, and whether virtual worlds can be used to develop core competencies that people with autism often struggle with (i.e. communication, confidence to initiate communication, testing socialising skills). This is a potential area for further pursuit in research agendas.

Overall, the area of technology used by people with autism and the potential benefits they hold, is still at an early stage in terms of research and an evidence-base. More so in relation to applied research and practice-based paradigms. In addition, and as highlighted above, no studies have yet applied a longitudinal or mixed-methods approach to this area; something that would help produce a far better picture in terms of the longer-term outcomes, frameworks for continued application of technology (updates, development, versions), and refined software/hardware, that might be most suitable and applicable in a variety of contexts (school, home, centres, etc...). Therefore, and while there is some evidence for the need to pursue this area of research, it is equally important to recognise and acknowledge this is an emergent field; one that is in the early stages of research outputs and projects. Virtual reality technology used with and by people with autism is an exciting one, with a positive future, but an area that warrants further research to yield a larger evidence-base.

REFERENCES

Alcorn, A., Pain, H., Rajendran, G., Smith, T., Lemon, O., Porayska-Pomsta, K., & Bernardini, S. (2011). Social communication between virtual characters and children with autism. In *Artificial intelligence in education* (pp. 7–14). Berlin: Springer. doi:10.1007/978-3-642-21869-9_4

Baird, G., Cass, H., & Slonims, V. (2003). Diagnosis of autism. *BMJ (Clinical Research Ed.), 327*, 488–493. doi:10.1136/bmj.327.7413.488 PMID:12946972

Baron-Cohen, S., & Bolton, S. (1993). *Autism: The facts*. Oxford, UK: Oxford University Press.

Benford, P. (2008). *The use of internet-based communication by people with autism*. (Unpublished doctoral dissertation). University of Nottingham, Nottingham, UK.

Bignell, S. (2008). *Autism and Asperger's in Second Life*. University of Derby. Retrieved from http://www.miltonbroome.com/2008/06/autism-aspergers-and-second-life.html

Bolte, S., Golan, O., & Goodwin, M. S., & Zwaigenbaum. (2010). What can innovative technologies do for Autism spectrum disorders? *Journal of Autism, 14*(3), 155–159. doi:10.1177/1362361310365028 PMID:20603897

Bolton, P. F., Macdonald, H., Pickles, A., Rios, P., Goode, S., & Crowson, M. et al. (1994). A case-control family history study of autism. *Journal of Child Psychology and Psychiatry, and Allied Disciplines, 35*, 877–900. doi:10.1111/j.1469-7610.1994.tb02300.x PMID:7962246

Boulos, M. N. K., Hetherington, L., & Wheeler, S. (2007). Second Life: An overview of the potential of 3-D virtual worlds in medical and health education. *Health Information and Libraries Journal, 24*(4), 233–245. doi:10.1111/j.1471-1842.2007.00733.x PMID:18005298

Charitos, D., Karadanos, G., Sereti, E., Triantafillou, S., Koukouvinou, S., & Martakos, D. (2000). Employing virtual reality for aiding the organisation of autistic children behaviour in everyday tasks. In *Proceedings of International Conference on Disability, Virtual Reality and Associated Technologies*, (pp. 147–52). Academic Press.

Cheng, Y., Chiang, H., Ye, J., & Cheng, L. (2010). Enhancing empathy instruction using a collaborative virtual learning environment for children with autistic spectrum conditions. *Computers & Education*, *55*(4), 1449–1458. doi:10.1016/j.compedu.2010.06.008

Cheng, Y., & Fan, Y. (2008). The 3D humanoid emotions in interactive learning environments for people with autism. In *Proceedings of World Conference on Educational Multimedia, Hypermedia and Telecommunications*, (pp. 5162–70). Academic Press.

Cheng, Y., & Ye, Y. (2010). Exploring the social competence of students with autism spectrum conditions in a collaborative virtual learning environment – The pilot study. *Computers & Education*, *54*(4), 1068–1077. doi:10.1016/j.compedu.2009.10.011

Cobb, S., Beardon, L., Eastgate, R., Glover, T., Kerr, S., & Neale, H. et al. (2002). Applied virtual environments to support learning of social interaction skills in users with Asperger's syndrome. *Digital Creativity*, *13*, 11–22. doi:10.1076/digc.13.1.11.3208

Cobb, S., Parsons, S., Millen, L., Eastgate, R., & Glover, T. (2010). Design and development of collaborative technology for children with autism: COSPATIAL. In *Proceedings of INTED2010 Conference*, (pp. 374–83). INTED.

Cobb, S. V. G. (2007). Virtual environments supporting learning and communication in special needs education. *Topics in Language Disorders*, *27*(3), 211–225. doi:10.1097/01.TLD.0000285356.95426.3b

Colby, K. M. (1973). The rational for computer-based treatment of language difficulties in non-speaking autistic children. *Journal of Autism and Childhood Schizophrenia*, *3*(3), 254–260. doi:10.1007/BF01538283 PMID:4800391

Craig, N. (2011). Autistic kids learn to fly in cyberspace. *The Age*. Retrieved from http://www.theage.com.au/victoria/autistic-kids-learn-to-fly-in-cyberspace-20110219-1b0fj.html

Cromby, J. J., Standen, P. J., Newman, J., & Tasker, H. (1996). Successful transfer to the real world of skills practised in a virtual environment by students with severe learning difficulties. In *Proceedings of the 1st International Conference on Disability, Virtual Reality and Associated Technologies (IDCVRAT)*. Reading, UK: IDCVRAT.

DeAngelis, T. (2009). Can Second Life therapy help with autism? *Monitor on Psychology*, *40*(8), 40–41.

Fabri, M., & Moore, D. (2005). The use of emotionally expressive avatars in collaborative virtual environments. In *Proceeding of Symposium on Empathic Interaction with Synthetic Characters, Artificial Intelligence and Social Behaviour Convention 2005* (AISB 2005). University of Hertfordshire.

Fabri, M., Moore, D., & Hobbs, D. (2004). Mediating the expression of emotion in educational collaborative virtual environments: An experimental study. *Virtual Reality (Waltham Cross)*, *7*, 66–81. doi:10.1007/s10055-003-0116-7

Fusar-Poli, P., Cortesi, M., Borgwardt, S., & Politi, P. (2008). Second Life virtual world: A heaven for autistic people? *Medical Hypotheses*, *71*(6), 980–981. doi:10.1016/j.mehy.2008.07.024 PMID:18783897

Grandin, T. (2002). *Teaching tips for children and adults with autism*. Autism Research Institute. Retrieved from http://www.autism.com/families/therapy/teaching_tips.htm

Guldberg, K., Porayska-Pomsta, K., Good, J., & Keay-Bright, W. (2010). ECHOES II: The creation of a technology enhanced learning environment for typically developing children and children on the autism spectrum. *Journal of Assistive Technologies*, *4*(1), 49–53. doi:10.5042/jat.2010.0044

Haswell, C., Izawa, J., Dowell, L., Mostofsky, S., & Shadmehr, R. (2009). Representation of internal models of action in the autistic brain. *Journal of Nature Neuroscience*, *12*(8), 970–972. doi:10.1038/nn.2356 PMID:19578379

Heimann, M., Nelson, K. E., Tjus, T., & Gillberg, C. (1995). Increased reading and communication skills in children with autism through an interactive multimedia computer program. *Journal of Autism and Developmental Disorders*, *25*(5), 459–480. doi:10.1007/BF02178294 PMID:8567593

Kandalaft, M., Didehbani, N., Krawczyk, D., Allen, T., & Chapman, S. (2012). Virtual reality social cognition training for young adults with high-functioning autism. *Journal of Autism and Developmental Disorders*, 1–11. PMID:21360019

Millen, L., Edlin-White, R., & Cobb, S. (2010). The development of educational collaborative virtual environments for children with autism. In *Proceedings of the 5th Cambridge Workshop on Universal Access and Assistive Technology*. Cambridge University.

Moore, D., Cheng, Y., McGrath, P., & Powell, N. J. (2005). Collaborative virtual environment technology for people with autism. *Focus on Autism and Other Developmental Disabilities*, *20*, 231–243. doi:10.1177/10883576050200040501

Murray, D. K. C. (1997). Autism and information technology: Therapy with computers. In *Autism and learning: A guide to good practice*. London: David Fulton Publishers.

Newbutt, N. (2013). *Exploring communication and representation of the self in a virtual world by young people with autism.* (Unpublished doctoral dissertation). University College Dublin, Dublin, Ireland.

Parson, S., Leonard, A., & Mitchell, P. (2006). Virtual environments for social skills training: Comments from two adolescents with autistic spectrum disorder. *Computers & Education*, *47*, 186–206. doi:10.1016/j.compedu.2004.10.003

Parsons, S. (2007). Virtual environments for social skills intervention: current findings and future challenges. In *El autismo en personas adultas: Nuevas perspectivas de futuro*. Ministerio de Trabajo y Asuntos Social.

Parsons, S., & Cobb, S. (2011). State-of-the-art of virtual reality technologies for children on the autism spectrum. *European Journal of Special Needs Education*, *26*(3), 355–366. doi:10.1080/08856257.2011.593831

Parsons, S., & Mitchell, P. (2002). The potential of virtual reality in social skills training for people with autistic spectrum disorder. *Intellectual Disability Research*, *46*(5), 430–443. doi:10.1046/j.1365-2788.2002.00425.x

Parsons, S., Mitchell, P., & Leonard, A. (2005). Do adolescents with autistic spectrum disorders adhere to social conventions in virtual environments? *Autism*, *9*, 95–117. doi:10.1177/1362361305049032 PMID:15618265

Rutten, A., Cobb, S., Neale, H., Kerr, S., Leonard, A., & Parsons, S. (2003). The AS interactive project: Single user and collaborative virtual environments for people with high-functioning autistic spectrum disorders. *Journal of Visualization and Computer Animation*, *14*, 1–8. doi:10.1002/vis.320

Salman, S. (2006). *Autism community forges virtual haven*. Retrieved from http://www.guardian.co.uk/society/2006/mar/08/guardiansociety-supplement1

Schmidt, C., & Schmidt, M. (2008). Three-dimensional virtual learning environments for mediating social skills acquisition among individuals with autism spectrum disorders. In *Proceedings of the 7th international Conference on interaction Design and Children* (pp. 85-88). Chicago, IL: Academic Press.

Schmidt, M., Laffey, J. M., Schmidt, C. T., Wang, X., & Stichter, J. (2012). Developing methods for understanding social behaviour in a 3D virtual learning environment. *Computers in Human Behavior*, *28*(2), 405–413. doi:10.1016/j.chb.2011.10.011

Scott, F. J., Baron-Cohen, S., Bolton, P., & Brayne, C. (2002). Brief report prevalence of autism spectrum conditions in children aged 5-11 years in Cambridgeshire, UK. *Autism*, *6*, 231–237. doi:10.1177/1362361302006003002 PMID:12212915

Silver, M., & Oakes, P. (2001). Evaluation of a new computer intervention to teach people with autism or Asperger syndrome to recognize and predict emotions in others. *Autism*, *5*, 299–316. doi:10.1177/1362361301005003007 PMID:11708589

Strickland, D., Marcus, L. M., Mesibov, G. B., & Hogan, K. (1996). Brief report: Two case studies using virtual reality as a learning tool for autistic children. *Journal of Autism and Developmental Disorders*, *26*(6), 651–659. doi:10.1007/BF02172354 PMID:8986851

Thomas, G. (2011). *How to do your case study: A guide for students and researchers*. London: Sage.

Van Rijn, H., & Stappers, P. J. (2008). The puzzling life of autistic toddlers: Design guidelines from the LINKX project. In *Advances in human-computer interaction*. Hindawi Publishing Corporation. doi:10.1155/2008/639435

Wallace, S., Parsons, S., Westbury, A., White, K., White, K., & Bailey, A. (2010). Sense of presence and atypical social judgements in immersive virtual environments: Responses of adolescents with autism spectrum disorders. *Autism*, *14*(3), 199–213. doi:10.1177/1362361310363283 PMID:20484000

Williams, L. K. (1996). *Caring and capable kids: An activity guide for teaching kindness, tolerance, self-control and responsibility*. ERIC Document, 395–697.

ADDITIONAL READING

Carr, D., & Oliver, M. (in press 2009) 'Second Life, Immersion and Learning, *Social Computing and Virtual Communitie*s. (Eds.) Panayiotis Zaphiris & Chee Siang Ang, Retrieved from http://learningfromsocialworlds.wordpress.com/immersion-and-sl/

Davidson, J. (2008). Autistic culture online: Virtual communication and cultural expression on the spectrum. *Social & Cultural Geography*, *9*(7), 791–806. doi:10.1080/14649360802382586

Gottschalk, S. (2010). The Presentation of Avatars in Second Life: Self and Interaction in Social Virtual Spaces. *Symbolic Interaction*, *33*(4), 501–525. doi:10.1525/si.2010.33.4.501

Mitchell, P., Parsons, S., & Leonard, A. (2007). Using Virtual Environments for Teaching Social Understanding to 6 Adolescents with Autistic Spectrum Disorders. *Journal of Autism and Developmental Disorders*, 37, 589–600. doi:10.1007/s10803-006-0189-8 PMID:16900403

Moore, D., Cheng, Y., McGrath, P., & Powell, N. J. (2005a). Collaborative Virtual Environment Technology for People with Autism. Pruski, A., & Knops, A. (Eds.) Assistive Technology: From Virtuality to Reality. Amsterdam: IOS Press, 442–48.

Parsons, S., Mitchell, P., & Leonard, A. (2004). The Use and Understanding of Virtual Environments by Adolescents with Autistic Spectrum Disorders. *Journal of Autism and Developmental Disorders*, 34(4), 449–466. doi:10.1023/B:JADD.0000037421.98517.8d PMID:15449520

Peña, J., & Sanchez, J. (2012). The Cowl Makes the Monk: How Avatar Appearance and Role Labels Affect Cognition in Virtual Worlds. *Journal of Virtual Worlds Research*, 5(3), 1–16.

Ramdoss, S., lang, R., Mulloy, A., Franco, J., O'Reilly, M., Didden, R., & Lancioni, G. (2011). Use of Computer-Based Interventions to Teach Communication Skills to Children with Autism Spectrum Disorders: A Systematic Review. *Journal of Behavioral Education*, 20(1), 55–76. doi:10.1007/s10864-010-9112-7

Short, J. Williams. E., & Christie, B. (1976). The Social Psychology of Telecommunications. United Kingdom, London: John Wiley

Spiker, D., & Ricks, M. (1984). Visual Self-Recognition in Autistic Children: Developmental Relationships. *Child Development*, 55(1), 214–225. doi:10.2307/1129846 PMID:6705623

Tjus, T., Heimann, M., & Nelson, K. E. (2001). Interaction patterns between children and their teachers when using a specific multimedia and communication strategy. *Autism*, 5(2), 175–187. doi:10.1177/1362361301005002007 PMID:11706865

UC Davis Medical Center. (2010). *Virtual Reality: An intervention for Autism*. Retrieved from http://www.ucdmc.ucdavis.edu/medicalcenter/features/2010-2011/09/20100916_MIND_virtual-autism.html

Williams, P., Jamali, H. R., & Nicholas, D. (2006). Using ICT with people with special educational needs: what the literature tells us. *Aslib Proceedings: New Information Perspectives*, 58(4), 330–345. doi:10.1108/00012530610687704

Yee, N., & Bailenson, J. N. (2009). The Difference Between Being and Seeing: The Relative Contribution of Self-Perception and Priming to Behavioral Changes via Digital Self-Representation. *Media Psychology*, 12, 195–209. doi:10.1080/15213260902849943

Yee, N., Bailenson, J. N., Urbanek, M., Chang, F., & Merget, D. (2007). The Unbearable Likeness Of Being Digital: The Persistence Of Nonverbal Social Norms In Online Virtual Environments. *Cyberpsychology & Behavior*, 10(1), 115–121. doi:10.1089/cpb.2006.9984 PMID:17305457

Yee, N., Ducheneaut, N., Yao, M., & Nelson, L. (2011). Do men heal more when in drag?: Conflicting identity cues between user and avatar. *In Proceedings of the 2011 annual conference on Human factors in computing systems* (pp. 773-776). ACM: 773–76.

Yin, R. K. (2003). *Case Study Research: Design and Methods* (3rd ed.). USA: SAGE Publications.

KEY TERMS AND DEFINITIONS

Autism: A condition defined by the American Psychiatric Association (2000), meaning people diagnosed will experience difficulties with social understanding and communication skills defined more specifically as: qualitative impairments in social communication, social interaction and social imagination.

Stakeholders: In this context reference is to schools, school-teachers, parents, care-providers, users, day centres.

Virtual Environment: A 3D computer program that simulates a situation (like a game). It ends and needs to be re-started; where similar scenarios are presented.

Virtual Reality Technology: A computer-simulated environment that can simulate physical presence in places in the real world or imagined worlds technology that involves immersion and interaction displayed through 3D rendered graphics.

Virtual World: A persistent virtual environment (3D) connected through computers. Engagement is through avatars that can represent the user. Communication with others is a feature of VWs.

Chapter 15
Realabilities:
The Development of a Research-Based Children's Television Program to Address Disability Awareness and a Stop-Bullying Platform in the Schools

Nava R. Silton
Marymount Manhattan College, USA

Rebecca Ruchlin
Marymount Manhattan College, USA

Senada Arucevic
Marymount Manhattan College, USA

Vanessa Norkus
Marymount Manhattan College, USA

ABSTRACT

This chapter explores Realabilities, a video-based children's television program featuring unique characters, each with a distinct disability. Beyond utilizing video technology to directly teach cognitive and social-emotional skills to children with autism, Realabilities demonstrates how video can be used to foster positive behavioral intentions and cognitive attitudes towards children with autism and other disabilities. Realabilities also reveals how a video medium can promote a stop bullying platform, especially since children with disabilities are at least two to three times more victimized by bullying than their typical peers. One hundred and sixty-six students from schools in Manhattan, NY, and Baltimore, MD, showed more favorable behavioral intentions and cognitive attitudes towards hypothetical peers with disabilities following a three episode viewing of Realabilities. Finally, Realabilities not only showcases the realities of disabilities but shares the potential strengths that children with disabilities possess. This is particularly illuminating, since the Affect/Effort Theory suggests that children are more motivated to interact with others when they possess positive expectancies of their social interaction partners.

DOI: 10.4018/978-1-4666-5792-2.ch015

INTRODUCTION

Realabilities is a video-based children's television program, which features unique characters, each with a distinct disability. Each episode presents a social story that heralds a pro-social anti-bullying message to viewers. Through this multimedia format, episodes of the show serve to enhance the sensitivity and understanding of typically developing children towards children with disabilities. The hope is that engaging typically developing students will foster positive attitudes and behavioral intentions of typical children towards individuals with disabilities.

It is instructive to teach typical children about disabilities that they may encounter at school and in the community in order for them to learn to be mindful and to make the environment as welcoming and safe as possible for their peers with disabilities. By encouraging typical children to be sensitive, take initiative, and engage in appropriate social interactions with children diagnosed with autism and other disorders, children with disabilities may be able to improve upon certain difficult features of their disorders. These relationships could enhance the school environment and ideally promote children with autism's interest and success in social interaction and social initiation as well as typical children's social-emotional intelligence, understanding and sensitivity (Kamps, Kravitz, Gonzalez-Lopez, Kemmerer, Potucek, & Harrell, 1998).

Autism is one of the most common developmental disorders in the United States, with prevalence rates consistently rising over the last 40 years. Currently 1 out of approximately 88 children is being diagnosed with an Autism Spectrum Disorder (ASD) (Autism Speaks, 2013). While there is no known cure for autism, many therapies have been proven to be beneficial in improving the day-to-day life functioning and quality of life of children with ASD and their families (Autism Speaks, 2013). However, one area that could benefit from greater scrutiny is how to enhance typical children's awareness, sensitivity and understanding towards their peers with ASDs. With the number of ASD diagnoses on the rise, the likelihood of a typically developing child encountering a child with this disorder is high. Providing typical children with the knowledge and tools to appropriately interact with and support their peers with disabilities would be highly beneficial for everyone involved.

Along with autism, there are countless other disabilities that typical children will likely encounter in school and in the community. These disabilities include: deafness, blindness, physical disability, Attention Deficit Hyperactivity Disorder, Down syndrome and others. Despite their limitations, many individuals with special needs possess special abilities and strengths. It is crucial that children who are typically developing appreciate that others with impairments have valuable strengths. Teaching positive behavioral intentions towards individuals with disabilities at a young age, therein fostering increased sensitivity is extremely beneficial in preventing bullying and other poor behaviors as children advance from elementary to junior high school. There is growing evidence that suggests that typical children may be effective agents for inducing change in their peers with developmental disabilities (Pierce & Schreibman, 1997). Research has also shown that without intervention, typically developing peers prefer to interact with one another rather than with children with disabilities (Disalvo & Oswald, 2002; Myles, Simpson, Ormsbee, & Erikson, 1993 & Goldstein, Kaczmarek, & Pennington, 1992). The importance of creating an intervention that encourages typically developing children to engage with their peers with disabilities would be beneficial for both children with disabilities and their typical peers alike.

Our video-based *Realabilities* intervention was designed to create a meaningful medium through which to inspire typical children to be more accepting and to encourage more positive attitudes and intentions towards their peers with disabilities. Children who view pro-social programs are often more altruistic, and involved in more pro-social behaviors (sharing, cooperation, manners) (Mares, 1996). The video intervention was not only created to promote these behaviors, but to challenge the often negative, pathetic portrayals of children with disabilities on television and to replace them with a focus on the special abilities and strengths that individuals with disabilities possess.

CHILDREN WITH DISABILITIES IN TELEVISION

Research suggests that children with disabilities are more at risk for developing negative attitudes towards television due to their pathetic portrayal on TV, where they are often depicted as sick, pitiful, aggressive or dangerous (Sprafkin, Gadow & Grayson, 1984). Wood (2012) explains that the representation and portrayal of individuals with disabilities on television is poor and progress towards improving the depiction of individuals with disabilities remains slow. A 2005 Skillset report states that there have been small changes in the employment rates of individuals with disabilities in the Broadcast Television sector. Within the media industry, individuals with disabilities account for only 2.3% of the workforce. The under-representation of these individuals within the media workforce strongly relates to how disabilities are portrayed within the media, which can have a negative impact on the public. The media is highly influential and a misrepresentation of individuals with disabilities may have great social implications (Wood, 2012).

Balter (1999) noted that individuals with disabilities remain a marginalized group who are rarely portrayed in a realistic manner on-screen and are rarely cast in primary roles despite expectations of the Americans with Disabilities Act.

Additionally, throughout the years, perceptions of individuals with disabilities remain stagnant and old stereotypes endure despite boons in technology and the participation of individuals with disabilities in sports (Day, 2000). Murphy (1995) stated that, "The greatest impediment to a person taking full part in his society is not his physical flaws, but rather the issue of myths, fears and misunderstandings that society attaches to them" (p. 140) (Hardin, 2001).

A study conducted by Wahl (2007) examined two hundred and sixty-nine hours of videotaped children's television programming and rated them. Nearly half of the viewed programs used mental health terms in which most of the terms were slang and disrespectful (e.g., crazy and nut) and were used to ridicule others. Twenty-one characters with a mental illness were identified, and they were depicted as aggressive and threatening. Other characters responded to these individuals with fear, exclusion, and disrespect. As indicated by this study, children's television programs appear to provide copious opportunities for children to create negative attitudes and behaviors towards individuals with mental illnesses or other disabilities (Wahl, 2007).

AT RISK FOR BULLYING AND STIGMATIZATION

Children tend to be observant, curious and inquisitive by nature. Meeting a peer with a disability or seeing someone with a disability portrayed on television might challenge their current schemas. It is important to teach children about various disabilities so that there is no room in school for misunderstanding or worse: teasing, bullying, and emotional pain (Pepler, 1993). Researchers Wall, Wheaton and Zuver (2009) reported that only ten studies have been conducted in the United States on bullying and disabilities, but each concluded that children with disabilities were two to three times more likely to be victims of bullying than their typical peers (Holmquist, 2011). Hoover and Stenhjem (2003) suggest how the continued failure of individuals with disabilities to participate in general education classes, mainstream educational clubs and organizations, and athletic programs perpetuates a lack of understanding and interaction among students with and without disabilities. Peer interactions and relationships are critical ingredients for developing social skills during childhood (Asher & Coie, 1990).

Bullying

Realabilities is catered to children between the ages of six and nine. Calvert & Kotler (2003) suggest that young viewers enjoy viewing actors, who are slightly older than they are. Thus, the show is catered to second and third grade children, since the *Realabilities* team members are in fourth and fifth grades (between nine and eleven years of age). Research has shown that 19% of students are bullied in U.S. elementary schools, with rates decreasing in the later school years (Dake, Price, & Telljohann, 2003). Thus, *Realabilities* is targeted to a slightly younger audience (second and third graders) to promote pro-social practices and to prevent negative bullying behaviors before they become commonplace in the classroom.

Olweus (2011) defines bullying as "when a student is being exposed, repeatedly and over time, to negative actions on the part of one or more students... negative actions must occur at least once a week for a month or more." Bullying can be explained as transpiring secondary to the existence of an imbalance of power. While anyone might be a target of bullying, the following student profiles are at a greater risk of becoming victims of bullying: smaller students, students with disabilities and mental health problems, and students who are lesbian, gay, bisexual, transgender and questioning (LGBTQ) (Lieberman & Cowan, 2011). Children who are bullied

often experience a variety of symptoms, including: bedwetting, difficulty sleeping, depression, low self-esteem, and discontentment at school (Kim & Leventhal, 2008). All forms of bullying and peer victimization are clear risk factors for depression and suicidal ideation but the specific groups mentioned are at a higher risk. According to the Center for Disease Control (CDC)'s Youth Risk Behavior Surveillance of 2011, bullying was associated with one of the leading causes of death among persons aged 10–24 years in the United States. It was reported that 20.1% have been bullied on school property, and 7.8% of those who have been victimized by bullying, have attempted suicide (Eaton et al., 2012).

Results from a review of eleven international studies indicated that students with disabilities, both visible and non-visible, were more victimized by bullying than their typical peers. The visible disabilities examined were cerebral palsy, muscular dystrophy and spina bifida, whereas the non-visible disabilities included ADHD and other learning disorders. Results indicated that the frequency with which students with disabilities, were being bullied was statistically significant compared to students without disabilities (Carter & Spencer, 2006). These students also reported having fewer friendships than their classmates, and 45% were moderately or severely victimized. Carter and Spencer (2006) intimate that classmates may be biased towards their peers with disabilities or towards children whom, in general, differ in appearance. These students struggle with a poor peer status and have fewer friends; making them more vulnerable to victimization.

Pepler et al. (1993) organized an anti-bullying intervention geared towards teaching students about bullying, specifically how to identify it as well as which actions to take to quell bullying. Activities like role-plays, drama and story-telling helped students begin to understand the perspective of the victim. Students who empathize with the victims are more likely to support them as well as to disapprove of bullying. *Realabilities* amplifies this message by employing all of these methods (storytelling, role-play and drama) through a video medium to encourage viewers to help prevent or combat bullying in their schools.

Efficacy of Video Technology in Addressing Bullying

Technology can unfortunately facilitate bullying via cyber-bullying (Campbell, 2005), but it can also facilitate anti-bullying efforts by capitalizing on its dissemination capabilities to promote stop bullying messages. In efforts to diminish the amount of bullying, in-vivo and ex-vivo, the use of technology has become a new means of behavioral training for children and adults against bullying and violence. Video technology use in bullying prevention and intervention has become more popular because of its low expense and simple training instructions for teachers and clinicians (Webster- Stratton, Kolpacoff, & Hollinsworth, 1988 as cited in Belnap, 2009).

There are various programs that have been used to help prevent bullying by focusing on its various causes. *Get Real about Violence* is a technology-based program focused on preventing bullying. It is composed of a twelve-course curriculum, which addresses three factors of violence: vulnerability to violence, contributors to violence, and alternatives to violence. Teachers are guided through lesson plans by a packet that consists of teachers' manuals, videos, audiotapes, and other tools (Belnap, 2009). The lessons are administered to children in grades K - 12 to learn about nonaggressive conflict resolution. This curriculum encourages students to actively participate before an argument progresses to a fight or confusion leads to bullying. The researchers demonstrated that aggressive communication is a prelude to bullying behaviors and reported that the intervention was instrumental in reducing verbal aggression (Meyer et al., 2004). *Get Real about Violence* is a preventative

approach teachers can use to educate students so that there is less aggression, fewer conflicts, and as a result, less bullying.

Another focus in anti-bullying studies involving technology relates to the bystander effect, or the "good Samaritan effect" and heroism. Rather than focusing solely on the perpetrators of bullying, it is instructive to consider the heroes, who aid victims of bullying or who assume other heroic roles. It is possible that there is a banality of heroism just as there is a banality of evil. In other words, each individual has the potential to do a heroic deed. The concept that there is a banality of heroism can be a helpful tool in teaching people how to evaluate conflicts which they witness, and how to act righteously to end them, at the time (Franco & Zimbardo, 2006-2007). In a study conducted in 2013 in the United Kingdom, the various conditions needed for bystanders to help others during a violent conflict were tested. Researchers used virtual reality technology to test 40 soccer supporters of the Arsenal Football Club in England to determine if they would help victims of confrontation of the same supporting team or victims of confrontation who supported a different team. The results showed that there was a significantly greater number of "heroes" when the supporter of the same team was in need of help than when a victim of another team needed assistance (Slater, Rovira, Southern, Swapp, & Zhang, 2013). By using technology, it was easy to control what the volunteers were seeing in order to merit results. Without technology, the researchers would have had to gather many more volunteers and actors to role-play an argument or a fighting scene which would inevitably involve more subjectivity and thus make it harder to uncover significant results.

Video media animation was selected as the medium for *Realabilities* since "stop bullying" is a key platform of the show and a video medium is often popular among children. Animation can often make stories more appealing and entertaining for children. Rieber (1991) discovered that fourth-grade students were capable of acquiring knowledge through incidental learning from a computer simulation of animated shapes. Seventy fourth-graders were tested to see if they could gather information learned incidentally. The students participated in an animated lesson on Newton's laws of motion and were able to understand a complex science principle through incidental learning. Children were also more likely to prefer the technological method of learning than to return to a more traditional method when given a choice (Rieber, 1991).

Over the course of numerous animated episodes of *Realabilities*, certain productive behaviors are shown to viewers through depicting realistic situations in elementary school such as during soccer practice, during spelling bees, school plays and at a heritage fair. By providing an example of how to behave in a bullying situation via this multi-sensory medium, children can more easily generalize and apply what they see and hear on-screen to their in-vivo life situations. Technology has shown itself to optimize this process since it seems to heighten children's interest in the programming and therefore to motivate their investment in this important platform. By capitalizing on technology to promote awareness of bullying and to demonstrate how to prevent it, important pro-social behaviors and alternatives to bullying behaviors are taught.

EDUCATIONAL PROGRAMMING AND VIDEO MODELING

Children's educational programming is a critical area of study in child development. A video tool which can build social skills development into its programming and offer a greater visibility of autism in children's educational programming may help children and society at large to better understand and optimally interact with children on the autism spectrum. These outcomes would both directly and indirectly alleviate some of the undue burdens and associated stress levels with which children with autism and their families contend.

Another benefit to consider in utilizing a video-based medium like *Realabilities* is that children's educational programming is one mass-media vehicle through which to teach key social skills to children with autism. Video tools are uniquely beneficial for children on the autism spectrum due to their anecdotal interests in TV and video mediums, to the success of video modeling (Charlop-Christy, 2000) for teaching various socialization and adaptive skills and to their great dissemination capabilities. Bellini & Akullian (2007) conducted a meta-analysis that examined intervention, maintenance and generalization effects of video modeling and video self-modeling interventions based upon three dependent variables: social-communication skills, functional skills, and behavioral functioning. Results demonstrated that individuals were capable of acquiring key skills after watching a video of an individual performing a task, communicating or behaving in a specific way. The skills acquired via video modeling and video self-modeling, more importantly are maintained over time and transferred across persons and settings (Bellini & Akullian, 2007). Bandura (1997) noted that children acquire a vast array of skills by observing others perform skills rather than through personal experiences. Therefore, observers will imitate behaviors with or without the presence of reinforcement.

Thus, a video medium can be used to teach social skills to children with ASD while also serving as a medium through which to reduce stigmatization by teaching the importance of sensitivity and positive behavioral intentionality. Knowledge and sensitivity training regarding children with disabilities would be useful for parents of children with autism and other less visible disabilities, since efforts towards social integration are critical for the healthy social-emotional development of typically developing peers and their peers with disabilities.

LITERATURE AND DISABILITIES

It is instructive to measure the degree to which typical peers tend to accept their peers with disabilities in integrated classrooms and to create an intervention tool that can help increase their knowledge and acceptance in a positive way. Smith-D'Arezzo and Moore-Thomas (2010) used the medium of literature to instill a sense of empathy towards those who face discrimination or other hardships. The researchers presented children's books which featured characters with disabilities to test fifth graders' perceptions of their peers with disabilities. Two books, each exhibiting a main character with a learning disability, were read to the children in a structured book discussion group. While the results were intended to improve children's attitudes towards the characters with disabilities, few positive results were recorded. In fact, the book intervention appeared to have a negative impact, reinforcing some of the poor views children have toward their peers with disabilities. One study explored the portrayal of disabilities within a sample of literature catered to primary-age children in the United Kingdom (Beckett, Ellison, Barrett, & Shah, 2010). It was hypothesized that the type of literature that children are exposed to is likely to influence their general perceptions of their daily lives. Therefore, it is essential to understand how disabilities are portrayed in the literature. The researchers discovered that despite the positive examples of inclusive literature, discriminatory language and negative stereotypes about disabilities continue to exist in children's books (Beckett et al., 2010). While using literature can have its advantages, it is clear that a different medium could be more effective in harnessing and disseminating positive feelings in typically developing children towards children with disabilities. Video technology can be used as an intervention tool that may produce these desired results; capturing the attention of children while educating them on the need to be accepting and understanding towards their peers with disabilities.

ASSESSMENT CONSTRUCTS OF BEHAVIORAL INTENTIONS AND COGNITIVE ATTITUDES

Researchers have attempted to enhance typical children's behavioral and cognitive attitudes towards their peers with disabilities and, as noted in the literature, this was ineffective. It is important to understand the assessment constructs of behavioral intentions and cognitive attitudes in order to better comprehend how to best improve the beliefs and actions of typical children. The affective component of attitudes that typical children have in perceiving their peers with disabilities involves statements about the individual child's feelings toward a target child with disabilities (Campbell et al., 2006). For instance, "I would be afraid of a new child with autism in my class" (Rosenbaum *et al.*, 1988). The behavioral component encompasses statements of intention in choosing whether or not to interact with a child with a disability. An example of a behavioral attitude would be, "I would sit next to a child with autism during lunch" (Gottlieb, 1977; Rosenbaum *et al.*, 1986a, 1986b; Swaim and Morgan, 2001). The cognitive aspect of intentions relates to a child's belief system about a child with a disability. It could pertain to the child's feelings or to a strength that he/she possesses. Examples include: "I think a child with autism is sad," or "Children with autism are good at reading."

According to a study conducted to determine parents' perceptions of attitudes towards their child with autism, it was concluded that parents felt their child was often portrayed in a negative light. Gray (1993) explains that often parents felt this negativity was due to the general public's failure to understand autism. Children with disabilities are frequently met with hostility and insensitivity. Along with a general lack of knowledge, parents felt that the community judged their children based on the way their children appeared. Most children with autism display disruptive behaviors that make them stand out relative to their typical peers. With the prevalence of autism increasing annually (Autism Speaks, 2013), the likelihood of individuals encountering an individual with autism is high. Providing information about autism and other disabilities through an effective medium to the public may have the capacity to increase positive attitudes and intentions towards individuals with disabilities.

VIDEO AND DISABILITIES

Swaim and Morgan (2001) capitalized on a video medium to help typical children visualize the differences in behavior of a typical child and a child on the autism spectrum. Typical children in third and sixth grades were shown a series of videos showcasing a child without autism, with autism, or a child on the autism spectrum with information about his disorder. The videos afforded typical children the opportunity to hear the unique speech of a child with autism and to visualize nonverbal cues that are often associated with autism spectrum disorders. The goal was to see if children rated their feelings about the child differently based on the information they did or did not receive. This study aimed to examine the factors that could potentially influence typical children's cognitive attitudes and behavioral intentions toward a peer with autism. Unfortunately the study results did not indicate a positive impact of the informational video on typical children's behavioral attitudes or their cognitive intentions towards the hypothetical peer presenting with autism. This type of video intervention, with short video clips, was ultimately ineffective at improving intentions and attitudes. Unfortunately, various other video-based interventions, which offered descriptive information about individuals with disabilities, have proven harmful, neutral or minimally helpful at enhancing behavioral intentions and cognitive attitudes towards individuals with disabilities. As per Heider's (1958) cognitive consistency theory,

descriptive information provides knowledge about similarities between a child with a disability and typical peers. The idea is that typical peers will learn to be more accepting and socially interested in their peer with a disability if they appear to be similar to their typical peers.

Campbell et al. (2004) added explanatory information to descriptive information to determine if explanatory information would create more positive intentions and attitudes of typical peers towards their peers with autism. Explanatory information provides causal information about the disorder at-hand (Kelley, 1967; Heider, 1958). This addition of explanatory information assumes that typical peers will become more accepting and demonstrate greater positive intentions towards children with autism if they feel that children with autism have little responsibility for their disorder (Juvonen, 1992). Typical peers were more likely to display anger and negative intentions towards their peers with autism if they attributed high levels of responsibility to their peers with autism. Campbell et al. (2004) found that the addition of explanatory information to descriptive information increased positive attitudes of younger typical children (third and fourth graders) towards children with autism. Older children (fifth graders) did not demonstrate significant increases in positive behavioral intentions towards individuals with autism following the video intervention. These findings correspond to studies that suggest that cognitive attitudes towards peers with disabilities become more negative as children grow older (Ryan, 1981).

In order to improve upon these previous interventions, Silton (2009) randomly assigned typical elementary school children to one of four video conditions: Descriptive and Explanatory information about autism, Descriptive, Explanatory and Peer Strategies Information about autism, Descriptive, Explanatory, and Strengths Information about autism, or to a video featuring all four forms of the aforementioned types of information. The inclusion of peer strategy information was based on the Social Learning Theory (Bandura, 1977), which suggests that individuals will learn behaviors if they are properly modeled and reinforced (Rosenthal, 1963). The inclusion of strengths information is based on affect/effect theory (Rosenthal, 1989), which posits that expectations influence an individual's affect and the amount of effort he/she puts forth. When a child is presented with a negative expectation of a social interaction partner, he/she makes less of an effort to interact, and is less friendly towards the social interaction partner, even if the social partner does not possess significant emotional or behavioral issues (Disalvo & Oswald, 2002; Harris, Milich, Corbitt; Hoover & Brady, 1992). However, if typical children are presented with positive strengths information about children with disabilities, they may have more positive expectancies of children with disabilities, and may thus take a more active social interest in them. When a typical child learns about the special strengths or abilities of a peer with disabilities, the typical child can focus on the unique strengths of the individual rather than on his/her disability. Silton's (2009) study suggested that the addition of peer strategies information was useful in enhancing typical children' behavioral intentions, while strengths information was more helpful at enhancing typical children's knowledge of autism.

Moreover, Silton's (2009) most fascinating incidental finding suggested that the actors who played the roles of children with autism in the video had achieved the greatest improvement in sensitivity and empathy following the filming. Thus, the simulation itself appeared to have a strong impact on enhancing sensitivity levels (Silton, 2009). Video interventions that encourage children to role-play an individual with a disability or the peer of an individual with a disability may be powerful at enhancing the interest and sensitivity of typical elementary and middle-school aged children towards children with autism and other disabilities.

A FOUR-PART CURRICULAR INTERVENTION

Silton (2011) created an additional video that included descriptive, explanatory, peer strategies, and strengths information on four distinct disabilities: autism, blindness, deafness, and paraplegia. The cognitive attitudes and behavioral intentions of the children who played the roles of individuals with disabilities in Silton's (2011) video were also assessed using the Shared Activities Questionnaire (SAQ; Morgan et al. 1996), a behavioral intention measure, as well as the Adjective Checklist (ACL; Siperstein, 1980, Siperstein & Bak, 1977), a cognitive attitude measure. Six actors (one fourth grader, one sixth grader and four eighth graders) from Baltimore, Maryland completed the SAQ and ACL both prior to and following a four-hour simulation of disabilities for the educational disabilities video. Four of the participants were male and two of the participants were female. Consistent with the research hypothesis, the video actors showed improved behavioral intentions towards individuals with disabilities following the video testing. More specifically, the actors were more eager to participate in recreational activities with children with disabilities on the SAQ Recreational ($p < .01$) and showed a trend of increasing interest on the SAQ Total ($p = .055$) following the video simulation. However, contrary to the research hypothesis, the video actors showed a decrease in their cognitive attitude scores on the ACL ($p < .05$) following the video simulation.

Silton's (2011) educational disabilities video was a portion of a four-part curricular intervention designed to bolster the positive expectancies of typical children towards their peers with special needs by portraying the strengths that many children with disabilities possess. Failing to expose typical children to peers with disabilities may prevent them from adequately comprehending such disabilities and may diminish their potential to maximize tolerance and appropriate social interactions towards individuals with disabilities in and outside of the school environment.

Fifty-four fifth and sixth grade students (26 fifth graders and 28 sixth graders) from a Jewish Day School in Manhattan, New York participated in the four-part curricular intervention over a two-week period, wherein each of the four sessions were 60 minutes in length. The SAQ and ACL were administered prior to the intervention. The students viewed Silton's (2011) video during the first session and then engaged in a simulation museum where students moved from one booth to the next, "trying on" four different disabilities during the second session. Each booth was monitored by an adult in order to ensure fidelity and that the participants were effectively carrying out the simulations. The students participated in the moral dilemma discussion during the third session and they were asked to create an invention that they felt would be beneficial to individuals with disabilities in the fourth and final session. At the end of the fourth session, the students were asked to present their invention and to explain its intended benefits for individuals with disabilities. The students completed the SAQ, ACL and open-ended questions pertaining to which sessions they prized most following the four-part curricular intervention.

Following a pre-post test design, the results of the four-part intervention suggested that twelve-year old participants were significantly less likely than ten and eleven year olds to report an interest in interacting socially and recreationally with individuals with disabilities. This finding is consistent with studies indicating an inverse relationship between age and attitudes (Bell & Morgan, 2000). Additionally, consistent with literature revealing girls' more positive intentions towards peers with disabilities (Friedrich, Morgan, & Devine, 1996), girls in this intervention were more willing to socially engage with children with disabilities than were boys. More importantly,

it was found that the students favored the video portraying all four forms of information and the simulation museum in comparison to the other activity sessions, which is likely due to the fact that technology was utilized (iPad displaying video, music, etc.). By having the children place themselves in the "shoes" of an individual with a disability, they may be more likely to gain more positive behavioral intentions and cognitive attitudes towards their peer with a disability. The notion that technology was favored by the students served as an impetus for *Realabilities*.

Realabilities

As mentioned previously, *Realabilities* is a proposed children's television program, designed to enhance the interest and sensitivity of typical children towards children with disabilities. It is a pro-social, stop-bullying program that features characters with disabilities as principal characters and portrays them in a strong and positive light. *Realabilities* seeks to replace typical negative portrayals of individuals with disabilities on TV with positive, strong depictions of characters with one of the following disabilities: autism, blindness, deafness, paraplegia, and attention-deficit/hyperactivity disorder (ADHD). Rather than solely focusing on the limitations of individuals with these disabilities, the strengths of each of the characters are highlighted and emphasized. The show contains pro-social messages not only to eradicate bullying, but to promote empathy, sharing, cooperation, and helping behaviors. The excitement of each episode derives from the various bullying obstacles the *Realabilities* team must cleverly traverse by creatively harnessing their special abilities. Each episode begins with a scenario where bullying is involved and one of the *Realabilities* team members intervenes and galvanizes his/her other team members to diffuse the situation in a creative, fun and remarkable way.

INTRODUCING STRENGTHS INFORMATION

Realabilities' focus on strengths information was inspired by the aforementioned affect/effect theory (Rosenthal, 1989), the success of Silton's (2009) and (2011) videos, which incorporated strengths information, and the success of an earlier study by Owen & Deschryver (2004), which found that offering strengths and preference information about children with autism coupled with peer strategies information, enhanced the social initiations and responses of both the typical peers and the peers with autism, alike.

The Realabilities show introduces five characters with disabilities: Uno (who has autism), Melody (who is visually impaired), Seemore (who is hearing impaired), Rolly (who is wheelchair-bound), Addy (who has ADHD) and Ezra (their typical friend). They all capitalize on their superior abilities to protect their elementary school from bullies.

Research suggests that some children with autism may display savant skills (Iavarone, Patruno, Galeone, Chieffi, & Carlomagno, 2007), enhanced spatial memory (Caron, Mottron, Rainville, Chouinard, 2004) and superior perceptual skills (Mottron, Dawson, Soulieres, Hubert & Burack, 2006). Individuals with hearing impairment may possess enhanced peripheral vision and other visual abilities (Bosworth & Dobkins, 1999), while individuals with visual impairment may exhibit a greater interest in, and/or talent for music than their sighted peers (Matawa, 2009). This reliance on sound by visually impaired individuals and interest in music helps to develop and strengthen their ability to sing, play instruments, and even to demonstrate exceptional pitch, sense of rhythm, and retention of melodies and lyrics. Finally, individuals who are wheelchair-bound often develop greater upper body strength due to exercising those muscles more frequently, which also helps prevent muscle atrophy. Thus, the *Realabilities* characters portray all of these potential strengths

of individuals with disabilities, rather than focusing on their potential limitations. *Realabilities* is designed to encourage typical children (without disabilities) to be more sensitive, interested, and to possess more favorable and positive images of their peers with disabilities. Additionally, it is intended to encourage children with varying disabilities to view themselves in a positive and strong light on the television canvas.

Autism

Uno, the character presenting with autism in *Realabilities,* benefits from special skills in the areas of mathematics and spatial orientation. As previously mentioned, these special abilities relate to the propensity of some children with autism to have savant abilities in math and superior perceptual skills.

Savant Syndrome

Savants are extremely gifted individuals who possess a disability yet prove to be highly skilled in certain areas. Studies show that nearly half of all savants have autism and that 10 percent of individuals with autism show signs of savant abilities (Miller, 1999). A savant is often described as a person "of low intelligence who possesses an unusually high skill in some special tasks like mental arithmetic, remembering dates or numbers, or in performing other rote tasks at a remarkably high level" (Miller, 1999). The most common types of savant skills include calendar calculating, musical ability, artistic talent, memorization, mathematical skills, and mechanical achievement (Cheatham, Rucker, Polloway & Edward, 1995). Individuals with autism who possess exceptional rote and visual memory for calendars are often referred to as "Savant Calendrical Calculators." These individuals are capable of identifying with speed the day of the week of any given date (Iavarone, Patruno, Galeone, Chieffi, & Carlomagno, 2007). Furthermore, individuals with autism with "Musical Savant Syndrome," often exhibit outstanding pitch processing and chord disentangling abilities along with an exceptional musical memory. Their ability to discriminate among pitches presented in the form of compound musical stimuli suggests that they may also excel at discriminating among frequencies of pure tones when presented in isolation (Bonnel, Mottron, Peretz, Trudel, & Gallun, 2003). Cheatham et al. (1995) identified the following as potential explanations for savant abilities: hereditary factors, eidetic memory, rote memorization, concrete versus abstract reasoning, sensory deprivation, reinforcement and cerebral dominance. While there is no clear explanation as to why these savant skills develop, evidence suggests that children who are particularly skilled in an area, also tend to be more interested in it, to work harder at it and to begin that activity at an early age (Winner, 2000).

While impairments in communication have been one of the major challenges children with autism encounter, visual memory has been found to be an area of particular strength for children with autism. In addition, children with autism demonstrate superior performance in pitch processing and memory (Caron, Mottron, Rainville, Chouinard, 2004). Children with autism also exhibit remarkable abilities in storage and manipulation components of spatial working memory, as well (Caron, Mottron, Rainville, Chouinard, 2004). This intact working memory is one of the many special abilities many children with autism appear to possess.

Superior Perceptual Abilities

Whatever the origin of savant skills, many of these savant abilities involve exceptional perceptual skills. Whether or not they possess savant skills, the literature suggests that a number of individuals with autism exhibit superior performance in both visual and auditory modalities while completing various cognitive tasks (Mottron, Dawson, Soulieres, Hubert & Burack, 2006). Compared to

typical controls, individuals with autism demonstrated superior performance in lab situations and showed an overall superior perceptual functioning (Mottron et al., 2006). Similarly, Bonnel et al. (2003) discovered that individuals with autism outperformed typically developing controls on a variety of low-level perceptual tasks.

Hearing Impairment

Seemore, the character presenting with a hearing impairment on *Realabilities,* benefits from exceptional visual abilities and perspective-taking. These special abilities derive from various studies which show that visual abilities in individuals with hearing impairment may be improved as a result of auditory deprivation and/ or because individuals who are deaf rely heavily on sign language (Bosworth & Dobkins, 2002). Since children with hearing impairments rely mainly on sign language to communicate with the outside world, signing is said to be responsible for their enhanced visual-cognitive abilities. Other studies note that individuals with hearing impairment may experience functional benefits from enhanced peripheral vision (Bosworth & Dobkins, 1999).

Visual Impairment

Melody, the character presenting with a visual impairment, benefits from special musical ability and from a beautiful voice, with perfect pitch and tone. This special musical ability derives from research that shows that music may play a more pivotal role in the lives of visually impaired children than in the lives of fully-sighted individuals. Therefore, individuals with visual impairment may exhibit a greater interest in, and/or talent for music than their sighted peers (Matawa, 2009). This reliance on sound and interest in music helps to develop and strengthen their ability to sing, play instruments, and even to acquire exceptional pitch, a sense of rhythm, and retention of melodies and lyrics.

Physical Impairment

Rolly, the character presenting with a physical impairment on *Realabilities,* benefits from upper body strength. Rolly's upper body strength derives from research, which suggests that individuals with physical impairments often develop greater upper body strength due to utilizing those muscles more frequently, which also helps prevent muscle atrophy.

Attention-Deficit/Hyperactivity Disorder (ADHD)

Finally, Addy, the character presenting with Attention-deficit/hyperactivity disorder (ADHD), benefits from her creativity and great problem-solving ability. ADHD is a neuropsychiatric disorder with an onset in childhood and affects 3% to 5% of all school-aged children. It is characterized by hyperactivity, inattentiveness, and impulsivity (Durston, 2003). This neurocognitive impairment in being unable to effectively filter stimuli is often the reason that children produce messy and careless work at school, interrupt tasks and are unable to focus attention on a particular task, have frequent shifts in conversation, as well as a difficult time waiting their turn. Addy's heightened creativity relates to studies like those by Healey and Rucklidge (2006), which suggest that children with ADHD display significantly higher levels of creativity. The presence of ADHD in a creative sample was first explored and then the relationship between cognitive functioning and ADHD symptomatology was observed by comparing four distinct groups ranging from 10 to 12 years of age: 1) Twenty-nine children with ADHD with low creativity, 2) twelve creative children with ADHD symptomatology, 3) eighteen creative children without ADHD symptomatology, and 4) thirty controls. Creativity, intelligence, processing speed, reaction time, working memory, and inhibitory control were measured. Results showed that 40% of the creative children displayed clinically elevated levels of ADHD symptoms (Healey & Rucklidge, 2006). While this connection between ADHD and creativity is still somewhat inconclusive, Carson et al.'s (2003) work on latent inhibition and creativity found that creative achievers had more difficulty filtering out possibly irrelevant information and suggested that this deficit, in combination with a high IQ, may be boosting the creativity of individuals with ADHD.

TESTING THE EFFICACY OF *REALABILITIES*

This research sought to determine whether viewing three episodes of the video-based *Realabilities* intervention would improve the behavioral intentions and cognitive attitudes of typical children towards children with disabilities. While some interventions have yielded modest improvements in behavioral intentions (Silton, 2009), very few interventions have been successful at enhancing cognitive attitudes (Swaim & Morgan, 2001).

The first three episodes, "The Real Goal", "Chemistry Craze", and "Play Nice" have corresponding storyboards that are displayed on YouTube and on a CD. Modified versions of the Shared Activities Questionnaire (SAQ) and the Adjective Checklist (ACL) were administered to second and third grade students in three elementary schools both before and after viewing these three show storyboards of *Realabilities*.

Participants

One hundred and sixty-six children (75 boys [45.7%] and 89 girls [54.3%]) in second (51.8%; n=86) and third grade (47.6%; n=79) participated in the *Realabilities* television show intervention. Three (1.8%) of the students were 6 years of age, 64 (38.6%) were 7 years of age, 66 (39.8%) were 8 years of age, and 31 (18.7%) were 9 years of age. All students identified themselves as "White," except one self-identified as Latino.

Seventy-nine children (36 boys [45.6%] and 43 girls [54.4%] in second [58.2%; n=46 and third grade [41.8%; n=33]) participated in the television show intervention. were from a Jewish Day School in Manhattan, New York and 87 (39 boys [45.9%] and 46 girls [54.1%] in first [1.1%; n=1], second [46.0%; n=40], and third [52.9%; n=46] of the children were from Jewish Day Schools in Baltimore, Maryland.

Instruments (Pre and Post-Tests)

Modified versions of the Shared Activities Questionnaire (SAQ), a behavioral intention measure, and the Adjective Checklist (ACL), a cognitive attitudinal measure were administered to one hundred and sixty-six elementary school children both prior to and following the viewing of three episodes of *Realabilities*. The children were then debriefed and were encouraged to discuss recommendations they would make for the show (See Table 1).

The Shared Activities Questionnaire (SAQ-Self; Morgan et al., 1996) is a 24-item experimental scale that evaluates the behavioral intentions and interest of a child in engaging in social, academic and recreational activities with a target child (Campbell et al., 2004; Morgan et al., 1996; Swaim & Morgan, 2001). An abridged eight-item version of the SAQ was used for the *Realabilities* testing to best cater to second and third grade elementary schoolchildren. The SAQ Self evaluates an individual's own preferences for engagement in activities with the target child. The Adjective Checklist (ACL) (Siperstein & Bak, 1977) is a commonly used measure for examining elementary school children's cognitive attitudes towards individuals with disabilities. It is a checklist composed of 32 adjectives, half of which feature positive values (e.g., smart, neat) and half of which feature negative values (e.g., dumb, sloppy). After reviewing the list of adjectives, the child rater circles which adjectives best describe the target child.

Results: Descriptive Analysis

Forty-six (28.0%) of the students preferred the "Pilot: Real Goal" Episode, 36 (21.3%) preferred "Chemistry Craze", starring Uno, the character with autism and 78 (46.7%) preferred the Play Nice Episode, starring Melody, the character with blindness. Fifty-nine (37.3%) of the students selected Melody, the female character who is visually impaired, as their favorite character in the show. The remaining students selected: Ezra (20.9%; n=33), the male typical character, Seemore (14.6%; n=23), the male character with a hearing impairment, Rolly (13.3%%; n=21), the male character with a physical impairment, and Uno (5.1%; n=8), the character with autism, as their favorite characters in the show.

Table 1. Realabilities SAQ and ACL results

	Autism	Blindness	Deafness	Paraplegia
SAQ Total	$t(141) = -5.326, p < .001$	$t(149) = -5.393, p < .001$	$t(142) = -3.878, p < .001$	$t(147) = -4.541, p < .001$
SAQ Academic Subtest	$t(142) = -5.327, p < .001$	$t(154) = -6.245, p < .001$	$t(149) = -4.131, p < .001$	$t(152) = -3.395, p < .001$
SAQ Social Subtest	$t(143) = -3.621, p < .001$	$t(153) = -4.398, p < .001$	$t(152) = -3.635, p < .001$	$t(153) = -3.106, p < .01$
SAQ Recreational Subtest	$t(143) = -4.385, p < .001$	$t(153) = -2.343, p < .01$	$t(151) = -1.913, p = .058$	$t(149) = -4.266, p < .001$
ACL	$t(151) = -2.101, p < .001$	$t(156) = -11.719, p < .001$	$t(155) = -10.694, p < .001$	$t(155) = -10.154, p < .001$

Main Analysis

Paired samples t-tests indicated that children reported significantly more positive cognitive attitudes on the Adjective Checklist (ACL) following the three-episode television show intervention. Children reported more positive cognitive attitudes on the ACL towards hypothetical children presenting with blindness, $t(156) = -11.719$, $p < .001$, deafness, $t(155) = -10.694$, $p < .001$, physical disability, $t(155) = -10.154$, $p < .001$ and towards children with autism, $t(151) = -2.101$, $p < .001$.

Qualitative Analysis

The administration of the post-tests included a qualitative portion wherein students were asked questions such as, "What was your favorite episode?", "Who was your favorite character?", and "Which future episodes and adventures would you recommend for the *Realabilities* team?" There was a largely positive response to these questions, which helped reveal what the young participants truly enjoyed about the show. Their thoughts and ideas for future proposals were unique and revealed their excitement about the subject matter and theme of the show. When asked, "What was your favorite episode and why?" one participant responded, "The Real Goal" because I like helping people," while another remarked, "The Real Goal" because when I played basketball, people were laughing at me". Another participant particularly enjoyed *Chemistry Craze* "because I know some kids have disabilities and they [children with disabilities] are always there for you".

With respect to which character was the students' favorite, many answered Melody, "Because she has a wand," "She sings beautifully", and "is really nice." Some reasons for why Rolly was a favorite were due to the fact that "He's so fast" and "he really believes in himself". Ezra was well liked "because he helps everyone", Uno "because he likes math and is really smart" and Seemore "because he can see into the future." It was noted that the students focused on the strengths of these characters and on the characters' pro-social interests in helping others and eradicating bullying as the primary reasons for favoring the characters. The students were motivated and enthusiastic in discussing their ideas for future episodes with the research team.

DISCUSSION

Following the three-episode intervention, the participants from three Jewish Day Schools in Manhattan, NY and Baltimore, Maryland showed significantly more favorable cognitive attitudes and behavioral intentions towards hypothetical children presenting with all four forms of disabilities. These findings are especially illuminating, since they are some of the first to show the success of a video intervention in improving cognitive attitudes in addition to behavioral intentions towards children with disabilities. This demonstrates that the use of a video medium was indeed an effective form of technology for enhancing the attitudes and behaviors of typical children towards children with disabilities.

CONCLUSION

Educational videos, as previously discussed, provide opportunities for students to increase their sensitivity towards not only children with autism, but to children with other disabilities as well. It is important that typically developing children receive proper instruction and lessons on how to optimally interact with individuals with disabilities in order to make the environment as safe and as welcoming as possible for children with disabilities. The famous twentieth century philosopher Levinas (1969) discusses the importance of welcoming the vulnerable other. *Realabilities* uses an appealing video medium to welcome the vulnerable other and to increase the positive expectancies that typical children have of children with disabilities by showcasing the strengths and special abilities of individuals with disabilities. It also attempts to promote empathy by promoting a "stop bullying" agenda in the schools and in society at large.

FUTURE RESEARCH DIRECTIONS

Due to the enhanced cognitive attitudes and behavioral intentions of the students tested, the future for *Realabilities* appears to be promising. A total of ten episodes of *Realabilities* have been scripted; each challenging the *Realabilities* team to harness their special abilities in order to combat bullying and to help their fellow students solve challenging dilemmas. These episodes are in the process of being animated in order to bring the show to life. Two comic books or graphic novel versions of the show have already been created to align with the animated episodes. We intend to conduct additional formative research to determine whether the animation, the graphic novels or the two mediums in combination are most efficacious in enhancing attitudes, behaviors and stop bullying sentiments. It is expected that testing the efficacy of the fully animated episodes and comic books of *Realabilities* will affect even greater change among our young viewers, since these modalities will be more appealing and clear means of communicating pro-social messages and values. All students will receive the pre and post-test behavioral intention, cognitive attitude and bullying questionnaires, and they will be divided into four experimental conditions: 1.) Those who will only view the *Realabilities* animated episode, 2.) Those who will only read the *Realabilities* comic book, 3.) Those who will both view the animated episode and read the comic book respectively, and 4.) Those will view the episode, read the comic book and participate in a brief instructional classroom activity pertaining to the episode. The results will help delineate which method is most effective at improving typical children's intentions, attitudes, and bullying behaviors. This effort would contribute greatly to the developmental, education and disability literature and would most importantly, improve the lives of children with disabilities.

A website has also been created for the show that displays information on the characters, the episodes, and on the research process and preliminary study results. This enables viewers to look beyond the show and understand the premise in a more didactic way. Each episode has a theme and teaches a key moral lesson; with the aid of teachers, students will be better able to understand the pro-social message that each episode is promoting. More research intends to be carried out with the new animated cartoons and comic books in elementary schools. The long-term goal is to pitch the show to network television or to stream it on Internet portals.

REFERENCES

Asher, S., & Coie, J. (1990). *Peer rejection in childhood*. New York: Cambridge University Press.

Autism Speaks. (2013). What is autism? *Autism Speaks*. Retrieved from http://www.autismspeaks.org/whatautism

Balter, R. (1999). From stigmatization to patronization: The media's distorted portrayal of physical disability. In L. L. Schwartz (Ed.), *Psychology and the media a second book* (2nd ed.). Washington, DC: American Psychological Association. doi:10.1037/10336-005

Bandura, A. (1977). *Social learning theory*. New York: Prentice Hall.

Bandura, A. (1997). *Self-efficacy: The exercise of control*. New York: Freeman.

Baseline Research. LLC. (2000). Get real about violence curriculum evaluation: Final report. Milwaukee, WI: Author.

Beckett, A., Ellison, N., Barrett, S., & Shah, S. (2010). Away with fairies? Disability within primary-age children's literature. *Disability & Society*, *25*(3), 373–386. doi:10.1080/09687591003701355

Bell, B., & Spencer, V. G. (2006). The fear factor: Bullying and students with disabilities. *International Journal of Special Education*, *21*(1), 11–22.

Bell, S. K., & Morgan, S. B. (2000). Children's attitudes and behavioral intentions toward a peer presented as obese: Does a medical explanation for the obesity make a difference? *Journal of Pediatric Psychology*, *25*, 137–145. doi:10.1093/jpepsy/25.3.137 PMID:10780140

Bellini, S., & Akullian, J. (n.d.). A meta-analysis of video modeling and video self-modeling interventions for children and adolescents with autism spectrum disorders. *Exceptional Children*, *73*(3), 264 – 287.

Belnap, B. B. (2009). *Effectiveness and acceptability of a bully prevention program with and without video supplements*. (Unpublished master's thesis). The University of Utah, Provo, UT.

Bonnel, A., Mottron, L., Peretz, I., Trudel, M., & Gallun, E. (2003). Enhanced pitch sensitivity in individuals with autism: A signal detection analysis. *Journal of Cognitive Neuroscience*, *15*(2), 226–235. doi:10.1162/089892903321208169 PMID:12676060

Bosworth, R. G., & Dobkins, K. R. (2002). The effects of spatial attention on motion processing in deaf signers, hearing signers and hearing nonsigners. *Brain and Cognition*, *49*, 152–169. doi:10.1006/brcg.2001.1497 PMID:12027400

Calvert, S. L., & Kotler, J. A. (2003). The children's television act: Can media policy make a difference? *Applied Developmental Psychology*, *24*, 375–380. doi:10.1016/S0193-3973(03)00066-2

Campbell, J. M., Cavanagh, S., Herzinger, C. V., Jackson, J. N., James, C. L., Marino, C. A., et al. (2006). *Peers' attitudes toward autism: Response to a student's self-introduction*. Paper presented at the Annual Meeting of the American Psychological Association. Washington, DC.

Campbell, J. M., Ferguson, J. E., Herzinger, C. V., Jackson, J. N., & Marino, C. (2005). Peers' attitudes toward autism differ across sociometric groups: An exploratory investigation. *Journal of Developmental and Physical Disabilities*, *17*(3), 281–298. doi:10.1007/s10882-005-4386-8

Campbell, J. M., Ferguson, J. E., Herzinger, C. V., Jackson, J. N., & Marino, C. A. (2004). Combined descriptive and explanatory information improve peers' perceptions of autism. *Research in Developmental Disabilities*, *25*, 321–329. doi:10.1016/j.ridd.2004.01.005 PMID:15193668

Campbell, M. A. (2005). Cyber bullying: An old problem in a new guise? *Australian Journal of Guidance & Counselling*, *15*(1), 68–76. doi:10.1375/ajgc.15.1.68

Caron, M., Mottron, L., Rainville, C., & Chouinard, S. (2004). Do high functioning persons with autism present superior spatial abilities? *Neuropsychologia*, *42*, 467–481. doi:10.1016/j.neuropsychologia.2003.08.015 PMID:14728920

Carson, S. H., Peterson, J. B., & Higgins, D. M. (2003). Decreased latent inhibition is associated with increased creative achievement in high-functioning individuals. *Journal of Personality and Social Psychology*, *85*(3), 499–506. doi:10.1037/0022-3514.85.3.499 PMID:14498785

Charlop-Christy, M. H., Le, L., & Freeman, K. A. (2000). A comparison of video modeling with in vivo modeling for teaching children with autism. *Journal of Autism and Developmental Disorders, 30*, 537–552. doi:10.1023/A:1005635326276 PMID:11261466

Cheatham, S., Rucker, H., Polloway, E., & Edward, A. (1995). Savant syndrome: Case studies, hypotheses, and implications for special education. *Education and Training in Mental Retardation and Developmental Disabilities, 30*(3), 245–253.

Dake, J. A., Price, J. H., & Telljohann, S. K. (2003). The nature and extent of bullying at school. *The Journal of School Health, 7*(5), 173–180. doi:10.1111/j.1746-1561.2003.tb03599.x PMID:12793102

Day, L. A. (2000). *Ethics in media communications: Cases and controversies*. Belmont, CA: Wadsworth/Thompson Learning.

DiSalvo, C. A., & Oswald, D. P. (2002). Peer-mediated interventions to increase the social interaction of children with autism: Consideration of peer expectancies. *Focus on Autism and Other Developmental Disabilities, 17*(4), 198–207. doi: 10.1177/10883576020170040201

Durston, S. (2003). A review of the biological bases of ADHD: What have we learned from imaging studies? *Mental Retardation and Developmental Disabilities Research Reviews, 9*(3), 184–195. doi:10.1002/mrdd.10079 PMID:12953298

Eaton, D. K. (2012). Youth risk behavior surveillance: United States, 2011. U.S. Department of Health and Human Services: Center for Disease Control and Prevention, 61(4).

Franco, Z., & Zimbardo, P. (2006-2007). The banality of heroism. *Greater Good: The Bystander's Dilemma, 3*(2).

Friedrich, S., Morgan, S. B., & Devine, C. (1996). Children's attitudes and behavioral intentions toward a peer with Tourette's syndrome. *Journal of Pediatric Psychology, 21*, 307–319. doi:10.1093/jpepsy/21.3.307 PMID:8935235

Gottlieb, J., & Gottlieb, B. W. (1977). Stereotypic attitudes and behavioral intentions toward handicapped children. *American Journal of Mental Deficiency, 82*, 65–71. PMID:142428

Gray, D. E. (1993). Negotiating autism: Relations between parents and treatment staff. *Social Science & Medicine, 36*, 1037–1046. doi:10.1016/0277-9536(93)90121-J PMID:8475419

Hardin, B. (2001). Missing in action? Images of disability in sports illustrated for kids. *Disability Studies Quarterly, 21*(2).

Harris, M. J., Milich, R. C., Corbitt, E. M., Hoover, D. W., & Brady, M. (1992). Self-fulfilling effects of stigmatizing information on children's social interactions. *Journal of Personality and Social Psychology, 63*, 41–50. doi:10.1037/0022-3514.63.1.41 PMID:1494984

Healey, D., & Rucklidge, J. J. (2006). An investigation into the relationship among ADHD symptomatology, creativity, and neuropsychological functioning in children. *Child Neuropsychology, 12*(6), 421–438. doi:10.1080/09297040600806086 PMID:16952888

Heider. (1958). *The psychology of interpersonal relations*. New York: Wiley.

Holmquist, J. (2011). Bullying prevention: Positive strategies. PACER Center, 1 – 6.

Hoover, J., & Stenhjem, P. (2003). Bullying and teasing of youth with disabilities: Creating positive school environments for effective inclusion. *National Center on Secondary Education and Transition, 2*(3), 1–6.

Iavaraone, A., Patruno, M., Galeone, F., Chieffi, S., & Carlomagno, S. (2007). Brief report: Error pattern in an autistic savant calendar calculator. *Journal of Autism and Developmental Disorders*, *37*, 775–779. doi:10.1007/s10803-006-0190-2 PMID:16900402

Juvonen, J. (1992). Negative peer reactions from the perspective of the reactor. *Journal of Educational Psychology*, *84*, 314–321. doi:10.1037/0022-0663.84.3.314

Kamps, D. M., Kravitz, T., Gonzalez-Lopez, A., Kemmerer, K., Potucek, J., & Harrell, L. G. (1998). What do peers think? Social validity of peer-mediated programs. *Education & Treatment of Children*, *21*, 107–134.

Kelley, H. H. (1967). Attribution theory in social psychology. In D. Levine (Ed.), *Nebraska symposium on motivation, 1967*. Lincoln, NE: University of Nebraska Press.

Kim, Y. S., & Leventhal, B. (2008). Bullying and suicide: A review. *Adolescent Medicine Health*, *20*(2), 133–154. PMID:18714552

Levinas, E. (1969). *Totality and infinity* (A. Lingis, Trans.). Pittsburgh, PA: Duquesne University Press.

Lieberman, R., & Cowan, K.C. (2011). Bullying and youth suicide: breaking the connection. *National Association of School Psychologists*, 12–17.

Mares. (1996). *Metanalysis of studies of prosocial portrayals*. Philadelphia: University of Pennsylvania.

Matawa, C. (2009). Exploring the musical interests and abilities of blind and partially sighted children and young people with retinopathy of prematurity. *British Journal of Visual Impairment*, *27*, 252. doi:10.1177/0264619609106364

Meyer, G., Roberto, A. J., Boster, F. J., & Roberto, H. L. (2004). Assessing the get real about violence curriculum: Process and outcome evaluation results and implications. *Health Communication*, *16*, 451–474. doi:10.1207/s15327027hc1604_4 PMID:15465690

Miller, L. K. (1999). The savant syndrome: Intellectual impairment and exceptional skill. *Psychological Bulletin*, *125*(1), 33–46. doi:10.1037/0033-2909.125.1.31 PMID:9990844

Morgan, S. B., & Wisely, D. W. (1996). Children's attitudes and behavioral intentions toward a peer presented as physically handicapped: A more positive view. *Journal of Developmental and Physical Disabilities*, *8*, 29–42. doi:10.1007/BF02578438

Mottron, L., Dawson, M., Soulieres, I., Hubert, B., & Burack, J. (2006). Enhanced perceptual functioning in autism: An update, and eight principles of autistic perception. *Journal of Autism and Developmental Disorders*, *36*(1), 27–43. doi:10.1007/s10803-005-0040-7 PMID:16453071

Murphy, R. (1995). Encounters: The body silent in America. In B. Instad, & S. R. White (Eds.), *Disability and culture* (pp. 140–158). Berkeley, CA: University of California Press.

Myles, B. S., Simpson, R. L., Ormsbee, C. K., & Erikson, C. (1993). Integrating preschool children with autism with their normally developing peers: Research findings and best practice recommendations. *Focus on Autistic Behavior*, *8*, 1–18.

NREPP. (2012). *Legacy program summary: Get real about violence*. Retrieved from http://www.nrepp.samhsa.gov/ViewLegacy.aspx?id=92

Owen-Deschryver, J. S. (2004). Promoting social interactions between students with autism and their peers in inclusive school settings. *Dissertation Abstracts International. A, The Humanities and Social Sciences*, *64*(9-A), 32–46.

Pepler, D. J., Craig, W. M., & Roberts, W. R. (1993). A school-based anti-bullying intervention: Preliminary evaluation. In D. Tattum (Ed.), *Understanding and managing bullying* (pp. 76–91). Heinemann Books.

Pierce, K., & Schreibman, L. (1997). Using peer trainers to promote social behavior in autism: Are they effective at enhancing multiple social modalities. *Focus on Autism and Other Developmental Disabilities*, *12*(4). doi:10.1177/108835769701200403

Rieber, L. P. (1991). Animation, incidental learning, and continuing motivation. *Journal of Educational Psychology*, *83*, 318–328. doi:10.1037/0022-0663.83.3.318

Rosenbaum, P. L., Armstrong, R. W., & King, S. M. (1988). Determinants of children's attitudes toward disability: A review of the evidence. *Children's Health Care*, *17*, 1–8. doi:10.1207/s15326888chc1701_5 PMID:10315759

Rosenthal, R. (1963). On the social psychology of the psychological experiment: The experimenter's hypotheses as unintended experimental results. *American Scientist*, *51*, 268–283. PMID:13974992

Rosenthal, R. (1989). *Experimenter expectancy covert communication and meta-analytic methods*. Paper presented at the 97th Annual Convention of the American Psychological Association. New Orleans, LA.

Ryan, K. M. (1981). Developmental differences in reactions to the physically disabled. *Human Development*, *24*, 240–256. doi:10.1159/000272685 PMID:6456979

Silton, N. R. (2009). Fostering knowledge, positive intentions and attitudes of typical children towards children with autism. Proquest Info and Learning Company, 1-108.

Siperstein, G. N. (1980). *Development of the adjective checklist: An instrument for measuring children's attitudes toward the handicapped*. Unpublished Manuscript

Siperstein, G. N., & Bak, J. (1977). *Instruments to measure children's attitudes toward the handicapped: Adjective checklist and activity preference list*. Unpublished Manuscript.

Slater, M., Rovira, A., Southern, R., Swapp, D., & Zhang, J. J. et al. (2013). Bystander responses to a violent incident in an immersive virtual environment. *PLoS ONE*, *8*(1), e52766. doi:10.1371/journal.pone.0052766 PMID:23300991

Smith-D'Arezzo, W.M., & Moore-Thomas, C. (2010). Children's perceptions of peers with disabilities. *TEACHING Exceptional Children Plus*, *6*(3).

Sprafkin, J. N., Gadow, K. D., & Grayson, P. (1984). Television and the emotionally disturbed, learning disabled, and mentally retarded child: A review. *Advances in Learning and Behavioral Disabilities*, *3*, 151–213.

Swaim, K. F., Morgan, S. B., Lenhart, J. A., Hyder, K., Zimmerman, A. W., & Pevsner, J. (2001). Children's attitudes and behavioral intentions toward a peer with autistic behaviors: Does a brief educational intervention have an effect? *Journal of Autism and Developmental Disorders*, *31*(2), 195. doi:10.1023/A:1010703316365 PMID:11450818

Swearer, S., Espelage, D. L., & Napolitano, S. A. (2009). *Bullying prevention and intervention: Realistic strategies for schools*. New York, NY: Guilford Press.

Wahl, O., Hanrahan, E., Karl, K., Lasher, E., & Swaye, J. (2006). The depiction of mental illnesses in children's television programs. *Journal of Community Psychology*, *35*(1), 121–133. doi:10.1002/jcop.20138

Winner, E. (2000). The origins and ends of giftedness. *The American Psychologist*, 55(1), 159–169. doi:10.1037/0003-066X.55.1.159 PMID:11392860

Wood, L. (2012). A critical analysis: Overview of the media. *Disability Planet*. Retrieved from http://www.disabilityplanet.co.uk/index.html

Compilation of References

AAPC Publishing. (2010). *Hidden curriculum to go: Version for kids: Version for adolescents and adults.* Shawnee Mission, KS: Author.

ABIresearch. (2013, January 31). *45 million Windows phone and 20 million BlackBerry 10 smartphones in active use at year-end, enough to keep developers interested.* Retrieved from http://www.abiresearch.com/press/45-million-windows-phone-and-20-million-blackberry

Achmadi, D. (2010). *Teaching a multi-step requesting sequence to two adolescents with autism using an iPod-based speech generating device.* (Unpublished master's thesis). Victoria University of Wellington, Wellington, New Zealand.

Adams, J. B. (2013). *Summary of dietary, nutritional, and medical treatments for autism-based on over 150 published research studies.* Arizona State University, Autism Research Institute.

Adkins, T., & Axelrod, S. (2001). Topography-versus selection-based responding: Comparison of mand acquisition in each modality. *Behavior Analyst Today, 2,* 259–266.

Adolphs, R., Sears, L., & Piven, J. (2001). Abnormal processing of social information from faces in autism. *Journal of Cognitive Neuroscience, 13*(2), 232–240. doi:10.1162/089892901564289 PMID:11244548

Ahn, C. H. (2012). *Big day.* Cupertino, CA: Author.

Alcorn, A., Pain, H., Rajendran, G., Smith, T., Lemon, O., Porayska-Pomsta, K., & Bernardini, S. (2011). Social communication between virtual characters and children with autism. In *Artificial intelligence in education* (pp. 7–14). Berlin: Springer. doi:10.1007/978-3-642-21869-9_4

Aldebaran Robotics. (2013). *Aldebaran robotics' NAO robot goes to school to help children with autism: ASK NAO initiative to revolutionize special education for children with autism.* Retrieved from http://asknao.aldebaranrobotics.com/media/article/download/Press%20release%20ASK%20NAO_RFB.pdf

Aljunied, M., & Frederickson, N. (2013). Does central coherence relate to the cognitive performance of children with autism in dynamic assessments. *Autism, 17,* 172–183. doi:10.1177/1362361311409960 PMID:21715547

Allen, R. E. (Ed.). (1990). *The concise Oxford dictionary of current English* (8th ed.). Oxford, UK: Clarendon Press.

Alpert, C. L., & Rogers-Warren, A. K. (1985). Communication in autistic person: Characteristics and intervention. In S. Warren & A. K. Rogers-Warren (Eds.), Teaching functional language: Generalization and maintenance of language skills (pp. 123–155). Academic Press.

American Psychiatric Association. (2000). Disorders usually first diagnosed in infancy, childhood, or adolescence. In *Diagnostic and statistical manual of mental disorders* (4th ed.). Washington, DC: American Psychiatric Association.

American Psychiatric Association. (2013). Autism spectrum disorder. *DSM-5 Autism Spectrum Disorder Fact Sheet.* Retrieved from http://www.dsm5.org/Documents/Autism%20Spectrum%20Disorder%20Fact%2Sheet.pdf

American Psychiatric Association. (2013). *Diagnostic and statistical manual of mental disorders* (5th ed.). Washington, DC: APA.

American Speech-Language-Hearing Association. (1991). Report: Augmentative and alternative communication. *ASHA, 33*(Suppl. 5), 9–12. PMID:1660275

Anderson-Hanley, C., Tureck, K., & Schneiderman, R. L. (2011). Autism and exergaming: Effects on repetitive behaviors and cognition. *Psychology Research and Behavior Management, 4*, 129–137. PMID:22114543

Andersson, U. Josefsson, & Pareto, L. (2006). Challenges in designing virtual environments training social skills for children with autism. In *Proceedings of the 6th International Conference on Disability, Virtual Reality, & Associated Technologies,* (pp. 35-43). Academic Press.

Andrews, J., & Andrews, M. (1990). *Family based treatment in communicative disorders.* Sandwich, IL: Janelle.

Annema, J. H., Verstraete, M., Abeele, V. V., Desmet, S., & Geerts, D. (2010). *Videogames in therapy: A therapist's perspective.* Paper presented at Fun and Games 2010. Leuven, Belgium.

Appelbaum, L. G., Cain, M. S., Darling, E. F., & Mitroff, S. R. (2013). Action video game playing is associated with improved visual sensitivity, but not alterations in visual sensory memory. *Attention, Perception & Psychophysics, 75,* 1161–1167. PMID:23709062

Apple, A. L., Billingsley, F., & Schwartz, I. S. (2005). Effects of video modeling alone and with self-management on compliment giving behaviors of children with high functioning ASD. *Journal of Positive Behavior Interventions, 7,* 33–46. doi:10.1177/10983007050070010401

Asher, S., & Coie, J. (1990). *Peer rejection in childhood.* New York: Cambridge University Press.

Ashwin, C., Ricciardelli, P., & Baron-Cohen, S. (2009). Positive and negative gaze perception in ASD spectrum conditions. *Social Neuroscience, 4*(2), 153–164. doi:10.1080/17470910802337902 PMID:18726820

Attwood, T. (2008). *The complete guide to Asperger's syndrome.* London, UK: Jessica Kingsley.

Aurora. (2000). *The Aurora project.* Retrieved June, 1, 2013 from http://www.aurora-project.com

Autism Emotion. (n.d.). Retrieved from http://www.autismspeaks.org/autism-apps/autism-emotion

Autism Society. (2011). *Facts and statistics.* Retrieved 6/25/2013 from http://www.autism-society.org/about-autism/facts-and-statistics.html

Autism Speaks. (2013). What is autism? *Autism Speaks.* Retrieved from http://www.autismspeaks.org/whatautism

Ayres, K. M., Mechling, L., & Sansosti, F. J. (2013). The use of mobile technologies to assist with life skills/independence of students with moderate/severe intellectual disability and/or autism spectrum disorders: Considerations for the future of school psychology. *Psychology in the Schools, 50,* 259–271. doi:10.1002/pits.21673

Bailey, J. S., & Burch, M. R. (2002). *Research methods in applied behavior analysis.* Thousand Oaks, CA: SAGE Publications.

Baio, J. (2012). *Prevalence of autism spectrum disorders – Autism and developmental disabilities monitoring network, 14 sites, United States, 2008.* Atlanta, GA: Centers for Disease Control and Prevention.

Baird, G., Cass, H., & Slonims, V. (2003). Diagnosis of autism. *BMJ (Clinical Research Ed.), 327,* 488–493. doi:10.1136/bmj.327.7413.488 PMID:12946972

Baker, M. J. (2000). Incorporating the thematic ritualistic behaviors of children with autism into games: Increasing social play interactions with siblings. *Journal of Positive Behavior Interventions, 2*(2), 66–84.

Balter, R. (1999). From stigmatization to patronization: The media's distorted portrayal of physical disability. In L. L. Schwartz (Ed.), *Psychology and the media a second book* (2nd ed.). Washington, DC: American Psychological Association. doi:10.1037/10336-005

Banda, D. R., & Grimmett, E. (2008). Enhancing social and transition behaviors of persons with autism through activity schedules: A review. *Education and Training in Developmental Disabilities, 43,* 324–333.

Banda, D. R., Matuszny, R. M., & Turkan, S. (2011). Video modeling strategies to enhance appropriate behaviors in children with autism spectrum disorders. *Teaching Exceptional Children, 39,* 47–52.

Bandura, A. (1977). *Social learning theory.* Englewood Cliffs, NJ: Prentice Hall.

Bandura, A. (1997). *Self-efficacy: The exercise of control.* New York: Freeman.

Baron-Cohen, S., & Bolton, S. (1993). *Autism: The facts.* Oxford, UK: Oxford University Press.

Baron-Cohen, S., Wheelwright, S., & Jolliffe, T. (1997). Is there a language of the eyes? Evidence from normal adults, and adults with autism or asperger syndrome. *Visual Cognition, 4*(3), 311–331.

Bartoli, L., Corradi, C., Garzotto, F., & Valoriani, M. (2013). *Exploring motion-based touchless games for autistic children's learning.* Paper presented at the Interaction Design and Children '13. New York, NY.

Baseline Research. LLC. (2000). Get real about violence curriculum evaluation: Final report. Milwaukee, WI: Author.

Bauminger-Zviely, N., Eden, S., Zancanaro, M., Weiss, P., & Gal, E. (2013). Increasing social engagement in children with high-functioning autism spectrum disorder using collaborative technologies in the school environment. *Autism, 17*, 317–339. doi:10.1177/1362361312472989 PMID:23614935

Bausch, M. E., & Hasselbring, T. S. (2004). Assistive technology: Are the necessary skills and knowledge being developed at the preservice and inservice levels? *Teacher Education and Special Education, 27*, 97–104. doi:10.1177/088840640402700202

Baxter, S., Enderby, P., Evans, P., & Judge, S. (2012). Barriers and facilitators to the use of high-technology augmentative and alternative communication devices: A systematic review and qualitative synthesis. *International Journal of Language & Communication Disorders, 47*, 115. doi:10.1111/j.1460-6984.2011.00090.x PMID:22369053

Beaudry, N. (2013). Best iPad apps for children with autism. *SheKnows Parenting.* Retrieved from http://www.sheknows.com/parenting/articles/953661/best-ipad-apps-for-children-with-autism

Beckett, A., Ellison, N., Barrett, S., & Shah, S. (2010). Away with fairies? Disability within primary-age children's literature. *Disability & Society, 25*(3), 373–386. doi:10.1080/09687591003701355

Bekele, E. T., Lahiri, U., Swanson, A. R., & Crittendon, J., A., Warren, Z. E., & Sarkar, N. (2013). A step towards developing adaptive robot-mediated intervention architecture (ARIA) for children with autism. *IEEE Transactions on Neural Systems and Rehabilitation Engineering, 21*(2), 289–299. doi: doi:10.1109/TNSRE.2012.2230188 PMID:23221831

Bell, B., & Spencer, V. G. (2006). The fear factor: Bullying and students with disabilities. *International Journal of Special Education, 21*(1), 11–22.

Bellini, S. (2008). *Building social relationships: A systematic approach to teaching social interaction skills to children and adolescents with autism spectrum disorders and other social difficulties.* Shawnee Mission, KS: Autism Asperger Publishing.

Bellini, S., & Akullian, J. (2007). A meta-analysis of video modeling and video self-monitoring interventions for children and adolescents with autism spectrum disorders. *Exceptional Children, 73*, 264–287.

Bellini, S., & Akullian, J. A. (2007). A meta-analysis of video modeling and video self-modeling interventions for children and adolescents with autism spectrum disorders. *Exceptional Children, 73*, 264–287.

Bellini, S., & Peters, J. (2008). Social skills training for youth with autism spectrum disorders. *Child and Adolescent Psychiatric Clinics of North America, 17*, 857–873. doi:10.1016/j.chc.2008.06.008 PMID:18775374

Bellini, S., Peters, J. K., Benner, L., & Hopf, A. (2007). A meta-analysis of school-based social skills interventions for children with autism spectrum disorders. *Remedial and Special Education, 28*, 153–162. doi:10.1177/07419325070280030401

Bell, S. K., & Morgan, S. B. (2000). Children's attitudes and behavioral intentions toward a peer presented as obese: Does a medical explanation for the obesity make a difference? *Journal of Pediatric Psychology, 25*, 137–145. doi:10.1093/jpepsy/25.3.137 PMID:10780140

Belnap, B. B. (2009). *Effectiveness and acceptability of a bully prevention program with and without video supplements.* (Unpublished master's thesis). The University of Utah, Provo, UT.

Ben-Avie, M., & Reichow, B. (2010). *Assistive technology national survey*. New Haven, CT: Center of Excellence on Autism Spectrum Disorders.

Bende, R. (2011). Kids and mobile devices: Half of kids under 8 use them. *PARENTS*. Retrieved from http://www.parents.com/blogs/red-hot-parenting/2011/10/25/health/kids-and-mobile-devices-half-of-kids-under-8-use-them/

Benford, P. (2008). *The use of internet-based communication by people with autism*. (Unpublished doctoral dissertation). University of Nottingham, Nottingham, UK.

Bereznak, S., Ayres, K., Mechling, L., & Alexander, J. (2012). Video self-prompting and mobile technology to increase daily living and vocational independence for students with autism spectrum disorders. *Journal of Developmental and Physical Disabilities, 24*, 269–285. doi:10.1007/s10882-012-9270-8

Bernard-Opitz, V., Sriram, N., & Nakhoda-Sapuan, S. (2001). Enhancing social problem solving in children with autism and normal children through computer-assisted instruction. *Journal of Autism and Developmental Disorders, 31*, 377–384. doi:10.1023/A:1010660502130 PMID:11569584

Bertrand, J., Mars, A., Boyle, C., Bove, F., Yeargin-Allsopp, M., & Decoufle, P. (2001). Prevalence of autism in a United States population: The Brick Township, New Jersey investigation. *Pediatrics, 108*, 1155–1161. doi:10.1542/peds.108.5.1155 PMID:11694696

Beukelman & Mirenda. (2005). *Augmentative and alternative communication: Supporting children and adults with complex communication needs* (3rd ed.). Baltimore, MD: Brookes Publishing Co.

Bignell, S. (2008). *Autism and Asperger's in Second Life*. University of Derby. Retrieved from http://www.miltonbroome.com/2008/06/autism-aspergers-and-second-life.html

Billstedt, E., Gillberg, I. C., & Gilbert, C. (2005). Autism after adolescence: population-based 13-22-year follow-up study of 120 individuals with autism diagnosed in childhood. *Journal of Autism and Developmental Disorders, 35*(3), 351–360. doi:10.1007/s10803-005-3302-5 PMID:16119476

Blair, K. C., Lee, I., Cho, S., & Dunlap, G. (2011). Positive behaviour support through family-school collaboration for young children with autism. *Topics in Early Childhood Special Education, 31*(1), 22–36. doi:10.1177/0271121410377510

Blum-Dimaya, A., Reeve, S. A., Reeve, K. F., & Hoch, H. (2010). Teaching children with autism to play a video game using activity schedules and game-embedded simultaneous video modeling. *Education & Treatment of Children, 33*(3), 351–370.

Bock, M. A. (1999). Sorting laundry: Categorization application to an authentic learning activity by children with autism. *Focus on Autism and Other Developmental Disabilities, 14*, 220–230. doi:10.1177/108835769901400404

Bock, M. A. (2007). A social-behavioral learning strategy intervention for a child with Asperger syndrome. *Remedial and Special Education, 28*, 258–265. doi:10.1177/07419325070280050101

Bolte, S., Golan, O., Goodwin, M. S., & Zwaigenbaum, L. (2010). Editorial: What can innovative technologies do for autism spectrum disorders? *Autism, 14*(3), 155–159. PMID:20603897

Bölte, S., Golan, O., Goodwin, M. S., & Zwaigenbaum, L. (2010). What can innovative technologies do for autism spectrum disorders? *Autism, 14*(3), 155–159. doi:10.1177/1362361310365028 PMID:20603897

Bolton, P. F., Macdonald, H., Pickles, A., Rios, P., Goode, S., & Crowson, M. et al. (1994). A case-control family history study of autism. *Journal of Child Psychology and Psychiatry, and Allied Disciplines, 35*, 877–900. doi:10.1111/j.1469-7610.1994.tb02300.x PMID:7962246

Bondy, A. S., & Frost, L. A. (1994). The picture exchange communication system. *Focus on Autistic Behavior, 9*, 1–19.

Bondy, A. S., & Frost, L. A. (1998). The picture exchange communication system. *Seminars in Speech and Language, 19*, 373–398. doi:10.1055/s-2008-1064055 PMID:9857393

Bonnel, A., Mottron, L., Peretz, I., Trudel, M., & Gallun, E. (2003). Enhanced pitch sensitivity in individuals with autism: A signal detection analysis. *Journal of Cognitive Neuroscience, 15*(2), 226–235. doi:10.1162/089892903321208169 PMID:12676060

Boraston, Z., Blakemore, S. J., Chilvers, R., & Skuse, D. (2007). Impaired sadness recognition is linked to social interaction deficit in ASD. *Neuropsychologia, 45*(7), 1501–1510. doi:10.1016/j.neuropsychologia.2006.11.010 PMID:17196998

Bosseler, A., & Massaro, D. W. (2003). Development and evaluation of a computer-animated tutor for vocabulary and language learning in children with autism. *Journal of Autism and Developmental Disorders, 33,* 653–672. doi:10.1023/B:JADD.0000006002.82367.4f PMID:14714934

Bosworth, R. G., & Dobkins, K. R. (2002). The effects of spatial attention on motion processing in deaf signers, hearing signers and hearing nonsigners. *Brain and Cognition, 49,* 152–169. doi:10.1006/brcg.2001.1497 PMID:12027400

Bouck, E. C., Okolo, C. M., & Courtad, C. A. (2008). Technology at home: Implications for children with disabilities. *Journal of Special Education Technology, 22*(3), 43–56.

Boulos, M. N. K., Hetherington, L., & Wheeler, S. (2007). Second Life: An overview of the potential of 3-D virtual worlds in medical and health education. *Health Information and Libraries Journal, 24*(4), 233–245. doi:10.1111/j.1471-1842.2007.00733.x PMID:18005298

Bowser, G. (2011, May 5). *Posting to QIAT listserv.* Retrieved from http://natri.uky.edu/assoc_projects/qiat/listserv.html

Bowser, G., & Reed, P. (2001). *Hey can I try that? A student handbook for choosing and using assistive technology.* Retrieved from www.wati.org/products/pdf/heycanitrythat.pdf

Briel, L. W., & Getzel, E. E. (2009). Postsecondary options for students with autism. In *Autism and the transition to adulthood: Success beyond the classroom* (pp. 189–207). Baltimore, MD: Paul H. Brookes.

Briody, J., & McGarry, K. (2005). *Beyond the journal: Young children on the web.* Retrieved from http://www.naeyc.org/files/tyc/file/TYC_V4N1_BriodyMcGarry.pdf

Browder, D. M., & Cooper-Duffy, K. (2003). Evidence-based practices for students with severe disabilities and the requirements for accountability in no child left behind. *The Journal of Special Education, 37,* 57–163. doi:10.1177/00224669030370030501

Bryant, B. R., & Kraft, G. (2012). Assistive technology devices to enhance speech communication. In D. P. Bryant, & B. R. Bryant (Eds.), *Assistive technology for people with disabilities* (pp. 104–125). Boston: Pearson Publishers.

Buggey, T. (2005). Video self-modeling applications with students with autism spectrum disorder in a small private school setting. *Focus on Autism and Other Developmental Disabilities, 20,* 52–63. doi:10.1177/10883576050200010501

Buron, K. D., & Curtis, M. (2012). The incredible 5-point scale: The significantly improved and expanded second ed: Assisting students in understanding social interactions and controlling their emotional responses (2nd ed.). Shawnee Mission, KS: AAPC Publishing.

Burton, C. E., Anderson, D. H., Prater, M. A., & Dyches, T. T. (2013). Video self-modeling on an iPad to teach functional math problems to adolescents and intellectual disability. *Focus on Autism and Other Developmental Disabilities, 28,* 67–77. doi:10.1177/1088357613478829

Cafiero, J. M. (2001). The effect of an augmentative communication intervention on the communication, behavior, and academic program of an adolescent with autism. *Focus on Autism and Other Developmental Disabilities, 16,* 179–189. doi:10.1177/108835760101600306

Cafiero, J. M. (2008). Technology supports for individuals with autism spectrum disorder. *Technology in Action, 3,* 1–12.

Calvert, S. L., & Kotler, J. A. (2003). The children's television act: Can media policy make a difference? *Applied Developmental Psychology, 24,* 375–380. doi:10.1016/S0193-3973(03)00066-2

Campbell, J. M., Cavanagh, S., Herzinger, C. V., Jackson, J. N., James, C. L., Marino, C. A., et al. (2006). *Peers' attitudes toward autism: Response to a student's self-introduction.* Paper presented at the Annual Meeting of the American Psychological Association. Washington, DC.

Campbell, J. M. (2011). Review supports use of aided augmentative and alternative communication (AAC) systems for improving communication skills for individuals with autism spectrum disorders: The role of moderators is not yet clearly established. *Evidence-Based Communication Assessment and Intervention, 5,* 187–192. doi:10.1080/17489539.2012.688624

Campbell, J. M., Ferguson, J. E., Herzinger, C. V., Jackson, J. N., & Marino, C. (2005). Peers' attitudes toward autism differ across sociometric groups: An exploratory investigation. *Journal of Developmental and Physical Disabilities, 17*(3), 281–298. doi:10.1007/s10882-005-4386-8

Campbell, J. M., Ferguson, J. E., Herzinger, C. V., Jackson, J. N., & Marino, C. A. (2004). Combined descriptive and explanatory information improve peers' perceptions of autism. *Research in Developmental Disabilities, 25,* 321–329. doi:10.1016/j.ridd.2004.01.005 PMID:15193668

Campbell, M. A. (2005). Cyber bullying: An old problem in a new guise? *Australian Journal of Guidance & Counselling, 15*(1), 68–76. doi:10.1375/ajgc.15.1.68

Cannella-Malone, H. I., DeBar, R. M., & Sigafoos, J. (2009). An examination of preference for augmentative and alternative communication devices with two boys with significant intellectual disabilities. *Augmentative and Alternative Communication, 25,* 262–273. doi:10.3109/07434610903384511 PMID:19883289

Cappadocia, M. C., Weiss, J. A., & Pepler, D. (2012). Bullying experiences among children and youth with autism spectrum disorders. *Journal of Autism and Developmental Disorders, 42*(2), 266–277. doi:10.1007/s10803-011-1241-x PMID:21499672

Cardon, T. A. (2012). Teaching caregivers to implement video modeling imitation training via iPad for their children with ASD. *Research in ASD Spectrum Disorders, 6*(4), 1389–1400. doi:10.1016/j.rasd.2012.06.002

Carlile, K. A., Reeve, S. A., Reeve, K. F., & DeBar, R. M. (2013). Using activity schedules on the iPod touch to teach leisure skills to children with autism. *Education & Treatment of Children, 36,* 33–57. doi:10.1353/etc.2013.0015

Caron, M., Mottron, L., Rainville, C., & Chouinard, S. (2004). Do high functioning persons with autism present superior spatial abilities? *Neuropsychologia, 42,* 467–481. doi:10.1016/j.neuropsychologia.2003.08.015 PMID:14728920

Carr, E. G., Levin, L., McConnachie, G., Carlson, J. I., Kemp, D. C., & Smith, C. E. (1994). *Communication-based interventions for problem behavior: A user's guide for producing behavior change.* Baltimore, MD: Paul H. Brookes.

Carrington, S., Templeton, E., & Papinczak, T. (2003). Adolescents with Asperger syndrome and perceptions of friendship. *Focus on Autism and Other Developmental Disabilities, 18*(4), 211–218. doi:10.1177/10883576030180040201

Carson, S. H., Peterson, J. B., & Higgins, D. M. (2003). Decreased latent inhibition is associated with increased creative achievement in high-functioning individuals. *Journal of Personality and Social Psychology, 85*(3), 499–506. doi:10.1037/0022-3514.85.3.499 PMID:14498785

Carter, A. S. et al. (2005). Social development in autism. In F. R. Volkmar, R. Paul, A. Klin, & D. Cohen (Eds.), *Handbook of autism and pervasive developmental disorders* (3rd ed., pp. 312–334). Hoboken, NJ: Wiley.

Carter, E. W., Trainor, A., Owens, L., Sweden, B., & Sun, Y. (2010). Self-determination prospects of youth with high-incidence disabilities. *Journal of Emotional and Behavioral Disorders, 18,* 67–81. doi:10.1177/1063426609332605

CAST. (2011). *About UDL.* Retrieved from http://www.cast.org/udl/index.html

CAST. (2011). *Universal design for learning guidelines – Version 2.0.* Wakefield, MA: Author. Retrieved from http://www.udlcenter.org/aboutudl/udlguidelines/downloads

CDC. (2013). *Autism spectrum disorders (ASD).* Retrieved from http://www.cdc.gov/ncbddd/autism/treatment.html

Centers for Disease Control and Prevention. (2007). Prevalence of autism spectrum disorders—Autism and developmental disabilities monitoring network, six sites, United States, 2000. *Surveillance Summaries, 56*(SS-1), 1–11.

Centers for Disease Control and Prevention. (2009). Prevalence of autism spectrum disorders–Autism and developmental disabilities monitoring network, United States, 2006. *Surveillance Summaries, 58*(SS10), 1–20.

Centers for Disease Control and Prevention. (2010). *Autism spectrum disorders (ASDs) data & statistics.* Retrieved 02/12/2011 from http://www.cdc.gov/ncbddd/autism/data.html

Centers for Disease Control and Prevention. (2012). *Autism spectrum disorders (ASDs) data & statistics.* Retrieved 10/28/2012 from http://www.cdc.gov/ncbddd/autism/data.html

Centers for Disease Control and Prevention. (2012). Prevalence of autism spectrum disorders – Autism and developmental disabilities monitoring network, 14 sites, United States, 2008. *Surveillance Summaries, 61*(SS03), 1–19. PMID:22456193

Centers for Disease Control and Prevention. (2012). Prevalence of autism spectrum disorders—Autism and developmental disabilities monitoring network, 14 sites, 2008, United States. *Morbidity and Mortality Weekly Monitoring Report, 61*(SS-3), 1–19.

Centers for Disease Control and Prevention. (2013). Changes in prevalence of parent-reported autism spectrum disorder in school-aged U.S. children: 2007 to 2011-2012. *National Health Statistics Reports, 5.*

Centers for Medicare and Medicaid Services. (2010). *Autism spectrum disorders: Final report on environmental scan.* Washington, DC: Author.

Ceranoglu, T. A. (2010). Star Wars in psychotherapy: Video games in the office. *Academic Psychiatry, 34,* 233–236. PMID:20431107

Ceranoglu, T. A. (2010). Video games in psychotherapy. *Review of General Psychology, 14*(2), 141–146.

Chamberlain, B., Kasari, C., & Rotheram-Fuller, E. (2007). Involvement or isolation? The social networks of children with autism in regular classrooms. *Journal of Autism and Developmental Disorders, 37*(2), 230–242. doi:10.1007/s10803-006-0164-4 PMID:16855874

Charitos, D., Karadanos, G., Sereti, E., Triantafillou, S., Koukouvinou, S., & Martakos, D. (2000). Employing virtual reality for aiding the organisation of autistic children behaviour in everyday tasks. In *Proceedings of International Conference on Disability, Virtual Reality and Associated Technologies,* (pp. 147–52). Academic Press.

Charlop-Christy, M. H., Carpenter, M., Le, L., LeBlanc, L., & Kellet, K. (2002). Using the picture exchange communication system (PECS) with children with autism: Assessment of PECS acquisition, speech, social-communication behavior, and problem behavior. *Journal of Applied Behavior Analysis, 35*(3), 213–231. doi:10.1901/jaba.2002.35-213 PMID:12365736

Charlop-Christy, M. H., & Daneshvar, S. (2003). Using video modeling to teach perspective taking to children with autism. *Journal of Positive Behavior Interventions, 5,* 12–21. doi:10.1177/10983007030050010101

Charlop-Christy, M. H., Le, L., & Freeman, K. A. (2000). A comparison of video modeling with in vivo modeling for teaching children with autism. *Journal of Autism and Developmental Disorders, 30,* 537–552. doi:10.1023/A:1005635326276 PMID:11261466

Chase, J. (2012). *A list of apps for social skills and autism spectrum disorders.* Academic Press.

Cheatham, S., Rucker, H., Polloway, E., & Edward, A. (1995). Savant syndrome: Case studies, hypotheses, and implications for special education. *Education and Training in Mental Retardation and Developmental Disabilities, 30*(3), 245–253.

Checkley, R., Reidy, L., Chantler, S., Hodge, N., & Holmes, K. (2012). Black white zebra orange orange: How children with autism make use of computer-based voice output communication aids in their language and communication at school. *Journal of Assistive Technologies, 6,* 245. doi:10.1108/17549451211285744

Cheng, Y., & Fan, Y. (2008). The 3D humanoid emotions in interactive learning environments for people with autism. In *Proceedings of World Conference on Educational Multimedia, Hypermedia and Telecommunications*, (pp. 5162–70). Academic Press.

Cheng, Y., Moore, D., & McGrath, P. (2002). Virtual learning environments for children with autism. In *Proceedings of the 6th Human Centred Technology Postgraduate Workshop*, (pp. 32-35). Academic Press.

Cheng, Y., Chiang, H., Ye, J., & Cheng, L. (2010). Enhancing empathy instruction using a collaborative virtual learning environment for children with autistic spectrum conditions. *Computers & Education*, *55*(4), 1449–1458. doi:10.1016/j.compedu.2010.06.008

Cheng, Y., & Ye, Y. (2010). Exploring the social competence of students with autism spectrum conditions in a collaborative virtual learning environment – The pilot study. *Computers & Education*, *54*(4), 1068–1077. doi:10.1016/j.compedu.2009.10.011

Chevallier, C., Kohls, G., Troiani, V., Brodkin, E. S., & Schultz, R. T. (2012). The social motivation theory of autism. *Trends in Cognitive Sciences*, *16*(4), 231–239. doi:10.1016/j.tics.2012.02.007 PMID:22425667

Chimiliar, L., & Cheung, B. (2007). Assistive technology training for teachers – Innovation and accessibility online. *Developmental Disabilities Bulletin*, *35*(1-2), 18–28.

Cihak, D. F. (2011). Comparing pictorial and video modeling activity schedules during transitions for students with autism spectrum disorder. *Research in Autism Spectrum Disorders*, *5*, 433–441. doi:10.1016/j.rasd.2010.06.006

Cihak, D., Fahrenkrog, C., Ayres, K., & Smith, C. (2010). The use of video modelling via a video iPod and a system of least prompts to improve transitional behaviors for students with autism spectrum disorders in the general education classroom. *Journal of Positive Behavior Interventions*, *12*(2), 103–115. doi:10.1177/1098300709332346

Clark, E., Kehle, T. J., Jenson, W. R., & Beck, D. E. (1992). Evaluation of parameters of self-modeling interventions. *School Psychology Review*, *21*, 246–254.

Cobb, S., Parsons, S., Millen, L., Eastgate, R., & Glover, T. (2010). Design and development of collaborative technology for children with autism: COSPATIAL. In *Proceedings of INTED2010 Conference*, (pp. 374–83). INTED.

Cobb, S. (2007). Virtual environments supporting learning and communication in special needs education. *Topics in Language Disorders*, *27*(3), 211–225. doi:10.1097/01.TLD.0000285356.95426.3b

Cobb, S., Beardon, L., Eastgate, R., Glover, T., Kerr, S., & Neale, H. et al. (2002). Applied virtual environments to support learning of social interaction skills in users with Asperger's syndrome. *Digital Creativity*, *13*(1), 11–22. doi:10.1076/digc.13.1.11.3208

Cobb, S., Kerr, S., & Glover, T. (2001). The AS interactive project: Developing virtual environments for social skills training in users with Asperger syndrome. In K. Dautenhahn (Ed.), *Robotic and virtual interactive systems in autism therapy*. Hatfield, UK: University of Hertfordshire.

Colby, K. M. (1973). The rational for computer-based treatment of language difficulties in nonspeaking autistic children. *Journal of Autism and Childhood Schizophrenia*, *3*(3), 254–260. doi:10.1007/BF01538283 PMID:4800391

Coleman-Martin, M. B., Heller, K. W., Cihak, D. F., & Irvine, K. L. (2005). Using computer-assisted instruction and the nonverbal reading approach to teach word identification. *Focus on Autism and Other Developmental Disabilities*, *20*, 80–90. doi:10.1177/10883576050200020401

Constantino, J. N., & Gruber, C. P. (2005). *Social responsiveness scale*. Los Angeles, CA: Western Psychological Services.

Copley, J., & Ziviani, J. (2004). Barriers to the use of assistive technology for children with multiple disabilities. *Occupational Therapy International*, *11*(4), 229–243. doi:10.1002/oti.213 PMID:15771212

Corbett, B. A., & Abdullah, M. (2005). Video modeling: Why does it work for children with autism. *Journal of Early and Intensive Behavior Intervention*, *2*(1), 2–8.

Coyle, C., & Cole, P. (2004). A videotaped self-modeling and self-monitoring treatment program to decrease off-task behavior in children with autism. *Journal of Intellectual & Developmental Disability, 29*, 3–15. doi:10.1080/08927020410001662642

Craig, N. (2011). Autistic kids learn to fly in cyberspace. *The Age*. Retrieved from http://www.theage.com.au/victoria/autistic-kids-learn-to-fly-in-cyberspace-20110219-1b0fj.html

Cromby, J. J., Standen, P. J., Newman, J., & Tasker, H. (1996). Successful transfer to the real world of skills practised in a virtual environment by students with severe learning difficulties. In *Proceedings of the 1st International Conference on Disability, Virtual Reality and Associated Technologies* (IDCVRAT). Reading, UK: IDCVRAT.

Dake, J. A., Price, J. H., & Telljohann, S. K. (2003). The nature and extent of bullying at school. *The Journal of School Health, 7*(5), 173–180. doi:10.1111/j.1746-1561.2003.tb03599.x PMID:12793102

Data Accountability Center. (2013). *Individuals with disabilities education act (IDEA) data*. Retrieved from www.ideadata.org

Dattilo, J., & Camarata, S. (1991). Facilitating conversation through self-initiated augmentative communication treatment. *Journal of Applied Behavior Analysis, 24*, 369–378. doi:10.1901/jaba.1991.24-369 PMID:1890052

Dautenhahan, K., & Werry, I. (2004). Towards interactive robots in autism therapy: Background, motivation and challenges. *Pragmatics & Cognition, 12*, 1–35. doi:10.1075/pc.12.1.03dau

Dautenhahn, K. (2003). Roles and functions of robots in human society: Implications from research in autism therapy. *Robotica, 21*, 443–452. doi:10.1017/S0263574703004922

Davis, M., Dautenhahn, K., Powell, S., & Nehaniv, C. (2010). Guidelines for researchers and facilitators designing software and software trials for children with autism. *Journal of Assistive Technologies, 4*, 38–48. doi:10.5042/jat.2010.0043

Dawe, M. (2006). Desperately seeking simplicity: how young adults with cognitive disabilities and their families adopt assistive technologies. In *Proceedings of the SIGCHI Conference on Human Factors in Computing Systems*, (pp. 1143-1152). ACM.

Dawson, G., Carver, L., Meltzoff, A. N., Panagiotides, H., McPartland, J., & Webb, S. J. (2002). Neural correlates of face and object recognition in young children with autism spectrum disorder, developmental delay, and typical development. *Child Development, 73*(3), 700–717. doi:10.1111/1467-8624.00433 PMID:12038546

Dawson, G., Jones, E. H., Merkle, K., Venema, K., Lowy, R., Faja, S., & Webb, S. J. (2012). Early behavioral intervention is associated with normalized brain activity in young children with ASD. *Journal of the American Academy of Child and Adolescent Psychiatry, 51*(11), 1150–1159. doi:10.1016/j.jaac.2012.08.018 PMID:23101741

Dawson, G., Toth, K., Abbott, R., Osterling, J., Munson, J., Estes, A., & Liaw, J. (2004). Early social attention impairments in Autism: Social orienting, joint attention, and attention to distress. *Developmental Psychology, 40*(2), 271–283. doi:10.1037/0012-1649.40.2.271 PMID:14979766

Day, L. A. (2000). *Ethics in media communications: Cases and controversies*. Belmont, CA: Wadsworth/Thompson Learning.

DeAngelis, T. (2009). Can Second Life therapy help with autism? *Monitor on Psychology, 40*(8), 40–41.

Dell, A. G., Newton, D. A., & Petroff, J. G. (2008). *Assistive technology in the classroom: Enhancing the school experiences of students with disabilities*. Upper Saddle River, NJ: Pearson/Merrill Prentice Hall.

Desch, L. W., & Gaebler-Spira, D. (2008). Prescribing assistive-technology systems: Focus on children with impaired communication. *Pediatrics, 121*(6), 1271–1280. doi:10.1542/peds.2008-0695 PMID:18519500

Dettmer, S., Simpson, R. L., Myles, B. S., & Ganz, J. B. (2000). The use of visual supports to facilitate transitions of students with autism. *Focus on Autism and Other Developmental Disabilities, 15*, 163–169. doi:10.1177/108835760001500307

Dew, D. W., & Alan, G. M. (Eds.). (2007). *Rehabilitation of individuals with autism spectrum disorders (Institute on Rehabilitation Issues Monograph No. 32)*. Washington, DC: The George Washington University, Center for Rehabilitation Counseling Research and Education.

Diehl, J. J., Cromwell, C. R., Villano, M., Wier, K., Tang, K., & Flores, J. … Van Ness, M. (2013). *Humanoid robots as co-therapists in ABA therapy for children with autism spectrum disorder.* Paper presented at the International Society for Autism Research. San Sebastián, Spain.

Diehl, J. J., Schmitt, L. M., Villano, M., & Crowell, C. R. (2011). The clinical use of robots for individuals with autism spectrum disorders: A critical review. *Research in Autism Spectrum Disorders, 6*, 249–262. doi:10.1016/j.rasd.2011.05.006 PMID:22125579

DiGennaro Reed, F. D., Hyman, S. R., & Hirst, J. M. (2011). Applications of technology to teach social skills to children with autism. *Research in Autism Spectrum Disorders, 5*, 1003–1010. doi:10.1016/j.rasd.2011.01.022

DiSalvo, C. A., & Oswald, D. P. (2002). Peer-mediated interventions to increase the social interaction of children with autism: Consideration of peer expectancies. *Focus on Autism and Other Developmental Disabilities, 17*(4), 198–207. doi:10.1177/10883576020170040201

Dodd, S. (2005). *Understanding autism.* Sydney, Australia: Elsevier Australia.

Dowden. (n.d.). *UW augcomm.* Retrieved from http://depts.washington.edu/augcomm/02_features/00_features_intro.htm

Dowden, P., & Cook, A. (2002). Choosing effective selection techniques for beginning communicators. In *Implementing an augmentative communication system: Exemplary strategies for beginning communicators.* Baltimore, MD: Paul H. Brookes Publishing Co.

Downing, J. E., & Peckham-Hardin, K. D. (2000). Daily schedules: A helpful learning tool. *Teaching Exceptional Children, 33*, 62–68.

Downs, A., & Smith, T. (2004). Emotional understanding, cooperation, and social behavior in high-functioning children with ASD. *Journal of ASD and Developmental Disorders, 34*(6), 625–635. doi:10.1007/s10803-004-5284-0

Dowrick, P. W. (1999). A review of self modeling and related interventions. *Applied & Preventive Psychology, 8*, 23–39. doi:10.1016/S0962-1849(99)80009-2

Duncan, H., & Tan, J. (2012). A visual task manager application for individuals with autism. *Journal of Computing Sciences in Colleges, 27*(6), 49–57.

Dunn, L. M., & Dunn, L. M. (1981). *Peabody picture vocabulary test, revised.* American Guidance Service.

Dunn, M. (2006). *S.O.S. social skills in our schools.* Shawnee Mission, KS: Asperger Publishing Company.

Duquette, A., Michaud, F., & Mercier, H. (2008). Exploring the use of a mobile robot as an imitation agent with children with low-functioning autism. *Autonomous Robots, 24*, 147–157.

Durkin, K. (2010). Videogames and young people with developmental disorders. *Review of General Psychology, 14*, 122–140. doi:10.1037/a0019438

Durkin, K., Boyle, J., Hunter, S., & Conti-Ramsden, G. (2013). Video games for children and adolescents with special educational needs. *Zeitschrift für Psychologie mit Zeitschrift für Angewandte Psychologie, 221*, 79–89. doi:doi:10.1027/2151-2604/a000138

Durston, S. (2003). A review of the biological bases of ADHD: What have we learned from imaging studies? *Mental Retardation and Developmental Disabilities Research Reviews, 9*(3), 184–195. doi:10.1002/mrdd.10079 PMID:12953298

Dymond, S. (2012). Community participation. In P. Wehman, & J. Kregel (Eds.), *Functional curriculum for elementary and secondary students with special needs* (3rd ed., pp. 351–387). Austin, TX: Pro-Ed.

Eaton, D. K. (2012). Youth risk behavior surveillance: United States, 2011. U.S. Department of Health and Human Services: Center for Disease Control and Prevention, 61(4).

Eaves, L. C., & Ho, H. H. (2008). Young adult outcome of autism spectrum disorders. *Journal of Autism and Developmental Disorders, 38*(4), 739–747. doi:10.1007/s10803-007-0441-x PMID:17764027

Edelson, S. M. (1998). *Learning styles and autism.* Retrieved January 16, 1998, from www.autism.org

Edyburn, D. L. (2010). Would you recognize universal design for learning if you saw it? Ten propositions for new directions for the second decade of UDL. *Learning Disability Quarterly, 33*(1), 33–41.

Edyburn, D. L. (2013). Critical issues in advancing the special education technology evidence-base. *Exceptional Children, 80*(1), 7–24.

Ekman, P. (1957). A methodological discussion of non-verbal behavior. *The Journal of Psychology, 43*, 141–149. doi:10.1080/00223980.1957.9713059

Ekman, P., & Friesen, W. V. (1976). *Pictures of facial affect*. Palo Alto, CA: Consulting Psychologist Press.

el Kaliouby, R., Picard, R., & Baron-Cohen, S. (2006). Affective computing and autism. *Annals of the New York Academy of Sciences, 1093*, 228–248. doi:10.1196/annals.1382.016 PMID:17312261

Element 84. (2009). *iHomework*. Alexandria, VA: Author.

Elkeseth, S. (2009). Outcome of comprehensive psycho-educational interventions for young children with autism. *Research in Developmental Disabilities, 30*(1), 158–178. doi:10.1016/j.ridd.2008.02.003 PMID:18385012

Ellwood, H. (2009). *Oh-my-goodness-moments*. Calgary, Canada: SMART Technologies ULC.

Ennis-Cole, D., & Smith, D. (2011). Assistive technology and autism: Expanding the technology leadership role of the school librarian. *School Libraries Worldwide, 17*(2), 86–98.

Escambia County Public Schools. (2013, July 7). Retrieved from www.escambia.k12.fl.us/pbis/data/Data%20Collection%20Guide_10-11-10.pdf

Fabri, M., & Moore, D. (2005). The use of emotionally expressive avatars in collaborative virtual environments. In *Proceeding of Symposium on Empathic Interaction with Synthetic Characters, Artificial Intelligence and Social Behaviour Convention 2005* (AISB 2005). University of Hertfordshire.

Fabri, M., Moore, D., & Hobbs, D. (2004). Mediating the expression of emotion in educational collaborative virtual environments: An experimental study. *Virtual Reality (Waltham Cross), 7*, 66–81. doi:10.1007/s10055-003-0116-7

Faja, S., Aylward, E., Bernier, R., & Dawson, G. (2008). Becoming a face expert: A computerize face-training program for high functioning individuals with autism spectrum disorders. *Developmental Neuropsychology, 33*, 1–24. doi:10.1080/87565640701729573 PMID:18443967

Fallon, K. A., & Katz, L. A. (2008). Augmentative and alternative communication and literacy teams: Facing the challenges, forging ahead. *Seminars in Speech and Language, 29*(2), 112–119. doi:10.1055/s-2008-1079125 PMID:18645913

Fan, T. (2012). *Enhancing learning with the use of assistive technology for children on the autism spectrum*. (Unpublished thesis for Master of Science in Education). Dominican University of California, San Rafael, CA.

Feil-Seifer, D., & Matarić, M. J. (2009). Toward socially assistive robotics for augmenting interventions for children with autism spectrum disorders. *Experimental Robotics, 54*, 201–210.

Fenner, G. H., & Renn, R. W. (2009). Technology-assisted supplemental work and work-to-family conflict: The role of instrumental beliefs, organizational expectations, and time management. *Human Relations, 63*, 63–82. doi:10.1177/0018726709351064

Fisher, K. W., & Shogren, K. A. (2012). Integrating augmentative and alternative communication and peer support for students with disabilities: A social-ecological perspective. *Journal of Special Education Technology, 27*(2), 23–62.

Fitzgerald, G., Koury, K., & Mitchem, K. (2008). Research on computer-mediated instruction for students with high incidence disabilities. *Journal of Educational Computing Research, 38*, 201–233. doi:10.2190/EC.38.2.e

Flores, M., Musgrove, K., Renner, S., Hinton, V., Strozier, S., Franklin, S., & Hil, D. (2012). A comparison of communication using the Apple iPad and a picture-based system. *Augmentative and Alternative Communication*. doi:10.3109/07434618.2011.644579 PMID:22263895

Fogg, B. J. (2003). *Persuasive technology: Using computers to change what we think and do*. San Francisco, CA: Morgan Kaufman Publishers. doi:10.1016/B978-155860643-2/50011-1

Fogg, B. J., & Eckles, D. (2007). *Mobile persuasion: 20 perspectives on the future of behavior change.* Stanford, CA: Stanford Captology Media.

Fornasari, L., Chittaro, L., Ieronutti, L., Cottini, L., & Dassi, S., Cremaschi, Brambilla, P. (2013). Navigation and exploration of an urban virtual environment by children with autism spectrum disorder to children with typical development. *Research in Autism Spectrum Disorders, 7*(8), 956–965. doi:10.1016/j.rasd.2013.04.007

Foster, E. M., Dodge, K. A., & Jones, D. (2003). Issues in the economic evaluation of prevention programs. *Applied Developmental Science, 7*(2), 76–86. PMID:20228955

Franco, Z., & Zimbardo, P. (2006-2007). The banality of heroism. *Greater Good: The Bystander's Dilemma, 3*(2).

François, D., Powell, S., & Dautenhahn, K. (2009). A long-term study of children with autism playing with a robotic pet: Taking inspirations from non-directive play therapy to encourage children's proactivity and initiative-taking. *Interaction Studies: Social Behaviour and Communication in Biological and Artificial Systems, 10,* 324–373. doi: doi:10.1075/is.10.3.04fra

Franzone, E., & Collet-Klingenberg, L. (2008). *Overview of video modeling.* Madison, WI: The National Professional Development Center on Autism Spectrum Disorders, Waisman Center, University of Wisconsin.

Friedrich, S., Morgan, S. B., & Devine, C. (1996). Children's attitudes and behavioral intentions toward a peer with Tourette's syndrome. *Journal of Pediatric Psychology, 21,* 307–319. doi:10.1093/jpepsy/21.3.307 PMID:8935235

Fullerton, A. (1996). Who are higher functioning young adults with autism? In A. Fullerton (Ed.), *Higher functioning adolescents and young adults with autism* (pp. 1–20). Austin, TX: PRO-ED, Inc.

Fusar-Poli, P., Cortesi, M., Borgwardt, S., & Politi, P. (2008). Second Life virtual world: A heaven for autistic people? *Medical Hypotheses, 71*(6), 980–981. doi:10.1016/j.mehy.2008.07.024 PMID:18783897

Gal, E., Bauminger, N., Goren-Bar, D., Pianesi, F., Stock, O., & Zancanaro, M. et al. (2009). Enhancing social communication of children with high-functioning autism through a co-located interface. *AI & Society, 24,* 75–84. doi:10.1007/s00146-009-0199-0

Ganz, J. B., Cook, K. E., & Earles-Vollrath, T. L. (2006). *How to write and implement social scripts.* Austin, TX: PRO-ED.

Ganz, J. B., Davis, J. L., Lund, E. M., Goodwyn, F. D., & Simpson, R. L. (2012). Meta-analysis of PECS with individuals with ASD: Investigation of targeted versus nontargeted outcomes, participant characteristics, and implementation phase. *Research in Developmental Disabilities, 33,* 406–418. doi:10.1016/j.ridd.2011.09.023 PMID:22119688

Ganz, J. B., Earles-Vollrath, T. I., Mason, R. A., Rispoli, M. J., Heath, A. K., & Parker, R. I. (2011). An aggregate study of single-case research involving aided AAC: Participant characteristics of individuals with autism spectrum disorders. *Research in Autism Spectrum Disorders, 5,* 1500–1509. doi:10.1016/j.rasd.2011.02.011

Ganz, J. B., Earles-Vollrath, T. L., & Cook, K. E. (2011). Video modeling: A visually based intervention for children with autism spectrum disorder. *Teaching Exceptional Children, 43*(6), 8–19.

Ganz, J. B., Earles-Vollrath, T. L., Heath, A. K., Parker, R. I., Rispoli, M. J., & Duran, J. B. (2012). A meta-analysis of single case research studies on aided augmentative and alternative communication systems with individuals with autism spectrum disorders. *Journal of Autism and Developmental Disorders, 42,* 60–74. doi:10.1007/s10803-011-1212-2 PMID:21380612

Ganz, J. B., Hong, E. R., & Goodwyn, F. D. (2013). Effectiveness of the PECS phase 111 app and choice between the app and traditional PECS among preschoolers with ASD. *Research in Autism Spectrum Disorders,* (7): 973–983. doi:10.1016/j.rasd.2013.04.003

Garreston, H. B., Fein, D., & Waterhouse, L. (1990). Sustained attention in children with autism. *Journal of Autism and Developmental Disorders, 20*(1), 101–114. doi:10.1007/BF02206860 PMID:2324050

Gartner. (2013). *Gartner says worldwide PC, tablet and mobile phone combined shipments to reach 2.4 billion units in 2013.* Retrieved from http://www.gartner.com/newsroom/id/2408515

Gastgeb, H. Z., Rump, K. M., Best, C. A., Minshew, N. J., & Strauss, M. S. (2009). Prototype formation in autism: Can individuals with autism abstract facial prototypes? *Autism Research, 2*(5), 279–284. doi:10.1002/aur.93 PMID:19877157

Gentile, D. (2009). Pathological video-game use among youth ages 8 to 18: A national study. *Psychological Science, 20*(5), 594–602. PMID:19476590

Gentile, D. A., Choo, H., Liau, A., Sim, T., Li, D., Fung, D., & Khoo, A. (2011). Pathological video game use among youths: A two-year longitudinal study. *Pediatrics, 127*, e319–e329. PMID:21242221

Gentry, T., Lau, S., Molinelli, A., Fallen, A., & Kriner, R. (2012). The Apple iPod touch as a vocational support aid for adults with autism: Three case studies. *Journal of Vocational Rehabilitation, 37*(2). doi: doi:10.3233/JVR-2012-0601

Gentry, T., Wallace, J., Kvarfordt, C., & Lynch, K. (2010). Personal digital assistants as cognitive aids for high school students with autism: Results of a community-based trial. *Journal of Vocational Rehabilitation, 32*(2), 101–107.

Gerhard, M. (2003). *A hybrid avatar/agent model for educational collaborative virtual environments.* (Unpublished Doctoral Dissertation). Leeds Metropolitan University, Leeds, UK.

Gerhard, M., Moore, D. J., & Hobbs, D. (2004). Embodiment and co-presence in collaborative interfaces. *International Journal of Human-Computer Studies, 61*(4), 453–480. doi:10.1016/j.ijhcs.2003.12.014

Gilotty, L., Kenworthy, L., Sirian, L., Black, D. O., & Wagner, A. E. (2002). Adaptive skills and executive function in autism spectrum disorders. *Child Neuropsychology, 8*, 241–248. doi:10.1076/chin.8.4.241.13504 PMID:12759821

Giusti, L., & Zancanaro, M. Gal, E., & Weiss, P. L. T. (2011). Dimensions of collaboration on a tabletop interface for children with autism spectrum disorder. In *Proceedings of Conference on Human Factors in Computing Systems* (CHI 2011). Vancouver, Canada: ACM.

Glenwright, M., & Agbayewa, A. S. (2012). Older children and adolescents with high-functioning autism spectrum disorders can comprehend verbal irony in computer-mediated communication. *Research in Autism Spectrum Disorders, 6*, 628–638. doi:10.1016/j.rasd.2011.09.013

Golan, O., Ashwin, E., Granader, Y., McClintock, S., Day, K., Leggett, V., & Baron-Cohen, S. (2010). Enhancing emotion recognition in children with ASD spectrum conditions: An intervention using animated vehicles with real emotional faces. *Journal of ASD and Developmental Disorders, 40*(3), 269–279. doi:10.1007/s10803-009-0862-9

Golan, O., & Baron-Cohen, S. (2006). Systemizing empathy: Teaching adults with Asperger syndrome or high-functioning ASD to recognise complex emotions using interactive multi- media. *Development and Psychopathology, 18*, 591–617. doi:10.1017/S0954579406060305 PMID:16600069

Goldsmith, T. R., & LeBlanc, L. A. (2004). Use of technology in interventions for children with autism. *Journal of Early and Intensive Behavior Intervention, 1*, 166–178.

Goldstein, A. P., & McGinnis, E. (1997). *Skillstreaming the adolescent: New strategies and perspectives for teaching prosocial skills.* Champaign, IL: Research Press.

Gomot, M., & Wicker, B. (2012). A challenging, unpredictable world for people with autism spectrum disorder. *International Journal of Psychophysiology, 83*, 240–247. doi:10.1016/j.ijpsycho.2011.09.017 PMID:21968196

Good Karma Applications. (2012). *Visual schedule planner.* San Diego, CA: Author.

Goodwin, M. S. (2008). Enhancing and accelerating the pace of autism research and treatment: The promise of developing innovative technology. *Focus on Autism and Other Developmental Disabilities, 23*, 125–128. doi:10.1177/1088357608316678

Gotsis, M., Piggot, J., Hughes, D., & Stone, W. (2010). SMART-games: A video game intervention for children with autism spectrum disorders. In *Proceedings of the 9th International Conference on Interaction Design and Children*. ACM.

Gottlieb, J., & Gottlieb, B. W. (1977). Stereotypic attitudes and behavioral intentions toward handicapped children. *American Journal of Mental Deficiency, 82*, 65–71. PMID:142428

Graham-Rowe, D. (2002). My best friend's a robot. *New Scientist, 176*, 30–33. PMID:12731520

Grandin, T. (2002). *Teaching tips for children and adults with autism*. Autism Research Institute. Retrieved from http://www.autism.com/families/therapy/teaching_tips.htm

Grandin, T. (1995). How people with autism think. In E. Schopler, & G. Mesibov (Eds.), *Learning and cognition in autism: Current issues in autism* (pp. 137–156). New York: Plenum Press. doi:10.1007/978-1-4899-1286-2_8

Grandin, T. (2010). *Thinking in pictures: My life with autism*. New York: Vintage Books.

Grandin, T. (2012). *Tablet computers: What they're good for, what they're not*. Autism Asperger's Digest.

Grandin, T. (2013). *The autistic brain: Thinking across the spectrum*. New York, NY: Houghton Mifflin Harcourt.

Grandin, T., & Scariano, M. M. (2005). *Emergence labeled autistic*. New York: Warner Books.

Gray, C. (2010). *The new social story book*. Arlington, TX: Future Horizons.

Gray, D. E. (1993). Negotiating autism: Relations between parents and treatment staff. *Social Science & Medicine, 36*, 1037–1046. doi:10.1016/0277-9536(93)90121-J PMID:8475419

Gray, L., Thomas, N., & Lewis, L. (2010). *Teachers' use of educational technology in U.S. public schools: 2009 (NCES 2010-040)*. Washington, DC: National Center for Education Statistics.

Greenhills, A. E. A. (2013, July 7). *Data collection resources*. Retrieved from https://sites.google.com/a/ghaea.org/challenging-behavior-team/data-collection-resources-1

Gregory, M. K., DeLeon, I. G., & Richman, D. M. (2009). The influence of matching and motor-imitation abilities on rapid acquisition of manual signs and exchange based communicative responses. *Journal of Applied Behavior Analysis, 42*, 399. doi:10.1901/jaba.2009.42-399 PMID:19949531

Grembe, Inc. (2013, February 28). *My pictures talk modeling application information*. Retrieved from https://itunes.apple.com/us/app/my-pictures-talk-video-modeling/id368388315?mt=8

Gresham, F. M. (2002). Best practices in social skills training. In A. Thomas, & J. Grimes (Eds.), *Best practices in school psychology* (4th ed.). Bethesda, MD: NASP.

Gresham, F. M., Sugai, G., & Horner, R. H. (2001). Interpreting outcomes of social skill training for students with high-incidence disabilities. *Teaching Exceptional Children, 67*, 331–344.

Grynszpan, O., Martin, J., & Nadel, J. (2008). Multimedia interfaces for users with high functioning autism: An empirical investigation. *International Journal of Human-Computer Studies, 66*, 628–639.

Guerra, N. G., Boxer, P., & Cook, C. B. (2006). What works (and what does not) in youth violence prevention: Rethinking the questions and finding new answers. *New Directions for Evaluation, 110*, 59–71. doi: doi:10.1002/ev.187

Guldberg, K., Porayska-Pomsta, K., Good, J., & Keay-Bright, W. (2010). ECHOES II: The creation of a technology enhanced learning environment for typically developing children and children on the autism spectrum. *Journal of Assistive Technologies, 4*(1), 49–53. doi:10.5042/jat.2010.0044

Habash, M. A. (2005). Assistive technology utilization for autism an outline of technology awareness in special needs therapy. In *Proceedings of the Second International Conference on Innovations in Information Technology*. Retrieved from http://www.autismarabia.com

Hagner, D., Kurtz, A., Cloutier, H., Arakelian, C., Brucker, D. L., & May, J. (2012). Outcomes of a family-centered transition process for students with autism spectrum disorders. *Focus on Autism and Other Developmental Disabilities, 27*(1), 42–50. doi:10.1177/1088357611430841

Hall, L. J. (2009). Autism spectrum disorders. In *From theory to practice*. London: Jessica Kingsley Publishers.

Hammond, D. L., & Whatley, A. D. (2010). Effectiveness of video modeling to teach iPod use to students with moderate intellectual disabilities. *Education and Training in Autism and Developmental Disabilities, 45*(4), 525–538.

Happe, F. (1994). Wechsler IQ profile and theory of mind in autism: A research note. *Journal of Child Psychology and Psychiatry, and Allied Disciplines, 35*, 1461–1471. doi:10.1111/j.1469-7610.1994.tb01287.x PMID:7868640

Happé, F., & Frith, U. (2006). The weak central coherence account: Detail-focused cognitive style in autism spectrum disorders. *Journal of Autism and Developmental Disorders, 36*, 5–25. doi:10.1007/s10803-005-0039-0 PMID:16450045

Hardin, B. (2001). Missing in action? Images of disability in sports illustrated for kids. *Disability Studies Quarterly, 21*(2).

Harms, M. B., Martin, A., & Wallace, G. L. (2010). Facial emotion recognition in ASD spectrum disorders: A review of behavioral and neuroimaging studies. *Neuropsychology Review, 20*(3), 290–322. doi:10.1007/s11065-010-9138-6 PMID:20809200

Harris, M. J., Milich, R. C., Corbitt, E. M., Hoover, D. W., & Brady, M. (1992). Self-fulfilling effects of stigmatizing information on children's social interactions. *Journal of Personality and Social Psychology, 63*, 41–50. doi:10.1037/0022-3514.63.1.41 PMID:1494984

Haswell, C., Izawa, J., Dowell, L., Mostofsky, S., & Shadmehr, R. (2009). Representation of internal models of action in the autistic brain. *Journal of Nature Neuroscience, 12*(8), 970–972. doi:10.1038/nn.2356 PMID:19578379

Hayes, G. R., Hirano, S., Marcu, G., Monibi, M., Nguyen, D. H., & Yeganyan, M. (2010). Interactive visual supports for children with autism. *Personal and Ubiquitous Computing, 14*(7), 663–680. doi:10.1007/s00779-010-0294-8

Healey, D., & Rucklidge, J. J. (2006). An investigation into the relationship among ADHD symptomatology, creativity, and neuropsychological functioning in children. *Child Neuropsychology, 12*(6), 421–438. doi:10.1080/09297040600806086 PMID:16952888

Heflin, L. J., & Alaimo, D. F. (2007). *Students with autism spectrum disorders: Effective instructional practices.* Upper Saddle River, NJ: Pearson Education, Inc.

Heider. (1958). *The psychology of interpersonal relations.* New York: Wiley.

Heimann, M., Nelson, K. E., Tjus, T., & Gillberg, C. (1995). Increasing reading and communication skills in children with autism through an interactive multimedia computer program. *Journal of Autism and Developmental Disorders, 25*, 459–480. doi:10.1007/BF02178294 PMID:8567593

Help, A. (2012). [*-point scale app.* Retrieved from http://www.ausm.org/index.php/autism-apps.html]. *Autism, 5*

Henninger, N. A., & Taylor, J. L. (2012). Outcomes in adults with autism spectrum disorders: A historical perspective. *Autism, 17*, 103–116. doi:10.1177/1362361312441266 PMID:22914775

Hess, K. L., Morrier, M. J., Heflin, L. J., & Ivey, M. L. (2008). Autism treatment survey: Services received by children with autism spectrum disorders in public school classrooms. *Journal of Autism and Developmental Disorders, 38*(5), 961–971. doi:10.1007/s10803-007-0470-5 PMID:17929155

Hetherington, S. A., Durant-Jones, L., Johnson, K., Nolan, K., Smith, E., Taylor-Brown, S., & Tuttle, J. (2010). The lived experiences of adolescents with disabilities and their parents in transition planning. *Focus on Autism and Other Developmental Disabilities, 25*(3), 163–172. doi:10.1177/1088357610373760

Hetzroni, O. E., & Harris, O. L. (1996). Cultural aspects in the development of AAC users. *Augmentative and Alternative Communication, 12*, 52–58. doi:10.1080/07434619612331277488

Higgins, K., & Boone, R. (1996). Creating individualized computer-assisted instruction for students with autism using multimedia. *Focus on Autism and Other Developmental Disabilities, 11*, 69. doi:10.1177/108835769601100202

Hill, E. L. (2004). Evaluating the theory of executive dysfunction in autism. *Developmental Review, 24,* 189–233.

Hiniker, A., Wong Daniels, J., & Williamson, H. (2013). *Go go games: Therapeutic video games for children with autism spectrum disorders.* New York, NY: IDC.

Hobson, R. P., Ouston, J. J., & Lee, A. A. (1988). What's in a face? The case of ASD. *The British Journal of Psychology, 79*(4), 441. doi:10.1111/j.2044-8295.1988.tb02745.x

Holmquist, J. (2011). Bullying prevention: Positive strategies. PACER Center, 1 – 6.

Holstein, J. (2013). *Tablets for autism: Tablet computers provide a voice for the autistic.* ViewSonic Corporation. Retrieved from www.viewsonic.com

Hoover, J., & Stenhjem, P. (2003). Bullying and teasing of youth with disabilities: Creating positive school environments for effective inclusion. *National Center on Secondary Education and Transition, 2*(3), 1–6.

Hopkins, I. M., Gower, M. W., Perez, T. A., Smith, D. S., Amthor, F. R., Wimsatt, F. C., & Biasini, F. J. (2011). Avatar assistant: Improving social skills in students with an ASD through computer-based intervention. *Journal of Autism and Developmental Disorders, 41,* 1543–1555. doi:10.1007/s10803-011-1179-z PMID:21287255

Horner, R. H., Carr, E. G., Strain, P. S., Todd, A. W., & Reed, H. K. (2002). Problem behavior interventions for young children with autism: A research synthesis. *Journal of Autism and Developmental Disorders, 32,* 423–446. doi:10.1023/A:1020593922901 PMID:12463518

Horowitz, B. (2013). *iPad app helps children with autism learn life skills.* Posted on the internet 2013-05-14.

Hourcade, J. J., Parette, H. P., & Huer, M. B. (1997). Family and cultural alert! Considerations in assistive technology assessment. *Teaching Exceptional Children, 30*(1), 40–44.

Hourcade, J. P., Bullock-Rest, N. E., & Hansen, T. E. (2012). Multitouch table applications and activities to enhance the social skills of children with autism spectrum disorders. *Personal and Ubiquitous Computing, 16*(2), 157–168. doi:10.1007/s00779-011-0383-3

Hourcade, J., Everhart, T., West, E., & Parette, P. (2004). A history of augmentative and alternative communication (AAC) for individuals with severe and profound disabilities. *Focus on Autism and Other Developmental Disabilities, 19*(4), 235–244. doi:10.1177/10883576040190040501

Howlin, P. (1998). Practitioner review: Psychological and educational treatments for autism. *Journal of Child Psychology and Psychiatry, and Allied Disciplines, 39*(1), 307–322. doi:10.1017/S0021963097002138 PMID:9670087

Howlin, P., Goode, S., Hutton, J., & Rutter, M. (2004). Adult outcome for children with autism. *Journal of Child Psychology and Psychiatry, and Allied Disciplines, 45*(2), 212–229. doi:10.1111/j.1469-7610.2004.00215.x PMID:14982237

Huang, A. X., & Wheeler, J. J. (2006). High-functional autism: An overview of characteristics and related issues. *Journal of International Special Education, 21,* 109–123.

Hume, K. (2008). *Transition time: Helping individuals on the autism spectrum move successfully from one activity to another.* Retrieved from http://www.iidc.indiana.edu/?pageId=399

Hume, K. (2009). *Visual schedules: How and why to use them in the classroom.* Retrieved from http://www.education.com/reference/article/visual-schedule-classroom autismASD/

Humphrey, N., & Symes, W. (2010). Responses to bullying and use of social support among pupils with autism spectrum disorders (ASDs) in mainstream schools: A qualitative study. *Journal of Research in Special Educational Needs, 10*(2), 82–90. doi:10.1111/j.1471-3802.2010.01146.x

Iavaraone, A., Patruno, M., Galeone, F., Chieffi, S., & Carlomagno, S. (2007). Brief report: Error pattern in an autistic savant calendar calculator. *Journal of Autism and Developmental Disorders, 37,* 775–779. doi:10.1007/s10803-006-0190-2 PMID:16900402

IES. (n.d.). Retrieved from http://ies.ed.gov/ncee/wwc/default.aspx

Illinois Autism/PDD Training and Technical Assistance Project. (n.d.). *Visual supports fact sheet.* Retrieved from http://autism.pbisillinois.org/iattap_Visual_Supports_Fact_Sheet_1_.pdf

Individuals With Disabilities Education Improvement Act of 2004, Pub. L. No. 108-446.

Innovative Ways the Autism Community Uses iPads. (2013). Retrieved online 9/5/13.

Inspiration Software Inc. (2008). *Kidspiration 3.* Beaverton, OR: Author.

Inspiration Software, Inc. (2010). *Inspiration 9.* Beaverton, OR: Author.

Iovannone, R., Dunlap, G., Huber, H., & Kincaid, D. (2003). Effective educational practices for students with autism spectrum disorders. *Focus on Autism and Other Developmental Disabilities, 18,* 150–165. doi:10.1177/10883576030180030301

Irish, J. E. N. (2013). Can I sit here? A review of the literature supporting the use of single-user virtual environments to help autistic adolescents learn appropriate social communication skills. *Computers in Human Behavior,* (29): A17–A24. doi:10.1016/j.chb.2012.12.031

Jacobson, J. W., & Mulick, J. A. (2000). Systems and cost research issues in treatments for people with autistic disorders. *Journal of Autism and Developmental Disorders, 30,* 585–593. doi:10.1023/A:1005691411255 PMID:11261469

Johnson, M. H. (2012). Executive function and developmental disorders: The flip side of the coin. *Trends in Cognitive Sciences, 16*(9), 454–457. PMID:22835639

Johnston, L., Beard, L. A., & Carpenter, L. B. (2007). *Assistive technology access for all students.* Upper Saddle River, NJ: Pearson/Merrill Prentice Hall.

Jones, M. (2008). *Animal agentz.* Liverpool, UK: Animal Agentz.

Jordan, R. (1995). Computer assisted education for individuals with autism. In *Proceedings from Autisme France 3rd International Conference.* Nice, France: Autisme.

Juvonen, J. (1992). Negative peer reactions from the perspective of the reactor. *Journal of Educational Psychology, 84,* 314–321. doi:10.1037/0022-0663.84.3.314

Kagohara, D. M., Achmedi, D., Meer, L., Lancioni, G. E., O'Reilly, M., & Lang, R. et al. (2013). Teaching two students with Asperger syndrome to greet adults using Social Stories™ and video modeling. *Journal of Developmental and Physical Disabilities, 25,* 241–251. doi:10.1007/s10882-012-9300-6

Kagohara, D. M., van der Meer, L., Achmadi, D., Green, V. A., O'Reilly, M. F., & Lancioni, G. E. et al. (2012). Teaching picture naming to two adolescents with autism spectrum disorders using systematic instruction and speech-generating devices. *Research in Autism Spectrum Disorders, 6,* 1224–1233. doi:10.1016/j.rasd.2012.04.001

Kagohara, D. M., van der Meer, L., Ramdoss, S., O'Reilly, M. F., Lancioni, G. E., & Davis, T. N. et al. (2013). Using iPods and iPads in teaching programs for individuals with developmental disabilities: A systematic review. *Research in Developmental Disabilities, 34,* 147–156. doi:10.1016/j.ridd.2012.07.027 PMID:22940168

Kamio, Y., & Toichi, M. (2000). Dual access to semantics in autism: Is pictorial access superior to verbal access? *Journal of Child Psychology and Psychiatry, and Allied Disciplines, 41,* 859–867. doi:10.1111/1469-7610.00673 PMID:11079428

Kamps, D. M., Kravitz, T., Gonzalez-Lopez, A., Kemmerer, K., Potucek, J., & Harrell, L. G. (1998). What do peers think? Social validity of peer-mediated programs. *Education & Treatment of Children, 21,* 107–134.

Kandalaft, M. R., Didehbani, N., Krawczyk, D. C., Allen, T. T., & Chapman, S. B. (2013). Virtual reality social cognition training for young adults with high-functioning autism. *Journal of Autism and Developmental Disorders, 43*(1), 34–44. doi:10.1007/s10803-012-1544-6 PMID:22570145

Kanda, T., Hirano, T., Eaton, D., & Ishiguro, H. (2004). Interactive robots as social partners and peer tutors for children: A field trial. *Human-Computer Interaction, 19,* 61–84.

Kanne, S. M., & Mazurek, M. O. (2011). Aggression in children and adolescents with ASD: Prevalence and risk factors. *Journal of Autism and Developmental Disorders*, *41*, 926–937. doi:10.1007/s10803-010-1118-4 PMID:20960041

Kelley, H. H. (1967). Attribution theory in social psychology. In D. Levine (Ed.), *Nebraska symposium on motivation, 1967*. Lincoln, NE: University of Nebraska Press.

Kent-Walsh, J. E., & Light, J. C. (2003). General education teachers' experiences with inclusion of students who use augmentative and alternative communication. *Augmentative and Alternative Communication*, *19*, 104–124. doi:10.1080/0743461031000112043

Kenworthy, L. E., Black, D. O., Wallace, G. L., Ahluvalia, T., Wagner, A. E., & Sirian, L. M. (2005). Disorganization: The forgotten executive dysfunction in high-functioning autism (HFA) spectrum disorders. *Developmental Neuropsychology*, *3*, 809–827. doi:10.1207/s15326942dn2803_4 PMID:16266250

Kerr, S. J. (2002). Scaffolding – Design issues in single and collaborative virtual environments for social skills training. In *Eighth eurographics workshop on virtual environments*. Academic Press.

Kimball, J. W., Kinney, E. M., Taylor, B. A., & Stromer, R. (2004). Video-enhanced activity schedules for children with autism: A promising package for teaching social skills. *Education & Treatment of Children*, *27*, 280–298.

Kim, E. S., Berkovits, L. D., Bernier, E. P., Leyzberg, D., Shic, F., Paul, R., & Scassellati, B. (2013). Social robots as embedded reinforcers of social behavior in children with autism. *Journal of Autism and Developmental Disorders*, *43*, 1038–1049. doi: doi:10.1007/s10803-012-1645-2 PMID:23111617

Kim, E. S., Paul, R., Shic, F., & Scassellati, B. (2012). Bridging the research gap: Making HRI useful to individuals with autism. *Journal of Human-Robot Interaction*, *1*(1), 26–54. doi:doi:10.5898/JHRI.1.1.Kim

Kim, Y. S., & Leventhal, B. (2008). Bullying and suicide: A review. *Adolescent Medicine Health*, *20*(2), 133–154. PMID:18714552

Kinney, E. M., Vedora, J., & Stromer, R. (2003). Computer-presented video models to teach generative spelling to a child with an autism spectrum disorder. *Journal of Positive Behavior Interventions*, *5*, 22–29. doi:10.1177/10983007030050010301

Klin, A., Jones, W., Schultz, R., Volkmar, F., & Cohen, D. (2002). Visual fixation patterns during viewing of naturalistic social situations as predictors of social competence in individuals with ASD. *Archives of General Psychiatry*, *59*(9), 809–816. doi:10.1001/archpsyc.59.9.809 PMID:12215080

Klin, A., Sparrow, S. S., de Bildt, A., Cicchetti, D. V., Cohen, D. J., & Volkmar, F. R. (1999). A normed study of face recognition in autism and related disorders. *Journal of Autism and Developmental Disorders*, *29*(6), 499–508. doi:10.1023/A:1022299920240 PMID:10638462

Knowledge by Design. (2010). *Text compactor*. Whitefish Bay, WI: Author.

Koch, A. (2012). *Assistive technologies for children with autism spectrum disorders*. Academic Press.

Koegel, L. K., Koegel, R. L., Harrower, J. K., & Carter, C. M. (1999). Pivotal response intervention I: Overview of approach. *Research and Practice for Persons with Severe Disabilities*, *24*(3), 174–185.

Koegel, L. K., Koegel, R. L., Shoshan, Y., & McNerney, E. (1999). Pivotal response intervention II: Preliminary long-term outcome data. *Research and Practice for Persons with Severe Disabilities*, *24*(3), 186–198.

Koegel, R. L., Fredeen, R., Kim, S., Danial, J., Rubinstein, D., & Koegel, L. (2012). Using perseverative interests to improve interactions between adolescents with autism and their typical peers in school settings. *Journal of Positive Behavior Interventions*, *14*(3), 133–141. PMID:24163577

Koegel, R. L., Koegel, L. K., & McNerney, E. (2001). Pivotal areas in intervention for autism. *Journal of Clinical Child Psychology*, *30*(1), 19–32. PMID:11294074

Kozima, H., Nakagawa, C., & Yasuda, Y. (2007). Children–robot interaction: A pilot study in autism therapy. *Progress in Brain Research*, *164*, 385–400. doi:doi:10.1016/S0079-6123(07)64021-7 PMID:17920443

Krantz, P. J., MacDuff, M. T., & McClannahan, L. E. (1993). Programming participation in family activities for children with autism: Parents' use of photographic activity schedules. *Journal of Applied Behavior Analysis*, *26*(1), 137–138. doi:10.1901/jaba.1993.26-137 PMID:8473254

Kurzweil Educational Systems. (2011). *Kurzweil 3000 reading writing learning education software*. Dallas, TX: Cambium Learning.

Kuusikko, S., Haapsamo, H., Jansson-Verkasalo, E., Hurtig, T., Mattila, M., Ebeling, H., & Moilanen, I. (2009). Emotion recognition in children and adolescents with ASD spectrum disorders. *Journal of ASD and Developmental Disorders*, *39*(6), 938–945. doi:10.1007/s10803-009-0700-0

Lacava, P. G., Golan, O., Baron-Cohen, S., & Myles, B. (2007). Using assistive technology to teach emotion recognition to students with Asperger syndrome: A pilot study. *Remedial and Special Education*, *28*, 174–181. doi:10.1177/07419325070280030601

Lancioni, G. E., O'Reilly, M. F., Cuvo, A. J., Singh, N. N., Sigafoos, J., & Didden, R. (2007). PECS and VOCAs to enable students with developmental disabilities to make requests: An overview of the literature. *Research in Developmental Disabilities*, *28*(5), 468–488. doi:10.1016/j.ridd.2006.06.003 PMID:16887326

Lányi, C. S., & Geiszt, Z., Károlyi, Tilinger, A., & Magyar, V. (2006). Virtual reality in special needs early education. *The International Journal of Virtual Reality*, *5*(4), 55–68.

Lányi, C. S., & Tilinger, A. (2004). Multimedia and virtual reality in the rehabilitation of autistic children. *Lecture Notes in Computer Science*, *3118*, 22–28. doi:10.1007/978-3-540-27817-7_4

Lasater, M. W., & Brady, M. P. (1995). Effects of video self-modeling and feedback on task fluency: A home-based intervention. *Education & Treatment of Children*, *18*, 389–408.

LeBlanc, L. A., Coates, A. M., Daneshvar, S., Charlop-Christy, M. H., Morris, C., & Lancaster, B. M. (2003). Using video modeling and reinforcement to teach perspective-taking skills to children with autism. *Journal of Applied Behavior Analysis*, *36*, 253–257. doi:10.1901/jaba.2003.36-253 PMID:12858990

Lee, H., & Templeton, R. (2008). Ensuring equal access to technology: Providing assistive technology for students with disabilities. *Theory into Practice*, *47*, 212–219. doi:10.1080/00405840802153874

Leonard, A., Mitchell, P., & Parsons, S. (2002). Finding a place to sit: A preliminary investigation into the effectiveness of virtual environments for social skills training for people with autistic spectrum disorders. In *Proceedings of the 4th International Conference on Disability*, (pp. 249-257). Academic Press.

Leonard, H. (2013). There will soon be one smartphone for every five people in the world. *Business Insider*. Retrieved on June 8, 2013, from: http://www.businessinsider.com/15-billion-smartphones-in-the-world-22013-2?IR=T

Lequia, J., Machalicek, W., & Rispoli, M. J. (2012). Effects of activity schedules on challenging behavior exhibited in children with autism spectrum disorders: A systematic review. *Research in Autism Spectrum Disorders*, *6*, 480–492. doi:10.1016/j.rasd.2011.07.008

Levinas, E. (1969). *Totality and infinity* (A. Lingis, Trans.). Pittsburgh, PA: Duquesne University Press.

Lieberman, R., & Cowan, K. C. (2011). Bullying and youth suicide: breaking the connection. *National Association of School Psychologists*, 12 – 17.

Light, J., & McNaughton, D. (2012). The changing face of augmentative and alternative communication: Past, present, and future challenges. *Augmentative and Alternative Communication*, *28*, 197–204. doi:10.3109/07434618.2012.737024 PMID:23256853

Locascio, G., Mahone, E. M., Eason, S. H., & Cutting, L. E. (2010). Executive dysfunction among children with reading comprehension deficits. *Journal of Learning Disabilities*, *43*, 441–454. doi:10.1177/0022219409355476 PMID:20375294

Logan, K. (2012, April 4). *Developing communication skills in children with autism spectrum disorder using Proloquo2go on the iPad: An aided language approach*. Paper presented at the ASPECT Research Forum. Sydney, Australia.

Lopez, B. R., Lincoln, A. J., Ozonoff, S., & Lai, Z. (2005). Examining the relationship between executive functions and restricted, repetitive symptoms of autistic disorder. *Journal of Autism and Developmental Disorders, 35*(4), 445–460. PMID:16134030

Lorah, Tincani, Dodge, Gilroy, Hickey, & Hantula. (2013, February). Evaluating picture exchange and the iPad™ as a speech generating device to teach communication to young children with autism. *Journal of Physical and Developmental Disabilities.*

Lord, C., & Bishop, S. L. (2010). Autism spectrum disorders: Diagnosis, prevalence, and services for children and families. *Social Policy Report, 24*(2), 1–26.

Lord, C., Wagner, A., Rogers, S., Szatmari, P., Aman, M., & Charman, T. et al. (2005). Challenges in evaluating psychosocial interventions for autistic spectrum disorders. *Journal of Autism and Developmental Disorders, 35*, 695–708. doi:10.1007/s10803-005-0017-6 PMID:16496206

Lotan, M., Yalon – Chamovitz, S., & Weiss, P. L. (2009). Improving physical fitness of individuals with intellectual and developmental disability through a virtual reality intervention program. *Research in Developmental Disabilities, 30*, 229–239. PMID:18479889

Loukusa, S., & Moilanen, I. (2009). Pragmatic inference abilities in individuals with Asperger syndrome or high-functioning autism: A review. *Research in Autism Spectrum Disorders, 3*(4), 890–904. doi:10.1016/j.rasd.2009.05.002

Loveland, K. A., & Tunali-Kotoski, B. (2005). The school-aged child with autistic spectrum disorder. In F. R. Volkmar, R. Paul, A. Klin, & D. Cohen (Eds.), *Handbook of autism and pervasive developmental disorders* (3rd ed., pp. 247–287). Hoboken, NJ: Wiley. doi:10.1002/9780470939345.ch9

Luckasson, R., & Schalock, R. L. (2012). Human functioning, supports, assistive technology, and evidence-based practices in the field of intellectual disability. *Journal of Special Education Technology, 27*(2), 3–10.

Ludicke, P., & Kortman, W. (2012). Tensions in home-school partnerships: The different perspectives of teachers and parents of students with learning barriers. *Australasian Journal of Special Education, 36*(2), 155–171. doi:10.1017/jse.2012.13

Macan, T. H. (1994). Time management: Tests of a process model. *The Journal of Applied Psychology, 79*, 381–391. doi:10.1037/0021-9010.79.3.381

MacDonald, R., Clark, M., Garrigan, E., & Vangala, M. (2005). Using video modeling to teach pretend play to children with autism. *Behavioral Interventions, 20*, 225–238. doi:10.1002/bin.197

Madsen, M. E., Kaliouby, R., Goodwin, M., & Picard, R. (2008). Technology for just-in-time in-situ learning of facial affect for persons diagnosed with an autism spectrum disorder. In *Proceedings of the 10th International ACM SIGACCESS Conference on Computers and Accessibility* (pp. 19–26). ACM.

Maione, L., & Mirenda, P. (2006). Effects of video modeling and video feedback on peer directed social language skills of a child with autism. *Journal of Positive Behavior Interventions, 8*, 106–118. doi:10.1177/10983007060080020201

Malecki, C. K., & Elliot, S. N. (2002). Children's social behaviors as predictors of academic achievement: A longitudinal analysis. *School Psychology Quarterly, 17*, 1–23. doi:10.1521/scpq.17.1.1.19902

Male, M. (2003). *Technology for inclusion: Meeting the special needs of all students.* Boston: Allyn and Bacon.

Mancil, R. G., Haydon, T., & Whitby, P. (2009). Differentiated effects of paper and computer-assisted Social Stories™ on inappropriate behavior in children with autism. *Focus on Autism and Other Developmental Disabilities, 24*, 205–215. doi:10.1177/1088357609347324

Marcu, G., & Hayes, G. R. (2010). Use of a wearable recording device in therapeutic interventions for children with autism. In *Proceedings of the First International Workshop on Interactive Systems in Healthcare,* (pp. 113-116). Academic Press.

Mares. (1996). *Metanalysis of studies of prosocial portrayals.* Philadelphia: University of Pennsylvania.

Martin, J. S., Poirier, M., & Dowler, D. M. (2010). Brief report: Impaired temporal reproduction performance in adults with autism spectrum disorder. *Journal of Autism and Developmental Disorders, 40*(5), 640–646. doi:10.1007/s10803-009-0904-3 PMID:19924521

Mason, T., & Stroud, D. (2012). iPads to support students with autism spectrum disorders: One districts' implementation. Academic Press.

Massey, G., & Wheeler, J. (2000). Acquisition and generalization of activity schedules and their effects on task engagement in a young child with autism in an inclusive preschool classroom. *Education and Training in Mental Retardation and Developmental Disabilities, 35,* 326–335.

Matawa, C. (2009). Exploring the musical interests and abilities of blind and partially sighted children and young people with retinopathy of prematurity. *British Journal of Visual Impairment, 27,* 252. doi:10.1177/0264619609106364

Matson, J. L., Hattier, M. A., & Belva, B. (2012). Treating adaptive living skills of persons with autism using applied behavior analysis: A review. *Research in Autism Spectrum Disorders, 6,* 271–276.

Matson, J., & Wilkins, J. (2007). A critical review of assessment targets and methods for social skills excesses and deficits for children with autism spectrum disorders. *Research in Autism Spectrum Disorders, 1,* 28–37. doi:10.1016/j.rasd.2006.07.003

MaxiAIDS. (1996). *Timer traffic light.* Farmingdale, NY: Author.

Mazefsky, C. A., Pelphrey, K. A., & Dahl, R. E. (2012). The need for a broader approach to emotion regulation research in autism. *Child Development Perspectives, 6,* 92–97. doi:10.1111/j.1750-8606.2011.00229.x PMID:22639681

Mazurek, M. O., & Engelhardt, C. R. (2013). Video game use and problem behaviors in boys with autism spectrum disorders. *Research in Autism Spectrum Disorders, 7,* 316–324.

Mazurek, M. O., & Engelhardt, C. R. (2013). Video game use in boys with autism spectrum disorder, ADHD, or typical development. *Pediatrics, 132*(2), 260–266. PMID:23897915

Mazurek, M. O., Shattuck, P. T., Wagner, M., & Cooper, B. P. (2012). Prevalence and correlates of screen-based media use among youths with autism spectrum disorders. *Journal of Autism and Developmental Disorders, 42,* 1757–1767. PMID:22160370

Mazurek, M. O., & Wenstrup, C. (2013). Television, video game and social media use among children with ASD and typically developing siblings. *Journal of Autism and Developmental Disorders, 43,* 1258–1271. PMID:23001767

McCoy, K., & Hermansen, E. (2007). Video modeling for individuals with autism: A review of model types and effects. *Education & Treatment of Children, 30,* 183–213. doi:10.1353/etc.2007.0029

McGinnis, E. (2011). *Skillstreaming the elementary school child: A guide for teaching prosocial skills* (3rd ed.). Champaign, IL: Research Press.

McGinnis, E. (2011). *Skillstreaming in early childhood: A guide for teaching prosocial skills.* Champaign, IL: Research Press.

McMillan, J. M. (2008). Teachers make it happen: From professional development to integration of augmentative and alternative communication technologies in the classroom. *Australasian Journal of Special Education, 32,* 199–211. doi:10.1080/10300110802047467

Meadan, H., Ostrosky, M. M., Triplett, B., Michna, A., & Fettig, A. (2011). Using visual supports with young children with autism spectrum disorder. *Teaching Exceptional Children, 43*(6), 28–35.

Mechling, L. C. (2011). Review of twenty-first century portable electronic devices for persons with moderate intellectual disabilities and autism spectrum disorders. *Education and Training in Autism and Developmental Disabilities, 46,* 479–498.

Mechling, L. C., & Ayres, K. M. (2012). A comparative study: Completion of fine motor office related tasks by high school students with autism using video models on large and small screen size. *Journal of Autism and Developmental Disorders, 42,* 2364–2375. doi:10.1007/s10803-012-1484-1 PMID:22354709

Merbler, J., Hadadian, A., & Ulman, J. (1999). Using assistive technology in the inclusive classroom. *Preventing School Failure, 43*(3), 113–118. doi:10.1080/10459889909603311

Mesibov, G. B. (1998). *Learning styles of students with autism.* Retrieved January 16, 1998, from http://www.autism-soceity.org/packages/edkids_learning-styles.html

Mesibov, G. B., Shea, V., & Schopler, E. (2004). The TE-ACCH approach to autism spectrum disorders. New York, NY: Springer Science+Business Media, Inc.

Mesibov, E., Schopler, G. B., & Hearsey, K. A. (1994). Structured teaching. In E. Schopler, & G. B. Mesibov (Eds.), *Behaviorial issues in autism* (pp. 195–207). New York: Plenum Press. doi:10.1007/978-1-4757-9400-7_10

Messinger-Willma, J., & Marino, M. (2010). Universal design for learning and assistive technology: Leadership considerations for promoting inclusive education in today'ssecondary schools. *NASSP Bulletin*, *94*(5). doi: doi:10.1177/0192636510371977

Meyer, G., Roberto, A. J., Boster, F. J., & Roberto, H. L. (2004). Assessing the get real about violence curriculum: Process and outcome evaluation results and implications. *Health Communication*, *16*, 451–474. doi:10.1207/s15327027hc1604_4 PMID:15465690

Mighty Kingdom. (2012, December 4). *iModeling application information.* Retrieved from https://itunes.apple.com/us/app/imodeling/id457539171?mt=8

Millar, D., Light, J., & Schlosser, R. (2006). The impact of augmentative and alternative communication on the speech production of individuals with developmental disabilities: A research review. *Journal of Speech, Language, and Hearing Research: JSLHR*, *49*, 248–264. doi:10.1044/1092-4388(2006/021) PMID:16671842

Millen, L., Edlin-White, R., & Cobb, S. (2010). The development of educational collaborative virtual environments for children with autism. In *Proceedings of the 5th Cambridge Workshop on Universal Access and Assistive Technology*. Cambridge University.

Miller, J. F., & Allaire, J. (1987). Augmentative communication. In M. A. Snell (Ed.), *Systematic instruction of persons with severe handicaps* (3rd ed., pp. 273–296). Upper Saddle River, NJ: Merrill.

Miller, L. K. (1999). The savant syndrome: Intellectual impairment and exceptional skill. *Psychological Bulletin*, *125*(1), 33–46. doi:10.1037/0033-2909.125.1.31 PMID:9990844

Mind Institute. (2013, July 7). *Self help and functional skills checklist.* Retrieved from http://media.mindinstitute.org/education/ADEPT/Notes/SelfHelpChecklist.pdf

Mintz, J. (2013). Additional key factors mediating the use of a mobile technology tool designed to develop social and life skills in children with autism spectrum disorders: Evaluation of the 2nd HANDS prototype. *Computers & Education*, *63*, 17–27. doi:10.1016/j.compedu.2012.11.006

Mirenda, P., & Iacono, T. (2009). *Autism spectrum disorders and AAC.* Baltimore, MD: Paul H. Brookes.

Mitchell, P., Parsons, S., & Leonard, A. (2007). Using virtual environments for teaching social understanding to 6 adolescents with autistic spectrum disorders. *Journal of Autism and Developmental Disorders*, *37*, 589–600. doi:10.1007/s10803-006-0189-8 PMID:16900403

Moore, D., Cheng, Y., McGrath, P., & Powell, N. J. (2005). Collaborative virtual environment technology for people with autism. *Focus on Autism and Other Developmental Disabilities*, *20*, 231–243. doi:10.1177/10883576050200040501

Moore, D., McGrath, P., & Thorpe, J. (2000). Computer-aided learning for people with autism: A framework for research and development. *Innovations in Education and Training International*, *37*, 218–228. doi:10.1080/13558000050138452

Moore, M., & Calvert, S. (2000). Brief report: Vocabulary acquisition for children with autism: Teacher or computer instruction. *Journal of Autism and Developmental Disorders*, *30*, 359–362. doi:10.1023/A:1005535602064 PMID:11039862

Morgan, S. B., & Wisely, D. W. (1996). Children's attitudes and behavioral intentions toward a peer presented as physically handicapped: A more positive view. *Journal of Developmental and Physical Disabilities*, *8*, 29–42. doi:10.1007/BF02578438

Mottron, L., Dawson, M., Soulieres, I., Hubert, B., & Burack, J. (2006). Enhanced perceptual functioning in autism: An update, and eight principles of autistic perception. *Journal of Autism and Developmental Disorders*, *36*(1), 27–43. doi:10.1007/s10803-005-0040-7 PMID:16453071

Müller, E., Schuler, A., & Yates, G. B. (2008). Social challenges and supports from the perspective of individuals with Asperger syndrome and other autism spectrum disabilities. *Autism*, *12*, 173–190. doi:10.1177/1362361307086664 PMID:18308766

Murdock, L. C., Ganz, J., & Crittendon, J. (2013). Use of an iPad play story to increase play dialogue of preschoolers with ASD spectrum disorders. *Journal of ASD and Developmental Disorders, 43*(9), 2174–2189. doi:10.1007/s10803-013-1770-6

Murphy, R. (1995). Encounters: The body silent in America. In B. Instad, & S. R. White (Eds.), *Disability and culture* (pp. 140–158). Berkeley, CA: University of California Press.

Murray, D. K. C. (1997). Autism and information technology: Therapy with computers. In *Autism and learning: A guide to good practice*. Academic Press.

Myles, B. S. (2005). *Children and youth with Asperger syndrome: Strategies for success in inclusive settings*. Thousand Oaks, CA: Corwin Press.

Myles, B. S. et al. (2005). *Life journey through autism: An educator's guide to Asperger syndrome*. Arlington, VA: Organization for Autism Research.

Myles, B. S., Endow, J., & Mayfield, M. (2012). *The hidden curriculum and getting and keeping a job: Navigating the social landscape of employment: A guide for individuals with autism spectrum and other social-cognitive challenges*. Shawnee Mission, KS: AAPC Publishing.

Myles, B. S., Grossman, B. G., Aspy, R., Henry, S. A., & Coffin, A. B. (2007). Planning a comprehensive program for students with autism spectrum disorders using evidence-based practices. *Education and Training in Developmental Disabilities, 42*, 398–409.

Myles, B. S., Simpson, R. L., Ormsbee, C. K., & Erikson, C. (1993). Integrating preschool children with autism with their normally developing peers: Research findings and best practice recommendations. *Focus on Autistic Behavior, 8*, 1–18.

Myles, B. S., & Southwick, J. (2005). *Asperger syndrome and difficult moments: Practical solutions for tantrums, rage, and meltdowns* (2nd ed.). Shawnee Mission, KS: AAPC Publishing.

Nally, B., Houlton, B., & Ralph, S. (2000). Researches in brief: The management of television and video by parents of children with autism. *Autism, 4*(3), 331–337.

National Autism Center. (2009). *Evidence-based practice and autism in the schools: A guide to providing appropriate interventions to students with autism spectrum disorders*. Randolph, MA: National Autism Center.

National Autism Center. (2009). *National standards project: Addressing the need for evidence-based practice guidelines for autism spectrum disorders*. Randolph, MA: National Autism Center.

National Center for Learning Disabilities, Inc. (2013). *Individualized education plan*. National Center for Learning Disabilities. Retrieved July 4, 2013 from http://www.ncld.org/students-disabilities/iep-504-plan/what-is-iep

National Institute of Mental Health. (2010). *What is autism spectrum disorders?* Retrieved from http://www.nimh.nih.gov/health/publications/autism/what-are-theautism...

National Professional Development Center on Autism Spectrum Disorders. (2010). *Evidence-base for computer-aided instruction*. National Professional Development Center on ASD, University of North Carolina, University of California, and the University of Wisconsin.

National Professional Development Center on Autism Spectrum Disorders. (n.d.). *Evidence based practice briefs*. Retrieved from http://autismpdc.fpg.unc.edu/content/briefs

National Research Council, Committee on Educational Interventions for Children with Autism, Division of Behavioral and Social Sciences and Education. (2001). *Educating children with autism*. Washington, DC: National Academy Press.

Neale, H. R., Kerr, S. J., Cobb, S. V. G., & Leonard, A. (2002). Exploring the role of virtual environments in the special needs classroom. In *Proceedings of the 4th International Conference Disability, Virtual Reality & Associated Technology,* (pp. 259-266). Academic Press.

Neale, H., Cobb, S., & Wilson, J. (2002). A front-ended approach to the user-centered design of virtual environments.[Los Alamitos, CA: IEEE.]. *Proceedings of IEEE Virtual Reality, 2002*, 191–198.

Newbutt, N. (2013). *Exploring communication and representation of the self in a virtual world by young people with autism*. (Unpublished doctoral dissertation). University College Dublin, Dublin, Ireland.

Newton, D., & Dell, A. G. (2011). Mobile devices and students with disabilities: What do best practices tell us? *Journal of Special Education Technology, 26*(3), 47–49.

Newton, D., Eren, R., Ben-Avie, M., & Reichow, B. (2013). Handheld technology for visual supports. *Journal of Special Education Technology, 27*(4), 53–56.

Nikopoulos, C. K., Canavan, C., & Nikopoulou-Smyrni, P. (2009). Generalized effects of video modeling on establishing instructional stimulus control in children with autism: Results of a preliminary study. *Journal of Positive Behavior Interventions, 11*, 198–207. doi:10.1177/1098300708325263

Nikopoulos, C. K., & Keenan, M. (2004). Effects of video modeling on social initiations by children with autism. *Journal of Applied Behavior Analysis, 37*, 93. doi:10.1901/jaba.2004.37-93 PMID:15154221

Nikopoulos, C. K., & Keenan, M. (2007). Using video modeling to teach complex social sequences to children with autism. *Journal of Autism and Developmental Disorders, 37*, 678–693. doi:10.1007/s10803-006-0195-x PMID:16897375

Nikopoulos, C. K., & Nikopoulou-Smyrni, P. (2008). Teaching complex social skills to children with autism: Advances in video modeling. *Journal of Early and Intensive Behavior Intervention, 5*, 30–43.

NREPP. (2012). *Legacy program summary: Get real about violence*. Retrieved from http://www.nrepp.samhsa.gov/ViewLegacy.aspx?id=92

O'Reilly, M. F., Lancioni, G. E., Lang, R., & Rispoli, M. (2011). Teaching functional use of an iPod-based speech-generating device to individuals with developmental disabilities. *Journal of Special Education Technology, 26*(3), 1–10.

Odom, S. L., Collet-Klingenberg, L., Rogers, S. J., & Halton, D. D. (2010). Evidence-based practices in interventions for children and youth with autism spectrum disorders. *Preventing School Failure, 54*(4), 275–282. doi:10.1080/10459881003785506

Office of Special Education Programs. (2011). *30ᵗʰ annual report to congress on the implementation of the individuals with disabilities education act, 2008*. Washington, DC: U.S. Department of Education.

Ogilvie, C. R. (2011). Step by step: Social skills instruction for students with autism spectrum disorder using video models and peer mentors. *Teaching Exceptional Children, 43*, 20–26.

Ogilvie, C. R. (2011). Ten steps to creating video models for students with autism spectrum disorders. *Teaching Exceptional Children, 43*, 8–19.

Ogilvie, C. R., & Dieker, L. A. (2010). Video modeling and peer-mediated instruction of social skills for students with autism spectrum disorders. *Journal on Developmental Disabilities, 16*, 48–59.

Ogletree, B. T. (2008). The communicative context of autism. In R. Simpson, & B. Myles (Eds.), *Educating children and youth with autism* (pp. 223–265). Austin, TX: PRO-ED, Inc.

Ohio State University. (2011, November 15). *InPromptu application information*. Retrieved from https://itunes.apple.com/us/app/inpromptu/id473450377?mt=8

Olive, M. L., de la Cruz, B., Davis, T. N., Chan, J. M., Lang, R. B., & O'Reilly, M. F. et al. (2007). The effects of enhanced milieu teaching and a voice output communication aid on the requesting of three children with autism. *Journal of Autism and Developmental Disorders, 37*, 1505–1513. doi:10.1007/s10803-006-0243-6 PMID:17066309

Olive, M. L., Lang, R. B., & Davis, T. N. (2008). An analysis of the effects of functional communication and a voice output communication aid for a child with autism spectrum disorder. *Research in Autism Spectrum Disorders, 2*, 223–236. doi:10.1016/j.rasd.2007.06.002

Omatsu, G. (2013, July 8). *Peer mentoring resource booklet*. Retrieved from http://www.csun.edu/eop/htdocs/peermentoring.pdf

Oppenheim-Leaf, M. L., Leaf, J. B., & Call, N. A. (2012). Teaching board games to two children with an autism spectrum disorder. *Journal of Developmental and Physical Disabilities, 24*, 347–358.

Ornitz, E. M. (1989). Autism at the interface between sensory and information processing. In G. Dawson (Ed.), *Autism: Nature, diagnosis, and treatment* (pp. 174–207). New York: Guilford Press.

Ortiz, J. M. (2011). *The five umbrellas: A strength-based framework for Asperger's, high functioning autism, and non-verbal learning disorder.* Dillsburg, PA: The Asperger's Syndrome Institute.

Owen-Deschryver, J. S. (2004). Promoting social interactions between students with autism and their peers in inclusive school settings. *Dissertation Abstracts International. A, The Humanities and Social Sciences, 64*(9-A), 32–46.

Pan, C. Y., & Frey, G. C. (2006). Physical activity patterns in youth with autism spectrum disorders. *Journal of Autism and Developmental Disorders, 36,* 597–606. PMID:16652237

Parette, H. P., & Angelo, D. H. (1996). Augmentative and alternative communication impact on families: Trends and future directions. *The Journal of Special Education, 30,* 77–98. doi:10.1177/002246699603000105

Parette, H. P., Brotherson, M. J., Hourcade, J. J., & Bradley, R. H. (1996). Family centered assistive technology assessment. *Intervention in School and Clinic, 32,* 104–112. doi:10.1177/105345129603200206

Parette, H. P., Brotherson, M. J., & Huer, M. B. (2000). Giving families a voice in augmentative and alternative communication decision-making. *Education and Training in Mental Retardation and Developmental Disabilities, 35,* 177–190.

Parsons, S., Beardon, L., Neale, H. R., Reynard, G., Eastgate, R., Wilson, J. R., & Hopkins, E. (2000). Development of social skills amongst adults with Asperger's syndrome using virtual environments: the 'AS interactive' project. In *Proceedings of the 3rd International Conference on Disability, Virtual Reality and Associated Technology* (pp. 163-170). Academic Press.

Parsons, S. (2005). Use, understanding and learning in virtual environments by adolescents with autistic spectrum disorders. In B. K. Wiederhold, G. Riva, & A. H. Bullinger (Eds.), *Annual review of cybertherapy and telemedicine* (pp. 207–215). Academic Press. doi:10.1037/e705572011-075

Parsons, S. (2007). Virtual environments for social skills intervention: current findings and future challenges. In *El autismo en personas adultas: Nuevas perspectivas de futuro.* Ministerio de Trabajo y Asuntos Social.

Parsons, S., & Cobb, S. (2011). State-of-the-art of virtual reality technologies for children on the autism spectrum. *European Journal of Special Needs Education, 26*(3), 355–366. doi:10.1080/08856257.2011.593831

Parsons, S., Leonard, A., & Mitchell, P. (2006). Virtual environments for social skills training: Comments from two adolescents with autistic spectrum disorder. *Computers & Education, 47,* 186–206. doi:10.1016/j.compedu.2004.10.003

Parsons, S., & Mitchell, P. (2002). The potential of virtual reality in social skills training for people with autistic spectrum disorders. *Journal of Intellectual Disability Research, 46*(5), 430–443. doi:10.1046/j.1365-2788.2002.00425.x PMID:12031025

Parsons, S., Mitchell, P., & Leonard, A. (2004). The use and understanding of virtual environments by adolescents with autistic spectrum disorders. *Journal of Autism and Developmental Disorders, 34*(4), 449–466. doi:10.1023/B:JADD.0000037421.98517.8d PMID:15449520

Parsons, S., Mitchell, P., & Leonard, A. (2005). Do adolescents with autistic spectrum disorders adhere to social conventions in virtual environments? *Autism, 9,* 95–117. doi:10.1177/1362361305049032 PMID:15618265

Partnership for 21st Century Skills. (n.d.). *Framework for 21st century learning.* Retrieved from http://www.p21.org/overview

Pennington, R. C. (2010). Computer-assisted instruction for teaching academic skills to students with autism spectrum disorders: A review of literature. *Focus on Autism and Other Developmental Disabilities, 25,* 239–248. doi:10.1177/1088357610378291

Pepler, D. J., Craig, W. M., & Roberts, W. R. (1993). A school-based anti-bullying intervention: Preliminary evaluation. In D. Tattum (Ed.), *Understanding and managing bullying* (pp. 76–91). Heinemann Books.

Phillips, B., & Zhao, H. (1993). Predictors of assistive technology abandonment. *Assistive Technology, 5*(1), 36–45. doi:10.1080/10400435.1993.10132205 PMID:10171664

Pierce, K., Conant, D., Hazin, R., Stoner, R., & Desmond, J. (2011). Preference for geometric patterns early in life as a risk factor for autism. *Archives of General Psychiatry*, *68*(1), 101–109. doi:10.1001/archgenpsychiatry.2010.113 PMID:20819977

Pierce, K., & Schreibman, L. (1997). Using peer trainers to promote social behavior in autism: Are they effective at enhancing multiple social modalities. *Focus on Autism and Other Developmental Disabilities*, *12*(4). doi:10.1177/108835769701200403

Pierno, A. C., Mari, M., Lusher, D., & Castiello, U. (2008). Robotic movement elicits visuomotor priming in children with autism. *Neuropsychologia*, *46*, 448–454. doi: doi:10.1016/j.neuropsychologia.2007.08.020 PMID:17920641

Plavnick, J. B. (2012). A practical strategy for teaching a child with autism to attend to and imitate a portable video model. *Research and Practice for Persons with Severe Disabilities*, *37*, 263–270. doi:10.2511/027494813805327250

Ploog, B. O., Banerjee, S., & Brooks, P. J. (2009). Attention to prosody (intonation) and content in children with autism and in typical children using spoken sentences in a computer game. *Research in Autism Spectrum Disorders*, *3*(3), 743–758.

Ploog, B. O., Scharf, A., Nelson, D., & Brooks, P. J. (2013). Use of computer-assisted technologies (CAT) to enhance social, communicative, and language development in children with autism spectrum disorders. *Journal of Autism and Developmental Disorders*, *43*, 301–322. doi:10.1007/s10803-012-1571-3 PMID:22706582

Porter, G., & Cafiero, J. M. (2009). Pragmatic organization dynamic display (PODD) communication books: A promising practice for individuals with autism spectrum disorders. *Perspectives on Augmentative and Alternative Communication*, *18*(4), 121–129. doi:10.1044/aac18.4.121

Prater, M. A., Carter, N., Hitchcock, C., & Dowrick, P. (2012). Video self-modeling to improve academic performance: A literature review. *Psychology in the Schools*, *49*, 71–81. doi:10.1002/pits.20617

Price, A. (2011). Making a difference with smart tablets: Are iPads really beneficial for students with autism? *Teacher Librarian*, *39*(1), 31–34.

Prizant, B. M., & Rubin, E. (1999). Contemporary issues in interventions for autism spectrum disorders: A commentary. *The Journal of the Association for Persons with Severe Handicaps*, *24*, 199–208. doi:10.2511/rpsd.24.3.199

Putnam, C., & Chong, L. (2008). Software and technologies designed for people with autism: What do users want? In *Proceedings of the 10th International ACM SIFACCESS Conference on Computers and Accessibility*. ACM.

Quill, K. (2000). *Do-watch-listen-say: Social and communication intervention for children with autism*. Baltimore, MD: Brookes Publishing.

Quill, K. A. (1995). Visually cued instruction for children with autism and pervasive developmental disorders. *Focus on Autistic Behavior*, *10*, 10–20.

Quill, K. A. (1997). Instructional considerations for young children with autism: The rationale for visually cued instruction. *Journal of Autism and Developmental Disorders*, *27*, 697–714. doi:10.1023/A:1025806900162 PMID:9455729

Quinn, M. (2013). Introduction of active video gaming into the middle school curriculum as a school-based childhood obesity intervention. *Journal of Pediatric Health Care*, *27*(1), 3–12. PMID:23237611

Ramdoss, S., Lang, R., Mulloy, A., Franco, J., O'Reilly, M., Didden, R., & Lancioni, G. (2011). Use of computer-based interventions to teach communication skills to children with autism spectrum disorders: A systematic review. *Journal of Behavioral Education*, *20*, 55–76. doi:10.1007/s10864-010-9112-7

Rao, P. A., & Beidel, D. C. (2009). The impact of children with high-functioning sutism on parental stress, sibling adjustment, and family functioning. *Behavior Modification*, *33*(4), 437–451. doi:10.1177/0145445509336427 PMID:19436073

Reed, P., & Lahm, E. A. (2005). *A resource guide for teachers and administrators about assistive technology*. Oshkosh, WI: Wisconsin Assistive Technology Initiative. Retrieved February 3, 2006 from http://www.wati.org

Rehfeldt, R. A., Kinney, E. M., Root, S., & Stromer, R. (2004). Creating activity schedules using Microsoft PowerPoint. *Journal of Applied Behavior Analysis, 37*, 115–128. doi:10.1901/jaba.2004.37-115 PMID:15154226

Reichle, J., Beukelman, D., & Light, J. (2002). *Exemplary practices for beginning communicators: Implications for AAC*. Baltimore, MD: Brookes Publishing Company.

Reichow, B., & Volkmar, F. R. (2010). Social skills Interventions for individuals with autism: Evaluation for evidence-based practices within a best evidence synthesis framework. *Journal of Autism and Developmental Disorders, 40*(2), 149–166. doi:10.1007/s10803-009-0842-0 PMID:19655240

Reichow, B., Volkmar, F., & Cicchetti, D. V. (2008). Development of the evaluative method for evaluating and determining evidence-based practices in autism. *Journal of Autism and Developmental Disorders, 38*, 1311–1319. doi: doi:10.1007/s10803-007-0517-7 PMID:18095149

RERC on Communication Enhancement. (2011, March 14). *Mobile devices and communication apps: An AAC-RERC white paper*. Retrieved from http://aac-rerc.psu.edu/index.php/pages/show/id/46

Retherford, K., & Sterling-Orth, A. (2009). Facilitating functional social communication skills in adolescents. *Journal of Autism and Developmental Disorders, 32*, 535–543.

Reynhout, G., & Carter, M. (2006). Social stories for children with disabilities. *Journal of Autism and Developmental Disorders, 36*, 445–469. doi:10.1007/s10803-006-0086-1 PMID:16755384

Reynolds, S., Bendixen, R. M., Lawrence, T., & Lane, S. J. (2011). A pilot study examining activity participation, sensory responsiveness, and competence in children with high functioning autism spectrum disorder. *Journal of Autism and Developmental Disorders, 41*, 1496–1506. PMID:21221753

Rice, C. (2006). Prevalence of autism spectrum disorders – Autism and developmental disabilities monitoring network, United States, 2006. *MMWR. Surveillance Summaries, 58*(10), 1–20.

Rieber, L. P. (1991). Animation, incidental learning, and continuing motivation. *Journal of Educational Psychology, 83*, 318–328. doi:10.1037/0022-0663.83.3.318

Rieffe, C., Terwogt, M. M., Mootz, S., Van Leeuwen, E., & Stockmann, L. (2011). Emotion regulation and internalizing symptoms in children with autism spectrum disorders. *Autism, 15*, 655–670. doi:10.1177/1362361310366571 PMID:21733959

Rigo, E. E. (2013). *Using an Apple iPad for self-monitoring of students with autism*. (Unpublished Masters of Arts Thesis). Department of Language, Literacy & Special Education at Rowan University, Rowan, NJ.

Rispoli, M., Franco, J. H., van der Meer, L., Lang, R., & Camargo, S. (2010). The use of speech generating devices in communication interventions for individuals with developmental disabilities: A review of the literature. *Developmental Neurorehabilitation, 13*(4), 276–293. doi:10.3109/17518421003636794 PMID:20629594

Ritterfeld, U., & Weber, R. (2005). Video games for entertainment and education. In P. Vorderer, & J. Bryant (Eds.), *Playing video games - Motives, responses, and consequences* (pp. 399–413). Mahwah, NJ: Lawrence Erlbaum.

Robotshop Distribution. (2013). *Aldebaran robotics*. Retrieved from http://www.robotshop.com/aldebaran-robotics-en.html

Rogers, S. J., & Dawson, G. (2010). *Early start denver model for young children with autism: Promoting language, learning, and engagement*. New York: Guilford.

Romski, M. A., & Sevcik, R. A. (1988). Augmentative and alternative communication systems: Considerations for individuals with severe intellectual disabilities. *Augmentative and Alternative Communication, 2*, 83–93. doi:10.1080/07434618812331274667

Rosenbaum, P. L., Armstrong, R. W., & King, S. M. (1988). Determinants of children's attitudes toward disability: A review of the evidence. *Children's Health Care, 17*, 1–8. doi:10.1207/s15326888chc1701_5 PMID:10315759

Rosenberg, N. E., Schwartz, I. S., & Davis, C. A. (2010). Evaluating the utility of commercial videotapes for teaching hand washing to children with autism. *Education & Treatment of Children, 33,* 443–455. doi:10.1353/etc.0.0098

Rosenfield, B. (2008). The challenges of teaching with technology: From computer idiocy to computer competence. *International Journal of Instructional Media, 35,* 157–166.

Rosenthal, R. (1989). *Experimenter expectancy covert communication and meta-analytic methods.* Paper presented at the 97th Annual Convention of the American Psychological Association. New Orleans, LA.

Rosenthal, M., Wallace, G. L., Lawson, R., Wills, M. C., Dixon, E., Yerys, B. E., & Kenworthy, L. (2013). Impairments in real-world executive function increase from childhood to adolescence in autism spectrum disorders. *Neuropsychology, 27*(1), 13–18. PMID:23356593

Rosenthal, R. (1963). On the social psychology of the psychological experiment: The experimenter's hypotheses as unintended experimental results. *American Scientist, 51,* 268–283. PMID:13974992

Rossi, P., Freeman, H., & Lipsey, M. (2004). *Evaluation: A systematic approach* (7th ed.). Thousand Oaks, CA: Sage.

Rothschild, B. (2011). *Special tool for special needs.* Retrieved from http://beta.courierpostonline.com

Rubin, E., & Lennon, L. (2004). Challenges in social communication in Asperger syndrome and high-functioning autism. *Topics in Language Disorders, 24,* 271–285. doi:10.1097/00011363-200410000-00005

Russoniello, C. V., O'Brien, K., & Parks, J. M. (2009). The effectiveness of casual video games in improving mood and decreasing stress. *Journal of CyberTherapy & Rehabilitation, 2*(1), 53–66.

Rutten, A., Cobb, S., Neale, H., Kerr, S., Leonard, A., Parsons, S., & Mitchell, P. (2003). The AS interactive project: single-user and collaborative virtual environments for people with high-functioning autistic spectrum disorders. *The Journal of Visualization and Computer Animation, 14,* 233–241. doi:10.1002/vis.320

Ryan, C., & Charragáin, C. (2010). Teaching emotion recognition skills to children with ASD. *Journal of ASD snd Developmental Disorders, 40*(12), 1505-1511.

Ryan, K. M. (1981). Developmental differences in reactions to the physically disabled. *Human Development, 24,* 240–256. doi:10.1159/000272685 PMID:6456979

Sachse, M., Schlitt, S., Hainz, D., Ciaramidaro, A., Schirman, S., & Walter, H. et al. (2013). Executive and visuo-motor function in adolescents and adults with autism spectrum disorders. *Journal of Autism and Developmental Disorders, 43,* 1222–1235. doi:10.1007/s10803-012-1668-8 PMID:23011252

Safran, S. P. (2008). Why youngsters with autistic spectrum disorders remain underrepresented in special education. *Remedial and Special Education, 29,* 90–95. doi:10.1177/0741932507311637

Salazar, M. J. (2012). Home-school collaboration for embedding individualized goals in daily routines. *Young Exceptional Children, 15*(3), 20–30. doi:10.1177/1096250612446870

Salman, S. (2006). *Autism community forges virtual haven.* Retrieved from http://www.guardian.co.uk/society/2006/mar/08/guardiansocietysupplement1

Sansosti, F. J. et al. (2004). A research synthesis of social story interventions for children with autism spectrum disorders. *Focus on Autism and Other Developmental Disabilities, 19,* 194–204. doi:10.1177/10883576040190040101

Sansosti, F. J., & Powell-Smith, K. A. (2008). Using computer-presented social stories and video models to increase the social communication skills of children with high-functioning autism spectrum disorders. *Journal of Positive Behavior Interventions, 10*(3), 162–178. doi:10.1177/1098300708316259

Sansosti, F. J., Powell-Smith, K. A., & Cowan, R. J. (2010). *High functioning autism/Asperger syndrome in schools: Assessment and intervention.* New York: Guilford.

Scassellati, B., Admoni, H., & Matarić, M. (2012). Robots for use in autism research. *Annual Review of Biomedical Engineering, 14,* 275–294. doi: doi:10.1146/annurev-bioeng-071811-150036 PMID:22577778

Schepis, M. M., Reid, D. H., & Behrmann, M. M. (1996). Acquisition and functional use of voice output communication by persons with profound multiple disabilities. *Behavior Modification, 20*, 451–468. doi:10.1177/01454455960204005 PMID:8875815

Schepis, M. M., Reid, D. H., Behrmann, M. M., & Sutton, K. A. (1998). Increasing communicative interactions of young children with autism using a voice output communication aid and naturalistic teaching. *Journal of Applied Behavior Analysis, 31*, 561–578. doi:10.1901/jaba.1998.31-561 PMID:9891394

Schlosser, R. W., & Blischak, D. M. (2004). Effects of speech and print feedback on spelling in children with autism. *Journal of Speech, Language, and Hearing Research: JSLHR, 47*, 848–862. doi:10.1044/1092-4388(2004/063) PMID:15324290

Schlosser, R. W., Sigafoos, J., Luiselli, J. K., Angermeier, K., Harasymowyz, U., & Schooley, K. et al. (2007). Effects of synthetic speech output on requesting and natural speech production in children with autism: A preliminary study. *Research in Autism Spectrum Disorders, 1*, 139–163. doi:10.1016/j.rasd.2006.10.001

Schlosser, R. W., & Wendt, O. (2008). Effects of augmentative and alternative communication intervention on speech production in children with autism: A systematic review. *American Journal of Speech-Language Pathology, 17*, 212–230. doi:10.1044/1058-0360(2008/021) PMID:18663107

Schlosser, R., & Lee, D. (2000). Promoting generalization and maintenance in augmentative and alternative communication: A meta-analysis of 20 years of effectiveness research. *Augmentative and Alternative Communication, 16*, 208–226. doi:10.1080/07434610012331279074

Schmidt, C., & Schmidt, M. (2008). Three-dimensional virtual learning environments for mediating social skills acquisition among individuals with autism spectrum disorders. In *Proceedings of the 7th international Conference on interaction Design and Children* (pp. 85-88). Chicago, IL: Academic Press.

Schmidt, M., Laffey, J. M., Schmidt, C. T., Wang, X., & Stichter, J. (2012). Developing methods for understanding social behaviour in a 3D virtual learning environment. *Computers in Human Behavior, 28*(2), 405–413. doi:10.1016/j.chb.2011.10.011

Schopler, E., & Mesibov, G. B. (1995). *Learning and cognition in autism*. New York, NY: Plenum Press. doi:10.1007/978-1-4899-1286-2

Schreibman, L., Whalen, C., & Stahmer, A. C. (2000). The use of video priming to reduce disruptive behavior in children with autism. *Journal of Positive Behavior Interventions, 2*, 3–11. doi:10.1177/109830070000200102

Schrum, L., & Glassett, K. F. (2006). Technology integration in P-12 schools: Challenges to implementation and impact of scientifically-based research. *Journal of Thought, 41*, 41–58.

Schwartz, I. S., Garfinkle, A. N., & Bauer, J. (1998). The picture exchange communication system: Communication outcomes for young children with disabilities. *Topics in Early Childhood Special Education, 18*, 144–159. doi:10.1177/027112149801800305

Scott, F. J., Baron-Cohen, S., Bolton, P., & Brayne, C. (2002). Brief report prevalence of autism spectrum conditions in children aged 5-11 years in Cambridgeshire, UK. *Autism, 6*, 231–237. doi:10.1177/1362361302006003002 PMID:12212915

Self, T., Scudder, R. R., Weheba, G., & Crumrine, D. (2007). A virtual approach to teaching safety skills to children with autism spectrum disorder. *Topics in Language Disorders, 273*(3), 242–253. doi:10.1097/01.TLD.0000285358.33545.79

Senju, A., & Johnson, M. H. (2009). Atypical eye contact in autism: Models, mechanisms and development. *Neuroscience and Biobehavioral Reviews, 33*, 1204–1214. PMID:19538990

Sennott, S., & Bowker, A. (2009). Autism, AAC, & Proloquo2Go. *Perspectives on Augmentative and Alternative Communication, 18*, 137–145. doi:10.1044/aac18.4.137

Seven Tips for Using iPads with Kids with Autism. (2013). Retrieved online 6/17/13.

Shamah, D. (2012, August 16). iPads and tablets could help autistic kids learn social skills. *Times of Israel.*

Shane, H. C., O'Brien, M., & Sorce, J. (2009). Use of visual graphic language system to support communication for persons on the autism spectrum. *Perspectives on Augmentative and Alternative Communication*, 130-136.

Shane, H. C., & Albert, P. D. (2008). Electronic screen media for persons with autism spectrum disorders: Results of a survey. *Journal of Autism and Developmental Disorders*, *38*, 1499–1508. doi:10.1007/s10803-007-0527-5 PMID:18293074

Shane, H. C., Laubscher, E. H., Schlosser, R. W., Flynn, S., Sorce, J. F., & Abramson, J. (2012). Applying technology to visually support language and communication in individuals with autism spectrum disorders. *Journal of Autism and Developmental Disorders*, *37*, 1228–1235. doi:10.1007/s10803-011-1304-z PMID:21691867

Shattuck, P. T., Narendorf, S. C., Cooper, B., Sterzing, P. R., Wagner, M., & Taylor, J. L. (2012). Postsecondary education and employment among youth with an autism spectrum disorder. *Pediatrics*, *129*, 1042–1049. doi:10.1542/peds.2011-2864 PMID:22585766

Sherer, M., Pierce, K. L., Paredes, S., Kisacky, K. L., Ingersoll, B., & Schreibman, L. (2001). Enhancing conversation skills in children with autism via video technology: Which is better, "Self" or "Other" as a model? *Behavior Modification*, *25*, 140–148. doi:10.1177/0145445501251008 PMID:11151482

Shipley-Benamou, R., Lutzker, J. R., & Taubman, M. (2002). Teaching daily living skills to children with autism through instructional video modeling. *Journal of Positive Behavior Interventions*, *4*, 165–175. doi:10.1177/10983 007020040030501

Shukla-Mehta, S., Miller, T., & Callahan, K. J. (2010). Evaluating the effectiveness of video instruction on social and communication skills for children with autism spectrum disorders: A review of the literature. *Focus on Autism and Other Developmental Disabilities*, *25*, 23–26. doi:10.1177/1088357609352901

Silton, N. R. (2009). Fostering knowledge, positive intentions and attitudes of typical children towards children with autism. Proquest Info and Learning Company, 1-108.

Silver, M., & Oakes, P. (2001). Evaluation of a new computer intervention to teach people with autism or Asperger syndrome to recognize and predict emotions in others. *Autism*, *5*, 299–316. doi:10.1177/1362361301005003007 PMID:11708589

Simpson, A., Langone, J., & Ayres, K. (2004). Embedded video and computer based instruction to improve social skills for students with autism. *Education and Training in Developmental Disabilities*, *39*, 240–252.

Simpson, R. L. (2005). *Autism spectrum disorders: Interventions and treatments for children and youth*. Thousand Oaks, CA: Corwin Press. doi:10.1177/10883 576050200030201

Simpson, R. L., Myles, B. S., & Ganz, J. B. (2008). Efficacious interventions and treatments for learners with autism spectrum disorders. In R. Simpson, & B. Myles (Eds.), *Educating children and youth with autism* (pp. 477–512). Austin, TX: PRO-ED, Inc.

Simpson, R. L., Myles, B. S., & LaCava, P. G. (2008). Understanding and responding to the needs of children and youth with autism spectrum disorders. In R. Simpson, & B. Myles (Eds.), *Educating children and youth with autism* (pp. 1–59). Austin, TX: PRO-ED, Inc.

Sinclair, J. (1992). Bridging the gaps: an inside-out view of autism. In E. Schopler, & G. B. Mesibov (Eds.), *High-functioning individuals with autism* (pp. 1–59). New York, NY: Plenum Press.

Siperstein, G. N. (1980). *Development of the adjective checklist: An instrument for measuring children's attitudes toward the handicapped*. Unpublished Manuscript

Siperstein, G. N., & Bak, J. (1977). *Instruments to measure children's attitudes toward the handicapped: Adjective checklist and activity preference list*. Unpublished Manuscript.

Slater, M., Rovira, A., Southern, R., Swapp, D., & Zhang, J. J. et al. (2013). Bystander responses to a violent incident in an immersive virtual environment. *PLoS ONE*, *8*(1), e52766. doi:10.1371/journal.pone.0052766 PMID:23300991

Smith Myles, B., & Simpson, R. L. (2001). Understanding the hidden curriculum: An essential social skill for children and youth with Asperger's syndrome. *Intervention in School and Clinic*, *6*, 279–286. doi:10.1177/105345120103600504

Smith Myles, B., Trautman, M. L., & Schelvan, R. L. (2004). *The hidden curriculum: Practical solutions for understanding unstated rules in social situations.* Shawnee Mission, KS: Autism Asperger Publishing.

Smith, B. R., Spooner, F., & Wood, C. L. (2013). Using embedded computer-assisted explicit instruction to teach science to student with autism spectrum disorder. *Research in Autism Spectrum Disorders, 7,* 433–443. doi:10.1016/j.rasd.2012.10.010

Smith, D. D., & Tyler, N. C. (2010). *Introduction to special education: Making a difference.* Upper Saddle River, NJ: Merrill.

Smith-D'Arezzo, W.M., & Moore-Thomas, C. (2010). Children's perceptions of peers with disabilities. *TEACHING Exceptional Children Plus, 6*(3).

Smith, T. (2001). Discrete trial training in the treatment of autism. *Focus on Autism and Other Developmental Disabilities, 16*(2), 86–92. doi:10.1177/108835760101600204

Smith, T., Scahill, L., Dawson, G., Guthrie, D., Lord, C., & Odom, S. et al. (2007). Designing research studies on psychosocial interventions in autism. *Journal of Autism and Developmental Disorders, 37,* 354–366. doi:10.1007/s10803-006-0173-3 PMID:16897380

Smyth, J. M. (2007). Beyond self-selection in video game play: An experimental examination of the consequences of massively multiplayer online role-playing game play. *Cyberpsychology & Behavior, 10*(5), 717–721. PMID:17927543

Snell, M., & Brown, F. (2011). *Instruction for students with severe disabilities* (7th ed.). Boston, MA: Pearson.

Soares, D. A., Vannest, K. J., & Harrison, J. (2009). Computer aided self-monitoring to increase academic production and reduce self-injurious behavior in a child with autism. *Behavioral Interventions, 24,* 171–183. doi:10.1002/bin.283

Social Skill Builder, Inc. (2011, October 24). *Social skill builder lite information.* Retrieved from https://itunes.apple.com/us/app/social-skill-builder-lite/id486116417?mt=8

Son, S. H., Sigafoos, J., O'Reilly, M., & Lancioni, G. E. (2006). Comparing two types of augmentative and alternative communication systems for children with autism. *Developmental Neurorehabilitation, 9,* 389–395. doi:10.1080/13638490500519984 PMID:17111565

Sprafkin, J. N., Gadow, K. D., & Grayson, P. (1984). Television and the emotionally disturbed, learning disabled, and mentally retarded child: A review. *Advances in Learning and Behavioral Disabilities, 3,* 151–213.

Steere, D. E., & DiPipi-Hoy, C. (2012). When you can't get out: Strategies for supporting community-based instruction. *Teaching Exceptional Children, 45,* 60–67.

Stokes, S. (n.d.). *Assistive technology for children with autism.* Retrieved from http://www.specialed.us/autism/assist/asst10.htm

Strickland, D. (1996). A virtual reality application with autistic children. *Presence (Cambridge, Mass.), 5*(3), 319–329.

Strickland, D. C., McAllister, D., Coles, C. D., & Osbourne, S. (2007). An evolution of virtual reality training designs for children with autism and fetal alcohol spectrum disorders. *Topics in Language Disorders, 27*(3), 226–241. PMID:20072702

Strickland, D., Marcus, L. M., Mesibov, G. B., & Hogan, K. (1996). Brief report: Two case studies using virtual reality as a learning tool for autistic children. *Journal of Autism and Developmental Disorders, 26*(6), 651–659. doi:10.1007/BF02172354 PMID:8986851

Strnadová, I., & Evans, D. (2007). Coping strategies in mothers of school-aged children with intellectual disabilities. *Australasian Journal of Special Education, 31*(2), 159–170. doi:10.1080/10300110701716196

Sumiyoshi, C., Kawakubo, Y., Suga, M., Sumiyoshi, T., & Kasai, K. (2011). Impaired ability to organize information in individuals with autism spectrum disorders and their siblings. *Neuroscience, 69,* 252–257. PMID:21129422

Swaim, K. F., Morgan, S. B., Lenhart, J. A., Hyder, K., Zimmerman, A. W., & Pevsner, J. (2001). Children's attitudes and behavioral intentions toward a peer with autistic behaviors: Does a brief educational intervention have an effect? *Journal of Autism and Developmental Disorders, 31*(2), 195. doi:10.1023/A:1010703316365 PMID:11450818

Swearer, S., Espelage, D. L., & Napolitano, S. A. (2009). *Bullying prevention and intervention: Realistic strategies for schools*. New York, NY: Guilford Press.

Takanori, K., & Hui-Ting, W. (n.d.). Review article: Use of activity schedule to promote independent performance of individuals with autism and other intellectual disabilities: A review. *Research in Developmental Disabilities, 32*, 2235-2242, doi:10.1016/j.ridd.2011.05.03

Tan, J., & Conway, T. (2012). iPAWS – Personal assistant web application system for autistic adults. Pennsylvania Computer and Information Science Educators, E. Stroudsburg.

Tanaka, J. W., Wolf, J. M., Klaiman, C., Koenig, K., Cockburn, J., & Herlihy, L. et al. (2010). Using computerized games to teach face recognition skills to children with autism spectrum disorder: The let's face it! program. *Journal of Child Psychology and Psychiatry, and Allied Disciplines, 51*(8), 944–952. PMID:20646129

Tapus, A., Matarić, M., & Scassellati, B. (2007). The grand challenges in socially assistive robotics. *IEEE Robotics & Automation Magazine, 4*, 35–42.

Tapus, A., Peca, A., Aly, A., Pop, C., Jisa, L., & Pintea, S. et al. (2012). Children with autism social engagement in interaction with nao, an imitative robot: A series of single case experiments. *Interaction Studies: Social Behaviour and Communication in Biological and Artificial Systems, 13*(3), 315–347. doi: doi:10.1075/is.13.3.01tap

Tasse, M. J., Aman, M. G., Hammer, D., & Rojahn, J. (1996). *The Nisonger child behavior rating form*. Columbus, OH: The Nisonger Center for Mental Retardation and Developmental Disabilities.

Tentori, M., & Hayes, G. (2010). Designing for interaction immediacy to enhance social skills of children with autism. In J. Bardram, M. Langhenreich, K. Truong, & P. Nixon (Eds.), *Proceedings of the 12th ACM International Conference on Ubiquitous Computing* (pp. 51–60). New York, NY: The ACM Press. http://dx.doi.org/10.1145/1864349.1864359

TextHelp, Inc. (2013). *Read&Write gold*. Antrim, Ireland: Author.

The iPad: A Useful Tool for Autism. (n.d.). Retrieved online 6/17/13.

Thiemann, K. S., & Goldstein, H. (2001). Social stories, written text cues, and video feedback: Effects on social communication of children with autism. *Journal of Applied Behavior Analysis, 34*, 425–446. doi:10.1901/jaba.2001.34-425 PMID:11800183

Thill, S., Pop, C., Belpaeme, T., Ziemke, T., & Vanderborght, B. (2012). Robot-assisted therapy for autism spectrum disorders with (partially) autonomous control: Challenges and outlook. *Palaydn: Journal of Behavioral Robotics, 3*(4), 209–217.

Thomas, G. (2011). *How to do your case study: A guide for students and researchers*. London: Sage.

Tien, K. C. (2008). Effectiveness of the picture exchange communication system as a functional communication intervention for individuals with autism-spectrum disorders: A practice-based research synthesis. *Education and Training in Developmental Disabilities, 43*, 61–76.

Timer, T. (1991). *Time timer*. Cincinnati, OH: Author.

Tincani, M. (2004). Comparing the picture exchange communication system and sign language training for children with autism. *Focus on Autism and Other Developmental Disabilities, 19*, 152–163. doi:10.1177/10883576040190030301

Tracy, J. L., Robins, R. W., Schriber, R. A., & Solomon, M. (2011). Is emotion recognition impaired in individuals with ASD spectrum disorders? *Journal of ASD and Developmental Disorders, 41*(1), 102–109. doi:10.1007/s10803-010-1030-y

Travers, J. C., Higgins, K., Pierce, T., Boone, R., Miller, S., & Tandy, R. (2011). Emergent literacy skills of pre-school students with autism: A comparison of teacher-led and computer-assisted instruction. *Education & Training in Autism & Developmental Disabilities, 46,* 326–338.

Trepagnier, C. Y., Sebrechts, M. M., Finkelmeyer, A., Coleman, M., Stewart, W. Jr., & Werner-Adler, M. (2005). Virtual environments to address autistic social deficits. *Annual Review of Cybertherapy and Telemedicine, 3,* 101–107.

Tsatsanis, K. D. (2004). Heterogeneity in learning style in Asperger syndrome and high functioning autism. *Topics in Language Disorders, 24,* 260–270. doi:10.1097/00011363-200410000-00004

Tsatsanis, K. D., Noens, I. L. J., Illman, C. L., Paul, D. L., Volkmar, F. R., Schultz, R. T., & Klin, A. (2010). Managing complexity: Impact of organization and processing style on nonverbal memory in autism spectrum disorders. *Journal of Autism and Developmental Disorders, 41,* 135–147. doi:10.1007/s10803-010-1139-z PMID:21128108

Tse, J., Strulovitch, J., Tagalakis, V., Meng, L., & Fombonne, E. (2007). Social skills training for adolescents with Asperger syndrome and high functioning autism. *Journal of Autism and Developmental Disorders, 37,* 1960–1968. doi:10.1007/s10803-006-0343-3 PMID:17216559

Tunney, R., & Ryan, M. (2012). Can iDevices help teaching assistants support pupils with ASD? *Journal of Assistive Technologies, 6*(3), 182–191. doi:10.1108/17549451211261308

U.S. Department of Health and Human Services, Interagency Autism Coordinating Committee. (2011). *2011 strategic plan for autism spectrum disorder research* (NIH Publication No. 10-7573). Retrieved from http://iacc.hhs.gov/strategic-plan/2011/index.shtml

United States Department of Education. (2012). *What works clearinghouse play-based interventions.* Washington, DC: Author.

University of Cambridge. (2003). *Mind reading.* Cambridge, UK: Author.

University of Maine Center for Community Inclusion and Disability. (2009). *A review of evidence-based practices for students with autism spectrum disorders.* Portland, ME: Kurtz.

Urinal Game. (n.d.). Retrieved from http://www.autismspeaks.org/autism-apps/urinal-game

Uxbridge Public Schools. (2013). *iPad initiative.* Retrieved Online 9/15/13.

van der Meer, L. A. J., & Rispoli, M. (2010). Communication interventions involving speech-generating devices for children with autism: A review of the literature. *Developmental Neurorehabilitation, 13,* 294–306. doi:10.3109/17518421003671494 PMID:20629595

van der Meer, L., Kagohara, D., Achmadi, D., O'Reilly, M. F., Lancioni, G. E., & Sutherland, D. et al. (2012). Speech-generating devices versus manual signing for children with developmental disabilities. *Research in Developmental Disabilities, 33,* 1658–1669. doi:10.1016/j.ridd.2012.04.004 PMID:22554812

Van der Meer, L., Sigafoos, J., O'Reilly, M. F., & Lancioni, G. E. (2011). Assessing preferences for AAC options in communication interventions for individuals with developmental disabilities: A review of the literature. *Research in Developmental Disabilities, 32,* 1422–1431. doi:10.1016/j.ridd.2011.02.003 PMID:21377833

Van Rijn, H., & Stappers, P. J. (2008). The puzzling life of autistic toddlers: Design guidelines from the LINKX project. In *Advances in human-computer interaction.* Hindawi Publishing Corporation. doi:10.1155/2008/639435

VanBiervliet, A., & Parette, H. P. (1999). *Families, cultures, and AAC.* [CD-ROM]. Little Rock, AR: Southeast Missouri State University and University of Arkansas for Medical Sciences.

Vanderborght, B., Simut, R., Saldien, J., Pop, C., Rusu, A. S., & Pintea, S. et al. (2012). Using the social robot Probo as a social story telling agent for children with ASD. *Interaction Studies: Social Behaviour and Communication in Biological and Artificial Systems, 13*(3), 348–372. doi: doi:10.1075/is.13/3/02van

Vedad, H., & Nirvana, P. (2012). LeFCA: Learning framework for children with autism. *Procedia Computer Science, 15*, 4–16. doi:10.1016/j.procs.2012.10.052

Vermeulen, P. (2012). *Autism as context blindness*. Shawnee Mission, KS: AAPC Publishing.

Vincent, T. (2012). *Evaluation rubric for iPod apps*. Retrieved from http://learninginhand.com/static/50eca8 55e4b0939ae8bb12d9/50ecb58ee4b0b16f176a9e7d/50 ecb595e4b0b16f176aaab8/1288148200553/AppRubric. pdf on 07-08-2013

VIRART. (n.d.). Retrieved from https://www.virart.nott. ac.uk/asi/b_design.htm

Volkmar, F. R., Lord, C., Bailey, A., Schultz, R. T., & Klin, A. (2004). Autism and pervasive developmental disorders. *Journal of Child Psychology and Psychiatry, and Allied Disciplines, 45*, 135–170. doi:10.1046/j.0021-9630.2003.00317.x PMID:14959806

Volkmar, F. R., Reichow, B., & Doehring, P. (2011). Evidence-based practices in autism: Where we are now and where we need to go. In *Evidence-based practices and treatments for children with autism* (pp. 365–391). New York: Springer. doi:10.1007/978-1-4419-6975-0_14

Wahl, O., Hanrahan, E., Karl, K., Lasher, E., & Swaye, J. (2006). The depiction of mental illnesses in children's television programs. *Journal of Community Psychology, 35*(1), 121–133. doi:10.1002/jcop.20138

Wainer, A. L., & Ingersoll, R. (2010). The use of innovative computer technology for teaching social communication to individuals with autism spectrum disorders. *Research in Autism Spectrum Disorders, 5*, 96–107. doi:10.1016/j.rasd.2010.08.002

Wainer, J., Ferrari, E., Dautenhahn, K., & Robins, B. (2010). The effectiveness of using a robotics class to foster collaboration among groups of children with autism in an exploratory study. *Personal and Ubiquitous Computing, 14*, 445–455. doi: doi:10.1007/s007/s00779-009-02660z

Walker, V., & Snell, M. (2013). Effects of augmentative and alternative communication on challenging behavior: A meta-analysis. *Augmentative and Alternative Communication, 29*, 117–131. doi:10.3109/07434618.2013.785 020 PMID:23705814

Wallace, L., & Happé, F. (2008). Time perception in autism spectrum disorders. *Research in Autism Spectrum Disorders, 2*, 447–455. doi:10.1016/j.rasd.2007.09.005

Wallace, S., Parsons, S., Westbury, A., White, K., White, K., & Bailey, A. (2010). Sense of presence and atypical social judgments in immersive virtual environments. Responses of adolescents with autism spectrum disorders. *Autism, 14*, 199–213. doi:10.1177/1362361310363283 PMID:20484000

Walton, K. M., & Ingersoll, B. R. (2012). Improving social skills in adolescents and adults with autism and severe to profound intellectual disability: A review of the literature. *Journal of Autism and Developmental Disorders, 43*, 594–615. doi:10.1007/s10803-012-1601-1 PMID:22790427

WatchMinder. (2013). *WatchMinder*. Irvine, CA: Author.

Webber, J., & Scheuermann, B. (2008). *Educating students with autism: A quick start manual*. Austin, TX: Pro-Ed.

Wehman, P. B. (2012). *Life beyond the classroom: Transition strategies for young people with disabilities*. Brookes Publishing Company.

Weinger, P. M., & Depue, R. A. (2011). Remediation of deficits in recognition of facial emotions in children with autism spectrum disorders. *Child & Family Behavior Therapy, 33*, 20–31. doi:10.1080/07317107.2011.545008

Weiss, P. L. T., Gal, E., Cobb, S., Millen, L., Hawkins, T., & Glover, T. … Eden, S. (2011). Usability of technology supported social competence training for children on the autism spectrum. In *Proceedings of International Conference on Virtual Rehabilitation 2011*. Zurich, Switzerland: Academic Press.

Weiss, P. L. T., Gal, E., Eden, S., Zancanaro, M., & Telch, F. (2011). Usability of a multi-touch tabletop surface to enhance social competence training for children with autism spectrum disorder. In *Proceedings of the Chais Conference on Instructional Technologies Research 2011: Learning in the Technological Era*. Raanana, Israel: The Open University in Israel.

Welsh, M. et al. (2001). Linkages between children's social and academic competence: A longitudinal analysis. *Journal of School Psychology, 39*, 463–482. doi:10.1016/S0022-4405(01)00084-X

Wendt, O. (2009). Research on the use of manual signs and graphic symbols in autism spectrum disorders: A systematic review. In P. Mirenda, & T. Iacono (Eds.), *Autism spectrum disorders and AAC* (pp. 83–140). Baltimore, MD: Paul H. Brookes.

Wert, Y. B., & Neisworth, J. T. (2003). Effects of video self-modeling on spontaneous requesting in children with autism. *Journal of Positive Behavior Interventions, 5*(1), 30–34. doi:10.1177/10983007030050010501

Westling, D. L., & Fox, L. (1995). *Teaching students with severe disabilities*. Englewood Cliffs, NJ: Prentice-Hall, Inc.

Wetherby, A. M., & Prizant, B. M. (2000). *Autism spectrum disorders: A transactional developmental perspective*. Baltimore, MD: Brookes.

Wheeler, J. J., & Carter, S. L. (1998). Using visual cues in the classroom for learners with autism as a method for promoting positive behavior. *B.C. The Journal of Special Education, 21*, 64–73.

Whelan, C., & Cernich, S. (2007). *Proceedings from the association for behavior analysis international (ABAI) conference '07: Assessment of motivation during reward games vs. learning trials using TeachTown: Basics*. ABAI.

Whelan, C., Cernich, S., Lockhart, D., Liden, L., & Vaupel, M. (2009). *Proceedings from the international meeting for autism research (IMFAR) '09: Analysis of usage of TeachTown: Basics with 1,100 subscribers*. IMFAR.

Whelan, C., Linden, L., Ingersoll, B., Dallaire, E., & Linden, S. (2006). Positive behavioral changes associated with the use of computer-assisted instruction for young children. *Journal of Speech and Language Pathology and Applied Behavioral Analysis, 1*(1), 11–26.

Whelan, C., Moss, D., Ilan, A. B., Vaupel, M., Fielding, P., & MacDonald, K. (2010). Efficacy of Teach-Town: Basics computer-assisted intervention for the intensive comprehensive autism program in Los Angeles Unified School District. *Autism, 14*, 179–197. doi:10.1177/1362361310363282 PMID:20484002

White, T. (2013). Tablets trump smartphones in global website traffic. *Adobe Digital Marketing Blog*. Retrieved on June 8, 2013 from: http://blogs.adobe.com/digital-marketing/digital-index/tablets-trump-smartphones-in-global-website-traffic/

Williams, L. K. (1996). *Caring and capable kids: An activity guide for teaching kindness, tolerance, self-control and responsibility*. ERIC Document, 395–697.

Williams, C., Wright, B., Callaghan, G., & Coughlan, B. (2002). Do children with autism learn to read more readily by computer assisted instruction or traditional book methods? A pilot study. *SAGE Publications and the National Autistic Society, 6*, 71–91. PMID:11918110

Wilson, K. P. (2013). Incorporating video modeling into a school-based intervention for students with autism spectrum disorders. *Language, Speech, and Hearing Services in Schools, 44*, 105–117. doi:10.1044/0161-1461(2012/11-0098) PMID:23087158

Wing, L., & Gould, J. (1979). Severe impairments of social interation and associated abnormalities in children: epidemiology and classification. *Journal of Autism and Developmental Disorders, 9*(1), 11–29. doi:10.1007/BF01531288 PMID:155684

Winner, E. (2000). The origins and ends of giftedness. *The American Psychologist, 55*(1), 159–169. doi:10.1037/0003-066X.55.1.159 PMID:11392860

Wisconsin Assistive Technology Initiative. (2009). *Assistive technology supports for individuals with autism spectrum disorder*. Author.

Wood, L. (2012). A critical analysis: Overview of the media. *Disability Planet*. Retrieved from http://www.disabilityplanet.co.uk/index.html

Works Clearinghouse, W. (2013). *Early childhood education interventions for children with disabilities – Social skills training*. Washington, DC: Institute of Education Sciences.

Works Clearinghouse, W. (2013). *Procedures and standards handbook, version 3.0*. Washington, DC: Institute of Education Sciences.

Works Clearinghouse, W. (2013). *WWC evidence review protocol for early childhood education interventions for children with disabilities, version 2.0.* Washington, DC: Institute of Education Sciences.

Works Clearinghouse, W. (2013). *WWC evidence review protocol for K-12 students with learning disabilities, version 2.0.* Washington, DC: Institute of Education Sciences.

World Health Organization. (1993). *The ICD-10 classification of mental and behavioural disorders diagnostic criteria for research.* Geneva, Switzerland: World Health Organization.

Wyman, B., & Stobbe, G. (2006). A case study. Presented at the Association for Behavior Analysis International (ABAI) Conference, Seattle, WA.

Yeargin-Allsopp, M., Rice, C., Karapurkan, T., Doernberg, N., Boyle, C., & Murphy, C. (2003). Prevalence of autism in a US metropolitan area. *Journal of the American Medical Association, 289,* 49–55. doi:10.1001/jama.289.1.49 PMID:12503976

Zabala, J. (2002). *A brief introduction to the SETT framework.* Retrieved from http://www.sbac.edu/~ese?AT/referralprocess/SETTUPDATE.pdf

Zabala, J. (2011, March 11). *Posting to QIAT listserv.* Retrieved from briohttp://natri.uky.edu/assoc_projects/qiat/listserv.html

Zabala, J., & Bowser, G. (2005). SETTing up staff and supporters to promote student achievement. *Closing the Gap: Computer Technology in Special Education and Rehabilitation, 24*(1), 1–3.

Zamfir, B., Tedesco, R., & Reichow, B. (2012). Handheld app offering visual support to students with autism spectrum disorders (ASDs). In *Computers helping people with special needs* (pp. 105–112). Berlin: Springer. doi:10.1007/978-3-642-31534-3_16

Zangari, C., Lloyd, L. L., & Vicker, B. (1994). Augmentative and alternative communication: An historic perspective. *Augmentative and Alternative Communication, 10,* 27–59. doi:10.1080/07434619412331276740

About the Contributors

Nava R. Silton, Ph.D., received her B.S. from Cornell University and her M.A. and Ph.D. from Fordham University. Silton has worked at Nickelodeon, Sesame Workshop, and Mediakidz. She has taught both undergraduate and graduate psychology courses at Fordham University, Hunter College, Touro College, and began a tenure-track line in the Department of Psychology at Marymount Manhattan College in the fall of 2010. She was a Postdoctoral Templeton Fellow at the Spears Research Institute at the Healthcare Chaplaincy from 2009-2010, and she has conducted research at the Autism Seaver Center at Mount Sinai Hospital and at Sesame Street Workshop. Her primary research interests include determining how best to enhance typical children's sensitivity to children with disabilities, how to teach social emotional skills to children on the spectrum, and looking at the interface between religion and health. She is currently producing a children's television show and a graphic novel series with disability awareness and stop bullying as primary platforms. She has written numerous peer-reviewed articles and chapters in the area of disabilities.

* * *

Kari A. Andersen is School Psychology Ph.D. student at Fordham University. She is a licensed school psychologist with a Master's degree from Touro College. Her research interests concern technology-based interventions for children in the context of academic and non-academic learning situations. Additionally, she holds interests in the development and employment of attentional strategies among preschool children.

Senada Arucevic is a senior of Marymount Manhattan College double majoring in biology and psychology. She is passionate about working with children and is working towards becoming a pediatric nurse practitioner. She has a strong interest in research and has worked alongside Nava Silton for the past three years. When Silton proposed the idea of Realabilities, Arucevic was eager to seize this opportunity. She has aided in the development of the characters, edited and written episodes, as well as contributed to the research design. Arucevic was selected to present her research projects at numerous conferences such as the American Psychological Association Conference and the Eastern Psychological Conference. Arucevic won the Professor-Student Collaboration Award in 2012 due to her work on the four-part intervention and Realabilities. She is also a member of the Psi Chi Honors Society in Psychology. Arucevic currently volunteers at Lenox Hill Hospital and spends her free time with her family.

Angela Barber (Ph.D. – Florida State) is an assistant professor of Communicative Disorders at the University of Alabama and the Research Director of the UA Autism Clinic. Her research focuses on early identification and social communication interventions for children with autism and improving access to services for children with autism in underserved communities.

Michael Ben-Avie, Ph.D., was the data analyst for Connecticut General Assembly Special Act 08-5: An Act Concerning the Teaching of Children with Autism and Other Developmental Disabilities (2008-2009). He is a senior researcher with the Center of Excellence on Autism Spectrum Disorders, and conducted research with his co-authors on a federal grant addressing "Handheld Technology to Improve Educational Outcomes for Students with Autism Spectrum Disorders" (2010-2013). He worked as a job coach at a school that serves students with Autism Spectrum Disorders and other Developmental Disorders. As Principal Investigator and Co-P.I., he conducted outcome evaluations of federal grants, including grants from the U.S. Department of Health and Human Services' Center for Substance Abuse Treatment; U.S. Department of Education; Substance Abuse and Mental Health Services Administration's Center for Mental Health Services; and a collaboration among the U.S. Departments of Education, Health and Human Services, and Justice. Dr. Ben-Avie is a nationally recognized expert on public education as co-editor of six books on educational change and youth development with James. P. Comer, M.D., Associate Dean of the Yale School of Medicine. He is chair of Tag Institute for Social Development.

Fran C. Blumberg received her Ph.D. in Developmental Psychology from Purdue University in 1988. She is an Associate Professor and in the Division of Psychological and Educational Services within Graduate School of Education at Fordham University. Her research interests concern the development of children's attention and attention strategies in the context of academic and non-academic learning situations. She has published and received funding for her research concerning children's attention and learning while playing video games and is editor of the forthcoming "Learning by Playing: Video Gaming in Education," to be published by Oxford University Press.

Terry Cumming is a Senior Lecturer in the School of Education at the University of New South Wales in Sydney, Australia. She has earned her PhD and MEd in Special Education (EBD) from the University of Nevada Las Vegas, and her BSED Special Education from Bloomsburg University of Pennsylvania. Her research interests include: educational technology, emotional and behavioural disorders, positive behavioural interventions, intellectual disabilities, and inclusive practices. Recent research projects include: using iPads to support students with language-based disabilities, using iPads to support adults with intellectual disabilities in being researchers, teachers' perspectives on student misbehavior, and using technology to enhance social skills instruction for students with emotional and behavioral disabilities. She has published a book and several journal articles and presented her work at both national and international conferences. Prior to her university and research work, Dr. Cumming has many years experience as a special educator and behaviour mentor.

Cathi Draper Rodriguez, Ph.D., NCSP, is an Associate Professor in the School of Education at California State University, Monterey Bay. Dr. Draper Rodriguez teaches curriculum, assessment, and introduction to research in the Special Education and Masters programs. Since earning her doctorate from the University of Nevada, Las Vegas, she has focused her research on using technology with English learners with and without disabilities, the diagnosis of disabilities in English learners, assessment in education and multicultural education. Dr. Draper Rodriguez is a Nationally Certified School Psychologist. Her previous work experience includes serving as a bilingual school psychologist in a public school setting and as an early interventionist providing services to young Latina mothers.

Gary Edwards (Ph.D. - Alabama) is the Chief Executive Officer of United Cerebral Palsy of Greater Birmingham, which provides a wide range of educational, therapeutic, medical, and vocational services to children and adults with disabilities. Gary is an expert on disabilities issues such employment and inclusion for people with disabilities in all aspects of life.

Jeff Gray (Ph.D. – Vanderbilt) is an Associate Professor in the Department of Computer Science at the University of Alabama. Jeff is a recipient of the NSF CAREER award and was named the 2008 Alabama Professor of the Year by the Carnegie Foundation. His research into assistive technologies and human-centered computing has been funded recently by Google and NSF. For more information, please see http://gray.cs.ua.edu/.

Julie E. N. Irish, M.Sc., is a Ph.D. student in the design graduate program in the College of Design at the University of Minnesota focusing on evidence-based design. Her previous graduate studies in Inclusive Environments from Reading University, England, U.K., have augmented her work as an interior designer of environments for people with disabilities. Projects in Wales, U.K., include the Ty Gwyn Special School, an environment for children with severe disabilities and autism. During her involvement with this project she became more keenly aware of the difficulties facing children with autism, particularly as they process and deal with their surroundings, and the effect on their parents, caregivers, and teachers. This prompted her desire to do more for this population and in Fall 2011, accompanied by her family, she moved to the States to pursue a research goal of exploring how the design of the educational environment affects children with autism in an adverse way, why that might be and how that environment could be improved to make their lives easier. She is also intrigued by virtual environments and the potential they could have as a design tool, particularly for those with ASD.

Allison Krupko, M.Ed. is an Educational Specialist (Ed.S.) student in the school psychology program at Kent State University. Currently, Ms. Krupko is completing her yearlong internship in school psychology in Ohio. Throughout her graduate training, Ms. Krupko has been active in assisting with research focusing on technology-based interventions for students with Autism Spectrum Disorders and assessing the efficacy of social skills interventions. Her professional interests include incorporating preschool and early elementary school students into a Response to Intervention (RTI) framework and assisting students who have experienced Traumatic Brain Injury (TBI) in transitioning back to the school setting.

Lauren Lambert is a Psychology student at the University of Alabama who has a passion for helping children with disabilities.

Cassidy Lamm is a student at the University of Alabama in the Department of Computer Science. She is currently supported by an NSF and College Board grant that is investigating the use of mobile computing as a context for a new Advanced Placement exam in collaboration with the College Board.

Lauren Levenson is a School Psychology Ph.D. student at Fordham University. Her research interests concern how family environment characteristics affect both behavioral and social-emotional outcomes in children with autism and other developmental disabilities. Other research interests are related to intervention techniques that may alleviate some of the difficulties associated with autism. She is currently working on a research project that will assess the relationship between parenting style and attachment style on the social-emotional outcomes of children ages three to five with autism.

Toby Mehl-Schneider, M.S., CCC-SLP, is a speech-language pathologist in New York City. She received a Bachelor of Arts, cum laude, in speech-language pathology and audiology and a Master of Science in speech-language pathology from Brooklyn College, The City University of New York. Toby is currently a doctoral student in the Department of Speech-Language-Hearing Sciences at The Graduate Center, The City University of New York. Toby Mehl-Schneider served as the lead researcher for the analysis, translation and standardization of the Preschool Language Scale (PLS-4) Hebrew Edition, adapting the PLS-4 English assessment materials to reflect the appropriate cultural and linguistic aspects of the Hebrew language. She has been providing therapeutic intervention to school-age children with various speech and language disorders in the New York City Department of Education for eight years.

Mary Lynn Mizenko, M.Ed. is a second year doctoral student in the school psychology program at Kent State University. Ms. Mizenko is currently analyzing and conducting research that utilizes technology to improve academic, behavioral, and social skills of students with Autism Spectrum Disorders (ASD). She has been actively involved in Kent State University's student school psychologist organization (SASP), and will assume the role as president for the upcoming school year. Ms. Mizenko also is a member of the Dean's Graduate Advisory Board for the School of Lifespan Development. She continues to hone her research and professional skills in the area of technology utilization for students with ASD.

Brenda Smith Myles Ph.D., a consultant with the Ohio Center for Autism and Low Incidence (OCALI) and the Ziggurat Group, is the recipient of the Autism Society of America's Outstanding Professional Award, the Princeton Fellowship Award, and the Council for Exceptional Children, Division on Developmental Disabilities Burton Blatt Humanitarian Award. Brenda has made over 1000 presentations all over the world and written more than 200 articles and books on ASD. In addition, she served as the co-chair of the National ASD Teacher Standards Committee; was on the National Institute of Mental Health's Interagency Autism Coordinating Committee's Strategic Planning Consortium; and collaborated with the National Professional Center on Autism Spectrum Disorders, National Autism Center, and the Centers for Medicare and Medicaid Services who identified evidenced based practices for individuals with autism spectrum disorders and served as Project Director for the Texas Autism Resource Guide for Teachers (TARGET). Myles is also on the executive boards of several organizations, including the Scientific Council of the Organization for Autism Research (SCORE) and ASTEP – Asperger Syndrome Training and Education Program. Further, in the latest survey conducted by the University of Texas, she was acknowledged as the second most productive applied researcher in ASD in the world.

Nigel Newbutt, BSc, MA, Ph.D., is a Senior Lecturer at Bath Spa University (UK) in Digital Cultures. His research interests are in the areas of autism, technology and the sociology of technology. His Ph.D. was completed at University College Dublin, Ireland, where he investigated the views of young people with autism and their engagement with a virtual world. His research to date has focused on participatory input and user-centered design approaches, as well as a qualitative approach to gathering data. His work sees him engaged in classrooms, working with children and teachers to design and develop virtual worlds, to help provide a platform that in many ways helps to provide a setting where social communication can be explored.

Deborah Newton, Ed.D. is the interim dean of the School of Education at Southern Connecticut State University (SCSU). She continues as coordinator of the Master Degree concentration and Sixth Year Diploma specialization in adaptive technology, and serves as a member of the internal advisory board for SCSU's Center of Excellence on Autism Spectrum Disorders. Dr. Newton holds teaching certifications in Elementary Education and Special Education and is a former assistive technology specialist. She continues to consult in assistive technology. Dr. Newton is a frequent presenter on a variety of assistive technology-related topics at national, regional, and state conferences. She is a co-author of Assistive Technology in the Classroom: Enhancing the School Experiences of Students with Disabilities, 2nd Ed.

Zandile Nkabinde is an associate professor and a chair person for the Department of Special Education at New Jersey City University. She was born and raised in South Africa. Dr. Nkabinde's areas of research interest include inclusive schooling for children with behavior disorders, high stake testing and its impact on minorities and persons with disabilities, and experiences of immigrant women scholars in higher education. Nkabinde has presented her scholarship throughout the world in both national and international professional gatherings. She has served in varied capacities in her field of interest including being a consulting editor for The Journal of the International Association of Special Education. She also served as a guest reviewer of Multiple Voices, the Journal of Division of Culturally and Linguistically Diverse Exceptional Learner (DDEL), the Council for Exceptional Children. She is currently a reviewer of multicultural Learning and Teaching. Dr. Nkabinde is affiliated with many professional organizations including: the Council for Exceptional Children (CEC), the Council for Children with Behavioral Disorders, and the International Association of Special Education. Nkabinde is the author of many articles in peer reviewed scholarly journals such as: The Journal of Special Education, European Journal of Special Needs, Journal of International Special Needs, International Encyclopedia of Education, Multicultural Learning and Teaching and The Negro Educational Review. Dr. Nkabinde has also written several book chapters on varied topics including one titled: Using assistive technology to educate students with developmental disabilities and autism in a book titled: Autism and Developmental Disabilities: Current practices and issue edited by Anthony F. Rotatori, Festus E. Obiakor and Sandra Burkhardt. Dr. Nkabinde is an active scholar who also enjoys doing community work and spending time with her family.

Vanessa Ioana Norkus graduated from Marymount Manhattan College with a B.A. in psychology in December of 2011. She has always had a keen interest in working with children who require extra attention. She has assisted Dr. Nava Silton since 2012 in researching how to improve typical children's behaviors towards children with disabilities. At the same time, Norkus has interned in social work with seniors at DOROT, a non-profit organization geared towards integrating people of different generations by helping provide services for the older generations. Norkus has also worked as a substitute teacher for a preschool. She has presented at the Hunter College Research Conference and looks forward to continue conducting research. Norkus holds that learning about different cultures is important in understanding human nature and hopes to use this to broaden her knowledge and improve the lives of people with mental and physical limitations.

Christine Ogilvie was a middle school teacher in Massachusetts and Vermont for 11 years before making the jump into higher education. A Ph.D. graduate of the University of Central Florida in Orlando, FL, Dr. Ogilvie has established a notable presence in the area of Autism Spectrum Disorders. Her specific focus is working with adolescents with High Functioning Autism and Asperger Syndrome in the area of social skills instruction. An avid supporter of the use of video modeling and simulation technology for social skills instruction, Dr. Ogilvie continues to pursue an active research agenda in order to impact the number of adolescents on the Autism Spectrum, their teachers, families, and the community at large.

Jody Marie Pirtle is an Assistant Clinical Professor at Northern Arizona University and completed her Ph.D. in Disability and Psychoeducational Studies with a major in early childhood special education and a minor in Family Studies and Human Development at the University of Arizona. As the aunt of two nephews with autism and a former special educator, Jody is known as a strong advocate and is passionate about ensuring inclusive educational opportunities, especially for children with significant support needs. Her research agenda includes studying the effects of family involvement as well as the impact of educational, community, medical, and familial collaboration on outcomes for children with special health care needs and disabilities.

Brian Reichow, Ph.D., BCBA-D, is an Assistant Professor in Community Medicine and Health Care and Director of Research at the AJ Pappanikou Center for Excellence in Developmental Disabilities at the University of Connecticut Health Center. He completed his doctoral studies in Special Education at Vanderbilt University, where he received the M.S. and Ph.D. degrees. Dr. Reichow completed his Undergraduate training in Elementary Education and Psychology at the University of North Carolina at Chapel Hill, and was a public school teacher for children with autism spectrum disorders for many years in the Durham Public Schools. As a researcher, Dr. Reichow has led numerous investigations of interventions for young children with autism and has led numerous systematic reviews and meta-analyses of autism interventions. Dr. Reichow's current research interests include methodological issues of meta-analytic techniques, identifying evidence-based practices and treatments for children with autism, and the translation of clinical and laboratory research findings into practice.

Jan Rogers, MS, OTR/L, ATP is currently the Program Director of the OCALI Assistive Technology Center. She is an occupational therapist and is also a RESNA certified ATP who has worked in a variety of agencies serving the needs of individuals with disabilities. She has taught assistive technology courses at The Ohio State University and currently teaches in the on-line AT certification and Master's program at Bowling Green State University. Additionally, she is a frequent presenter at local, state and national conferences on the topic of assistive technology.

Rebecca Ruchlin is a senior at Marymount Manhattan College, studying Speech-Language Pathology. She has been a part of the Realabilities project as of March 2012, and has aided in conducting research for the show. She has maintained her status on the dean's list throughout her undergraduate career and has presented at Marymount Manhattan College's Honors Day in 2012 and 2013. Ruchlin created a children's story, Chicken Nuggets in the Freezer, discussing what life is like having a brother with autism. She draws much of her interest and passion for disability awareness, especially autism, from her brother Matthew who has autism. When she is not at school, Ruchlin can be found volunteering her time with the special needs community. Upon graduating, Rebecca hopes to attend graduate school and to pursue her degree in Speech-Language Pathology. She hopes to become certified in Applied Behavioral Analysis.

Frank J. Sansosti, Ph.D., NCSP is an Associate Professor and Coordinator of School Psychology at Kent State University. He has extensive experience working with individuals with autism spectrum disorders (ASD) in both school and clinic settings. As a practitioner he provided coaching and technical assistance for early intervention and best practice approaches for students with ASD in inclusive settings, and coordinated efforts between parents, teachers, administrators, and district level personnel. Currently, Dr. Sansosti's primary research and professional interests focus on the development and implementation of behavioral and social skills interventions for individuals with ASD and best practice approaches for the inclusion of students with low-incidence disabilities. In addition, Dr. Sansosti has been active in conducting professional workshops for educators working with students with ASD at local, regional, national, and international venues and he serves as a consultant to multiple school districts/agencies.

Peggy J. Schaefer Whitby is an assistant professor in special education and Program Coordinator for the graduate certificate in Autism Spectrum Disorders at the University of Arkansas. Prior to coming to Fayetteville, Dr. Whitby was an assistant professor at the University of Nevada Las Vegas and the director of the Center for Autism Spectrum Disorders. Dr. Whitby is a board certified behavior analyst at the doctoral level. Her research interests include the education and academic achievement of children with autism spectrum disorders. She has multiple publications in peer reviewed journals and book chapters on educating children with autism.

Amie Senland received her Bachelor of Arts in psychology from the University of Saint Joseph in West Hartford, Connecticut. She earned her M.A. in Applied Developmental Psychology at Fordham University in Bronx, New York, where she is now a Ph.D. Candidate, working under the mentorship of Dr. Ann Higgins-D'Alessandro. Her research interests include autism spectrum disorder and moral development. More specifically, her dissertation investigates moral reasoning, empathy, and the transition to adulthood in young adults with high functioning autism spectrum disorder. Amie's master's thesis research on a similar topic, but with adolescents, was recently published in a flagship moral development journal, Journal of Moral Education.

Shimon Steinmetz is a historian, editor, bibliographer and researcher.

Iva Strnadová is a Senior Lecturer in Special Education at the University of New South Wales in Sydney, Australia. She is also an Honorary Senior Lecturer at the University of Sydney, Faculty of Education and Social Work, Australia. Iva has a strong history in securing national and international research grants. She has published two professional books in the field of special education, co-authored eight other books and co-edited two books. She has also written thirty-six book chapters and twenty-five peer-refereed journal articles in prestigious journals in this area. Iva's previous research and ongoing research interests include ageing with intellectual disabilities, women with intellectual disabilities, well-being of people with developmental disabilities (intellectual disabilities and autism) and their families over the life span, and transitions in lives of people with developmental disabilities.

Joo Tan holds a B.A. in Computer Science from the University of New Mexico and the M.S. and a Doctoral degree from Kansas State University. Prior to academia, Dr. Tan worked at various companies such as BELLCORE and Lucent Technologies for over 6 years. He had a previous teaching stint at Mansfield University before moving to Kutztown University of Pennsylvania in 2005. Dr. Tan has a strong background in Software Engineering and Web Design. His current research interest is primarily in the latest technology that can be adapted in Web design and programming of user interfaces for special needs groups.

Elizabeth West is an Associate Professor at the University of Washington in the Area of Special Education. Dr. West's research agenda focuses on transforming communities to increase access and to improve outcomes for students with low incidence disabilities. Specific research interests include: a) identifying instructional variables that will facilitate and enhance skill acquisition and generalization by students with low incidence disabilities, b) developing effective practices to positively influence outcomes for students with low incidence disabilities who are culturally and linguistically diverse, c) online course development, implementation, and use of technology to facilitate teacher and student learning and, d) establishing positive behavioral supports for a diverse society. Dr. West has established an exciting and productive scholarly agenda with numerous published articles on diversity, skill acquisition for individuals with autism, assistive technology and teacher learning. Dr. West has a wide range of experience in a variety of instructional settings, both in the private sector and in the public school setting.

Joshua Wolfe is a student at the University of Alabama in the Department of Computer Science. Works at Science Application International Solution (SAIC) as an Engineering Co-op/intern in Huntsville, Alabama developing mobile applications systems.

Index